2 CORINTHIANS

THE NIV
APPLICATION
COMMENTARY

From biblical text . . . to contemporary life

THE NIV APPLICATION COMMENTARY SERIES

2 CORINTHIANS

THE NIV APPLICATION COMMENTARY

From biblical text . . . to contemporary life

SCOTT J. HAFEMANN

ZondervanPublishingHouse
Grand Rapids, Michigan

A Division of HarperCollinsPublishers

The NIV Application Commentary: 2 Corinthians
Copyright © 2000 by Scott J. Hafemann

Requests for information should be addressed to:

⛭ Zondervan Publishing House
Grand Rapids, Michigan 49530

Library of Congress Cataloging-in-Publication Data

Hafemann, Scott J.
    2 Corinthians / Scott J. Hafemann.
        p. cm.—(NIV application commentary)
    Includes bibliographical references and indexes.
    ISBN: 0-310-49420-6
    1. Bible. N.T. Corinthians, 2nd—Commentaries. I. Title: Second Corinthians.
II. Title. III. Series.
BS2675.3.H24 2000
227'.3077—dc21   00–029000
                                         CIP

This edition printed on acid-free paper.

Printed in the United States of America

---

00 01 02 03 04 05 06/ ❖ DC / 10 9 8 7 6 5 4 3 2

To Paul House
ἐπιστολὴ Χριστοῦ

Contents

The NIV Application Commentary Series

When complete, the NIV Application Commentary
will include the following volumes:

Old Testament Volumes

Genesis, John H. Walton

Exodus, Peter Enns

Leviticus/Numbers, Roy Gane

Deuteronomy, Daniel I. Block

Joshua, Robert Hubbard

Judges/Ruth, K. Lawson Younger

1-2 Samuel, Bill T. Arnold

1-2 Kings, Michael S. Moore

1-2 Chronicles, Andrew E. Hill

Ezra/Nehemiah, Douglas J. Green

Esther, Karen H. Jobes

Job, Dennis R. Magary

Psalms Volume 1, Gerald H. Wilson

Psalms Volume 2, Gerald H. Wilson

Proverbs, Paul Koptak

Ecclesiastes/Song of Songs, Iain Provan

Isaiah, John N. Oswalt

Jeremiah/Lamentations, J. Andrew Dearman

Ezekiel, Iain M. Duguid

Daniel, Tremper Longman III

Hosea/Amos/Micah, Gary V. Smith

Jonah/Nahum/Habakkuk/Zephaniah
    David M. Howard Jr.

Joel/Obadiah/Malachi, David W. Baker

Haggai/Zechariah, Mark J. Boda

New Testament Volumes

Matthew, Michael J. Wilkins

Mark, David E. Garland

Luke, Darrell L. Bock

John, Gary M. Burge

Acts, Ajith Fernando

Romans, Douglas J. Moo

1 Corinthians, Craig Blomberg

2 Corinthians, Scott Hafemann

Galatians, Scot McKnight

Ephesians, Klyne Snodgrass

Philippians, Frank Thielman

Colossians/Philemon, David E. Garland

1-2 Thessalonians, Michael W. Holmes

1-2 Timothy/Titus, Walter L. Liefeld

Hebrews, George H. Guthrie

James, David P. Nystrom

1 Peter, Scot McKnight

2 Peter/Jude, Douglas J. Moo

Letters of John, Gary M. Burge

Revelation, Craig S. Keener

To see which titles are available,
visit our web site at http://www.zondervan.com

NIV Application Commentary
Series Introduction

THE NIV APPLICATION COMMENTARY SERIES is unique. Most commentaries help us make the journey from our world back to the world of the Bible. They enable us to cross the barriers of time, culture, language, and geography that separate us from the biblical world. Yet they only offer a one-way ticket to the past and assume that we can somehow make the return journey on our own. Once they have explained the *original meaning* of a book or passage, these commentaries give us little or no help in exploring its *contemporary significance*. The information they offer is valuable, but the job is only half done.

Recently, a few commentaries have included some contemporary application as *one* of their goals. Yet that application is often sketchy or moralistic, and some volumes sound more like printed sermons than commentaries.

The primary goal of the NIV Application Commentary Series is to help you with the difficult but vital task of bringing an ancient message into a modern context. The series not only focuses on application as a finished product but also helps you think through the *process* of moving from the original meaning of a passage to its contemporary significance. These are commentaries, not popular expositions. They are works of reference, not devotional literature.

The format of the series is designed to achieve the goals of the series. Each passage is treated in three sections: *Original Meaning, Bridging Contexts,* and *Contemporary Significance.*

THIS SECTION HELPS you understand the meaning of the biblical text in its original context. All of the elements of traditional exegesis—in concise form—are discussed here. These include the historical, literary, and cultural context of the passage. The authors discuss matters related to grammar and syntax and the meaning of biblical words.[1] They also seek to explore the main ideas of the passage and how the biblical author develops those ideas.

---

1. Please note that in general, when the authors discuss words in the original biblical languages, the series uses a general rather than a scholarly method of transliteration.

After reading this section, you will understand the problems, questions, and concerns of the *original audience* and how the biblical author addressed those issues. This understanding is foundational to any legitimate application of the text today.

*Bridging
Contexts*

THIS SECTION BUILDS a bridge between the world of the Bible and the world of today, between the original context and the contemporary context, by focusing on both the timely and timeless aspects of the text.

God's Word is *timely*. The authors of Scripture spoke to specific situations, problems, and questions. The author of Joshua encouraged the faith of his original readers by narrating the destruction of Jericho, a seemingly impregnable city, at the hands of an angry warrior God (Josh. 6). Paul warned the Galatians about the consequences of circumcision and the dangers of trying to be justified by law (Gal. 5:2–5). The author of Hebrews tried to convince his readers that Christ is superior to Moses, the Aaronic priests, and the Old Testament sacrifices. John urged his readers to "test the spirits" of those who taught a form of incipient Gnosticism (1 John 4:1–6). In each of these cases, the timely nature of Scripture enables us to hear God's Word in situations that were *concrete* rather than abstract.

Yet the timely nature of Scripture also creates problems. Our situations, difficulties, and questions are not always directly related to those faced by the people in the Bible. Therefore, God's word to them does not always seem relevant to us. For example, when was the last time someone urged you to be circumcised, claiming that it was a necessary part of justification? How many people today care whether Christ is superior to the Aaronic priests? And how can a "test" designed to expose incipient Gnosticism be of any value in a modern culture?

Fortunately, Scripture is not only timely but *timeless*. Just as God spoke to the original audience, so he still speaks to us through the pages of Scripture. Because we share a common humanity with the people of the Bible, we discover a *universal dimension* in the problems they faced and the solutions God gave them. The timeless nature of Scripture enables it to speak with power in every time and in every culture.

Those who fail to recognize that Scripture is both timely and timeless run into a host of problems. For example, those who are intimidated by timely books such as Hebrews, Galatians, or Deuteronomy might avoid reading them because they seem meaningless today. At the other extreme, those who are convinced of the timeless nature of Scripture, but who fail to discern its timely element, may "wax eloquent" about the Melchizedekian priest-hood to a sleeping congregation, or worse still, try to apply the holy wars of the Old Testament in a physical way to God's enemies today.

The purpose of this section, therefore, is to help you discern what is time-less in the timely pages of the Bible—and what is not. For example, how do the holy wars of the Old Testament relate to the spiritual warfare of the New? If Paul's primary concern is not circumcision (as he tells us in Gal. 5:6), what *is* he concerned about? If discussions about the Aaronic priesthood or Melchizedek seem irrelevant today, what is of abiding value in these passages? If people try to "test the spirits" today with a test designed for a specific first-century heresy, what other biblical test might be more appropriate?

Yet this section does not merely uncover that which is timeless in a passage but also helps you to see *how* it is uncovered. The authors of the commentaries seek to take what is implicit in the text and make it explicit, to take a process that normally is intuitive and explain it in a logical, orderly fashion. How do we know that circumcision is not Paul's primary concern? What clues in the text or its context help us realize that Paul's real concern is at a deeper level?

Of course, those passages in which the historical distance between us and the original readers is greatest require a longer treatment. Conversely, those passages in which the historical distance is smaller or seemingly nonex-istent require less attention.

One final clarification. Because this section prepares the way for dis-cussing the contemporary significance of the passage, there is not always a sharp distinction or a clear break between this section and the one that fol-lows. Yet when both sections are read together, you should have a strong sense of moving from the world of the Bible to the world of today.

THIS SECTION ALLOWS the biblical message to speak with as much power today as it did when it was first written. How can you apply what you learned about Jerusalem, Ephesus, or Corinth to our present-day needs in Chicago, Los Angeles, or London? How can you take a message originally spoken in Greek, Hebrew, and Aramaic and com-municate it clearly in our own language? How can you take the eternal truths originally spoken in a different time and culture and apply them to the sim-ilar-yet-different needs of our culture?

In order to achieve these goals, this section gives you help in several key areas.

(1) It helps you identify contemporary situations, problems, or questions that are truly comparable to those faced by the original audience. Because

contemporary situations are seldom identical to those faced by the original audience, you must seek situations that are analogous if your applications are to be relevant.

(2) This section explores a variety of contexts in which the passage might be applied today. You will look at personal applications, but you will also be encouraged to think beyond private concerns to the society and culture at large.

(3) This section will alert you to any problems or difficulties you might encounter in seeking to apply the passage. And if there are several legitimate ways to apply a passage (areas in which Christians disagree), the author will bring these to your attention and help you think through the issues involved.

In seeking to achieve these goals, the contributors to this series attempt to avoid two extremes. They avoid making such specific applications that the commentary might quickly become dated. They also avoid discussing the significance of the passage in such a general way that it fails to engage contemporary life and culture.

Above all, contributors to this series have made a diligent effort not to sound moralistic or preachy. The NIV Application Commentary Series does not seek to provide ready-made sermon materials but rather tools, ideas, and insights that will help you communicate God's Word with power. If we help you to achieve that goal, then we have fulfilled the purpose for this series.

The Editors

General Editor's Preface

THREE ELEMENTS NEED TO BE RECONCILED to one another in order to understand Paul's second letter to the Corinthians: weakness, sufficiency, and the Holy Spirit. The weakness is Paul's personal inability to succeed; the sufficiency is the fact that Paul does succeed (i.e., glorifies God) in spite of his weakness. And the Holy Spirit is the power that enables this sufficiency in spite of weakness to occur.

What Scott Hafemann shows us in his excellent commentary in the pages that follow is that in both Paul's day and ours, this argument is novel. One might even call it radical. For us, weakness is rarely seen as a precursor to sufficiency, sufficiency is almost never defined as the glorification of someone else, and the Holy Spirit, if discussed at all, is considered an occult power who, if cajoled in just the right way, facilitates health, wealth, and fame, not spiritual growth of the kind proclaimed in the gospel.

In both Paul's day and in ours the definition of each of these elements has changed and the relationship among them is skewed. Weakness, for example, is disparaged and its opposite, strength, worshiped. We consider our God-given gifts to be stored in clay jars, easily breakable and considered common by worldly standards.

Or consider sufficiency. By putting the word "self" in front of sufficiency, pride and greed replace a proper sense of self and contentment with what God faithfully provides. The message is be strong and self-reliant, not dependent on the Holy Spirit. Paul's argument and the form it takes is heavily dependent on the Holy Spirit as our source of strength.

Yet in championing his own apostleship and authority, Paul seems to violate an increasingly sacred position these days. He says with no little gusto that this is right and that is wrong. And he does more than that: He says I am right and you are wrong. In a day and age when vigorous argument is almost always called arrogant, triumphalistic, and imperialistic, Paul tramples all over what passes for total acceptance; he draws moral and doctrinal lines in the sand.

Yet Paul is not arrogant or triumphalistic. He is weak, and he suffers. What kind of argument is this? Several years ago, a colleague and I interviewed a great pastor in Brooklyn, Gardner Taylor. Dr. Taylor was selected by *Time* magazine as one of the seven greatest preachers in America, so we asked him what preaching was like. He replied it was one of the greatest joys in his life and also one of his greatest agonies. We ended up titling the interview, "The Sweet Sorrow of Sunday Morning."

General Editor's Preface

What Paul does in 2 Corinthians is to tell us how Christian ministry can be one of life's greatest joys and greatest sorrows at the same time. What he does is properly order what one might call "mis-filed feelings": joy, pathos, anger, anxiety, pain. We all experience them. There is no avoiding them. So we try to make sense of them by evaluating them against some rational principle or standard. Too often we choose the wrong standard. We mis-file our feelings.

Some of the improper standards we use are personal well-being, social success, even psychological health. According to these standards, if a feeling contributes to personal well-being, social success, or psychological health, it is good. If it does not seem to contribute to one of these three, it is bad. Paul does not claim that personal well-being, social success, and psychological health are bad. Indeed, in many ways, Paul endorses all three. But what he does say is that these are secondary, not primary evaluation tools. He insists that the primary measuring stick is the glorifying of God through whatever ministry we have. When this outside and ultimate measuring tool is used, we can see both joy and anxiety as positive contributors to ministry. Once we get our feeling filing system straight, we can understand Gardner Taylor's seemingly ambiguous feelings about his great preaching gift.

Paul can say I am right and you are wrong without being arrogant because he understands that he is weak, that he is sufficient only because the Holy Spirit works in and through him and his weaknesses to reveal God's great glory. This is a much needed message we all need to hear more regularly.

Terry C. Muck

Author's Preface

IN A REAL SENSE, I owe the writing of this commentary, under God, to my "Doktorvater," Prof. Dr. Peter Stuhlmacher, who on a late afternoon in 1980 directed me to write my doctoral thesis on "2 Corinthians 3." At the time, that is all he said. Little did I know then that this would launch me into a twenty-year study of this letter. Nor did I know what I have often read from others and experienced myself since then, that of all Paul's letters, 2 Corinthians is probably the most difficult to understand. To get to the bottom line of both its meaning and significance has not been easy. Part of the reason for this is that in these pages Paul's "pastor's heart" comes to the surface. This letter is, without a doubt, the most personal of Paul's letters. In it, Paul's theology is embedded in his passion for the gospel and in his joy and agony over those who do and do not embrace it.

Second Corinthians is a letter stained with Paul's blood, sweat, and tears. To know this letter is to be moved by Paul's life. What is most striking, however, is not what this letter reveals about Paul, but what it says about God. Even after twenty years of reading these thirteen chapters, I am still struck by the radical way in which Paul evaluates everything theologically. For him, all things derive from and relate back to the sovereign and good hand of God. This "Godward" orientation remains true whether he is speaking about his intense suffering or his change in travel plans, the coming of the new creation of the new covenant or the repentance and rebellion of the Corinthians, the collection of money for Jerusalem or the future of his own ministry. Thus, in the end, the most personal of all Paul's letters, in which his struggles and triumphs ooze out of every paragraph, becomes a letter about God. In writing this commentary, I found my own "practical atheism" constantly called into question.

Unlike the apostle Paul, I am not good at expressing my joy and gratitude for those, under God, who have extended to me their support and help. Let me take this opportunity to do so. First, and foremost, I would like to thank the many scholars and pastors who have given their lives to the study of this letter and to the study of the Bible in general, without whom I would have missed so much of what Paul is saying. There could be a thousand more footnotes in the pages that follow; as is so often the case, these scholars remain the unsung heroes of the church.

I also want to give a special word of thanks to my former teaching assistant, Chris Beetham. Chris read the manuscript carefully and checked my references. He also had words of encouragement during the long months in which I labored to put my thoughts down on paper. Chris's gentle spirit and deep faith, mixed with his genuine love for the Scriptures, kept reminding me of why such labor is worthwhile.

Another gift came from the editors of this series, who showed great patience with my slow progress and did not give up on me. Jack Kuhatschek helped me with sound advice at the end, Terry Muck encouraged me, and Verlyn Verbrugge put the finishing editorial touches on the work. Above all, I am indebted to Klyne Snodgrass, whose pages of single spaced questions forced me to rethink my conclusions one by one. The limitations and perspectives of this commentary remain my own, but my thoughts are much clearer because of his friendly and constructive criticism.

I am greatly indebted to the administration of Wheaton College and to the donors behind the Gerald F. Hawthorne Chair of New Testament Greek and Exegesis, which I am honored to occupy, for their generous support of my research and writing. I am grateful daily for this amazing provision. Thanks to Mark Talbot, a soulmate on our faculty, for our 3:15 discussions and lunches. I am also grateful to John Armstrong and to his ministry, Reformation and Revival, for their friendship and encouragement in the gospel, and for the opportunity to share aspects of this work in their conferences.

It is not merely a matter of custom to say that my wife, Debara, deserves more than a simple word of thanks. She has supported my work in so many ways that this project, like my life itself, would never have been possible without her. Her artistic and pedagogical gifts inspire me to try to be creative in my own limited ways. My two sons, John and Eric, now young men, continue to enrich my life by carving out their own. And I am sure that I owe more to my mother's daily prayers than I will know this side of eternity.

Finally, this book is dedicated with deep admiration to my friend, Paul House, a professor of the Scriptures in and for the church. In his life and life's work I have seen fleshed out what it means "to be led to death" for the sake of the gospel (cf. 2 Cor. 2:14). Friendship is a rare gift of grace. Our countless phone calls and times together down through the years (especially in the tired, third week of November) have been tools of encouragement in the hand of God. Thanks, Paul, for everything!

Scott J. Hafemann
Wheaton College
Wheaton, Illinois

Abbreviations

AB	Anchor Bible
ABD	*Anchor Bible Dictionary*
ASV	American Standard Version
BAGD	*A Greek-English Lexicon of the New Testament*, ed. W. Bauer, trans. and rev. W. F. Arndt, F. W. Gingrich, and F. W. Danker, 2d ed.
BDF	*A Greek Grammar of the New Testament*, F. Blass and A. Debrunner, trans. and rev. R. W. Funk.
BETL	Bibliotheca ephemeridum theologicarum lovaniensium
CTJ	*Calvin Theological Journal*
DPHL	*Dictionary of Paul and His Letters*, ed. G. F. Hawthorne, R. P. Martin, and D. G. Reid
HNTC	Harper New Testament Commentary
HTR	*Harvard Theological Review*
ICC	International Critical Commentary
JSNTSup	Journal for the Study of the New Testament Supplement Series
LXX	Septuagint
MT	Masoretic text of the Hebrew Old Testament
NIBC	New International Biblical Commentary
NIV	New International Version
NICNT	New International Commentary on the New Testament
NIVAC	NIV Application Commentary
NovT	*Novum Testamentum*
NRSV	New Revised Standard Version
RevExp	*Review and Expositor*
RSV	Revised Standard Version
SBJT	*Southern Baptist Journal of Theology*
SBLDS	Society of Biblical Literature Dissertation Series
SNTSMS	Society of New Testament Studies Monograph Series
TDNT	*Theological Dictionary of the New Testament*, ed. G. Kittel, trans. G. W. Bromiley
TynBul	*Tyndale Bulletin*
WBC	Word Biblical Commentary
WMANT	Wissenschaftliche Monographien zum Alten und Neuen Testament
WUNT	Wissenschaftliche Untersuchungen zum Neuen Testament
ZNW	*Zeitschrift für die neutestamentliche Wissenschaft*

Introduction

"THEOLOGICALLY DRIVEN PASSION for the purity of God's people." This, in a word, encapsulates the motivation behind the writing we call "2 Corinthians." At the same time, the letter before us is, without a doubt, the most personal of all Paul's correspondence. As a result, his last letter to the church in Corinth, more than any of his other letters, is "theology in the flesh." Still under severe attack because of his suffering and weakness, with even his identity as a Christian being called into question (cf. 10:7), Paul is now forced to defend his apostolic authority and lifestyle with all his might. In doing so, his burden is to make it clear that in his suffering he is the aroma of the crucified Christ (2:14b–16b); that in the "jar of clay" that was his weakness Paul carried the treasure of God's glory (4:6–7).

Thus, Paul fights for his authority as an apostle not for his own sake, but because the gospel itself, and hence the very life of the Corinthians, are at stake (12:19). To reject Paul's apostolic ministry is to reject Christ (2:14–16a); to refuse to see the glory of God in Paul's suffering is to reveal one's own blindness (4:4; 11:1–4). Here we see, then, in the most autobiographical of terms, that Paul's message, ministry, and manner of life are one.

All was not in turmoil, however. In the midst of his self-defense, Paul is overjoyed because of the majority in Corinth who, having spurned Paul for a season, have now repented (7:2–16). But under the continuing pressure of his opponents, those who stand with the apostle must persevere in loving God alone (6:14–7:4) and in loving their neighbor as themselves (chs. 8–9). Otherwise, they too will have "received God's grace in vain" (6:1). In defending himself, therefore, Paul is fighting not only to win back the rebellious, but also to support the repentant. The deep emotion in this letter reflects Paul's conviction that eternity is tucked between the lines of what he writes (cf. 4:13–5:10). Paul's heart is torn open, both in joy and in fear over the future (2:4; 4:13–15; 5:11; 6:11–13; 7:2–4; 12:21), since the stakes could not be higher in his "war" for legitimacy as an apostle (7:1; 10:1–6; 13:10). "Writing 2 Corinthians must have come near to breaking Paul, and . . . a church that is prepared to read it with him, and understand it, may find itself broken too."[1]

The Purpose of 2 Corinthians

THE LETTER WE call "2 Corinthians" is widely recognized as the most difficult to understand among Paul's letters. It is actually at least the *fourth* letter Paul

---

1. C. K. Barrett, *Second Epistle to the Corinthians*, vii.

wrote to his church in Corinth, together with the churches in the surrounding region of Achaia (1 Cor. 1:2; 2 Cor. 1:1; cf. Rom. 16:1): the previous letter mentioned in 1 Corinthians 5:9, canonical 1 Corinthians itself, the tearful, severe letter referred to in 2 Corinthians 2:3–4, and canonical 2 Corinthians.[2] More importantly, these letters reflect that Paul had stayed in touch with his churches in and around Corinth and knew well their history, character, and problems. After his initial stay in Corinth for a year and a half, during which he founded the church (cf. 1 Cor. 4:14–15; 2 Cor. 10:13–14; cf. Acts 18:1–17), Paul continued on as their "father" in the faith from afar. First Corinthians is a product of this pastoral concern. Written in the spring of A.D. 54 or 55, approximately three years after Paul's founding visit, it provides the most detailed example of the way in which Paul applied his theological convictions to the practical problems of the church (for Paul, practice and profession are inextricably linked!).

At the time he wrote 1 Corinthians, Paul intended to return to Corinth after his stay in Ephesus and after passing through Macedonia, to proceed from Corinth to Jerusalem with the collection (cf. 1 Cor. 16:5–9). In the meantime, he sent Timothy to visit the Corinthians on his behalf (16:10–11; cf. Acts 19:22). Upon his arrival, Timothy found that the problems in Corinth had escalated, most probably a result of the recent appearance of Paul's opponents from outside the city. In response, Paul decided to visit Corinth immediately himself in order to shore up the church, after which he would go on to Macedonia and then return for a second visit en route to Jerusalem (the double "benefit" of 2 Cor. 1:15–16). At this point, Paul assumed that once in Corinth, his holy and sincere conduct toward the Corinthians would be vindicated (1:15a). Nothing could have been further from the truth.

When he arrived for what soon became a very "painful visit" (2:1), the church called into question Paul's authority and gospel, while one of its leaders severely attacked Paul himself (cf. 2:1, 5–8; 7:8–13; 11:4). Indeed, the false teaching of Paul's opponents had led a great number, if not most, of the Corinthians to accept another view of Jesus, a contrary spirit, and hence a different gospel altogether (cf. 11:4)! So, faced with this confrontation to his ministry, Paul left Corinth and returned to Ephesus in the midst of a large-scale rebellion against his apostolic authority (1:23–2:5; 7:12), determined not to make another "painful visit" (2:1–2).

---

2. What follows is an adaptation of my "Corinthians, Letters to the," *DPHL*, 164–79, which includes a summary of the contents of 1 and 2 Corinthians, section by section. See too the helpful introduction by Craig Blomberg, *1 Corinthians* (NIVAC; Grand Rapids: Zondervan, 1994), 17–27.

Paul's leaving, however, was not the act of a weak coward, as the false apostles no doubt portrayed it (cf. 10:10–11; 11:20–21). Far from being scared by his opponents, Paul suffered humiliation without retaliating, in order to extend mercy to the Corinthians (1:23–24). Once in Ephesus, and still distraught over the plight of his spiritual children, Paul sent Titus back to Corinth with a tearful and severe letter in which he warned the Corinthians of God's judgment and called them to repent (2:3–4; 7:8–16).

After Titus left for Corinth, Paul himself went on to Troas to pursue his own ministry and to wait for Titus to return with news about the church. But when Titus delayed in returning, Paul feared both for Titus's safety and for the condition of the Corinthians. Filled with anxiety, Paul left the open door he had in Troas and went on to Macedonia to find Titus (2 Cor. 2:12–13). There he met Titus and received the joyful news that God had used his letter written "with many tears" (2:4) to bring about the repentance of the majority of the church (2:5–11; 7:5–16). Unfortunately, Paul also heard that, under the continuing influence of his opponents, there was still a rebellious minority who continued to reject Paul's authority. In response, Paul wrote "2 Corinthians" from Macedonia, a year or so after the writing of 1 Corinthians (ca. A.D. 55/56), and began to make final plans to return to Corinth for his "third visit" (2 Cor. 12:14; 13:1).

As a result, whereas in 1 Corinthians we see Paul the pastor, striving to fill in the cracks in the Corinthians' way of life, in 2 Corinthians we encounter Paul the apologist, fighting for the legitimacy of his own apostolic ministry. His goal in doing so, because of his confidence in the power of the Spirit in those in whom Christ dwells (cf. 2 Cor. 3:18; 5:17; 13:1–5), is to give the rebellious one more chance to repent, thereby showing that they are in fact a new creation (5:16–6:2). Thus, like Paul's earlier tearful letter, 2 Corinthians aims, yet again, at the repentance of those who have accepted a different gospel in order to spare them God's judgment (cf. 2:9; 10:6; 12:19; 13:1–10). At the same time, Paul's apology provides an opportunity for those who have already repented to demonstrate the genuine nature of their faith (6:14–7:4). Specifically, he calls the repentant to separate from the unbelievers in their midst and to participate in the collection for Jerusalem (6:14–7:4; 8:1–9:15).

This dual purpose explains the mixed nature of 2 Corinthians. In it, Paul strengthens the repentant majority, while at the same time seeking to win back the resistant minority. Moreover, behind the Corinthians stand Paul's opponents, whom he addresses indirectly throughout his letter as the immediate source of the current problem. His goal in writing is to prepare for his upcoming visit to the Corinthians, at which time he will punish those who persist in rejecting him and his gospel (6:1; 10:6–8; 13:1–10). This is their last chance to repent, just as Paul's letter also provides a concrete opportunity for those who have already repented to demonstrate their faith.

As part of the ongoing history of the Corinthian church's stormy relationship with Paul, her apostle, 2 Corinthians is anything but an abstract treatise written into a vacuum. Neither is it merely an expression of "practical theology" aimed at the "bottom line." It is simply impossible to divorce Paul the theologian from Paul the missionary pastor. But neither is it adequate to speak of Paul as a theologian *and* a missionary, as if Paul's theological reflection and pastoral ministry operated out of two separate spheres. As we will see throughout this letter, his apostolic ministry and his reflections on the history of redemption form an inseparable unity. As Peter O'Brien has observed:

> The notion that Paul was both a missionary and a theologian has gained ground among biblical scholars.... Yet Paul's theology and mission do not simply relate to each other as "theory" to "practice." It is not as though his mission is the practical outworking of his theology. Rather, his mission is "integrally related to his identity and thought," and his theology is a missionary theology.[3]

Paul was a theologically driven missionary and a missiologically driven theologian. His theology was missiological and his missionary endeavors were theological.

The History and People of Corinth

FIRST-CENTURY CORINTH WAS located at the bottom of a 1,886-foot hill, called the "Acrocorinth," on the southern side of the four-and-a-half mile isthmus that connected the Peloponnesus with the rest of Greece, thereby separating the Saronic and Corinthian gulfs. Corinth thus controlled part of the overland movement between Italy and Asia, as well as the traffic between the two ports of Lechaeum, one and a half miles to the north, and Cenchrea, five and a half miles to the east, a portage that made it possible to avoid sailing the treacherous waters around the Peloponnesus. As a result, its location was strategic militarily and profitable commercially. Ever since the sixth century B.C., a paved road existed across the isthmus, making Corinth a wealthy city because of its tariffs and commerce and a crossroads for the ideas and traffic of the world (cf. Strabo, *Geography* 8.6.20–23).

The history of ancient Corinth is really the history of two cities. As a political entity, Corinth goes back to the eighth century B.C., and it flourished as

---

3. Peter T. O'Brien, *Consumed by Passion, Paul and the Dynamic of the Gospel* (Homebush West, NSW: Lancer Books, 1993), 62.

a Greek city-state until 146 B.C., when it was destroyed by Rome. Corinth lay in ruins for more than a century, until Julius Caesar reestablished the city in 44 B.C. as a Roman colony, after which it once again quickly rose to prominence (cf. Appian, *Roman History* 8.136). By the first century, "Roman Corinth had roughly eighty thousand people with an additional twenty thousand in nearby rural areas.... In Paul's day, it was probably the wealthiest city in Greece and a major, multicultural urban center."[4] Beginning in 27 B.C., it was also the seat of the region's proconsul, and it was the capital of the senatorial province of Achaia until A.D. 15, when the region became an imperial province. Hence, Corinth soon became the third most important city of the empire, behind only Rome and Alexandria in status.

After Corinth had been reestablished as a Roman city, it experienced a rapid influx of people. In addition to the military veterans and those from the lower classes who moved to Corinth because of the infant city's new economic and social opportunities, the largest group of new settlers came from among the "freedmen" from Rome, whose status as manumitted servants would have remained just above that of a slave. The repopulation of Corinth consequently provided Rome with a way to ease her overcrowding and the new settlers with new possibilities for upward mobility. Corinth also boasted a significant community of Jews, who exercised the right to govern their own internal affairs (cf. Acts 18:8, 17). Philo lists Corinth as one of the cities of the Jewish Diaspora (cf. *On the Embassy to Gaius* 281–282), and scholars have discovered a lintel inscribed with the words, "Synagogue of the Hebrews," on the ruins of a synagogue in the city, though its date cannot be determined with certainty.[5]

Thus, by Paul's day, Corinth had become a pluralistic melting pot of subcultures, philosophies, lifestyles, and religions. This is reflected in the various Jewish, Roman, and Greek names mentioned in 1 and 2 Corinthians (e.g., the Jews: Aquila, Priscilla, Crispus; the Romans: Fortunas, Quartus, Justus, etc.; the Greeks: Stephanus, Achaicus, Erastus). And we know from 1 Cor. 7:20–24 that some of the believers in Corinth were still slaves. However, most of the church was apparently from the middle, working classes of tradesmen, with only a few wealthy families (cf. 1:26–27). Nevertheless, since no landed aristocracy existed in Roman Corinth, an "aristocracy of

---

4. Blomberg, *1 Corinthians*, 19 (following the work of Donald Engels, *Roman Corinth* [Chicago: Univ. of Chicago Press, 1990], 84). This will become an important point when Paul uses the generosity of the much poorer Macedonians as an example for the Corinthians (cf. 8:1–7; 9:1–5)!

5. Jerome Murphy-O'Connor, *St. Paul's Corinth: Texts and Archaeology* (Wilmington, Del.: Michael Glazier, 1983), 79. This text is the most accessible collection of the relevant material concerning the history and culture of Corinth in Paul's day.

money" soon developed (both among those who had wealth and those who wanted it!), with a fiercely independent spirit.

The resultant class distinctions based on acquired wealth, not birth, are reflected in the social tensions that came to a head during the celebration of the Lord's Supper (1 Cor. 11:17–34). Corinth was a free-wheeling "boom town," filled with the materialism, pride, and self-confidence that come with having made it in a new place and with a new social identity. The "pull-your-self-up-by-your-own-bootstraps" mentality that would become so characteristic of the American frontier filled the air.

Thus, Corinth's place and people combined to create a diverse public life that pulsated with all that the ancient world had to offer. Although Roman law, culture, and religion dominated in Corinth, and Latin was the city's official language, Greek traditions and philosophies, together with the mystery cults from Egypt and Asia, were also strongly represented (cf. 1 Cor. 1:20–22). For example, Diogenes, the founder of the Cynics, was associated with Corinth and Craneum, a residential area near it. Indeed, it is judged that Corinth was "the most thoroughly Hellenistic city in the NT."[6]

In addition to this, there was the city's ever-present entertainment and sports culture, with its love of public rhetoric and human achievement. The Corinthian theater in Paul's day held 14,000–18,000 people, the concert hall, 3,000, while the thoroughfares of the city saw the constant ebb and flow of street-corner philosophers. Among the three hundred athletic games held every year throughout Greece, the Isthmian Games, celebrated biennially in Corinth, were second only to the Olympics in size and prestige. At the same time, as can be expected in a city that was a seaport, entertainment center, and sports capital all in one, with its teeming tourists and travelers, Corinth had its share of sexual immorality and vice.[7] First Corinthians 5:1–2; 6:9–20; and 2 Corinthians 12:21 reflect just such an atmosphere.

---

6. Gordon D. Fee, *The First Epistle to the Corinthians* (NICNT; Grand Rapids: Eerdmans, 1987), 4n.12.

7. This was nothing new. As a wealthy hub for commerce and seafarers, Greek Corinth was renowned for its vice, especially its sexual corruption. In view of the city's reputation, Aristophanes (ca. 450–385 B.C.) even coined the term *korinthiazo* (i.e., to act like a Corinthian, which meant to commit fornication), and Plato used the term "Corinthian girl" as an euphemism for a prostitute (Murphy-O'Connor, *St. Paul's Corinth*, 56). Although its historical accuracy is disputed, Strabo's account of a thousand prostitutes in the temple of Aphrodite does reflect the city's image, in which the many temples played their own role in the immoral tenor of its life (cf. *Geography* 8.6.20, first written in 7 B.C. and revised slightly in A.D. 18). While the texts reflecting the widespread sexual immorality that characterized Greek Corinth cannot be taken to apply directly to the Corinth of Paul's day, certainly such a problem also came to be prevalent in the new, Roman city.

Right in the middle of all of this were the ubiquitous religious sites that filled first-century Corinth (cf. 1 Cor. 8:4–6; 10:14, 20–30). Pausanias (d. ca. A.D. 180), who gives us our earliest guide book to Corinth in his *Description of Greece*, Book 2, refers to at least twenty-six sacred places for the Greco-Roman pantheon and mystery cults alone. Archaeologists have unearthed physical evidence of no less than thirty-four different deities among the ruins of the city. For the time of Paul, this includes a temple of Fortune and temples or shrines to Neptune, Apollo, Arphrodite (on the Acrocorinth), Venus, Octavia, Asclepius, Demeter, Core, and Poseidon. Pluralism in North America pales in comparison to Paul's experience in Corinth.

Christ Confronts Culture in Corinth

AGAINST THIS BACKDROP, Timothy Savage has analyzed how Paul and his ministry would have been viewed in Corinth by outlining the ways in which contemporary Greco-Roman culture evaluated social status and the significance of religion for everyday life.[8] In regard to sizing up one's peers, Savage observes that in Paul's day Greco-Roman society stressed (1) a rugged individualism that valued self-sufficiency; (2) wealth as the key to status within society; (3) a self-display of one's accomplishments and possessions in order to win praise from others; (4) a competition for honor that viewed boasting as its natural corollary; and (5) a pride in one's neighborhood as a reflection of one's social location. These values combined to create a populace for which self-appreciation became the goal and self-gratification the reward.

In addition, since one-third of urban populations in Paul's day was indigent or slaves, and only one percent belonged to the aristocracy by birth, the large "middle class" could move up within the social scale primarily through acquiring wealth. Hence, the drive for upward social mobility by advancing economically became the obsession of the middle class. It could even be said that it worshiped wealth. For with wealth came the other significant markers of social advancement, such as reputation, occupation, neighborhood, education, religious status, political involvement, and athletic achievement. In short, the culture was openly materialistic in its quest for praise and esteem. Unfortunately, in reading such a description we are not sure whether we are hearing about life in Corinth in the first century, or about life in the Western world today, even within most middle class, evangelical churches!

The corollary to this search for status was that superstition and magic dominated Greco-Roman religious practice. There was little emphasis on

---

8. See his *Power Through Weakness*, 19–53.

doctrine or learning in the religions of Paul's day, and little mention of the after-life. "Salvation" was defined primarily in terms of provision and protection for the present. The motivation for participating in "organized religion" was the promise it held for health, wealth, and social standing. In turn, the value of a religion was measured by the amount of "power" displayed by the deity, as seen through the consequent cultural, physical, and economic power of its followers. The various religions attracted followers by providing visible displays of their gods at work, as seen in the "success" of their members. "The more powerful one's god the more strength one expected to receive and manifest."[9] In the same way, on the popular level orators gained a following not primarily by virtue of their content, but by their ability to captivate their audiences with powerful and entertaining deliveries. In Savage's words, "They honoured the one who preached with flair, force and pride."[10]

In such a milieu, the vast majority of religious people had little or no theology and no interest in gaining any more. For all intents and purposes, their religion remained contentless, apart from the rituals needed to influence the deity. Consequently, since religion was not driven by ideas but by experience, there was little friction between the various cults and temples. Toleration was practiced, since all religious experience was fundamentally the same. Most people sought salvation from suffering now, power in daily life, and entertainment.

As a group, first-century worshipers, regardless of their religious affiliation, wanted "health, wealth, protection and sustenance, not moral transformation."[11] Religious services, like other social gatherings, were simply ways to gain fellowship, especially as they revolved around lavish banquets. Indeed, regardless of one's religion of choice, "the cults seemed to exact little appreciable change in a convert's manner of life . . . religion served not as a critic of, but as a warrant for, society. It uplifted, entertained, prospered and confirmed those it was designated to serve."[12]

All of these cultural trends were intensified in Corinth (as they are in the Western world), since Corinth was the young and prosperous "New York, Los Angeles, and Las Vegas of the ancient world,"[13] where old money and family connections meant little and where social location and status meant every-

---

9. Ibid., 29.

10. Ibid., 34.

11. Ibid. The point of the cults was not the doctrine of the religion. As Savage puts it, "It mattered little who the gods were or what the cults taught. What was important was . . . whether everyday desires for health, wealth and safety and, more importantly, power and esteem, were being fulfilled" (52).

12. Ibid., 34.

13. Blomberg, *1 Corinthians*, 20 (quoting Fee, *First Corinthians*, 1987, 3).

thing. The "self-made" Roman "freedmen," who had applied the hard labor of their former slave status to the business of making it in this new Roman colony, were known for being crassly materialistic, self-confident, and proud. The atmosphere of sports that filled the air with its pride, competition, and exaltation of heroes, not to mention that Corinth was the entertainment center of Greece, exacerbated all of this.

> Corinth had become the envy of the Empire—a city of pleasure, a tribute to human-made splendour, a place where assertiveness and pride reaped great reward. . . . Consequently, [the Corinthians] placed a *higher* premium on social prominence and self-display, on personal power and boasting. . . . In Corinth, perhaps more than elsewhere, people looked to the cults for satisfaction, and satisfaction as they defined it, as personal exaltation and glory.[14]

Into this world God sent Paul to suffer as an apostle of the crucified Christ, carrying his treasure in a "jar of clay" (4:7). As such, Paul's message and life were an affront to Hellenistic Jews and Gentiles. The materialism and self-serving individualism that dominated Corinth, together with the reigning pluralism and status-oriented civil religion of the day, all fueled by the self-glorifying entertainment and sports subculture, presented a formidable front for the gospel of the cross and for its cruciform messenger (cf. 1 Cor. 1:17–19 with 2 Cor. 2:14–17).

Thus, both in founding the church and in pastoring it thereafter, Paul had to deal head-on with the social identity that Corinth's history had created. Though culturally Corinthian, Paul no longer viewed the Corinthian Christians "from a worldly point of view" (2 Cor. 5:16). Instead, they were a "new creation" in Christ, who "no longer live for themselves but for him who died for them and was raised again" (5:15, 17). But the Corinthians came from a powerfully attractive culture that, for all its diversity, centered on the worldly desire for security and social status. As both 1 and 2 Corinthians make clear, the church in this city had a difficult time being in the world, but not of it.

Driven by their culture, the key issue in the Corinthian church was what it meant to be "spiritual."[15] Filled with the Spirit, but still heavily influenced by their society, the Corinthians were prone to intellectual pride. Instead of seeking a Spirit-empowered conformity to the self-giving character of Christ,

---

14. Savage, *Power Through Weakness*, 52 (emphasis his).

15. Cf. Paul's use of *pneumatikos* ("spiritual") 14 times in 1 Corinthians alone, over against only 4 times in the other undisputed Pauline letters, and the centrality of the new covenant "ministry of the Spirit," as outlined in 2 Cor. 3:1–18, for the argument of the present letter.

they placed a high value on their newfound "knowledge" and spiritual experiences in and of themselves (cf. 1 Cor. 1:5; 4:7; 8:1, 7, 10, 11; 12:8; 13:2; etc.).

The result was a self-serving attitude of boasting and moral laxity, further fed by their culture's admiration of the public power, persona, and polish of the Sophist rhetorical tradition.[16] They buttressed this cultural captivity of the gospel with a triumphalist, "over-realized eschatology." From this perspective, the Corinthians misinterpreted the coming of the kingdom of God, the resurrection power of the Holy Spirit, and the dawning of the *new* age of the *new* creation under the *new* covenant in terms of a super-spirituality in which believers viewed themselves as *already* participating in the fullness of the heavenly reality still to come. Such a view further inflated the Corinthians' estimation of their spiritual knowledge, gifts, and experiences, especially that of tongues, which they viewed as indicating that they were already sharing in the spiritual existence of the angels (cf. 1 Cor. 13:1). It also downplayed the need for moral transformation, since on the "spiritual" plane they were already fully raised with Christ.

The Situation in Corinth

AS A RESULT, life in Corinth and the Corinthians' previous spiritual problems provided the cultural and religious seedbed for the subsequent, tragic influence of Paul's opponents. With their "health and wealth" gospel and public image of strength and power, these "false apostles" and "servants of Satan" (11:13–15) capitalized on the Corinthian "middle class" love of money and prestige, on their self-understanding as "super-spiritual," and on their desire for self-aggrandizing spiritual experiences.

Another reason it was so difficult to meet the challenge posed against the gospel in Corinth was that "the church" in Corinth and in the surrounding villages of Achaia actually met in small groups in various houses (cf. 1 Cor. 16:19; also Rom. 16:5, 23; Col. 4:15; Phlm. 2). There was no possibility for a newly constituted religious movement that still lacked government recognition to secure a public meeting place. Though often romanticized today, these house churches made it difficult to respond with one voice to

---

16. The Sophists were a movement that stressed philosophy for the masses and made much of the form and persuasive power of rhetoric as the expression of their "wisdom," priding themselves on the public appeal, social status, influence, and acclaim to be garnered through the masterful display of rhetorical prowess. For two significant studies of this background and its impact on the problems in Corinth and on Paul's response, see Duane Litfin, *St. Paul's Theology of Proclamation: 1 Corinthians 1–4 and Greco-Roman Rhetoric* (SNTSMS 79; Cambridge: Cambridge Univ. Press, 1994), and Bruce W. Winter, *Philo and Paul among the Sophists* (SNTSMS 96; Cambridge: Cambridge Univ. Press, 1997).

the various concerns and rumors that were dispersed throughout the various groups.[17]

As pointed out above, Paul's purpose in writing the present letter of 2 Corinthians to this network of small groups was vastly different than the motivation behind 1 Corinthians. Unlike 2 Corinthians, Paul's intention in 1 Corinthians was not primarily apologetic, but *didactic*.[18] In writing 1 Corinthians Paul continues to bank on the fact that the Corinthians recognize him as their founder and as a legitimate apostle, even though others might not (1 Cor. 4:15; 9:1–2). So Paul writes to "remind" the Corinthians of "my way of life in Christ" (4:17) and to call their attention to the fact that, as their "father" (4:15), it is his way—that is, the way of the cross—that is to be imitated (4:16; 11:1).

The appropriateness of Paul's suffering is therefore nowhere defended in 1 Corinthians. Instead, his suffering, including that which comes from his commitment to support himself in Corinth, functions as a foundational premise for his arguments,[19] which are applied to the Corinthians on the basis of his parental authority over them in Christ (1 Cor. 4:14–21; 9:3–23; 11:1). Throughout 1 Corinthians, the focus of Paul's arguments is on the Corinthians and their behavior, not on his own legitimacy. The mode of his address is directive, not apologetic. The problems that 1 Corinthians addresses are essentially *within* the church, not between the church and her apostle.

By the time of 2 Corinthians, however, Paul's opponents had arrived from outside Corinth, preaching a view of Christ and the Spirit that the Corinthians wanted to hear (2 Cor. 11:4). Instead of calling the Corinthians

---

17. Based on the excavation of the four houses in Corinth from the Roman period (one from Paul's time) and the listing of the fourteen male members of the church in 1 and 2 Corinthians, Murphy-O'Connor, *St. Paul's Corinth*, 158, estimates the base figure of the Corinthian church to be fifty members, though it may have been much larger, since larger villas certainly existed in the city.

18. Contra Fee, whose excellent commentary represents a thoroughgoing presentation of the "apologetic" view of the problem behind 1 Corinthians. In this view, the historical situation behind 1 Corinthians, like that of 2 Corinthians, was also fundamentally one of conflict between Paul and the church as a whole. Hence, the heart of the problem is taken to be the Corinthians' rejection of Paul's authority as the founder of the church. The letter as a whole is therefore taken to be combative, and Paul's references to his apostleship are seen to be apologetic (cf. esp. 1 Cor. 4:1–21; 9:1–27; 15:8–11).

19. Paul's argument seems to go like this: He is a true apostle; he preaches the cross of the resurrected Christ and suffers for the sake of others; therefore his experience makes it clear that the kingdom of God, though here in power, is not yet here in all its fullness, and that true spirituality involves the willingness to give up one's own rights for the good of others. Hence, Paul's most basic advice is to "imitate me" (1 Cor. 4:16; 11:1; cf. 1:17–19; 8:1–3, 11–13; 9:15–23; 10:23–24; 10:31–11:1; 13; 14:4–5, 18–19).

to a life of faithful endurance and love in the midst of adversity, Paul's opponents promised them deliverance from suffering and a steady diet of spiritual experiences. Instead of demonstrating the fruit of the Spirit in their own lives, they supported their claims to be true apostles with letters of recommendation from other churches (cf. 3:1), by trumpeting their ethnic heritage as Jews (3:4–18; 11:21–22), by displaying professional rhetorical flash (10:10; 11:6), and by boasting in their spiritual experiences and supernatural signs (10:12; 11:12, 18; 12:12).

Furthermore, Paul's apologetic in 3:3–18 suggests that they also tied their ministry in some way to the ministry of Moses, although, unlike in Galatians, the issues of ritual purity, circumcision, and the law itself are not explicitly mentioned in 2 Corinthians. Finally, Paul's opponents sealed their claims by demanding money from the Corinthians as evidence of the value of their message (2:17; 11:19–21). In order to make these claims and demand this payment, they had to attack Paul, since his message and manner of ministry called into question their "gospel," their lifestyle, their grounds for boasting, their demand for money, and their desire to receive letters of recommendation from the Corinthians (cf. 2:14–3:3; 10:12–18; 11:10–12; 12:11–16).

Hence, at the writing of 2 Corinthians, Paul finds himself in a new situation: His own legitimacy as an apostle has been severely called into question and is still being doubted by a significant minority within the church. Under the influence of his opponents, many in the church have come to believe that Paul simply suffers too much personally and that he is too weak and unimpressive in his public manner to be a Spirit-filled apostle. To make matters worse, the apparent shame brought to the church because of Paul's practice of self-support (cf. 11:7–9), his seemingly fickle change of plans—not once, but three times (cf. 1:12–2:4; 2:12–13)—and the suspicion that he preached for free as part of a scam in which he was using the collection to line his own pockets (cf. 8:16–24; 12:16–18), all appear to support this conclusion. Consequently, by the time Paul writes 2 Corinthians, his apostolic authority is no longer common ground between him and his church as a whole. The church stands divided over Paul and his legitimacy as an apostle.

Some Critical Questions

Authorship

BOTH 1 AND 2 Corinthians are attributed to Paul in their salutations and show every historical and literary evidence of Pauline authorship. Although 2 Corinthians is not clearly documented until Marcion's canon (A.D. 140), it is undisputed as part of the Pauline corpus. Even the most critical scholarship has consistently accepted 2 Corinthians as genuine. The only exception is

6:14–7:1, whose distinct vocabulary and subject matter have led some to conclude that it derives from a Jewish source (often associated with Qumran documents), or from a Jewish-Christian tradition. However, its unique character is more likely determined simply by the string of Old Testament texts that Paul quotes in this section (see comments on this section). Even if it were an interpolation, Paul or some other editor has integrated this passage fully into the train of thought of 2 Corinthians.

The Unity of 2 Corinthians

BESIDES THE QUESTION of 6:14–7:1, the literary unity of 2 Corinthians as a whole has also been disputed because of the seemingly abrupt transitions and change of subject matter within the letter. The majority of scholars argue that 2 Corinthians is a composite document of at least two or more Pauline fragments that were written at different times and later amalgamated into a single letter. The key issues are the apparent breaks in thought between 2:13 and 2:14 and between 7:4 and 5, and between 6:13 and 14 and between 7:1 and 2; the seemingly separate treatments of the collection in chapters 8 and 9; and the distinct nature of 10:1–13:14. If each of these transitions marks out a separate document, 2 Corinthians becomes a composite of as many as six fragments: 1:1–2:13 and 7:5–16; 2:14–6:13; 6:14–7:1; chapter 8; chapter 9; and chapters 10–13!

In line with this partition theory, scholars have sought to assign these various fragments to the history of Paul's interaction with the Corinthians. For example, some view chapters 10–13 to be part of the "tearful letter"; 2:14–6:13 to be part of a lost letter of defense; 1:1–2:13 and 7:5–16 to be Paul's letter of reconciliation after Titus' report; and 6:14–7:1 to be part of yet another lost Pauline writing, part of the "tearful letter," or even part of the "previous letter" of 1 Corinthians 5:9. The growing consensus, however, is that 2 Corinthians 1–9 (minus perhaps 6:14–7:1) is a unified composition written after Paul's encounter with Titus (cf. 7:5–13). Chapters 10–13 are taken as part of a subsequent work, now otherwise completely lost, which was written after a fresh outbreak of trouble in Corinth or in response to Paul's reception of further information about the situation. It was then appended to the previous section at some time early on in the history of these traditions.[20]

---

20. Hence, because V. Furnish, *II Corinthians*, 397, views chapters 10–13 to be a response to subsequent events, he must conclude that Paul's encouragement and Titus's joy over the Corinthians in chapter 7 were "probably a false perception, whether due to Titus's overly optimistic report or to Paul's overly optimistic interpretation of that report." According to Furnish, 7:16 could not have stood in the same letter as the "worried polemic of chaps. 10–13" (p. 398).

However, a minority of scholars still maintains the literary unity of the entire letter. This is the position taken here. There is no manuscript evidence that 2 Corinthians ever contained less than or more than its present content or that its sections were ever in any other order than they are now. Nevertheless, the question of the integrity of the letter is, in the end, an exegetical one. In order to defend the unity of the letter, we must be able to explain the nature of the transitions at each point in the letter. In doing so, we will argue that the transitions make sense internally and that the changes in subject matter throughout 2 Corinthians are the result of the mixed nature of the Corinthian community.[21] Moreover, James Scott has observed a basic, chronological progression within 2 Corinthians: Chapters 1–7 reflect on past events, chapters 8–9 prepare for the completion of the collection in the present, and chapters 10–13 look forward to Paul's third visit in the future.[22]

Within this framework, Paul begins with a prologue, setting forth the main theme and points of the letter (1:3–11), reviews his past history with the Corinthians (1:12–2:11), and then sets forth the most extensive apologetic for the legitimacy of his apostolic ministry found anywhere in his letters (2:12–7:1). On this basis, Paul then draws out the implications of his apologetic, first for the repentant (7:2–9:15), and then for the rebellious (10:1–13:10). Thus, although each of three main sections prepares for Paul's third visit in some way, in chapters 10–13 Paul confronts head-on the persistent problem posed by the arrival of his opponents. The ambassador of reconciliation (cf. 5:18–6:2) becomes the warrior against those still in rebellion (cf. 10:1–6). Just as 8:1–9:15 is Paul's application of his previous arguments to the repentant (with one eye on the rebellious), chapters 10–13 present Paul's final appeal to the rebellious (with one eye on the repentant).[23] The

---

21. Against the theory that chs. 10–13 were originally part of the tearful letter, this section contains no instruction to punish the offenders, nor do chapters 1–7 anticipate that the offenders have all been judged already, as chs. 10–13 anticipates. Against the theory that chs. 10–13 were written after 1–9, there is no mention in chs. 10–13 that Paul had received more information from Corinth, that there had been a significant period of time between chs. 1–9 and 10–13, or that the situation had worsened, which those who hold this view must assume. Thus, Scott, *2 Corinthians*, 7, is right that, as a matter of principle, "a historical reconstruction that can operate with the unity of 2 Cor. has the advantage over partition theories, since it works with fewer unknowns."

22. Ibid., 208–9.

23. In support of this reading, Ben Witherington III, *Conflict and Community in Corinth*, 430–32, offers a rhetorical argument for the unity of 2 Corinthians. Witherington points out that the issue of Paul's opponents and their charges that is taken up directly in chs. 10–13 was already insinuated in chs. 1–9. Indeed, there are already nine such allusions to Paul's opponents in chapters 1–9 (the charge of fickleness in chapter 1; 2:17; 3:1; the use of Moses by his opponents as reflected in 3:7–18; 4:2; 5:12; 6:3; 6:4–10; 7:2). Thus, the con-

complex character of 2 Corinthians derives from the fact that in chapters 1–9 the repentant are addressed directly and the rebellious indirectly, whereas in chapters 10–13 the opposite is the case.

Paul's Opponents

IT IS APPARENT that the identity and theology of Paul's opponents played a strategic role in the writing of 2 Corinthians. The key passages for identifying Paul's opponents have traditionally been 3:1–18; 11:4; and 11:22–23. From these texts it is clear that they were Jews familiar with the Hellenistic world and its values and that they relied on their own ethnic and spiritual heritage as Jews. Beyond this bare sketch, however, the exact identity and theology of the opponents must remain a matter of scholarly reconstruction, since 2 Corinthians itself provides our only available evidence, and it is all secondhand.

Scholars have offered three basic theories concerning the identity of Paul's opposition in 2 Corinthians, arrived at for the most part by a "mirror reading" of his letter. That is to say, Paul's arguments are seen to be a direct contrast or mirror image of the positions taken by his opponents. As a result, Paul's opponents have been identified as gnostics, as legalistic Judaizers on a par with those fought elsewhere by Paul, or as super-charismatics or "divine men" who represented a mixture of legalistic and pneumatic elements of various persuasions.

Given the circularity and subjectivity of these past approaches and its resultant stalemate in recent scholarship, Sumney's proposal of a "minimalist approach" to identifying Paul's opponents is to be welcomed. Sumney rightly emphasizes a "text-focused method," with a "stringently" limited application of the "mirror technique," rejecting all attempts to approach 2 Corinthians with a previously determined, externally based reconstruction of the nature of Paul's opposition.[24] We must start with what we have (i.e., Paul's text) before trying to reconstruct what we do not have (i.e., a picture

---

tention that the situation described in chs. 1–9 *differs* from that in chs. 10–13 fails (p. 431n.5). Moreover, the difference in tone between chs. 1–9 and 10–13 merely reflects a common rhetorical strategy in which one invokes strong emotion at the end in order to make a lasting impression on one's audience. Finally, Witherington points to the work of Bjerkeland, who observed that those sections of Paul's letters in which he exhorts his readers using the verb *parakaleo* regularly follow thanksgivings or doxologies (cf. Rom. 11:33–36 to 12:1; 1 Thess. 3:11–13 to 4:1). In accordance with this pattern, Paul's exhortation in 10:1 follows naturally on the praise of 9:12–15.

24. Jerry L. Sumney, *Identifying Paul's Opponents*. When Sumney applies his own method to the text, he ends up agreeing in substance with the previous proposal of Käsemann that the opponents behind 2 Cor. 10–13 were pneumatics rather than Judaizers, gnostics, or self-styled "divine men." Moreover, the short time span between the letter fragments of 1–9 and 10–13 leads one to "reasonably conclude" that the opponents in both cases are part of the same group (p. 183).

of Paul's opponents). The absence of direct evidence from Paul's opponents renders all attempts to *begin* by reconstructing the identity of Paul's opposition, based on a few tips from 2 Corinthians itself, and then using this reconstruction to interpret 2 Corinthians, uncontrollably circular.

Following Sumney's admonition, a close reading of 2 Corinthians itself leads at least to the following fundamental fact: The concern of Paul's opponents with their Jewish heritage was inextricably tied to their promise of providing what they considered a more powerful experience of the Spirit than that found in Paul's gospel. The artificial divorce between the law and the Spirit, which has led scholars to posit two distinct types of opponents behind Paul's letters (e.g., Judaizers behind Galatians and some kind of pneumatics behind 1 Corinthians), must therefore be overcome. The question raised by Paul's opponents, based on their Jewish heritage, was essentially the same one being raised by the Corinthians, based on their Hellenistic worldview: How does one participate fully in the power of the Spirit?

The opponents' answer to this question was based on a theology of "over-realized glory," in which participation in their gospel, with its tie to the old covenant, was said to grant freedom from suffering. From their perspective, being a member of the new covenant *and a Jew* was the key to experiencing the full spiritual blessing that God has for his people. This meant that for the Gentiles to become full-fledged members of God's people they had to trust in Jesus as the Jewish Messiah *and* become part of God's chosen people, Israel, in accordance with the Sinai covenant. Only then could they expect to experience God's covenant promises completely. What made such an appeal to Judaism attractive, therefore, was its promise of more of the Spirit. As a result, the debate between Paul and his opponents centered on the relationship between the old and new covenants as this came to expression in the ministry of Moses in comparison to Paul's ministry as an apostle of Christ and mediator of the Spirit (cf. 2:16b; 3:4–18).

The Central Theme of 2 Corinthians

AS THE COROLLARY to this reconstruction, a close reading of the text also makes clear that the central theological theme of 2 Corinthians is the relationship between suffering and the power of the Spirit in Paul's apostolic experience. Paul's point concerning this theme is as simple as it is profound. Rather than calling his sufficiency into question, Paul's suffering is the revelatory vehicle through which the knowledge of God manifest in the cross of Christ and in the power of the Spirit is being disclosed.[25] The clearest direct

---

25. For this thesis, with 2 Cor. 2:14 as its centerpiece, see my *Suffering and the Spirit, An Exegetical Study of II Cor 2:14–3:3 Within the Context of the Corinthian Correspondence* (WUNT 2.19;

statements of this point are found in the thesis-like affirmations of 1:3–11, 4:7–12, 6:3–10, 11:23b–33, 12:9–10, 13:4, and, by way of metaphor, 2:14–17. In these passages Paul's suffering, as the embodiment of the crucified Christ, is the very instrument God uses to display his resurrection power (cf. also 1 Cor. 2:2–5; 4:9; 1 Thess. 1:5).

This revelation took place in two ways. Either God rescued Paul from adversity when it was too much to bear, as in 2 Corinthians 1:8–11 (cf. Phil. 2:25–30), or he strengthened Paul in the midst of adversity that he might endure his suffering *with thanksgiving to the glory of God* (2 Cor. 4:7–12; 6:3–10; 12:9; 13:4; cf. 2 Tim. 2:10). Thus, Paul's call to suffer as an apostle is the very means by which God makes his love and power known in the world *for the proclamation and praise of his glory* (2 Cor. 1:3, 11, 20; 3:8–11; 4:4–6, 15; 9:11–15). If Paul's suffering is the means of God's self-revelation, then the manifestation of God's glory is its ultimate goal. Moreover, Paul affirms that whenever God's people endure the same sufferings to which he was called as an apostle, they too manifest the power and glory of God in the midst of their adversity (cf. 1:7). In support of these points, Paul outlines the nature of the new covenant in relationship to the old (3:6–18), the nature of the new creation in the midst of the old (4:6–5:21), and the call, for the sake of Christ, to embody the new creation of the new covenant by living for the sake of others (5:15; 8:1–9:14).

Applying 2 Corinthians Today

AS AN APOLOGY for Paul's apostolic ministry, 2 Corinthians is filled with challenges for the people of God in the twenty-first century. Paul's experience of God, his understanding of Christ, his authority as an apostle, and his willingness to suffer for the sake of the gospel because of his love for Christ's people call into question the easy believism of our contemporary Christian culture. His gospel unmasks the cheap grace of today's repentant-less forgiveness, the legalism of those who attempt to remedy this problem by calling for more "obedience to God," and the complacency we feel over the spiritual condition of others. Moreover, Paul's letter reveals that ministering Christ to others is not a matter of technique, program, and performance, but of mediating to others the same truth, mercy, and comfort we have experienced in trusting the God "who raises the dead" (1:9).

Paul's apology thus makes us painfully aware that the primary problem in communicating 2 Corinthians today is our failure to comprehend that his the-

Tübingen: J. C. B. Mohr [Paul Siebeck], 1986), slightly abridged as *Suffering and Ministry of the Spirit, Paul's Defense of His Ministry in II Corinthians 2:14–3:3* (Grand Rapids: Eerdmans, 1990).

ology and experience are God-determined, Scripture-based, and love-soaked. These are hard realities to bring to bear on a church that is dominated by a culture of science-driven technology, biblical illiteracy, and the cult of the "self." Hence, in a symposium on "Recapturing the Evangelical Mind," held in honor of the reissuing of Carl F. H. Henry's magisterial work, *God, Revelation, and Authority*, Dr. Henry himself wisely said that what is needed at the beginning of the twenty-first century is "the articulation of an enduring Christian life and worldview with revelatory excitement that transcends technological science and heralds an unrevisable truth claim that replies to critics who decry reason."[26] This is precisely what a careful application of Paul's second letter to the Corinthians both gives and demands of us today.

---

26. Spoken in the author's presence by Carl F. H. Henry on January 22, 1999, on the occasion of his eighty-sixth birthday, at the Inaugural Summit Conference of The Carl F. H. Henry Institute for Evangelical Engagement, Southern Baptist Theological Seminary, Louisville, Kentucky. Henry's work is now published by Crossway Books, Wheaton, 1998.

Outline

I. **Letter Opening: The Identity of Paul and His Church** (1:1–2)

II. **Prologue** (1:3–11)
   A. Paul's Prayer of Praise for the Comfort of God (1:3–7)
   B. Paul's "Sentence to Death" As the Pattern of His Suffering (1:8–11)

III. **Letter Body** (1:12–13:10)
   A. Paul's History with the Corinthians (1:12–2:11)
      1. The Content of Paul's Boast (1:12–14)
      2. The Reason for Paul's First Change of Plans (1:15–22)
      3. The Reason for Paul's Second Change of Plans (1:23–2:4)
      4. The Application of Paul's Example to the Corinthians (2:5–11)
   B. Paul's Apologetic for His Apostolic Ministry (2:12–7:1)
      1. The Reason for Paul's Last Change of Plans (2:12–13)
      2. Paul's Sufficiency As an Apostle (2:14–3:3)
         a. "Led Unto Death" in the Ministry (2:14–16a)
         b. Paul's Sufficiency for the Ministry (2:16b–17)
         c. Paul's Letter of Recommendation for the Ministry (3:1–3)
      3. Paul's Boldness As a Minister of the New Covenant (3:4–18)
         a. Paul's Confidence As a Minister (3:4–6a)
         b. Paul's Ministry of the New Covenant (3:6b)
         c. The Ministry of the Spirit, Not the Letter (3:6c)
         d. The Old Covenant Ministry of Death (3:7a–b)
         e. The Glory of Moses' Ministry (3:7c)
         f. The Glory of the Ministry of the Spirit (3:8)
         g. The Contrast Between the Two Ministries (3:9–11)
         h. The Boldness of the New Covenant Ministry (3:12–13)
         i. The Continuing Hardening of Israel (3:14–15)
         j. The Conversion of the Remnant (3:16–18)
      4. Paul's Confident Boldness in Spite of Rejection (4:1–6)

D.The Application of Paul's Apologetic to the Rebellious (10:1–13:10)
  1. Paul's Apostolic Authority (10:1–18)
      a. Paul's Warfare on Behalf of His Authority (10:1–6)
      b. The Purpose of Apostolic Authority (10:7–11)
      c. The Basis of Apostolic Authority (10:12–18)
  2. Paul's Apostolic Boast (11:1–12:13)
      a. The Necessity of Paul's Boast (11:1–21a)
      b. Paul's Boast in His Weakness and the Boasting of a Fool: Part 1 (11:21b–33)
      c. Paul's Boast in His Weakness and the Boasting of a Fool: Part 2 (12:1–6)
      d. Paul's Strength in His Weakness (12:7–10)
      e. The Superfluous Nature of Paul's Boast (12:11–13)
  3. Paul's Final Appeal (12:14–13:10)
      a. Paul's Final Appeal Regarding His Legitimacy as an Apostle (12:14–21)
      b. Paul's Final Appeal for the Repentance of the Rebellious (13:1–10)

IV. Letter Closing: Exhortation and Benediction (13:11–14)

Annotated Bibliography
of Selected Commentaries
and Monographs

Selected Commentaries on 2 Corinthians

Barnett, Paul. *The Second Epistle to the Corinthians*. NICNT. Grand Rapids: Eerdmans, 1997. Based on the NIV, with reference to Greek in footnotes; evangelical in perspective; views the letter as a unity; a detailed exegesis of the
flow of the argument and of all the individual interpretive issues; of the
four major English-language commentaries (i.e., together with Furnish,
Martin, and Thrall), Barnett's presents the most consistent blend of close
textual analysis and general theological development; also provides sug-
gestions for contemporary application.

Barrett, C. K. *A Commentary on the Second Epistle to the Corinthians*. HTNC. New
York: Harper & Row, 1973. Based on his own translation; moderately
critical; views chs. 1–9 and 10–13 as separate letters; theologically and
historically insightful; offers a more general, semitechnical overview of
the argument.

Betz, Hans Dieter. *2 Corinthians 8 and 9: A Commentary on Two Administrative Letters of the Apostle Paul*. Hermeneia. Philadelphia: Fortress, 1985. Based on
the Greek text; critical in its perspective; views both chapters as independent letters; a wealth of background material from Greco-Roman
sources on the meaning of key terms; focuses on the basic outline of
Paul's argument from the standpoint of ancient rhetoric; nontheological
and technical in its approach.

Furnish, Victor Paul. *II Corinthians*. AB 32A. Garden City, N.Y.: Doubleday,
1984. Based on his own translation, with transliterated Greek; moderately
critical; views chs. 1–9 and 10–13 as separate letters; a thorough and
exhaustive treatment of the interpretive issues; approaches the text phrase
by phrase, with helpful syntheses of the argument; of the four major English-language commentaries, more thematic than Martin and Thrall,
though not as theologically oriented as Barnett.

Hughes, Philip Edgcumbe. *Paul's Second Epistle to the Corinthians*. NICNT. Grand
Rapids: Eerdmans, 1962. Based on the ASV; evangelical and exegetical in
approach; views letter as a unity; focuses on phrases and words as well as
themes; excellent treatment of the flow of the argument; though dated,
still a helpful treatment of Pauline theology.

Lambrecht, Jan. *Second Corinthians*. Sacra Pagina 8. Collegeville, Minn.: Liturgical Press, 1999. Based on the author's own translation; exegetical and theological in its approach; views the letter as a unity; focuses on exposition of the text without extended discussion of secondary literature; presents a concise overview of the interpretive issues and themes in the letter; written by one of the leading experts on 2 Corinthians.

Martin, Ralph P. *2 Corinthians*. WBC 40. Waco, Tex.: Word, 1986. Based on the Greek text, with its own translation; evangelical in its perspective; views chapters 1–9 and 10–13 as separate letters; an encyclopedia of exegetical detail, with a near exhaustive account of the secondary literature; focuses on the various interpretive options for each word and clause, though overall structure of the argument is not as well developed; of the four major English-language commentaries (with Furnish, Thrall, and Barnett) Martin provides the standard reference work for the history of interpretation.

Scott, James M. *2 Corinthians*. NIBC 8. Peabody, Mass.: Hendrickson, 1998. Based on the NIV; evangelical in its perspective; views 2 Corinthians as a unity; especially helpful in drawing out background material from the Old Testament and Judaism; nontechnical in its presentation, with a focus on the significance of Paul's argument of his self-understanding as an apostle; brief in scope, but filled with helpful exegetical and theological insights.

Thrall, Margaret E. *The Second Epistle to the Corinthians. Vol. 1: Introduction and Commentary on II Corinthians I-VII*. ICC. Edinburgh: T. & T. Clark, 1994. Based on the Greek text; focuses on grammar and syntax; moderately critical; reads the text verse by verse; strong emphasis on outlining the interpretive options for each verse; historical and exegetical in approach, but not very theological; of the four major English-language commentaries (with Barnett, Furnish and Martin), Thrall's offers the closest treatment of the Greek text.

Witherington, Ben III. *Conflict and Community in Corinth: A Socio-Rhetorical Commentary on 1 and 2 Corinthians*. Grand Rapids: Eerdmans, 1995. An important companion commentary to more traditional approaches; focuses on the social and cultural background to Paul's thought and interaction with the Corinthians; treats the text in terms of rhetorical categories, rather than its intrinsic argument.

Selected Monographs on 2 Corinthians

Fitzgerald, John T. *Cracks in an Earthen Vessel: An Examination of the Catalogues of Hardships in the Corinthian Correspondence*. SBLDS 99. Atlanta: Scholars, 1988. A study of the texts on this theme in view of the Greco-Roman tradition concerning the suffering of sages and philosophers.

Annotated Bibliography

Georgi, Dieter. *Remembering the Poor: The History of Paul's Collection for Jerusalem.* Nashville: Abingdon, 1992 (1965). A critical reconstruction of the history behind chapters 8–9.

Hafemann, Scott J. *Suffering and Ministry in the Spirit: Paul's Defense of His Ministry in II Corinthians 2:14–3:3.* Grand Rapids: Eerdmans, 1990. An exegetical study of the themes of suffering and the power of the Spirit in Paul's ministry.

———. *Paul, Moses, and the History of Israel. The Letter/Spirit Contrast and the Argument from Scripture in 2 Corinthians 3.* WUNT 81. Tübingen: J. C. B. Mohr (Paul Siebeck), 1995 [published in the U.S. by Peabody, Mass.: Hendrickson, 1996]. An exegetical study of 3:4–18 against the background of Exodus 32–34, Jeremiah 31, Ezekiel 36, and the development of these themes in postbiblical Judaism.

Harvey, A. E. *Renewal Through Suffering: A Study of 2 Corinthians.* Studies of the New Testament and Its World. Edinburgh: T. & T. Clark, 1996. A development of this theme throughout 2 Corinthians, taking 1:3–9 to be the key to its meaning and unity.

Pate, C. Marvin. *Adam Christology As the Exegetical and Theological Substructure of 2 Corinthians 4:7–5:21.* Lanham: Univ. Press of America, 1991. A helpful approach to the vexed question of the meaning of 5:1–10 in its context and against the backdrop of the Old Testament and postbiblical Judaism.

Peterson, Brian K. *Eloquence and the Proclamation of the Gospel in Corinth.* SBLDS 163. Atlanta: Scholars, 1998. An analysis of chapters 10–13 from the standpoint of ancient rhetorical theory and practice.

Savage, Timothy B. *Power Through Weakness: Paul's Understanding of the Christian Ministry in 2 Corinthians.* SNTSMS 86. Cambridge: Cambridge Univ. Press, 1996. A helpful study of 4:7–18 within its cultural and theological context.

Sumney, Jerry L. *Identifying Paul's Opponents: The Question of Method in 2 Corinthians.* JSNTSup 40. Sheffield: Sheffield Academic, 1990. An insightful analysis of the pitfalls encountered in trying to determine the identity and theology of Paul's opponents, together with a presentation of his own helpful, text-based method.

Young, Frances, and David F. Ford. *Meaning and Truth in 2 Corinthians.* Grand Rapids: Eerdmans, 1987. A thematic study of various hermeneutical issues raised by the argument of 2 Corinthians by doing exegesis with an eye toward its theological significance.

2 Corinthians 1:1–2

❦

PAUL, AN APOSTLE of Christ Jesus by the will of God, and Timothy our brother,

To the church of God in Corinth, together with all the saints throughout Achaia:

²Grace and peace to you from God our Father and the Lord Jesus Christ.

LETTER OPENINGS IN the first century followed the typical pattern, "(Sender) to (recipient): Greetings!" Paul customarily followed this form, but expanded these standard elements in order to indicate his own authority for writing, the recipient's qualification(s) for receiving what is written, and the Christian perspective on what we desire for one another.[1] In 2 Corinthians, however, Paul foregoes a detailed elaboration of his own authority and the status of the believers in Corinth (cf. 1 Cor. 1:1–3) in favor of a nearly standard salutation. His only expansions are the reminders that he is "an apostle of Christ Jesus by the will of God" and that the Corinthians are the "church of God," who exist "together with all the saints throughout Achaia."

This unusual simplicity serves to emphasize that Paul *is* an "apostle" (Gk. *apostolos*) and that he owes his calling as an apostle to the "will *of God*." An *apostolos* is an emissary who is authorized and commissioned to carry out a personal mission on someone else's behalf.[2] Paul's use of the genitive, "an apostle *of Christ Jesus*," indicates that Christ is the one who has *directly* and *ultimately* sent him, while the reference "by the will of God" asserts that God is the *intermediate* agent of Paul's apostleship.[3] Christ is the one responsible for sending

---

1. For examples of ancient letters and their forms and an analysis of this genre in the New Testament, see John L. White, *Light From Ancient Letters* (Philadelphia: Fortress, 1986), and Stanley K. Stowers, *Letter-Writing in Greco-Roman Antiquity* (Philadelphia: Westminster, 1986).

2. The discussion that follows is indebted at several points to the helpful summary by P. W. Barnett, "Apostle," *DPHL*, 45–51, and to the standard article by Karl H. Rengstorf, "ἀποστέλλω," *TDNT* 1:398–447.

3. See Daniel B. Wallace, *Greek Grammar Beyond the Basics, An Exegetical Syntax of the New Testament* (Grand Rapids: Zondervan, 1996), 82n.30, 434n.79. This use of "by the will of God" (*dia thelematos theou*) to express the intermediate agency of an action, here the intermediate agent of the passive action implied in the noun "apostle," occurs exclusively in Paul's writings; cf. Rom. 15:32; 1 Cor. 1:1; 2 Cor. 8:5; Eph. 1:1; Col. 1:1; 2 Tim. 1:1.

Paul, but God is the one who has made this sending possible. In other words, Christ sends Paul in accordance with God's will.

Separated from Paul's tradition and culture, it is easy to miss the significance of Paul's self-designation. There is no parallel in the Greco-Roman world for the use of the noun "apostle" to refer to an emissary who carried an authorized commission as a matter of sovereign appointment. Rather, the New Testament concept derives from the Old Testament, where the verb *apostello* occurs approximately 696 times in the LXX to refer to sending someone out on a mission or special task (the noun *apostolos* occurs only once in the LXX in 1 Kings 14:6). In all but twelve of these passages it renders the Hebrew verb *šalaḥ* (= "to commission with a mission or a task"; cf. Gen. 32:4; Num. 20:14; Josh. 7:22; Judg. 6:35; 2 Chron. 36:15; Mal. 3:1).[4]

Although *apostello* is not a specifically religious term, in the LXX it becomes a technical designation for "the sending of a messenger with a special task" in which "the one who is sent is of interest only to the degree that in some measure he embodies in his existence as such the one who sends him."[5] This meaning anticipates a later rabbinic aphorism, that "the one sent by a man is as the man himself" (*m. Ber.* 5:5). Rengstorf consequently concludes that in contexts where sending with a religious purpose is in view, *apostello* begins to become "a theological term meaning 'to send forth to service in the kingdom of God with full authority (grounded in God).'"[6]

In line with this development, Paul's own use of the term corresponds most closely to the use of *apostello* in regard to Moses and the prophets, where it signifies that they had been sent with an official commission as a representative of Yahweh and were thus unconditionally subordinate to God's will (cf. Ex. 3:10; Judg. 6:8, 14; Isa. 6:8; Jer. 1:7; Ezek. 2:3; Hag. 1:12; Zech. 2:8–9; 4:9; Mal. 3:1; 4:5). This is confirmed by the use of the verb in the New Testament as a whole, where it occurs 135 times, only twelve of which are found outside of the Gospels and Acts.[7] Whereas in secular literature there

---

4. As Rengstorf observes ("ἀποστέλλω," 400), the exceptions occur only when the Hebrew idiom will not allow it (cf. Gen. 3:22; 22:12). Rengstorf points out that the nuance of *apostello*, over against *pempo* (to send), is not in the nature of the sending as such, but in the fact that *apostello* "unites with the sender either the person or the object sent" (398). Hence, in both secular and religious contexts, *apostello* implies a commission and "associated authorization," typically from either a king or a deity. "The men thus described are representatives of their monarch and his authority," or carry divine authorization that grants them "full religious and ethical power" (399, cf. its use by Cynics and Stoics, e.g., Epictetus, *Disc.* 1.24.6; 3.22.23, 69; 3.23.46; 4.8.31).

5. Ibid., 400–401.

6. Ibid., 406.

7. Cf. Rom. 10:15; 1 Cor. 1:17; 2 Cor. 12:17; 2 Tim. 4:12; Heb. 1:14; 1 Pet. 1:12; 1 John 4:9, 10, 14; Rev. 1:1; 5:6; 22:6.

is no essential distinction between *pempo* (to send) and *apostello*, in the NT *pempo* usually occurs when the emphasis is on the sending as such (cf. Rom. 8:3; 2 Thess. 2:11), whereas *apostello* carries the nuance of a commission.[8]

This same emphasis on being sent with a commission is found in the seventy-nine uncontested uses in the New Testament of the corresponding noun, "apostle" (*apostolos*), where all ten of its occurrences in the Gospels refer to the twelve "apostles" who were commissioned and sent out by Christ.[9] Hence, although Paul's letters are the earliest writings of the New Testament, and although he uses the word *apostolos* more than any other New Testament writer, the origin of its specific use for Christian emissaries almost certainly goes back to Jesus, who himself was "sent" (*apostello*) by the Father (cf. Mark 9:37; Luke 4:43; John 5:36) and can therefore also be called an "apostle" (Heb. 3:1).

Moreover, the transition from the ministry of Jesus to that of the apostles is reflected in the fact that in the Gospels and Acts the action of "sending" (*apostello*) is emphasized, whereas in the letters the emphasis is on the one sent (*apostolos*). These statistics point to the unique meaning of "apostle" within early Christianity as a designation of those commissioned to preach and act in the *authority* of Christ's name (cf. Matt. 10:1, 7–8; Mark 3:14; 6:30; Luke 9:1–2). Paul's point in 2 Corinthians 1:1 is that the will of God that sent Jesus is the same will that Christ enacts in sending Paul to represent him as his "apostle."

The simple declaration in 1:1 thus reminds Paul's readers of his divinely appointed role and authority among God's people, thereby opening the way for the defense of his apostolic ministry that will be the focus of so much of 2 Corinthians (see Introduction). Indeed, Paul's self-designation in 1:1 is the first salvo in the battle to reaffirm his apostolic legitimacy (cf. 10:1–6). There can be no compromise between Paul's claim here and the claims of those whom Paul will unmask as "pseudo-apostles," "deceitful workmen," and "servants" of Satan (cf. 11:13–15). This affirmation of Paul's own authority as an apostle is most likely the reason why he also mentions Timothy, his "brother," as a cosender of the letter.[10] By associating Timothy with

---

8. Cf. Rengstorf, "ἀποστέλλω," 402, 404, for the points concerning the use of the two verbs. In John's Gospel *pempo* occurs thirty-three times and takes on a theological significance in regard to the sending of Jesus by the Father that is unique to this Gospel.

9. Cf. Matt. 10:2; Mark 3:14 [textually uncertain]; 6:30; Luke 6:13; 9:10; 11:49; 17:5; 22:14; 24:10; John 13:16.

10. The fact that Timothy is identified as "our brother" (lit., "the brother") indicates that he is considered a coworker alongside Paul, but not a fellow "apostle" of equal status with Paul. "On the contrary," Ralph Martin suggests, "it is more probable that Timothy is mentioned in the letter's prescript because he needed Paul's endorsement of all he had sought to do as he undertook an intermediate mission between the visits of Acts 18:3 and 20:4" (*2 Corinthians*, 2). On Timothy, see Acts 16:1–3; 17:13–15; 18:5; 19:22; 20:4; Rom. 16:21; Phil. 1:1; 2:19–23; Col. 1:1; 1 Thess. 1:1; 3:2, 6; 2 Thess. 1:1; 1 Tim. 1:2, 18; 6:20; 2 Tim. 1:2; Phlm. 1; Heb. 13:23.

himself in this way, Paul reaffirms the legitimacy of Timothy's ministry among them, both in his helping Paul to establish the church (cf. Acts 18:5) and in his recent visits on Paul's behalf (cf. 1 Cor. 4:17; 16:10). This too underscores the validity of the gospel the Corinthians have received through Paul's coworkers (cf. 2 Cor. 1:19).

Having asserted his own authority and the validity of Timothy's earlier ministry among them, Paul turns to the Corinthians as his addressees (v. 1b). His warrant for writing (i.e., he is "an apostle of Christ Jesus") is matched by their reason for receiving it (i.e., they are the "church of God"). Despite their past problems and recent rebellion, the repentance of the majority of the Corinthians (cf. 2:6; 7:2–16) has demonstrated that they continue to be God's people (cf. 7:2–16). The designation "church" (ekklesia) is one of two terms used in the LXX to define the local gathering of God's chosen people (cf., e.g., Deut. 9:10; Judg. 20:1–2; 1 Kings 8:14; Ps. 22:22; 26:5; 35:18; 40:9).[11] Thus, just as Paul owed his life as an apostle to the same will of God that had called Moses and the prophets (cf. 2 Cor. 2:16b; 3:4–5), so too the Corinthians owed their existence as Christians to the same mercy of God that had chosen Israel.

Hence, these twin designations, "apostle ... by the will of God" and "church of God," connote a continuity with the people of God and her leaders under the old covenant. At the same time, they also underscore the reality of the *new* covenant, since Paul is an apostle "of Christ [i.e., Messiah] Jesus," and they are the *church* of God, not the synagogue (cf. 3:14–18). Moreover, the Corinthians are part of a larger gathering of "all the saints" (hagioi; i.e., "holy ones") scattered throughout the Roman province of Achaia, an area roughly equivalent with modern-day Greece. Corinth was the capital of Achaia and the home of the first of the interrelated churches in the region (cf. Acts 18:1–11; 1 Cor. 16:15).

Paul's specific reference to Corinth in relationship to this wider network of churches reflects the primacy and significance of Corinth as the center of the Pauline mission in the region, from which the gospel spread like spokes on a wheel (cf. 10:15–16). In writing to Corinth, Paul is therefore writing to *all* of the churches in Achaia, not only because he viewed them as belonging to one another, but also because he knew that as things go in Corinth,

---

11. It was used exclusively to translate the Hebrew term qahal, which was also sometimes translated by the Greek term "synagogue" (synagoge). But unlike ekklesia, synagoge was also used to translate the Hebrew word ʿedah, which overlapped in meaning with qahal, but could also be used as a more general term to refer to non-Israelites or wicked Israelites. In contrast, qahal, with its Greek equivalent ekklesia, was the more specific term, always being used of Israel in a positive or neutral sense. The Jewish use of synagoge no doubt led the early Jewish Christians to use ekklesia as their designation of choice.

so too in Achaia (cf. 9:2; 11:10). The problems in Corinth, past and present, were bound to impact the surrounding churches.

Given these problems, Paul's use of "saints" to describe the believers in Achaia, including by implication the Corinthians (!), often surprises modern readers, since our word "saint" has come to designate those who have attained such a high degree of spirituality that they are set apart from the "normal" rank and file of Christians. Indeed, to be "holy" is to be "set apart." But Paul uses it to refer to *all* believers as those who have been set apart as belonging to God. Far from describing a special class of Christians, all believers, as saints, are to live "holy" lives (for the Old Testament roots of the calling to be "saints," see Ex. 19:5–6; Lev. 11:44; 20:24–26; Num. 23:9; Deut. 7:6; 14:2; Ps. 147:20).

Hence, just as Paul's self-designation as an apostle began the battle for his own legitimacy, so too his describing the Corinthians as saints lays the foundation for his subsequent appeals throughout the letter (cf. 2 Cor. 6:13; 6:14–7:1; 7:2–3; 13:1–10). Those who are truly *saints* will show themselves to be so by responding positively to Paul's self-defense. For, in reality, it is not Paul's apostleship that is now on the line, but the faith of those who continue to reject his gospel and its embodiment in his calling to suffer on behalf of God's people (cf. 5:20–6:2; 10:8; 12:19).

Finally, the play on words that exists in Greek between the normal word for "hello" (*charein*) and the Christian term for "grace" (*charis*) is lost in the English translation of Paul's greeting (cf. Rom. 1:7; 1 Cor. 1:3). At the point where Paul's hearers would have expected to hear "hello!" (*charein*), Paul wishes them "grace" (*charis*). Paul wishes his readers a continuing experience of God's merciful gifts, from forgiveness and justification to deliverance from the power of sin and eternal life. Paul can do so because Christ's death on the cross for those who deserve only God's wrath makes such grace possible.

Accordingly, Paul's desire that they experience "peace" is not primarily a wish for untroubled circumstances. Rather, he wishes them that comprehensive *shalom* or well-being that characterizes the lives of believers, individually and corporately, when all is right with God, a possibility also granted by the grace of God through Christ. Paul's two wishes are therefore inextricably interrelated. "Peace" is an expression of the "grace" of God in the life of the believer. The significance of this grace and the peace of reconciliation that it engenders will be detailed in 5:11–6:2. But in view of the controversy still raging in Corinth, Paul's otherwise standard wish takes on from the beginning an added sense of poignancy and pain. Only those who accept Paul's greeting as an expression of his genuine apostolic authority will receive what "God our Father and the Lord Jesus Christ" desire for them.

Bridging
Contexts

PAUL IS AN "Apostle" and an "apostle." In applying this text, it is important to keep in mind that
there were two types of apostles within the early
church. On the one hand, there were the original
"twelve Apostles," who were sent out by Jesus himself during his earthly ministry and were later confirmed in their calling by witnessing the resurrected
Christ (cf. Mark 3:14; 6:7, 30; 9:35; 10:32; 11:11; cf. Acts 1:2, 22; 1 Cor.
15:5). As a result, their authority was derived *directly* from Christ himself. The
replacement of Judas with Matthias according to the qualifications reported
in Acts 1:12–26 indicates that this class of apostles was fixed both in number
and in kind in order to maintain the parallel between the twelve Apostles and
the twelve tribes of Israel (cf. Luke 6:13; Acts 8:1; Rev. 21:12–14).

These Apostles of Christ made up the nucleus of the new covenant people of God, establishing the continuity between Israel and the church. But
whereas physical lineage determined the twelve patriarchs, the twelve Apostles, like the faithful remnant within the nation of Israel, existed by virtue of
Christ's calling. The role of the twelve Apostles was not to initiate and receive
a blessing for their physical descendants, but to represent Christ by providing the authoritative leadership and foundational teaching for the church,
God's "children" (cf. Acts 2:42; 6:2; 15:2, 22–23; 1 Cor. 12:28; Gal. 1:18–19;
Eph. 2:20; 3:5; 4:11; 2 Peter 3:2; Jude 17; Rev. 18:20; 21:14). These were
"Apostles" with a capital "A."

On the other hand, there were those "apostles" who may not have seen
the risen Christ, but who were sent out by the early churches to preach and
administer in Christ's name. Not all who saw the risen Christ were sent out
as apostles (cf. 1 Cor. 15:6), just as not all those sent out as apostles by the
churches had seen the risen Christ (cf. 2 Cor. 8:23). Moreover, no matter how
much authority these church-commissioned apostles possessed, they were still
distinguished from the "twelve Apostles" (e.g., James; cf. 1 Cor. 15:7; Gal.
1:19). In contrast to the latter, their number was not fixed, nor did they carry
the same *intrinsic* authority. Instead, such apostolic missionaries derived their
authority from the other apostles and the churches that sent them (see, e.g.,
Acts 14:4, 14; Rom. 16:7; Phil. 2:25).

Against this backdrop, it is striking that Paul stands in *both* classes; or better, *between* both classes. Like the "twelve Apostles," the resurrected Christ
himself commissioned Paul to be an apostle. He was thus an "apostle *of Christ
Jesus*" (1:1). As the *last* (!) of those commissioned in this way (cf. 1 Cor. 15:8),
he too represented Christ directly and authoritatively (see too Rom. 1:1, 5;
1 Cor. 1:1; 9:1; Gal. 1:1; Eph. 1:1; Col. 1:1; 1 Thess. 2:6; 1 Tim. 1:1; 2 Tim.
1:1; Titus 1:1). So like the "twelve," he too claimed an intrinsic authority.

Moreover, just as the "twelve" symbolized and were called primarily to the Jews (and hence had to be with Jesus during his earthly ministry to Israel), Paul, as the "thirteenth" apostle (cf. 1 Cor. 15:9), was called to the Gentiles (Gal. 1:16; 2:7–9; cf. Rom. 11:13; 15:14–22).

Thus, unlike the "twelve Apostles," Paul had not been with Jesus during his earthly ministry; indeed, prior to his conversion call on the road to Damascus, Paul had been an enemy of the church. He was also different from the "twelve" in that, in addition to his commission by Christ, a local church sent him out (see Acts 13:1–3). This combination of Paul's calling by the risen Christ to be "the Apostle to the Gentiles" and his commission by the church to be a missionary among the Gentiles made Paul unique within the early church. As we will see, it also caused Paul problems (see 2 Cor. 3:1–6). Those who rejected Paul's apostolic authority denied his calling by the resurrected Christ, since Paul had not been among the original disciples of Jesus, at the same time decrying his missionary status because of his refusal to provide letters of recommendation from his churches. Nevertheless, Paul's conviction was firm. He was "an apostle of Christ Jesus by the will of God," that is, by the distinct call of God in his life on the road to Damascus (cf. Acts 9:15; 1 Cor. 9:1–2; Gal. 1:1–2, 11–12). His "letter of recommendation" was the very existence itself of his churches (2 Cor. 3:1–3; 10:12–18).

Without this historical context, modern readers often miss the fact that the comparative brevity of Paul's present greeting bears a poignant message in and of itself. In view of all that had transpired since Paul penned the letter we call "1 Corinthians" (see Introduction), Paul honed his opening words to focus the Corinthians' attention on the divine origin of his apostleship and on their own identity and responsibility as Christians. In both cases much more is at stake than merely repairing Paul's reputation. As an Apostle, Paul is conscious that he is speaking with divinely commissioned *authority*, and that his apostolic ministry, in that it represents *Christ*, is the appropriate manifestation of this authority in the world. As James Scott puts it:

> Paul wants to stress from the beginning that he does not write as a private person who happened to choose a ministerial "profession," but rather in his official capacity as an apostle, a position to which God himself has appointed Paul. This shows that the apostle does not speak or act in his own authority, but in the commission and authority of the one who sent him.[12]

Hence, to reject Paul is to reject Christ, which, in turn, is to reject God.

---

12. 2 Corinthians, 17.

From our present distance, it is easy to read right past this brief letter opening without realizing the gravity of the claims Paul is making. The battle over Paul's legitimacy as an Apostle may seem foreign and overblown to us today, but it reflects the early Christian conviction that the Apostles formed the authoritative foundation of the church. The church was, and still is, built on their proclamation of the gospel, their teaching of the Scriptures, and their preservation of the traditions concerning Jesus (cf. 1 Cor. 12:28; Eph. 2:20; 3:5; 4:11; Rev. 21:14; cf. 2 Peter 3:2; Jude 17).[13] Hence, it was the apostolate that made the continuation of the early Christian community possible, since the Apostles "became [Christ's] representatives in the sense that they took his place and thus assumed an authoritative position," their missionary calling and authority being the essential hallmarks of their identity.[14]

The Apostles under the new covenant can therefore best be understood as the equivalents of the old covenant prophets. Hence, as Jan-A. Bühner has pointed out, the meaning of apostle must include both his *representative function* and his *authoritative office*, with its accompanying prophetic role of mediating between God and his people.[15] For, as Barnett has warned us:

> Some modern scholars have attempted to broaden the definition of "apostle" in such a way [e.g., as "missionary" or "church planter"] that Paul's distinctive authority is dissipated. Paul strenuously resisted attempts to downgrade him in this way. If Paul's apostleship meant and means no more than that, then he had and continues to have little real authority in the churches.[16]

There is simply no equivalent in the ancient Greco-Roman world at large, or in the modern world of today, to the inspired authority and founding function of the Apostles. With the death of the "thirteen Apostles" (the "twelve" plus Paul), the apostolic age came to an end, as did their authorita-

---

13. This is confirmed by the five occurrences of "apostle" in the Pseudepigrapha. Cf. *GrApEzra* 2:1, where the Christian Apostles are referred to, together with Michael and Gabriel, as messengers of God; *Apoc. Sedrach* 14:10, where the Apostles, together with the Gospels, are seen as repositories of God's Word, and 15:4, 7, where their conversion is paralleled to that of the Gospel writers; and *Paraleipomena Jeremiou* 9:18 (9:20), where the mission of the Son of God is summarized in terms of his death on the cross and his choosing of the twelve Apostles to proclaim the news among the nations.

14. Rengstorf, "ἀποστέλλω," 431.

15. See his *Der Gesandte und sein Weg im 4. Evangelium* (WUNT 2, Reihe Bd. 2; Tübingen: J. C. B. Mohr [Paul Siebeck], 1977), 285–314. Bühner argues for this both on the basis of postbiblical and rabbinic literature and in view of the LXX use of *apostello* to describe Moses' being sent by God in Ex. 3:10, 12; 4:13, 28.

16. Barnett, "Apostle," 50.

tive function and inspiration, though the missionary role of the apostles continues on into the present.

The Corinthians are the church of God. The corollary to Paul's self-understanding as an apostle is his conviction that the Corinthian church is a local gathering of God's people. In applying 2 Corinthians to our own day, it is therefore paramount to keep in view that this letter is God's abiding Word for his people, not a general treatise on the nature of religious conflict in the ancient world. At the same time, no one would dispute, of course, that our cultural expressions of the church are vastly different from those of the churches in Corinth in the first century. We cannot be nonchalant in bridging contexts, as if we still lived in the first century.

But apply the text we must, for the continuity between the church in Corinth and our own church does not derive from our common culture. Rather, it is based on our common identity as the people of the same God, who live under the lordship of the same Christ. As the people of God, the church universal is constituted by the grace and peace she has received from God in Jesus as her Messiah and Lord (1:2). In this sense, the church through the ages is not an institution, but a family organically related to the same "Father" (1:2).

In bringing this text into the twenty-first century, therefore, we must keep in mind that although our cultural identities are radically different, the unchanging character of God and the abiding nature of his covenant bind us together with the "saints" in Corinth and Achaia. This is what makes it possible to move from Paul's context to our own. As Paul put it earlier to the Corinthians, "for us there is but one God, the Father, from whom all things came and for whom we live; and there is but one Lord, Jesus Christ, through whom all things came and through whom we live" (1 Cor. 8:6). For this reason, as Paul expressed it in Ephesians 4:4–6, "there is one body and one Spirit—just as you were called to one hope when you were called—one Lord, one faith, one baptism; one God and Father of all, who is over all and through all and in all."

INTERPRETING THE BIBLE **in a postmodern world.** We must be careful not to make a mountain out of a molehill when applying biblical texts. As profound as Paul's understanding of his own identity as an apostle and of the identity of the church as God's people is, this caution is certainly true here. By form and function this text is simply Paul's opening greeting to his church.[17] Thus, it is important to resist the temptation

---

17. See Blomberg's wise words on applying Paul's opening in 1 Cor. 1:1–2 in *1 Corinthians*, 37–39.

to use this passage, for example, as a platform from which to expound on everything we know about God, his will, the nature of sanctification, the contours of grace, and the need for peace.

At the same time, we should not underestimate its significance. It is one thing to work hard at understanding the meaning and significance of Paul's claim to be an "apostle of Christ Jesus by the will of God." It is quite another, however, to submit to such a claim from the past, since it confronts our very identity and central assumptions as "modern" and "postmodern" men and women. In regard to the former, Paul's claim to speak authoritatively on Christ's behalf calls into question the "modern" propensity to worship (i.e., to depend on) "scientific progress" as the solution to our problems. Ever since the Enlightenment, the modern mindset has assumed that, since science has succeeded in leading us into a healthier and more prosperous future, people are getting better as well. In the end, therefore, the latest scientific discovery will save us. Under the power of this belief system, progress in technology is trusted to mean progress in moral development. The assumption is that increased control of our environment, more effective medicine, everexpanding scientific understanding, and amazing new inventions must be the result of superior people thinking higher thoughts. A world filled with personal computers and cell phones must be getting better!

Ironically, at the same time the modern world often believes in a "negative" progress as well. If "good" is getting better, "evil" is also getting worse; just as our potential for weal is taken to be greater than ever before, so too our potential for woe is unmatched by anything the ancients could imagine—and hence understand. We have both the promise of nuclear medicine and the peril of nuclear war. Thus, since the goal of life is seen simply to be survival for the future and pleasure in the present, the stakes appear much higher now and the moral choices more dramatic than ever before. The "good ol' days" are quaint, and they fill us with nostalgia, but, in the end, they are irrelevant. We are convinced that our problems are much more profound than they were in those "simpler" days, and that the answers they require must be that much more sophisticated, scientific, technological, and "up to date." In this culture, Paul's claim to speak for Christ in accordance with God's will appears small and old, naïve and outdated, a religious relic from the past with little relevance for today.

Such modern assumptions are, of course, open to serious criticism, even by those who share the scientific outlook.[18] But the pride of the modern paradigm has attracted many adherents. Most people in the West presume that

---

18. For a critical look at these assumptions, see Neil Postman's work, *Technopoly: The Surrender of Culture to Technology* (New York: Vintage, 1992).

our age is superior to the past, both positively and negatively, especially to the prescientific past. As a result, when we encounter a claim to authority like that found in this passage, even Christians have trouble taking it seriously. Our cultural values clash with our confessions. Although as Christians we reject the modernist antisupernaturalism that views the universe as a closed, evolutionary continuum of cause and effect, we are not immune to the pervasive influence of modernism's faith in the future rather than faith in God.

We may assert Paul's historical importance, and even assent to his apostolic authority, but we flinch at having to submit to his teaching as binding in all matters of contemporary faith and practice. *Sola scriptura* may not be a problem in the realm of religion, but the sufficiency of Scripture certainly is when it comes to the realm of "real life"! Can Paul's teaching really be adequate for the questions posed by the ethical, social, and scientific complexities of today? Do the words of Paul to a cluster of house churches in ancient Corinth really have a word for the age of AIDS and nuclear bombs, of artificial intelligence, cloning, and space travel, of psychoanalysis, nationalism, and religious pluralism?

This, of course, is a *modern* question. It assumes that Paul can be understood, evaluated, and then accepted or rejected on the basis of our own comparative analysis of his views compared to ours. For many, however, these very assumptions and the questions they pose are themselves outdated, naïve, and irrelevant. Indeed, this skepticism concerning the validity of the "modern" mindset is bringing about a massive cultural shift, at least for the moment. The *modern* worldview, with its confident belief in discovery and progress, is increasingly being rejected in favor of a *postmodern* evaluation of history and society.

Under the influence of Kantian idealism and the social science paradigm of cultural relativity, modernism's search for the Truth is being replaced by postmodernism's affirmation that all "scientific" and "universal" truths of reason are, in fact, merely local and private interpretations, derived from the socialization and experiences of the "self." Instead of the "objective" world determining us, our "self" determines the world in which we live, whether that self be the individual, or the individual ethnic group, gender, social class, political party, or religious subculture to which we belong. The modern search for universals is thus replaced with a postmodern celebration of the particular; the modern focus on analyzing the world "out there" gives way to a fixation on articulating one's own social location. As a result, "truth" is not objective and universal (which is merely a modern myth), but personal and relative.

In other words, postmoderns see no such thing as Truth, only different "truths" from different perspectives and for different purposes. "The" Truth has been replaced with "my truth" or "our truth." Indeed, for many within the postmodern camp, the claim that something is true in any objective and universal sense is merely a political tool of conquest used by those in power to force their views on others. Moreover, the emphasis on one's social location as the source of truth has led to questioning whether significant communication between individuals and social groups is even possible. After all, if meaning is not derived from reality but imposed on it in accordance with our own relative frames of reference, then we can never really understand anybody else, since *we* are the ones who determine what is meant when someone else speaks or writes.

Hence, the only words we can really hear and understand are those we speak to ourselves. Within the field of biblical studies, this has meant that the old maxim that "interpretation without presuppositions is impossible" is being replaced by the new maxim that interpretation is nothing *but* presuppositions. Unlike the old maxim, which served as a necessary call to evaluate one's "self" and its interpretations critically, this new "truth" enthrones one's "self" as the only interpreter that exists.

> Where modern critics delve into the text to get something out of it, we will now acknowledge that meaning—to the extent that there is such a thing—does not inhere in a text any more than it might inhere in a dream.... Meaning is what we make of texts, not an ingredient in texts.[19]

Many scholars have seriously challenged the encroachment of postmodernism into the realms of theology and exegesis.[20] But the false humility of the postmodern paradigm, with its relativism concerning the nature of truth and its skepticism concerning the validity of the interpretive process, has won many converts, even among evangelicals.[21] Indeed, as a consequence of the growing influence of postmodernism, even those who affirm that Paul's writings are apostolic begin to wonder if they can ever *really* understand

---

19. A. K. M. Adam, *What Is Postmodern Biblical Criticism?* (Minneapolis: Fortress, 1995), 33.

20. For recent responses to "postmodernism" from within the evangelical camp, see David S. Dockery, ed., *The Challenge of Postmodernism: An Evangelical Engagement* (Wheaton: Victor, 1995); Millard J. Erickson, *The Evangelical Left: Encountering Postconservative Evangelical Theology* (Grand Rapids: Baker, 1997); and D. A. Carson, *The Gagging of God: Christianity Confronts Pluralism* (Grand Rapids: Zondervan, 1996). For a more technical assessment, see Brian D. Ingraffia, *Postmodern Theory and Biblical Theology: Vanquishing God's Shadow* (Cambridge: Cambridge Univ. Press, 1995) and Keven J. Vanhoozer, *Is There a Meaning in This Text? The Bible, the Reader, and the Morality of Literary Knowledge* (Grand Rapids: Zondervan, 1998).

21. See, for example, the discussion in Stanley Grenz, *Revisioning Evangelical Theology: A Fresh Agenda for the 21st. Century* (Downers Grove, Ill.: InterVarsity, 1993).

them, and if so, whether Paul's truth has any relevance for their own particular social situation, racial identity, gender, or life experience. "Paul has his
culture and its truth and we have ours."

In this regard, modernism and postmodernism end up strange bedfellows
when it comes to accepting an authority from the past. For modernism, the
advent of science, with its discovery of the "real" world, separates us from the
ancient world; for postmodernism, the rise of the self, with its discovery of
its own "cultural" world, separates us from *everyone* else. Thus, whether read
from the lofty heights of progress or under the shadow of the self, Paul's second letter to the Corinthians (like the Bible as a whole) increasingly functions merely as a stimulus to reflect on our own experience. In either case,
we protect ourselves by assuming that our perspective is either better than
or simply different from Paul's.

Nevertheless, Paul's claim to speak authoritatively as Christ's representative calls into question the postmodern worship of the self as the source of
truth just as decisively as it does the modern worship of scientific progress.
Paul assumed that his experience and perspectives, even though he was a
Diaspora Jew from Cilicia, ought to be understood and accepted as norma-
tive by the Corinthians, even though they were predominantly urban Gentiles in a Greek culture. Paul's understanding of what it means for him to be
writing the Corinthians as an apostle flows from his conviction that he speaks
for God authoritatively, fully confident that its truth will be understood adequately and that it will resonate in those in whom God is at work.

When preaching and teaching from Paul's letters, we too must not shrink
back from their intrinsic and abiding authority (Paul is an *apostle*), or from their
ability to communicate persuasively to God's people (Paul *writes* to the
Corinthians as the *church*). For this reason, the NIV Application Commentary series takes as its working presupposition that Paul's intention is accessible and that it is relevant and authoritative for today. Because of our
confidence in the authority and sufficiency of Scripture, we seek to move *from*
the original meaning of the text *to* its contemporary significance. Second
Corinthians is not presented here merely as an interesting and classic example of first-century Christian piety. It is interpreted and applied as a writing
that imparts to us a truth from God that confronts our most cherished ideas
and ways of life.

Thus, Paul's deviations from the standard elements in ancient letter openings do reveal important aspects of his self-understanding, of the nature of
his recipients, and of his reasons for writing. In this regard, it is imperative
to stress the unique nature of the apostolic office and its authority for the
church today. In short, Paul writes with the authority of God himself. As an
apostle, he represents not his own will, but the will of God and the character

of Christ. To reject Paul is therefore to reject the Messiah who sent him. These fundamental truths, implicit in Paul's use of the title "apostle," cannot simply be assumed in our day. They must be recovered in an age in which the natural impulse is to flee from external authority to the autonomy of the self and its experience, whether it be the modern "scientific self" or the post-modern "cultural self."[22]

Clearly, then, to read 2 Corinthians without reflecting on the assumptions of authority with which Paul wrote would be to miss one of the essential points of the text. In studying this letter, we are studying God's Word, and in studying God's Word we are obligated to submit to its truth and relevancy for our lives. Paul's apostolic authority was not the product of his own initiative, cleverness, people skills, political savvy, or education. In 2 Corinthians Paul is not the CEO of a corporation fighting to keep his career or a personnel manager struggling with administering his human resources. Although 2 Corinthians contains a powerful polemic on behalf of Paul's ministry, the urgency of his self-defense derives from the fact that, as "an apostle of Christ Jesus," he represents Christ himself rather than his own personal interests. Paul is not on an ego-trip. He is defending himself so vehemently not for the sake of his own career or reputation, but for the sake of the truth of the gospel that he preaches and embodies—and hence for the sake of the eternal welfare of the Corinthians (cf. 5:20–6:2; 10:8; 12:19; 13:9–10).

The call to be holy. Our responsibility to submit to Paul's teaching derives from our identity as part of the church of God. As members of God's people, we too are "saints," "sanctified in Christ Jesus" by the Spirit as "holy" (1 Cor. 1:2; cf. Acts 20:32; 26:18; Rom. 15:16). In Greek, the word for "holy" (hagios) and the verb "to sanctify" (hagiazo; i.e., to make holy) are part of the same family. To be a saint means that God has already made us his own by his redeeming grace (cf. 2 Cor. 5:16–19), that he has graciously begun the process of transforming us into his own image (cf. 3:18), and, by that same grace, that he will bring us into his presence for all eternity (cf. 4:13–5:18, esp. 4:13–15).

Paul can consequently speak of the Corinthian believers as *already* having been sanctified, that is, *made* holy, while at the same time being called *to become* holy (1 Cor. 1:2; 6:11). To be called a "saint" is not to say something about our own intrinsic character, but to declare what the love and power of the God who "sanctifies" has done and is doing for us (cf. Rom. 8:29; 2 Cor. 5:17; Eph. 1:4; 5:26–27; Phil. 1:6; 1 Thess. 4:3–7). Hence, since it reflects

---

22. For a development of the philosophical roots of this cultural impulse, see Jeffrey Stout, *The Flight From Authority: Religion, Morality, and the Quest for Autonomy* (Notre Dame: Univ. of Notre Dame Press, 1981).

the reality of having been called, forgiven, redeemed, and empowered by Christ, the term *saints* (Gk. *hagioi*) becomes one of the most common designations for God's people in the New Testament.[23] Addressed to saints, Paul's opening wish for his readers retains its power through the ages as it reminds us that what we ultimately need in life to be profoundly happy is not more scientific discoveries or celebrations of the self, but an increasing experience of God's grace and peace in every area of our lives. It was this simple but profound awareness that led Paul to labor on behalf of the church of God as "an apostle of Christ Jesus."

---

23. See, e.g., Matt. 27:52; Acts 9:13; Rom. 1:7; 15:25–26; 1 Cor. 1:2; 6:1–2; 14:33; 2 Cor. 8:4; 13:12; Eph. 1:18; 2:19; 5:27; Phil. 1:1; 4:21; Col. 1:26; 3:12; 1 Thess. 3:13; Heb. 3:1; 13:24; 1 Peter 1:15–16; 3:5; Rev. 5:8; 13:7; 20:9.

2 Corinthians 1:3–11

PRAISE BE TO the God and Father of our Lord Jesus Christ, the Father of compassion and the God of all comfort, [4]who comforts us in all our troubles, so that we can comfort those in any trouble with the comfort we ourselves have received from God. [5]For just as the sufferings of Christ flow over into our lives, so also through Christ our comfort overflows. [6]If we are distressed, it is for your comfort and salvation; if we are comforted, it is for your comfort, which produces in you patient endurance of the same sufferings we suffer. [7]And our hope for you is firm, because we know that just as you share in our sufferings, so also you share in our comfort.

[8]We do not want you to be uninformed, brothers, about the hardships we suffered in the province of Asia. We were under great pressure, far beyond our ability to endure, so that we despaired even of life. [9]Indeed, in our hearts we felt the sentence of death. But this happened that we might not rely on ourselves but on God, who raises the dead. [10]He has delivered us from such a deadly peril, and he will deliver us. On him we have set our hope that he will continue to deliver us, [11]as you help us by your prayers. Then many will give thanks on our behalf for the gracious favor granted us in answer to the prayers of many.

IT WAS CUSTOMARY in ancient letters to follow the opening address with a brief thanksgiving to a deity. Paul usually follows this pattern in his letters; but as with his letter openings, he expands its content in order to introduce the main perspectives and purposes of his letter. As O'Brien has shown, in Paul's letters the reasons listed for thanksgiving serve an epistolary, instructive, and directive function that sets "the tone and themes of what is to follow."[1]

---

1. Peter Thomas O'Brien, *Introductory Thanksgivings in the Letters of Paul* (Leiden: Brill, 1977), 263.

Second Corinthians 1:3–7 is no exception.[2] Thus, Paul's prayer of praise introduces the main topic of his letter (its "epistolary" function), expresses his controlling perspective (its "instructive" function), and carries an implicit appeal to his readers to join him in his convictions (its "directive" function). In other words, rather than being a spontaneous outburst of unreflected piety, Paul's prayer in 1:3–7 is a carefully crafted expression of his main points, which provides a crucial key to the theme, perspective, and purpose of his letter. Moreover, the opening declaration, "Praise be to … God" (1:3), follows the blessing (*berakah*) formula found in Jewish prayers of thanksgiving, in which God is declared blessed for benefits in which the speaker *himself* has participated.[3] From the beginning, therefore, the focal point of Paul's letter is on himself, thereby reflecting the apologetic character of the letter as a whole.

Though focused on his own experience as an apostle, Paul's opening prayer of praise reflects the fact that the letter as a whole is theologically orientated. God the Father is praised in verse 3, and God is the subject of the action throughout verses 4–6. It is also Christologically qualified. The God who comforts in suffering is "the God and Father *of our Lord Jesus Christ*," just as the sufferings and comfort experienced are both explicitly associated with Christ (cf. v. 5). This twofold emphasis reflects Paul's fundamental conviction that God is sovereign and that he is to be known ultimately in Christ, through whom we come to know the "compassion" (or "mercy") and "comfort" (or "consolation") that characterize the Father. Indeed, the vocabulary in this section confirms that the main theme of 2 Corinthians is the "comfort" that comes from God in the midst of affliction and suffering (cf. the climax of this theme in 12:7–10).

The concept of "comfort" (*paraklesis*) and "comforting" (*parakaleo*) occurs ten times in this short passage. The density of this concentration is even more striking in view of the fact that of the approximately thirty-one times these two words are found with this meaning in the New Testament as a whole, twenty-five of them are in Paul's writings.[4] Of these twenty-five occurrences,

---

2. This section and the commentary sections on 1:8–11 and 1:12–2:11 are based on the analysis presented in my "The Comfort and Power of the Gospel: The Argument of 2 Corinthians 1–3," *RevExp* 86 (1989): 325–44.

3. See O'Brien's analysis of the form and function of Paul's thanksgivings, *Thanksgiving*, 233–40.

4. The verb *parakaleo* actually occurs 109 times in the NT, 54 of them in Paul's writings, while the noun *paraklesis* occurs 29 times, 20 of which are found in Paul's writings; see Kurt Aland, ed., *Vollständige Konkordanz zum Griechischen Neuen Testament, Band II: Spezialübersichten* (Berlin: Walter De Gruyter, 1978), 208–11. But besides "to comfort" and "comfort," the verb and noun have a wide range of meanings, including "to call to one's side," "to appeal to," "to exhort," "to request," and "to conciliate," and for the noun, "encouragement," "exhortation," "appeal, "request" (cf. BAGD, 617–18). I have therefore counted only those verbal and noun meanings judged by their contexts to mean "to comfort" and "comfort" respectively.

seventeen occur in 2 Corinthians and ten in this short introduction. If Paul is the *apostle* of comfort within the New Testament, then 2 Corinthians is the *letter* of comfort, with 1:3–7 being the *paragraph* of comfort.

As its counterpart, the theme of comfort is matched by the theme of suffering. The Greek word for "affliction" (*thlipsis*) occurs forty-five times in the New Testament, but is mentioned more often by Paul than by any other New Testament author (twenty-four times in the seven undisputed letters), yet more often in 2 Corinthians than in any other letter (nine times), and more often in 1:3–11 than in any other section (three times, plus one occurrence of the verb "to be distressed" [*thlibo*] in 1:6). Similarly, the related word "suffering" (*pathema*) is found sixteen times in the New Testament, nine times in Paul, and three times in 2 Corinthians, all in 1:3–7.[5]

In other words, Paul talks about comfort more than any other author because he talks about suffering more than any other author, and he does so more often in 2 Corinthians than in any other letter, and more densely in 1:3–11 than in any other section of this letter. There is no doubt that the passion with which he writes 2 Corinthians is matched by the pathos of the subject matter that distinctly characterizes this letter. From its very beginning, the reader's attention is fixed on the problem of suffering and the promise of God's comfort.

The focus of Paul's discussion, however, is not on suffering and pain in general, or even on the suffering of Christians in particular. Paul's use of the *berakah*-formula in 1:3, the structure of the argument in verses 4–6, and the continuation of his thought in verses 8–11 all indicate that he is referring primarily to his *own* suffering as an apostle. Paul's use of first person plural pronouns throughout this section is part of his custom of employing a "literary plural" (often called the "apostolic 'we'") to reflect his awareness that he is not speaking merely as an individual, but as a representative of the apostolic office. Paul's purpose in 2 Corinthians is not to reflect philosophically on the problem of evil (though his insights are no less profound). Nor is he intending to describe the character of Christian experience in general (in 1:7, the suffering of the Christian in view is that patterned on the suffering of Paul). Rather, Paul's desire is to defend his apostolic ministry in the face of those who called his legitimacy into question, primarily because of his weakness and suffering (10:10; 11:7; 13:3).

Paul's ultimate goal in doing so is not to guard himself, but to strengthen the faithful (cf. 5:12) and win back the wayward (cf. 12:19). His perspective in this letter is therefore not abstract, but concrete. Paul understands that the gospel itself is embodied in his own experience as Christ's apostle, so that in

---

5. Aland, *Vollständige Konkordanz*, 130–31, 206–7.

---

defending his legitimacy he is fighting for the salvation of the Corinthians. As a result, Paul's hope is that the Corinthians will come to understand the divinely ordained role that suffering plays in the life of the one concerning whom Jesus said, "This man is my chosen instrument to carry my name before the Gentiles and their kings and before the people of Israel. I will show him how much he must suffer for my name" (Acts 9:15–16).

Given his theme and perspective, Paul's exhortations to the Corinthians are sometimes direct and forceful (cf. 2:5–11; 5:20–6:2; 7:2; 12:11; 13:5). But his basic plea to accept his legitimacy as an apostle also runs implicitly throughout the letter, beginning already in 1:3–11. Paul begins his letter by praising God for the very thing his opponents maintain calls his ministry into question: his suffering. In doing so, Paul's praise itself contains the primary appeal of the letter. Rather than rejecting Paul for his suffering, the Corinthians should join Paul in praising God for the afflictions Paul continues to experience on behalf of Christ and the church (1:3, 11).

Paul's tone in 2 Corinthians is, therefore, at once not only apologetic, but also confrontational. The motivation for his appeals is clear: On the horizon stands God's judgment in Christ (5:10–11), to be exacted in advance when Paul makes his third and decisive visit to Corinth (13:1–10). The only hope for those still in rebellion against him is to repent, even as the majority has done already (cf. 2:5–11; 7:2–16). As for that majority, they must demonstrate the validity of their repentance by continuing to support Paul, by separating from those who will not repent, and by participating in the collection as part of the fruits of righteousness characteristic of the people of God (cf. 2:5–11; 3:18; 5:17; 6:1; 6:14–7:1; 8:1–9:15).

Paul's Prayer of Praise
for the Comfort of God (1:3–7)

PAUL BEGINS BY praising God because he is "the Father of compassion" and "the God of all comfort" (better: "consolation"). As verses 8–11 will make clear, the "compassionate comfort" in view here is not merely a subjective feeling of relief or psychological support. Rather, Paul is referring to his present state of peace in the midst of adversity because of his confidence in God's willingness and ability to deliver his people. The experience of God's deliverance in the *past* and the corresponding surety of his deliverance in the *future* (cf. 1:10) is the "comfort" of his people in the *present*. God is "the God of all comfort" because he is the one who is "our refuge and strength, an ever-present help in trouble" (Ps. 46:1; cf. also 23:4–6; 71:20–21; 94:17–18; Isa. 12:1; 40:1; 49:13; Jer. 31:13; 38:9). Our emotional comfort comes not from within ourselves, but from God's commitment to sustain and save his people, no matter what.

For this reason, Paul moves from a statement of who God *is* in verse 3, to a declaration of what God *does* in verse 4a, to God's *goal* for doing it in 4b. Because God is "the God of *all* comfort" (i.e., true comfort comes from God), he comforts Paul in all his troubles so that, in turn, Paul has the ability ("we can") to comfort others no matter what comes their way. The resource Paul uses to comfort others is the same comfort he himself has experienced from God. It is God's faithfulness to Paul that enables him to pass on to others the same assurance of God's commitment to deliver them as well. For this reason, *God* is the one who is to be praised (1:3), even though *Paul* is the one through whom others are comforted (1:4).

There is a type of "spiritual algebra" here. The measure of God's comfort matches the measure of Paul's suffering, with the result that others may be comforted to that same degree ("Paul's suffering + God's comfort = comfort for others"). This is the point of verse 5, which functions to support the principle stated in verse 4. No matter how great the affliction, it has never outweighed the comfort Paul has received from God. This is true because, as verse 5 now explicitly indicates, Paul's trouble can be *equated* with the sovereignly superintended "sufferings of Christ" (for the way in which this is the case, see 1:8–11; 2:14–16a; 4:7–12).

The word translated "trouble" (*thlipsis*) in verse 4 can refer to distress or pain brought about either by outward circumstances (cf. Rom. 2:9; 5:3; 8:35; 1 Cor. 7:28; 2 Cor. 4:17; Eph. 3:13; Col. 1:24) or by mental and spiritual states of mind (cf. 2 Cor. 2:4; 7:4–5; Phil. 1:17), while the "suffering" (*pathema*) of verse 5 refers to misfortune, physical pain, and death (cf. Rom. 8:18; Phil. 3:10; Col. 1:24). So Paul views his troubles of every kind as an expression of the same kind of sufferings Christ experienced under God's hand.

Likewise, the divine comfort Paul experiences also comes "through Christ," that is, through Christ's own experience of God's commitment and ability to deliver him, even from death. Just as Christ's experiences of suffering are replicated in Paul's life, so too Paul is greatly comforted by his confidence in sharing in Christ's resurrection (cf. 2 Tim. 3:11). In this sense, Paul participates in the dying and rising of Christ, the twin pillars of his gospel. Paul is confident, moreover, that the comfort that comes from being convinced of God's ability and commitment to deliver his people, seen in Christ and now experienced by Paul himself, can be passed on to others. What God did for Jesus in his suffering, Paul is confident God will do for him; and what God will do for Paul, he will do for all who trust in God. This is the comfort the apostle has "through Christ" that he passes on to others.

Verse 6 applies the principle of "from comfort to comfort" to the Corinthians directly. The result of both Paul's distress and his comfort is the same: The Corinthians are comforted. It is important to notice that this movement is not reciprocal. Paul does not say that when they suffer, *he* comforts *them*, and when he suffers, *they* comfort *him*. While the Corinthians' comfort comes through Paul, Paul's comfort does not come through the Corinthians, but through Christ. As Barnett points out, "According to vv. 4–5 the 'comfort' is not mediated directly to both parties, but given in the first instance to Paul, that he might 'comfort' them, which he does through his ministry. . . ."[6]

This "one-way street" from God to Paul to the Corinthians will be developed throughout the letter (cf. 1:8–11; 2:14–3:3; 4:7–15; 6:3–10; 11:7–33; 12:7–13). Yet already here we see an important clue to its significance. The identification of Paul's troubles (v. 4) with the sufferings of Christ (v. 5) as a means of mediating the comfort of the resurrection to the Corinthians (v. 6) reveals that Paul considered his suffering as an apostle to be a sovereignly ordained vehicle for mediating God's presence in the lives of his people, just as Christ suffered on the cross and was raised from the dead for the sake of the church.

The ultimate consequence of Paul's suffering and comfort is spelled out in verses 6b–7. At the first level, Paul's experience of God's comfort is to produce "endurance" among the Corinthians whenever they undergo the same sufferings that befall Paul (cf. 4:10–12). Like Paul, they too can rely on God to "comfort" them. Conversely, the Corinthians' ability to endure patiently the same sufferings Paul endures will be evidence that they have indeed experienced God's comfort through Paul. This ability to endure in the midst of adversity because of the comfort they have received is Paul's "hope" for the Corinthians.

Moreover, Paul's hope for the Corinthians is certain *because* he knows that their participation in his suffering, like his own participation in the sufferings of Christ, will never outdistance their common share in God's comfort (v. 7b).[7] Wherever God is present, there exists a sense of security and peace in the midst of our afflictions that derives from God's commitment to deliver his people since God is, by the very definition of his nature, the "God of all comfort" (v. 3c). Therefore, the ultimate purpose of Paul's argument in verses 3b–7 is not to comfort the Corinthians, but to bring honor to God as the one who has shown himself in and through Paul's afflictions to be the faithful Father of the Lord Jesus Christ (v. 3a). The end of all experience and theology is doxology.

---

6. Paul Barnett, *The Second Epistle to the Corinthians*, 80.

7. It is important to keep in mind that in the New Testament "hope" (*elpis*) and the related verb "to hope" (*elpizo*) do not refer to "wishful thinking," but to a certainty and confidence concerning the future.

Paul's "Sentence to Death"
As the Pattern of His Suffering (1:8–11)

PAUL'S ARGUMENT IN 1:3–7 raises the question of how his suffering and comfort actually produce this endurance among the Corinthians so that he can justifiably equate his experience with that of Christ's. Against the backdrop of his opponents' accusation that Paul's suffering disqualifies his ministry, it is striking that he answers this question in verses 8–11 not only by calling attention to his suffering in Asia,[8] but also by revealing just how drastic the situation really was. He knew that, humanly speaking, he was in over his head, both physically and emotionally (v. 8).

Indeed, Paul's suffering was so severe that he saw no way out but death (cf. 1:9). In other words, the apostle felt as if he had received a "sentence of death" (v. 9a), which most likely refers to an official decision concerning his fate.[9] But God's purpose was not to kill Paul. Instead, the apostle was brought to what he thought was the end of his life *in order that* (see *hina*, v. 9) he would in no way rely on himself, but only "on God, who raises the dead" (cf. the outcome of this lesson in 4:7–9, esp. v. 8). Building on his prior identification in verse 5 of his suffering with the sufferings of Christ, this somewhat standard Jewish confession consequently becomes an intentional allusion to the resurrection of Christ.[10]

In making this link, Paul takes the decisive step of interpreting the death of Christ as a type of his own "death" experience in Asia, so that Christ's "comfort" on the cross as a result of hoping in the resurrection becomes a type of Paul's own experience. Like Christ, Paul too was called in his "death" (i.e., his overwhelming suffering in Asia) to trust the God who raises the dead. And just as God raised Christ from the dead, so too God delivered Paul (1:10a).

---

8. Though many have suggested that this refers back to Paul's suffering in Ephesus as recounted in 1 Cor. 15:32, the precise location within the Roman province of Asia and the exact nature of his "hardships" are no longer known to us, though they would have been to the Corinthians.

9. See Margaret E. Thrall, *The Second Epistle to the Corinthians*, 1:118–19, who points out that *apokrima* (NIV "sentence") means "official report" or "decision," often in response to a petition. If this connotation of a response is to be emphasized here, then "one might suppose Paul to be saying that he had asked himself what his prospects were, and had received the inward reply . . . that he must die" (p. 119).

10. Ibid., 119. Following Windisch, Barrett, Furnish, and Martin, Thrall points out that the description of God as the one who raises the dead "comes in all probability from the Jewish synagogue liturgy, since it occurs in the Eighteen Benedictions." There, in the second blessing, we read: "Thou art mighty, strong, that livest for ever, that raisest the dead, that sustainest the living, that quickenest the dead. Blessed are thou, O Lord, who quickenest the dead!" (p. 119n.275; quoted from W. Förster, *Palestinian Judaism in New Testament Times* [London: Olives and Boyd, 1964], 228).

Thus, just as Christ's resurrection points forward to and secures our hope in God's final deliverance of all his people (cf. 1 Cor. 15:20–28), so too God's past deliverance of Paul establishes his confidence in the deliverance to come (2 Cor. 1:10b). Hence, this replay of Christ's death and resurrection in Paul's own life leads him to be confident that God can be trusted to deliver him in the future. This confidence for the future is the biblical notion of "hope," a hope that Paul will continue to maintain with the help of the Corinthians' prayers (1:10–11a).

Far from calling his apostleship into question, it thus becomes clear that Paul's past deliverance and present endurance in the midst of suffering are the means by which God continues to display that he is both willing and able to deliver and sustain his people. Paul's experience in Asia was an object lesson of the same divine faithfulness and power portrayed in the cross and resurrection of Christ. As such, it should draw others to join Paul in trusting and praising God in the present as they look to the future. Hence, since Paul's suffering is the platform for the display of God's resurrection power, the Corinthians should not reject Paul for his weakness. Rather, they ought to pray for Paul that, having learned to hope in God, he may continue to trust God in the midst of his adversities. And as a result of the many prayers being offered up on Paul's behalf, others will join in praising God for displaying his great mercy and comfort to his apostle (v. 11).

Paul therefore ends in verse 11 where he began in verse 3, with thanksgiving and praise to God. This is not an accident or merely the result of a careful rhetorical strategy. The goal of Paul's ministry, like that of his life itself, including his suffering, is to bring about thanksgiving to God, since this is the fundamental reversal of the heart of sin (cf. Rom. 1:21). In calling the Corinthians to join him in thanking God, Paul is calling them to express the heart of gratitude that comes from living a life of faith in the God who creates and creates anew. In short, he is calling them, as saints within the church of God (2 Cor. 1:1), to reverse the effects of sinful self-dependence and self-glorification in their lives (cf. Rom. 1:22).

In returning to the praise of God, Paul has fulfilled the three purposes of his opening thanksgiving. (1) In fulfillment of his epistolary purpose, Paul has made it clear that the comfort of God in the midst of adversity is the main theme of the letter. (2) By way of instruction, Paul has stated his corresponding thesis, namely, that his suffering, rather than calling his legitimacy into question, is the very means by which God's comfort is mediated to others. (3) In mounting his consequent appeal, Paul invites the Corinthians to join him in thanking God for his suffering and deliverance, thus fulfilling Paul's initial call to praise God in verse 3. If the Corinthians should spurn this invitation, their very refusal becomes an indictment of their rebellion against the gospel (cf. 12:19–21; 13:1–10).

Bridging
Contexts

PAUL'S VIEW OF GOD. In order to move from Paul's context to our own, there are at least three fundamental perspectives to keep in mind, all of which are increasingly alien to our worldview. We note first Paul's view of God.[11] The movement in Paul's thought from verse 3a to verses 3b–11 demonstrates that although God is known by his actions, his actions derive from his character, not the reverse. *Because* God is the God of *all* comfort, therefore he comforts Paul, and the comfort Paul experiences must come from God.

This has at least two important implications. (1) God's character is not in flux or in a process of development in response to his own unfolding actions or as a consequence of the actions of others. Though we know God's character through his acts *within* history, his character is not derived *from* that history. Instead, Paul teaches that history itself is dependent on the display of God's absolute sovereignty and freedom from constraint, whether in creation (cf. Rom. 1:18–25; 1 Cor. 11:9; Col. 1:16; 1 Tim. 2:13), in providence (cf. Acts 17:24–31; Eph. 1:9–11; Col. 1:17), or in redemption (cf. Rom. 11:33–36; 1 Cor. 10:11; Eph. 1:3–8). Even more striking is Paul's conviction that God's character is also manifest in and through the circumstances of Paul's own personal life (cf. Gal. 1:15; Eph. 3:1–6; Phil. 1:12–26).

(2) The ultimate purpose not only of history in general, but also of our own history in particular, is to reveal the majestic character of God, to which his people respond with the praise and thanksgiving due his name (1:3, 11). Moreover, Paul's emphasis in this passage on God's "comfort" reflects his conviction that the glory of God's sovereignty is most profoundly displayed in his merciful goodness toward those who trust in his "compassion" no matter what the circumstances (cf. Rom. 8:28–39; 9:22–29). In moving from Paul's worldview to ours, we must therefore maintain the "Godness" and "God-centeredness" of God in a world that is prone to place humanity at the epicenter of the universe. Contemporary popular theology does not often contain such an emphasis on the centrality and sovereignty of God, but bringing Paul's perspective into our own age is virtually impossible without it. For when Paul speaks of "God," it is in the light of his conviction, well known to the Corinthians, that

> there is no God but one. For even if there are so-called gods, whether
> in heaven or on earth (as indeed there are many "gods" and many

---

11. It is my conviction that Paul's views are consonant with the developing views of the biblical canon as a whole. As such, they can also be called "biblical views." But our purpose here is to restrict ourselves to a development of Paul's thought in particular.

"lords"), yet for us there is but one God [cf. Deut. 6:4; 10:17], the Father, from whom all things came and for whom we live; and there is but one Lord, Jesus Christ, through whom all things came and through whom we live. (1 Cor. 8:4–6)

Paul's view of suffering. The second controlling perspective is Paul's view of suffering. The apostle will develop his understanding of the purpose of suffering more fully as the letter unfolds. But already we have seen that the words he chooses to refer to his troubles (*thlipsis* and *pathema*) were general terms that could be used to signify both physical and emotional distress, as well as the suffering caused by persecution.

Hence, Paul's full-orbed definition of suffering speaks against those who, whether in Paul's day or our own, attempt to limit the kinds of suffering that can legitimately be experienced by those who are filled with the Spirit. In such a "health and wealth gospel," those who truly live by faith may be persecuted, but they will not be subject to emotional illness, physical sickness, or financial distress. Yet the general terminology Paul uses in this context to describe affliction, together with his own experiences of physical suffering, persecution, natural deprivations, economic hardships, and the emotional distress of anxiety (see 1 Cor. 4:11–13; 2 Cor. 2:12–13, 17; 4:8–9; 6:4–10; 11:23–28; 12:7; Gal. 4:12–16), makes such a limitation impossible.

At the same time, Paul never glorifies suffering per se. There is no evidence that he sought it or encouraged others to do so, as if it were a sign of special spirituality. Hence, the emphasis among some of the early church fathers on actively seeking martyrdom as the highest form of Christian witness is a dangerous misapplication of Paul's view of suffering.[12] For Paul, suffering is not intrinsically good, nor is it a Christian virtue. Rather, suffering is a page in the textbook used in God's school of faith (cf. vv. 8–10). It is not suffering *itself* that teaches us faith, but *God*, who uses it as a platform to display his resurrection power in our lives, either through deliverance from suffering or by comfort within it (vv. 4–6, 10).

Paul's view of the ministry. Third, and most important for Paul's present purpose, we must keep before us Paul's view of the ministry. This theme too will be developed as the letter continues (cf. 2:14–3:3; 4:1–6, 10–12; 5:11–6:2; 10:7–18). Here Paul's implicit appeal is that his readers praise God for the very suffering his opponents think will call Paul's ministry into question. Far from being ashamed of his suffering, Paul testifies that his afflictions are the very means God uses to reveal himself in and through Paul's life as an

---

12. Cf. the desire of Ignatius (d. ca. A.D. 115) to be devoured by the wild beasts in Rome so that he might "truly be a disciple of Jesus Christ," quoting 1 Cor. 15:32 in his *Letter to the Romans*, 4–5.

apostle. Like the suffering righteous in the Old Testament and *the* Suffering Righteous One, Jesus Christ, Paul is led into situations of suffering in order that God may display his resurrection power through Paul *to others.*

Through Paul's ministry, characterized as it is by his experience of God's past deliverance and present comfort in the midst of his suffering, believers come to experience the peace that comes from hoping in God's resurrection power. Hope for the future is the engine that creates comfort in the present. As a result, Paul's suffering is an essential, legitimizing characteristic of his ministry as an apostle (cf. again Acts 9:16). It is not *in spite of,* but *in and through* Paul's suffering that his legitimacy is established. As we have seen, this is the major theme of 2 Corinthians.

One of the most difficult aspects of reading 2 Corinthians, therefore, is to know how to apply Paul's suffering as an apostle to general Christian experience. To begin with, we must remember that the mediation of God's comfort is not reciprocal between Paul and his church. The movement is a "one-way street" from God through Paul to the Corinthians (cf. 1:6). This reflects Paul's conviction that as an apostle, unlike believers in general, he was *called* to suffer as the revelatory means by which God's power in Christ is portrayed to others (cf. also Phil. 1:12; 3:10–11; Col. 1:24; 1 Thess. 3:3–4, 7; 2 Tim. 2:9; 3:10–11). In return, God comforts Paul through the positive response of the Corinthians to his ministry (cf. 7:6–7; cf. Rom. 1:11–12).

Moreover, having learned the lesson of faith, whenever believers do in fact suffer (and Paul promises them that they will), they too are to exhibit the same hope-driven endurance manifested in Paul's life, thereby joining him in becoming an example to others (1:6–7; cf. Acts 14:22; Phil. 1:29; 2 Tim. 3:12). There is therefore a qualitative and quantitative difference between the suffering that will come their way periodically (cf. Phil. 2:26–27; 1 Thess. 1:6; 2 Thess. 1:4–7; 1 Peter 1:6–9; 4:12–19; Heb. 10:32–34; 12:4–13), and the daily experience of suffering that was an essential aspect of Paul's calling as an apostle.

We must be careful, then, not to move directly from these passages concerning Paul's suffering as an apostle to our suffering as believers. We must not conclude from Paul's calling that all Christians must suffer alike. Nor should we assign a revelatory role or higher degree of spirituality to those who suffer more than others. In the providence of God, some believers live significantly more peaceful and healthy lives than others. Furthermore, when we do draw a parallel between Paul's suffering and our own (as in 1:6–7), we should not trivialize Paul's suffering for the gospel by equating it with our experiences of inconvenience, ego-deflation, or lack of middle-class material comforts. Nevertheless, all Christians must face the last enemy, death.

And God calls all believers to experience the lack that comes from daily considering the needs of others more important than their own (cf. Mark 8:34–35; 10:43–44; Phil. 2:3–5).

> In fact, the way of life that comes from living by faith in future grace [cf. Paul's emphasis on his hope in God's future rescue in 1:10] will very likely involve *more* suffering, not *less*. When you know that your future is in the hands of an all-powerful, all-knowing, all-wise God who promises to work all things for your good, you are free to take any risk that love demands—no matter what the cost. It is a biblical truth that the more earnest we become about being salt of the earth and the light of the world, and the more devoted we become to reaching the unreached peoples of the world, and exposing the works of darkness, and loosing the bonds of sin and Satan, the more we will suffer.[13]

So those who are not suffering should not seek to do so. Rather, they should seek to be faithful to God, banking their hope on his promises so that meeting the needs of others becomes more important than securing their own future. Though such a call will no doubt involve suffering, the circumstances surrounding this life of faith are up to God.

In applying Paul's example it is also important to stress that the apostolic age is over. When drawing parallels between Paul's relationship to his churches and the ministry of contemporary pastors, we must distinguish between Paul's *functions* as an apostle and his *office* as an apostle. Pastors and missionaries today fulfill many of the same functions that Paul performed, and for this reason we may rightly ask whether they too might not be called to suffer on behalf of their people in essentially the same way Paul was. Certainly the age-old dictum that the blood of the martyrs is the seed of the church is often true.[14]

But neither our pastors nor our missionaries, nor even contemporary martyrs, occupy the intrinsically authoritative office held by Paul as an apostle (see comments on 1:1). The authority of the pastor and missionary remains derivative from and subordinate to Scripture as the deposit of the prophetic and apostolic witness. A person's suffering in and of itself, though it may reveal the purity of one's motives (cf. 1:12–14), should never be used as a reason to accept the authority of his or her teaching. Only the revelation of God's Word in the Scriptures can be the plumb line of truth.

---

13. John Piper, *Future Grace: The Purifying Power of Living by Faith in Future Grace* (Portland: Multnomah, 1995), 341–42.

14. Originally found in Tertullian, *Apologeticus* 50, who was himself converted in A.D. 193 by witnessing the courage of Christians who were facing torture and death for their faith.

THE CHARACTER OF WORSHIP. As we have seen, Paul employs the standard Jewish *berakah*-formula in 1:3–11, grounding his praise in 1:3 with reasons garnered from his own experience, an experience permeated with the will and presence of God. Paul's use of this form carries an important lesson for the nature of prayer. As this structure indicates, praise is the expression of our adulation of God's character that flows from a serious reflection on the way in which he works to accomplish his purposes for the good of his people. There must be reasons for prayer.

Moreover, the transition from verses 3–7 to 8–11 indicates that a primary purpose for corporate prayer, even when it focuses on the experience of an individual, is the incorporation of others into our praise. Paul's thanksgiving in verses 4–7 leads to the Corinthians' joining him in verse 11, which in turn is a fulfillment of Paul's admonition to declare God's praise in verse 3. Biblical worship therefore avoids two extremes: contentless expressions of praise on the one hand, and human-centered "testimonies" on the other. Genuine praise is not a mindless act designed to escape thinking about our daily lives, nor is it a means of sugarcoating our circumstances. Our praise of God should never be transformed into some sort of Christian "mantra," nor should it be used to make things look better than they really are. We praise God in the midst of our adversity not because things are not as bad as they seem (they could be worse!), but because of who God is and of what he does in and through the reality in which we live.

It is not the command to praise God per se that gives birth to true worship, but an encounter with the living God. As 1:3–11 illustrates, therefore, the way to bring about praise for God is to ground our call to praise (1:3) with declarations and illustrations of the praiseworthy character of God himself (1:4–11). For the same reason, testimonies should not degenerate into news reports about how bad the circumstances really were (note the lack of details in verses 8–11), or into thinly veiled vehicles for displaying one's "accomplishments," good or bad (cf. 11:18, 23). Nor should "leading worship" call attention to the abilities of the worship leaders. Instead, those who testify to God's mercies should present a God-centered display of his character and attributes as seen in his works on behalf of his people (1:11; cf. Isa. 64:4). The goal of worship, after all, is not to display our performance or experience, but to enlarge the circle of those who enjoy the comfort and therefore praise the glory of God (cf. 2 Cor. 1:3, 11).

The character of God. As a prayer of thanksgiving, this opening passage, though concerned with Paul's suffering as an apostle, is ultimately about God. A moment's reflection will reveal just how countercultural this is in our day and age. Such a theocentric perspective is difficult to recover and maintain in our cultural milieu. Few today focus attention first and foremost on the character of God; doing so does not seem to have relevance for our daily lives.

For example, in the contemporary church the popularity of topical talks concerning our "felt needs" far outweighs any interest in contemplating the nature of God as revealed in the Scriptures. When was the last time you heard a sermon series on the attributes and purposes of God as revealed in the history of redemption? "Theology" as the study of the nature and purposes of the transcendent God is viewed as arcane, abstract, and out of touch. Instead, surrounded by a "new age" Gnosticism that champions personal enlightenment through private "spiritual experiences" as the pathway to knowing the god within each of us,[15] even the church finds herself self-absorbed.

Thus, in order to regain the significance of Paul's worldview, we must recover his affirmation that the comfort of God so desperately needed in our day derives not from within, but from knowing the transcendent God as the one who has delivered and will deliver his people. In order to restore the Pauline gospel, God himself must become the central subject of our worship, of our conversation, and of our theology. Only then will we be able to combat the tyranny of subjectivity that is seeping into our churches through the cracks of our theology as it spreads throughout our culture. For as David Wells has documented, we have "bought cultural acceptability by emptying [ourselves] of serious thought, serious theology, serious worship, and serious practice. . . ." Hence, "the fundamental problem in the evangelical world today is that God rests too inconsequential upon the church. His truth is too distant, his grace is too ordinary, his judgment is too benign, his gospel is too easy, and his Christ is too common."[16]

Ironically, then, given the pervasive influence of our own culture, one of the best ways to gain contemporary significance is to return to the theological reflections of earlier periods. Hearing a word from the past often enables us to gain perspective on our own cultural situation, with its own particular forms of idolatry. In regard to regaining a sense of God-centeredness in all we do and experience, including our suffering, a serious reflection on Chapter 2 of *The Westminster Confession of Faith* (1646) is extremely helpful:

---

15. For a concise look at the parallels between ancient Gnosticism and modern day "new age" religions, see Peter Jones, *The Gnostic Empire Strikes Back: An Old Heresy for the New Age* (Phillipsburg, N.J.: Presbyterian & Reformed, 1992).

16. D. Wells, *God in the Wasteland: The Reality of Truth in a World of Fading Dreams* (Grand Rapids: Eerdmans, 1994), 27, 30.

I. There is but one only living and true God, who is infinite in being and perfection, a most pure spirit, invisible, without body, parts, or passions, immutable, immense, eternal, incomprehensible, almighty, most wise, most holy, most free, most absolute, working all things according to the counsel of his own immutable and most righteous will, for his own glory; most loving, gracious, merciful, long-suffering, abundant in goodness and truth, forgiving iniquity, transgression, and sin; the rewarder of them that diligently seek him; and withal most just and terrible in his judgments; hating all sin, and who will by no means clear the guilty.

II. God hath all life, glory, goodness, blessedness, in and of himself; and is alone in and unto himself all-sufficient, not standing in need of any creatures which he hath made, nor deriving any glory from them, but only manifesting his own glory in, by, unto, and upon them: he is the lone foundation of all being, of whom, through whom, and to whom are all things; and hath most sovereign dominion over them, to do by them, for them, or upon them whatsoever himself pleaseth. In his sight all things are open and manifest; his knowledge is infinite, infallible, and independent upon the creature; so as nothing is to him contingent or uncertain. He is most holy in all his counsels, in all his works, and in all his commands. To him is due from angels and men, and every other creature, whatsoever worship, service, or obedience, he is pleased to require of them.

The contemporary relevance of such a focus on God himself is well illustrated by the life and thought of Karl Barth, in most people's estimation the greatest theologian of the twentieth century. Barth's renewed emphasis on the doctrine of God turned an entire generation of church leaders away from the Protestant liberalism of the late nineteenth and early twentieth centuries. As Eberhard Jüngel, perhaps the leading interpreter of Barth's thought, put it:

The freedom of God: for Barth, that was God himself. The unmistakable greatness of his theology arises from his unwavering intention to think of God himself. The polemical aspect of his theology is directed against all surrogates. No idea, no ideology, no pious postulate, and especially no theological concept may take the place of God. God confides in no one. He speaks for himself. He reveals himself. Barth uncompromisingly demanded that we think of God himself![17]

---

17. Eberhard Jüngel, *Karl Barth: A Theological Legacy* (Philadelphia: Westminster, 1986), 21, from Jüngel's lecture "A Tribute at His Death," given at the University of Zurich on Dec. 11, 1968, the day after Barth died.

Unfortunately, the re-escalation of a human-centered epistemology brought about by the rise of postmodern thought has once again made personal experience, whether that of the individual or the individual's social class, gender, or culture, the all-determinative matrix by which truth is determined (see Contemporary Significance section of 1:1–2). This has transformed our view of God into a view of ourselves and recast thought about God into an exercise in self-discovery. Those most in need of God's comfort are thus shut off from its only source, the "God of all comfort" himself.

Paul's call in 1:3 to praise God as the one who comforts us is not a cold, lifeless theological formula, but the very means by which we find the rest that comes from knowing God's sovereign commitment to deliver his people. So Paul's prayer of praise in 1:4–7 stands not only as a needed corrective to the cultural currents of our day, but also, and more critically, as the pathway to a true experience of God's comforting presence. To seek our comfort in God is to glorify him as the God of all comfort. Hence, our search for comfort is, in the end, a search for the glory of God, who shows himself glorious by comforting his people.

Seen in this light, Paul's call in 1:3 to praise God's character is, in effect, a call to be comforted, since in doing so we are affirming in the midst of our adversity that God is the one who can do so. God's commitment to show forth his glory is, therefore, the comfort of his people. The most comforting thing God can do is to call us to praise him as the one worthy of our honor. John Piper's exposition of the significance of this crucial perspective is again helpful:

> But is it loving for God to exalt his own glory? Yes it is . . . *God is most glorified in us when we are most satisfied in him.* . . . Therefore God's pursuit of his own glory is not at odds with my joy, and that means it is not unkind or unmerciful or unloving of him to seek his glory. In fact it means that the more passionate God is for his own glory the more passionate he is for my satisfaction in that glory. . . . Therefore when we read hundreds of texts in the Bible that show God passionately exalting his own glory, we no longer hear them as the passions of an overweening, uncaring ego. . . . God is utterly unique. He is the only being in the universe worthy of worship. Therefore when he exalts himself he thus directs people to true and lasting joy. "In your presence is fullness of joy; at your right hand are pleasures for evermore" (Psalm 16:11).[18]

---

18. John Piper, *Let the Nations Be Glad! The Supremacy of God in Missions* (Grand Rapids, Baker, 1993), 16–28.

The character of God's sovereignty in suffering. The other reason Paul praises God in this passage is because of his confidence that the Corinthians too will be recipients of God's comfort in the midst of their suffering (1:6–7, 11). The basis for his confidence is his own past experience of God's comfort (here experienced as an actual deliverance from his suffering). Paul's entire argument, however, is built on his underlying conviction that God's sovereignty extends over *all* circumstances. To curtail the extent of God's power or purposes in the world is to cut off the possibility of comfort in the midst of adversity.

For Paul there are no such things as "luck" or "accident." To follow his thought we must resist limiting God's sovereignty in the face of suffering. The comfort of God in this text is not his empathy with us as someone who feels the tragedy of evil but is helpless in it. Nor does the comfort of God reside in his actions as a "fourth-quarter quarterback," who is brought in after things have fallen apart to save the day just before the whistle blows. There is no comfort in suffering if God is not sovereign over it. To pare down God's sovereignty is to render suffering a triumph of evil and sin against the limited will and power of God. But, for Paul, *God* is the one who leads Paul into suffering, sustains him in its midst, and delivers him from it—all to the glory of God himself and for the eternal good of his people (cf. 2:14; 4:7–18; 12:9–10).

Against all "down-sizings" of God in order to cope with the "problem of evil," Paul confesses that one divine purpose in suffering is the glory of God (1:3, 11) *by* the sanctification of his people (1:4–10). Although we cannot understand fully God's ultimate intent in the tragic events of life (or even in the normal, routine matters!), it *is* possible to say that an essential part of God's purpose in all things is to honor himself by creating a people who, like Christ, trust him in every circumstance (1:9–10; cf. Rom. 8:28–30; Phil. 3:10 with Heb. 5:8). As a result, Paul's hope derives from his confidence in God's ability to rescue his people in their affliction for the purpose of creating faith in his comforting sovereignty and love. And it is this confidence that leads Paul to prayer and praise rather than to resignation and self-pity.[19] In a similar way, listen to the confession of Dietrich Bonhoeffer from New Year's Day, 1943, as it reminds us of Paul's own experience recounted in 1:8–11:

> I believe that God can and will bring good out of evil, even out of the greatest evil. For that purpose he needs men who make the best use of everything. I believe that God will give us all the strength we need

---

19. For a helpful application of the sovereignty of God to situations of suffering, see Jerry Bridges, *Trusting God* (Colorado Springs: NavPress, 1988). For an excellent treatment of the biblical texts concerning suffering, see D. A. Carson, *How Long, O Lord? Reflections on Suffering and Evil* (Grand Rapids: Baker, 1990).

to help us to resist in all time of distress. But he never gives it in advance, lest we should rely on ourselves and not on him alone. A faith such as this should allay all our fears for the future. I believe that even our mistakes and shortcomings are turned to good account, and that it is no harder for God to deal with them than with our suppos- edly good deeds. I believe that God is no timeless fate, but that he waits and answers sincere prayers and responsible actions.[20]

It was this bedrock conviction that enabled Bonhoeffer to endure his subse- quent imprisonment and eventual death at the hands of the Nazis.[21]

The character of endurance in view of the comfort of God. Our response to the comfort of God's sovereign presence is to endure the suffering that comes our way, confident that it is a divinely orchestrated aspect of our school of faith. Under God's sovereignty, the "endurance" spoken about in 1:6 as the goal of Paul's apostolic suffering cannot be reinterpreted as some sort of Stoic self-discipline, in which we attempt to conquer suffering by controlling our emotions. Paul is not talking about will power in this passage. Nor should Paul's thought be perverted into the "power of positive thinking," in which we try to "psyche ourselves up" into believing that things are really not as bad as they seem (they are usually worse), so that we can overcome our circumstances if we would "only put our mind to it." Moreover, nothing could be farther from Paul's thought than the "new age" conviction that all we have to do is to get in touch with "the god within us."

In stark contrast to all such self-help strategies, by "endurance" Paul means that trust in *God's* power and purposes in the midst of adversity expresses itself in a steady not giving up. His words in 1:6 must have reminded the Corinthians of what he had said earlier in 1 Corinthians 10:13: We endure in faith because of our confidence that "God is faithful," so that "he will not allow you to be tempted beyond what you can bear. But when you are tempted, he will also provide a way out so that you can stand up under it." Note that in this verse Paul again makes it clear that God is active both before temptation strikes and in the midst of it. Note too that the "way out" is not necessarily an immediate deliverance from temptation, since God pro- vides the "way out" in order that we might persevere, not escape.

This means that when suffering strikes, we can be sure that God will either deliver us from it to show himself powerful and teach us faith, as he did for Paul in Asia, or, as our faith grows, will give us the strength to endure in order to show himself even *more* powerful, as he did for Paul in regard to

---

20. D. Bonhoeffer, *Letters and Papers From Prison*, ed., Eberhard Bethge, enlarged ed. (New York: Macmillan, 1972 [1953]), 11.

21. Cf. his poem "Who Am I," from July, 1944, found in *Letters and Papers*, 347–48.

his "thorn in the flesh" (2 Cor. 12:7–10; cf. 4:7–12; 6:3–10). In either case, God will not allow us to suffer beyond what we can handle. Indeed, Paul knew that God had spared the life of Epaphroditus not only for Epaphroditus's sake, but also for Paul's own sake, since Paul would not have been able to handle it if Epaphroditus had died (cf. Phil. 2:27).

Nevertheless, our passage makes clear that God did not rescue Paul in Asia or spare Epaphroditus in order to encourage others to seek a miracle. Paul's deliverance from his suffering in Asia was intended to encourage the Corinthians to endure suffering in their own lives (1:6). This side of Christ's return (cf. the future deliverance of 1:10), God is glorified in our lives *not* primarily by performing miracles, but by enabling us to persevere because of our trust in him as the one who raises the dead. God rescued Paul in the *past* so that he might trust in God's *future* rescue while he suffered in the *present* (1:10). God spared Epaphroditus, Paul's fellow worker and soldier in the causes of Christ, in order that Paul might learn to be content no matter what, knowing that the Lord was committed to doing whatever it took to meet his real needs (Phil. 2:30; 4:12, 19).

Anybody can worship Santa Claus. But hanging in there with God in the midst of intense suffering, as Christ hung on the cross, magnifies the worth of God as the one who sustains us. God's goal in suffering, therefore, is to teach us that in life and in death, as in all eternity, he himself is all we ultimately need. God never intends to destroy his people, nor will he allow anyone or anything else to do so. Nothing can separate us from the love of God in Christ (Rom. 8:31–39). In placing Paul in a situation in which he despaired even of life itself (2 Cor. 1:8), the only thing God destroyed was Paul's self-confidence. In return, Paul received God himself. In response, the apostle gave God praise. To return to the past again, this focus and foundation of comfort finds an enduring expression in the first question of *The Heidelberg Catechism* (1563):

Question 1. What is your only comfort, in life and in death?

That I belong—body and soul, in life and in death—not to myself but to my faithful Savior, Jesus Christ, who at the cost of his own blood has fully paid for all my sins and has completely freed me from the dominion of the devil; that he protects me so well that without the will of my Father in heaven not a hair can fall from my head; indeed, that everything must fit his purpose for my salvation. Therefore, by his Holy Spirit, he also assures me of eternal life, and makes me whole-heartedly willing and ready from now on to live for him.[22]

---

22. Quoted from Mark A. Noll, ed., *Confessions and Catechisms of the Reformation* (Grand Rapids: Baker, 1991), 137 (following the 1962 translation of Miller and Osterhaven).

The priority Paul places on endurance as our response to God's sovereign power and will points to two important implications for modern Western culture. (1) On the one hand, contrary to the movement made popular by Elisabeth Kubler-Ross, we must resist "accepting" affliction and "welcoming" death as merely a normal part of life.[23] For Paul, death is still "the last enemy" (1 Cor. 15:26) and the result of sin in the world (Rom. 5:12). The gospel is not a coping mechanism, but the promise of resurrection life in the future, the inauguration of which is God's power for a new life in the present. In destroying the stranglehold of sin, Christ vanquishes the "sting" of death. (2) On the other hand, we must also resist at all costs the "health and wealth gospel" (on this "gospel" as a perversion of the true gospel, see comments and application to 4:7–12 and 11:1–6, below). The glory of the gospel is its declaration that the message of the cross is the power of God.

The former attempt to sanitize suffering and death expects *too little* from God, as if the kingdom of God has not been inaugurated (i.e., it operates with an *"under*realized eschatology"). In this view, all we can hope for in life is the status quo. Thus, we must have faith to accept things the way they are. The latter attempt to purge suffering from the life of the Christian expects too *much* from God in the present, as if the kingdom of God has been inaugurated in all its fullness (i.e., it operates with an *"over*realized eschatology"). In this view, true believers can expect to experience almost all the glories of heaven already on earth. Thus, we must have faith to ignore the way things are.

In contrast, Paul proclaims an endurance of faith that lives in the tension of the "overlapping of the ages," in which the kingdom of God is certainly here, but is not yet here in all its fullness (i.e., we operate with an *"inaugurated* eschatology"). In Paul's view, we must have faith in the sovereignty *and* goodness of God in and through the way things are—expectant, enduring, full of praise, confident that God is glorified through comforting his people in himself.

The character of the pastor. Finally, Paul's experience as an apostle leads to the conclusion that those called to proclaim and embody the kingdom of God are called to a unique role within the church. Through their lives of trust (1:9), integrity (see the next section, 1:12–2:4), and mercy (2:5–11), *in the midst of adversity*, the saints entrusted to their care will see displayed before them the reality of Christ's death and resurrection. This implies that the life of the pastor will normally be characterized by a quality (and even quantity?) of suffering not usually experienced in the lives of those gifted for other, equally important roles within the church (see esp. 11:28). If bringing about the endurance of faith in the lives of God's people is the goal of Paul's ministry,

23. See her *Death, The Final Stage of Growth* (Englewood Cliffs, N.J.: Prentice Hall, 1975).

his own life of faith as a servant of the new covenant (3:4–6), lived out publicly before them (4:7–15; 6:3–10), is the means to that end.

In watching their apostle, the Corinthians see the comfort of God enfleshed in Paul's experience. Hence, the movement in this passage *from* God *to* Paul *to* the Corinthians illustrates that God calls those in ministry, especially through leading them into afflictions of all kinds, to be an example to the church in a way that cannot be said of the church as a whole. The suffering of the pastor or missionary functions as a primary vehicle through which the truth of the gospel is mediated to God's people (cf. 2:14–3:3; 4:7–12; 6:3–10; 12:9–10). To quote Barnett again:

> Paul's experience of suffering and comfort in the course of his ministry is replicated in every generation in the lives of godly missionaries and pastors in their interrelationships with their congregations. While both minister and people suffer as they bear witness to Christ in an alien culture, there remains a distinctive role and therefore a distinctive suffering to the Christian leader. As the comfort of God is experienced in the life of the leader, so it will be passed on through ministry to the people.[24]

In the midst of a contemporary church that is often caught up in techniques and technology as the way to grow, Paul's message in 1:3–11 reminds us that just as redemption took place through the coming of Christ, so too God's plan for strengthening the faith of his people is not ultimately a program, but a person. The life and proclamation of the pastor, replicated in the faith of his people in the midst of their own sufferings, is the primary way God grows his church.

One of the central messages of 2 Corinthians is the centrality and significance of the pastoral office. And at the heart of the pastoral office is the suffering of the pastor, even as Christ came as the suffering servant who was obedient to the point of death. In an age when pastors are being increasingly reconfigured as professional therapists, business managers, and coaches in the game of life, such an understanding seems as strange as it is needed. It is this high view of the ministry in particular, and at the same time the surprising character of that same office, that informs the next sections of Paul's letter.

---

24. Barnett, *Second Corinthians*, 80.

2 Corinthians 1:12–2:11

NOW THIS IS our boast: Our conscience testifies that we have conducted ourselves in the world, and especially in our relations with you, in the holiness and sincerity that are from God. We have done so not according to worldly wisdom but according to God's grace. [13]For we do not write you anything you cannot read or understand. And I hope that, [14]as you have understood us in part, you will come to understand fully that you can boast of us just as we will boast of you in the day of the Lord Jesus.

[15]Because I was confident of this, I planned to visit you first so that you might benefit twice. [16]I planned to visit you on my way to Macedonia and to come back to you from Macedonia, and then to have you send me on my way to Judea. [17]When I planned this, did I do it lightly? Or do I make my plans in a worldly manner so that in the same breath I say, "Yes, yes" and "No, no"?

[18]But as surely as God is faithful, our message to you is not "Yes" and "No." [19]For the Son of God, Jesus Christ, who was preached among you by me and Silas and Timothy, was not "Yes" and "No," but in him it has always been "Yes." [20]For no matter how many promises God has made, they are "Yes" in Christ. And so through him the "Amen" is spoken by us to the glory of God. [21]Now it is God who makes both us and you stand firm in Christ. He anointed us, [22]set his seal of ownership on us, and put his Spirit in our hearts as a deposit, guaranteeing what is to come.

[23]I call God as my witness that it was in order to spare you that I did not return to Corinth. [24]Not that we lord it over your faith, but we work with you for your joy, because it is by faith you stand firm. [2:1]So I made up my mind that I would not make another painful visit to you. [2]For if I grieve you, who is left to make me glad but you whom I have grieved? [3]I wrote as I did so that when I came I should not be distressed by those who ought to make me rejoice. I had confidence in all of you, that you would all share my joy. [4]For I wrote you out of great distress and anguish of heart and with many tears, not to grieve you but to let you know the depth of my love for you.

⁵If anyone has caused grief, he has not so much grieved me as he has grieved all of you, to some extent—not to put it too severely. ⁶The punishment inflicted on him by the majority is sufficient for him. ⁷Now instead, you ought to forgive and comfort him, so that he will not be overwhelmed by excessive sorrow. ⁸I urge you, therefore, to reaffirm your love for him. ⁹The reason I wrote you was to see if you would stand the test and be obedient in everything. ¹⁰If you forgive anyone, I also forgive him. And what I have forgiven—if there was anything to forgive—I have forgiven in the sight of Christ for your sake, ¹¹in order that Satan might not outwit us. For we are not unaware of his schemes.

THIS SECTION BEGINS the body of Paul's letter (cf. outline). The first two topics to be discussed are Paul's recent changes in travel plans (1:12–2:4) and the situation now facing the church in regard to the repentant offender (2:5–11). At first glance, these two topics appear unrelated. In reality, however, they are intimately connected. Paul turns his attention to the motivation behind what appears to be his arbitrary change of mind so that, by applying this same rationale to his readers, he might encourage them to respond in the same way to the one who has caused the community so much pain. Rather than calling his own legitimacy into question, Paul's sudden change in plans (1:12–2:4) becomes a *model* for the change in behavior he expects from the Corinthians (2:5–11).

In this letter Paul is engaged on three fronts (see the Introduction). He is concerned primarily with the Corinthians themselves, who are divided into those who have already repented from their rebellion against Paul (cf. 2:5, 8–9; 5:12; 7:7–16) and those who are still questioning his legitimacy as an apostle (chs. 10–13). In addressing the Corinthians as a whole, he seeks to encourage the former while trying to win back the latter. At the same time, Paul must counter the influence among those still questioning his legitimacy of the "false apostles," who have recently arrived in Corinth (cf. 2:17; 10:12–18; 11:1–15).

Nowhere is this threefold dialogue more evident than in this section of the letter. Against his opponents and those still under their influence, Paul must answer the objection that his change in travel plans reveals his overall weakness because of his lack of the Spirit's guidance. But Paul must also make his motives clear to those who support him so that they will not only have confidence in his behavior, but even emulate it. To accomplish this task,

Paul's argument falls naturally into four parts: 1:12–14; 1:15–22; 1:23–2:4; and 2:5–11.

The Content of Paul's Boast (1:12–14)

PAUL MAKES THE transition to this next section by indicating another reason he is so confident in calling the Corinthians to praise God for his life of faith in the midst of adversity (cf. 1:3–11). In 1:8–11, his confidence derived from God's work of rescuing Paul in order to sustain his hope personally. In 1:12–14, it now derives from God's work of establishing Paul's ground for boasting publicly. Specifically, Paul's conscience is clean concerning his behavior in the world in general and toward the Corinthians in particular since in both regards he has acted "in the uprightness[1] and sincerity that are from God" (v. 12a).

"Uprightness" (haplotes) and "sincerity" (eilikrineia) are concepts that carry the connotation of moral purity. From their use elsewhere in Paul's writings it is clear that, given humanity's bankrupt nature and the dominance of sin in the lives of those outside of Christ (see, e.g., Rom. 6:16–20; 8:5–8), the presence of such uprightness and sincerity cannot be attributed to Paul's own moral ability (for haplotes, see esp. 2 Cor. 11:3 as well as Rom. 12:8; Eph. 6:5; for eilikrineia, 1 Cor. 5:8; 2 Cor. 2:17). Where such attributes exist, they are "from God," the result of the transforming work of God's Spirit in the lives of his "new creation" (2 Cor. 5:17; cf. 3:18).

The contrast in 1:12 between conduct carried out according to "worldly [lit., fleshly] wisdom" and that which derives from "God's grace" thus reflects the difference between Paul's own condition apart from Christ and his new standing as an apostle (cf. 1:1; 3:4–6; 5:20; 6:1). Apart from God's grace, one's only recourse is to the wisdom that comes from the values, worldview, and societal structures associated with life devoid of the Spirit's power and guidance. This is what Paul refers to as living or thinking according to "the flesh" (cf. 1:17; 5:16; 10:2; also Rom. 8:3–17; Gal. 5:13–26; Eph. 2:1–3) or according to this "world" (cf. 1 Cor. 1:20; 2:12; 3:19; Eph. 2:2; Titus 2:12).

---

1. The NIV follows the textual variant that reads hagiotes ("holiness"), rather than those texts that read haplotes ("uprightness" or "simplicity"). The external evidence is evenly divided between the two possibilities, but the context favors the reading haplotes for two reasons. (1) Paul never uses hagiotes anywhere else (its only other New Testament use is found in Heb. 12:10), but he does use haplotes all seven of the times it occurs in the New Testament, five of them in 2 Cor. (1:12; 8:2; 9:11, 13; 11:3; see also Rom. 12:8; Eph. 6:5). Thus, the theme of "uprightness" or "honesty" is a key theme in this letter and is introduced here. This means that hagiotes is a more difficult reading, but too difficult for this context. (2) The contrast with "worldly wisdom" in v. 12b and Paul's emphasis on openness in v. 13 favors the fact that he is stressing his honesty in v. 12a, not his holiness (see Martin, 2 Corinthians, 18).

For this reason, the NIV often translates Paul's use of "flesh" (*sarx*) as "sinful nature" (cf. Rom. 8:3, 4, 5, 8, 9, 12, 13; Gal. 5:13, 16, 17, 19; Eph. 2:3; Col. 2:11), while it understands the "mind of the flesh" to refer to "the mind of sinful man" (Rom. 8:6–7). In 1:12 the NIV captures well the meaning of the phrase "fleshly wisdom" with its "*worldly* wisdom."

Paul's point in verse 12 is that his outward behavior, rather than calling his ministry into question, actually confirms the grace of God's call in his life. In his "boast" about a clean conscience, Paul is therefore not engaging in the self-glorification and self-dependence that he himself so strongly condemns (cf. Rom. 3:27; 1 Cor. 1:29; 3:21; 4:7; 5:6; 2 Cor. 5:12; 11:12, 16, 18; 12:1–5; Eph. 2:9). To boast in one's honesty and sincerity, or in any other evidence of God's grace, is to boast or glory properly in what *God* has done in and through one's life, that is, to "boast in the Lord" (1 Cor. 1:31; 15:9; 2 Cor. 10:17; cf. 10:8; 11:10; Rom. 5:2; 15:17; 1 Cor. 9:15; Gal. 6:4; Phil. 3:3). The content of one's boast, not the act of boasting as such, determines whether it is legitimate or not.

Hence, Paul's reference to the testimony of his conscience is, in fact, a reference to the objective work of God in his life as manifest in his outward behavior; it is not a retreat to a private and hidden sense that nobody else can judge. Of course, Paul knows that the conscience can deceive, so that ultimately it is the Lord who judges (cf. 1 Cor. 4:4–5; 2 Cor. 5:10). At the same time, the Lord testifies to his grace in the lives of his people by changing their behavior. The testimony of Paul's conscience will consequently find resonance in the conscience of those in whom the Spirit is also at work (cf. 2 Cor. 4:2; 5:11).

Paul's confidence that his actions reflect God's work in his life is supported by his willingness to write openly and clearly, that is, to "boast" about his recent change of plans, which he proceeds to do in 1:15–2:4. The transparency of his report reflects God's grace manifested in the truthfulness of his actions (1:13a). He has nothing of which he needs to be ashamed. Paul thus has confidence (i.e., "hope") that when the Corinthians hear the rest of the story, they too will no longer doubt his credibility, but will join him in boasting in what God has done in his life as their apostle. In doing so they will testify to God's grace in their own lives. As a result, their boast in *Paul* will match Paul's boast about *their* genuine spiritual nature on the day of final judgment, that is, "in the day of the Lord Jesus" (v. 14; for Paul's boast in and about his people, cf. 7:4, 14; 8:24; 9:2–3; 1 Cor. 15:31; Phil. 2:16; 1 Thess. 2:19).[2]

---

2. James Scott, *2 Corinthians*, 54, rightly points out that in using the Old Testament prophetic expression, "the day of the Lord" (= Yahweh), which refers to that time in which God would judge Israel and the nations and establish his own kingdom of righteousness (cf. Joel 1–3; Zech. 12–14), to refer to "the day of the Lord *Jesus*," Paul equates Christ's work with God's (cf. 1 Cor. 1:8; 5:5; Phil. 1:6; 1 Thess. 5:2).

It is not too much to conclude, therefore, that the Corinthians' acceptance of Paul becomes the criterion by which their own genuine conversion will be measured. If they boast in Paul as a genuine apostle, he will be able to boast in them as genuine believers (1:14). In both cases, however, the proof of their respective legitimacy is to be found in the manner of their lives. For Paul this entails the way in which he behaved toward the Corinthians as their apostle; for the Corinthians it means the way in which they respond to Paul as his "dear children" in the Lord (cf. 1 Cor. 4:14–15).

The Reason for Paul's First Change of Plans (1:15–22)

EVIDENTLY, PAUL'S OPPONENTS had pointed to his apparent change in plans regarding coming to Corinth as further evidence of his illegitimacy as an apostle. They also seem to have argued that Paul's first change in plans, in which he decided to come to Corinth twice instead of making one extended visit, was part of an elaborate scheme to use the collection for the believers in Jerusalem as a front to defraud the Corinthians (cf. 1 Cor. 16:5–7 with 2 Cor. 7:2; 8:20–21; 11:7f.; 12:13–18). After all, if Paul were a true, Spirit-filled apostle and not merely after their money, he should be able to rely on the guidance of God, rather than changing his mind concerning his itinerary, not only once, but even two and three times! Paul's plans should reflect the very surety of the God who never changes, his word should be as reliable as the God who never lies, and his authority should be as unassailable as that of God's himself. Hence, Paul's opponents viewed his failure to carry through with his original plan as an indication that the Spirit was not at work in his ministry, but that he made his decisions "in a worldly manner" (1:17; lit., "according to the flesh," i.e., devoid of the Spirit).

Nevertheless, despite Paul's opponents' criticism, the rhetorical questions of verse 17 expect a negative answer. So he reminds the Corinthians that his first change in plans derived not from a lack of God's guidance, but from the confidence that his actions were being carried out in response to God's grace in his life (taking the "this" of v. 15 to refer back to vv. 12–14). His motives for acting were pure and his conscience was clear. Since Paul acted according to God's grace, he need not swear an oath to establish the truth of his word by declaring "yes, yes" and "no, no" (1:17).[3] In Jewish tradition, given

---

3. The NIV of 1:17, "so that in the same breath I say, 'Yes, yes,' and 'No, no'" adds the idea of simultaneous action (i.e., "in the same breath") to make sense of this difficult passage. But such an idea is not explicit in the text. It simply reads, "in order that from me it might be 'yes, yes' and 'no, no.'" This was an oath formula commonly used among Jews, especially those who wanted to avoid swearing by the name of God. See L. L. Welborn, "The Dangerous Double Affirmation: Character and Truth in 2Cor 1:17," ZNW 86 (1995): 34–52, 41–48.

the "inconstancy of human nature," the repetition "guarantees that the 'yes' of the speaker is truly 'yes,' as his 'no' is truly 'no,'" whereas "the 'yes' of the righteous should be truly 'yes' and the 'no' should be 'no'"[4]

Against this backdrop, Paul's change of plans was not the expression of a vacillating character, but a display of God's faithfulness (1:18). Grounded in God's grace as proclaimed in the gospel, the apostle's speech, like his preaching, was straight and pure, so that his message and his plans were a simple "yes" (1:19; cf. 1:12–14).[5] Instead of coming to Corinth only once on his way to Jerusalem from Macedonia (cf. 1 Cor. 16:1–9), Paul would visit Corinth twice, once on his way to Macedonia and then again on his way back to Jerusalem (2 Cor. 1:15–16). That such a change in plans did not reflect a lack of the Spirit is evident in Paul's purpose for the extra visit: that the Corinthians, not Paul, might "benefit twice" (v. 15).

The word translated "benefit" here (charis) is the same word used to refer to "grace" and its gifts. Paul's purpose in wanting to visit the Corinthians twice was that they might have (lit.) "a second [expression of] grace." As chapters 8–9 make clear, this twofold experience of grace refers to the Corinthians' being able to have two opportunities to contribute financially to the collection. In 8:1, 4, 6–7, 19, "grace" is used to describe the act of contributing to the collection since, according to 9:6–11, the ability to give to others is a manifestation of God's gracious ability to meet one's own needs. The Corinthians' willingness and ability to give to those who cannot repay is a demonstration that they too have received "grace." For this reason, when Paul planned this unanticipated second visit it was not an act of the "flesh" (i.e., "making plans in a worldly manner") by which he had hoped to benefit personally (v. 17). He did it for the Corinthians, fully aware that to provide them an opportunity to give twice would benefit them twice as much, since "God loves a cheerful giver" (9:7).

Seen in this light, Paul's change of plans was not a duplicitous act of vacillation, but a reflection of God's own faithfulness (1:8–19). Here too Paul supports his bold counterpunch by relating his experience to the revelation of God in Christ (cf. 1:9). Just as God has shown himself faithful by fulfilling his promises in Jesus Christ, so too Paul has acted in accordance with this same gospel as it was preached and confirmed to the Corinthians by several witnesses (v. 20a).

---

4. Ibid., 46.

5. For an analysis of 1:17–18 against the backdrop of Matt. 5:37 and James 5:12 that illustrates how Jesus' prohibition against oaths may have been wrongly used by Paul's opponents against Paul, see David Wenham, "2 Corinthians 1:17, 18: Echo of a Dominical Logion," NovT 28 (1986): 271–79.

Paul's open-ended description in verse 20 of these promises ("no matter how many promises God has made") reflects his conviction that Jesus is both the midpoint and climax of redemptive history. There is no event in Israel's history or promise granted to God's people that does not find its significance or fulfillment in Christ. God's unchanging commitment to pour out his grace toward his people by meeting their needs reached its climax in the sending of Christ for their sins (cf. 5:21). So too God's promise to deliver his people from sin and evil, the ultimate fulfillment of which is their resurrection from the dead, also takes place in Christ (cf. 4:14). And God's intention to judge the world is likewise brought about by Christ (cf. 5:10). Hence, God's apparent change of plans in first sending Christ to the cross (cf. Mark 10:45) before he comes to judge (cf. 1:14; 5:10) was, in reality, a consistent fulfillment of his promises to bless the nations (cf. Gen. 12:1–3; Rom. 3:21–26; 4:11; Gal. 3:13–14).

The unexpected nature of Christ's first coming was, in reality, the unfolding of God's overarching plan and promise to pour out his grace on his people. Similarly, Paul's commitment in Christ to meet the needs of the Corinthians led him to change his plans in order that they might experience God's grace or "benefit" as much as possible (not once, but twice). In other words, because Paul's intention remained the *same*, his plans *changed*! Paul utters his agreement (his "amen") to what God has done in Christ (i.e., meet their needs), not only in word by preaching the gospel, but also in deed by acting like Christ himself toward the Corinthians.

"Amen" is a transliterated form of a Hebrew word that means "to confirm" or "to establish." Jews regularly declared "amen" in response to prayers or statements with which they agreed. Thus, by his own change of plans toward the Corinthians, Paul "amens" God's demonstration in Christ of his divine faithfulness toward his people. In doing so, he expresses God's own commitment to keep his promises in and through Christ.

The object of Paul's "amen" is "to the glory of God" (v. 20b). Again he reminds the Corinthians that the purpose of all things is to glorify God (cf. 1:3, 11). God is the one who is to be honored for their good works (cf. Matt. 5:16), whether it be Paul's decision to visit the Corinthians twice or the Corinthians' decision to give to the collection. The reason for giving God the credit is expressed in the three images set forth in verses 21–22, which are best taken as referring to both Paul and the Corinthians (note the explicit inclusion of the Corinthians in 1:21a). (1) God is to be praised because he is the one who enables both Paul and the Corinthians to "stand firm in Christ." This is a reference to their conversion, by which God establishes them securely as Christians.

(2) God is the one who has "anointed" them. To be in Christ, "the Anointed One," leads in turn to being anointed by God.[6] This is a reference to their calling as Christians by which God has set them apart and equipped them by the gifting of the Spirit to accomplish his special purpose for them.

(3) God is the one who, like an ancient king, has "set his seal of ownership" on them and "put his Spirit in their hearts as a deposit, guaranteeing what is to come." Here Paul is referring to God's commitment to their consummation, sealed and certified by his having given them his Spirit as an *arrabon.* This is a technical, financial term referring to a "first installment" or "down payment" paid out as a pledge of faithfulness to a commitment. In this context it refers to the pouring out of the Spirit as God's pledge to "pay in full" the promise he has already begun to keep by granting his presence and power to his people. Paul's praise in 1:20 consequently reflects his Trinitarian theology and his understanding of God's promise to save, sanctify, and glorify his people: *God* is praised for his work in and through *Christ* as effected and secured by the gifting of the *Spirit.*

We have seen already that Paul's praise carries a polemic purpose (cf. 1:3–11). As 1:20b makes clear, the experience of conversion, calling, and consummation outlined in verses 21–22 comes about through Paul's apostolic ministry. In other words, the "amen" uttered to the glory of God comes about *through Paul* (lit., "through us," as an apostolic plural). This means, in turn, that the very existence of the Corinthians as believers authenticates the character and conduct of Paul's life, since it is Paul's ministry as an apostle that mediates God's presence and power to the Corinthians (cf. 3:7–18). Hence, if they doubt Paul's motives, they will be casting doubt on the reality of their own life in Christ (for the explicit development of this point, see 3:1–3).

The Reason for Paul's Second Change of Plans (1:23–2:4)

AS IF PAUL'S original change of plans was not confusing enough, he changed them yet again after his first planned visit. Paul's visit on his way to Macedonia turned out to be extremely difficult because of the rebellion against his authority that took place at that time (see the Introduction). Rather than going on directly to Macedonia and then risking yet another such "painful visit" (2:1), Paul decided to return to Ephesus. Once there, he wrote a letter out of "distress and anguish of heart and with many tears, not to grieve [the Corinthians] but to let [them] know the depth of [his] love for [them]" (2:4). To those opposing Paul, this new change of plans appeared to be motivated

---

6. There is a wordplay in 1:21 based on the derivation of the title "Christ" (*Christos,* i.e., "anointed one") from the verb "to anoint" (*chrio*) that is missed in translation. Verse 21 reads: God establishes them "in Christ" (*eis Christon*) and has "anointed" (*chrisas*) them.

by his fear of rejection in Corinth. In their view, Paul was a coward who refused to face his accusers.

In reality, however, the same Christological principle that motivated Paul's first change of plans motivated his second, namely, a desire to extend mercy to others. But whereas earlier Paul had wanted to give the Corinthians a double opportunity to extend grace to *others* (by giving money twice), this time Paul acts to extend mercy to the Corinthians *themselves*. Paul reminds them in 13:1–10 that he is both willing and able to exercise his authority to judge those who claim Christ but live in sin (cf. 1 Cor. 4:21; 5:1–13). Nevertheless, before judgment comes mercy. God is long-suffering. Just as God has extended one more opportunity for repentance and restoration to the world by separating the two comings of Christ, Paul too wanted to extend this same opportunity to the Corinthians.

The gravity of what Paul is saying in this section is reflected in his willingness to confirm it by a solemn oath, which calls God to be his "witness," as in a court of law, thereby inviting divine judgment on himself should he be lying (1:23a). Indeed, Paul is so serious about this assertion that he even puts his own life on the line in support of it (the NIV does not translate the full text, which reads, "I call God as my witness against my life").[7] In 1:23 Paul is testifying in the most earnest way possible that it was not his fear of rejection that kept him from returning to Corinth, but his wish to "spare them" the judgment of God. In 13:2, Paul issues the same warning that he will not "spare" those who are still rebelling when he comes again (like the second coming of Christ). Had Paul come to them in the midst of their rebellion, he would have been compelled to pronounce God's condemnation and to put them out of the church (cf. again 1 Cor. 5:1–5 and the principle in 5:12–13).

In explaining his motives, Paul is not trying to be heavy-handed or to flaunt his authority. Just the opposite! His decision not to come to Corinth a second time was an act of humble restraint in which he refused to exercise his authority toward them, even when it would have meant his own vindication. Rather than fight for his own reputation, Paul's purpose was "to work with [them] for [their] joy" (1:24a). Paul's goal as an apostle was not to establish his authority for its own sake, but to establish their faith so that they might stand "firm" as God's people (1:24b).

So Paul canceled his return visit (2:1) because he recognized that his own happiness as an apostle was wrapped up in the Corinthians' progress in faith, not in their judgment and ensuing grief (2:2). Paul was willing to deny himself

---

7. See again James Scott, *2 Corinthians*, 55–56, for a development of the theme of God as a witness for and against the actions of people (cf. Gen. 31:44, 50; 1 Sam. 12:5–6; 20:23, 42; 1 Kings 17:12; Isa. 43:10, 12; Jer. 42:5).

the immediate pleasure of his own vindication for the greater satisfaction of seeing the Corinthians experience the joy of a renewed faith. In this sense, Paul changed his plans not solely for the sake of the Corinthians, but for his own sake as well (2:3). Moreover, in making this decision, Paul had the confidence that his mercy toward the Corinthians would have its desired result: The Corinthians would repent and once again share Paul's joy in Christ (2:3b). The very existence of 2 Corinthians is itself testimony to the fact that Paul's confidence, if not fully realized (note his emphasis on "all of you" in 2:3), was not misplaced. Paul's love for the Corinthians, expressed in the severe warnings and calls to repentance of his previous letter (2:4), was the instrument God used to bring the majority of the Corinthians back to Paul (cf. 7:8–12). Paul's hope is that his present letter will do the same for the rest (cf. 13:5–7).

The Application of Paul's Example to the Corinthians (2:5–11)

HAVING EXPLAINED HIS rationale for his changes in plan, Paul now turns his attention back to the Corinthians. His goal is to admonish them to use the same rationale in dealing with the one who caused grief not only to Paul, but also "to some extent" to the community as a whole (2:5). Paul's inclusion of the church at this point is crucial. Had the offense been against Paul alone, he would have been compelled to heed his own advice in 1 Corinthians 6:7 and "rather be wronged" than pursue personal vindication. But in opposing Paul the integrity of the congregation was at stake, since the legitimacy of the Corinthians is inextricably bound up with that of Paul as their apostle (cf. 2 Cor. 3:1–3). Paul therefore felt it was warranted to take up this offense (cf. 2:3–4; also 1 Cor. 4:14–21).

Though Paul nowhere mentions the specifics of the offense itself, it must have involved some sort of slander against him and his apostolic relationship with the Corinthians. Perhaps the offender had been a person of influence who had sided with Paul's opponents and led the opposition against Paul. Whatever the case, most of the Corinthians had initially sided with this slanderer. Later, after the majority had repented as a result of his "tearful letter" (2:4; 7:8–13), they grieved with Paul because of the offender's influence over them. They consequently punished the offender (2:6), most likely by excluding him from the fellowship of the Christian community in accordance with the precedent set in 1 Corinthians 5:2, 5, 13.

The punishment had its intended, salutary impact. The offender had repented. He was ready to rejoin the congregation. In response, Paul calls the Corinthians to follow in his footsteps not only in pouring out punishment on those who deserve it, but also in showing mercy to the repentant. Paul's purpose is redemptive, not the reestablishment of reputations. The same desire to extend mercy to others that guided Paul's relationship with the Corinthians is to guide the Corinthians' relationships with one another. Paul's concern is that if forgiveness, comfort, and love are not extended to the offender, that person will be "overwhelmed by excessive sorrow" (2:7–8). As Victor Furnish observes, "any further discipline would be strictly punitive and could only lead to grief of a worldly sort, unrelieved by any redemptive value" (cf. 7:9–11, where such "worldly grief" leads to death).[8]

This is why Paul makes it clear that his confrontational letter was intended to "test" them to determine whether they would be "obedient in *everything*" (2:9). This obedience includes not only a willingness to repent and to judge the offender as needed (2:6), but also an eagerness to forgive him once he too has repented (2:7, 10). By exercising such obedience, they will be following Paul's example in extending mercy to the Corinthians themselves, just as he follows the example of Christ (1 Cor. 11:1). In turn, Paul's willingness to submit to the Corinthians' extending forgiveness to the offender is yet another expression of this same Christ-like obedience (2 Cor. 2:10a).

Even though Paul was the one who suffered first and foremost, he considers the Corinthians to be the ones primarily injured in this rebellion against his apostolic authority, so that they must take the lead in reconciliation. In other words, in following the offender's lead in rejecting Paul they were, in reality, injuring *themselves*. As they now welcome back the repentant sinner (Paul fully expects that they will pass this test), so will he, aware that he is acting "in the sight of Christ," that is, under Christ's judgment and for the sake of his approval (2:10b). Like Christ, Paul's concern is not for his own reputation, but for the good of the Corinthians (cf. 1:24; 12:19). Paul's forgiveness is extended "for [their] sake" (2:10), not his own. Throughout 1:15–2:10, the model of Christ motivates Paul's relationship with the Corinthians.[9]

---

8. *II Corinthians*, 162. For the persuasive reasons against the traditional approach in which 2:5–11 is taken to refer to the offender from 1 Cor. 5:1–5, so that the "tearful letter" becomes identified with 1 Corinthians itself, see Furnish's discussion on pp. 163–68. Of the nine arguments Furnish details, the most telling are: (1) In 1 Cor. 5 the mourning in view is for the offender's sin; in 2 Cor. 2:5–11 and 7:7–8 it is for their own and leads to their own repentance as well as that of the offender; (2) in 1 Cor. 5:3–5 Satan's role is to punish the offender; in 2 Cor. 2:5–11 it is to threaten the congregation itself; (3) in 1 Cor. 5 Christ is the authority behind Paul's judgment; in 2 Cor. 2 Christ is the eschatological judge; and (4) in 1 Cor. 5 the concern is for the moral purity of the congregation; in 2 Cor. 2 the concern is for harmony within the congregation.

9. See, too, Jan Lambrecht, *Second Corinthians*, 32, who comments on 2:10: "Through the rather strange wording of this verse one feels Paul's sensitiveness, but also his Christian and apostolic passion: the minimalizing of the injustice he personally experienced, his forgiving, his concern for the Corinthians (they should follow his example), and his union with Christ (cf. 'in the presence of Christ')."

As Paul concludes this section, his seriousness is striking. He ends by indicating that the ultimate purpose for his admonitions is to prevent Satan from using this situation against the church (note the purpose clause in 11a). Satan's "schemes" (v. 11b) revolve around destroying the mutual acceptance and forgiveness that is to characterize God's people, since they are the evidence of God's redeeming work in Christ and of the unity of the Spirit that it creates (1:19–22; cf. 1 Cor. 12:3, 12–13). And no early church had struggled with the unity of the Spirit in Christ more than the Corinthians. In fact, most of the commands throughout 1 Corinthians center on some aspect of church unity (e.g., 1 Cor. 1:10; 3:1–3; 4:14, 16; 5:4a, 5a, 7a, 8b; 6:1, 4, 6–7, 18, 20; 8:9, 13; 10:14; 11:33–34).

Once again, therefore, Paul reminds the Corinthians of the spiritual battle that is raging as they fight the temptation to bear a grudge and to transform their punishment into an act of revenge by extending it beyond what is needed. The majority of the Corinthians have demonstrated their renewed allegiance to Paul by showing righteous anger against the one who caused him grief and harmed the church. Now it is time to pass the ultimate test of whether their repentance is indeed legitimate. Nothing less than the validity of their own salvation is on the line in the call to forgive others. Those who have repented and experienced mercy from God have no choice but to extend the same mercy to those who have done likewise (Matt. 6:12, 14–15).

Bridging Contexts

WE HAVE SEEN that throughout this passage Paul responds to the problems at hand theologically. In 1:12–2:4, he described how his own decision-making was based on principles derived from the way in which God himself has acted in redemptive history. In changing his plans in regard to the Corinthians Paul was practicing what he preached when he admonished others to be "imitators of God" (Eph. 5:1). Then, in 2 Corinthians 2:5–11, Paul applied these same principles to the Corinthians.

This was nothing new on Paul's part. As he had admonished the Corinthians before, he expected them to "follow my example, as I follow the example of Christ" (1 Cor. 11:1). They had also seen this imitation of Christ illustrated in Paul's willingness to give up his rights for the sake of others (cf. 9:1–23; 10:33), which he then applied to the Corinthians (8:1–13; 10:23–32). In the same way, Paul's theological convictions concerning God's work in Christ, not the specifics of his circumstances, provide the guidance we need in moving from his context to our own. The key, then, to applying this passage is to isolate the theological principles Paul adduces to justify his actions.

Theology (1:12–14). The basis of Paul's boast in 1:12–14 was his clear conscience concerning his conduct. His theological support for this confidence was his doctrine of God (*theology*), since it was God's grace that made his ethical behavior possible. For Paul there is a direct link between theology and ethics, between the dynamic nature of God's presence in one's life and how one actually lives. Rather than copying Paul's behavior per se, in applying his example we too should evaluate whether or not our way of life reflects the sincerity and uprightness that flow from the presence of God's grace in our lives.

Paul's decision to be transparent about his suffering (1:8–11), and now about his change in plans (1:12–14), reflects a confidence concerning God's transforming grace that remains relevant in any context. If our decisions flow from an honest attempt to reflect God's work in our lives, not from the ways of the world, then we will not need to hide our actions or motives behind a cloak of secrecy, even when we are wrong (1:13). This combination of humility before others and confidence before God becomes the strength and boast of those who know that Christ is their judge (1:14).

Christology (1:15–22). In 1:15–22, Paul explains his behavior by appealing to salvation history, in which the sending of Jesus as the Christ demonstrates God's faithfulness and ultimate purpose toward his people. Thus, if theology provides the basis for our conduct, Christology becomes the key to evaluating its content. The coming of Christ as the verification and fulfillment of God's promises is the turning point in the history of the world (1:20). As such, it is the most important datum for Christian ethics.

But as Paul's argument illustrates, this does not mean that we simply ask, "What would Jesus think or do in our situation?" When dealing with issues that are specifically addressed by Jesus' moral admonitions and theological affirmations, we may extend these teachings to our circumstances by way of correspondence or implication. But when discerning God's will in ambiguous situations, such as Paul's travel plans, it is almost always impossible to transport Jesus from his first-century context in Roman-occupied Palestine into our own circumstances. Nor can we assume that in our finite, sinful state we should do everything that Jesus did as the messianic Son of Man and the incarnate, divine Word.

Moreover, most attempts to discover "what Jesus would have done" degenerate into an attempt to get behind the texts of the Gospels into the "mind of Christ." To do so, one must either psychologize the text by trying to recreate what Jesus "felt" or desired at the time, or fall prey to the fallacy of what E. D. Hirsch called "intuitionism."[10] In either case, the reader has

---

10. For the problems of subjectivity and the inherent claims to power that reside in such an assumed "direct spiritual communion with a god or another person," so that the

removed the meaning of Christ's words from the words themselves and taken them captive to his or her own subjective imagination. In applying texts, however, we must keep in view that the only intention that can be recovered from a passage is that which is explicitly expressed in the language of the text itself, understood within its own historical and literary context. We cannot get "behind" the text to what an author was thinking or feeling apart from what the author himself tells us about those thoughts or feelings.

Thus, in appealing to Christ in this passage, Paul does not attempt to reconstruct Christ's mindset or to imagine what plans Christ would have made had he been in Ephesus. Paul does not say that he changed his plans because of what Christ would have done in Paul's place, but because of what Christ had already done as the Son of God (1:19). Rather than providing a short-cut to discerning God's will, the fact that Paul justifies his actions by referring to Christ, whom he had preached as the fulfillment of God's promises, pushes us to ponder the nature of redemptive history as a framework for making ethical decisions.

When Paul earlier reminded the Corinthians that they had "the mind of Christ" (1 Cor. 2:16), he was not promising them a pipeline to Christ's inner thoughts and feelings. He was assuring them that the coming of Jesus now makes clear the inscrutability of God's ways in history (cf. the quote of Isa. 40:13 in 1 Cor. 2:16). As Craig Blomberg has pointed out, 1 Corinthians 2:13–16 does not

> justify attempts at interpreting God's will, including his revelation in the Scriptures, apart from standard, common-sense principles of hermeneutics.
>
> ... the Spirit never teaches that which is contrary to the plain meaning of passages interpreted in their original historical and literary contexts. And this meaning is accessible to anyone—believer or unbeliever—willing and able to put in the necessary study time.... The "understanding" these non-Christians do not possess is what the Bible consistently considers to be the fullest kind of understanding: a willingness *to act on and obey* the word of God (cf. v. 14a).[11]

In our passage, therefore, in order to act ethically in a complex situation for which there is no direct scriptural mandate, Paul does the hard work of reflecting theologically on the significance of Christ within God's plan of redemption.

---

reader begins with the words of the text but then transcends them based on an uncontrollable intuitive certainty, see E. D. Hirsch, *The Aims of Interpretation* (Chicago: Univ. of Chicago Press, 1976), 20ff.

11. Blomberg, *1 Corinthians*, 67.

Such a strategy for making decisions is not unique here. For example, in Romans 15:2–3 Paul grounds his ethical principle that in matters of personal, Christian liberty those who are strong in their faith should please their neighbors rather than themselves in the fact that Christ did not please himself in going to the cross. Similarly, in 15:7 Paul admonishes the Romans to accept one another "just as Christ accepted [them], in order to bring praise to God." In Philippians 2:1–18, the ethical admonitions of 2:2–5 and 2:12 are grounded in the incarnation, crucifixion, and exaltation of Christ as outlined in 2:6–11. This same Christological orientation is found in 2 Corinthians 1:20 and can be multiplied throughout Paul's letters.

This means that the key question to be asked in evaluating ambiguous moral situations is not primarily, "What would Jesus do in my place?" but, "What course of action best reflects what Christ has accomplished for us in redemptive history, so that the Trinitarian God will be honored for his merciful actions toward us?" (cf. Rom. 12:1). In Paul's situation, this meant changing his original plans so that the Corinthians would have the opportunity to contribute twice to the collection being taken up for the poor believers in Jerusalem (1:15). As we will see in chapters 8–9, such an opportunity fits the criterion outlined above, since in showing mercy to those in Jerusalem the Corinthians will be extending to others the very mercy they themselves have received from God in Christ (cf. 8:9).

Paul's change in plans, in other words, was motivated by his desire to enable those who had received such abundant mercy to be abundantly merciful to others to the glory of God. So too, our actions ought to reflect the character of God's grace as we have come to know it in Christ. Specifically, our decisions should be motivated by a desire to see the church benefit by extending to others the same mercy she has experienced from God.

Soteriology (1:23–2:4). In 1:23–2:4, Paul makes it clear that, unlike his first change of plans, his second change of plans was not driven by his desire for the Corinthians to be merciful *to others*, but by his desire to be merciful to the Corinthians *themselves*. Though the Corinthians had rebelled against Paul and his gospel during the first of his two proposed visits, Paul was willing to give them the benefit of the doubt that the opponents were temporarily misleading them, rather than concluding that they were definitively rejecting Christ. Accordingly, the theological principle guiding Paul's actions at this point was an extension of his Christology from 1:15–22 into its corresponding soteriology.

The gap between Christ's coming to die on the cross and his coming again to judge the world demonstrates that God's purpose is to extend the gospel to the ends of the earth by creating a final opportunity for mercy. Moreover, the instrument of God's mercy between Christ's two comings is the proclamation of the gospel itself. In it the good news of God's grace takes shape against the backdrop of the warning that God's judgment is sure to come against those who do not trust in Christ, thereby bringing about repentance and reconciliation with God in those in whom the Spirit is at work (cf. 3:3–6; 4:3–6; 5:6–6:2).

In the same way, Paul's decision not to return to Corinth immediately after his "painful visit" was an act of mercy on his part (1:23). It was not the act of a coward, the expression of anger, or the protective response of someone whose feelings had been hurt. Rather, it was done to spare them God's wrath, allowing the preaching of the gospel contained in the "sorrowful letter" written in his absence (2:3–4). Both Paul's delay and his reaffirmation of the implications of the gospel were intended to bring about the Corinthians' repentance in order that they might be spared the eventual judgment of God (cf. 13:1–10). Paul changed his plans in order to act toward the Corinthians in the same way that God is now acting between the first and second comings of Christ. Like those of Christ, Paul's actions consequently become a conduit for the revelation of the glory of God's mercy.

To make the transition from Paul's context to our own in this regard means, therefore, that we must follow Paul in making two fundamental evaluations. (1) In dealing with opposition within the church, we must discern whether there is any ground for holding open the possibility that those who are currently rejecting the gospel might in fact not be "enemies of the cross of Christ," whose destiny is "destruction" (Phil. 3:18–19), but merely deceived disciples. When making this evaluation, it is important to keep in mind that Paul erred on the side of thinking the best of the Corinthians, not the worst (cf. 2 Cor. 2:3). And he did so even when the injury was to him.

(2) We must discern whether extending mercy yet again expresses the character of God in Christ, or whether it makes a mockery of God's character by presuming upon his grace. Paul stresses in chapter 13 that in order to preserve the honor of God's own character, God's patience eventually comes to an end. When it does, God's long-suffering becomes the very ground for his wrath against those who persistently fail to trust in him (see Num. 14:10–35 for the paradigmatic expression of this principle). Faced with unbelief, even among those who claim to follow Christ, our response must therefore always be to warn of the judgment of God rather than to offer a false comfort in the midst of sin (cf. 13:1–10). At the same time, the offer of forgiveness and reconciliation to those who return to Christ must be equally strong. Such a serious and gracious call will be the very means God uses to bring his people to repentance (cf. 7:8–13). Moreover, we must also examine ourselves, to make sure that we too are not presuming on God's grace in the face of flagrant sin.

Ecclesiology (2:5–11). In 2:5–11, the overarching principle that guided Paul's application of his own experience to the Corinthians was his understanding of the church. The theology, Christology, and soteriology that informed Paul's own actions (1:12–2:4) led to an ecclesiology that demanded similar actions and attitudes from the Corinthians. In particular, there are at least four ecclesiological principles guiding Paul's admonitions in this passage.

(1) Paul's argument assumes the essential interconnectedness of the body of Christ. One of the implications of this unity had already been expressed to the Corinthians in 1 Corinthians 12:26: "If one part suffers, every part suffers with it; if one part is honored, every part rejoices with it" (cf. 2 Cor. 11:29 for another outworking of this same principle). In our present passage too, Paul's concern derives from his conviction that the grief, punishment, and forgiveness taking place in the church are not individual matters of private conscience and experience. Paul's grief is their grief (2:5), and their willingness to forgive others will be matched by his own (v. 10). We too, like the Corinthians, must understand that being part of the Christian community is not simply a slogan. Our local gathering of God's people is the basis and extension of our own identity. Like a family (we are brothers and sisters in Christ), our fortunes are inextricably intertwined. Such a corporate self-understanding is not easy to maintain in the West, with its transient communities and isolating individualism.

(2) Paul assumes that there will be judgment and ensuing punishment within the body of Christ, just as there will be forgiveness and reconciliation. We must regain the seriousness that surrounds being a member of God's people. To be part of the community of faith entails a responsibility to hold each other accountable to Christ as judge, under whom and in whose name we are called to a growing obedience and to an open admission of our faults. Such a responsibility will also entail punishing those whose continual and flagrant sin casts scorn on Christ's call and character as the Lord of the church.

Such a punishment, of course, will require wise and humble discernment. If any doubt remains over whether such a punishment is necessary, our life together calls for the kind of intentional patience that grants the offender yet another opportunity to repent (see above on 1:23–24). In Paul's day, the Corinthians struggled with knowing when to *stop* the punishment; in our time we struggle with whether we should ever *start*. The very mention of "church discipline" makes us uneasy (to say nothing of being concerned about secular lawsuits). Living up to Paul's expectations in our day will therefore be difficult, given our view of the church as a "club" we have "joined," rather than a family into which we have been born again.

(3) Paul operates on the assumption that the exercise of genuine faith included not only the courage to punish the offender, but also the willingness

to forgive the repentant. As Jesus' qualifications to prayer demonstrate (cf. Matt. 6:12, 14–15), this twofold test of faith is intimately intertwined. Not to forgive the repentant is evidence that we have not repented and experienced forgiveness ourselves (cf. Jesus' parable of the unmerciful servant in Matt. 18:21–35). This principle is as relevant today as it has ever been, especially in a litigious society such as ours. But its acceptance as a way of life will depend on regaining a sense of our own sin and need for repentance, a recognition of what it means to be forgiven by a just God and an appreciation of the way in which our attitudes toward others reflect our attitude toward the Lord.

(4) Most fundamental is Paul's reminder in verse 10 that the lordship of Christ leads to forgiving others for their sake, not to seeking vengeance for one's own. The power to forgive comes from a God-given recognition that the one who fulfilled God's promises by being the means of God's mercy is also the one who fulfills God's purposes by becoming the agent of God's judgment. He who has had mercy on us will be the one to judge us, with Christ's own righteous and merciful character being the essential criterion for evaluation. Those who have received mercy *in Christ* will be merciful to others, receiving mercy *from Christ* on the day of judgment.

Hence, motivated by our hope in Christ for the *future* (1:21–22) because of what he has done for us in the *past* (1:19–20), we discipline and forgive others in the *present*, both for the sake of our own spiritual health and for the good of the church (2:10–11). For the spiritual growth of others and the unity of the church are the true source of joy for those being made into the image of Christ (cf. Phil. 2:1–2). As a result, God's plan for his people is to make punishment the pathway to repentance so that discipline, rather than leading to "excessive sorrow" (2:6–7), purifies our devotion. This is the countercultural message of the gospel. Punishment for the sake of repentance and renewal stands in direct opposition to what in our culture appears to be only "natural," namely, to punish for the sake of revenge.

THE STRANGENESS OF Paul's theological justification for his actions reveals just how worldly the church has become. As David Wells points out, "worldliness is that system of values and beliefs, behaviors and expectations, in any given culture that have at their center the fallen human being and that relegate to their periphery any thought about God. Worldliness is what makes sin look normal in any age and righteousness seem odd."[12]

---

12. David Wells, *God in the Wasteland: The Reality of Truth in a World of Fading Dreams* (Grand Rapids: Eerdmans, 1994), 29.

How odd it seems to us in our pragmatism or private piety to realize that, for Paul, God's self-revelation in Christ, the significance of Christ for history, and Christ's example of mercy and judgment are the guiding principles of his decision-making. We desperately need to regain a God-centered view of our own lives, in which what we do is measured by what God has done and will do in and through Christ.

Paul's concern was not whether this or that itinerary corresponded to some hidden "will of God" that he must set out to discover, but whether his itinerary would reflect the character and purposes of God in Christ. In the midst of the many "how to" guides for discovering God's plan for our lives, we must rediscover the Bible itself as the focal point for finding God's purposes for our lives. But in turning to the Bible, we must not pervert it into some kind of "Ouija-board" filled with secret messages for our future. The Bible is not fundamentally about us, but about God. Its message is not about my future but about *the* Future. We should read it not to unearth a new message for this afternoon per se, but to get to know the character and purposes of God for eternity. When confronted with major decisions in life, the question is not, "Do I have a personally revealed word from God about this situation?" but, "What does God's Word say about the God of this situation?" Paul's perspective calls us to worry less about finding God's will for my circumstances and more about discovering God's character as the pattern for my life.

The worldliness of easy believism. With the rise of modern relativism, our culture increasingly assumes a radical separation between the private and public spheres, that is, between merely personal convictions and public performance. Paul's argument in this passage makes it clear that it is impossible to draw such a distinction between who we are personally (our "private morality") and what we do publicly. A genuine experience of God's grace, with its down payment of the Spirit, will inevitably impact the way we live by revolutionizing what we hope in for our future. Knowing God converts the goals and purposes of our lives as it transforms our values.

Thus, as this passage illustrates so vividly, being re-created by God to "stand firm in Christ" (1:21) changes what makes us happy and what grieves us because it transforms what we love (2:2–4). In the face of the cultural pressures around us, we must therefore resist the counterfeit "easy believism" that downsizes biblical faith into a decision of the will based on an intellectual assent to the truths of history. We must maintain Paul's understanding of *faith* as that dependence or trust in God in the *present*, because of his acts in the *past*, that leads inevitably to banking our *hope* on his promises for the *future* (cf. 1:20–22). Moreover, those who hope in God's promises *love* one another (2:4–11). This means that we must fight against what Stephen Carter has shown is the not-so-subtle assumption of our society that whenever our religious convictions "conflict with what one has to do to get ahead, one is expected to ignore the religious demands and act . . . well . . . *rationally.*"[13] Within Western society at large, to act on religious principles is simply irrational.

> In contemporary American culture, the religions are more and more treated as just passing beliefs—almost as fads, older, stuffier, less liberal versions of so-called New Age—rather than as the fundamentals upon which the devout build their lives. . . . If you can't remarry because you have the wrong religious belief, well, hey, believe something else! If you can't take an exam because of a Holy Day, get a new Holy Day! If the government decides to destroy your sacred lands, just make some other lands sacred! If you must go to work on your sabbath, it's no big deal! It's just a day off! Pick a different one! If you can't have a blood transfusion because you think God forbids it, no problem! Get a new God! And through all of this trivializing rhetoric runs the subtle but unmistakable message: pray if you like, worship if you must, but whatever you do, do not on any account take your religion seriously.[14]

What a different perspective pervades the present passage. While "we often seem most comfortable with people whose religions consist of nothing but a few private sessions of worship and prayer, but who are too secularized to let their faiths influence the rest of the week,"[15] Paul strove to evaluate all his behavior in view of the character of God. He was convinced that only those actions that correspond to God's actions in Christ make sense. In our contemporary context, however, doing what "makes sense" in relationship to Christ will increasingly feel "odd" indeed.

In view of this cultural pressure, we need a new boldness for theologically informed conduct within the church, especially for the demonstration of mercy to those who are struggling (1:15–2:4), for the courage to separate from those who continue to claim the name of Christ but deny him with their lifestyles (2:6), and for the willing extension of forgiveness to those who repent (2:7–11). This will entail rejecting our culture's attempt to privatize morality. We must resist all attempts to drive a wedge between a public pragmatism for the sake of "getting along" in the world and one's private conscience and personal values. Nowhere is this privatization more evident than in the values reflected in American politics at the end of the twentieth

---

13. Stephen Carter, *The Culture of Disbelief: How American Law and Politics Trivialize Religious Devotion* (New York: BasicBooks, 1993), 13.

14. Ibid., 14–15.

15. Ibid., 29.

century.[16] In radical contrast, Paul's example in this text illustrates that our theological and moral commitments at the level of character directly determine our behavior. For Paul, the test of faith is the test of obedience (2:9); rather than a chasm between the two, there should be an ever-narrowing convergence between our Christian confession and our conduct.

The worldliness of competition and corruption. Closely related to the previous point is the fact that Paul's example and his expectations for the Corinthians directly confront the competition for position and prestige that exists in so many quarters of the contemporary church. Instead of displaying the open transparency that comes from knowing the reality of God's grace, the greed and immorality of many of our public figures have scandalized the church around the world.[17] Rather than operating secretly for the sake of preserving one's power, Paul's practice in this passage calls Christian leaders and administrators to a forthright declaration of the reasons for their decisions.[18]

This is especially needed in a day when people "in high places deceive themselves very easily into believing that they are protecting the confidentiality of their high office when in fact they are only covering up their covert corruption."[19] Too many of our leaders have been more concerned with their own reputations than with the restoration of God's people. Paul's practice is a sober reminder that what counts in the church is building the faith of others, not building one's own "career" (1:24).

The worldliness of self-generated, self-centered joy. In stark contrast to the "me first" mantra of our culture, Paul's motivation for acting makes clear that within the body of Christ the joy or grief of one is the joy or grief of the other (2:2–4, 5–10). Indeed, as this passage illustrates, Paul worked for his own vindication only to the degree that the faith of others was at stake. What drove Paul was not his own status, but the Corinthians' participation in the joy that comes from faith (1:24). In turn, the goal of Paul's ministry was to build up the faith of the Corinthians because this, not the magnification

---

16. In this regard, see the evaluation, pro and con, of President Clinton's understanding of "repentance" in Gabriel Fackre, ed., *Judgment at the White House: A Critical Declaration Exploring Moral Issues and the Political Use and Abuse of Religion* (Grand Rapids: Eerdmans, 1999).

17. For example, 32 percent of Americans think that they have been lied to by a pastor; see James Patterson and Peter Kim, *The Day America Told the Truth: What People Really Believe About Everything That Really Matters* (New York: Prentice Hall, 1991), 48–49.

18. There are, of course, situations in which it is right to remain silent in order to avoid the risk of violence or personal hurt to others or to avoid violating a confidence created for the good of others; for these and other helpful principles for evaluating when the truth must be told or not told, see Lewis B. Smedes, "On Being Truthful," paper published by Center for Applied Christian Ethics, Wheaton College, Wheaton, Ill., 1991.

19. Ibid., 17.

of his own ministry, was also his own source of joy. It was *their* joy that made Paul glad (2:2). Paul acted as he did because he knew that it would be the restoration of the Corinthians that would make him "rejoice" (2:3a). In short, Paul's joy was wrapped up with the Corinthians' progress in faith. Thus, he canceled his second visit because to judge them at that point would not have honored Christ's purpose in their lives, thereby destroying his joy.

But the converse is also true. Paul wrote the painful letter instead of visiting because he also knew that the joy of the Corinthians was wrapped up in his own joy as well. His love for the Corinthians was driven by his desire that they would share his joy, thereby making his joy complete (cf. Phil. 2:1–4). This is the point of 2 Corinthians 2:3b. Just as Paul's joy is linked to the restoration of the Corinthians' faith, the happiness of the Corinthians is intimately tied to the restoration of Paul's honor, and hence to his joy as an apostle, since as his spiritual children they have been united with him in Christ. Thus, as 2:4 makes clear, both Paul's changes in plan and his tearful letter are expressions of his love for the Corinthians, even as their repentance is an expression of their love for Paul.

In both cases, their mutual joy is at stake. When one member of the body of Christ suffers, all suffer; when one is honored, all rejoice (1 Cor. 12:26). This is the opposite of being self-centered, in which we use others as a means to our own ends with no thought about their welfare. Instead, the loving person seeks the happiness of others because he knows that his own joy is inextricably wrapped up in their welfare. To be loving, therefore, does not require losing interest in oneself, as if love were a disinterested benevolence. But it does require recognizing that my own needs, in the end, are most profoundly satisfied in meeting those of others.

> So what is love? Love abounds between us when your joy is mine and my joy is yours. I am not loving just because I seek your joy, but because I seek it as mine.
>
> ... love is what exists between people when they find their joy in each other's joy, [both of which come from] knowing and resting in God's grace.... When this joy abounds in his converts, Paul feels great joy himself.
>
> So [2:3] is the converse of [2:2]. In verse two the point is that *their* joy is his joy; that is, when they are glad he feels glad in their gladness. And the point of verse three is that *his* joy is their joy; that is, when he is glad they feel glad in his gladness.[20]

---

20. John Piper, *Desiring God, Meditations of a Christian Hedonist*, 2d ed. (Sisters, Ore.: Multnomah, 1996), 105, 106, 105. I owe the insights of these surrounding paragraphs to Piper as well.

Paul's profound insight that the pathway to our own happiness is found in working for the happiness of others stands against the common assumption of our day that true love means giving up our welfare for the sake of others. The basic insight that we all naturally strive to be happy, and that this striving is not frustrated but fulfilled by working for the genuine happiness of others, will revitalize Christian charity by removing the false guilt people are made to feel over wanting to be happy. Seeking the welfare of others does not entail giving up our desire to be happy but is, in reality, the way to meet it. Without this insight, Paul's call to extend mercy and forgiveness to others will remain an idealistic and unintelligible goal that appears beyond the reach of "normal" people with "real needs." Of course, Paul's argument makes no sense unless he is right that only God can meet our deepest needs. Hence, it is only "by faith" that we "stand firm" in joy, since true and lasting happiness comes from knowing God intimately so that we trust him completely (1:24).

While Paul's admonitions in this passage certainly necessitate serious acts of self-denial, there is no hint of a sad sacrifice in anything Paul says. Only a desire for delight in Christ, not the doing of one's duty, can motivate extending grace and forgiveness to others in the face of ongoing grief and wrongdoing. In working hard for the restoration of the Corinthians, even at great cost to his own reputation, Paul is no hero or martyr. In suffering for the Corinthians, Paul is a recipient of comfort from God (cf. 1:4–6, 11). Paul's purity is the product of the grace he received (1:12). The apostle has given up what the world holds dear, but he has gained a greater treasure (cf. Matt. 6:19–21). The only hero worthy of praise is God, since he is the one who makes our lives of grace and love possible by mercifully loving us.

This is why Paul's theology and ethics lead to doxology (cf. 1:3, 11, 20). As Piper has pointed out, God's "aim is to ravish our affections with irresistible displays of glory. The only submission that fully reflects the worth and glory of the King is glad submission. . . . When the kingdom is a treasure, submission is a pleasure."[21] And when submission is pleasure, its greatest act of "service" is praise. This is also why Paul is not shy about the fact that his own motivation to act like Christ toward the Corinthians is the joy he derives from doing so (cf. 2:3)! Piper again puts it well:

> Gladness and gravity should be woven together in the life and preaching of a pastor in such a way as to sober the careless soul and sweeten the burdens of the saints. . . . Love for people does not take precious realities lightly (hence the call for gravity), and love for people does

21. John Piper, *The Supremacy of God in Preaching* (Grand Rapids: Baker, 1990), 25.

not load people with the burden of obedience without providing the strength of joy to help them carry it (hence the call for the gladness).[22]

Thus, our applications of this passage must reflect the fact that Paul's actions in ministry were not a random series of ad hoc responses dictated by his circumstances, but the outworking of deep-seated theological principles and convictions. In this regard, Ben Witherington has summarized an important aspect of the overarching significance of this passage:

> It is essential that Christian ministers take stock with some regularity and be clear in their own minds about the proper priorities in ministry, especially for those occasions when two important obligations suddenly and undeniably come into conflict with one another. This is a matter not just of being careful not to promise too much, but also of making clear to the congregation of the minister's identity as a person under authority and of being ready in any given situation to do what through God's word, circumstance, conscience, or godly counsel the Holy Spirit is leading toward. Nor is this a matter of providing for oneself an escape clause to justify any sort of action. If a minister makes clear what the priorities will be in ministry in a given situation, the congregation will better understand what they can expect and ought to expect from the minister.
>
> Sometimes a foolish consistency leads away from what God is urging in a particular situation. Paul's example suggests that one must learn when to follow a plan and when to depart from it. This wisdom comes partly through experience, partly through the Word and the Spirit's guidance, and partly from knowing ahead of time what the priorities are in one's ministry.[23]

But none of the principles for bridging contexts or the suggestions concerning specific applications outlined above will be either relevant or possible unless we reconstitute the church as a Christian community. Paul's attitudes and admonitions in this passage are all predicated on his presupposition that the Corinthians are the one people of God whose life together constitutes the platform for and firstfruits of the outworking of God's purposes in history. Throughout this section "one sees again how reluctant Paul is to acknowledge that the injury had been to him as an individual. At every turn and in every way he is extraordinarily insistent that the real danger had been not to himself but to the whole Corinthian church."[24]

---

22. Ibid., 52.

23. Witherington, *Conflict and Community in Corinth*, 363–64n.10.

24. Furnish, *II Corinthians*, 163.

What is ultimately at stake is not Paul's personal reputation as an apostle, but the work and witness of God in the world. For that reason, his warning must be equally heeded today: Satan's scheme is to destroy the unity of the church in Christ (2:11), a unity forged by grace (1:12) and forgiveness (2:7). This is his target, since it is the unity of forgiven sinners forgiving one another that embodies and manifests the love of Christ "in the world ... in the holiness and sincerity that are from God" (1:12).

2 Corinthians 2:12–3:3

N OW WHEN I went to Troas to preach the gospel of
Christ and found that the Lord had opened a door
for me, ¹³I still had no peace of mind, because I did
not find my brother Titus there. So I said good-by to them
and went on to Macedonia.

¹⁴But thanks be to God, who always leads us in triumphal
procession in Christ and through us spreads everywhere the
fragrance of the knowledge of him. ¹⁵For we are to God the
aroma of Christ among those who are being saved and those
who are perishing. ¹⁶To the one we are the smell of death; to
the other, the fragrance of life. And who is equal to such a
task? ¹⁷Unlike so many, we do not peddle the word of God for
profit. On the contrary, in Christ we speak before God with
sincerity, like men sent from God.

³⁻¹Are we beginning to commend ourselves again? Or do
we need, like some people, letters of recommendation to you
or from you? ²You yourselves are our letter, written on our
hearts, known and read by everybody. ³You show that you are
a letter from Christ, the result of our ministry, written not
with ink but with the Spirit of the living God, not on tablets
of stone but on tablets of human hearts.

Original Meaning
IN 2:12–3:18, PAUL lays the foundation for the
most sustained defense of his apostolic ministry
found anywhere in his letters (i.e., 2:14–7:16 and
10:1–13:10). The importance of 2:14–3:18,
which we will treat in accordance with its three sections (2:12–3:3; 3:4–6;
3:7–18), is further reflected in that it marks the transition in Paul's argument
from his past dealings with the Corinthians to the issues presently confronting the church. Second Corinthians 2:14–3:18 is therefore both the
theological heart and structural turning point of the letter (see outline).

Its interpretation, however, is highly controversial, since this passage is
among the most dense and difficult to understand in all of Paul's writings.[1]

---

1. The understanding of the original meaning of this section is based on my previous
works, *Suffering and Ministry in the Spirit*, and "Paul's Argument From the Old Testament and

The meaning of almost every clause is contested. This difficulty is compounded by the fact that Paul develops his argument by offering the most extended interpretation of an Old Testament text found anywhere in his letters. It will therefore be necessary to devote more time to our exposition of its original meaning than is otherwise the case, especially since our applications of it will only be as solid as the exegetical foundation on which they are built.

The disproportionately large amount of space devoted to the original meaning of 2:14–3:18 in comparison to its application is therefore intentional. It reflects Paul's own strategy, in which he begins his apology for his apostolic ministry by marshalling a massive biblical and theological argument in support of a few fundamental points. The application of 2:14–3:18 is not difficult to apprehend, once we are convinced of the reality that supports it. Moreover, in a real sense, all applications throughout Paul's letter derive from this foundational passage.

The Reason for Paul's Last Change of Plans (2:12–13)

IN MAKING THE TRANSITION from the past to the present, Paul's recent experience in Troas (2:12–13) once again raises the question of the significance of his suffering for the spread of the gospel in general (2:14–16a) and for the life of the Corinthians in particular (2:17). Paul's sudden switch back to his travel plans in 2:12 thus performs a twofold function. Materially, it provides Paul's last example of how his changes in travel plans were expressions of Christ-like suffering on behalf of the Corinthians. Structurally, it provides the transition to his direct response to the issues now being raised in Corinth.

Indeed, Paul's last change of plans appears to be his worst. In anticipation of meeting Titus in order to receive word of how the Corinthians had responded to Paul's "tearful" letter (cf. 2:4), Paul moved back toward Macedonia by traveling up from Ephesus to Troas. Then, when Titus failed to show up, Paul's anxiety (lit., Paul had "no rest in [his] spirit") over Titus and the Corinthians forced him to move on from Troas in spite of the open door for the gospel that he encountered there. The apostle was simply too concerned over Titus and the spiritual condition of the Corinthians to carry on his ministry. Certainly, then, Paul's opponents could point to this anxiety-ridden decision as apparently incontrovertible evidence that he lacked the power of the Spirit. How else could one explain the fact that Paul's anxiety drove him away from a clear opportunity to preach the gospel?

Christology in 2 Cor. 1–9: The Salvation-History/Restoration Structure of Paul's Apologetic," in R. Bieringer, ed., *The Corinthian Correspondence* (BETL 125; Leuven: Leuven Univ. Press, 1996), 277–303.

By now, Paul's answer is not surprising. His anxiety over Titus, who was bringing news about whether or not the Corinthians had repented of their rebellion, was yet another concrete example of the suffering God called Paul to bear as an apostle. In fact, his experience in Troas was part of the hardest suffering Paul had to endure. According to 11:28, the climax of the litany of suffering that characterized Paul's life is the daily "pressure" on him of "concern for all the churches." Just as Paul's concern for Titus and the Corinthians originally led him to Troas, so too his concern for them led him on to Macedonia (cf. 7:5–7). Nothing was more important to Paul than their welfare, not even an opportunity to expand his own ministry!

This is why Paul emphasizes in 2:13 that he first said "good-by" before he left Troas. He was not ashamed of leaving. He did not try to sneak out at night when no one was looking. Rather, he took his leave publicly, no doubt making clear his reasons for having to depart. Hence, by filling in the rest of Paul's recent itinerary, 2:12–13 bring us back to the central theme of Paul's letter: his suffering as an apostle. In doing so, these verses also prepare the way for the powerful restatement of Paul's central thesis in 2:14.

"Led Unto Death" in the Ministry (2:14–16a)

MOST STUDENTS OF this passage maintain that it is impossible to move smoothly from Paul's anxiety over Titus in 2:12–13 to his praise for God in 2:14. The transition from anxiety and apparent failure to praise seems too abrupt. It is therefore often posited that Paul's praise in 2:14 anticipates prematurely the good news Paul received from Titus as outlined in chapter 7. Others argue that 2:14–7:4 is a fragment from a different letter altogether, usually viewed as having been written earlier than the rest of chapters 1–7 and then inserted later between 2:13 and 7:5.

However, once the reason for Paul's praise in 2:14 is clearly ascertained, it becomes clear that 2:14 does not pose a break in Paul's thought at all. Rather, it introduces the necessary and logical response to the suffering introduced in 2:12–13. Without 2:14, Paul's continuing honesty in 2:12–13 would play right into the hands of his opponents as yet another evidence of his weakness. So before his opponents can utter a word against Paul because of his anxiety over Titus, Paul praises God for it as part and parcel of his apostolic life of suffering, through which God's power and presence are being revealed.

In 2:14 Paul begins by praising God with a characteristic thanksgiving formula, "but thanks be to God, who . . ." (cf. 1 Cor. 15:57; 2 Cor. 8:16). Peter O'Brien has demonstrated that these thanksgiving formulas, like their counterparts in other Jewish prayer texts from antiquity, serve a twofold purpose:

to set a tone and to establish the themes for what is to come.[2] Thus, the thanksgiving formula in 2 Corinthians 2:14 performs the same thesis-like function as the blessing formula of 1:3. In both cases, the reasons given for the praise introduce the main themes to follow. Like 1:3, 2:14 is not an unanticipated explosion of gratitude, but a carefully crafted statement that introduces a major new section in his letter by encapsulating the main points to come. In turning to praise God, Paul turns his attention to the main point of his defense against those who have called his ministry into question because of his suffering.

The content of Paul's thesis, first introduced in 1:3–11, is summarized in the two participles that follow his statement of thanks: "leading in triumph" (*thriambeuonti*) and "making known" (*phanerounti*). Paul thanks God because (1) God always "leads us in triumphal procession in Christ," and, in so doing, (2) "through us spreads [makes known] everywhere the fragrance of the knowledge of him." As the NIV rightly indicates, the verb often rendered "lead in triumph" (*thriambeuo*) is actually a technical term that refers to the Roman institution of the triumphal procession. This portrayal of God's leading Paul in such a procession is the key to the meaning of 2:14 and therefore to what follows.

The triumphal procession was a lavish parade conducted in Rome to celebrate great victories in significant military campaigns. Like a St. Patrick's Day parade in Chicago, these were major cultural and civic events. Everybody in the Roman empire knew about these parades, which were represented on Roman arches, reliefs, coins, statues, medallions, paintings, and cameos, not to mention the approximately 350 triumphs that are recorded in ancient literature.[3] They were ostentatious celebrations, filled with valiant soldiers, the spoils of war, and the most theatrical pomp and circumstance Rome could muster.

Moreover, the triumphal procession demonstrated Rome's prowess as the victor not only by parading the spoils of war, but also by leading in triumph the most important leaders and intimidating warriors of the enemy, now presented as conquered slaves. The highest honor any Roman Caesar or general could receive would be to lead one of these parades. Conversely, to be led as a prisoner in such a triumphal procession signaled one's utter defeat. Once the verb *thriambeuo* is understood as referring to leading or being led in the Roman triumphal procession, we are confronted with the uncomfortable

---

2. This type of thanksgiving also occurs in a modified form in Rom. 7:25; 2 Cor. 9:15; 1 Tim. 1:12ff.; 2 Tim. 1:3ff. See Peter T. O'Brien, *Introductory Thanksgivings in the Letters of Paul*, NovTSup 49 (Leiden: Brill, 1977), 100–101, 233–240.

3. See Scott, *2 Corinthians*, 90–91.

fact that in these parades, "prisoners are said to be led in triumph when to disgrace them they are bound in chains and dragged before the chariot of the conqueror."[4]

This fact is so startling because in 2:14 Paul is the direct object of the verb, not its subject. Paul is not the one leading the triumphal procession; he is the one being led in it like a prisoner of war! This image is so gruesome that Calvin could not imagine that Paul could praise God for such a thing. Thus, for theological reasons, Calvin changed the meaning of the verb, declaring that "Paul means something *different* from the common meaning of this phrase."[5] Instead of translating 2:14a, "Thanks be to God who always *leads us in the triumphal procession*," Calvin gave the verb a causative sense and rendered the text, "Thanks be to God *who causes us to triumph*." To Calvin it made better sense to think of Paul praising God because he shared in God's triumph, like a general walking alongside of the chariot, than to picture Paul being paraded around as a conquered enemy.

Calvin's translation won the day for almost three hundred years. It is still preserved in the KJV and in the many popular expositions of this passage that speak about our "triumph" in Christ.[6] But today it is widely recognized that Calvin's interpretation is linguistically impossible. Paul's statement can only mean, "Thanks be to God, who always leads us in a triumphal procession." The only remaining question is what Paul intended this metaphor to signify.

Faced once again with the image of the triumphal procession, the solution to understanding Paul's metaphor is not to soften the image in some way, but to recognize fully what it meant to "be led in triumph." The portrayals from the ancient world of these processions make clear that those led in triumphal processions were in fact being led to their *death*.[7] At the end of the parade, the Romans publicly slaughtered as a sacrifice to their god(s) those prisoners who had been led in the procession (or at least a represen-

---

4. As recognized already by Calvin in his commentary on 2 Corinthians; this quote is taken from his *The Second Epistle of Paul the Apostle to the Corinthians and the Epistles to Timothy, Titus and Philemon*, trans. T. A. Smail (Grand Rapids, Eerdmans, 1964), 33.

5. Ibid.

6. See the note to 2 Cor. 2:14 in *The NIV Study Bible*, ed. Kenneth Barker, et al. (Grand Rapids: Zondervan, 1985), 1765, for an example of an interpretation of this passage in terms of Paul's "triumphant faith": "So the Christian, called to spiritual warfare, is triumphantly led by God in Christ." Such an interpretation misses the point of the imagery here as well as the fact that the focus of the text is on Paul's ministry as an apostle, not on Christian experience in spiritual warfare.

7. For the history and significance of the triumphal procession, see H. S. Versnel, *Triumphus: An Inquiry Into the Origin, Development and Meaning of the Roman Triumph* (Leiden: Brill, 1970).

tative sample thereof, selling the rest into slavery). Though a gruesome thought to us, what better way to magnify one's victory, while at the same time offering a sacrifice of gratitude to the gods, than to kill publicly the leaders and the most valiant of the vanquished warriors as the final act of triumph over them?

Ironically, then, Paul's image of "being led in a triumphal procession" is even more repugnant than usually recognized. The role of those led in triumph was to reveal the glory of the one who had conquered them, ultimately through their public execution and death. By using this well-known cultural event to describe his own life as an apostle, Paul's point is that, as the one "being led in triumph," God is leading Paul to his death. This meaning of the metaphor is confirmed by its parallel use in Colossians 2:15, the only other passage where *thriambeuo* is used in the New Testament. There God, as the victor, having disarmed the rulers and authorities of this age, has led them in a triumphal procession, the result of which is his public display of their defeat and destruction.

Read against the background of the triumphal procession, Paul's metaphor in 2:14 may be "decoded" as follows: As the enemy of God's people, God had conquered Paul at his conversion call on the road to Damascus and was now leading him, as a "slave of Christ" (his favorite term for himself as an apostle), to death in Christ, in order that Paul might display or reveal the majesty, power, and glory of God, his conqueror.

But why use such a gruesome metaphor to describe his apostolic life? And why use it here? The answer becomes clear in the light of the other passages within the Corinthian correspondence in which Paul discusses his experiences as an apostle. There too Paul consistently uses the image of being given over to or sentenced to death as a metonymy for his suffering (1 Cor. 4:8–13 [cf. 4:9]; 2 Cor. 1:3–11 [cf. 1:9]; 4:7–12 [cf. 4:10]; 6:3–10 [cf. 6:9]). A metonymy is a figure of speech in which the name of one thing is used for that of another with which it is usually associated. For example, we use "crown" as a metonymy for the queen of England, the royal family, and all that that tradition implies when we say, "This land belongs to the crown." In the same way, Paul could use "death" and images of death as a metonymy for his suffering, since death is an essential part of suffering and suffering's crowning achievement. This is why, against the backdrop of the danger and suffering he endured in Ephesus, including fighting with wild beasts, Paul could declare in 1 Corinthians 15:31, "I die every day."

Furthermore, in all these passages, as in 2:14, Paul's suffering, as the corollary to and embodiment of his message of the cross, is the very thing God uses to make himself known (in addition to the texts listed above, cf. 1 Cor. 2:2–5). Far from calling his apostleship into question, Paul's point in 2:14 is that his suffering, here portrayed in terms of being led to death in the Roman triumphal procession, is the means through which God is revealing himself. This revelation of God's power and glory took place in two ways. Either God rescued Paul from adversity when it was too much to bear (cf. 1:8–11), or, having strengthened Paul's hope through such experiences of deliverance, enabled him to endure his adversity with thanksgiving to God (cf. 4:7–12; 6:3–10). The latter way was even more glorious than the former (cf. 12:9). In other words, God continually leads Paul *to death* in a triumphal procession and in this way everywhere reveals the knowledge of him (2:14a).[8]

In 2:14b–16a, Paul continues to describe the nature and function of his ministry metaphorically, this time under the images of a "fragrance" and "aroma." Through Paul's suffering, the "fragrance" of the knowledge of God is being spread everywhere (v. 14b) because Paul is the "aroma of Christ" to God (v. 15; again taking the "we" of v. 15 to be a literary plural referring to Paul in his role as an apostle). Many have suggested that these references continue the image of the triumphal procession by picturing the incense that was often carried through the streets as part of the celebration. But both in Judaism and elsewhere in Paul's writings, the images of "fragrance" and "aroma" are sometimes used together or sometimes separately, as synonyms (as they are here), to refer in a technical sense to the odor of a sacrifice pleasing to God.[9]

---

8. Not everyone has been convinced by this reading. There have been two substantial criticisms of it. Jens Schröter, *Der versöhnte Versöhner: Paulus als unentbehrlicher Mittler im Heilsvorgang zwischen Gott und Gemeinde nach 2 Kor 2:14–7:4* (Tübingen: Francke Verlag, 1993), has argued that this view goes too far. He posits that in using the triumphal procession metaphorically Paul is referring only to the revelation of the victor's glory and that he does not imply a reference to the death of those led in triumph. Paul only has in mind here his ministry as an apostolic mediator of the knowledge of God in a general sense. Schröter thus suggests translating 2:14a, "God triumphs *in relation to* Paul" (p. 21). James M. Scott, by contrast (*2 Corinthians*, 60–64, 90–92), criticizes this view for making too little of the metaphor. He argues that central to the metaphor is not Paul's being led to death as a slave, but God's riding in the chariot as a conquering general. As one being led in the procession, Paul is looking at the chariot in front of him. Scott then equates this with the mysticism of the throne chariot of God (e.g., Ezek. 1:4–28; possibly, Ps. 68:17–18; also Jewish *merkabah* mysticism). Hence, in 2 Cor. 2:14 Paul is not speaking primarily of his suffering. Rather, Paul is speaking of being led into mystical experiences of God's glory. Thus, Paul's statement here should be related to those texts that speak of his visions of Christ and God (e.g., 2 Cor. 12:1–5). But it makes far more sense, when one takes into view the immediate context and the more far-reaching content of several of Paul's letters, to see 2:14 as a reference to his suffering as an apostle.

9. Cf. Gen. 8:21; Ex. 29:25, 41; Lev. 1:13, 17; Num. 15:3; Ezek. 16:19; 20:40–41; Judith 16:16; esp. Sir. 24:15, where the two terms are split apart and used as synonyms as in 2:14–15. For the parallels in Paul, see Phil. 4:18; Eph. 5:2. Scott, *2 Corinthians*, 64, extends the imagery of *merkabah* mysticism into the image of the aromas, but his explanation lacks convincing evidence.

In view of these parallels and given Paul's biblical frame of reference, it is better to read 2:14b–16a as a reference to Old Testament sacrifice. Taken in this way, Paul is practicing effective cross-cultural communication. First he introduces the familiar image of the Roman triumphal procession in order to portray the role his suffering plays as an apostle, and then he uses sacrificial imagery from the Scriptures in order to unpack its significance.

As 2:15 makes clear, the knowledge being spread through Paul's suffering is the "fragrance" of Christ himself that rises up to God from Paul's life. More specifically, Christ is pictured as the sacrifice and Paul as the odor that arises from it. The knowledge of God manifest in the cross of Christ is now being revealed through Paul's suffering among those to whom he is sent (cf. Col. 1:24). To encounter Paul in his suffering on behalf of his churches is to encounter a picture of the crucified Christ, who died for his people. For this reason, Paul supports his praise in verse 14 by pointing in verses 15–16b to the twofold impact that God's self-revelation in Christ brings about through Paul's suffering: Those who are being saved welcome his suffering as an expression of the glory of God revealed in the crucified Christ, while those who are perishing reject Paul's suffering as foolishness, just as they reject the cross of Christ.

Furthermore, 2:16a declares that the character of a person's moral disposition determines the nature of his or her response (v. 16a reads lit., "to the latter, an aroma from death unto death; to the former, an aroma from life unto life"). Paul is merely an instrument that, like a litmus-paper test, makes manifest the true nature of a person's heart. The implied admonition to the Corinthians in this passage is therefore striking. How they respond to Paul's declaration in 2:14 is a clear indication of where they stand concerning the divide between life and death created by the cross of Christ and manifest through Paul's ministry.

This reading of Paul's argument is confirmed by the parallels between 1 Corinthians 1:17–18 and 2 Corinthians 2:14–16a. Paul's ministry and message were one; what Paul could say about the cross of Christ in 1 Corinthians 1:17–18, he could reaffirm about his own life as an apostle in 2 Corinthians 2:14–16. Hence, as the "aroma of Christ," Paul's suffering brings about the same twofold effect caused by his proclamation of the cross:

1. Paul is sent to preach in a mode that corresponds to the cross of Christ (1:17; cf. 2:1, 4).	1. Paul is "being led to death," which is a mode of existence that reveals the cross of Christ (2:14).
2. For (*gar*) (18a)	2. For (*hoti*) (15a)
3. the word of the cross (15a)	3. we are an aroma of Christ to God

| 4. is foolishness to those who are perishing (18a) | 4. among those who are perishing . . . to those a fragrance from death to death (15c, 16a) |
| 5. to us who are being saved it is the power of God (18c). | 5. among those who are being saved . . . to those a fragrance from life to life (15b, 16a). |

For Paul, therefore, the cross of Christ determined both the manner of his life and the content of his message. Conversely, his manner of life embodied and displayed his message. As a result, Paul recognized that his life and ministry functioned to further the process of salvation ("life") and judgment ("death") in the lives of others. To reject Paul and his message as "foolishness" confirmed that one was already "perishing." To accept Paul and his message demonstrated that the power of God was already at work to save. As an extension of the cross of Christ, Paul's life and message are the means God uses to propagate the process of salvation and judgment in the world by revealing the character of people's hearts.

Paul's Sufficiency for the Ministry (2:16b–17)

THE SIGNIFICANCE PAUL attaches to his ministry in 2:14–16a can hardly be overemphasized. His ministry manifests and moves along a person's eternal destiny. The magnitude of such a calling naturally leads to the rhetorical question of 2:16b: "And who is equal to [lit., sufficient for] such a task?" In view of Paul's high calling, it is often suggested that the implied answer to this question is "no one," as if Paul's question indicated a humble resignation in the face of such a responsibility.[10] Others suppose that Paul answers the question negatively because he has *self*-sufficiency in view, even though there is no hint of such a concept in the word *hikanos* ("sufficient"). Although such views may seem natural to us, Paul's implied answer to the question, "Who is sufficient for these things?" is better understood as, "I am!" In being "led to death" as the "aroma of Christ," Paul is confident that God *is* making himself known.

---

10. This view was made popular by the influential commentary of Hans Windisch, *Der zweite Korintherbrief* (KeK 6; Göttingen: Vandenhoeck & Ruprecht, 1970), 100, who, based on the work of Loesner from 1777, suggested a parallel between 2:16b and Joel 2:11, and between this verse and Mark 10:26; Rom. 11:34; Rev. 6:17. But it is difficult to link Joel's resignation in the face of God's judgment to Paul's confidence in his sufficiency as an apostle (cf. 2 Cor. 3:4–6, 12; 4:1) or his confident hope for the salvation of those in Christ in general (cf., e.g., Rom. 1:16–17; 8:1; 2 Cor. 4:13–17; 5:14–21; Phil. 1:6; 1 Thess. 3:11–13). In the same way, the resignation in Rev. 6:17 is not that of the faithful, but of those faced with "the wrath of the Lamb" (cf. 6:15–16). The same is true of Mark 10:26, while the parallel between Rom. 11:34 and 2 Cor. 2:16b is difficult to establish.

This interpretation is confirmed by two factors. (1) The language of "sufficiency" used here alludes to the call of Moses in Exodus 4:10, where in the LXX Moses responds to God's call by declaring that he is not "sufficient" (*hikanos*) for the task. In the context of Exodus 4, Moses is then *made sufficient* by God himself. Paul too sees his sufficiency as coming from God (cf. 2 Cor. 3:4–6). By alluding to Moses' call, Paul's point is that, as in the case of Moses, God is the one who has made Paul sufficient for his ministry (cf. 1 Cor. 15:9–10, where the same "sufficiency" motif is used). Only if Paul expected a positive answer to 2:16b—that is, "I am, by God's grace"—does the argument in 3:4–6, based on Paul's call to be an apostle, make sense.

(2) The logical relationship between the implied answer to the question of 2:16b and the statement of verse 17 confirms this interpretation. Verse 17 is intended to support the implied answer of verse 16b (unfortunately, the NIV does not translate the conjunction *gar* ["for, because"] that introduces v. 17). Such a move only makes sense if Paul has just declared that *he*, not his opponents, is the one who is sufficient for the apostolic ministry. The very suffering that his opponents have argued calls Paul's ministry into question is the means by which he shows himself sufficient as an apostle. If Paul had just denied his sufficiency for the apostolic ministry, the comparison in the following verse makes no sense.

In verse 17, therefore, Paul supports his sufficiency for the ministry by comparing his practice of preaching the gospel free of charge to that of the "many" who accept, even demand, money for their ministry. Unlike them, Paul does not "peddle the word of God for profit." Though a matter of debate, the fact that Paul contrasts himself negatively to this group, together with the image he uses to do so, indicates that he is not referring to the apostles listed in 1 Corinthians 9:5, or to their counterpart, the "super-apostles" of 2 Corinthians 11:5 and 12:11. In each of these cases, Paul compares himself *positively* to these other genuine apostles, and nowhere does he call into question their receiving financial support for their ministry (in 1 Cor. 9, Paul explicitly defends their right to do so). In contrast, Paul is referring here to those opponents who have recently arrived in Corinth (i.e., the "false apostles" of 2 Cor. 11:4, 13–15).

No doubt Paul's opponents had interpreted his practice of preaching the gospel without charge as a sign of the worthlessness of his message (if it were valuable, he would have charged a high price for it; after all, you get what you pay for).[11] In 2:17, Paul responds by reminding the Corinthians that

---

11. Anticipating Paul's counterargument, his opponents also alleged that, by providing a smokescreen to cover up his intention to skim money from the collection, Paul's practice of self-support was part of his plan to defraud the Corinthians (cf. 2 Cor. 11:7–9; 12:14–18).

he had freely given up his right to financial support in Corinth in order, out of love for the Corinthians, to avoid erecting a stumbling block for the gospel (cf. 1 Cor. 9:1–23; 2 Cor. 11:7–15; 12:13–16). That Paul's decision to preach in Corinth for free was motivated by love can be seen in the many sufferings that he willingly underwent as a direct result of this decision (cf. 1 Cor. 4:11– 13; 2 Cor. 6:4–5; 11:26–27). Only a genuine love for the Corinthians and Paul's commitment to the gospel could lead to such voluntary suffering. Paul's actions testify to the sincerity of his speech.

In contrast, Paul's choice of words in 2:17 indicates that it was his opponents' practice, like that of a retailer in the market, that was suspicious (Gk. *kapeleuo* means to peddle for profit like a retailer). In Paul's day, to compare his opponents to those who sold wares in the market was no compliment. Retailers in the ancient world were infamous for their dishonesty. Such a comparison was thus a common way to cast doubt on someone's character and motives, without calling into question the fact of being paid, which was legitimate for those worthy of their hire.[12]

Paul's opponents presumably claimed and took pride in the fact that their practice of receiving money for their ministry paralleled that of the pillar apostles themselves (cf. 1 Cor. 9:3–6). Paul counters by comparing them not to the pillar apostles but to peddlers. In so doing, he uses their own boast against them. In taking money, like retailers in the market, it was their motives, not his, that smacked of "shady business," a "sham" built around the gospel itself (cf. 2 Cor. 11:20). If anyone is trying to con the Corinthians, it cannot be Paul. His manner of life, including his suffering for the sake of the Corinthians, is a window to his sincere motives, which in turn are a manifestation of the grace of God in his life (cf. 1:12).

Moreover, Paul is aware that as an apostle (i.e., he speaks "in Christ"), he preaches the gospel under the judgment of God (i.e., he speaks "before God"), since God is the one who has called him (i.e., he speaks as one "sent from God"). Paul's entire life as an apostle is contained in these prepositional

---

12. For a survey of the evidence for these points, see my *Suffering and Ministry in the Spirit*, 106–25. Cf., e.g., Plato, *Protagoras* 313CD; *Sophist* 223D–235A; Isocrates, *Against the Sophists* 4, who criticize the Sophists not for "selling" their message per se, but for appearing with their rhetorical skill to sell what they do not have, namely true wisdom. Plato, *Laws* XI.915D– 920C, cautions against the temptation to greed that surrounds retail business. Isaiah 1:22; Sir. 26:29; 27:1–3; Philo, *On the Giants* 39; *Life of Moses* II.212; Josephus, *Ant.* 3.276; Lucian, *The Wisdom of Nigrinus* 25; *Hermotimus* 59; and Philostratus, *Life of Apollonius* 1.13–14 all use "selling as a retailer" as a metaphor for casting into question someone's motives, trading on the negative connotation surrounding merchants in the ancient world. Didache 12.5 warns the early church about those who wish to live off of her generosity without working, i.e., those who are "making traffic of Christ."

phrases! Just as God's call is the foundation of his apostolic ministry, so too the reality of God's judgment is its refining fire. Paul, like all believers, lives before God, who is both his gracious provider and his sovereign ruler. The motivation for Paul's preaching is therefore the same: God himself as the source (cf. 1 Cor. 1:30; 7:7; 8:6; 11:12; 12:7ff.; 2 Cor. 5:18) and judge (cf. 2 Cor. 4:2; 5:9–11; 12:19) of all things. Thus, it is Paul's practice of self-support in Corinth, not his opponents' insistence on being paid for their preaching, that is the true expression of God's grace and calling. And it is his ministry, not theirs, that will be vindicated before God's judgment. Talk is cheap. But Paul's declaration of his sufficiency is supported by his willingness to preach for free.

Understood as a reference to his practice of self-support, verse 17 continues Paul's argument for the legitimacy of his ministry introduced in 2:12–13. In other words, the description of his ministry in 2:14–16 is framed by two examples of his love for the Corinthians: his willingness to leave Troas and his willingness to preach the gospel in Corinth without charge. Both occasioned great suffering on his part that he nevertheless embraced for their sake and for the sake of the gospel in response to God's call in his life. In short, Paul ministers as one "sent from God" (2:17c).

At the same time, far from calling his apostleship into question, Paul's apostolic suffering "in Christ," as the embodiment of his proclamation, is that which shows him approved by God. In Paul's words, knowing that he speaks "before God" as judge, Paul does so with the "sincerity" that comes from the grace of God himself (2:17b; cf. 1:12). As a result, Paul's assertion that he is not like his opponents is an evidential argument for the divine origin and approval of his apostolic ministry.

Paul's Letter of Recommendation for the Ministry (3:1–3)

PAUL'S ARGUMENT NOW takes a decisive turn. Up to now, he has argued for the legitimacy of his ministry based on his suffering as the divinely ordained means for mediating the comfort of God to believers (1:3–11) and the knowledge of God to the world (2:14–17). Beginning in 3:1–3, Paul vies for the validity of his apostleship based on the presence and power of the Spirit as the specific content of his mediation. If the means of Paul's apostolic ministry is his suffering, the Spirit is its content as the one who converts and comforts the Christian and convicts the world (1:21–22; 2:15–16a). By embodying the gospel, Paul mediates the Spirit.

The transition in Paul's train of thought is marked by the two rhetorical questions of 3:1, both of which anticipate a negative response (he introduces them in 3:1a with the negative particle *me*). In view of his suffering and weakness, Paul's opponents had evidently dismissed his exalted claims as an apostle to be nothing more than unsubstantiated "hot air." His rhetorical questions and their implied answer anticipate this charge once again. Paul is not engaging in mere self-commendation when he claims that his suffering is the divinely orchestrated vehicle of God's self-revelation, as if he had no evidence to back up what he said.[13] After all, his leaving Troas and his practice of self-support are clear evidence of his genuine nature as an apostle.

Nor, for the same reasons, does he have to rely on letters of recommendation from others to validate his claims, as his opponents do for theirs. In the ancient world, like today, the need for letters of recommendation indicated that someone lacked his own evidence to back up the claims being made. Letters of recommendation are a substitute source of credibility. But Paul's work as an apostle speaks for itself, especially his founding of the church in Corinth (10:12-18; cf. 1 Cor. 4:14-17; 15:10). Thus, the Corinthians themselves are Paul's "letter of recommendation" (2 Cor. 3:2; cf. 1 Cor. 9:1-2). It is this "letter" (i.e., the Corinthians themselves as Christians) that Paul carries around "written on our hearts," so that it can be "known and read by everybody."

That the Corinthians are "written" (lit., engraved) on Paul's heart does not mean that he has warm feelings for them, but that he is committed to act on their behalf as their "father" in the faith (cf. 1 Cor. 4:15). Paul's willingness to support himself for the sake of the gospel (1 Cor. 4:11-12; 9:12-23; 2 Cor. 2:17; 6:3, 11-13; 12:14-15), his concern for the Corinthians' welfare (1 Cor. 4:14-15; 2 Cor. 11:2-4), and his anxiety for their salvation (2 Cor. 1:12-2:13; 7:4; 11:28) make it obvious to all that these believers are on his heart as his children (cf. 7:3). Once again, his way of life reveals the content of his heart.

Conversely, the very existence of the Corinthians as Christians testifies to the power of the Spirit in and through Paul's ministry. This is the point of 3:3. The Corinthians are Paul's "letter of recommendation" (3:1) *because* they show themselves to be "a letter from Christ," that is, those whom Christ has "written," a metaphor referring to their conversion (3:3a). The force of Paul's

---

13. In 3:1 Paul frontloads the reflexive pronoun in the Gk. expression "to commend oneself" (*heauton sunistano*), thus emphasizing that he has in view a negative "*self*-commendation." When Paul speaks of commending himself in a positive sense, he uses the normal word order, *sunistano heauton* (cf. 4:2; 6:4; 12:11). I owe this insight concerning the difference in emphasis between the two forms of the expression in 2 Corinthians to J. H. Bernard, *The Second Epistle to the Corinthians, The Expositor's Greek Testament*, Vol. 3, ed. W. Robertson Nicoll (Grand Rapids: Eerdmans, 1979 reprint), 52. My rendering of 3:1 as a "self-commendation" rather than "to commend oneself" is an attempt to reflect this distinction. For the resolution of the apparent conflict between the fact that three times Paul denies that he in engaging in self-commendation (cf. 3:1; 5:12; 10:18), only to turn around and commend himself three times (cf. 4:2; 6:4; 12:11), see comments on 10:12-18.

argument resides not in their having become Christians per se, but in their having done so as "the result of our ministry" (3:3b; lit., "you are a letter of Christ, having been ministered[14] by us"). Since the church in Corinth is a direct result of Paul's ministry, to deny him now would be tantamount to denying their own spiritual experience as Christians (something the pride-prone Corinthians are not inclined to do).

Paul's statement in 3:2 leads him to refer in 3:3a-b to the status of the Corinthians as believers, which in turn leads him in 3:3c to picture their new identity in terms of the Old Testament imagery of Ezekiel 11:19 and 36:26–27: The Corinthians, as Christ's "letter," have been written "not with ink but with the Spirit of the living God," and written "not on tablets of stone, but on tablets of human hearts." Paul here establishes *two* contrasts, not one: a contrast between the two *means* of writing (human agency of ink versus the Spirit) and a contrast between the two *spheres* of the writing (the old covenant tablets of the law versus the new covenant "tablets" of the human heart).[15] The apostle's ministry of "writing" with the Spirit, who is at work in the human heart, is contrasted with the old covenant ministry of the "writing" that took place on the stone tablets of the law (cf. Ex. 24:12; 31:18; 32:15; 34:1; Deut. 9:10).

It is crucial to see that this contrast is essentially not one of kind, but of time within the history of redemption.[16] Under the old covenant, the locus

---

14. Paul's use of the verb *diakoneo* ("to serve, minister") in 3:3 to describe his activity of bringing Christ to the Corinthians indicates that he is much more than simply a courier delivering a letter (cf. 1 Cor. 4:15; 9:1–2; 2 Cor. 10:14; 11:2). Cf. Paul's use of words from the same root to refer to the collection as an expression of the gospel in 2 Cor. 8:4; 9:1, 12, 13; also Rom. 15:25, 31; to his "ministry" in general in 3:6, 7–9; 4:1; and to his ministry of the gospel among the Gentiles in Rom 11:13; 2 Cor. 5:18; 6:3; 11:8.

15. This reading differs from the common attempt to read 3:3c as a single contrast between writing with ink on tablets of stone (!) verses the Spirit writing on the heart. To do so mixes Paul's metaphors to the point of self-destruction.

16. This becomes clear once we take our starting point from the Old Testament texts themselves rather than from our own views of the nature of the contrasts between "ink" and "Spirit," "stone" and "flesh." Paul's contrast is not an abstract one between "outward" and "inward," between "externality" and "internality," between "ritualism" and "a living experience of the Spirit," or between "rigidity" and "spontaneity," etc., as is often suggested. Nor is Paul making a negative statement about the nature or content of the law by associating it with "stone," which seems to be the common denominator undergirding these interpretations. The reference in 3:3 to the "tablets of stone" is part of a long tradition in which this designation is at the least a normal, neutral way of referring to the law, and more likely functions to emphasize its permanence, divine authority, honor, and glory (cf. 3:7, 9, 11!). See Ex. 24:12; 31:18; Deut. 9:10; 1 Kings 8:9; 2 Chron. 5:10, etc. and my discussion of this motif within postbiblical Judaism in *Suffering and Ministry in the Spirit*, 214–20. The fact that the law was engraved on stone is not associated in Ezekiel or anywhere else with "stone hearts" as something to be done away with under the new covenant.

of God's activity was in the law; in the new age promised by Ezekiel, God will be at work in human hearts by the power of the Spirit. Paul's ministry is therefore nothing less than a fulfillment of the promise of the new covenant as prophesied by Ezekiel. The Corinthians need look only at themselves for proof that the new age of the new covenant has dawned (cf. Isa. 32:15; 44:3; 59:21; Joel 2:28–29; also the use of Jer. 31:31–34 in 2 Cor. 3:6). Their rejection of Paul's ministry, therefore, means not only a denial of their own genuine existence as believers, but also a disavowal of God's work in Christ as the fulfillment of the prophetic hope.

As a result, to reject Paul's apostleship is to place oneself outside of the work of God in the world (cf. 2 Cor. 13:5, 10). If Moses is the "lawgiver," who mediates the Sinai covenant as a result of the Exodus, Paul is the "Spirit-giver," who mediates the new covenant as a result of the "second-exodus" that has come about through Christ. *Like* Moses, Paul is called to be a mediator between God and his people. *Unlike* Moses, the essential content of Paul's mediation is not the law, but the Spirit.

INASMUCH AS THIS section develops the theme and thesis of 1:3–11, the same principles are in play here that governed Paul's earlier discussion. But while 1:3–11 focused on Paul's suffering as the vehicle for displaying the *power* of God for the *comfort* of believers, 2:12–3:3 focuses on Paul's suffering as the vehicle for revealing the *knowledge* of God for the *proclamation* of the gospel. In line with this switch in focus, our present passage reveals five bedrock convictions that further undergird Paul's self-understanding and support the legitimacy of his apostolic ministry. These pillars of Paul's thought should likewise undergird any application of this passage.

(1) Paul is convinced that God is sovereign over the circumstances of his life, even his suffering. *God* is the one who "leads [him to death] in the triumphal procession" (2:14a).

(2) Paul understands that for believers, and especially for his own calling as an apostle, the suffering of this life becomes a conduit for the revelation of God's presence and power (2:14b). Far from calling his apostleship into question because of the "missed opportunity" it caused in Troas (2:12–13), Paul's anxiety is the very means God ordained to express Paul's sufficiency for the gospel ministry (2:16a). Paul is sufficient for the life- and death-producing proclamation of the cross because in his suffering he embodies the "fragrance" of Christ's death. It is precisely through Paul's suffering that the reality of Christ's person, the reliability of God's Word, and the restoration of the Spirit

are made known. Paul's life is an embodiment of the gospel he preaches. It follows then that those who reject the cross of Christ as the power of God (cf. 1 Cor. 1:17–25) will also reject Paul because of his suffering (2:15–16a). Hence, one's reaction to Paul is a reflection of one's spiritual condition.

(3) Paul is confident that his sufficiency as an apostle can also be seen in his willingness to endure the inevitable suffering that came from preaching the gospel for free in Corinth (2:17). The motives of the heart are manifest in the manner of one's life (3:2).

(4) Paul can point to the Corinthians' Christian experience as evidence for his own legitimacy as an apostle because the presence of the Spirit in the life of the believer is undeniable (3:2–3). Consequently, they cannot reject Paul without at the same time rejecting their own spirituality. Conversely, Paul is sufficient for the ministry of life and death (2:16), not because of his own natural aptitudes, but because of the Spirit's work in and through him (3:3b). Paul's confidence therefore ultimately derives from the dawning of the new age of the new covenant (3:3), a reality that impacts all he does and expects.

(5) Though the focus of this passage is on Paul's own legitimacy as an apostle, the ultimate goal of the text was to cause the Corinthians to be confident in their own standing as believers (cf. 1:24). The point was not to vindicate Paul per se, but to vindicate Paul *for the sake of* vindicating those who have placed their trust in his gospel and ministry. In a real sense, then, in focusing on himself Paul is calling for his readers to focus on their own standing "before God" (2:17). Paul and his message become the instrument for measuring where one stands with God.

Hence, given their foundational nature in Paul's argument, we too may appropriate the same perspectives employed in this passage when discerning the validity of our Christian claims. To do so, Paul's five convictions may be expressed in a series of questions, which together help expose the nature of our spiritual condition: (1) Do we show a growing trust in God's sovereignty over the circumstances of life? (2) Do we increasingly reflect the peace and praise that come from understanding the role of suffering in the lives of Christians? (3) Do we progressively demonstrate the kind of loving actions that flow from a willingness to give up our rights for the sake of others? (4) Do we give evidence of the transforming work of the Spirit in our willingness to stand for the truth as God's people? (5) Do our lives model for others what it means to imitate Christ?

Ultimately, of course, the issue is not Paul at all. As he himself indicates, the overarching perspective that governs all such evaluations is the awareness that *God* is the judge, since he alone knows the true nature of our actions and the motives that drive them (cf. 2:17). Paul is not calling us to pass judgment on one another according to our own standards and experiences, but to live in the knowledge that we all stand before God's righteous judgment. In the end, we are all measured by *his* character as revealed in his Word and embodied in his Son.

 THE NATURE OF **Christian ministry.** Paul's argument for his legitimacy as an apostle calls into question the prevailing view of the ministry in our day. It was the character of Paul's life and the transforming work of the Spirit, not his personality and his "success" in growing large churches, that recommended him as a true representative of Jesus Christ. In direct defiance of his opponents' criticism, Paul's argument in 2:12–3:3 reflects his persuasion that the condition of the heart, not the performance of the preacher, determines a person's response to the proclamation of the gospel (2:14–15a; cf. 1 Cor. 1:17–19; 2:1–5; 2 Cor. 4:3–4; 10:10; 11:6).

Paul's understanding of the nature of Christian ministry strikes a piercing blow against all attempts, whether in Paul's day or our own, to fashion ministries and messages around techniques and technology. As children of the entertainment age, our culturally conditioned reflex is to make creating right environments for hearing the gospel our priority, instead of relying first and foremost on the power of the Spirit to call people to repentance. Our tendency is to concentrate on "working the angles" instead of relying on Christ to work. Rather than viewing the pastor as a mediator of the Spirit in conjunction with the proclamation of the Word, the minister becomes a "professional" whose job it is to manage the corporate life of the congregation and oversee the creation of meaningful worship "events." David Wells has poignantly pointed out the dangerous consequences of this movement in contemporary American culture:

> As the technological world has encroached upon the pastorate, management by technique has come to replace management by truth. . . .
> The result, according to Stanley Hauerwas and William Willimon, is practical atheism. . . . It is an atheism that reduces the Church to nothing more than the services it offers or the good feelings the minister can generate. In other words . . . the ministry will typically be deprived of its transcendence and reduced to little more than a helping profession. . . . It is under this guise of piety—indeed, of professionalization—that pastoral unbelief lives out its life.[17]

17. David Wells, *No Place for Truth or Whatever Happened to Evangelical Theology* (Grand Rapids: Eerdmans, 1993), 248–49, following Hauerwas and Willimon, "Ministry As More Than a Helping Profession," *Christian Century* (March 15, 1989), 282.

In response, our congregations often no longer view themselves as those whom God has called in Christ to seek and worship the Lord in the power of the Spirit. Nor does the church view herself through the lens of redemptive history as the people called to mediate God's glory to the ends of the earth (note the argument from the fulfillment of Scripture in 3:3). Instead, she becomes a conglomerate of consumers held together only by its common view that this or that particular church happens to be the institution in the area best designed to provide the services sought. Going to church is more like going to a supermarket than like getting together with family. As in Paul's day, so too today, the popular preachers are frequently those who give the people what they "want," religiously speaking, thereby confirming them in their own self-understanding and self-reliance. As Wells points out:

> What this means in practice is that the minister . . . has become vulnerable to a multitude of perils. Within the Church, strong winds are blowing from a range of religious consumers who look to the churches and ministers to meet their needs—and who quickly look elsewhere if they feel those needs are not being met. Basically, these consumers are looking for the sort of thing the self movement is offering; they just want it in evangelical dress. A genuinely biblical and God-centered ministry is almost certain to collide head-on with the self-absorption and anthropocentric focus that are now normative in so many evangelical churches. The collisions take place in the soul of the minister and at the expense of his or her career.[18]

The nature of being Christian. As the corollary to his own suffering *and* the power of the Spirit in his life (not suffering *versus* the Spirit), Paul's portrayal of his ministry also calls into question our image of the Spirit-filled Christian. Like Paul's opponents, we too find it hard to shake the "health and wealth gospel," with its promise of God's physical and financial blessing for the faithful. In our age of materialism, we find it almost impossible to fathom that God would not only use suffering as the vehicle for manifesting the presence and power of his Spirit, but also actually lead someone to death for the sake of revealing his glory and spreading the gospel (2:14). Instead, we strive hard to give the impression that Christians overcome suffering and want, rather than finding Christ strong in their very evident weakness.

Though we do not often express it overtly, deep down we are still convinced that if we just had enough faith, we should be able to beat or avoid the adversity around us. We believe, somehow, that true followers of Christ should not have to endure the kind of health problems and heartache known

---

18. Ibid., 256.

to our neighbors. At least our marriages should work and all our children should be Christians. This "health and wealth" assumption is even more evident in regard to pastors, both in terms of our expectations for them and in regard to their own self-understandings. We naturally assume that the handsome and healthy are strong in the Lord, especially if they are skilled rhetorically. Yet from Paul's perspective the dominant characteristic of those in whom God is mightily at work is their confident endurance in the midst of adversity. Our pastors are to model perseverance, not personality; morality, not miracles.

Moreover, with Paul as their example, pastors should not be surprised when God's leading takes them into deeper waters of suffering than those experienced by their people. This is especially true of suffering caused by the anxiety they will experience over the spiritual health of their churches (cf. 2:12–13; cf. 6:3–10; 11:28). A pastor's heart is a broken heart.

Although the church in the West is not presently suffering the persecution so common elsewhere in the world, many pastors today, like Paul in Corinth, have to endure the low-grade but discouraging suffering that comes from financial uncertainty, underpayment, and cultural disdain. This may lead in turn to the unnecessary burden of having to work to support themselves in addition to carrying on the work of the ministry. Whereas Paul supported himself voluntarily in order to avoid placing a stumbling block in the way of the gospel, today such "tent-making" in the West often results from the materialism of believers and their lack of esteem for the ministry.

The inability of many congregations to support their pastors adequately or to support the planting of churches elsewhere is often a consequence of people's unwillingness to part with their money for the sake of the ministry. In other cases, this unwillingness is caused by the low value associated with the ministry itself. This is derived in part from the fact that the minister has allowed himself to be viewed as a low-grade personnel manager, a free alternative to expensive counseling, a purveyor of moral values for the children, a programmer of healthy activities for the youth, and an emotional cheerleader in times of crisis. In this sense, we pay our pastors what we think they are really worth.

The nature of faith. Paul's ability in 2:17 to determine the motives of his opponents by their actions, together with his insistence in 3:2 that his own love for the Corinthians can be seen in his willingness to suffer on their behalf, confronts the "easy believism" that marks so much of the church today. In view of Paul's teaching, we simply must not continue to deceive ourselves into thinking that lifestyles of self-serving greed, sexual impurity, self-preserving dishonesty, and prestige-seeking careerism are merely the result of "not yet becoming who we are in Christ." Nothing less than the integrity of our message is at stake in the manner of our lives. Our actions are a manifestation of our moral condition.

There is no dichotomy between the private and public spheres of our lives. Paul would not accept that those who use the goodwill and Christian charity of others for personal gain, privilege, and prestige are preaching and living out the gospel of Christ, no matter how strong their claims. At the same time, Paul's own willingness to forgive the offender and his admonition to the Corinthians to do the same in 2:5–11 demonstrates that he is not a perfectionist. His emphasis in 3:18 on the continuous process of transformation shows that his expectation is not perfection over night, but progression over a lifetime. The pathway to becoming more like Christ is paved with repentance (cf. 2 Cor. 7:9–12).

The manner of our lives, including repentance, must increasingly match the character of the gospel we profess. The need for maturity in this matter is especially true for those who claim to be leaders of God's people. It should go without saying that pastors must practice what they preach, including repentance. That many still do not is itself an indictment of our times. As Richard Baxter (1615–1691) put it in his classic work from 1656, *The Reformed Pastor*, and modeled in his life: "Take heed to yourselves, lest your example contradict your doctrine, and lest you lay such stumbling-blocks before the blind, as may be the occasion of their ruin; lest you unsay with your lives, what you say with your tongues."[19] Indeed, as J. I. Packer observes, "the Puritans were *men of the Spirit;* lovers of the Lord, keepers of his law, and self-squanderers in his service, which are in every age the three main elements of the truly Spirit-filled life."[20]

The nature of the Spirit's presence. The flip-side to Paul's insistence that those who preach the gospel must live its virtues, including repentance and the forgiveness of the repentant, is his expectation that the Spirit's presence in the world is not invisible or private, but palpable and powerful. Paul's "holiness" theology is not a call to pull ourselves up by our own spiritual bootstraps. The life of faith is the work of the Spirit. But the Spirit does not invade our lives in order to go on vacation! For those in whom the Spirit dwells, we must be able to taste the "fruit of the Spirit" (Gal. 5:22) or "the fruit of righteousness" (Phil. 1:11) in our attitudes and actions.

Paul would never accept the modern attempt to relegate religion to a private affair of one's innermost thoughts and beliefs. He casts the purpose of

---

19. Richard Baxter, *The Reformed Pastor*, ed. William Brown (Edinburgh: The Banner of Truth Trust, 1974; from the 1862 ed.), 63.

20. J. I. Packer, *A Quest for Godliness: The Puritan Vision of the Christian Life* (Wheaton: Crossway, 1990), 75.

his ministry in terms of unveiling and praising the glory of God (cf. 1:3, 11, 20; 2:14). To do so reflects his assumption that God is not an Idea to be believed, but a Person to be encountered and trusted; or better, a Person who encounters us with the same power that raised Jesus from the dead (1:9, 22; 2:14b; 3:3). The Spirit raises us from the deadness of our sinful lives and makes us "a letter from Christ," who speak of his transforming grace in our own words and display his power by our deeds. For as we have seen, Paul's argument in 3:1–3 was based on his certitude that the promise from Ezekiel 36:25–26 is now being fulfilled in and through his own ministry of the gospel. Certainly this is still the case today.

Thus, Paul's emphasis in this passage on the transforming power of the Spirit supports the recently renewed focus in many circles on the formation of Christian character within the community of faith as the central task of Christian ethics. As Stanley Hauerwas argues, Christian ethics should be viewed under the metaphor of life as a "journey," in contrast to the prevailing Lutheran view of life as a "dialogue." The latter view emphasizes "the dual nature of the self, the 'internal,' justified self divorced from the 'external,' sinful self—the passive self from the active. This has been more than just a theological description, for it has frequently implied that what a man does and how he acts have relatively little to do with his real 'internal,' justified self."[21] Such a dichotomy cannot be maintained in view of Paul's argument in this passage concerning the significance of his own suffering and the testimony of the Corinthians' experience of the Spirit.

Paul's point, in the end, is that what makes one a member of God's people, whether Moses in the tent of meeting or Suzie and Jim in the church on the corner, is a life-transforming encounter with the glory of God (1:18–22; cf. 3:16–18). This is the basis for the next stage of Paul's argument: "With unveiled faces" (3:18) we are irresistibly drawn to the beauty and majesty of the sovereign Lord, whose image we take on by trusting in his all-sufficiency to such a degree that we are free to love others in obedience to his commands. This is the "letter of recommendation" brought about through the gospel by the Spirit of the living God (3:2), who, in fulfillment of Ezekiel's promise, causes us to walk in God's statutes as "a letter from Christ" (3:3).

Therefore, those who minister the gospel are not technicians trained to provide services (not even worship services). They are mediators of the Spirit, who preach Christ in accordance with the Scriptures and embody his character in their own faithful endurance and love for others. The contemporary

---

21. Stanley Hauerwas, *Character and the Christian Life: A Study in Theological Ethics* (Notre Dame: Univ. of Notre Dame Press, 2d. ed., 1994), 4; see esp. his new introduction, xiii–xxxiii.

significance of Paul's perspective is its call to recover our awareness of and dependence on the reality of the Spirit, convinced that the Spirit is vital, not supplemental, to the life and witness of the church (3:1–3).

Together with this, Paul's self-understanding must cause us, especially as Christian leaders, to pray for a renewed willingness to suffer for the sake of others and, in faithfulness to God's calling, to be led into suffering for the sake of the gospel. Only in this way will the knowledge of God, in the cross and by the Spirit, be made known in every generation (2:12–17). We cannot "manage" the kind of suffering, divine self-revelation, and transformation Paul envisions in this text. It is the result of a miraculous invasion of our lives by the power and presence of God himself. Only the glory of God can drive out the glitter and tinsel of this world. For Paul's confidence and hope do not reside in his own power as a motivational speaker, but in the power of the Spirit (3:4, 12; cf. again 1 Cor. 2:1–5).

2 Corinthians 3:4–6

 ❧

SUCH CONFIDENCE AS this is ours through Christ before God. ⁵Not that we are competent in ourselves to claim anything for ourselves, but our competence comes from God. ⁶He has made us competent as ministers of a new covenant—not of the letter but of the Spirit; for the letter kills, but the Spirit gives life.

IN 2:12–3:3, PAUL POINTED to his ministry of suffering and the Spirit as two arguments for his sufficiency as an apostle. This evidence, however, was not the *source* of his ministry or the *basis* of his sufficiency, as if Paul's adequacy ultimately derived from his own experiences. Rather, in 2:16b, Paul grounded the legitimacy of his ministry in his *calling* to be an apostle by picturing his sufficiency in terms of the call of Moses. Like Moses, Paul too was called by God. Hence, Paul's suffering and sincerity derive from the fact that he speaks "in Christ," "before God," and "from God" (2:17). But Paul is an apostle of Christ, not a prophet of the old covenant. Hence, in 3:3, Paul also contrasted his calling to that of Moses by stressing that his ministry of the Spirit is part of the new covenant promised by the prophets.

In 3:4–6, Paul returns to the theme of his "Mosaic" calling introduced earlier in 2:16b–17 in order to make explicit that the origin and foundation of his ministry is God himself. In doing so, Paul completes his self-defense by reminding the Corinthians that the genuine results of his ministry (3:1–3) make up his "confidence" *as* an apostle (3:4) precisely because his ministry, and hence its results, are based on his prior call *to be* an apostle (3:5). Paul's suffering and the presence of the Spirit are twin supports of his sufficiency since they are also evidence that God is the one who has "made [him] sufficient" (NIV "competent," 3:6a). For Paul, therefore, his confidence concerning his competence (2:16b; 3:4), as evidenced by the work of the Spirit in and through his apostolic suffering (3:2–3; 3:6b), is based on the call of God in his life (2:17b; 3:5–6a).

Paul's Confidence As a Minister (3:4–6a)

SECOND CORINTHIANS 3:4 marks a transition in Paul's argument by summarizing his previous affirmation that Paul's suffering (2:14–17) was the vehicle through which God was pouring out his Spirit (3:1–3). This, in a word, is the "confidence" Paul has "through Christ before God."[1] Paul's "confidence" is the subjective assurance he possesses because of the objective content of what God is doing through his life as an apostle (cf. 10:18). Paul wants to make it clear that although he is confident he is sufficient for the ministry (2:16b; 3:4), his sufficiency (NIV competence) comes from God, not himself (3:5), since God is the one who made him sufficient as a minister of the new covenant (3:6a).

This qualification is all-important. Just as Paul was careful in 2:17 to emphasize that his sufficiency to preach the word of God came about as a result of his call "from God," now too he stresses in 3:5 that he is not sufficient to consider this aspect of his ministry or anything else as originating from himself (note again the use of the apostolic plural in 3:1–6 to emphasize that Paul represents the apostolic office).

To underscore this point, Paul alludes again to the call of Moses (cf. 2:16b), now presented in a way that also evokes the call of the prophets. Beginning with Moses' own call in Exodus 4:10 (cf. Ex. 3:1–4:17), the ensuing calls of Gideon (Judg. 6:11–24), Isaiah (Isa. 6:1–8), Jeremiah (Jer. 1:4–10), and Ezekiel (Ezek. 1:1–3:11) all reflect the same pattern: The prophet is not sufficient (competent) in himself (because of an obstacle to be overcome), but is nevertheless made sufficient by God's grace.

From a canonical perspective, the fact that these prophetic "call narratives" all parallel the call of the prophet Moses carries with it an implied apologetic force. Since the prophet is called like Moses, he can claim the same "sufficiency-in-spite-of-insufficiency-by-the grace of God" that Moses had. If Yahweh called and used Moses in spite of his speech defect, no one can point to the military insignificance of Gideon, the sin of Isaiah, the youth of Jeremiah, or the timidity of Ezekiel as reasons to doubt the validity of their respective calls. In spite of their insufficiency, God made them sufficient. Indeed, the call of Moses demonstrates that these very obstacles are an essential part of the call itself, illustrating clearly that God's grace, not the prophet's strength, is the source of his sufficiency.

When Paul says God "made us competent as ministers of a new covenant" (3:6a), he is therefore referring to his Moses-like call on the road to Damascus as a legitimizing principle. Like Moses and the Old Testament prophets after him, Paul too was made "sufficient in spite of insufficiency by the grace of God." Rather than calling his ministry into question, Paul's insufficiency

---

1. The detailed support for the understanding of the original meaning of 3:4–18 presented here is found in my earlier work, *Paul, Moses, and the History of Israel: The Letter/Spirit Contrast and the Argument From Scripture in 2 Corinthians 3* (Peabody, Mass.: Hendrickson, 1996).

thus provides the counterpart to God's elective grace. Such a strategy was not without precedent. This use of Moses in order to legitimize one's own authority was a common move in the Judaism of Paul's day. That Paul has this motif in mind is confirmed by Galatians 1:15–16, where he portrays his call in "Mosaic" terms as they were crystallized in the call of Jeremiah.[2]

Nevertheless, although Paul has been called in the pattern of Moses like a prophet, he is not a prophet, but an apostle of Jesus Christ. In the words of 3:6a, Paul has been made sufficient to be a "minister [or servant; Gk. *diakonos*] of a new covenant." In presenting himself as a minister of the *new* covenant rather than as a prophet under the old, Paul declares that his ministry fulfills the Old Testament office of prophet. Phenomenologically, Paul's ministry is like that of a prophet, while eschatologically he is an apostle of Christ Jesus (1:1).[3]

Yet here Paul does not refer to himself as an apostle, but as a "minister." A survey of Pauline usage makes clear that the emphasis in the term *diakonos* is not on an office,[4] but on the function or act of mediation and representation assigned by God in regard to a particular work of service (*diakonia*).[5] In using

---

2. For confirmation of this fundamental point, see Karl Olav Sandnes, *Paul—One of the Prophets? A Contribution to the Apostle's Self-Understanding* (WUNT 2, Reihe 43; Tübingen: J. C. B. Mohr [Paul Siebeck], 1991), 7–8, 16n.6, 64–65, 68–69. Sandnes demonstrates that in the central passages in which Paul presents his self-understanding as an apostle, he consistently does so in terms of common *prophetic* motifs (Rom. 1:1–5; 10:14–18; 1 Cor. 2:6–16; 9:15–18; 2 Cor. 4:6; Eph. 2:19–3:7; 1 Thess. 2:3–8). Hence, although Paul never refers to himself as a prophet, he understood his apostleship to be a continuation of the Old Testament prophetic calling, conducted under the same kind of compulsion and inspired speech that characterized the prophets (cf. pp. 2–3, 15, 18, 20, 115, 129, 152).

3. Ibid., 18.

4. When Paul wants to emphasize his office, he uses the word "apostle," which points directly to the divinely granted authority of his ministry (cf. Rom. 1:1; 11:13; 1 Cor. 1:1; 9:1–2; 2 Cor. 1:1; Gal. 1:1; Eph. 1:1; Col. 1:1; 1 Tim. 1:1; 2:7; 2 Tim. 1:1, 11; Titus 1:1).

5. For Paul's use of *diakonos*-terminology to describe his apostolic ministry in service to the gospel, cf. Rom. 11:13; 2 Cor. 3:3, 6, 8–9; 4:1; 5:18; 6:3–4; 11:8; Eph. 3:7; Col. 1:23, 25; 1 Tim. 1:12. For a treatment of this terminology in the New Testament within its historical and linguistic environment, see John N. Collins, *DIAKONIA: Re-interpreting the Ancient Sources* (New York: Oxford Univ. Press, 1990), esp. 195–215 on Pauline usage. Collins' central thesis is that Paul's terminology refers to the function of proclaiming the gospel ("spokesman") and, specifically in 2 Cor. 2:14–6:13, to Paul's role as a "medium" of God's revelation and glory, rather than to a general Christian service undergone by the church as a whole or to the work of "deacons" (cf. 197–98, 203–5). Moreover, Paul can share this title more broadly with those who are preaching the gospel or representing a church: Rom. 16:1 (with Phoebe); 1 Cor. 3:5 (with Apollos); 16:15 (with the household of Stephanas); 2 Cor. 11:23 (ironically with his opponents); Col. 1:7 (with Epaphras); Eph. 6:21; Col. 4:7 (with Tychicus); Col. 4:17 (with Archippus); 1 Tim. 4:6 (with Timothy). Indeed, in 2 Cor. 11:15 even Satan has his "servants" (*diakonoi*), while a pagan ruler used by God to accom-

this designation here, Paul is not pulling rank, but is calling attention to the way in which his ministry actually works as evidence for his authority. Because he is an apostle (i.e., his office, cf. 1:1), he is a minister of the new covenant (i.e., his function). As a minister, he mediates the Spirit in establishing the church (cf. the use of the corresponding verb "to minister" [*diakoneo*] in 3:3 and the reference to Paul's "ministry" [*diakonia*] of the Spirit in 3:8). This ministry, as the outworking of his office, is his confidence "through Christ before God." In other words, Christ is the one who has made Paul's confidence possible, and God is the one before whose judgment Paul ministers (cf. 2:17).

Paul's Ministry of the New Covenant (3:6b)

THE CONTENT OF Paul's activity as a minister is the "new covenant" (3:6a). As is well known, the only explicit use of the expression "new covenant" in the Old Testament is found in Jeremiah 31:31.[6] The conclusion that Paul is alluding to this background here, though disputed by some, is accepted by most. The framework for understanding Paul's conception of the church is his conviction that she constitutes the community of the new covenant. His only other explicit reference to the "new covenant" (1 Cor. 11:25) occurs in relationship to the death of Christ as the foundation of the church, a tradition deriving from Jesus himself.

Paul's reference to the tradition of the church in 1 Corinthians 11:23 and 15:1–3, together with his introduction of the new covenant terminology without explanation in 3:6, indicates that the Corinthians were well aware of the significance of the new covenant. Specifically, they understood that Jesus' death had inaugurated the new covenant and that, as believers, they were members of it (cf. 1 Cor. 1:2, 17–18, 23–24, 26–31; 2:2; 3:16; 6:19; 7:23; 12:13, 27; 2 Cor. 6:14–7:1). As William Lane has observed, "Paul's pastoral response to the disruptive situation at Corinth" entailed "an appeal to the New Covenant and the administration of its provisions." Like an Old Testament prophet, called to be a "messenger of the covenant lawsuit of God," Paul was called to proclaim the "divine complaint against the rebellious Corinthians and to call them back to the stipulations of the covenant."[7]

---

plish his purposes can be called a "servant" (*diakonos*) of God in Rom. 13:4. Christ himself in the function of his earthly ministry is described as a *diakonos* to the circumcised in Rom. 15:8, and Moses' ministry of the law is called a *diakonia* in 2 Cor. 3:7, 9.

6. Much of this section and the Bridging Contexts section below are taken from my earlier attempt to summarize my work in "The Temple of the Spirit' As the Inaugural Fulfillment of the New Covenant Within the Corinthian Correspondence," *Ex Auditu* 12 (1996): 29–42.

7. William Lane, "Covenant: The Key to Paul's Conflict with Corinth," *TynBul* 33 (1982): 3–29, 6, 10. God's "covenant lawsuit" against the Corinthians therefore provides a necessary key for understanding the character, content, and unity of 2 Corinthians.

This is confirmed by Paul's portrayal of his ministry in 2 Corinthians 10:8 and 13:10 (cf. Gal. 2:18) in terms of the covenantal tasks of "building up" and "tearing down" (see Jer. 1:10; 31:28). How we understand Paul's self-understanding as a minister of the "new covenant" (2 Cor. 3:6) will therefore primarily be informed by our understanding of the meaning of the new covenant itself as found in Jeremiah 31:31–34 (see Bridging Contexts section).

The Ministry of the Spirit, Not the Letter (3:6c)

IF PAUL'S AUTHORITY as an apostle is based in part on the parallel between his sufficiency and the sufficiency of Moses (3:4–6a), it is equally supported by the contrast between his "ministry" (*diakonia*) and the "ministry" (*diakonia*) of Moses (3:6, as unpacked in 3:7–18). Paul is called like Moses, but with a distinctively different function. In the end, then, the character of Paul's ministry as an apostle, compared and contrasted to the ministry of Moses, becomes the key to understanding Paul's self-conception and defense. The heart of this comparison and contrast is the famous letter/Spirit contrast of 3:6.

The use of the "letter/Spirit" contrast as a proof text for a literal (= "letter") versus allegorical (= "Spirit") reading of the Scriptures has a long history in the church, going back as far as Origen (d. 254). It has even survived in modern times as an idiom for considering the "spirit" of a law more important than its "letter." Since the Reformation, however, interpreters have recognized that the letter/Spirit contrast does not signify two different ways of reading the Scriptures (with the church herself determining the "spiritual" meaning of the text). Rather, it refers to the distinction between the law and the gospel, either as two manners of relating to God or as two epochs within redemptive history.

Under the influence of the law/gospel contrast so central to Reformation thinking, the letter/Spirit contrast is often taken to refer to the law (= "letter") and the gospel (= "Spirit") themselves. Read in this way, the law is said to "kill" because of its demand for sinless perfection as a means of works righteousness and its corresponding condemnation of all those who fail to keep it perfectly (which is everybody!). All is not lost, however, for the law forces the sinner to despair under its demands and judgment, thereby driving a person to the life-giving promise of forgiveness and power found in the gospel. The "letter" (= law) kills *in order that* the "Spirit" (= gospel) might make alive. The unity of God's message in the Bible is found by virtue of the fact that the demand for works righteousness leads, through our failure, to the promise of the gospel.

Yet many students of the Bible have become uncomfortable with attributing such a negative function to the law itself, realizing that within the covenant structure of the Old Testament the law was an expression of the election and salvation of Israel, not a precondition for it. As a response to God's acts of deliverance and commitment to provide for his people, obedience to his commands became an outward expression of trust in his promises. Keeping the covenant stipulations is the way God's people demonstrate that they belong to him, not a way to become his people. Moreover, the Old Testament law itself provided for forgiveness, since its call for obedience is clearly given within the provisions of the sacrificial system. That is, the law itself recognizes that given our sinful nature, a key component of our obedience is repentance.

Consequently, many today argue that the "letter" does not refer to the law as such, but to its later perversion into legalism by the Judaism of the post-exilic period. It is not the law that kills, but legalism. Others maintain that the "letter" terminology is Paul's reference to some smaller subset of the law, such as purity regulations, food laws, the calendar, or circumcision. Read in this way, it was not the law as a whole, but an inappropriate emphasis on some aspect of the law (usually in order to maintain a Jewish separatism or self-reliance) that killed, while the Spirit, given to both Jew and Gentile alike, gives life. In both cases the Spirit brings one back to a proper understanding of the true intent of the law.

But this interpretation is not entirely satisfying either, since it is hard to demonstrate that Paul has such a subset or perversion of the law in view in his letters, while others note that Judaism itself was not always as legalistic as many assume. The law, for Paul, is a whole, and in the end the issue is the relationship between God's work in Christ and his saving work under the Sinai covenant, not what this or that Jewish community may have thought.

The key to the meaning of the letter/Spirit contrast, therefore, is its immediate context. In 3:3b, Paul had established a contrast between God's work in the past under the old covenant, in which he engraved his covenant document on stone tablets, and his present work under the new covenant, in which he engraves his "letter of Christ" on the "tablets of human hearts." Moreover, God's present work by means of the Spirit was seen to be fulfillment of Ezekiel 11:19 and 36:26–27. Against this backdrop, Paul's concern is not with two distinct messages, but with the two materials on which God wrote, corresponding to the two basic ages within the history of salvation. If anything is to be assumed as implicit in Paul's contrast in regard to the law, it is that those who have received the Spirit are now keeping the law, just as Ezekiel prophesied.

The flow of Paul's argument from 3:3 to 3:6 demonstrates that Paul understood the coming of the Spirit as promised by Ezekiel to be equated with the promise of the new covenant from Jeremiah. Paul's allusion to Ezekiel 11:19 and

36:26–27 in 2 Corinthians 3:3b, whose main point is that God will pour out the Spirit on those whose hearts were previously made of stone *so that he might cause them to observe his statutes and ordinances*, calls attention to the corresponding new covenant promise from Jeremiah 31:31–34 in 2 Corinthians 3:6a. The "law written on the heart" from Jeremiah 31:33 is equivalent to the obedience to God's statutes that, according to Ezekiel, the Spirit will bring about at the time of the final restoration of God's people. As was true for Jeremiah, for Ezekiel too this promise of a new heart, with its Spirit-caused obedience to the law, is a reversal of the hard-heartedness that characterized Israel since the Exodus (cf. the stone heart imagery in Ezek. 11:19b; 36:26b with Ezek. 2:1–8; 20:1–31). Finally, for Ezekiel, like Jeremiah, this new relationship to God's law will be made possible only by a divine act of redemption and forgiveness, which for Ezekiel is pictured in the priestly terms of God's cleansing his people from their uncleanness and idolatry (Ezek. 36:25, 29).

Once Ezekiel 36:25–26 and Jeremiah 31:31–34 are seen to be the keys to Paul's thinking in 2 Corinthians 3:6, the meaning of the letter/Spirit contrast becomes readily apparent. The passages from Ezekiel supply Paul's references to the work of the Spirit in 3:3b, while the Jeremiah passage provides the focus on the new obedience to the law in 3:6. Within the framework created by these two texts, Paul's role as a servant of the new covenant involves mediating the Spirit, which in turn brings about the transformation of the "heart" that makes obedience to the law possible.

For this reason, Paul is careful in 3:6 *not* to establish a contrast between the law itself and the Spirit. Nor is the Spirit to be read as a code-word for the gospel, so that the letter/Spirit contrast is transformed into a law/gospel contrast. The problem with the Sinai covenant was not with the law itself, but, as Ezekiel and Jeremiah testify, with the people whose hearts remained hardened under it. The law remains for Paul, as it did for the Jewish traditions of his day, the holy, just, and good expression of God's covenantal will (Rom. 7:12). Indeed, Paul characterizes the law itself as "spiritual" (7:14). As the expression of God's abiding will, it is not the law per se that kills, or any aspect or perversion of it, but the law *without the Spirit*, that is, the law as "letter." Devoid of God's Spirit, the law remains to those who encounter it merely a rejected declaration of God's saving purposes and promises, including its corresponding calls for repentance and the obedience of faith. Although the law declares God's will, it is powerless to enable people to keep it. Only the Spirit "gives life" by changing the human heart. In this regard, Paul can say that the gospel too kills when it encounters those who are perishing (cf. 2:16)!

The "letter/Spirit" contrast encapsulates this distinction between the role of the law within the Sinai covenant, in which it effects and pronounces judgment on Israel, and its new role within the new covenant in Christ, in which it is kept by the power of the Spirit. The contrast here is not between the law and the Spirit, as if the Spirit now replaces this expression of God's will, but between the law *as letter* and the Spirit. By choosing the designation "letter" (*gramma*) Paul brings out the nuance of the law under the old covenant (cf. 3:14) as that which remained expressed merely in writing, acknowledged as God's Word but not kept, rather than being obeyed from the heart by the power of the Spirit. The law without the Spirit remains merely a lifeless "letter."

Under the old covenant, Israel as a whole received the law, but only the remnant received the Spirit (see comments on 3:7–18). In accordance with the establishment of the new covenant, the pouring out of God's Spirit on all those within the covenant community reverses this state of affairs. In Christ it is no longer possible to be a member of the covenant people ethnically or corporately, but not spiritually. Those who are members of the new covenant community are so only by virtue of having been made alive by the Spirit. Hence, the letter/Spirit contrast is a contrast between *the law itself without the Spirit*, as it was and still is experienced by the majority of Israelites under the Sinai covenant (cf. 3:14–15), and *the law with the Spirit*, as it is now being experienced by those under the new covenant in Christ. At the center of this contrast is the determinative role played by the Spirit as the mark of the new covenant reality.

Accordingly, Paul's assertion in 3:6b that God made him sufficient to be a servant of the Spirit, in contrast to serving the letter, points to his assumption that just as Moses was called to be the mediator between God and Israel, Paul has been called to be an apostle of Christ to the church. Accordingly, the function of their ministries is radically different. Moses was called to mediate the law to a stiff-necked people who could not obey it, whereas Paul is called to mediate the Spirit to a transformed people who are being empowered to keep the law as appropriated under the new covenant. The startling implication of the letter/Spirit contrast, therefore, is that Israel's promised restoration is now beginning to take place in and through Paul's new covenant ministry within the church.

THE NATURE OF **the covenant.** Our exposition of this passage makes clear that how one understands Jeremiah 31:31–34 will determine to a great degree how one reads and hence applies this passage. For all are agreed that our expectations and self-understanding as people of the new covenant must be derived from the scriptural contours of that covenant relationship. The decisive question is what those contours actually are. In approaching this question it is important to make clear that the operating assumption of this commentary is that Paul did not rip scriptural passages out of their original contexts in order to use them as isolated proof texts for his own theology in service to his own polemical ends. Rather, Paul derived his thought and self-understanding from the Scriptures themselves, read soberly in their own literary and canonical contexts. Thus, to bridge contexts we cannot merely read Paul's letters in isolation from that canonical context. Instead, we must return to the biblical sources of Paul's own theology. To understand and apply Paul's calling to be an apostle of the "new covenant" in our own context thus necessitates understanding the new covenant within its own original setting.

What, then, are the contours of Jeremiah 31:31–34? It may be outlined in four main points. (1) The new covenant is the divinely promised answer to the perennial problem of Israel's hard-hearted rebellion against Yahweh, which, apart from the remnant, continues to characterize the people as a whole.[8] What is needed is nothing less than a new beginning, a new (or renewed) covenant, in which Israel's relationship with God will be decisively changed.

(2) The nature of this new covenant is described in Jeremiah 31:32–33 by contrasting it to the Mosaic/Sinai covenant (cf. 11:1–11; cf. 22:9–10), a covenant that both the fathers (11:7) and the Israel and Judah of Jeremiah's own day (11:9–10; cf. 22:9–10) had broken in "the stubbornness of their evil hearts" (11:8). Hence, according to 31:32, the essential difference between the Sinai covenant and the new covenant is that the latter will not be broken (though, of course, God had remained faithful to his covenant commitments under the Sinai covenant; the problem was with the people; cf. 2:5–8). The new covenant is an "everlasting covenant that will not be forgotten" (50:5). Jeremiah 31:33 gives the reason for this confidence: In this new covenant God will place his law (LXX reads the plural, "laws") within them ("in their minds") and "write it on their hearts."

In doing so, God will bring about a reversal of the present situation in which, instead of the law, "Judah's sin is engraved with an iron tool, inscribed with a flint point, on the tablets of their hearts" (Jer. 17:1). In view of Jeremiah's emphasis on Israel's stubborn rebellion, beginning from the Exodus, this reversal of what is written on the heart implies that in the new covenant Israel's rebellious nature will be fundamentally transformed. As a result, her

---

8. For the stubbornness of Israel's evil heart and her perpetual disobedience as a people within Jeremiah, see, e.g., Jer. 2:21–22; 3:17; 5:20–25; 7:24–26; 8:7; 9:12–16; 11:14; 13:10, 23; 14:11, 22; 15:1; 16:12; 17:1, 23; 18:12–15a; 19:15; 23:17. For the corresponding point that the covenant people and their leaders have continued to break the covenant, see Jer. 2:8; 5:31; 6:13, 17; 10:21; 14:18; 23:13–14; 27:16; 28:2.

disobedience will be replaced by an open compliance with God's covenant stipulations in his law. In describing the law as written "on their hearts," Jeremiah is picturing a people who accept God's law as their own and obey it willingly, rather than merely paying lip service to it, obeying it begrudgingly, or spurning it altogether (cf. Deut. 6:4–5; 10:16; 11:18; Ps. 40:8; Isa. 51:7). In the words of the covenant formula, Yahweh "will be their God, and they will be [his] people" (Jer. 31:33c).

(3) The movement of thought from Jeremiah 31:32 to 31:33 reveals that the covenant relationship between God and his people, whether under the Sinai covenant or the new covenant to come, is maintained by keeping the law *in response to* God's prior act of redemption. It must be emphasized that this is no truer of the new covenant than it was of the Sinai covenant before it (cf. Deut. 6:20–25). Rather than suggesting that the law is somehow negated or replaced in the new covenant, Jeremiah 31:31–33 emphasizes that it is the ability to keep the law as a result of having a transformed nature, not its removal, that distinguishes the new covenant from the covenant at Sinai. The contrast between the two covenants remains a contrast between two different conditions of the people and their correspondingly different responses to the same law. The Israelites broke the Sinai covenant, being unable to keep it because of their stubborn, evil hearts; the people of the new covenant will keep God's law because of their transformed nature.

(4) Jeremiah 31:34 depicts the result of the transformation of God's people promised under the new covenant and its ultimate ground. As a result of having God's law written on their hearts, the people of the new covenant will *all* know him directly. Unlike the role played by the prophets and remnant within Israel, there will no longer be any need to admonish others to "know the LORD." The call to repentance will no longer need to be issued within the community, but will go out instead from the covenant community to the world.

Against the backdrop of the Sinai covenant, this also points to a time when the role of Moses as the mediator of the will, knowledge, and presence of God will no longer be necessary. In the new covenant, God will renew the people's ability to encounter him directly, whereas under the Sinai covenant, beginning with the sin of the golden calf, the presence of God had to be kept completely separated from the people in order to protect them from destruction because of their "stiff-necked" state (cf. Jer. 7:26; 19:15 with Ex. 32–34 [esp. 33:3, 5]; Deut. 9:6, 13). It indicates as well that under the new covenant there will no longer be a distinction between those within the community who have a transformed heart and those who do not. By definition, all those who belong to the new covenant community do so by virtue of their transformed nature.

The people of the new covenant, in other words, are an extension of the faithful remnant within Israel who knew the Lord, not a continuation of the "mixed multitude" that constituted Israel's life as a nation and ethnic people (cf. Rom. 11:1–24). All of this is based on the fact that, despite Israel's past rebellion, God will "remember their sins no more" (Jer. 31:34). The changed condition of God's people and their resultant obedience to the covenant, together with their renewed access to the knowledge of God, are based on the divine forgiveness that makes the new covenant possible.

Consequently, in moving from Paul's day to our own, it is crucial to keep in view the covenant structure and promise of Jeremiah 31:31–34, both of which informed Paul's understanding of the gospel: The foundation of the covenant is forgiveness; the provision of the covenant is the Spirit; the consequence of the covenant is obedience; the promise of the covenant is to be in God's presence forever as his faithful people:

> I will make an everlasting covenant with them; I will never stop doing good to them, and I will inspire them to fear me, so that they will never turn away from me. (Jer. 32:40)

GOD AS THE source and supply of our lives. The contemporary significance of our passage revolves around one central, all-determining point: God is the source and supply of our lives, as demonstrated by his calling and equipping his people for service in a covenant relationship with him. The call of God takes place in Christ; the service takes place by means of the Spirit. This is true whether one is an apostle called to be a minister of the new covenant in the first century or a believer called to be faithful in service to others in the twenty-first. Though inherently offensive to the self-reliance and self-glorification that are so much a part of modern culture (and every culture since the Fall), Paul's stark reminder is that we cannot claim anything as coming from ourselves (cf. Rom. 11:36; Eph. 2:8–10). *All* things come from God (cf. 1 Cor. 8:6; 2 Cor. 1:21). Nothing we have is earned; everything is a gift (1 Cor. 4:7).

This fundamental reality is embedded in the nature of the covenant relationship that has always existed between God and his people. In referring to his own identity as a minister of the new covenant, Paul is bringing to bear on his self-understanding the history of God's covenant relationship with his people. In the same way, as called by God and sealed by the Spirit, this covenant relationship becomes determinative for our lives as well. "In Christ," we are people of the new covenant.

It is imperative for our relationship with God, therefore, that we keep in view that the "new covenant" (*kaine diatheke*) referred to in 3:6 is not an "agreement" or "treaty" (*syntheke*) that is mutually initiated, arranged, or disposed. We are not, as it were, God's junior partners, who are called to make our contributions to his plans. There is no synergism in the covenant in which God contributes his part and we do ours in order to accomplish something together that is greater than either of us. God is not looking for help. Rather, Paul's emphasis on the priority of the cross in salvation and on the work of the Spirit in justification and sanctification makes it evident that the initiative, inauguration, and sustenance of the new covenant, like the Sinai covenant before it, is due solely to the unilateral and merciful work of God on behalf of his people (cf. 1 Cor. 1:17–31; 2:1–5; 15:3–4; 2 Cor. 1:19–20; 3:5–6; 4:1–3; 5:18–9).

It is the Spirit, in bringing one to Christ for the forgiveness of sins, who brings into being the new life of the "new creation" (2 Cor. 5:17; cf. 1 Cor. 2:6–16 in light of the wisdom of God in the cross; 12:13 in light of baptism into the body of Christ by the Spirit; and 15:17 in light of the Spirit's testimony to the lordship of Christ). One can swear allegiance to Christ and remain faithful to him only by the power of this same Spirit (cf. 1 Cor. 2:9–13; 6:11; 12:3, 13; 2 Cor. 3:3, 17–18; 4:13–14). Our covenant relationship with God is, from beginning to end, based on God's *previous* act of redemption and *continuing* acts of provision, whether they are anchored in the Exodus from slavery in Egypt or in the "second exodus" from our slavery to sin. This is the great indicative reality of the gospel.

Faith-generated obedience. At the same time, Paul's reminder that we are people of the new covenant drives home the absolute necessity of living in obedience to God's commands as the expression of our faith in his promises. Keeping God's commands is what trusting in God as the source and supply of our lives looks like in everyday life. In response to God's gracious act of deliverance, both parties are obligated to remain faithful to their covenant commitments. For his part, God will continue to glorify himself by delivering and preserving and providing for his people (cf. 4:13–5:10). The Giver receives the glory. Having freely committed himself to his people, God cannot break his covenant promises without dishonoring his character. God's commitment to his own glory thus gives his people the confidence needed to persevere in the midst of adversity (1 Cor. 1:8–9; 10:13; 2 Cor. 1:7; 6:16; cf. Phil. 1:6; 4:10–19; 1 Thess. 5:9).

For their part, the Corinthians must keep the covenant stipulations as the natural expression of their continuing dependence on God (cf. 1 Cor. 3:1–3; 6:9–11; 2 Cor. 5:10; 13:5). In the new covenant, "what counts" is not ethnic identity (i.e., whether one is physically circumcised), but "keeping God's commands" (1 Cor. 7:19; i.e., whether one has experienced the spiritual circumcision of the heart; cf. Lev. 26:41; Deut. 10:16; 30:6; Jer. 4:4; 9:23–26). From Paul's perspective, given God's justifying and sanctifying work in the lives of his people *as guaranteed and brought about by the presence and power of the Spirit*, there is no excuse for habitually failing to trust God's gracious provisions and promises in Christ (cf. 1 Cor. 1:20; 5:7; 6:11, 19–20; 10:13; 13:1–3; 2 Cor. 1:22). Faith that trusts God to meet one's needs invariably "expresses itself through love" as the fulfillment of the law (Gal. 5:6, 14; cf. Rom. 13:10).

The *indicatives* of what God has done, is doing, and will do for his people are therefore inextricably linked to the *imperatives* that flow from them. For example, God commands his people not to steal because he has committed himself to meet their needs. To steal is to disbelieve God's promise in this regard. God commands his people not to covet because he has already promised to satisfy their deepest longings, ultimately in himself (note Paul's equation of idolatry with covetousness in Eph. 5:5; Col. 3:5). To say, "All I need to be happy is Jesus and something my neighbor has" is to commit idolatry by failing to trust God's covenant commitment that he will be enough for us. Idolatry is looking to something or someone other than God as the source of our happiness and contentment for the future.

In the same way, God commands his people not to retaliate against evil because he will vindicate the righteous and seek their vengeance. God commands his people to love others because he first loves them. In short, God commands the Corinthians to flee the life of sin described in 1 Corinthians 6:9–11 because they have been "washed ... sanctified ... justified in the name of the Lord Jesus Christ and by the Spirit of our God" (v. 11). In short, God calls us in all areas of our lives simply to trust in him as our God, the source and supply of all things.

The fundamental point concerning our covenant relationship with God in this regard is that every command from him is a call to trust in his promises and provisions, culminating in his greatest provision, namely, the purification and profound delight that come from enjoying his presence.[9] For this reason, although God's provisions and promises are all undeserved as unconditional gifts of grace, they are at the same time conditional upon the "obedience that comes from faith" (Rom. 1:5; cf. 15:18; 16:26).

Paul's job description as an apostle of the new covenant was to bring about this life of faith-generated obedience. For as he warned the Corinthians, "Do you not know that the wicked will not inherit the kingdom of God?" (1 Cor. 6:9). We are saved "by grace ... through faith" as the "gift of God,"

---

9. This perspective has been insightfully set forth in Daniel P. Fuller's important work, *The Unity of the Bible: Unfolding God's Plan for Humanity* (Grand Rapids: Zondervan, 1992).

a gift that includes being re-created in Christ Jesus in order that we might do "good works, which God prepared in advance for us to do" (Eph. 2:8–10). The necessity of obedience to God's commands, as the expression of faith in God's promises, is therefore not works righteousness, since both the promises of God and the power to trust them are gifts of God's unmerited, saving grace. God gives what he demands, and what he demands is the obedience that flows from faith (Rom. 1:5; 16:26). The threefold covenant structure may thus be outlined as follows:

God's unconditional act of redemption to establish the covenant relationship (the indicative provisions and promises of the covenant, given as an act of grace in the *past*)

which leads to

the covenant stipulations or "conditions"
upon which the covenant relationship is maintained
(the imperatives of the covenant
to be kept in the *present*)

which leads to

the fulfillment of the covenant promises of the covenant
(the consummation of the covenant promises or curses,
to be imparted in the *future*)

In the new covenant, as in the Sinai covenant before it, obedience to God's will is the inextricable manifestation of trusting in God's promises. Paul's ethical admonitions are grounded both in the past indicative of justification and in the future indicative of eschatological judgment and vindication, which, rather than being in conflict, flow inextricably from one another (cf. 2 Cor. 5:11–16). God judges according to our works because the expression of our having been forgiven, justified, and sealed in the Spirit (1:22) is the growing life of the obedience of faith that flows from the presence and power of the Spirit in our lives. Our obedience demonstrates publicly the validity of God's justifying act and saving actions on our behalf. All of this is from God. The fruit in our lives is the fruit of the Spirit.

This is why the Corinthians, if they persist in their unfaithfulness, will suffer God's ultimate judgment. Persistent disobedience, without concern for repentance, is the life of unbelief. God's wrath is meted out on all who dishonor God by a hardened refusal to acknowledge his provisions and trust in his promises (cf. Rom. 1:18–21), which shows itself in an inability to obey and callousness toward his commandments (cf. 1 Cor. 4:7, 19–21; 5:9–13; 6:9–11; 11:27, 30–32; 15:1–2; 16:22; 2 Cor. 5:10–11; 6:1–3; 12:19–21;

13:2–10). Conversely, as "the righteous Judge," God will reward those who "fight the good fight" with the "crown of righteousness," promised to all who "long for [the Lord's] appearing" and who trust God to bring them "safely to his heavenly kingdom" (2 Tim. 4:7–8, 18). In either case, for God not to judge the wicked or vindicate the righteous would be to denigrate his own glory as the sovereign Creator and Redeemer.

The church in Corinth was consequently well aware of the inextricable link in the new covenant between the redemptive work of Christ on the cross and the ethical admonitions of the gospel. They also understood that the driving assumption of the new covenant is that those who possess the Spirit as their "seal" and "guarantee" of salvation (2 Cor. 1:22; 5:5; cf. Rom. 8:23) will grow in faith from being "mere infants in Christ" to becoming "spiritual" people (1 Cor. 3:1; cf. 6:20; 9:24; 10:7–10, 14; 15:58; 16:13–14; 2 Cor. 7:1; 8:7–8; 9:13). For Paul, to speak about the saving power of the new covenant is to speak about the Spirit. Viewed from this covenant perspective, Paul's admonitions throughout 2 Corinthians are examples of the essential unity that exists between justification by faith (the indicative of the gospel) and an eschatological judgment on the basis of works (the imperative of the gospel). For Paul consistently argues throughout his letters from the evidence of the Spirit to the legitimacy of one's faith.[10]

The contemporary significance of this passage is therefore as straightforward as it is troubling. Have we downsized the indicative realities of the new covenant into abstract notions about God's activities in the past, or do we recognize God's sufficiency to supply all our needs, from forgiveness from sins to deliverance from death? Have we traded in the work of the Spirit under the new covenant for our own best efforts and feeble attempts to do the right thing for God? Do we break the link between faith and obedience in our daily lives, as if God's commands no longer apply to us as long as we "believe" in Jesus? Do we pray for the power of the Spirit to change our lives more and more, or are we content with our current spiritual plateau? Do we offer ourselves cheap grace when we sin, or do we fight the fight of faith in rooting out sin in our lives by serious grief and repentance over our unbelief? What evidence do we have that we belong to Christ as a member of the new covenant community?

---

10. For this same argument from the evidence of God's work in the lives of believers to the genuine nature of their faith, see Rom. 1:5; 8:3–4; 15:18; 2 Cor. 13:5; Gal. 5:16–26; Phil. 1:6; 2:12–13; 1 Thess. 1:3–6.

2 Corinthians 3:7–18

NOW IF THE ministry that brought death, which was engraved in letters on stone, came with glory, so that the Israelites could not look steadily at the face of Moses because of its glory, fading though it was, [8]will not the ministry of the Spirit be even more glorious? [9]If the ministry that condemns men is glorious, how much more glorious is the ministry that brings righteousness! [10]For what was glorious has no glory now in comparison with the surpassing glory. [11]And if what was fading away came with glory, how much greater is the glory of that which lasts!

[12]Therefore, since we have such a hope, we are very bold. [13]We are not like Moses, who would put a veil over his face to keep the Israelites from gazing at it while the radiance was fading away. [14]But their minds were made dull, for to this day the same veil remains when the old covenant is read. It has not been removed, because only in Christ is it taken away. [15]Even to this day when Moses is read, a veil covers their hearts. [16]But whenever anyone turns to the Lord, the veil is taken away. [17]Now the Lord is the Spirit, and where the Spirit of the Lord is, there is freedom. [18]And we, who with unveiled faces all reflect the Lord's glory, are being transformed into his likeness with ever-increasing glory, which comes from the Lord, who is the Spirit.

ONCE AGAIN WE must invest a substantial amount of exegetical labor in order to arrive at the primary point of this passage. Although the significance of 3:7–18 itself may seem slight in comparison to the mountain of historical and theological reflection on which it sits, we must keep in mind that in this passage Paul is putting in place the third and final plank of the foundation he has been laying for his apology as a whole (cf. 2:12–3:3; 3:4–6). Indeed, the remainder of the letter rests on the argument of 2:14–3:18, the theological heart and structural turning point of the letter (see comments on 2:12–3:3).

Moreover, Paul's commentary on and application of the Scriptures in the two paragraphs now before us (his own "application commentary" on

Ex. 32–34) were necessitated by his argument thus far, while at the same time pointing forward to his argument to come. In this sense, 3:7–18 is a hinge between Paul's argument for his legitimacy in 2:14–3:6 and its resumption in 4:1, offering support in both directions. Looking back, Paul maintained that the *similarity* between his call and that of Moses, which *legitimated* his apostolic ministry (cf. 2:16b; 3:4–5), was matched by the *difference* between their respective ministries, formulated in terms of the letter/Spirit contrast (cf. 3:6), which made up the distinctive *content* of his apostolic ministry. Called as a mediator of the covenant, Paul was a minister of the new covenant, not the old.

Paul must now clarify and substantiate this thesis. For as the history of the church demonstrates, the thesis-like nature of Paul's dramatic statement in 3:6 was open to misunderstanding. Indeed, Romans 7:6–7 (written from Corinth!) illustrates that from the very beginning there were those who took Paul's letter/Spirit contrast to mean that the law was sin. Thus, in order to support his thesis, Paul turns in 3:7–18 to the Old Testament narrative in Exodus 32–34 to explicate the essential difference between the ministries of the old and new covenants. We must, therefore, review this Old Testament backdrop before turning our attention to Paul's use of it.[1]

Exodus 32–34 as the Backdrop for 3:7–18

MOSES' BREAKING THE tablets of the law in response to Israel's sin with the golden calf demonstrated that the Sinai covenant was broken from the beginning (cf. Ex. 32:7–9, 19). Although Israel had been rescued from slavery, her idolatry revealed that her "neck" remained "stiff," enslaved to sin (32:9; 34:9; cf. Deut. 29:1–4). As a result, the Sinai covenant failed in its purpose, in which Israel's ongoing experience of the glory of God had been intended to purify them to become a holy "kingdom of priests" (cf. Ex. 19:5–6; 20:20). Instead, faced with the sin of the nation, God proclaimed a desire to destroy the people and to start over with Moses (cf. 32:10). Nevertheless, based on God's unswerving commitment to maintain his own glory (32:11–13), Moses interceded three times on Israel's behalf in order to keep Israel from being destroyed, to regain God's promise to lead the people into the Promised Land, and to secure God's presence with them as they went (32:11–33:17).

God responds positively to Moses' request to preserve the honor of his reputation, since, by virtue of his own promises to the patriarchs, it is now intertwined with the destiny of Israel (cf. Ex. 2:24–25; 9:16; 14:4, 17–18, 25; 15:1, 6, 11, 21; 16:6–7, 10; 32:13). At the same time, God's glory consists in

---

1. For the detailed support of the interpretation of Ex. 32–34 and 2 Cor. 3:7–11 presented here, see my *Paul, Moses, and the History of Israel*.

his sovereign freedom from all human claims, a freedom he demonstrates by showing mercy to whomever he desires (33:19). Therefore, although God grants Moses' request to preserve Israel as a nation, the people as a whole remained spiritually hardened. Consequently, in accordance with the covenant stipulations and curses of the law, the judgment of death falls on the three thousand directly involved in the idolatry—so that, in Paul's words, the "letter kills" (2 Cor. 3:6; cf. Ex. 32:26–28).

Ironically, it is now a faithful remnant, the sons of Levi, who executes God's judgment against the faithless nation. The Levites, who will now become priests *within* the people, bring about God's judgment *on* the very people who had once been called to be priests. From now on God's presence will bring punishment for Israel herself, not transformation, since she remains "stiff-necked" (Ex. 33:3, 5). When Yahweh comes to visit his people, that visit will no longer be to bless Israel, but to judge (cf. 3:16; 4:31; 13:19 with 32:34).

This leads to the pressing theological problem of the passage: How can God's glory continue to dwell in the midst of Israel without destroying her? Initially, God's glory was forced to dwell outside the camp in the "tent of meeting," lest God's presence destroy the people (cf. Ex. 33:7–11). Only Moses, as part of the faithful "remnant," could approach the presence of God. Moses is not happy with such a solution, however. He recognizes that God's presence in Israel's midst is the only thing that distinguishes Israel from the nations around her (33:16). So Moses has no desire to enter the Promised Land without the God of the promise in their midst.

Yet Moses also knows that God cannot dwell in the midst of a stiff-necked people. In his final petition, Moses consequently pleads that he himself, as the mediator of the covenant, might experience God's glory as the solution to Israel's dilemma (33:18–23). Because Moses has found favor (grace) before him, Yahweh grants Moses' startling request. In the end, therefore, Moses becomes the answer to his own prayers and the covenant is restored (34:1–10). Moses receives the law a second time and, with the glory of God beaming on his face, mediates God's presence to his people (34:11–35).

The narrative makes it clear, however, that although the Sinai covenant is renewed in a second giving of the law (Ex. 34:1–28), the people remain hardened (34:9). As a result, although the Ten Commandments are reestablished (cf. 34:1, 27–28), this time the public declaration of the covenant stipulations focuses on the so-called "cultic commands," since Israel's sin with the golden calf was a cultic sin of idolatry (34:12–26). The laws in Exodus 34 highlight Israel's propensity to sin in view of her sinful condition. The people who were to be a "kingdom of priests" mediating God's glory to the nations must now be ever mindful of the idolatry of their own hearts and of God's pronouncement of judgment against them.

God's covenant with Israel has been restored, but its context has been significantly altered. Thus, when Moses descends from God's presence on Mount Sinai, his face radiating with the glory of God, Aaron and the people *fear* his arrival (Ex. 34:29–30). This reaction is best explained as a reflection of God's prior declaration in 33:3, 5: The presence of God's glory means Israel's death. In response, after speaking God's word to the people, Moses veils his face, not to hide the fact that the glory is fading (there is no evidence for such a supposition in the text), but *in order to protect Israel from being destroyed* (34:32–33). Given Israel's "stiff-necked" condition, this remained Moses' practice from then on (34:34–35).

Moses' veiled mediation of God's glory permits his presence to remain in Israel's midst without destroying her. In this regard, Moses' veiling himself is an act of mercy. At the same time, the very fact that Moses must veil his face is an act of judgment because of the hardness of Israel's heart. This veil not only preserves Israel from being destroyed; it also keeps her from being transformed. For as Exodus 20:20 makes clear, the fear of God in response to the revelation of his glory was intended to purify the nation and to keep her from sinning.

From the very beginning, therefore, Israel was separated from the transforming glory of God: first at Mount Sinai (albeit much to Moses' surprise!), then in the tent of meeting, then behind the veiled face of Moses, and finally within the Most Holy Place in the tabernacle and temple. Eventually, in fulfillment of the covenant curses, Israel's continuing idolatry leads to a separation even from the Promised Land itself through the destruction of the northern kingdom in 722 B.C. and the exile of the southern kingdom in 586 B.C. (cf. Deut. 27:1–29:29; 31:16–32:44). Hence, the need for a "new covenant," articulated in Jeremiah 31:31–34 from the brink of the Exile, becomes apparent from the very beginning of Israel's history (cf. Deut. 30:1–20).

The Old Covenant Ministry of Death (3:7a-b)

AGAINST THIS OLD Testament backdrop, Paul's argument in 3:7–18 falls naturally into two parts: the interpretation of Exodus 32–34 in verses 7–11 and its application in verses 12–18. The first section is built around a series of three comparisons, all of which follow the *qal wahomer* (Hebrew) or *a fortiori* (Latin) style of argument. This type of comparison was well known in both the Jewish and Hellenistic literature of Paul's day. In it the truth of a greater assertion is based on a corresponding, lesser reality commonly agreed upon by both parties (i.e., "*if* this is so, then *how much more* so that . . ."; cf. vv. 7–8, 9–10, and 11).

Here the focus of these comparisons is between the "glory" of the ministries of the old and new covenants. Within five verses the term "glory" occurs eight times and the corresponding verb "to glorify" twice, and each time, for the sake of emphasis, they are placed in the Greek wording of the text at the end of their respective statements. There can be no doubt: The subject matter of this text is the glory of God.

In introducing this theme, 3:7–11 supports Paul's apology in two directions: Looking back, it grounds the thesis statement of 3:6b; looking forward, it undergirds the declaration of Paul's confidence in 3:12, which will in turn support Paul's not losing heart in 4:1. Moreover, here too, as in 2:16b– 3:3, Paul argues for his sufficiency as an apostle on the basis of his "ministry of the Spirit" as a fulfillment of the Scriptures. Paul's argument thereby exhibits the following parallel structure:

2:16b: Paul's sufficiency	3:5–6a: Paul's sufficiency
2:17: First support (Paul's suffering)	3:6bc: First support (Paul's ministry of new covenant)
3:1–3: Subsequent support (Paul's ministry of the Spirit in view of the Scriptures)	3:7–11: Subsequent support (Paul's ministry of the Spirit in view of the Scriptures)

Just as 3:1 began with a rhetorical question in support of 2:17, so too 3:7– 8 begins with a rhetorical question in support of 3:6. But this time Paul expects a positive answer: Since Moses' ministry came in glory, the ministry of the Spirit surely exists so much more in glory. With this comparison, Paul is not denigrating the character of Moses' ministry. Just the opposite! Given his *a fortiori* mode of argument, Paul's conclusion is only as strong as the premise on which it is built, that is, that Moses' ministry also "came with glory." Rather than attributing some inferior quality or lesser quantity to the glory associated with Moses' ministry, Paul bases his entire argument on the similarity between the glory of Moses' ministry and that of Paul's "ministry of the Spirit."

What *is* unsettling here is that Moses' ministry, though glorious, is associated with *death*. How can Paul affirm that Moses' ministry was one of glory and at the same time assert that it "brought death"? The foundation of Paul's argument appears to be self-contradictory and hence self-defeating. In order to make his case, Paul must therefore support the validity of both of these declarations.

In support of his first pronouncement, Paul reminds his readers that the law came "engraved in letters on stone." This reference to the law as "letter" recalls 3:6, pointing back to the function of the law as that which sets forth God's covenant stipulations, while at the same time "killing" those who, without the Spirit, cannot fulfill them. The reference to the law being "engraved on stone" points back to the fuller expression "tablets of stone" in 3:3, a description that highlights the law's divine origin, authority, and permanence (cf. Ex. 24:12; 31:18; Deut. 4:13; 5:22; 9:9–11).

But now, in 2 Corinthians 3:7, Paul is specifically referring to the *second* giving of the law in Exodus 32–34, which contains the only other mention in the Pentateuch of the stone nature of the tablets (see Ex. 34:1, 4). There the law is described in this way three times in order to underscore that the second giving of the law is like the first. Moreover, 34:1–28 both begins and ends with a reference to the tablets. Just as Moses first received the law within the cloud of God's glory (cf. 24:15–18), so too Moses' reception of the second set of stone tablets provides the framework for the renewed manifestation of the glory of God.

In support of his second and pivotal point—namely, that the ministry of the glorious law nevertheless "brought death"—Paul reminds his readers of the result of the law's coming: "so that the Israelites could not look steadily at the face of Moses because of its glory." Against the backdrop of Exodus 34:29–35, the significance of this statement is readily apparent. Paul is careful to point out that although the people saw God's glory for short periods of time, most likely to authenticate Moses' message (cf. 34:34–35), it was impossible for them to "look steadily" (*atenisai*[2]) into Moses' face, since doing so would mean their destruction (33:3, 5). Here Paul follows the LXX's translation of Exodus 34:29–30, 35, where the Hebrew reference to the "radiance" of Moses' face is rendered as the "glory" (*doxa*) of God. This translation rightly indicates that more is at stake in their inability to gaze at Moses than simply the condition of their eyes. As a "stiff-necked people," Israel cannot endure the glory of God (32:9–10, 22; 33:3, 5; 34:9).

Viewed in this light, the switch in terminology from the depiction of the law under the old covenant in 3:6 as a "letter," because of its function as that which killed, to the depiction of the law in 3:7a as "the ministry that brought death," is motivated by Paul's desire to express carefully the exact locus of the comparison between the old and the new covenants. The issue at stake is not a contrast between the law and the gospel understood as two qualitatively distinct means of salvation. It is neither the law nor the gospel itself that kills or makes alive, but the absence or presence of the Spirit (3:6c). Apart from the Spirit, the gospel too brings death to those whose hearts are hardened (cf. 2:16; 4:1–6). The issue at stake is the distinct consequences brought about by the respective "ministries" of Moses and Paul. Paul associates Moses' ministry,

---

2. Paul's use of *atenisai* (to gaze intently, continually, or directly) in 3:7 reflects his careful, contextual reading of the Old Testament; for its meaning, cf. Luke 4:20; 22:56; Acts 3:4, 12; 6:15; 11:6; 13:9; 14:9; 23:1. In Acts 1:10 and 7:55 it is used with reference to the glory of God as well (now in the form of the glorified Christ), and in 10:4 in reference to an angel of God.

not the law as such, with "death," since it was Moses' mediation of the glory of God that brought the judgment of God on a rebellious people. This realization leads Paul to his final point concerning the glory of the ministry of death in 3:7.

The Glory of Moses' Ministry (3:7c)

PAUL'S FINAL STATEMENT in 3:7 is to describe the glory on Moses' face with the passive participle *katargoumenen*, which is usually translated here and elsewhere throughout the passage as "fading away" (cf. 3:7, 11, 13). Paul is thus understood to be saying that Moses veiled himself to keep Israel from discovering that the glory was passing away in order to protect his own authority. When Moses subsequently returned to the tent of meeting, he removed the veil, thereby "recharging" the glory on his face. After again showing his face to the people, Moses would then quickly veil himself to hide the fact that the glory was fading away. Rather than protecting Israel from the judgment of God that would have ensued from encountering God's glory, Moses' veiling himself was an act of duplicity. Rendered in this way, it is obvious why readers have concluded that Paul radically reinterprets Exodus 34:29–35 *against* its original context, for there is no indication in 34:29–35 whatsoever that the glory on Moses' face was fading or that Moses veiled himself to hide something from Israel.

The evidence, however, does not warrant such a translation and conclusion concerning Paul's argument. A study of *katargeo* throughout Paul's writings reveals a narrow semantic field for its meaning and a uniform context for its use. Its Pauline context is consistently eschatological and its meaning is best translated in accordance with its rare, but unvaried use elsewhere in the ancient world, "to render (something) inoperative, ineffective, powerless," or "to nullify (something) in terms of its effects or impact."[3]

The consistency of this usage is striking. Indeed, Paul's use of this verb warrants its consideration as a Pauline *terminus technicus* (technical term), usually used to express the significance of the coming and return of Christ for the structures of this world.[4] In most of Paul's uses, *katargeo* expresses that which the

---

3. This is my own definition. The verb occurs 27 times in the New Testament, 25 of which are in Paul's writings (the exceptions are Luke 13:7 and Heb. 2:14). In contrast, there are less than 20 occurrences of the verb in all the literature prior to or outside of the New Testament and its circle of influence, including its four uses in 2 Esdras 4:21, 23; 5:5; 6:8. *Katargeo* is a rare word with a specific meaning that Paul introduced into the vocabulary of the early Christians (cf. its approximately 250 uses in the early church fathers, all of which derive from allusions to or quotes from Paul!). For a detailed study of this term, see my *Paul and Moses*, 301–9.

4. Besides the four occurrences in 2 Cor. 3:7, 11, 13, 14; cf. esp. Rom. 3:3, 31; 7:6; 1 Cor. 1:28; 2:6; 6:13; 13:11; 15:24, 26; Gal. 3:17.

---

gospel does and does not abolish and that which does and does not continue to be in effect as a result of the dawning of the new age of the new covenant. Paul's characteristic use of this word, therefore, poses in itself the question of the continuity and discontinuity between this age and the age to come.

In no case, however, does *katargeo* refer to the gradual "fading away" of some aspect of reality. The only evidence pointed to by NT Greek dictionaries and scholars who adopt this reading is 2 Corinthians 3 itself. Nevertheless, when read against the backdrop of Exodus 32–34, there is no indication that Paul himself was creating a new meaning for the word, that is, "to fade away." Instead, if the universally attested meaning of *katargeo* is assigned to 3:7c, Paul's result clause becomes, "so that the Israelites could not look steadily at the face of Moses because of its glory, *which was being rendered inoperative* (with special regard for the effects of such an action)."

This rendering is in full accord with the intention of Exodus 34:29–35, to which Paul is referring and which makes sense within 2 Corinthians 3 as well. Thus, there is no need to suggest that here and only here *katargeo* means "to fade away." Paul's point is that the glory on Moses' face was continuously being brought to an end or cut off in regard to its impact (note the passive voice of the verb). Within the context of Exodus 32–34, this reference to the glory on Moses' face being stopped points to the fact that, if left unattended, Moses' mediation of God's glory would have destroyed Israel because of their "stiff-necked" condition (cf. again 33:3, 5).

Once this interpretation is adopted, the natural question posed by Paul's statement in 3:7 is the identity of the unexpressed agent of this passive action. Who or what was rendering the glory inoperative? Within the context of Exodus 32–34 and in view of Paul's explicit statement in 2 Corinthians 3:13, the answer must be Moses' veiling himself. Hence, instead of going beyond the text, and by no means against it, Paul's interpretation of Exodus 34:29–35 remains faithful to its original meaning. The veiling of Moses' face in 34:34–35 underscores Paul's point that because of Israel's hardened nature as manifested in her sin with the golden calf, Moses' mediation of the glory of God was a ministry of death. The very need itself for Moses' veil manifests Yahweh's judgment against his rebellious people.

The fact that Israel could not gaze into Moses' face and the consequent necessity of the veil provide the evidence needed to support the propriety of Paul's description of Moses' ministry as a glorious ministry of death in support of his earlier statement that the "letter kills." It is clear that the glory of the letter "kills" because Moses had to veil his face. Moreover, this reading of Exodus 34:29–35 is not novel. It stands at the end of a long line of canonical interpretations of Exodus 32–34 in which Moses' ministry was interpreted not only as an act of divine mercy and grace, but also as a ministry of judgment on a rebellious people (cf., e.g., Num. 14:26–35; Deut. 1:3, 34–46; 2:14–16; 9:6–8; 29:4; Ps. 78:21–22; 95:10; 106:23, 26; Jer. 7:24–26; Ezek. 20:21–26).

The Glory of the Ministry of the Spirit (3:8)

BY CALLING ATTENTION to God's judgment embodied in Moses' veil, Paul's interpretation of Exodus 32–34 in the result clause of 2 Corinthians 3:7 provides the point of comparison on which his argument in verse 8 now turns. The comparison in 3:7–8 is based on the *similarity* between the glory of Moses' ministry of death and that of Paul's ministry of the Spirit. What drives the argument, however, is not the similarity between the two ministries, but their *differences*. For the argument to work, the glory of Moses' ministry cannot be the main point of verse 7, but rather its function as that which brought death. This is reflected in the syntax of verse 7 itself, where the result clause ("so that . . .") is the main point. The assertion of verse 8 is based on the fact that Moses' ministry was a ministry of death, *so that* the sons of Israel could not gaze into the glory of Moses' face, which because of their hardened condition had to be veiled to prevent them from being destroyed. Given Israel's "death" experience under Moses' ministry, Paul concludes in 3:8 that the ministry of the Spirit mediates the glory of God "even more."

The structure of Paul's argument in 3:7 thus makes it clear that the point of the "even more" comparison in 3:8 is not that Paul's ministry possesses God's glory in a greater quality or quantity, as if God's glory is given out in varying degrees. Rather, Paul argues that since the old covenant ministry, which brought death, came in glory, as testified to by its having been veiled, "then how much more must the ministry of the Spirit exist in *glory*" (3:8, lit. trans.),[5] since it brings life (3:6c). Paul is arguing for the very existence of glory in the ministry of the new covenant, despite the absence of visible displays of God's presence, not its degree or kind. The basis of his argument is the consequence (i.e., life) brought about by the ministry of the Spirit, in contrast to that of the ministry of the letter (i.e., death).

In this way, Paul's comparison in 3:7–8 reflects the difference between the old and new covenants themselves. Just as Israel's *inability* supports the glorious nature of Moses' ministry (if there were no glory in Moses' ministry, there would be no need for Moses' veil), the church's *ability* supports the glorious nature of Paul's ministry (if there were no glory in Paul's ministry, there

---

5. The NIV translation of 3:8, 9, 11 is misleading, since it wrongly indicates that the point of comparison in each case is the qualitative or quantitative *extent* of the glory. But in each case the comparison modifies the verb "to be" (3:8, 11) and "abounds" (3:9; trans. "is" in the NIV), not the nature of the glory per se.

would be no new life among the Corinthians). Given the distinct purposes of the old and new covenants as encapsulated in the letter/Spirit contrast, the *different* consequences of their respective ministries demonstrate that Moses and Paul mediate the *same* glory.

Thus, to support his assertions in 3:7–8, Paul appeals to two sources of uncontested validity. For his description of Moses' ministry, Paul rests his case on Israel's experience of death in response to the second giving of the law. For his contrasting description of his own ministry, Paul points to the Corinthians' experience of life in response to the apostolic mediation of the Spirit. The basis of Paul's argument for the past is the Old Testament account; for the present it is the reality being experienced in the church. In both cases, Paul's audience cannot deny either of these presuppositions. Hence, Paul's ultimate purpose in drawing this comparison is not to demonstrate the superiority of the new covenant over the old (though this is the implied basis of his argument), but to demonstrate his own qualifications to be its minister. At stake is Paul's legitimacy as an apostle and the reality of the glory of the new covenant he mediates.

The Contrast Between the Two Ministries (3:9–11)

VERSE 9 SUPPORTS verse 8 by reminding Paul's readers of why the Spirit is now able to live in their midst and in their lives without destroying them (though not translated in the NIV, verse 9 begins with *gar*, "for"). Moses' ministry brought about death to those who received the law (v. 7) because it declared and effected God's sentence of condemnation on those who broke the covenant (v. 9a). In contrast, Paul's ministry of the Spirit brings life (v. 8) because it declares and effects God's "righteousness" to those who keep the new covenant by the power of that same Spirit (vv. 6b, 8, 9b). The ministry of the Spirit in 3:8 is parallel to the ministry of righteousness in 3:9, the latter supporting the former. In the same way, the ministry of condemnation in 3:9 supports the ministry of death in 3:7.

Hence, if God's glory was associated with the ministry that brought condemnation (v. 9a), then all the more the ministry that brings God's "righteousness" *abounds* in glory (v. 9b; the NIV translation of *perisseuei* as "is" is too weak). If God's presence is the instrument of condemnation, it is also surely the means of salvation. The glory on Moses' face, by virtue of its having to be veiled, was the means used to carry out God's condemnation on Israel for her hard-hearted idolatry. In the same way, the glory that now abounds in the new covenant, by virtue of its now being unveiled, is the instrument by which God's righteousness in Christ is declared and effected in the church. The righteousness bestowed on God's people as a result of Christ's death makes it possible for God to dwell in the midst of his people without destroying them, thereby bringing about their righteousness.

Through the experience of God's glory that it makes possible, the righteousness of God granted to the believer also brings about the believer's growing transformation into that same righteousness (cf. 3:12, 18). This real experience of God's glory, here associated with the ministry of the Spirit (3:8) and righteousness (3:9), is an essential aspect of Paul's apostolic preaching of the cross of Christ (cf. Rom. 5:1–5; 8:2–10; 14:17; Gal. 2:20–21; 3:1–5; 1 Cor. 1:17–19; 2 Cor. 2:15–16a). The presence of God's glory in the believer's life, evidenced by his or her new life in and through the Spirit (2 Cor. 3:8), is at the same time an expression of God's righteousness revealed in the death of Christ for the ungodly (3:9; cf. Rom. 3:21–26; 2 Cor. 5:14–21).[6]

Before introducing the last of his three comparisons, Paul pauses in verse 10 to explain the meaning of the comparison established in verse 9. In turning our attention to this statement we must keep in mind that for Paul, God's glory remains God's glory, whether revealed in connection with the law or with the gospel. It is not as if the glory in the new covenant ministry is a substance that is better, stronger, or more brilliant than the revelation of that glory on the face of Moses, as often maintained. Rather, the key to Paul's thinking is his choice in verse 10 of the summarizing neuter designation, "what was glorious" (to dedoxasmenon). This designation denotes that the apostle is not referring to the law (which in Greek is masculine), or to the glory of the old covenant itself (which in Greek is feminine), or even to the ministry of the glory as such (also feminine). Instead, the abstract or collective use of the neuter indicates[7] that Paul's reference is to the ministry of the old covenant as a whole, especially its theological purpose (v. 9a), results (v. 7), and function (v. 6b).

Literally translated, verse 10 reads: "For indeed that which has been glorified is not glorified in this respect because of the surpassing glory." Paul's point

---

6. This inextricable link between judicial and ethical righteousness in Paul's thought, which undergirds this text, is well summarized by Hughes, *Paul's Second Epistle to the Corinthians*, 104–5, in commenting on 3:9: "Christ is the believer's righteousness (1 Cor. 1:30): first of all in justification, whereby Christ's obedience is reckoned to the sinner on the ground that the penalty of the sinner's disobedience has been borne by Christ, who suffered the Righteous for the unrighteous (1 Pet. 3:18); and then in sanctification, whereby the Holy Spirit causes the believer to grow more and more in obedience and likeness to Christ (Eph. 4:13, 15; Gal. 4:19). In accordance with the promises of the new covenant . . . God's law is written on the believing heart and the power is granted . . . to fulfil it."

7. So A. T. Robertson, *A Grammar of the Greek New Testament in the Light of Historical Research* (Nashville: Broadman, 1934), 1109, who takes to dedoxasmenon in 3:10 to be an example of the use of the neuter participle as an abstract substantive (cf. also Luke 8:56; 9:7; John 16:13; Acts 24:25; 1 Cor. 1:28; 14:7).

is not that the ministry of the old covenant as a whole, which has been glorified, is now finally seen to be less glorious in view of the greater glory that has
arrived. This view is often supported by interpreting Paul's statement in terms
of an analogy taken from the sun and moon. As a result, the glory of the old
covenant is said to be eclipsed by the new, just as the reflected light of the
moon pales in the direct light of the sun. Instead, the comparison here is one
of divine purpose within redemptive history, not of quality or quantity. The
glory of the new covenant surpasses the old in time and intent, not in kind.

As in 3:3, 6, the point of verse 10 is an eschatological one (on the meaning of "surpassing" as a reference to the quality of the new age, cf. 9:12–15).
Paul is not saying that the glory of the old covenant pales in comparison to
the new, but that the "surpassing glory" of the new covenant now brings
"that which had been glorified," that is, the old covenant, to an end. When
one compares the purposes and results of the two covenants, *in this respect*
(the NIV misleadingly reads: "now in comparison") the former has no glory
at all. The meaning of 3:10 can therefore be paraphrased as follows: *Because
God's purpose and its results in the new covenant surpass what he has accomplished thus far in the old covenant, therefore that which formerly was the
vehicle of revelation of God's glory is in this respect no longer the means
through which God is revealing his glory. Once the new covenant arrives,
with its primary purpose of granting new life in the Spirit, the old covenant,
with its primary purpose of condemnation, is no longer the locus of God's
glory in the world.

In verse 11 Paul brings this section of his argument to a close by introducing a third comparison. In doing so he continues his use of the neuter designations introduced in verse 10. Paul's focus is still on the purpose and results
of the old and new covenants respectively, with the neuters referring in a
broad, encompassing sense to "that which was being rendered inoperative"
(*to katargoumenon*) over against "that which is remaining" (*to menon*). The introduction of verse 11 with yet another *gar* ("because") follows Paul's stylistic tendency of stringing together assertions in order to undergird his main point
with a series of step-by-step supports (the NIV simply translates this "and").[8]
The assertion in verses 7–8 is supported by verse 9, which in turn is supported
by verse 10, which in turn is supported by verse 11. But how does verse 11
support Paul's assertion that his ministry as an apostle is the vehicle through
which the surpassing glory of the new covenant is now being revealed (3:10)?

The answer is found in the two new, interrelated elements in verse 11.
(1) Paul transfers the *katargeo* terminology from its use in verse 7 as a direct

---

8. Cf. the chains of *gar* in Rom. 1:16–21; 2:11–14; 4:1–3, 13–15; 5:6–7; 7:14–15, 18–19;
8:1–6, 12–15, 18–24; 1 Cor. 1:18–21; 3:2–4; 9:16–17; 12:12–14; 2 Cor. 5:1–4; 13:4; etc.

reference to the glory on Moses' face to the old covenant ministry conceived as a whole. The Sinai covenant's mediation of God's glory, which as a result of Israel's "stiff neck" had to be continually rendered inoperative by the veil (3:7), is now itself described as that which was continually being rendered inoperative (3:11). The veiling of Moses' face (v. 7) demonstrates that the Sinai covenant, *from its very beginning*, was hindered from accomplishing its purpose of establishing God's immediate and abiding presence among a sanctified people (v. 11; cf. Ex. 19:5–9; 20:20).

(2) Paul describes the new covenant ministry as that which "remains," "lasts," or "persists" (*meno*). This verb recalls its earlier use in 1 Corinthians 3:14, where it referred to that work that "survives" beyond the eschatological judgment, and in 13:13, where it referred to faith, hope, and love as the three things that "remain" in the future eschatological era. In this latter context, as in 2 Corinthians 3:11, *katargeo* again forms the counterpart to *meno* as a description of those things that are abolished or do not "remain" eschatologically (cf. 1 Cor. 13:8, 10, 11).

Moreover, Paul's quote from Psalm 111:9 (LXX) in 2 Corinthians 9:9 indicates that he can link the notion of being abolished (*katargeo*) or remaining (*meno*) at the eschatological judgment to the psalmist's declaration that the Lord's "righteousness endures [*meno*, remains] forever." Only those things based on God's own righteousness can stand the test of his "righteous judgment" (Rom. 2:5; cf. 3:4–5; 2 Cor. 5:10; 2 Thess. 1:5). What remains eschatologically in 1 Corinthians 3 and 13 does so because it corresponds to God's "righteousness" that "remains." Thus, the new covenant "remains" in force since it reveals the righteousness of God that lasts forever (cf. Jer. 32:37–40).[9] It is this "remaining" (2 Cor. 3:11) new covenant (3:10) of the Spirit (3:8), based on the righteousness of God (3:9), that Paul was called to minister (3:4–6).

The Boldness of the New Covenant Ministry (3:12–13)

IN 3:12–18 PAUL draws out the implications of his argument from 3:7–11 concerning the "glory" of the two ministries. In doing so he switches his focus from a *comparison* between the ministries of the old and new covenants to

---

9. See F. Hauck, "μένω," *TDNT* 4:574–88, esp. 574–76, for the use of the verb in Jewish and non-Jewish religious texts, where in both cases "μένειν is a mark of God and what is commensurate with Him" (574). Hauck also outlines the key Old Testament eschatological background of the word (cf. Ps. 102:12; Isa. 40:8; 66:22; Dan. 4:26; 11:6; Zech. 14:10; Wis. 7:27; Sir. 44:13; 4 Esdras 9:37). He then points out that in John's Gospel the eschatological promise of that which remains is realized in that God "remains" in Christ, Christ "remains" in believers, and believers "remain" in Christ (cf. John 6:56; 8:35; 15:4–7, 9–10; 14:10; 1 John 2:26–28; 3:6, 24; 4:16).

their essential *difference*. Paul derives this difference from the necessity of Moses' veil over against his own "unveiled" apostolic ministry. Accordingly, Paul's assertions concerning his boldness (v. 12), the hardness of Israel's minds (v. 14a), Israel's current relationship to the old covenant and Moses (vv. 14b–15), and the contrast between Israel's situation and the experience of Christians (vv. 16–18) are all based on the meaning and significance of Moses' veil.

As the inference ("therefore"; Gk. *oun*) and summary statement "since we have such a hope" indicate, in 3:12 Paul draws the conclusion to which 3:7–11 naturally leads. Based on 3:8, the main point of 3:7–11, Paul's confident expectation (i.e., his "hope"; cf. the parallel between 3:4 and 3:12) is that through his own life and message as a minister of the new covenant (3:6) the glory of God is being mediated to God's people in the Spirit (3:11). Because he has this "hope," Paul is therefore "very bold" (note the continuation of the apostolic plural "we" in 3:12).

The word translated "bold" (*parresia*) in 3:12 is a technical term from the political realm that was associated with freedom and truth. In moral contexts such as this, it refers to a shamelessness in one's behavior that leads to a free, courageous, and open manner of speech.[10] The power of the Spirit in Paul's ministry (3:8) has made Paul fearless and forthright in his proclamation of the gospel (3:12; cf. Rom. 1:16–17). Ultimately, this boldness arises from his assurance that his life and labors derive from God's grace in his life, that they are being carried out in God's presence, and that they will be vindicated before God's judgment (cf. 2 Cor. 1:12; 2:17b–3:3, 7–11; cf. 1 Cor. 4:1–5; Phil. 1:20).

In 3:13, Paul illustrates the bold character of his ministry by drawing a contrast between his own ministry and Moses' need to veil himself. Here too, as in 3:7, the dominant approach has been to take verse 13 to refer to Moses' practice of hiding from Israel the fact that the glory on his face was coming to an end (*to telos*) because of its fading nature (*katargeo*). Read in this way, Moses is pictured as being less than honest with Israel, while Paul is able to speak the truth boldly to the church. Since there is no mention in Exodus 34:29–35 of any such motive for Moses' action or that the glory was fading, it is therefore common to conclude that in making this point Paul willfully goes beyond, or even against, the Old Testament text. The contrast in 3:13 is consequently seen to be Paul's clever attempt to denigrate his opponents' position by devaluing Moses' ministry.

---

10. For the evidence for this meaning, see my *Paul, Moses, and the History of Israel*, 338–47, and texts such as Philo, *On Sacrifices* 35; *On the Confusion of Tongues* 165; *Who Is the Heir* 5–6; *On Dreams* II.83, 85; Plutarch, *Demosthenes* 12, 14; *Cato* 33, 35; *Ep. Arist.* 125; *Joseph and Aseneth* 17:9; 23:10; *T. Reub.* 4:2; Wis. 5:1; and Mark 8:32; John 7:13, 26; 10:24; 11:14; Acts 2:29; 4:13, 29, 31; 9:28; 13:46; 14:3; 26:26; 28:31; Eph. 6:19–20; Phil. 1:20.

Nevertheless, when interpreted within the context of Exodus 32–34 already picked up by Paul in 3:7–11, and with a more appropriate understanding of *katargeo* (see comments above), Paul's affirmation is different from what is usually portrayed. Like 3:7, 3:13 refers to Moses' practice of veiling himself as a result of Israel's hard-heartedness. Now, however, Paul turns his attention from the consequences of Moses' ministry, which formed the heart of the comparison in 3:7–11, to the distinction in *purpose* between Moses' veiling himself and Paul's own ministry of preaching the gospel openly.

In 3:7a, the glory of Moses' ministry itself, with its effect of death, resulted in Israel's inability to gaze into the face of Moses (Gk. *boste* plus infinitive). As its corollary, in 3:13 it is Moses' practice of veiling himself that brings about Israel's inability (Gk. *pros to* plus infinitive). Because Israel was not able to gaze into Moses' face (3:7), Moses veils himself in order that they might not do so (3:13). Whereas in 3:7–11 Paul based his comparisons on their different results, in 3:13 he bases his comparison on their different intentions or goals. In the first instance, Israel was not able to gaze continuously into the glory on the face of Moses because in her "stiff-necked" condition it would have destroyed her (3:7). In the present instance, Moses veiled himself both to embody this judgment and to mediate the mercy of the renewed covenant.

In verse 13b Paul makes this purpose explicit by calling attention to Moses' intention in veiling the glory of God (pers. trans.): "in order to keep the Israelites from gazing at *the outcome* [NIV "it"; Gk. *to telos*[11]] of that which was being rendered inoperative in terms of its consequences [*tou katargoumenou*; again in the neuter as an abstract reference to the old covenant as a whole]." In our context, this outcome or *telos* can only refer to the death-dealing judgment of God's glory on his "stiff-necked" people.

In 3:12, Paul is not declaring that he is open and honest in contrast to Moses' conscious or unconscious deception. Rather, unlike Moses, he is free to preach the gospel in the knowledge that the present revelation of God's glory need not be veiled from those to whom he is sent, since its outcome (*telos*) is life, not death (cf. 3:6). Whereas Moses had to veil himself as an act of judgment toward a rebellious people, Paul need not "veil himself" before a people whose disposition toward God has been radically changed by the Spirit (3:3–6).

---

11. The well-established range of meaning for *telos* includes the idea of "end," both in the sense of "abolishment" or "termination," and in the sense of "outcome," "consequence," "goal," or even "purpose." Here the latter is more appropriate contextually. See BAGD, 811–812, and its confirmation in W. Bauer, K. Aland, and B. Aland, *Griechisch-deutsches Wörterbuch* (Berlin/New York: Walter de Gruyter, 1988[6]), 1617–18. The NIV translation "it" for the Greek *to telos* misses the point of the text. *To telos* is not a pronoun referring back to Moses' face, but a noun best translated as "the goal."

Paul is keenly aware of the implications of what he has just said, not only for the significance of his own ministry, but also for those whom he encounters (cf. 2:15–16a). The contrast established between Moses and Paul in 3:12–13 means that only those who are accepting Paul's bold message number among the people of God to whom his glory is now being revealed. Paul's argument therefore raises some troubling questions. If Paul is openly mediating God's glory among his people in fulfillment of the promises of the new covenant, why are the "Israelites" not accepting Paul's ministry? Does Israel's rejection of Paul's message not call into question his legitimacy as an apostle? If not, why has Israel failed to respond to the gospel? Is Israel no longer the locus of God's presence in the world?

The Continuing Hardening of Israel (3:14–15)

COMMENTATORS HAVE LONG struggled with the transition from 3:13 to 3:14. Where we would expect a supporting statement (i.e., "Moses veiled himself to keep the Israelites from gazing into the goal of that which was being rendered inoperative *because* their minds were hardened"), Paul introduces a strong contrast (cf. *alla* in v. 14a; "but" in NIV).[12] This difficulty derives from attempting to relate the strong contrast of 3:14 directly back to 3:13b. Though possible, there is another option grammatically. Instead of relating 3:14a directly to the purpose clause of 3:13b, the contrast of 3:14 may be taken back to 3:12–13a as part of a "not ... but" (*ou ... alla*), negative-positive construction. Read in this way, 3:13b becomes a parenthetical reflection on the significance of 3:7.

The flow of the argument from 3:12–14 then reads as follows: "We are very bold. That is to say, we are *not* like Moses (who would put a veil over his face ...). *But* their minds were hardened [NIV dull[13]]. ...." Since the Spirit is being poured out through his ministry, Paul can only conclude that "the Israelites" continue to reject the gospel because, from the very beginning of her covenant history, "their minds were hardened" (3:14a). In spite of his bold proclamation, Israel is not responding to Paul for the same reason she did not respond to Moses: From Sinai on, Israel has been hardened [by God!]

---

12. There have been numerous attempts to get around this difficulty by suggesting novel readings for the conjunction itself or by supplying supposedly missing assertions between 3:13 and 3:14 (e.g., "not that Moses sought to deceive, but their minds were hardened"; or, "the glory should have impacted Israel positively, but their minds were hardened").

13. The verb translated "dull" in the NIV is better translated, "hardened," alluding to Ex. 32–34 as picked up in Jer. 5:21 and Ezek. 12:2 in parallel to Isa. 6:9 and against the backdrop of Deut. 29:3–4. Cf. Rom. 11:7–10 and Acts 28:26–27, where the same verb is used against this same Old Testament background to explain the Jews' rejection of Paul's ministry, and the related passages in Matt. 13:15 and Mark 4:12.

to the revelation of God's glory in her midst (taking the aorist "were hard-ened" to be gnomic[14] and a divine passive).

The evidence for this evaluation is given in 3:14b–15, where Paul again turns to the veil of Moses from Exodus 34:29–35. This time Paul uses Moses' veil as a metonymy.[15] Israel's hardened nature as manifested in her sin with the golden calf is represented by Moses' veil, employing the consequence for its underlying cause.[16] As a result, the veil can now move in Paul's argument from that which originally resided on Moses' face to that which now lies over the reading of the old covenant in 3:14 to that which lies over Israel's heart in 3:15.

Decoded, Paul's symbolism is clear. Because Israel's hardened condition can only be rendered inoperative in terms of its impact (NIV "taken away"; Gk. *katargeo*) "in Christ" (3:14d), Israel's large-scale rejection of the gospel indi-cates that she remains in the same hardened condition that has characterized her history ever since the golden calf (3:14c, 15a). The very one whom they reject is the only one who can remove their blindness. Only "in Christ" can the Spirit remove the heart of stone (cf. 3:2–3, 8–9). This has consequences both for Israel's reading of the Scriptures and for her own spiritual state.

(1) The first implication of Israel's hardened condition is hermeneutical. Even though the age of the new covenant has dawned, "to this day" Israel remains veiled, that is, hardened to the significance of the very law that was intended to lead her to the Messiah (vv. 14b, 15a). As 3:14b and 15a make clear, this is not because the real meaning of the Sinai covenant is somehow hidden or veiled, but because Israel is veiled (= hardened) whenever "Moses is read." Here too we have a metonymy. Just as Moses' "veil" now represents Israel in her hardened state, "Moses" himself represents the old covenant as codified in the law.

Again the meaning is clear. When Israel reads the Scriptures in her hard-ened condition, she stubbornly refuses to go where the biblical text leads. For as the metonomy of the "veil" signifies, Israel's "hermeneutical problem" is not intellectual, but moral. The "veil [that] covers [Israel's] heart" (v. 15b) does not refer to a cognitive inability because of a lack of a special spiritual endow-ment, but to a volitional inability as a result of a hardened disposition. The meaning and significance of the old covenant is not an esoteric secret to be

---

14. I.e., the use of the aorist to represent "an act which is valid for all time . . . because (originally at least) the author had a specific case in mind in which the act had been real-ized," BDF, §333. The specific case in mind here is Israel's sin with the golden calf.

15. Metonymy is a figure of speech in which one thing is called by another thing asso-ciated with it; e.g., we can use "bottle" to refer to drunkenness, as in "he is off the bottle."

16. For a discussion of this use of metonymy, see G. B. Caird, *The Language and Imagery of the Bible* (Philadelphia: Westminster, 1980), 136–37, with many biblical examples.

unlocked by a special "Christian" revelation. In other words, the issue in 3:14–15 is not that Israel *cannot* understand intellectually the implications of her history under the old covenant and her consequent need for the death of the Messiah. Rather, the problem is that she *will not* accept it as true for her. Israel's "stiff-necked" condition continues to "veil" her response to the Sinai covenant.

(2) The second implication of Israel's hardened condition is spiritual. The description of Israel's condition in 3:14–15 indicates that her large-scale rejection of Christ does not call into question the legitimacy of Paul's own apostolic ministry or the validity of his gospel as the revelation of God's glory. To make this point, Paul has used the scriptural pattern of seeing Israel's current rejection of God's work as evidence that Israel remains in the same hardened state that has characterized her from the beginning.[17] This interpretation of Israel's present state as a reflection of her past history of rebellion is reflected in Paul's incorporation into his own argument of the biblical phrases "to this day" and "even to this day" (3:14–15). These phrases recall the parallel designation in Deuteronomy 29:4 (v. 3 in LXX), where Moses declares that, despite the Lord's deliverance from Egypt, "the LORD has not given [Israel] a heart to know, and eyes to see, and ears to hear *until this day*."

Within its original context, this divine prerogative not only explains Israel's past disobedience, but also grounds Moses' proclamation that Israel will continue to break the covenant in the future, suffering the judgment of the Exile as a result. Further confirmation that Paul's use of the phrase "(even) to this day" is a reference to the scriptural pattern of viewing Israel's present in terms of her past is found in Jeremiah and Ezekiel. Both prophets use the same designation to underscore that Israel's plight in their time was evidence that Israel's rebellion was continuing unabated from the days of their fathers.[18] So too in Paul's day, as in the days of Moses and the prophets, the problem is not with Paul's gospel, but with Israel herself.

Thus, in supporting the legitimacy of his ministry, Paul again builds his argument on the testimony of the law and the prophets (note that his language in 3:14–15 comes from Moses and the same two prophets referred to

---

17. For the pattern of arguing from Israel's current rebellion (and consequent judgment in the Exile) to her being hardened from the beginning, see Neh. 9:16–31; Ps. 78:5–8, 54–64; 106:6–39; Isa. 63:7–19; 65:2–7; Jer. 3:25; 7:18–26; 11:7–10; 15:1 (where not even Moses himself could prevent the ensuing judgment of God); 16:11–13; 17:23; 19:15; 44:9–10; Lam. 5:7; Ezek. 2:3; 20:8–36; Amos 2:4; Zech. 1:2–4; 7:11–14; Mal. 3:7. See too Paul's own mixed citation of Deut. 29:3 and Isa. 29:10 in Rom. 11:8, where the latter prophetic text concerning Israel's hardening in Isaiah's day is explicated in terms of Israel's hardening during the days of Moses.

18. For the use of this motif see Jer. 3:25; 7:25; 11:7 (MT); 32:20–21 (MT); 44:10 (MT); Ezek. 2:3.

in 3:3–6). Rather than calling Paul's ministry and message into question, Israel's rejection of the gospel is evidence that she remains in the same hardened state that Moses encountered and predicted would continue into the Exile and that the prophets consequently met in their own lifetimes. Hence, as Paul explicitly puts it for the first time in Christian literature, Israel continues to subscribe to the "old covenant," even though the new covenant has been established (3:14).

Paul's introduction of the terminology "old covenant" is a declaration of his eschatology, not a denigration of the law. He refers to the Sinai covenant as "old" only because he is convinced that Jesus, as the Christ, has inaugurated the "new covenant" of Jeremiah 31:31–34 and Ezekiel 36:26–27 (cf. again the allusions to these two texts in 2 Cor. 3:3, 6). The designation "old" is not a pejorative evaluation of the content of the Sinai covenant, but an eschatological designation of its fulfillment. To speak of it as "old" is to view the covenant ministered by Moses through the lens of the dawning of the "new covenant" ministered by Paul.

The Conversion of the Remnant (3:16–18)

HAVING SPOKEN TO the issue of Israel's rejection of the gospel in 3:14–15, in 3:16–18 Paul returns to Moses' experience with the veil one last time. Now, however, he brings out its significance not for unbelieving Israel, but for those who have responded to Christ. Paul begins by paraphrasing Exodus 34:34a, which contrasts Moses' veiling himself before the people with his practice of removing the veil when he spoke with the Lord in the tent of meeting. This again highlights the contrast between Israel's inability to encounter God's glory because of her "stiff-necked" state, which necessitated the use of the veil, and Moses' ability to encounter the glory of God unveiled as one whose heart had been transformed by the Spirit. But whereas in Exodus 34:34 it was Moses who entered before the Lord unveiled, in 2 Corinthians 3:16 "anyone [who] turns to the Lord" has the veil taken away. And whereas in Exodus 34:34 Moses removes the veil, in 2 Corinthians 3:16 "the veil is taken away" by God (note the divine passive).

The switch in subject in 3:16 indicates that Paul regards Moses' experience to be the prototype of those believers under the new covenant who follow Moses "to the Lord." This reading is confirmed by the connotation of conversion introduced by the use of the verb "to turn"[19] and the emphasis on

---

19. Cf. the use of this same verb, *epistepho*, to refer to "turning to the Lord" in the sense of conversion in Luke 1:16–17; Acts 3:19; 9:35; 11:21; 14:15; 15:19; 26:18 (in the context of Paul's ministry to the Jews and Gentiles in fulfillment of Isa. 42:7, 16; cf. Isa. 35:5); 26:20; 1 Thess. 1:9; 1 Peter 2:25.

the passive nature of the veil's removal. For believers, as for Moses, the veil has been removed from their "hardened mind" (3:14) as a result of having their "heart of stone" removed by the Spirit (cf. 3:6).

Against the backdrop of Exodus 34, the "Lord" (*kyrios*) in view in verse 16 is not Christ, *in whom* the veil of hard-heartedness is taken away (2 Cor. 3:14b), but Yahweh, *to whom* one turns once the veil has been removed. Although *kyrios* in Paul's writings generally refers to Christ, this is not the case when Paul is quoting Scripture or working with a scriptural context.[20] Paul's use of "the Lord" to refer to Yahweh in 3:16 corresponds to the other ten times in Pauline citations of the Old Testament in which *kyrios* reflects the Septuagint's use of this word to translate Yahweh in the Hebrew text.[21] At this point in his argument, Paul is thinking theologically, not Christologically. Like Moses, so too the one who "turns to the Lord" in conversion encounters the glory of God without fear of destruction. The hard heart of rebellion has been removed (3:3, based on Ezek. 11:19; 36:26–27) and forgiveness received (2 Cor. 3:6, based on Jer. 31:31–34)—all based on the righteousness that comes from Christ (2 Cor. 3:9).

The age-old problem of the apparent identification of Jesus with the Spirit in 3:17a can now be seen to be the creation in large measure of interpreting this statement apart from its Old Testament background. As a further development of 3:16, there is no indication that in verse 17a Paul has suddenly substituted Christ for Yahweh. Since the *kyrios* of 3:17a is still Yahweh, the "is" of 3:17a is therefore better rendered "means."[22] In 3:17, Paul is not identifying Christ and the Spirit. Rather, he is making it abundantly clear that Moses' experience of Yahweh in the tent of meeting is equivalent to the current experience of the Spirit in Paul's ministry, just as Paul referred earlier to the Spirit mediated through his ministry as the "Spirit of the living God" (3:3). Paul's point is that those who are presently living under the new covenant in Christ are in direct continuity with the revelation of Yahweh begun at Sinai.

In this context, the "freedom" spoken of in 3:17b implies a freedom from the veil of hard-heartedness that is unable to enter into the presence of the Lord (3:7, 9, 13–14). Nevertheless, this *negative* reading of the freedom in view in 3:17a as a "freedom *from*" is most likely not the major thrust of Paul's statement. In contexts such as this one, where he is not referring to the political

---

20. Following Furnish, *II Corinthians*, 211.

21. See Rom. 4:8; 9:28, 29; 10:13; 11:34; 14:11; 15:11; 1 Cor. 2:16; 3:20; 10:26. To these may be added 2 Cor. 8:21, in which the LXX reads *kyrios*, but the MT reads *elohim* ("God").

22. For this same use of the verb "to be" in the sense of "means" or "implies" when referring to an interpretation of Scripture, see 1 Cor. 10:4; Rom. 10:6–8; Gal. 3:16; 4:24.

and social status of being "free,"[23] Paul uses the concept of "freedom" primarily to refer to the *positive* results of having been "set free" from sin (cf. Rom. 6:16–23; 1 Cor. 7:39; 9:1; 10:29). In our present passage, this positive result is a freedom *for* an obedience to the law that flows from the power of the Spirit as promised by Jeremiah and Ezekiel (2 Cor. 3:3, 6).

As such, this freedom is the reversal of the state of affairs illustrated in Exodus 32–34. The force of Paul's argument in 2 Corinthians 3:17 can now be uncovered. Just as Israel's persistent hardening to the demands of the old covenant could be adduced in 3:14–15 as evidence of her continuing separation from God, so too the Christians' "freedom" for obedience to the law can be adduced as evidence of their being in the presence of Yahweh.

In 3:18 Paul closes his argument by drawing the conclusion that naturally follows from his identification of Yahweh with the Spirit, who is the power of new life (3:6b). The meaning of Paul's statements in 3:18, despite their complicated mode of expression, can be paraphrased as follows. Since the Lord is the Spirit, as demonstrated by the freedom (from the veil) for obedience that the Spirit creates (v. 17), "we all"[24]—that is, all members of the new covenant community, both Jews and Gentiles—"are being transformed into the same image" (NIV "into his likeness"). In other words, by the power of the Spirit we are experiencing in a progressive sense more and more of this freedom to obey God, and as a result we are being changed into God's own image by becoming obedient to his will. To be in the image of God is to manifest his "likeness" by acting in accordance with his commands as an expression of God's own nature.

This moral transformation of God's people marks the decisive difference between the ministries of the old and new covenants. Moreover, the allusion in 3:18 to the image of God from Genesis 1:26–27 points forward to Paul's later identification of the new covenant with the new creation (cf. 4:6; 5:17). Just as those in Adam disobey God's will, those in Christ, the second Adam, are being brought back into the relationship of faith-generated obedience that characterized Adam and Eve before the Fall. As in the Garden of Eden before the Fall and at the Exodus before the golden calf, the new creation is characterized by encountering God himself.

---

23. For one's social status as "free" over against being a slave, cf. 1 Cor. 7:21–22; 12:13; Gal. 3:28; Eph. 6:8; Col. 3:11. Cf. Gal. 4:22–31, where the social status of the "free woman" is loaded with theological significance as representing the "children of promise" down through Israel's history and into the present.

24. The NIV translates this simply as "we," which misses Paul's transition from speaking of his own apostolic role (apostolic we) to that of all believers. This switch in subject is indicated by his explicit use of "we all" (*hemeis pantes*) in 3:18a (which is the best attested reading), in contrast to the use of the first person plurals alone in the previous paragraphs.

In Paul's words, this transformation is taking place "with ever-increasing glory" (lit., "from glory unto glory"). To say that we are being transformed into his likeness *"from glory"* means that the believer's gradual growth in obedience pictured in 3:18 takes place in response to God's presence. To say that we are being transformed into his likeness *"unto glory"* means that the final result of becoming more and more like him in anticipation of the final consummation of this age is that we will one day participate in his glory in all its fullness. Our life with God begins and ends by entering into his glorious presence—now in the Spirit, then face to face.

For this reason, the present transformation of God's people "comes from the Lord, who is the Spirit," since the Spirit is the down payment of God's presence and power in our lives (1:20–22; 3:3–6, 8). Finally, this transformation takes place because, from beginning to end—that is, from glory unto glory—"we behold as in a mirror" (not "reflect," as in the NIV[25]) the glory of the Lord without being destroyed by it, since we do so "with unveiled faces."

The spiritual and moral transformation pictured in 3:18 is the final support for Paul's prior assertion that Israel continues to be hardened "to this day" (3:14a, 15b), which in turn supports the validity of Paul's bold ministry in spite of his lack of success among his fellow Jews (3:12–13). If the people of Israel in Paul's day had not continued to be hardened like their "fathers" before them, they too would be able to behold the glory of God on the face of Christ and be transformed by it. Moreover, that Moses provides a type of the believer's experience (3:16–17), in contrast to the ongoing experience of Israel in her stiff-necked condition (3:14–15), demonstrates that a remnant of Jews and Gentiles is still being saved (3:18; 5:17).

Furthermore, this restoration of God's people in Christ is taking place through the gospel as embodied and proclaimed in Paul's own ministry. As a mediator of the glory of God on the face of Christ (cf. 4:4, 6), Paul's "ministry of the Spirit" (3:6, 8) is the means by which the prophetic expectation of the new creation under the new covenant is already beginning to be realized. At the center of the "new creation" is the manifestation of God's presence in the midst of his people, both Jew and Gentile, in anticipation of the final redemption of all creation.[26]

---

25. In the active voice, the verb used here (*katoptrizo*) means "to show as in a mirror or by reflection," and in the passive, "to be mirrored," while the middle means "behold (something) as in a mirror" (H. G. Liddell, R. Scott, and H. S. Jones, *A Greek-English Lexicon* [Oxford: Clarendon, 1940], 929). The middle voice is used here. As Furnish, *II Corinthians*, 214, has pointed out, to read this middle form to mean "reflecting as a mirror" clearly goes against the linguistic evidence.

26. Cf. Isa. 2:2–3; 24:23; 25:6–9; 43:21; 56:6–8; 60:1–3; 65:19, 24; 66:18–21, 23, for the revelation of God's glory in the midst of Israel and among the nations, and 43:19–20; 65:25 for its revelation among the animals and created order.

The result of this present revelation of God's glory is a life of growing obedience to God's commands, in stark contrast to Israel's present rebellion and the continuing wickedness of the nations. It is this transformation "from glory unto glory" that supports Paul's legitimacy, so that he needs no "letter of recommendation" beyond the Corinthians themselves (3:1–3). As new creatures in Christ (cf. 5:17) under the new covenant (3:6; cf. 6:16–18), the Corinthians testify by their Spirit-induced obedience that the glory of God is now being revealed in their midst, unveiled, through Paul's apostolic ministry.

RECOVERING THE THEOLOGICAL purpose of this passage is the key to its application. The danger that confronts us when we encounter a passage that is as carefully argued and conceptually rich as this one is that we will not invest the necessary time and effort to understand it on its own terms. Instead, in our haste to be "practical" and "relevant," we fall prey to the temptation to isolate individual statements from their context and to extrapolate from them abstract, theological principles that will "preach" (such as a "law/gospel contrast," "the glory of the ministry," or a rallying cry for "freedom in the Spirit"). In doing so in this passage, we will miss the fact that, as the very heart of Paul's apology for the legitimacy of his apostolic ministry, the purpose of his argument in 2:14–3:18 is to support his statements of confidence and hope in 3:4 and 3:12.

Thus, in order to apply this passage appropriately, we must make Paul's main points our main points. On the one hand, Paul is confident that as a minister of the gospel he mediates the Spirit through his suffering (3:3–6, 8). On the other hand, Paul's hope as a servant of the new covenant is that his ministry of the Spirit will transform God's people into the very character of God himself (3:9, 16–18). Paul is fully aware, therefore, that his sufficiency derives not from himself, but from God through Christ (3:5–6). Conversely, the evidence of his legitimacy is not his own abilities and accomplishments, but the transforming work of the Spirit in the lives of God's people (3:3, 18). This means that those who reject his gospel do so because of the hardness of their own hearts (3:13–15).

These realities have universal application. We too must derive our sense of sufficiency for the tasks to which God has called us from the power of his Spirit in and through us. The confidence that undergirds the ministry of the pastor and the life of the believer does not come from techniques or training, but from God's call and the reality of God's Spirit. This is the great news of the gospel and the foundation of our "hope," that is, of our absolute confidence for the future.

Bringing Paul's message in this passage from his day to our own is thus more a matter of patient interpretation than it is of recovering historical or cultural insights, either from Paul's day or our own. This section is one of theological exposition, not theological application. Paul's argument climaxes with indicatives, not imperatives. The implications are therefore implied, not explicit, and have to do with gaining right perspectives, not developing specific practices. Nevertheless, the perspectives that the apostle develops in this passage, being foundational to his entire letter, are of fundamental significance in and of themselves, both theologically and in terms of Paul's method of argument.

Moreover, Paul's recourse to the history of Israel *as taught in the Scriptures* and his recognition of a "hermeneutic of the heart," in which only those who want to accept the message of Scripture will go where the text leads, restrains our own source and means of application. We too, like Paul, must strive to view our present context through the lens of the history of redemption, beginning with the history of Israel as interpreted in the Bible. God has revealed his authoritative Word in a space and time that is not our own. The Scriptures, not our own private, mystical experiences, constitute revelation. Hence, we too, like Paul, must find the justification for our own self-understandings in the message of Scripture itself. At the same time, we must remain mindful that without the work of the Spirit in softening our hearts, we too may twist Paul's often difficult-to-understand words in order to justify ourselves, to our own destruction (cf. 2 Peter 3:16).

IN A REAL sense, therefore, the contemporary significance of this text is in the original meaning of the text itself, since it maps out the historical framework for understanding who Paul was as an apostle of Christ and who we are as people of the new covenant. In regaining this perspective, we regain a sense of our own place and privilege in the world and within the history of redemption, without which we are doomed to drown in the passing currents of contemporary culture. In particular, the passage before us grounds the specific applications that Paul will draw from it throughout his letter by establishing two fundamental perspectives, one theological and one methodological, both of which are of crucial significance for today.

The implications of Paul's theological worldview: living in the midst of an inaugurated eschatology. Though we are almost two thousand years farther down the road of redemptive history, we too live under the same "new covenant" that marked out Paul's ministry and determined the life of his church (see Contemporary Significance section to 3:4–6). Accordingly, we too live in the tension that now exists between the inauguration of the new covenant and its consummation. In Christ, the deliverance of God's people has taken a giant step forward toward its climax, but this climax has not yet been realized. The kingdom of God is here, but it is not yet here in all of its fullness. The age of the new creation has dawned (2 Cor. 5:17), but the "present evil age" still continues (cf. Gal. 1:4). As a result, believers find themselves between the first and second comings of Christ.

In our present passage, there are two negative consequences of this overlapping of the ages. (1) Israel's current rejection of Christ means that as a nation she continues under the same condition that has characterized her history ever since the golden calf (3:13–15). In this regard, God's promises concerning Israel's restoration still await fulfillment, while the church suffers the pain of being separated from her own spiritual ancestors. Even more painful is that Israel's rejection of Christ sometimes calls into question the truth of the gospel itself, in this case as taught and embodied in Paul's ministry. Faced with Israel's unbelief, Christians often wonder if the gospel of salvation in Christ alone as the Messiah is just as true and necessary for the Jews, the descendants of Israel, as it is for Gentiles. Paul's argument for the legitimacy of his boldness in 3:12–15, as harsh as it may appear in our age of pluralism, is intended to silence such doubts.

(2) There is also the realization that the remnant of God's people from among both Jews and Gentiles is still in the process of being transformed into God's image (3:18). In this regard, the promises of God concerning the redemption of his people still await fulfillment, while the church suffers the pain of her own sin, both personal and corporate. What is even more tragic, however, is that in many cases those within our churches show no such pain at all over their sin, but have simply succumbed to an easy-believism in which lip-service has replaced lifestyle as the mark of a Christian. Faced with the impotence of the church itself, Christians often wonder whether the promises of new life in Christ really apply to this day and age at all, or whether our only hope for deliverance from the power of sin is death. Paul's argument for the legitimacy of his boldness in 3:16–18, as convicting as it may be to us in our age of repentance-less Christianity, reminds his readers of the upward call in Christ, "from glory unto glory."

Hence, it is important to realize that the main thrust of Paul's argument is not negative but positive. His point is his confidence and boldness as an apostle because of the life-changing reality of the Spirit. Though the old age continues, the new age of the new covenant is here. Though those around us have veils on their hearts, we all, like Moses, can enter into the presence of God with unveiled faces. Though some have fallen prey to Satan, now disguised as an angel of light, those who know Christ are being transformed by God's glory into the glory of God's likeness.

In view of these tensions, the church today, like the Corinthians of Paul's day, is often tempted by the lure of an "over-realized eschatology" that promises an escape from the consequences of living in the midst of a sinful world. Like Paul's opponents, we too are often convinced that Paul suffered too much to be a Spirit-filled apostle of Christ. Nevertheless, God *is* creating a "remnant" from among both Jews and Gentiles who, by their ongoing moral transformation, testify to the presence and power of God's Spirit in their lives. For those who have benefited from the "ministry of the Spirit" and "righteousness," conformity to Christ in the midst of adversity, not miracles and minimizing the glory in the gospel, is the primary evidence that the kingdom of God is here (1:7; 2:12–14; 3:18). Their "obedience that comes from faith" (Rom. 1:5) makes it evident that only "in Christ" can such a salvation take place, since only Christ's death can make it possible for the *Holy Spirit* of God to invade our lives with mercy rather than judgment (3:15–16).

As the "letter from Christ" written "with the Spirit of the living God" (3:3), the church is therefore a local outpost of the kingdom of God and his righteousness in the midst of this evil age. As such, she lives in confident anticipation of her final redemption, having received the Spirit as God's own "deposit" or down payment (1:22). Having received the Spirit, the believer has also received a revelation of God's righteousness (cf. 3:8 with 3:9). This righteousness is his just character, as demonstrated in the consistency of his actions toward his creation. Specifically, this righteousness consists in his unswerving commitment to glorify himself by maintaining his moral standards in judgment, by revealing his sovereignty in election, and by showing his mercy through meeting the needs of his sinful people.

Because of Christ's life and death, these displays of God's righteousness are not in conflict with one another. In Christ, God's righteousness toward his sinful people can begin with their election, work itself out in the forgiveness of their sins, and culminate in their deliverance from sin. The display of God's righteous activity toward his sinful people thus includes both their redemption because of Christ and their transformation in Christ, as well as their final restoration into the image of Christ in the age to come (cf. 3:18; 4:4–6; 5:21; 8:9). The death of Christ makes possible the righteousness of God in all three of these ways.

Hence, the flip side and expression of God's righteousness displayed on our behalf is our transformation into the likeness of God himself. The evidence that we have been sealed in the Spirit is the growing life of the obedience of faith that flows from the presence and power of the Spirit in one's life. All of this is from God. None of this is works righteousness, since in no place does God ever call for and anticipate that anybody can or should try to merit grace. He never says, "Get your act together for six weeks and then I will bless you." The indicatives always precede the imperatives. But there are no bare, naked indicatives without the imperatives that flow from them. For this reason and from our perspective, God's work of transforming us into his image is manifest in the perseverance of the saints, even in the face of suffering and death. This, then, is the central theme to be developed throughout the letter.

A fundamental principle thus emerges from the content of Paul's argument and the structure of the covenant that lies beneath it. Despite the vast cultural differences between Paul's day and our own, his conviction that the Spirit's work in transforming God's people is *the* distinguishing characteristic of the church, including his apostolic ministry of the gospel, remains a constant. In contrast to the mixed character of Israel under the old covenant, by definition the apostles and people of the new covenant are those whose values and corresponding way of life are being converted by the power and presence of God. Paul's confidence that the Spirit is being poured out on God's people under the new covenant (3:4) leads directly to his conviction that God's people will become increasingly more like God himself (3:12, 16–18; cf. Eph. 5:1).

The implications of Paul's method: a call back to the Bible. In addition to *what* Paul says, a key principle for doing theology emerges from *how* Paul goes about saying it. Not merely his message, but his method is instructive for our contemporary context. In short, Paul's mode of argumentation in this strategic text makes it clear that although he argued from the presence and power of the Spirit in his ministry, the Scriptures are the final court of appeal for adjudicating disputes. For this reason, he turns to the Mosaic law and the Old Testament prophets in 3:3–18 to establish the criterion by which he defines the character and purposes of his new covenant ministry, as well as what it means to be members of this covenant.

For this same reason, to move forward from Paul's day to our own entails moving backward to the same Scriptures that Paul read as the sourcebook for his Christian identity and understanding (plus, today, the New Testament). In any context, the ministry of the gospel must derive its impetus and contours from the power and presence of the Spirit *in conjunction with the intention of the Scriptures.* The Spirit (3:8) and the Word (3:14–15) are one. Paul's convictions concerning his ministry in 3:7–18 are all based on his interpretation of the Scriptures.

Naturally, then, Paul's return to the Scriptures as the foundation for his apology not only provides a model for us; it also raises the question of how the Scriptures are to be read. As we have seen, the "letter/Spirit" contrast in

3:6 is not a proof text for an allegorical method of reading the Scriptures, but a shorthand description of the two epochs within redemptive history. Paul did not resort to some kind of special "Christian" reading of the Old Testament that was available only to those who had the Spirit. Nor is Paul's use of Scripture in this passage (and throughout his writings) an example of special pleading based on Christian presuppositions for the sake of his Christian polemic. Paul did not derive "the right doctrine from the wrong text," legitimizing noncontextual readings by attributing them to the Spirit.[27] Rather, our study of 3:7–18 has demonstrated that Paul offered a sober, contextual interpretation of the original intention of the Scriptures, viewed from the perspective of Christ's coming as the turning point within the history of redemption.

In thinking of our own cultural context, Paul's argument from Scripture reminds us that the original intention of the Scriptures is the locus of divine revelation. God's intention cannot be discovered apart from the intention of the biblical authors. This is a sober truth in view of the contemporary challenges of postmodernism (see the Contemporary Significance section of 1:1–2). Paul's presupposition concerning the divine authority and accessibility of the Scriptures and his method of interpretation here and elsewhere offer no support for the postmodern version of the allegorical method, with its own "letter/spirit" contrast. For under the influence of postmodernism, the supposedly true, spiritual meaning of the text is once again being determined not by the author's statements read within their own context, but by one's own spiritual, ethnic, gender, or sociopolitical experience.

Postmodernism justifies this relocation of meaning from the author to the reader by stressing that the attempt to recover the author's expressed intention is, in the end, an act of self-deception. According to postmodernists, the attempt to submit oneself to the text does not recognize the inherent ambiguity of human perception, the all-pervasiveness and controlling nature of our cultural conditioning, the multivalence of words and symbols, the existence of concealed, ideological motives behind all supposedly neutral statements of universal truth, and the indebtedness that reason has to a particular tradition for the definition of what is "reasonable." Hence, in postmodernism, what is needed to understand the Bible is not a thorough knowledge of the ancient world and its languages, but a self-conscious reflection on one's own social status, gender relationships, community traditions,

---

27. For a helpful presentation of the various contemporary views on the nature of the use of the Old Testament in the New, including the idea that the Spirit led the apostles to read the Scriptures in ways illegitimate for us today, see G. K. Beale, ed., *The Right Doctrine From the Wrong Texts? Essays on the Use of the Old Testament in the New* (Grand Rapids: Baker, 1994).

and political aspirations. For in the end, the purpose of reading the Bible is to better understand ourselves from our own perspective. From the perspective of postmodernism, there is nothing more subjective and ideologically driven than the violent act of reading.

There is much positive that evangelicals can learn from postmodernism, insofar as it rightly points out the influence of culture, ideology, and social location on interpretation. It poses a needed challenge to what is often (though not always) an unreflective hubris within scholarship. Postmodernism's willingness to rethink even the most cherished interpretive conclusions is a welcomed stimulus to look at overly familiar texts with new eyes. And there is no doubt that a black or feminist or socialist or freewill reading of the text *may* uncover aspects of the author's original intention that my white, male, Calvinist reading has missed (though it may also obscure it all the more!). Two heads or cultures or perspectives are often better than one. The warning raised by postmodernism that interpretations of a text are often thinly veiled expressions of our own ideologies is a sobering wake-up call to be self-critical in reading the Bible.

But as my qualifications indicate, postmodernism's hermeneutical relativism and often radical rejection of a subject-object distinction cannot be assimilated into the biblical conception of revelation within history. Whereas postmodernism despairs over the possibility of ascertaining an author's original intention, the very fact that God has chosen to reveal himself in a space- and time-bound collection of writings means that cross-cultural, cross-linguistic, and cross-temporal communication is possible.

Postmodernism is, in essence, atheism applied to literature. Many evangelicals have gravitated toward it, believing that its celebration of diversity, its skepticism concerning the reigning scientific paradigms, and its openness to all forms of community-based hermeneutics enable us once again to sit at the academic table without being ashamed of our belief in the Bible. Yet once we share our conviction that our particular, historically revealed truth claims, derived through reading an ancient book, are universally valid, we find ourselves marginalized as silent partners who must be tolerated but cannot be allowed to speak. The destructive force of postmodernism's pluralism is just as strong as secular modernism's antisupernaturalism.

Moreover, like postmodernism, Paul too is painfully aware that people believe what they *want* to believe and that what they want to believe, often a product of their history or social identity, determines what they *can* believe. In 3:14–15, he therefore reminded the Corinthians of his "hermeneutic of the heart." Israel's problem was not intellectual but a matter of spiritual disposition. Paul recognizes that only those whom Christ has redeemed will accept his argument from Scripture in 3:7–13. Although anyone who does the hard work of reading the Bible carefully can adequately understand its message, only those in whom the Spirit is at work will receive its truths into their lives (cf. 1 Cor. 2:14). Though being willing to go where the text leads is in itself no guarantee that one's interpretation will be sound (one must still be a careful, informed reader), without such a willingness the chances that the interpretation will be seriously skewed are increased dramatically. Empathy for the author is an essential ingredient in understanding, though it brings with it its own perils.

This realization is especially important for those who, like Israel in 3:14–15, are already committed in principle to the Scriptures as God's Word. Unlike outsiders, who simply reject the divine authority of the Scriptures, those committed to the truth of the Bible feel compelled to submit to its teachings. Hence, when the Scriptures call our worldview or way of life into question, our first response will not be to reject Scripture outright. Instead, our inclination as Bible-believers will be to "reinterpret" the text in line with our own most cherished convictions.

Thus, Paul's recognition of the root problem behind Israel's rejection of the gospel demonstrates that the Spirit must create within us a willingness to accept God's Word so that, being receptive to its message, we will be more apt to comprehend its meaning. Paul's argument from the Scriptures as common ground with his opponents assumes that the role of the Holy Spirit in biblical interpretation is not to provide God's people with hidden information or insights into the Scriptures, but to change their moral disposition (cf. 3:14).

What is needed is not a private illumination to open our eyes to the secret meaning of the text, as if the gospel were a gnostic truth that only the initiated can understand. The issue is not one of content, but of character.[28] The "veil" in 3:14–15 is a metonymy for hard-heartedness, not intellectual inability. In Fuller's words,

> Apart from regeneration ... men do not welcome the reasonableness of the teaching that fulfillment for their deepest yearnings comes from

---

28. For these points and one of the clearest expositions of the role of the Spirit in biblical interpretation, including Paul's key statement in 1 Cor. 2:13–14 as a reference to "welcoming" or "accepting what the Bible teaches with pleasure," see Daniel P. Fuller, "The Holy Spirit's Role in Biblical Interpretation," in *Scripture, Tradition, and Interpretation: Essays Presented to Everett F. Harrison by His Students and Colleagues in Honor of His Seventy-Fifth Birthday*, ed. W. Ward Gasque and William Sanford LaSor (Grand Rapids: Eerdmans, 1978), 189–98. As Fuller observes (p. 190), the problem with relying on the illumination of the Spirit as the means to understanding the Bible "is that the words of the text can play no essential role in conveying its intended meaning, even though it is these very words which the writers were inspired to use in transmitting God's message."

delighting in God's goodness by trusting his promises and thereby rendering him honor. People prefer instead to accomplish things that supposedly provide reasons for delighting in how much they can trust themselves.

... Only God, working through the Holy Spirit, has the power to replace one's foolish desire for ego-fulfillment with the reasonable, well-advised desire to find peace and joy in depending on God to stand by his promises.[29]

Finally, Paul's method of mounting a careful argument from the Scriptures in order to support his claims to apostolic authority throws in sharp relief the waning emphasis in the contemporary church on original language exegesis and expository preaching. In place of the serious study and proclamation of the Scriptures as the foundation and focal point of ministry, pastors are increasingly turning to "talks" on general themes, sprinkled with biblically phrased words of advice, in order to respond to the "felt needs" of their congregations.[30] In response to the cry for cultural relevance (assuming that people know best what they need), most seminaries have bowed to the pressure of their constituency (i.e., tuition-paying students and high-profile churches) by relaxing or eliminating altogether the requirement to gain a working knowledge of the biblical languages.[31]

This crisis in our seminaries has direct consequences for our churches.[32] Though many are hailing the above as the curriculum for the next millennium,

---

29. Ibid., 196–97.

30. Note, e.g., the 1989 survey sponsored by the Lilly Endowment of 205 alumni/ae from Gordon Conwell Theological Seminary, South Hamilton, Massachusetts. Though the respondents ranked "proclamation of God's Word" the number one "personal spiritual gift" needed for effectiveness in the ministry, they ranked "able to do Greek and Hebrew exegesis" eleventh in importance when it came to the "academic abilities" needed for the ministry! The only things deemed less important to know were "the major themes of adult life cycles" and the "major themes of Christian education."

31. For example, a 1994 survey sponsored by the Murdock Charitable Trust of more than 800 laypeople, pastors, and seminary professors revealed that the first priority for pastors, according to laypeople, was "spirituality," while pastors responded that their first priority was "relational skills" (*Christianity Today* [Oct. 24, 1994], 75). For professors, in contrast, it was "theological knowledge." Conversely, both laypeople and pastors ranked "theological knowledge" last among their five priorities, while professors listed "counseling skills" as their fifth priority. For the most part, seminaries have not been able to resist the pressure brought about by this mismatch concerning priorities in the pastorate.

32. See, e.g., the perceptive essay by Dennis Johnson, "The Peril of Pastors Without the Biblical Languages," *Presbyterian Journal* (Sept. 10, 1986), 23–24. As Johnson points out, Hebrew and Greek are in fact *"practical* subjects for pastors"* (23). Indeed, given "the labyrinth of modern translations" and the false teaching that plagues the church, "this is one time when the church needs pastors who can study God's Word in the languages in which he gave it" (ibid.).

the rejection of a classical theological education has produced a crisis of confidence in the pastoral office in which pastors are forced to become the second-hand purveyors of the opinions of "experts," our new priestly class. To the degree that they are unable to enter into the exegetical discussion themselves, pastors inevitably end up offering their congregations a smorgasbord of opinions in response to the panorama of views with which they are confronted. In the end, since "even the experts can't agree," knowledge of the Bible is trivialized. In its place, the subjective experience of the individual, the pastor, or the community, often baptized as the movement of the Spirit, becomes determinative.

In other words, while decrying the influence of postmodernism on our ethics, we become the ultimate postmoderns in our handling of the Bible, hoping that our theological traditions will keep us from error. Over against this trend, Paul's boldness was derived from his experience of the Spirit, understood within the framework of redemptive history that he gained from reading the Scriptures and from applying them to his own context.

Thus, unless we regain a serious study of the Scriptures in our pulpits and pews, we will end up redefining the role of the Protestant pastor altogether by denying in practice the authority of the very Bible we are purporting to preach. If the pastor, not to mention those of us in the congregation, no longer struggles to decide for himself what the text means, the authority for preaching will once again reside in our pope, wherever we find him. The pastor then downsizes his role into that of a book reviewer. What is worse, since the pastor is still going to "preach" from the Bible, the authority for preaching now resides in the rhetorical power of the presentation, not in its content. So instead of wrestling with the text, he invests time in searching out illustrations for a basic, thematic, generalized, and pietistic sounding message. This approach makes popular, entertaining preachers, but it loses the Bible altogether.

This does not mean that we must all be able to out-expert the experts. We all have different gifts and callings. It does mean, however, that we must be able to explain to ourselves and to others why people disagree, what the real issues are, and what are the strengths of our own considered conclusions. We must have reasons for what we believe and preach, without having to resort to the papacy of scholarship or the papacy of personal experience.

A serious study of the text reaffirms the nature of biblical revelation and communicates to the church that the locus of meaning and authority of the Scriptures does not reside in us, but in the text that we labor so hard to understand. In his weakness, Paul argued for his authority from the Scriptures, in contrast to his opponents, who relied on their personal power, mystical experiences, rhetorical prowess, and public reputations. So too, we turn to the Scriptures because we are convinced that the authority of our gospel derives from the inerrancy, sufficiency, and power of the Word of God.[33]

In addition to all that Paul actually says in this passage, the scriptural foundation of his argument calls the church to regain its commitment to a serious exegesis of the biblical text as the basis of its authority and ministry in the modern world. As Daniel Fuller put it, the essential role of the Holy Spirit in biblical interpretation urges "the exegete always to acknowledge his complete dependence on the Holy Spirit, and at the same time ... to develop his skill in using valid exegetical means to determine the meanings that were intended by the words which the Holy Spirit inspired the biblical writer to use."[34]

We must pray that our Spirit-inspired willingness to go where the text leads us will be matched by a corresponding willingness to take up the task of studying the Scriptures under the conviction that in these writings alone God has spoken to his people. Given the subjectivity that reigns both in our culture and in the church, this second willingness will necessitate a dramatic work of the Spirit of no less magnitude than the first.[35]

---

33. For these points and the practical and theological reasons why pastors should learn the biblical languages as the basis for preaching, see my "Why Use Biblical Languages in Preaching?" *SBJT* 3 (1999): 86–89.

34. "The Holy Spirit's Role in Biblical Interpretation," 190. The work of the Holy Spirit is essential in reading the Bible because, as Fuller insightfully observes, our deep-seated desire to exult in ourselves and glory in our own abilities and achievements will otherwise keep us from the fundamental truth of the Bible that everything we have is a gift (cf. 1 Cor. 4:7).

35. For an analysis of the crisis of authority caused by our culture of subjectivity and its implications for our lack of willingness to pursue a serious exegesis of the text, see my "Seminary, Subjectivity, and the Centrality of Scripture: Reflections on the Current Crisis in Evangelical Seminary Education," *JETS* 31 (1988): 129–43.

2 Corinthians 4:1–18

THEREFORE, SINCE THROUGH God's mercy we have this ministry, we do not lose heart. [2]Rather, we have renounced secret and shameful ways; we do not use deception, nor do we distort the word of God. On the contrary, by setting forth the truth plainly we commend ourselves to every man's conscience in the sight of God. [3]And even if our gospel is veiled, it is veiled to those who are perishing. [4]The god of this age has blinded the minds of unbelievers, so that they cannot see the light of the gospel of the glory of Christ, who is the image of God. [5]For we do not preach ourselves, but Jesus Christ as Lord, and ourselves as your servants for Jesus' sake. [6]For God, who said, "Let light shine out of darkness," made his light shine in our hearts to give us the light of the knowledge of the glory of God in the face of Christ.

[7]But we have this treasure in jars of clay to show that this all-surpassing power is from God and not from us. [8]We are hard pressed on every side, but not crushed; perplexed, but not in despair; [9]persecuted, but not abandoned; struck down, but not destroyed. [10]We always carry around in our body the death of Jesus, so that the life of Jesus may also be revealed in our body. [11]For we who are alive are always being given over to death for Jesus' sake, so that his life may be revealed in our mortal body. [12]So then, death is at work in us, but life is at work in you.

[13]It is written: "I believed; therefore I have spoken." With that same spirit of faith we also believe and therefore speak, [14]because we know that the one who raised the Lord Jesus from the dead will also raise us with Jesus and present us with you in his presence. [15]All this is for your benefit, so that the grace that is reaching more and more people may cause thanksgiving to overflow to the glory of God.

[16]Therefore we do not lose heart. Though outwardly we are wasting away, yet inwardly we are being renewed day by day. [17]For our light and momentary troubles are achieving for us an eternal glory that far outweighs them all. [18]So we fix our eyes not on what is seen, but on what is unseen. For what is seen is temporary, but what is unseen is eternal.

As the "therefore" in 4:1 indicates, Paul begins this new section by once again drawing a conclusion based on his previous argument (cf. 3:4, 12), which he sums up as "this ministry." Because of "this ministry," Paul does "not lose heart." The apostle will return to this same conclusion in 4:16, thereby framing this unit of his letter with two declarations of his encouragement. In spite of the rejection he experiences (4:1–6), the suffering he must endure (4:7–15), and the death he faces (4:16–18), Paul still does not lose heart (4:16).

Paul supports this resolve by outlining yet again the foundation, purpose, and assurance of his apostolic ministry. Now, however, his focus is not on his *suffering* as an embodiment of the *knowledge* of God revealed in the cross (cf. 2:14–16a), but on his *endurance* as an expression of the *power* of God revealed in the resurrection (cf. 4:7–12). Thus, Paul's suffering manifests the gospel of the death and resurrection of Christ in two ways: as a corollary to the cross that it embodies and as an antithesis to the glory of God that is revealed through it.

Paul's Confident Boldness in Spite of Rejection (4:1–6)

In 3:4, Paul's "confidence" was based on God's revealing knowledge of himself through Paul's suffering (2:14–3:3). In 3:12, his boldness was founded on his assurance that the glory of God will continue to be unveiled in his ministry of the Spirit (3:8). In 4:1, his encouragement is therefore based on this same "ministry" (*diakonia*) of suffering and the Spirit (cf. this same terminology in 3:3, 6, and 7–11 as a summary of the main points of 3:3–18). Paul does not lose heart because *God* has commended him through the pouring out of the Spirit in fulfillment of the promises of the new covenant through Paul's life of suffering "in Christ."

Hence, in surveying his ministry, Paul reminds the Corinthians that, as the former persecutor of the church, he owes his apostleship solely to "God's mercy" (cf. 1 Cor. 15:9–10). Within its present context, this refers specifically to Paul's experience of God's grace both in his call to preach (2:14–16a; 3:4–6; cf. 1 Cor. 9:16–17) and in his ministry of the Spirit (cf. 2 Cor. 2:17; 3:1–3, 7–18; cf. 1 Cor. 9:18). The very existence of his ministry is evidence of God's reality in his life, from which he derives great encouragement. The mercy granted to Paul in the past undergirds his confidence for the future.

Paul has already shown that a person's conduct reveals the content of his or her character (cf. 2:17; 3:1–2). Accordingly, the evidence of Paul's not losing heart is that he renounces the "secret and shameful ways" of his opponents, who were attempting to cover up their true motives with a veneer of apparent piety and counterfeit spiritual power (4:2a; cf. 11:1–15). Since Paul is confident of his mercy-generated motives and the Spirit-led character of his ministry, he has no need for such cover-up tactics in his ministry (cf. 1:12–14).

This is confirmed by the parallel between 4:2 and 2:17b, which makes it clear that Paul's preaching with sincerity has resulted from God's conversion-call in his life and from the knowledge that he stands "in the sight of God," that is, before God as judge. Paul goes on to delineate three ways in which he has renounced the duplicitous maneuvers of his opponents, two negative and one positive. Negatively, Paul need not "use deception" (lit., walk around in a cunning way) or "distort the word of God" (4:2b). Positively, "by setting forth the truth plainly," Paul can "commend [himself][1] to every man's conscience" (4:2c). Because of his own clear conscience (cf. 1:12), he can boldly appeal to the conscience of others (cf. 3:12). Conversely, all whose consciences are likewise clean because of God's mercy will accept this divine commendation of Paul's ministry (cf. 2:15–16a).

For this reason, Paul does *not* engage in *self*-commendation, since *God* is the one who recommends Paul by the very existence of the Corinthians as Christians (3:1–3). Nevertheless, Paul *does* commend *himself* by pointing to the evidence that God has had mercy on him, namely, to his open life and pure presentation of the gospel (4:1–2).[2] The difference between these two kinds of commendation is whether there is concrete evidence of God's mercy in one's life. Because the motives of Paul's opponents remain impure, they demand payment from the Corinthians, preach a "different gospel" of health and wealth, and live boastful lives of arrogant self-promotion (cf. 11:4). Because, as a result of God's mercy, Paul's motives are pure, he preaches for free, proclaims the cross, and lives a life of suffering for their sake (cf. 2:17; see also 1 Cor. 4:8–13; 9:12–23).

Given the evidence supporting Paul's commendation, a failure to respond to his proclamation of God's word does not call into question the validity of his ministry. Instead, "even if [Paul's] gospel is veiled, it is veiled to those who are perishing" (4:3a; cf. 2:15–16a; cf. 1 Cor. 1:18). This evaluation of the reason for the rejection of Paul's life and message is the main point of 2 Corinthians 4:1–6. The problem is not with Paul but with those who spurn

---

1. Here too, as in 2:14–3:17, the use of the plurals in 4:1–18 refer to Paul in his apostolic office as a continuation of his apology for the validity of his ministry.

2. The italics here are an attempt to bring out the difference in content between the negative self-commendation of 3:1 and the positive commendation of oneself in 4:2, which is clearly indicated in the Greek text by the position of the pronoun. In the former, negative case it precedes the verb (*heautous synistanein*), in the latter it follows it (*synistanein heautous*). See comments on 3:1 for more on this grammatical point.

him. In making this point, Paul continues to use Moses' veil as a metonymy for the hardness of one's heart (cf. 3:14–15a). Thus, those who fail to see God's glory in Paul's ministry do so because of their spiritual blindness.

The cause for this hard-heartedness is given in 4:4. Those who repudiate the gospel do so because of their inability to accept that it owes its existence to Satan's rule over the present evil age (cf. Gal. 1:4; Eph. 2:1–3). Like Israel in 2 Corinthians 3:13–15a, "they cannot see the light of the gospel of the glory of Christ, who is the image of God" (4:4; cf. Col. 1:15). People are not blinded because they choose to renounce the gospel; rather, they choose to renounce the gospel because they are blind. And they are not blind because they choose to be so, but because Satan has made them so.

The description Paul uses in 4:4 to depict the glory now being veiled from those who are perishing is one of the most important Christological statements in the New Testament. Since in the Old Testament the concept of an "image" can never be understood without a connotation of physical representation, "the conception of Christ as the *eikon tou theou* [the image of God] both in 2 Cor. 4:4 and Col. 1:15 clearly conveys the sense that Christ is the [visible, therefore material] manifestation of [the invisible] God, and therefore his likeness to God is strongly implied in it."[3] Christ is the embodiment of God's own character, the prototype and representation of what all those who see God's glory will become (3:18).

The entire history of redemption is encapsulated in this statement. Adam was created in the glorious image of God, but fell from it. God consequently barred Adam and Eve from his presence. Israel encountered the glory of God on Mount Sinai, but fell from it. Moses consequently veiled his face. Christ did not fall, but is the revelation of the glory of God to his people. Paul, as an apostle, encountered the glory of God in Christ on the road to Damascus and was converted. As a result, he mediates the glory of God in Christ, unveiled, in order to reverse the effects of the Fall as manifested in Israel's history of hard-heartedness. Paul's experience and ministry are therefore part of the "second exodus" and "new creation" brought about by Christ as the "second Adam."

This explains Paul's stress on a person's inability in 4:4. He draws this conclusion because he is convinced that those who, by the power of the Spirit, "see" God's glory will inevitably be transformed by it (3:8, 18). God delivers his people by removing their blindness to his glory (cf. 2:16b; 3:9–11). Conversely, the underlying cause for moral inability to behold God's

---

3. Seyoon Kim, *The Origin of Paul's Gospel* (WUNT 2.Reihe, Vol. 4; Tübingen: J. C. B. Mohr [Paul Siebeck], 1981), 219. Kim's study is the most definitive study of 2 Cor. 4:4, 6 in view of Paul's Damascus Road "Christophany" (see esp. 6–13, 137–268).

glory is Satan, who "blinds the minds of unbelievers" (for the way in which he accomplishes this, see 11:3).

Yet Paul is not teaching a dualism in which competing gods battle one another for the lives of men and women. Paul describes Satan as limited, that is, he is only "the god of this age." When taken together with the use of the "divine passive" of 3:14 and Paul's emphasis on the active work of the Spirit in removing the "veil" in 3:17, Satan's work is clearly seen to be subordinate to the sovereignty of the "one God" (cf. 1 Cor. 8:6; also Rom. 11:36). "Those who are perishing" (2 Cor. 4:3) do so because God leaves them in their blinded state, cut off from his glory and without the power of the Spirit needed to escape Satan's reign over their lives.

Paul's final argument that those who refuse his ministry are not revealing his insufficiency but their own "blindness" is given in 4:5 (note "for" [*gar*] in v. 5a), which in turn is supported by 4:6 (note "for" [*gar*] in v. 6a). The Corinthians will not be surprised to hear that Paul does not preach himself (or any human leader) as the foundation or object of faith. Jesus, the Messiah, is alone Lord, both over the church and over the world (for the former, see, e.g., 1 Cor. 1:13; 2:5; 3:4–9; 4:1; for the latter, see, e.g., 1 Cor. 1:2, 3, 7, 23; 5:4; 6:11; 8:6; 9:1; 11:26–27; 12:3; 15:11–12, 31, 57; 16:22; 2 Cor. 1:2–3, 19). What is surprising is that Paul also preaches himself as the Corinthians' "servant" (Gk. *doulos*, slave). He himself is an essential aspect of his preaching! This is the case since the gospel that he preaches is embodied in his own Christ-like willingness to consider the needs of others more important than his own "rights."

As the Corinthians' "slave," Paul is willing to forego financial support as an apostle (1 Cor. 9:12–18; 2 Cor. 2:17) and to submit his own freedom in Christ to their religious-ethnic distinctives and level of maturity in the faith (1 Cor. 9:19–23; cf. 8:9–13). Paul does this "for Jesus' sake" (lit., "because of Jesus"), that is, in accordance with the pattern of the cross in which Jesus himself counted the needs of his people more important than his own position as God's Son (cf. Mark 8:34–38; 10:45 as applied in Phil. 2:1–13). Because of Jesus, Paul too must be a "slave" to those to whom he is sent. As an extension of the cross of Christ, he is called to suffer in service to the Corinthians (see comments on 1:3–11; 2:14–16a). For this reason, Paul can and, given the polemic situation in which he now finds himself, *must* include his own apostolic ministry as an essential part of his message. To reject Paul is to reject the gospel of Jesus Christ as Lord—the message he preaches.

That many were rejecting Paul in spite of the pattern of Christ exhibited in his ministry is further evidence of their hardened nature. What is true for Israel as a people (3:14–15) is true for the Gentiles as well (4:3–5). Their rejection of Paul exposes their own spiritual blindness, since his legitimacy has been established in accordance with the twofold criteria from 1 Corinthians 12–13 for determining the genuine nature of spiritual gifts. On the one hand, "no one who is speaking by the Spirit of God says, 'Jesus be cursed,' and no one can say, 'Jesus is Lord,' except by the Holy Spirit" (12:3). On the other hand, the purpose of a spiritual gift is the common good of the church (12:7, 13; 14:12).

Hence, both the content of Paul's message (he preaches Jesus as Lord) and the manner of his ministry (his change of plans and practice of self-support, both resulting from his love for the Corinthians as their "slave") have already demonstrated the genuineness and divine origin of his calling. In contrast, Paul's opponents have made the Corinthians *their* slaves (cf. 2 Cor. 11:4–20). Moreover, his opponents' refusal to take up their cross on behalf of the Corinthians clearly reveals that they preach another Jesus (11:4, 18–20). Indeed, they water down the gospel for the sake of their own financial gain (4:1–2 in view of 2:17).

In 2:16b and 3:4–6a Paul upheld the legitimacy of his suffering for the sake of the Corinthians by pointing to his conversion-calling. In the same way, in 4:6 Paul supports his role as a "slave" to the Corinthians by pointing to his calling. Paul has become a slave to others because he was taken captive to Christ on the road to Damascus, where he encountered "the knowledge of the glory of God in the face of Christ." As a result, through his suffering Paul mediates the same "knowledge" of God's glory in Christ as the "image of God" that converted him. Hence, "the Damascus event is the basis of both his theology and his existence as an apostle."[4]

In 2:16b and 3:4–5 Paul depicted his call in terms of the call of Moses and the prophets, thereby highlighting the "second exodus" framework for his own ministry of the new covenant in fulfillment of Jeremiah 31:31–34 and Ezekiel 36:25–27. This prophetic motif is continued in 4:6 in Paul's reference to seeing "the glory of God in the face of Christ," which recalls Ezekiel's vision of God's glory in human form (cf. Ezek. 1:26, 28; cf. 2:1–7; 3:12, 23; 8:2–4; 9:3; 10:1–4; 11:22–23; 43:2–5; 44:4).[5] Now, however, Paul portrays this call in terms taken from the creation of light in Genesis 1:3 ("Let there be light") as this was picked up in Isaiah 9:2. The latter is a prophecy of redemption in which the coming new creation is pictured as a "light" that will shine on those dwelling in darkness.

---

4. Kim, *Origin*, 31. This is the central thesis of Kim's work.

5. I owe this point to Kim, *Origin*, 205–7, 212, 230. See too James Scott, *2 Corinthians*, 82–83, 88–89, who takes this to indicate a mystical interpretation of Paul's experience in 3:18 and 4:6 in line with the Jewish *"merkabah"* (= "chariot") mysticism that used Ezek. 1 as its proof text. But Paul's encounter with Christ on the road to Damascus does not fit the pattern of mystical experience.

Paul's point is that his own conversion-call on the road to Damascus and resultant apostolic ministry express the dawning of the new creation now taking place in Christ (once again taking the plurals in 4:6 to be apostolic plurals, referring to Paul himself).[6] As such, Paul's experience is a paradigm for the experience of all believers. Inasmuch as "the god of this age" has blinded people to the glory of God in Christ, only the God of creation, the one who originally called forth light out of darkness, can overcome this blindness. The same power that created the world is now being unleashed in recreating God's people by shining "in [their] hearts."

Against the backdrop of the veil in 3:16–18 and 4:3–4, this shining in the heart most naturally refers to God's work of changing the moral disposition and spiritual condition of his people. Paul is a living example of this new creation. Only a new creation in Christ can account for such a conversion from persecutor to persecuted one (cf. Acts 9:15–16; 1 Cor. 15:8–10; Gal. 1:13–16; 1 Tim. 1:12–16; 2 Tim. 1:11–12). Encountering God's glory in Christ changed Paul's life.

This can be seen in the parallel between 3:18 and 4:4, 6. The "glory" of the "image/likeness of God" from Genesis 1:26 that is equated with Christ in 4:4, 6 is the same glory of God's image/likeness that provides both the basis and goal of transformation in 3:18. To be transformed by the Spirit into the image of God's glory (3:18) is to be conformed to the "image of God" as manifest in Christ as the second Adam (4:4; cf. 1 Cor. 15:42–49; Rom. 5:12–21; 8:28–30). In the first creation we were made in the image of God; in the new creation we are made into the image of God in Christ. This is why the "light" of the new creation used by God to transform his people is not the glory of God seen in the firmament (cf. Ps. 19:1–2), but "the light of the knowledge of the glory of God in the face *of Christ*" (2 Cor. 4:6b).

As in the theophanies under the old covenant, it was a blinding revelation of God's glory, now "in the face of Christ," that removed Paul's spiritual blindness.[7] Against the backdrop of Genesis 1:3 as read through the lens of Isaiah 9:2, the knowledge of the glory of God revealed to Paul in the face of

---

6. So already Anton Fridrichsen, *The Apostle and His Message* (Uppsala: Lundequistska Bokhandeln, 1947), 16, who in writing on 4:6, said that Paul "cannot find a stronger expression for his conviction that he has received a revelation of unique importance and of cosmic scope, a knowledge which is a main element in the development of the eschatological situation. It is very significant that Paul's thought here goes back to creation in the beginning. He himself is with his gospel active in the new creation at the end of time."

7. Cf. the narratives of Paul's conversion-call in Acts 9:1–19; 22:3–16; 26:9–18. Note esp. the play on Paul's blindness versus his call to "see" the Righteous One in 22:14 (cf. 2 Cor. 3:16–18) and his call to open the eyes of others in Acts 26:17–18, turning them from darkness to light and from the power of Satan to God (cf. 2 Cor. 4:4–6).

Christ is the means and goal of the new creation (2 Cor. 4:6) in fulfillment of the new covenant (3:3, 6). To "see" the glory of God in Christ (4:4, 6) with an "unveiled face" (3:16–18) is to begin to come face to face with the presence of God as enjoyed by Adam before the Fall. "Thus, the gospel of faith simply repeats in a new guise the word spoken at creation (1 Cor. 1:28; cf. Rom. 4:17; 2 Cor. 4:6)."[8] Paul's argument is therefore emphatically *theocentric*.[9] It is the "glory of *God*" that is being revealed in "the glory of Christ" as "the image of *God*."

It is this glory, spoken in God's word at creation and enfleshed in Jesus, that is proclaimed in the gospel (2 Cor 4:4 in view of 4:6; cf. Phil 4:19), embodied in the suffering of Paul (2 Cor 1:3–11; 2:14 in view of 4:6; 4,7–12; 6:3–10; 7:2–16), and experienced in the church (3:18; 4:13–18; 6:14–7:1). Thus, the antithetical parallels between 4:4 and 4:6[10] demonstrate not only Paul's redemption, but also his ensuing ministry as the means by which the new creation of the new covenant is being inaugurated in the midst of this present evil age (cf. Gal. 1:4):

The god	God
of this age	of creation ("Let light . . .")
has blinded	made his light shine
the minds of unbelievers	in our hearts
so that they cannot see	to give us
the light of the gospel	the light of the knowledge
of the glory of Christ	of the glory of God
who is the image of God.	in the face of Christ.

Paul's gospel declares the light of the new creation by showing forth how Christ himself manifests the glory of God's image, that is, his righteous and merciful character (4:4). When in conjunction with this gospel God shines his presence into the lives of those whom he is now re-creating in Christ, he makes it clear how Christ himself embodies in his death and resurrection on behalf of those who were living in the darkness of sin the very glory of God (4:6). Because of the reality of this mercy, both in Paul's own life and in the lives

---

8. Günther Bornkamm, *Paul* (New York: Harper & Row, 1971), 161.

9. Clearly seen by Philip Hughes, *Paul's Second Epistle to the Corinthians*, 133, concerning 4:6: "At the dawn of creation the darkness was dispelled by the word of Almighty God (see Gen. 1:2–3); and it is the same God who, in the spiritual sphere, drives back the darkness of sin and unbelief from the hearts of men." Hughes then equates the light of Acts 26:13 with the "light of the gospel of the glory of Christ" and the "light of the knowledge of the glory of God in the face of Jesus" from 4:4–6, taking 4:6 to be a reference to Paul's conversion.

10. For these parallels, see Timothy B. Savage, *Power Through Weakness*, 127, whose work offers an insightful analysis of 4:1–18 against its cultural background (see below).

of those to whom he is sent, Paul does not lose heart (4:1). Those who reject Paul do so because they remain blind to the reality of God in Christ. For the very glory of God himself is now being revealed through Paul's ministry.

Paul's Confident Boldness in the Midst of Suffering (4:7–12)

SINCE PAUL'S CONFIDENCE (4:1–2) is based on the reality of God's glory in and through his life (4:5–6), he counters his opponents' influence on the Corinthians by again reminding them that this glory is not mediated through a "health and wealth" gospel and lifestyle. Rather, Paul carried his "treasure" in a "jar of clay," a reference to his weakness and sufferings (1:3–11; 2:14–16a; 6:3–10; 11:23–33), especially his concern for his churches (2:12–13; cf. 11:28). This is God's design in order to make it evident that the power of the gospel does not reside in Paul, but belongs to God (4:7). The power of the gospel is so great and its glory so profound that it must be carried in a jar, lest people put their trust in Paul himself (cf. 1 Cor. 2:1–5).

Within its context, the "treasure" in view in 4:7 refers most directly back to "the knowledge of the glory of God in the face of Christ" from 4:6. But the link between 4:6 and 4:4, where the glory of Christ is seen to be the content of the gospel, suggests that it can also refer to Paul's entire ministry as this is embodied in his life of suffering. The idea of picturing humans as "jars of clay" ("earthen vessels" NASB) as a metaphor for human weakness was common in the ancient world, including the Qumran writings (cf. the references to clay pots as weak and prone to break in Ps. 31:12; Isa. 30:14; 1QS 11:22; 1QH 1:21–22; 3:20–21; 4:29). Read in this way, Paul's image points to a contrast between his own weakness and suffering and the power of God.

Others, however, see "jars of clay" as a metaphor of cheapness, based on Lamentations 4:2 (LXX), thereby establishing a contrast between Paul's lack of significance or worth and the surpassing value of the treasure. Still others argue that both ideas are present here, so that 4:7 provides a contrast to both the "treasure" and the "power of God." As Timothy Savage puts it, "the glorious gospel is borne about by those who are comparatively inferior, the powerful gospel by those who are weak."[11] Of these options, the purpose clause in 4:7b seems to indicate that the point of contrast is God's power, so that the intention of the image is to highlight the weakness of Paul (for this same contrast, but without the metaphorical dress, cf. 1 Cor. 2:3–5).

The purpose clause in 4:7b is often translated with the idea of "making manifest" or "demonstrating" (cf. NIV: "to show that ... is"). But literally it reads, "in order that the all-surpassing power might *be* from God and not from us."

11. Ibid., 165–66 (quote from 166).

As Savage points out, if we take the verb "to be" in this formal sense, then Paul's point is even more striking: "It is only in weakness that the power may *be* of God, that [Paul's] weakness in some sense actually serves as the grounds for divine power."[12] Since the emphasis in 3:1–18 was on the glory of God and power of the Spirit, Paul now emphasizes that his mediation of the Spirit takes place in the "earthen vessel" of his suffering. He does this so that the power and glory that he mediates might not be associated with his own person or talent in any way. Paul's weakness ensures that the power *is* from God and not from Paul (cf. 12:1–10).

The series of four adversative contrasts in 4:8–9 all modify 4:7 by illustrating *how* this divine power comes to expression in Paul's life. In spite of Paul's being "hard pressed," nevertheless he is not "crushed"; he is "perplexed, but not in despair," and so on. Paul's not being done in by his circumstances, suffering, or persecution is to be attributed directly to God's ability or "power" to sustain him in the midst of his adversity. In making this point, these four contrasts confirm that the "power" manifested in the "treasure" of the gospel ministry belongs to God. Given Paul's weakness, his perseverance can be attributed only to God. Paul's suffering provides the platform for the display of God's power.

In 4:10–11 Paul then interprets the experiences of 4:8–9 in terms of the death *and* resurrection of Jesus in order to indicate the Christological purpose of his suffering. The power of God revealed in Paul's suffering is, in fact, the same power revealed in the experience of Jesus. Just as Jesus was put on the cross in order to be raised from the dead, so too Paul is "carry[ing] around in [his] body the death of Jesus" (4:10), "always being given over to death for Jesus' sake" (4:11), *in order that* the "life of Jesus may also be revealed in [his mortal] body." Here, too, the categories of Jesus' death and resurrection are used to interpret Paul's experience of suffering and sustenance, thereby demonstrating that his life mediates the knowledge of God to the world embodied in Christ (cf. 2:14–16a):

the dying of Jesus	*the life of Jesus*
hard pressed	but not crushed
perplexed	but not in despair
persecuted	but not abandoned
struck down	but not destroyed

Moreover, the verb translated "[not] in despair" in 4:8 is the same word found in 1:8, where Paul recounts that in the past he *did* despair of his life. This move from 1:8 to 4:8 shows that Paul learned his lesson in Asia. God

---

12. Ibid., 166.

proved himself faithful to rescue his people. And God's rescuing Paul in the *past* gave him confidence that God could and would rescue him in the *future*, so that this hope enabled Paul to endure in the *present* (cf. 1:8–10). Within this framework, the reference to not being "abandoned" in 4:9 is especially significant. Its background in the LXX indicates that this is a "divine passive," which speaks of being abandoned by God (cf. Gen. 28:15; Deut. 31:6, 8; 1 Chron. 28:20; Ps. 16:10; 37:25, 28; Sir. 2:10).[13] Just as God did not ultimately abandon Jesus in the grave, so too God's resurrection power sustains Paul in his own experiences of "death."

The contrasts of 4:8–9 underscore that during this evil age it is endurance in the midst of adversity, not immediate, miraculous deliverance from it, that reveals most profoundly the power of God. Paul's deliverance in Asia (1:8–10) leads to the daily endurance of 4:8–9. This is confirmed by Paul's use in 4:10 of *nekrosis* (dying), rather than *thanatos* (death), which indicates that he is thinking of the process of dying rather than its final condition (cf. 1:9, 10; 2:16; 3:7; 4:12; 7:10; 11:23). Paul's focus on endurance in the midst of adversity may also explain his emphasis in this passage on *Jesus*, recalling his earthly life that culminated in the cross, rather than on his royal title, *Christ*.[14] He carries around "the dying of *Jesus*" (4:10) as he is given over to "death" (4:11). Finally, the present participles in 4:8–9, together with the emphasis on "always" in 4:10, add to this emphasis on the continual process of "dying" that takes place in his life as an apostle.

In 4:11 Paul gives the theological basis for his conviction that his suffering, like the "death of Jesus," mediates the resurrection power of God, that is, the "life of Jesus." By using the divine passive, "we are always being given over to death" (by God), Paul again asserts that his sufferings are not merely coincidental, but part of the divine plan for the spread of the gospel. Like Jesus, Paul too is delivered over to his own death (cf. 2:14; for Jesus, see Mark 10:33; Rom. 4:25; 8:32). In verse 10, Paul "carries" the death of Jesus in his own body; in verse 11, Paul himself is the living one who is given over to death by God. But this does not lead Paul to the conclusion that the "life" he mediates is his own—it remains the "life of *Jesus*" (4:11b).

As in 1 Corinthians 4:12–13, here too God's power is therefore expressed *through* Paul's weakness. Moreover, as in 1 Corinthians 4:9 and 2 Corinthians 2:14, in 4:11 Paul's suffering is again portrayed under the image of death. In the first two passages this was done by means of a metaphor (1 Cor. 4:9: being

---

13. I owe this insight to Savage, *Power Through Weakness*, 169.

14. Paul uses "Jesus" by itself (i.e., apart from the common expression "Jesus Christ" or with the title "the Lord") six times in this passage (4:5, 10, 11, 14). In all the rest of Paul's writings combined, it is used by itself only nine times (Rom. 3:26; 1 Cor. 12:3; 2 Cor. 11:4; Gal. 6:17; Eph. 4:21; Phil. 2:10; 1 Thess. 1:10; 4:14 [2x]).

sentenced to death in the arena; 2 Cor. 2:14: being led to death in the triumphal procession). Here Paul explicitly associates his suffering with the death of Jesus itself (4:10–11). In each case, Paul views his suffering to be a divinely orchestrated death that, like the cross of Christ, performs a revelatory function. The exact parallels between 1 Corinthians 4:9; 2 Corinthians 2:14; and 4:11 thus demonstrate not only that our interpretation of the triumphal procession in 2:14 is accurate, but also that it provides a thematic key to Paul's self-understanding as an apostle:

2 Cor. 4:11a	*2 Cor. 2:14a*	*1 Cor. 4:9a*
1. Divine passive	1. Thanks be to God	1. God
2. constantly (cf. "always" in v.10a)	2. always	2. (cf. "to this very hour," v. 11, and "up to this moment," v. 13)
3. we the living	3. us	3. us apostles
4. are being handed over to death	4. leads us in a triumphal procession to death	4. exhibited last of all as those sentenced to death
5. on account of Christ	5. in Christ	5. (cf. "for [i.e., on account of] Christ," v. 10)

2 Cor. 4:11b	*2 Cor. 2:14b*	*1 Cor. 4:9b*
1. in order that the life of Jesus might be revealed	1. and reveals the fragrance of the knowledge of him	1. because we became a spectacle
2. in our mortal flesh	2. through us	2. _____
3. _____	3. in every place	3. to the world, that is, to angels and to men

Unlike 1 Corinthians 4:8–14, however, where Paul's purpose was instructional, in 4:7–18 Paul's intent is apologetic. Rather than providing an example for the Corinthians to follow, Paul must now defend why the glory of his ministry must be contained in his weakness.[15] As a result, the context within which Paul interprets his ministry has also changed. In 1 Corinthians 1:4–4:13, Paul's suffering was shown to be the means by which God attests (cf. 1:17–18; 2:1–5) and makes known (4:9–13) the wisdom and power of God *as revealed in the cross*. In 2 Corinthians 4:7–12, Paul's suffering is now shown

---

15. For a delineation of the similarities and differences between 1 Cor. 4:8–13 and 2 Cor. 4:7–12 as these reflect the essential difference between the situations behind the two letters, together with the parallels between 1 Cor. 4:9; 2 Cor. 2:14 and 4:11 outlined above, see my *Suffering and Ministry in the Spirit,* 59–71.

to attest (4:7) and reveal (4:11) the power of God *as revealed in the resurrection* (4:10–11). Hence, instead of Paul's "death" being linked to the cross of Christ as its corollary, it is now contrasted with the resurrection of Christ as its antithesis.

Taken together, these twin emphases of Paul's "theology of the cross" and "theology of glory" are not contradictory, but complementary. He is not combating a theology of glory with a theology of the cross, but showing their essential unity. In 2 Corinthians 1–4, Paul's task has been to show how his apostolic experience of being "led to death" supports his preaching of both the cross and the resurrection of Christ. His suffering embodies the cross as a revelation of the knowledge of God (2:14–16a), but it also demonstrates that the resurrection power in the gospel is not his own, but God's (4:7–11). If Paul's suffering is a sign that the kingdom of God has *not yet* been consummated, his endurance is evidence that it *has been* inaugurated. The power of the new creation (4:6) is being mediated in the midst of this evil age (4:3) through Paul's suffering (4:7–11), which is itself an expression of God's triumph over Satan.

In 4:7 Paul stated the purpose for his weakness: in order that the power might be from God; in 4:8–11 he illustrated the way in which this purpose is fulfilled: through his carrying around the "death of Jesus" (4:10a) in his own "death" (4:10b) in order that the "life of Jesus" might be revealed in his body (4:10b, 11b). In 4:12 Paul draws the consequence of this purpose for the Corinthians: He is given over to death in the present so that God's resurrection power might be at work in their lives (cf. 1:3–6, 10–11).

The relationship between Paul and his church is not reciprocal when it comes to Paul's call as an apostle to share abundantly in the sufferings of Christ (cf. 4:15). Paul is called to suffer on behalf of and for the sake of the Corinthians; they are not called to suffer for him. Nevertheless, Paul's suffering and experience of God's deliverance are always derivative, since Jesus' death and resurrection provide the pattern for Paul's experience and the content of his proclamation. Paul's life is not a "second atonement," but a mediation of the death and life of Jesus. In his preaching and suffering, Paul stands between the glory of God and the life of his congregation as an instrument in God's hand to bring about new life among his people.

Paul's Confident Boldness in Light of the Experience of the Righteous (4:13–15)

RENDERED LITERALLY, THE opening clause of 4:13 reads, "having the same spirit of faith according to what has been written. . . ." This is the same construction found in 3:4; 3:12; 4:1; and 4:7 (the NIV obscures this correspondence). In each case, Paul sums up what has just been said with the expression, "we have [or having] this . . ." in order to provide a transition to a new unit of thought. Here Paul begins his new paragraph by referring to what has just been said in 4:7–12 as the "same spirit of faith." His point is that the profound character of his life as an apostle described in 4:7–12 is not new. He stands in the long line of the suffering righteous from the past, here expressed in terms of Psalm 116:10.[16]

Moreover, since it is the Spirit who creates faith and conforms one to Christ's faithfulness in the midst of adversity, the "spirit" in view here is most likely the Holy Spirit as the source of faith, not the "spirit" as a reference to the "essence" or "nature" of faith (cf. 1 Cor. 12:9). As with the psalmist, it is the Spirit who empowers Paul to believe and therefore also to preach (2 Cor. 4:13b; cf. 3:3, 6). For like the psalmist, Paul's preaching not only takes place in the midst of adversity, but also leads to even more adversity itself (Ps. 116:10b). It is therefore not surprising that in 116:3–4 the psalmist too is in a situation of "death," only to be rescued by the Lord in response to his desperate cry for help (cf. 116:1–2, 4–9). The psalmist's response is to fulfill a corresponding "vow" of thanksgiving (116:12–14) as his "sacrifice" of praise (116:17).

An essential aspect of this praise is the psalmist's conclusion from this experience of suffering and divine rescue that he is indeed God's servant (Ps. 116:16). So, too, Paul's experience of God's rescuing him from death leads to this same response of praise (cf. 2 Cor. 1:3, 11; 2:14; 4:8–9, 15) in response to the same conclusion concerning his own validity as God's servant (3:1–6; 4:1–7). Paul's citations of Scripture are not isolated "proof texts," but "footnotes" to their original context, from which he builds his own argument. Far more than merely a pious outburst or scriptural coloring, Psalm 116 provides an interpretive lens through which the apostle understands the significance of his experience in Christ, *the* suffering Righteous One.

(1) The first reason for Paul to persevere in his preaching, in spite of and in the midst of the adversity that engulfs him, is his knowledge that the God

---

16. That Paul pictures his proclamation and suffering in 4:13 in terms of the biblical tradition of the suffering of the righteous is confirmed by his use of related OT passages concerning the suffering of the righteous in 1 Cor. 1:19, 31; 2:9; 3:19–20. For the OT sources of Paul's understanding of his suffering, see Karl Theodor Kleinknecht, *Der leidende Gerechtfertigte: Die alttestamentlich-jüdische Tradition vom 'leidenden Gerechten' und ihre Rezeption bei Paulus* (WUNT 2.Reihe 13; Tübingen: J. C. B. Mohr [Paul Siebeck], 1984), 242–84. Kleinknecht points to the Old Testament tradition of the suffering righteous, now interpreted Christologically, as the backdrop to Paul's thought in 2 Cor. 1:3–11 (cf. Ps. 71:20–21; 94:19; 23:4–5; 69:33–4; Jer. 16:7; 2 Cor. 4:7–18 (in addition to 116:10, cf. Jer. 19:11; Ps. 2:9; esp. 31:12; 37:28; 4 Ezra 4:11; 7:88–89; *Test. Jos.* 1:3–7; 2:3–7); 2 Cor. 6:1–10 (cf. *1 Enoch* 66:6; Ps. 139; 118; Isa. 49:8a; in addition to Ps. 118:17–18); and 2 Cor. 8:9 (cf. Isa. 53:5).

who raised the Lord Jesus from the dead will also raise Paul with Jesus, together with all who will likewise stand resurrected in God's presence (4:14). This is the surety that comes from the Spirit as a "deposit" or "down payment" of the salvation yet to come (cf. 1:22; 5:5). No matter what the circumstance, Paul's commitment to preach derives from his assurance for the future, the initial fulfillment of which he has already experienced in the Spirit. As in Psalm 116:9, the experience of having been preserved by God in the past leads one to declare defiantly: "[I will] walk before the LORD in the land of the living" (cf. 2 Cor. 1:8–11).

But beyond his own experience and that of the psalmist, Paul can point all the more to Jesus' empty grave as the solid foundation for trusting God's sovereignty, love, and power for the future, despite the suffering of the present. If the cross of Christ explains why Paul suffers, it is the resurrection of Christ that gives him the confident hope needed to persevere as he suffers.

(2) Paul's second support for his perseverance in preaching is his surety concerning the present impact of his ministry (4:15). Paul keeps preaching, no matter what, because he knows that the purpose of his life is exhibited in the lives of others. As in 1:3, 11 and 2:14, here too Paul reminds his readers that the purpose of his ministry is to display God's glory through the thanksgiving that has increased among many as a result of Paul's ministry. The specific cause and object of this thanksgiving is the grace of God experienced in Christ through Paul. The more people who experience grace, the greater the thanksgiving. A life rescued by God produces a heart filled with gratitude, thereby reversing the fundamental sin of self-glorifying ingratitude that lies at the root of all sins (cf. Rom. 1:21; 3:23).

Thus, Paul keeps preaching because he is confident that this very redemption is now taking place through his ministry of the Spirit under the new covenant (3:3–6). Through his unveiled boldness (3:12), an unveiled encounter with God's "surpassing glory" is transforming God's people into those who praise his glory (cf. 3:10, 16–18; 4:6, 15). In 3:10, Paul referred to the new covenant manifestation of God's glory as "surpassing" (*hyperbal-louses*) that of the old, since the age of the new covenant had dawned. This point was confirmed by Paul's use of the related noun "all-surpassing quality" (*hyperbole*) in 4:7 to describe God's power as seen in "the light of the knowledge of the glory of God in the face of Christ" (4:6).

This present experience of God's glory, however, is merely the beginning of the consummation to come. Hence, in 4:17 Paul uses the same terminology to refer to the future "eternal glory" that "far outweighs" (*kath' hyperbolen eis hyperbolen*) all afflictions. Accordingly, as in 3:10 and 4:7, so too in 4:17 the future revelation of God's glory remains explicitly tied to Paul's suffering, endured by the power of the Spirit (cf. 4:1, 7, 13 with 2:14–3:3).

In fulfillment of God's goal in redemptive history, Paul's proclamation of the gospel reveals God's glory in Christ and, in so doing, the grace of God is causing thanksgiving to overflow among many others (4:13, 15; cf. 9:12–15 for these same themes). As a result, following in the footsteps of the righteous who suffered before him, including Christ himself, Paul's delight in the manifestation of God's glory is the ultimate reason that he does not lose heart in the ministry.

Paul's Confident Boldness in Light of the Resurrection (4:16–18)

IN 4:16 PAUL returns to the point where he began in 4:1. There the parallel was between not losing heart and ministering with integrity in spite of his suffering (cf. 4:1–2). Here the corresponding parallel is between not losing heart and the daily renewal of Paul's "inner self" (NIV: "inwardly") in spite of the "wasting away" of his "outer self" (NIV: "outwardly"). The correspondence between 4:1 and 16 makes it clear that "outer" and "inner" do not refer to a dualistic body/soul dichotomy. Rather, they point to the moral transformation of Paul's life as a believer (his "inner self") in the midst of his life within the suffering and sin of this present evil age (his "outer self").[17] In both cases, the "inner" and "outer self" refers to Paul in his *entirety* as one who lives eschatologically in this "overlapping of the ages."[18]

Pate's study of this text against the backdrop of the common Jewish conception that in the coming age Adam's lost glory will be restored to the righteous who suffer has confirmed this eschatological interpretation of the inner self/outer self contrast.[19] Against this backdrop, the allusion to Genesis 1:26–28 in 2 Corinthians 4:4, 6 is again picked up in 4:16, now associated with Psalm 8:5–6. The outer self refers to the believer's existence under

17. For the "inner"/"outer" distinction as parallel moral categories to the "old self"/"new self," cf. Rom. 6:5–6; Eph. 3:16; 4:20–24; Col. 3:5–14. Most students of Paul no longer believe that he had a dualistic conception of the nature of humanity (for the texts usually adduced to support such a view, see Rom. 7:22–25; 1 Cor. 5:5; 7:34; 2 Cor. 7:1).

18. For a concise presentation of this central, eschatological concept in the teaching of Jesus, see still George Eldon Ladd, *The Gospel of the Kingdom, Scriptural Studies in the Kingdom of God* (Grand Rapids: Eerdmans, 1959). For its application in Paul's thought, see William J. Dumbrell, *The Search for Order: Biblical Eschatology in Focus* (Grand Rapids: Baker, 1994), 259–316, and C. Marvin Pate, *The End of the Age Has Come: The Theology of Paul* (Grand Rapids: Zondervan, 1995). For inaugurated eschatology and the new creation as the unifying center of New Testament theology as a whole, see Greg K. Beale, "The Eschatological Conception of New Testament Theology," in *"The Reader Must Understand:" Eschatology in Bible and Theology*, ed. K. E. Brower and M. W. Elliott (Leicester: Apollos, Inter-Varsity, 1997), 9–52.

19. C. Marvin Pate, *Adam Christology*, 61, 106, 126. For the implications of Pate's study for 5:1–10, see comments on these verses.

the decaying mortality inherited from Adam, while the inner self is the believer's existence in the new age already inaugurated by Christ as the "last Adam."[20] "In Christ" Paul belongs to the age to come ("inwardly") at the same time that he continues to live in the midst of this evil age ("outwardly"). Therefore, he does not lose heart, but instead is encouraged by the way in which his life is being renewed into the character of Christ (cf. Rom. 8:28–30, within the context of the suffering outlined in 8:18–25 and 8:35–39).

The result of this renewal is that God will use these "light and momentary troubles" to achieve for Paul "an eternal glory that far outweighs them all" (4:17; cf. Rom. 8:18). Instead of destroying Paul, his sufferings "outwardly" are the very instrument God uses to reveal the glory of his presence and power in Paul's life "inwardly." Second Corinthians 4:17 thus supports 4:16 (see the "for" in 4:17a), so that Paul himself is a beneficiary of what he mediates to others. Paul's own experience testifies that the present revelation of the glory of the Lord (cf. 4:4, 6) is the means to the future enjoyment of the incomparable eternal weight of glory (cf. 4:17) that is being prepared for God's people, who in the meantime must patiently endure "the same sufferings [Paul] suffers" (1:6; cf. 3:18; Phil. 3:11, 20–21; Col. 1:27; 3:3–4; also Rom. 5:2; 8:18, 21).

This insight and assurance did not come naturally. Paul had to learn this profound truth (cf. 1:8–11), the process of which is itself an essential part of his inward renewal (4:16). That Paul can testify to this conviction in 4:17 thus implicitly undergirds his encouragement that he is, in fact, being renewed into the image of Christ. Unbelievers do not experience God's glory or the faith it engenders (4:3–4). This is born out by the parallel between 4:17 and 1:8. We saw that Paul's description of no longer despairing when perplexed in 4:8 refers back to 1:8. So too, Paul uses the same image of "weight" (*baros*) to describe God's glory in 4:17 that he used earlier in 1:8 to describe being "weighed down" (*bareo*) by his suffering.[21] Just as Paul has grown to trust God to sustain him under the "weight" of his afflictions, so too Paul has come to see that the "weight" of his glory far surpasses that of his afflictions. "The affliction which once felt like a lethal weight round his neck now seems weightless in comparison to his eternal load of glory."[22]

This change of perspective brought about by Paul's encounter with the surpassing value of God's glory is evidence that God is renewing Paul in and through his suffering. It is this "eternal perspective" that leads Paul to his final

---

20. Following Pate, ibid., 110, 112.

21. The NIV obscures this link by not translating this noun separately in 4:17 or the verb in a related manner in 1:8.

22. Timothy Savage, *Power Through Weakness*, 183.

conclusion in 4:18. In view of the future glory he anticipates inheriting, Paul no longer focuses on the visible, temporary things of the present, that is, the suffering and adversity of the evil age in which he still lives (cf. Rom. 8:24–25). Instead, Paul's focus is on the unseen things to come, that is, on his growing, Spirit-empowered participation in the image of God, culminating in his final transformation into God's likeness as manifest in Christ (cf. 3:18; 4:4, 6).

This is Paul's response to God's presence in his life. The power of God that sustains Paul in his weakness (4:7–12) causes him to remain confident in his proclamation (4:13) and in his suffering for the sake of others (4:16). All that God has done and is doing through the adversities of his life (4:1–15) leads him to focus on all that God will do (4:16–18), which in turn gives him confidence to endure the daily consequences of sin (4:1–15). This is the cycle of faith.

THE SECULAR AND the sacred: first century and twenty-first century. Moving from Paul's context to our own requires an understanding of both. Concerning the former, Savage has provided a significant study of the cultural values and religious ideals that were current in the Greco-Roman society of Paul's day, particularly in Corinth.[23] In doing so, Savage paints a picture of how the pattern of "power through weakness" associated with the Christian ministry in 4:7–18 would have been perceived by the Corinthian church.

It is important to keep in mind, first of all, that in Paul's day no self-conscious wall of distinction existed between the sacred and the secular. Society's social values permeated the many religions of Corinth, just as the more narrowly defined religious expectations of the day permeated the culture. As Savage observes, "the cults supplied the heart of daily life. They arranged the social, inspired the cultural, stimulated the commercial and assisted the political . . . cult and society were inseparable, hardly to be distinguished."[24]

Thus, Paul had to fight the culture at large in order to establish the counterculture of the church. This meant having to fight the cultural conception of what it meant to be "religious" as a "Corinthian," since Paul's ministry, embodied as it was in his suffering, called into question both of these identities. Paul's

---

23. Ibid., 19–53. What follows in regard to Corinthian culture is a summary of his helpful study. The reflections on contemporary society and evangelical Christianity are my own, except where noted.

24. Ibid., 34. As Savage points out (51), the cults did not offer a sacred perspective in a secular world, but formed the nucleus of that world itself. Society's social, cultural, commercial, political, athletic, and medical values all came together in its religious experience.

defense of his ministry was, in reality, a defense of the values and worldview of the gospel of Christ over against the culture of his day, since to be Corinthian and to be religious were one and the same thing. It was therefore difficult, if not impossible, for the Corinthians to separate what they understood from their culture concerning what it meant to be normal from what they learned religiously, since the two were part of one reality and self-identity.

At first glance, most contemporary, evangelical Christians in the "post-Christian" West appear to live in a very different cultural context, at least at the formal level. The distinction between sacred and secular, between church and state, is embedded in our cultural identity. Indeed, at the formal level, evangelical churches in North America most often derive their identity by contrasting themselves with the secular culture around them. In the modern (and even more so in the postmodern) world, unlike the world of Paul's day, our very starting point is to draw a distinction between the "world" and the "kingdom of God." This becomes all the more true as the ethos around the church becomes increasingly dominant and secularized in its perspective and practice, while the religious space within society shrinks more and more into our private world of personal opinion. In this context, the difference between the secular world and the church is championed as a matter of theological orthodoxy.

At the formal level of self-definition, this awareness of the inherent differences between the church, alternative religions, and secular society is itself an indication of how far we have come in carving out a specifically Christian identity and worldview. Most believers understand at the intellectual level that being Christian entails a different way of thinking and living. We affirm, with Paul in 4:18, that our reason for living is radically different from that offered by the culture around us. In this way, after almost two thousand years of Christian history, we are far ahead of the Corinthians. In ministering to new converts, Paul's first battle was to get the Corinthians to see that there was a difference to begin with (cf. 1 Cor. 5–7).

At the same time, the ability to reflect on our unique identity makes us aware that our attempts to define ourselves over against our culture often fail both in what we esteem and in how we act. While still oblivious to many of our cultural values (objectivity toward the self is never perfect), we nevertheless know all too well that many of the godless values of the dominant culture impact us as Christians. In this light, Savage's study is all the more significant. His survey of the dominant cultural values in Corinthian society reveals a haunting similarity to the values often implicitly and explicitly espoused within the church today. In spite of our attempts to separate ourselves from the modern/postmodern culture around us, we look surprisingly like the Corinthians of Paul's day in our way of life and values. When making the transition from Paul's context to our own, we are therefore chagrined by how immediately relevant Paul's central message remains for us (see the Introduction: "Christ Confronts Culture in Corinth").

The root issue in Corinth. Nevertheless, we must exercise caution in applying this text in our context. We must be careful to distinguish between Paul's explication of the gospel and his example of suffering as its embodiment. The former is universally true at all times; the latter is to be followed only as God himself orchestrates the circumstances of our lives. Given Paul's understanding of God's sovereignty and the distinction in calling between his role as an apostle and the life of the Corinthians, Paul did not call the Corinthians to try to suffer more. There is no martyrdom theology in Paul's writings, in which the cross is applied literally to the life of the church as the path of true discipleship. For believers in general, suffering will happen in their lives (cf. 1:6—7), but they are not called to a life of suffering per se.

The root problem in Corinth was not that the Corinthians were not suffering enough, though they no doubt were quick to reject its necessary role in the life of the Christian. Rather, their basic problem was their prideful refusal to consider all that they had to be gifts from God (1 Cor. 4:7), so that their spiritual experiences, leaders, and endowments became grounds for boasting and pride (cf. 3:3, 18, 21; 4:6—7; 8:1; 12—14). Consequently, in 1 Corinthians Paul pointed to his own suffering as an apostle to illustrate that they ought to imitate him in principle by humbly considering the needs of others more important than their own (cf. 4:15—17; 10:31—11:1). To adopt Paul's Christ-like attitude would not necessarily mean going without food and shelter, as Paul did, though it might. But it should lead to serving one another, rather than boasting and using each other for their own ends (cf. chs. 12—14).

If suffering for the sake of the gospel is the essential characteristic of Paul's apostolic ministry, on which the very lives of the Corinthians are based, then how much more should the Corinthians give up their own rights for the sake of others (cf. 1 Cor. 9:1—27 within the argument of 8:1—11:1). Paul's life of carrying around the "death of Jesus" for the sake of the Corinthians should lead to their own dying to self and living for others in whatever circumstance God places them. Being raised with Christ in this life does not refer to the ability to escape suffering, but to the power to endure it for the sake of Christ and his church. As Paul's children, the Corinthians' lives should not be characterized by boasting in their own spiritual attainments, leaders, or status (1:10—13; 3:21).

By the time of 2 Corinthians, however, Paul could no longer call his people to imitate him. Instead, Paul had to argue for the legitimacy of his ministry itself, both to shore up the repentant and to rescue the rebellious. Between the writing of 1 and 2 Corinthians, the Corinthians' propensity to boast, fueled by their culture's esteem for the status associated with health and wealth, had led them to accept Paul's opponents and their false gospel. Paul's opponents not only promised such "glory" on earth, but also paraded their own religious "accomplishments," ethnic pedigree, rhetorical flair, and materialism as evidence of their validity.

For a while, their manner of life and message proved too hard to resist for the majority of the church. The supposed super-spirituality of Paul's opponents, with its health and wealth gospel, played directly into the Corinthians' cultural propensity for self-reliance and glorification. The only obstacle in their way was Paul himself, since the life and ministry of the apostle who had founded the church and through whom they received the power of the Spirit in Christ was marked by suffering, weakness, and a willingness to preach for free. If the false apostles were to win in Corinth, they had to destroy the credibility of Paul's ministry.

It is at this point that we can apply Paul's writing directly to our present context by maintaining our allegiance to his model and message through resisting any attempt to redefine the gospel in terms of success and serenity in this life. Paul does not call all Christians to suffer as such. Yet those who embrace his gospel *will* suffer as they take their stand for Christ and as they give up the comforts of contemporary culture in response to the call to serve others wherever and however God should lead them to do so.

Paul's appeal. In the end, therefore, Paul's suffering is not to be sought but accepted as the valid and indeed necessary embodiment of the gospel of the glory of God, as it was made known "in the face of Christ" (4:6). Through the example of Paul's apostolic ministry and the writings he has left behind, God will sanctify his people, through whom he will continue to make his appeal to the world (cf. 5:20).

At the heart of this appeal is the declaration that the value of the glory of God in Christ, now and in the future, "far outweighs" any and all of the "light and momentary troubles" of this life (4:17). To believe in this gospel of grace is to "fix [one's] eyes" on what is still "unseen" (4:18), so that, even in the midst of affliction, we react with the overflowing thankfulness that honors God for granting to us in his mercy his "surpassing" glory (4:15). For such thankfulness reflects the knowledge that experiencing God's glory in Christ is of infinitely more value than anything this world has to offer, positively or negatively. This can only mean that to reject Paul and his message is to manifest one's own blindness to the power and glory of God now being revealed in "the face of Christ" (4:1–6; cf. 1 Cor. 1:17–19; 2 Cor. 2:15–16a).

These reflections on what it means to bring this passage into our contemporary culture, beginning and climaxing as it does with Paul's reflections on the glory of God, lead to a sobering realization. Thinking about and interpreting and preaching this text should never be reduced to some kind

of "armchair theology," in which discussions are pursued for the sake of intellectual dispute or banter. In the end, the glory of God, which is both the foundation and final goal of Paul's reflections, is not a theorem to be analyzed.
Nothing less than eternity is at stake. In turning to the contemporary significance of this passage, J. I. Packer's perspective, which he said he learned
from the Puritans, is therefore worth contemplating:

> All theology is also spirituality, in the sense that it has an influence,
> good or bad, positive or negative, on its recipients' relationship or
> lack of relationship to God. If our theology does not quicken the con-
> science and soften the heart, it actually hardens both; if it does not
> encourage the commitment of faith, it reinforces the detachment of
> unbelief; if it fails to promote humility, it inevitably feeds pride. So one
> who theologises in public, whether formally in the pulpit, on the
> podium or in print, or informally from the armchair, must think hard
> about the effect his thoughts will have on people—God's people, and
> other people. Theologians are called to be the church's water engineers
> and sewage officers; it is their job to see that God's pure truth flows
> abundantly where it is needed, and to filter out any intrusive pollution
> that might damage health.[25]

FROM PAUL'S PERSPECTIVE, God's power and glory
are not abstract theological postulates, but realities to be experienced. Conversion and transformation are brought about not by putting two and
two together and making the right decision, but by an encounter with the
living God (3:3, 7–11, 16–18; 4:1–6). Men and women are created anew
when they come face to face with the presence of God's Spirit (1 Cor. 1:26–
31; 2:5, 12–16; 3:16; 5:4–5; 6:19; 2 Cor. 3:17–18; 4:6; 5:17). Our attempts
to psychologize Paul's thought or to relegate it to the realm of feelings are
not a reflection of Paul's perspective, but a reaction to the poverty of our own
knowledge of God.

The glory of godliness. Thus, in drawing out the contemporary significance
of Paul's theocentric worldview, we need to keep in focus the ways in which
Paul sees the glory of God in Christ at work among the church. Otherwise, it
is simply too easy to become enamored with the false glory of the health and
wealth gospel. In our day and age, as in Paul's, the moral transformation into

---

25. J. I. Packer, *A Quest for Godliness: The Puritan Vision of the Christian Life* (Wheaton: Crossway, 1990), 15.

God's character pictured in 3:18 and the endurance in the midst of adversity modeled in 4:1–8 seem too mundane to be miraculous. To consider health more important than holiness, however, is to slight God himself and his work in bringing about the new creation in our midst. For Paul, the reality of the resurrection is already being inaugurated in the conversion of believers into the body of Christ.[26]

As a result, the power of Christ in establishing his reign as the Son of God (1 Cor. 15:25) is already taking hold in the lives of believers, who, as children of God, wage war against the flesh (3:9, 16–18; 6:14–7:1; cf. Rom. 8:14 in the context of 8:9–16; Gal. 5:17). And the return of Christ will consummate God's kingdom with the resurrection of those who are owned by God, as signified by the down payment of the sanctifying Spirit in their lives (1 Cor. 15:23; 2 Cor. 1:23; 3:18; 4:14–18). We thus live in the overlapping of the ages (the kingdom is here, but not yet here in all its fullness). The life of faith therefore takes place within the context of the suffering of God's people, who, being "saved in hope" (Rom. 8:17–25), live and endure by the power of the Spirit while they await the future consummation.

In view of this emphasis on growth in holiness and the endurance of faith as the present demonstration of God's power, there is a twofold application of Paul's thought to the experience of Christians in general. (1) Paul's portrayal of his apostolic ministry calls us to accept his authority and embodiment of the gospel as legitimate. There is a dangerous tendency among Christians to pick and choose their religious authorities according to their own likes and dislikes. For many today, Paul is no longer popular. Nonetheless, his claim to authority throughout these chapters is unmistakable. To reject his person and message is to reject the gospel of Christ. As challenging as Paul's message may be, we turn away from it at our own peril (cf. 13:1–10).

(2) Paul's understanding of God's sovereign design for affliction, once embraced, will dramatically transform our own experience whenever we too find ourselves in situations of suffering. When Christians suffer, they too, like Paul, can take courage from the fact that their lives will mediate to others the power of the resurrection, either through God's act of deliverance or, even more profoundly, through the testimony of their endurance and holiness. Even though the circumstantial suffering that was an essential part of Paul's call may be an occasional aspect of God's will for all believers, all of us can follow Paul's example of incurring the suffering that comes from considering the needs of others more important than our own.

---

26. 1 Cor. 12:12–13; 15:45; 2 Cor. 1:18–22; cf. Rom. 1:4; 8:11; compare Jesus as the "firstfruits" of the resurrection in 1 Cor. 15:20, 23 with believers who possess the Spirit as the "firstfruits" of the future restoration in Rom. 8:23.

Moreover, there are those among us whom God will call into the ministry and mission of the gospel, in which the proclamation of the cross and resurrection of Christ will necessarily be embodied in a willingness to suffer for the sake of others. In either case, we too, like Paul, are called to trust God to sustain us in the midst of our adversity (4:8–15) in the confidence that he will ultimately deliver us (4:16–18), so that God's power may be manifest in our weakness (4:7; cf. 12:7–10).

The glory of the world to come. The kingdom of God has already broken into this "present evil age" (Gal. 1:4; cf. 2 Cor. 1:20–22). But it is not yet here in all its fullness. This means that our enjoyment of the fullness of God's presence and the blessings this entails are still a future reality. Our experience of the Spirit today, as great as it is, is still just a "down payment" of the glories to come. Only such an "already/not yet" view of the kingdom, with its hope in the consummation still to come, can resist the temptation to fall prey to the health and wealth gospel. We must resist all forms of "overrealized eschatology," in which God's promises for the future are transported into the present.

At the same time, it must be emphasized that suffering in and of itself is not the revelation of God's power. Paul never glorifies affliction. Although the revelation of Christ's power takes place in the paradox of Paul's suffering, this paradox is not absolute. The cross is not itself glory, death is not itself life, weakness is not power (cf. 4:8–11, 16–18). Instead, Paul posits that deliverance, power, and renewal also exist in, through, and after suffering. Paul's suffering is not the glory of Christ; Christ's glory is mediated *through* Paul's suffering. Believers are therefore to avoid circumstantial suffering and persecution whenever such avoidance does not hinder or compromise their calling, and to pray for healing and deliverance when sick (cf. Rom. 12:17–18; 1 Cor. 7:15; Phil. 4:4–7; 1 Tim. 5:23).

But the righteous do suffer (cf. Ps. 116:10 in 2 Cor. 4:13). And some, like Paul, are even called to do so for the sake of the gospel. God makes known his sovereignty and love by handing Paul over "to death for Jesus' sake" (4:11–12; cf. 1 Cor. 4:9; 2 Cor. 2:14) and then by sustaining him through it so that he may be able to endure in faith (2 Cor. 4:8–10; cf. 1 Cor. 10:13; Phil. 2:15–28). It is Paul's ability to endure and rejoice in the midst of adversity that reveals "the life of Jesus" to others. Anyone can worship Santa Claus. In stark contrast, the ultimate testimony to God's power is the praise that arises in the midst of affliction because of our conviction that God is at work in and through our suffering for a future good so great that all present suffering seems "light and momentary" (4:14–17).

Paul's words in 4:14 and 4:16–18 remind us that this future focus of our faith is the key to resisting the "Corinthianization" of the church. The structure of

Paul's thought in this passage makes clear that whatever we long for and expect in the future inevitably determines how we live in the present. Hope and its desires are the engine that drives us. The pursuit of a greater good in the future is the sole motive strong enough to bring about a willing and persevering self-denial in the present. Only the "eternal glory" can outweigh the burdens of this world. If what we consider to be good remains identified with what this world has to offer, perhaps even rationalized as the blessing of God, our lives will inevitably become worldly. Such an outcome is inescapable. As Paul put it from the perspective of his own culture, if all we have to look forward to is life on earth, then "let us eat and drink, for tomorrow we die" (1 Cor. 15:32).

Without confidence in our future resurrection and a growing longing for what exaltation with Christ will mean, the call of the gospel loses its transforming power. Our hopes determine our habits. Made for God's presence, we are a future-determined people. In order not to lose heart now, the world to come, not this one, must captivate our minds. Only those who are heavenly minded are any earthly good.

> It is partly because [Paul] believes in a future resurrection of the dead that he is presently willing to carry about in his body the dying of Jesus (4:10–11). It is because he trusts in a future exaltation that he submits now to the condition of a "slave" (4:5). It is because he looks forward to a future heavenly life that he is willing to die daily (1 Corinthians 15:30). It is because he anticipates reigning with Christ in the future that he can speak so boldly in the present (2 Corinthians 4:13). Without faith in a future resurrection Paul's present suffering would be not only intolerable, but also meaningless (1 Corinthians 15:30–32). He would, on his own admission, be a man most to be pitied (1 Corinthians 15:17–19).[27]

Modern and postmodern culture revolves around a this-world orientation; the only long-term future our culture conceives to be important enough to plan for consistently is retirement. This pervasive preoccupation with living as long as possible, as healthy as possible, and as wealthy as possible has dramatically impacted the church in the West. Our knowledge and experience of God are so weak, and our desire for the pleasures of the present so strong, that we find it almost impossible to imagine that life with God in the world to come could be incomparably better than what we hope to experience in this world.

This worldliness is reflected in our worship, since people always praise what they value. Though we have a multitude of contemporary worship songs celebrating God's presence in our lives here and now, when was the last

---

27. Savage, *Power Through Weakness*, 181.

time you were deeply moved by a heartfelt and thoughtful song about the glories of heaven? When was the last time you even sang one? Are there any such hymns or choruses being written today in the West? We are simply too happy with the world to think seriously about the world to come. The longing expressed in Psalm 42:1–2 and 84:1–12 is foreign to us. The reality of the resurrection that the Corinthians denied explicitly (cf. 1 Cor. 15:12), we deny by default. In both cases the consequence is the same: a life lived in pursuit of the temporary rewards of this world.

Sheep go where their shepherds lead. Congregations take on the vision and values of their pastors. Paul's argument in this passage, focused on his own ministry as an apostle, thus provides the antidote to the church's this-worldly shortsightedness. Rather than portraying the persona of the successful leader, pastors are to take the lead in suffering for the sake of the gospel because of their confidence in the surpassing worth of the glory that "outweighs our light and momentary troubles" (4:18). Unfortunately, in many quarters of the church today Christian leaders have perverted the gospel into a magical attempt to gain physical healing and material comforts through "name-it-and-claim-it" faith formulas and "positive confessions" of healing in spite of one's apparent "symptoms." As D. R. McConnell observes, this so-called "Faith gospel" is

> without question the most attractive message being preached today or, for that matter, in the whole history of the Church. Seldom, if ever, has there been a gospel that has promised so much, and demanded so little. The Faith gospel is a message ideally suited to the 20th-century American Christian. In an age in America characterized by complexity, the Faith gospel gives simple, if not revelational answers. In an economy fueled by materialism and fired by the ambitions of the "upwardly mobile," the Faith gospel preaches wealth and prosperity ... in an international environment characterized by anarchy ... the Faith gospel confers an authority with which the believer can supposedly exercise complete control over his or her own environment.[28]

---

28. D. R. McConnell, *A Different Gospel: A Historical and Biblical Analysis of the Modern Faith Movement* (Peabody, Mass.: Hendrickson, 1988), xvii. McConnell (15–76) demonstrates that the origin of this movement can be traced back to the metaphysical teachings of E. W. Kenyon (1867–1948), esp. as derived from Christian Science and popularized by Kenneth E. Hagin (b. 1917). Central to this perversion of the gospel is a doctrine of God in which he "is not a personal god who sovereignly governs the universe," but "an impersonal force" who rules through spiritual laws that can be operated through the "faith" or "mind" of the believer (cf. 136–37). Ultimately, this false gospel has substituted a faith in "faith," redefined as the power of right thinking and a "power force" of words, for a humble dependence on the biblically defined promises and leading of God (140–41).

Indeed, the cultural ethos of materialism surrounding us is so pervasive that even those who do not advocate this perversion of the gospel explicitly find themselves expecting that circumstances should go well for godly followers of Jesus Christ. Anything less than peace (at least within the nuclear family), prosperity (at least a middle-class lifestyle), and health (at least most of the time) becomes a disappointment with God. Within this context, it is imperative that we constantly remind ourselves that endurance with praise, not avoidance of pain, is the evidence that the kingdom of God is here (4:8–9).

The glory of self-denial. Such endurance in faith is not wishful thinking. It is not being a Pollyanna about our circumstances. It is not the heroic act of those endowed with great fortitude and willpower, nor is it simply resignation. For those who can see the glory to come, it is the only thing that makes sense. Paul's evaluation of his present suffering in the light of his future hope makes clear that following Jesus entails both perseverance in the midst of suffering and self-denial for the sake of others, and perhaps even suffering for Christ. But such suffering is never a sacrifice. As believers we never give up more than we receive in Christ.

"Comparison shopping" between the suffering of earth and the glory of heaven, between losing this world and gaining the world to come, leads to the conclusion that nobody ever outserves or outgives God. Whatever we give up in the present, even life itself, pales in comparison to what God will grant us in the future (4:17–18). The worst the world can do to us is kill us. In Paul's view, however, to die in Christ is "gain" (Phil. 1:21). Yet only those who wish to gain their lives with God will be able lose their lives for Christ and the gospel (Mark 8:34–35). Hence, in order to follow in the footsteps of Jesus and Paul, an intimate relationship with God ("our Father in heaven"), a desire for the glory of his character to be manifest ("hallowed be your name"), and a longing for the coming of his kingdom in all its fullness ("your kingdom come, your will be done on earth as it is in heaven") must replace our cravings for what the world has to offer.

Changed desires come through altered appetites. What is needed in every generation is an acquired taste for God in all his majesty and for what it will mean to live and reign with Christ forever. To live holy lives here and now, we must do whatever it takes in our preaching, worship, and life together to regain a sense of the glory of being in the presence of God (Matt. 6:19–24). Only in this way can the stranglehold of materialism that chokes out a vibrant walk with Christ be broken. As Richard Sturch has observed, when the Bible uses images to speak about heaven,

> they are images of a strong reality. Heaven is like the literal heaven, the sky; it is like a garden; like a city, a *garden* city, even; like music; like a solemn liturgy of praise; like a great feast; like the goal of a pilgrimage;

like kingship, priesthood, and a victory celebration. To try to reduce such images to a literal and prosaic level is folly not only artistically but theologically.... And at the centre of each image is he who is the heart and source of all reality, God himself.... God's presence with his people is the heart of their reward.... And since God is the supreme goodness, surely to see and know him is our supreme bliss....[29]

God himself and God alone makes heaven, heaven. In order to honor his name and protect his people from a second-rate joy, he tolerates no rivals. As a minister of the gospel, Paul mediated this glory and happiness of heaven in the midst of the sin-soaked realities of his world. The corresponding affirmation that he derived his encouragement from the eternal value of his ministry is particularly poignant for pastors today, who must resist the invasion of our churches by the "success syndrome" of our culture. A helpful counteroffensive is David Hansen's work, *The Art of Pastoring: Ministry Without All the Answers*. Hansen provides a moving, first-person portrayal of Paul's vision of the ministry as it applies to the pastorate today and by extension to all Christians who are used by God in pastoral ways. By reflecting theologically on his own experiences, Hansen demonstrates how the following principles from 2 Corinthians 1–4 work themselves out in the contemporary life of a pastor:

1. Reading biblical studies, theology, and church history is more "practical" and helpful in the ministry than the mountain of "how-to" books on the market, since our primary need is for a greater sense of who we are and why we act, not more skills....
2. Ministry is a way of life, not a technology....
3. Those called to minister serve the church, but they do not work for the church. Instead, Jesus is their boss....
4. Ministry is not to be employer-driven, trend-driven, or task-driven, but is a following of Jesus Christ as the one who calls his pastors, so that the act of following Jesus *is* the act of pastoral ministry....
5. The Jesus whom we follow has a "general narrative direction" in his life, namely, the way of the cross....[30]

---

29. Richard Sturch, "On Being Heavenly Minded," in Anthony N. S. Lane, ed., *The Unseen World: Christian Reflections on Angels, Demons and the Heavenly Realm* (Carlisle, Eng.: Paternoster; Grand Rapids: Baker, 1996), 65–74, 65–68. Sturch (66–70) unpacks the biblical images of "heaven" as indicating God's superior power, omniscience, goodness (the positive associations of light; cf. James 1:17), bliss (cf. 2 Cor. 12:2), and the final state of the redeemed, including a state of mind attuned to God's presence in awareness and fulfilled desire (see John 17:3; 1 Cor. 13:12; 1 John 3:2; Rev. 21:3–4).

30. David Hansen, *The Art of Pastoring: Ministry Without All the Answers* (Downers Grove, Ill.: InterVarsity, 1994), 10, 11, 17, 20, 22–23, 27. Hansen (19) points out that academic

Not surprisingly, Hansen concludes these observations by pointing to Paul's words in 2 Corinthians 4:10–11:

> Jesus specifically directed us to follow him in his life's general direction, the Way of the Cross. Lest we object to bearing the cross as pietistic nonsense in a world of "scientific" management principles and psychological method, simply observe that virtually all the trouble that the best, and most talented pastors get into comes from not following the Way of the Cross. The best and most talented in the pastoral ministry and in denominational hierarchies harm themselves and harm the church most through their unrestrained ego and unwillingness to step off the high places. Sexual sin gets the press, but ego sin kills the church. Jesus told us exactly what direction our lives are to take: "If anyone would come after me, he must deny himself and take up his cross and follow me" (Mark 8:34).
>
> The power to do pastoral ministry and its central focus ... lies specifically in the everyday, concrete following of Jesus, led by him on the Way of the Cross.... Paul recognized this when he told the Corinthians: "We always carry around in our body the death of Jesus, so that the life of Jesus may be revealed in our body. For we who are alive are always being given over to death for Jesus' sake, so that his life may be revealed in our mortal body" (2 Cor. 4:10–11).[31]

The glory of future grace. As we have seen, it was not primarily Paul's gratitude for what Christ had done for him in the past that sustained him (though he certainly was profoundly thankful), but his hope for the future (cf. 4:14). In our "now" generation, Paul's orientation toward the future, which is such an essential aspect of a biblical worldview, is a desperately needed corrective. What God has done for us in the past is the foundation of our faith, not its focus. We do not live in the past. Looking back, we gain confidence in God for the future. It is this hope for the future, whether it be for this afternoon, as we depend on God to protect us in the midst of the temptations and

---

theology itself is much to blame for the current crisis in the ministry because of its having separated "practical theology" from the other disciplines and then defining the ministerial task in terms of what pastors "do." In his words, "professional theologians wonder why pastors don't read theology. The fault lies with them. Since theologians describe pastors as people who do things in the church, pastors don't have time to read theology. Since pastors are taught to be task doers, academic theology has sent pastors to the quick and lightweight how-to books. If theologians lament that pastors are not sufficiently interested in eschatology, it is because time management is the new eschatology. Theology's venerable 'already and not yet' has become 'what needs to be done today and what can be left until tomorrow'" (19–20).

31. Ibid., 27–28.

suffering to come, or for our death bed, as we depend on God to deliver us into his presence for all eternity, that empowers God's people not to lose confidence, but to live like Christ.

The faith Paul exhibits in 4:13 is not mental assent to the truth of historical facts, though it is certainly based on such facts. Nor is it a magic formula designed to get things from God, though God certainly rewards faith by bringing his people into his presence for all eternity. Rather, it is a growing trust in the promises of God because of God's proven trustworthiness. This faith begins when we first bank our hope on God's promise of forgiveness in Christ. It continues through the ups and downs of life as we grow increasingly confident in God's wisdom and power to lead, sustain, and sanctify us. And it culminates on that day in which we trust God to take us home to himself. Having been saved by faith from beginning to end, faith also lasts forever, as we depend on God for all we are and ever hope to be throughout all eternity (cf. 1 Cor. 13:13).

John Piper pinpoints for us the heart of the matter.[32] Like Paul (cf. 4:15), Piper realizes that the goal of the Christian life is that

> God be *prized* above all things. I could also say that the ultimate purpose is the *praise* of the glory of God's grace. The reason both are aims, and both are ultimate, is that *prizing* is the authenticating essence of *praising*. You can't praise what you don't prize. Or, to put it another way, *God is most glorified in us when we are most satisfied in him.* . . .
>
> Sin is what you do when your heart is not satisfied with God. No one sins out of duty. We sin because it holds out some promise of happiness. That promise enslaves us until we believe that God is more to be desired than life itself (Psalm 63:3). Which means that the power of sin's promise is broken by the power of God's. All that God promises to be for us in Jesus stands over against what sin promises to be for us without him. This great prospect of the glory of God is what I call *future grace*. Being satisfied with that is what I call *faith*. And therefore the life I write about in this book is called *Future Grace: The Purifying Power of Living by Faith in Future Grace.* . . .
>
> The promises of future grace are the keys to Christ-like Christian living. . . . By *future* I do not merely mean the grace of heaven and the age to come. I mean the grace that begins now, this very second, and sustains your life to the end of this paragraph. By *grace* I do not merely mean the pardon of God in passing over your sins, but also the power

---

32. For a profound depiction of the "practical" implications of Paul's future orientation in 4:16–18 in view of 4:7–12, see Piper's important work, *Future Grace: The Purifying Power of Living by Faith in Future Grace* (Sisters, Ore.: Multnomah, 1995).

and beauty of God to keep you from sinning. By *faith* I do not merely mean the confidence that Jesus died for your sins, but also the confidence that God will "also with him freely give us all things" (Romans 8:32). Faith is primarily a future-orientated "assurance of things hoped for" (Hebrews 11:1). Its essence is the deep satisfaction with all that God promises to be for us in Jesus—beginning now![33]

This expectation of "future grace" is at the center of how Paul coped with his own wasting away in this life. When all is said and done, why did Paul not lose heart? What was it that made the renewal of Paul's "inner self" possible? The answer is the future orientation of 4:16–18. As Piper again puts it:

> The renewing of his heart comes from something very strange: it comes from looking at what he can't see. . . . This is Paul's way of not losing heart: looking at what you can't see. What did he see? A few verses later in 2 Corinthians 5:7, he says, "We walk by faith, not by sight." This doesn't mean that he leaps into the dark without evidence of what's there. It means that the most precious and important realities in the world are beyond our physical senses. We "look" at these unseen things through the gospel. By the grace of God we see what Paul called "the light of the gospel of the glory of Christ who is the image of God" (2 Corinthians 4:4). We strengthen our hearts—we renew our courage—by fixing our gaze on the invisible, objective truth that we see in the testimony of those who saw Christ face to face.[34]

The "unseen reality" that sustains Paul's faith is the glory of God he saw imaged in the crucified and risen Christ (cf. 4:5–6). Paul's confidence in God's promise that he too would one day share beyond measure in this eternal glory kept him persevering in faith in the midst of adversity. As a result, he was being transformed "with ever-increasing glory" (3:18). God had opened Paul's eyes to the glory of God himself in Christ, so that he had come to see that knowing God was of more value than anything the world has to offer. Thus, to listen to Piper yet again:

> This means that the decaying of his body was not meaningless. The pain and pressure and frustration and affliction were not happening in vain. They were not vanishing into a black hole of pointless suffering. Instead, this affliction was "producing for [him] an eternal weight of glory far beyond all comparison."

---

33. Ibid., 9–13.
34. Ibid., 359.

The unseen thing that Paul looked at to renew his inner man was the immense weight of glory that was being prepared for him not just *after*, but *through* and *by*, the wasting away of his body. . . . When he is hurting, he fixes his eyes not on how heavy the hurt is, but on how heavy the glory will be because of the hurt.[35]

Paul's understanding of how "heavy" this promised "future grace" actually is and what this means for the ministry of the gospel become the subject of 5:1–6:2.

---

35. Ibid., 359–60.

2 Corinthians 5:1–10

🕊

NOW WE KNOW that if the earthly tent we live in is destroyed, we have a building from God, an eternal house in heaven, not built by human hands. ²Meanwhile we groan, longing to be clothed with our heavenly dwelling, ³because when we are clothed, we will not be found naked. ⁴For while we are in this tent, we groan and are burdened, because we do not wish to be unclothed but to be clothed with our heavenly dwelling, so that what is mortal may be swallowed up by life. ⁵Now it is God who has made us for this very purpose and has given us the Spirit as a deposit, guaranteeing what is to come.

⁶Therefore we are always confident and know that as long as we are at home in the body we are away from the Lord. ⁷We live by faith, not by sight. ⁸We are confident, I say, and would prefer to be away from the body and at home with the Lord. ⁹So we make it our goal to please him, whether we are at home in the body or away from it. ¹⁰For we must all appear before the judgment seat of Christ, that each one may receive what is due him for the things done while in the body, whether good or bad.

Original Meaning

THE CONNECTION BETWEEN 4:16–18 and 5:1–5 is a matter of dispute, primarily because of the several meanings that the Greek conjunction *gar*, which introduces 5:1, can signify (the NIV renders it "now").[1] Paul often refers to something known in support of other affirmations he makes.[2] Thus, "we know" in 5:1 suggests that *gar* introduces

---

1. See BAGD, 151–52. This conjunction usually introduces a cause or reason (meaning "for"), but can also indicate a further interpretation (meaning "that is"), a conclusion ("therefore"), or merely a continuation of what is being said ("indeed," "but then").

2. For Paul's other uses of *gar* ("for") plus something said to be known, see Rom. 7:14, 18; 8:26; 2 Cor. 9:2; Eph. 5:5; Phil. 1:19; 1 Thess. 2:1; 3:3; 4:2; 5:2; 2 Thess. 3:7; 2 Tim. 1:12; for Paul's related use of the participle "knowing" in support of what has just been said, see Rom. 5:3; 6:9; 13:11; 1 Cor. 15:58; 2 Cor. 1:7; 4:14; 5:6, 11; Gal. 2:16; Eph. 6:8, 9; Phil. 1:16; Col. 3:24; 4:1; 1 Thess. 1:4; 1 Tim. 1:9; 2 Tim. 2:23; 3:14; Titus 3:11; Philem. 21; for the parallel use of "to know" (*oida*) with *de* ("but") to introduce support, see Rom. 2:2; 3:19; 8:28; 1 Tim. 1:8; and for his use of "to know" rhetorically in support of what he has just said (i.e., "Do you not know . . . ?"), see Rom. 6:16; 1 Cor. 3:16; 5:6; 6:2–3, 9, 15, 16, 19; 9:13, 24.

---

the ground or reason for what he has just affirmed in 4:16–18. The ambiguous rendering of *gar* in 5:1 as "now" is therefore better translated "for" or "because": "For what is seen is temporary, but what is unseen is eternal [4:18], *because* [*gar*] we know that if the earthly tent we live in is destroyed, we have a building from God, an eternal house in heaven, not built by human hands [5:1]." The eternal nature of the unseen world is based on the fact that it is built by God as our eternal dwelling place in his presence. When we understand 5:1 in this way, it becomes evident that the theme from chapter 4 of Paul's confidence in the present, based on his convictions concerning the future, continues on in 5:1–10.

As important as the conjunction in 5:1 is for tracing Paul's argument in 5:1–10, the key to understanding his thought here is determining the subject matter of the paragraph itself. The apparent simplicity of this text dissipates as soon as one realizes that the meaning of the contrast in 5:1 between what is "earthly" and what is "eternal" is by no means immediately clear. To what do the figures of an "earthly tent" (lit., "an earthly house, i.e., a tent") that is destroyed, in contrast to a "building from God, an eternal house in heaven not built by human hands" refer? How can this eternal house or building "clothe us," so that we will not be "found naked," *in order that* "what is mortal may be swallowed up by life" (5:2–4)? What is the "nakedness" that Paul wants to avoid? What is Paul longing for that causes him to "groan" as he waits for it, and when will his longing be fulfilled (5:2, 4)? Of the many answers that have been given to these questions, two interpretations have won the most support.[3]

(1) The most common interpretation is that Paul is expressing his certainty concerning the resurrection (5:1) and his longing to be alive when Jesus returns, so that he may go directly from his present life (= the "earthly tent" or being "at home in the body") into his resurrected state (= the "building from God," the "eternal house," the "heavenly dwelling"; 5:2, 4) without experiencing death. Nevertheless, if one should die, Paul acknowledges a disembodied, "intermediate state" (= "being found naked" or being "unclothed"), which occurs between the death of a believer (= losing his earthly tent/body or being "unclothed") and the future resurrection of the body (5:3–4). Though dying before Christ returns is not Paul's first desire, if it should happen, he will "be away from the body and at home with the Lord" (5:8) until that time when believers receive their new resurrected bodies at the final "judgment seat of Christ" (5:10). Thus, dying is still preferable to remaining on in this life, since it means being with Christ (5:8).

---

3. For a helpful survey of the extensive literature on this passage, see C. Marvin Pate, *Adam Christology*, 1–31.

This reading views Paul's argument as primarily indebted to Jewish eschatology with its belief in a bodily resurrection, though Paul is also seen as influenced by the body/soul dichotomy common to the Hellenism of the age. The basis of this interpretation is the parallel between this passage and 1 Corinthians 15:50–55, where the concept of "being clothed" also appears in relationship to the resurrection of believers at Christ's second coming (cf. 2 Cor. 5:2–4 with 1 Cor. 15:53–54).

There are modifications within this first view. Some argue that 5:1–5 speaks only of the final resurrection at the return of Christ, while the intermediate state described in 5:6–10 is also one of resurrection. In this view, there are only two kinds of existence (the earthly body and the resurrected body), so that those who die before Christ returns are already experiencing the resurrection of the age to come. At death, believers enter directly into their resurrected state. In contrast to Hellenistic thought, Paul's point is to *deny* that there will be an intermediate period of "nakedness" without a resurrected body, which he would not desire (5:3–4).

Still others within this basic perspective argue that 5:1–5 describes the intermediate state itself. In this view, the "building from God" or "heavenly dwelling" of 5:1–2 does not refer to the resurrection body, but is Paul's attempt to describe a temporary dwelling or clothing in the intermediate state that will keep believers from being found "naked" (i.e., as a disembodied spirit), something that Paul could not imagine (5:3–4). In this view, Paul is still affirming the intermediate state as different from that of the final bodily resurrection, but rejecting the idea of being "naked" during it.

(2) In stark contrast to this first view and its variations, an influential group of scholars has followed the lead of Earle E. Ellis in arguing that the subject matter here is not the *future* of the *individual* at all, as it is in 1 Corinthians 15, but the Jewish temple as a symbol for the *present* incorporation of believers into the *collective* body of Christ.[4] Instead of describing death and the afterlife, Paul is referring to becoming a Christian in this life. Taking the parallels in terminology between 5:1 and Mark 14:58 as its clue, this view argues that the eternal, heavenly building from God in 5:1–2 refers to God's people as the new temple in which he now dwells (for this use of the building imagery for the people of God, cf. 1 Cor. 3:9; Eph. 2:21; 4:12, 16).

In 2 Corinthians 5:1–2, therefore, Paul is talking about those who have been incorporated into the church as the body of Christ, who alone is now present in heaven. The "destruction" in view in 5:1 is not the individual believer's death, but the whole process of dying spoken of in 4:7–11 and

---

4. See Earle E. Ellis, "The Structure of Pauline Eschatology (II Corinthians V:1–10)," *NTS* 6 (1959–1960): 211–24.

4:16–18. Paul's point and confidence is that, even though the mortal bodies of believers are being destroyed, they are now members of Christ's body. The image of "being clothed"/"putting on" in 5:2, 4 does not refer to gaining some kind of heavenly existence, but to taking on Christ in baptism.[5] In 5:3, Paul is not thinking about being "naked" during an intermediate state, but about being found exposed "before the judgment seat of Christ" without the necessary good deeds spoken of in 5:10.[6]

Paul is not personally worried about being found wanting on the day of judgment, since he has been incorporated into "the heavenly body," which is Christ, so he makes it his goal to please the Lord (5:9). According to this interpretation, Paul's groaning and longing in 5:2, 4 refer to the tension that now exists between being in Christ in the midst of the suffering and sin of this world and the longing to be "found" in him rather than being "found" judged by God. Only in 5:6–10 does Paul turn to the future, and then to the return of Christ, not to some kind of intermediate state. In 5:8, Paul is therefore referring to being "at home" with Christ at his second coming.

This "corporate identity in Christ" perspective is insightful in many respects. It only succeeds completely, however, if one dissociates 2 Corinthians 5:1–5 from its close parallels in 1 Corinthians 15:53–55. Yet this is the backdrop that the Corinthians would have before them in reading Paul's current letter. Although the idea of "putting on"/"clothing oneself" is closely related thematically to our present context (only as a "new self" [Eph. 4:24] "in Christ" [Gal. 3:27] does one inherit the "heavenly dwelling"), this view has difficulty dealing with the fact that Paul presently *longs for* this "dwelling" (2 Cor. 5:2), which is hard to reconcile with his insistence that we are now *already* "in Christ."

Moreover, 5:1 is best read as an event (cf. the use of the aorist tense), not as a parallel to the ongoing process of 4:16–18, where the verbs "wasting away," "being renewed," and "achieving" were all in the present, continuous tense. The future orientation of 5:1–5, as well as 5:6–10, is difficult to deny

---

5. For the related image of "putting on"/"being clothed" as a reference to putting on Christ, see Rom. 13:14; Gal. 3:27; Eph. 4:22–24; Col. 3:9–10.

6. For the idea of "nakedness" as a reference to the shame of standing condemned before judgment, cf. Gen. 3:7, 10, 11; Isa. 20:2–5; 32:11; 47:3; Ezek. 16:36–39; 23:10, 26, 29; Hos. 2:3, 8–13; Amos 2:16; 4:3 (LXX); Micah 1:8, 11; for the idea of "being found" as a reference to standing before judgment, cf. 1 Cor. 4:2; 15:15; Gal. 2:17; 2 Peter 3:10. This same metaphorical use of nakedness to refer to being judged or condemned is used in Rev. 3:17; 16:15; 17:16. In this regard, it is important to see that the "nakedness" of Gen. 3:7, 10, 11 (Heb. ʿyrm), with its negative nuance of shame and judgment, is not equated in the biblical narrative with the "nakedness" of 2:25 (Heb. ʿrum), with its positive nuance of openness and unity.

as well. Thus, the idea that Paul is referring directly to the believer's incorporation into the body of Christ as the temple in 5:1–4 cannot be sustained.

In view of such objections, C. Marvin Pate has developed this "corporate identity" view further in an attempt to overcome its weaknesses. Following the basic insight of Ellis that Paul is speaking of the believer's corporate identity in Christ, Pate argues that the "nakedness" in view in this passage is an allusion to Adam's experience in Genesis 3:1–7, thus reestablishing a link between this text and Paul's "Adam-Christology" in 1 Corinthians 15:21–55 (cf. Rom. 5:11–21). Against this backdrop, Christ as the "second Adam" forms the theological foundation for 2 Corinthians 5:1–10, supported by the larger context of 4:7–5:21 (cf. the allusion to Gen. 1:26–27 in 2 Cor. 4:4, 6, 16). Paul's fundamental point is that "the primeval glory that the first Adam lost has been restored through the righteous suffering of Christ, the last Adam."[7] The "nakedness" of 5:3 therefore refers to our participation in Adam's nakedness after the Fall.[8] In Adam, we too are "naked" of our bodily glory, a condition that continues in the "bodiless" intermediate state. Paul fears the continuation of this "glory-less" state after death and longs for the full manifestation of divine glory in his mortal body, which has already begun in his heart.

Thus, Pate's reading corrects the corporate view by bringing it more into line with 1 Corinthians 15, as well as maintaining a body/soul dualism within a Jewish, eschatological framework. However, Pate's view is weakened by his attempt to relate this passage almost exclusively to Paul's "Adam Christology," which is merely a secondary allusion in this context. Moreover, this background cannot explain 5:6–10. In the end, Pate too falls back on the traditional view of "nakedness" as a description of the intermediate state, where being naked is still taken to refer to being "bodiless," now viewed in terms of lacking the glory of God.

Against the backdrop of the strengths and weaknesses of these interpretations, the view proposed here takes its starting point from (1) the contrast

---

7. Pate, *Adam Christology*, 22. For a description and evaluation of Pate's thesis, see my review of his work in *JBL* 113 (1994): 346–49. Cf. *Adam Christology*, 33–106, where Pate traces the tradition of the restoration of Adam's glory throughout postbiblical Judaism and early rabbinic thought.

8. Pate, *Adam Christology*, 115–16, in support of which Pate points to 3 *Apoc. Bar.* 6:16; 2 *Enoch* 22:8; 30:12; *Gen. Rab.* 20:12, where Adam's nakedness as a result of losing his glory is interpreted in terms of a garment or "clothing" that was lost at the Fall. In 1 *Enoch* 90:28–36; 2 *Bar.* 4:2–7; 4 *Ezra* 10:22–55; 13:36, a future, glorious building/temple with Adamic overtones is used to describe the future glory of the righteous. For the general motif of Adam's loss of glory at the Fall, see 1 *Enoch* 32:3–6; *Apoc. Mos.* 20:1. For the idea that the glory of the righteous in the age to come was already possessed by Adam before the Fall, see Sir. 49:16 (cf. Ps. 8:5; Ezek. 28:11–17); Dan. 12:3; 4 Ezra 8:51; 1 *Enoch* 39:9; 50:1; 58:2; 69:11, 13; 85:3; 103:2–3; 2 *Bar.* 15:8; 54:15, 21; 2 *Enoch* 30:10–11; *Lev. R.* 30:2.

in 4:18 between the temporary and the eternal that 5:1–10 is designed to support, (2) the corresponding reference to only two periods of time in this passage—an earthly time in which we are "at home in the body" and an eternal, heavenly time in which we are "at home with the Lord," (3) the explicit reference to the judgment seat of Christ in 5:10 as the decisive factor separating these two epochs, and (4) the direct parallels between 1 Corinthians 15:50–54 and 2 Corinthians 5:1–10. As these points indicate, the framework of 5:1–10 is Paul's two-age conception in which life in this age (i.e., the "mortal" of 5:4) will one day be "swallowed up" by the life of the age to come, when all people will stand before Christ as judge (5:1, 4, 10).

In contemplating this future, Paul's longing is not for death per se, but to be transformed into his resurrection body (5:2, 4). There is therefore no explicit reference in this passage to an intermediate state. Ellis has convincingly argued that the "nakedness" in view is an ethical term, referring to the shame of exposure before the judgment of God, not an anthropological term that refers to a state of human existence (the common view), or a material term that refers to the absence of God's glory (Pate's view). Paul's focus is exclusively on the future resurrection at the judgment seat of Christ. Finally, Pate's emphasis on the restoration of God's glory to those who are now "in Christ" as the "second Adam" provides an important though secondary conceptual background to Paul's thought.

Paul's Confident "Groaning" for the Future (5:1–5)

THE MAIN POINT of 4:13–18 was that, in the midst of his adversities, Paul focuses on those things that are not presently seen (4:18b), because these unseen things are what count, for they are eternal (4:18d). Paul supports this conviction in 5:1: "*because [gar]* we know that if the earthly tent we live in is destroyed [= life in the perishable, mortal body of this age of suffering, the temporary things now being seen from 4:18], we have a building from God, an eternal house in heaven, not built by human hands [= life in the glory of the imperishable resurrection body, the eternal, unseen things from 4:18]." These equations are confirmed by the direct parallels between 5:1–3 and 1 Corinthians 15:50–54, as well as the reference to the resurrection in 2 Corinthians 4:14 (see also Phil. 3:21).

The wasting away and affliction that Paul now sees at work in his life may even lead to his destruction in death, but his confidence in the coming "*eternal* weight of glory" (4:17) cannot be shaken, since it is based on what God himself will provide; that is, it is "not built by human hands." Paul's switch in metaphors in 5:1 from an "earthly tent" to a "building" is intended to communicate this difference between impermanence and permanence.[9] Paul knows that whatever this life may bring in terms of suffering and destruction, the life of the age to come will just as surely be filled with the glory of God. This confidence, expressed in 5:1, is the main point of 5:1–5, with verses 2–5 serving to support Paul's confident knowledge of the future.

In 5:2, Paul's confidence in God's future provision (4:13–5:1) causes him, like all believers, to "groan" in the midst of his present suffering as he longs to inherit the glory God has in store for him in Christ—that is, "to be clothed with our heavenly dwelling" (see Rom. 8:22–25).[10] Hence, the "building from heaven" that is the object of Paul's longing in 5:2 is the same "building from God" referred to in 5:1, namely, resurrection life in the eternal age to come.

Paul's point is that the groaning of anticipation that comes from this longing is itself evidence that God has promised believers more to come than the moaning of suffering and death. For this reason, the NIV rendering of the *gar* in 5:2 as "meanwhile" is to be rejected in favor of "because" or "for," indicating another ground clause. Just as 5:1 supported 4:18 by pointing to what God will do, 5:2 supports the confidence expressed in 5:1 by pointing to the response of the believer. In spite of the suffering Paul currently experiences and the prospect of destruction on the horizon, he is confident that he will inherit the glory of the resurrected life because of his God-given longing for it. If God had not planted this seed of hope in his heart, his current suffering would be all that could be expected (cf. 1:22; 4:13–16; 5:5).

Paul longs to "be clothed with" his heavenly dwelling because he can assume that he "will not be found naked" (like Adam after the Fall); that is, that he will not be condemned by God in the final judgment (5:3). Inasmuch as the image of "being clothed" in 5:2–3 refers primarily to the resur-

---

9. It is at this point that the "temple" imagery comes to the fore in this passage. As James M. Scott, 2 Corinthians, 110, points out, "the expression that Paul uses for his mortal body is not just *the earthly tent* (NIV) but rather 'our earthly house of the tent.' The language is drawn from 1 Chronicles 9:23 LXX, which refers to the tabernacle as 'the house of the tent' (cf. also 1 Chron. 6:17 LXX). Just as the tabernacle was the temporary dwelling of God from the time of the wilderness wanderings and until the building of a permanent temple in Jerusalem, so also Paul's mortal body is merely temporary." Scott (111) also points out that the word "house" (oikos) is frequently used of the temple of God (cf. 1 Kings 7:31; Matt. 21:13; Mark 11:17; Luke 19:46; John 2:16; Acts 7:47, 49), while the designation "eternal house" is a common name for the Solomonic temple in Jerusalem (cf. Josephus, Ant. 8.107; Gen. Rab. 54:4; 99:1; Num. Rab. 9:26, 32, 42; b. Yoma 44a, 53a, 67b).

10. See Paul Barnett, The Second Epistle to the Corinthians, 261, who observes that this is not the groaning of fear or even of mortality, but of hopeful longing as in childbirth (cf. Rom. 8:23–25), since Paul uses the same verb in 5:2 that is used to express a longing for absent friends in Rom. 1:11; Phil. 1:8; 2:26; 1 Thess. 3:6; 2 Tim. 1:4.

---

rection body, it is important to see that believers receive this body "in Christ." Being raised to new life by faith in Christ as the second Adam, symbolized in baptism (cf. Rom. 5:15–6:23), anticipates being raised to new life in Christ at the resurrection (cf. 1 Cor. 15:20–28, 45–49). Indeed, being clothed with Christ is the theological foundation to being clothed with our eternal dwelling from God. The believer's union with the resurrected Christ inaugurated in baptism is consummated in the resurrection from the dead. Or, in the terms of 2 Corinthians 3:18, the believer's encounter with the transforming glory of God in Christ as the "image of God" (cf. 4:4, 6) culminates in the final glorification of the believer into that same image (i.e., the believer is being transformed "with ever-increasing glory").

The positive groaning of 5:2–3 is matched by a negative one, expressed in 5:4, the presence of which supports Paul's anticipation in 5:3 (note again *gar*, "for,"[11] in 5:4). Paul's confident longing to inherit the eternal life of the age to come is supported by his desire to escape God's judgment. In terms of his metaphor, the apostle is "burdened" because he does "not wish to be unclothed" (i.e., found naked or condemned at the judgment of God), but "clothed" (i.e., vindicated at the judgment of God by his resurrection). If "nakedness" is seen as a metaphor for being under God's judgment, then there is no reference to an intermediate state in this verse. Moreover, Paul focuses on his longing in the present, not his whereabouts between his death and the final resurrection. The desire not to be "unclothed" when judgment takes place is supporting evidence that the believer will indeed be "clothed" when it occurs (5:5, 9–11).

To fear God's judgment is a sign that God is at work to save a person from it. Unbelievers do not fear that judgment in a way that causes them to repent (cf. 6:14–7:1; 7:9–11). The purpose of Paul's desire to avoid being naked on the Judgment Day is cited at the end of 5:4: "so that what is mortal may be swallowed up by life" (an allusion to the consummation of redemption as pictured in Isa. 25:8; see 1 Cor. 15:54). The "life" in view here is the resurrection life of the age to come (cf. 2 Cor. 4:14).

To end the first section of his argument, Paul makes explicit in 5:5 that the basis of his groaning, both positively and negatively, is God himself, since he is the one who has "made us for this very purpose." God is the one who brought about Paul's longing for the resurrection, since he is the one who "has given the Spirit as a deposit, guaranteeing what is to come." Furthermore, this Spirit-wrought longing takes place in the midst of the very adversities that fuel this same desire (cf. 1:22; Rom. 8:23).

---

11. Note how Paul uses a string of *gar*-clauses here. For his pattern of using such a string to support his contentions, see 3:9–11 and the list of examples given on p. 152n.8.

The NIV obscures the fact that the same verb used in 5:5 to refer to God's having prepared Paul for the future by granting him the Spirit (*katergazomai*) is used in 4:17 to describe his "achieving . . . an eternal glory" through his present afflictions. Here too, as in 2:14–3:3, suffering and the Spirit come together. Without the Spirit, the adversities of 4:17 would not seem temporary and slight. But without the adversities, the hope generated by the reception of the Spirit would lose its force. So God prepares his people by giving them a foretaste of the glory to come, in order that the suffering of this present age might be put into its proper perspective. And he gives them suffering so that the glory to come might be put into its proper perspective as well.

In 5:1–5, therefore, Paul is developing what he stated earlier. Both his confident longing for the future (his "positive" groaning) and his burden to put off the sin and suffering of the present (his "negative" groaning) are derived from the presence and power of the Spirit (for the role of the Spirit as the "deposit" on God's future promises, see 1:22; for the role of the Spirit as the power of new life en route to the fulfillment of these promises, see 3:3, 6, 8–9, 18). This "groaning" is not a natural response to suffering and sin, but the supernatural gift of God. God prepares his people for the future by giving them a longing for it. And he does this by granting them his Spirit as a down payment of his presence. Only those who have begun to experience the glory of God long for its consummation in the midst of their adversities.

The Consequence of Paul's Confidence (5:6–10)

PAUL NOW DRAWS the first conclusion that flows from his knowledge concerning the future: the ethics inherent in 5:6–10. Because Paul knows that his future with God is secure no matter what takes place in the present, including his complete destruction, "therefore" (*oun*) Paul remains "confident" (better, "courageous"; cf. 3:12; 4:1; 4:16). Paul knows "that as long as we are at home in the body we are away from the Lord." His point here is not intended to be a tautology, nor is it a denial of the possibility of being in communion with Christ while still on earth. It is a caution against absolutizing the significance of our present "location"—that is, of our lives on earth. Paul is reminding his readers that the source of a Christian's confidence is the recognition that to be "at home in the body" (parallel to being in "the earthly tent," 5:1, 4) is not the end-all of life. Life in this world is not the believer's final reality. It must be seen for what it is, namely, being "away from the Lord" (as a parallel to the "heavenly dwelling" or "house from God" in 5:1, 4). It is the penultimate, relative significance of the present, no matter how adverse its circumstances, that gives Paul courage (cf. comments on 4:13–18).

Therefore[12] Paul, like all believers, lives "by faith, not by sight" (5:7). This is the first consequence of Paul's confidence. Paul's lack of "sight" refers to what is now being experienced in this "earthly tent" (cf. 4:18–5:1). In the present, it is impossible to see the fullness of the resurrection glory still to come. Nevertheless, he trusts in God's promises as the ultimate reality and lives accordingly; he does not live as if his present suffering were the sum of life. It is Paul's confidence in God's future (i.e., faith focused on God's promises) that determines how he lives in the present. In other words, the apostle

fixes his gaze on what cannot be seen (4:18), his inner glory, not his outer affliction (4:17), his inward renewal, not his external decay (4:16), the new age, not the old (4:18), resurrection life, not present dying (4:10, 11), the weighty, not the trifling (4:17), the eternal, not the temporal (4:18), the heavenly, not the earthly (5:1–2). In short, he adopts a perspective of faith ... of trusting that, for the present eschatological moment, glory really does come to expression through affliction.[13]

Verses 6–7 thus provide a healthy corrective to the misunderstanding concerning what it meant to be "in Christ" that was so much a part of the Corinthian church. Unfortunately, their spiritual experiences led them to believe that they were already experiencing the fullness of the age to come (cf. 1 Cor. 4:8; 15:12[14]). In turn, the Corinthians' self-important, super-spirituality made the triumphalistic message of Paul's opponents so attractive, especially when it excused and even legitimized their materialism and moral laxity. Once again, however, the impossibility of such a winking at sin because of one's supposed spirituality (cf. 1 Cor. 5:1–6:20; 2 Cor. 12:21) becomes clear as Paul's argument continues. Rather than downplaying God's judgment, the Spirit actually discloses it and then prepares us for it by transforming our desires, which in turn alters our actions.

Verses 8–9 restate verses 6–7, unpacking the implications of what it means to know that one is still "away from the Lord" and of what living by

---

12. 2 Cor. 5:7 begins with the conjunction *gar*, here taken not as a ground clause, but as an inference, based on the structural parallel in the argument between vv. 6–7 and vv. 8–9, in which v. 9a begins with *dio* ("therefore"); the NIV omits translating the *gar* in 5:7.

13. Timothy B. Savage, *Power Through Weakness*, 184.

14. So Craig Blomberg, *1 Corinthians*, 90, 295, on the irony and sarcasm of 1 Cor. 4:8: "Here is one of the key texts that discloses the prevailing 'overly realized eschatology' (the idea that all of the blessings of the messianic age had already arrived) that afflicted the church at Corinth"; and on 15:12: "In keeping with their overly realized eschatology ... and like some later Gnostics, they may have applied the language of resurrection to the state of spiritual transformation they believed they had already achieved in this life."

faith looks like. In regard to the former, viewing the present from the perspective of the future means that our values and desires are radically altered. Instead of desiring a prolonged life on earth, we prefer to be "at home with the Lord" (cf. Phil. 1:23). Concerning the latter, living by faith is being confident that the eternal glory of "what is unseen" is certain and secure for believers and that it "far outweighs" any suffering of this world (4:17–18), so that the believer would trade this world for the world to come in a moment (5:8). Hence, to live by faith also means that, "whether we are at home in the body or away from it"—that is, whether we live or die—we aim to please the Lord, not ourselves (5:9; cf. 5:15; Phil. 3:1–13; cf. Rom. 12:1–2; 14:17–18; Eph. 5:10; Phil. 4:18; Col. 3:20).

The basis ("for," once again, *gar*) for this ambition to please the Lord is given in 5:10: Believers are aware that all people must appear before Christ as judge (cf. 1:14). Since in Romans 14:10–12 Paul signifies God as the judge, this identity of function between Christ and God highlights the divine sovereignty of Christ in a dramatic way. The purpose of Christ's divine judgment is to grant to each person his or her due, based on what was done while living "in the body," that is, while in the "earthly tent" of this life. The image of the "judgment seat" (*bema*) in 5:10 comes from the practice of the Roman governors, who sat on such tribunal benches to render judgment in legal cases. Just as the Corinthians were aware that Paul had stood before the "judgment seat" of the Roman governor Gallio in Corinth (cf. Acts 18:12, 16–17), so too Paul reminds them that they will stand before the "judgment seat" of Christ.

The main point of 5:1–10, therefore, is Paul's ambition to please the Lord in walking by faith (5:7a, 9). This ambition is rooted in his courage during this life (5:6a, 8a) because of his confidence in the resurrection of the righteous (5:1–5) *and* his awareness of the universal judgment to come (5:10). He is thus motivated both by the positive appeal of God's promises and by the negative prospect of Christ's judgment against all that is "bad." The explicit use of "we ... all" in 5:10 indicates a widening focus to include all believers (cf. 3:18). Paul's own way of life is based on his conviction that all believers will stand before Christ as judge. That unbelievers are also in view in 5:10 goes without saying.

The conviction that the judgment for all people is according to one's deeds is a common theme in Paul's letters.[15] The affirmation of this principle in the midst of his discussion of his hope of sharing in the eternal, resurrection life

15. Cf. Rom. 2:5–11; 1 Cor. 5:12–13; 6:9–10; Gal. 6:7–10; Eph. 6:8; Col. 3:24–25; 1 Thess. 4:1–8; 2 Thess. 1:3–10; etc., and Paul's positive affirmation that our work in the Lord is not in vain (1 Cor. 15:58; Gal. 6:9). For this same emphasis in the teachings of Jesus, see Matt. 7:16–23; 12:33–37; 16:27; 25:31–46; Mark 4:13–20; Luke 6:43–45; 19:12–27; John 5:28–29; 15:2, 16; Rev. 2:18–25; 22:12; cf. also 1 Peter 1:17; Rev. 20:12.

of Christ makes it clear that salvation itself is in view in Christ's judgment, not merely giving believers "rewards" for their faithfulness. Paul's confidence in the face of such judgment consequently reflects the reality of the new covenant in bringing about salvation, with its promise of righteousness and forgiveness in Christ, power for obedience through the Spirit, and deliverance from God's condemnation and wrath to come (cf. 3:3, 6, 8–9).

What renders one "naked" on the Judgment Day is a lack of good deeds done while still "in the body." What "clothes one" *in Christ* before the judgment seat *of Christ* is a life filled with acts pleasing to God (cf. Rom. 2:5–11; 14:17–18; cf. 1 Cor. 6:9–11; Gal. 5:16–26; Phil. 1:6, 11). The good deeds of 5:10 reveal what was stated in 3:3, namely, that one is "a letter from Christ ... written ... with the Spirit of the living God." Thus, Paul's statements in 5:9–10 should not be reduced to refer merely to rewards given to believers for righteous living after conversion.

Bridging Contexts

MUCH OF THE "bridge work" in this text revolves around determining controversial issues of interpretation. However, once Paul's unfamiliar metaphors are decoded, bringing his thought here to our own day presents no real problems at the conceptual level. Given our exposition of the text, we may simply point out the obvious. Death is the perennial problem of human existence. Thus, our greatest deception remains the thought that this life is all there is or that there is no judgment at the gateway to eternity. The profound and all-encompassing impact of knowing that there is a future reality beyond "being at home in the body" (5:9) and that there is a judgment yet to come in the presence of Christ (4:14; 5:10) remains as radical in the twenty-first century as it was in the first. It is this knowledge that fuels a life lived not for the present, but for the Lord (cf. 5:1, 10).

In view of the central role Paul's hope for the future plays in his life as a believer and in his ministry as an apostle, it is important to note that this text does not present a timetable for Christ's coming or a treatise on the precise contours of heaven. For Paul, "eschatology" is not primarily a series of doctrines or predictions about what will happen, but a longing for the resurrection and a certainty of heaven's eternal glory. The promises for which he longs are made real not by trying to figure out when Christ will return, but by an encounter with the risen Christ and by an experience of the Spirit's power and presence. It is Paul's knowledge of God in the present, not a calendar of end-times events, that makes him long to be with God for all eternity.

Moreover, a focus on the future that is fueled by a foretaste of God's presence leads to a life of faith aimed at pleasing the God in whose presence we already find ourselves. The goal and consequence of eschatology is ethics! Thus, this passage is another expression of the "already/not yet" tension that runs throughout the New Testament: Our experience of God in the present creates in us a craving for the full revelation of his glory in the future, which in turn creates a deep desire to live now in light of realities yet to come.

The personal obstacle. Having interpreted our text and seen its immediate relevance, our work at bridging contexts is still far from finished. Though there may be no difficulty in bringing this passage to our day at the conceptual level (the significance of the text is all too clear!), there are several serious impediments to appropriating Paul's message at the volitional level. Sometimes we may have to destroy old foundations at the personal, cultural, and/or theological level before we can build a biblical edifice. This is the case here.

The first difficulty is a personal one. Though we understand what Paul is saying, our now-centered culture makes it difficult for us to relativize the importance of the present by measuring it against the significance of the future. Since our churches seldom confront our saturation with the present, Paul's vision of the surpassing value of being "at home with the Lord" (5:8) strikes us as foreign and uncomfortable. Much of the contemporary Western church has lost sight of Paul's perspective that the glorious fulfillment to be gained from pleasing the Lord cannot be compared to the puny pleasures to be strained out of this life if lived for itself. Glutted on the second-rate happiness of this world, we are too full to hunger after God.

Moreover, we lack the spiritual "exercise" needed to make us hungry again. Filled with the sights and sounds around us, we think little about—indeed, we are embarrassed to spend time—cultivating a confident vision of the glories to come. As David Van Biema questions in *Time* magazine's 1997 Easter essay, "Does Heaven Exist?": "It used to be that the hereafter was virtually palpable, but American religion now seems almost allergic to imagining it. Is paradise lost?"[16] The answer, in a word, is "yes." Van Biema reports that for most people "the current generic heaven still delivers when people need it most ... at the death of a loved one. Why bother with it any other time?"[17] He observes, "Modernist attacks on God's place in this world made people allergic to bold predictions about his kingdom in the next ... 'scientific, philosophical and theological skepticism has nullified the modern heaven and replaced it with teachings that are minimalist, meager and dry.'"[18]

---

16. *Time* (March 24, 1997), 71–78 (p. 71).

17. Ibid., 73.

18. Ibid., 75, quoting McDannell and Lang from their social survey entitled, *Heaven: A History*.

David Wells points out that this intellectual skepticism has a corollary at the person level: "It's difficult for some people to conceive of anything that is really much better than this life. Sure, they go to bed appalled by the 11 o'clock news. But those buddies on the beer commercial saying, 'It doesn't get much better than this' are speaking more deeply than we realize."[19] No wonder there is so little moral courage or self-giving left in our culture of expediency and self-love. In stark contrast, Paul's bold certainty concerning the resurrection and his corresponding comparison between the values of the present and those of the future give him courage in this world (5:6, 8), precisely because they cause him to long for his life "from God . . . in heaven" (5:1).

The absence of a longing for heaven in our churches therefore represents much more than merely a shift in doctrinal emphasis, as if the difference is merely one of personal preference. It is not as if Paul focuses on the future as central to life in the present, but we, given the needs of the day, prefer instead to focus on Christology or the doctrine of justification by faith. Rather, Paul's reminder in 5:5 that his courage in the present and longing for the future both derive from the "deposit" of the Spirit in his life reveals the poverty of contemporary experience of the life-changing power of God's holy presence (see comments on 3:16–18). If the granting of the Spirit prepares us for and guarantees our future in God's unmediated presence, our dim view of the glory to come means that we have far too little genuine knowledge of God here and now. Not having tasted much of heaven, all we can imagine is earth.

Over against our weak desires, Paul's ambition is to please Christ, not because he has convinced himself that he "ought" to do so, but because he is convinced that the Christ he has already come to know will one day also judge him (5:9–10). Inasmuch as his experience of God has already proved so valuable (5:5; cf. 1:22), he will not risk doing anything that may keep him from being "at home with the Lord." By contrast, our jokes about heaven being filled with our greatest pleasure on earth (e.g., "heaven is the great golf course in the sky"; or, "when I get to heaven I am going to eat all the pizza I can without worrying about my cholesterol") simply show how blind we are to the reality that it is the Lord himself who makes heaven our rightful home, and that it is this same Lord who will welcome us there. To make the central focus of heaven anything or anyone beside God himself is ludicrous; to add something to God as heaven's pleasure is idolatrous.

The cultural obstacle. Our exposition of this passage makes clear that Paul's emphasis on the "eternal" nature of the glory he anticipates seeing (4:17), on the "eternal" nature of the "unseen" things he therefore focuses on

---

19. Quoted by Van Biema, "Does Heaven Exist?" 76.

(4:18), and on the "eternal" quality of the dwelling he will inherit (5:1) ties this passage together with 4:13–18. In Paul's thinking, "eternal" (*aionios*) does not refer to an ethereal region or an atemporal manner of existence, but to a span of time—in this case, to the unending age to come. "Eternal" is a temporal term for Paul, not a mystical one.[20] What makes something "eternal" is its unending nature over against the finite nature of the historical age in which we live.

Though we read in Paul's letters about eternal realities, as members of the "now generation" the difficulty of escaping our love affair with the present is made all the more difficult by the dominant cultural ethos of "progress" in which we live. To quote van Biema again: "When heaven comes up in public debate these days, it is often just a metaphor for the concerns of a perfectible secular kingdom of man."[21] Therefore, if we are to resist such cultural pressure in order to live by faith so that Christ is pleased (5:7, 9), we must keep in mind the dramatic distinction between the biblical view of history and the modern notion of progress. In the latter, the world is somehow getting "better" as it marches into unending time. In the worldview of the Bible, history, under the providence of God, is moving toward its appointed end, which will culminate with a personal and world-transforming day of reckoning. The end of history is the judgment of God, meted out on the basis of a faith-induced obedience to God's will. In the modern view of progress, the world is run by natural law alone; in the biblical view of providence, the world is under the grace and law of God.

In his important study, *The True and Only Heaven: Progress and Its Critics*, Christopher Lasch has portrayed in great detail this difference between the biblical and modern worldviews and its implications.[22]

---

20. Cf. the summary of this point by Scot McKnight, "Eternal Consequences or Eternal Consciousness?" in *Through No Fault of Their Own? The Fate of Those Who Have Never Heard*, ed. by William V. Crockett and James G. Sigountos (Grand Rapids: Baker, 1991), 147–157: "The standard Greek lexicons divide the meaning of *aionios* into two major categories: (1) lasting for a long but definite period of time (aeonial), an age or lifetime, and (2) perpetual, immeasurable time (eternal), forever, or a temporally unlimited period. Context must decide.... But the matter is largely resolved when one recognizes that this present age is temporally limited ... and the future age is temporally unlimited (because it shares in God's immortality). The distinction between 'this age' (limited time) and 'the age to come' (unlimited time) is central to New Testament eschatology.... God's time is essentially endless and eternal, and it follows that the final age is an eternal (endless) age. In the exegesis of New Testament texts, this distinction must be observed." McKnight therefore argues that the final vindication of the righteous and judgment of the wicked are both "eternal" in the sense of being unending in their consciousness, not just in their consequences.

21. Van Biema, "Does Heaven Exist?" 73.

22. cf. esp. 44–46.

Once we recognize the profound differences between the Christian view of history, prophetic or millenarian, and the modern conception of progress, we can understand what was so original about the latter: not the promise of a secular utopia that would bring history to a happy ending but the promise of steady improvement with no foreseeable ending at all. The expectation of indefinite, open-ended improvement, even more than the insistence that improvement can come only through human effort, provides the solution to the puzzle that is otherwise so baffling—the resilience of progressive ideology in the face of discouraging events that have shattered the illusion of utopia.... The modern conception of history is utopian only in its assumption that modern history has no foreseeable conclusion. We take our clue from science, at once the source of our material achievements and the model of cumulative, self-perpetuating inquiry....[23]

Hence, although the idea of a utopian future has been given up in modern thought, the populace and modern politics, not to mention our personal ambitions, are still driven by a conviction that things will somehow improve, at least for those in the privileged classes of power. Lasch traces this belief in unending progress, "in the face of massive evidence that might have been expected to refute the idea of progress once and for all," to the eighteenth century, when it began to be argued that

human wants, being insatiable, required an indefinite expansion of the productive forces necessary to satisfy them. Insatiable desire ... came to be seen as a powerful stimulus to economic development ... a continual redefinition of ... standards of comfort and convenience led to improvements in production and general increase of wealth. There was no foreseeable end to the transformation of luxuries into necessities. The more comforts people enjoyed, the more they would expect. The elasticity of demand appeared to give the Anglo-American idea of progress a solid foundation that could not be shaken by subsequent events, not even by the global wars that broke out in the twentieth century. Those wars, indeed, gave added energy to economic development.[24]

The modern notion of progress is so enduring because it is so intimately tied up with our boundless appetite for more. In fact, progress itself is defined as that which helps satisfy our cravings. Our love of money, with its promise

---

23. Christopher Lasch, *The True and Only Heaven: Progress and Its Critics* (New York: W. W. Norton & Company, 1991), 47–48.
24. Ibid., 13–14. In short, "the modern conception of progress depends on a positive assessment of the proliferation of wants" (45).

of ever-increasing comforts in this life, is the engine that drives our self-deluded optimism in a better tomorrow on earth. We assume that getting more money will mean getting a better life; our optimism that we can make more money brings with it a confidence in a better life to come. This is the American dream, best epitomized by our modern, materialistic conception of retirement, in which the hope is to live as long as we can, as healthy as we can, and as wealthy as we can.

Increased life span, along with increased health and wealth, deceive us into thinking that we are making progress toward what is good and right and pleasing. Even those who are the most realistic or pessimistic among us still cling to some notion of an eventual progress, in spite of the economic, health, and social crises that seem to be mounting all around us, especially if we view life on planet earth from a global vantage point.[25] After all, the very fact that more people than ever are enjoying middle class lifestyles is itself progress!

Yet Paul's argument makes clear that true ethics are not derived from a materialistic understanding of progress but from a biblically informed view of the future. Such an eschatology is prophetic in nature, as an expression of God's sovereignty over his creation, and not progressive, as an expression of humanity's creative ingenuity and will to survive. The biblical view of the future *ends* with a judgment according to the character of one's life as lived by faith and measured by Christ, not with the accumulation of goods or the development of some this-worldly civic virtue. The biblical view of history is personal, ending with the judgment of Christ, not impersonal, ending with the fatalism of progress or disaster.[26] History is not unending progress, but the goal-driven culmination of God's purposes.

---

25. Lasch argues that the signs are already evident, both economically and environmentally, that such a belief in progress is misplaced, unrealistic, and ultimately self-destructive (cf. his summary on ibid., 528–529). In his words, "The belated discovery that the earth's ecology will no longer sustain an indefinite expansion of productive forces deals the final blow to the belief in progress" (529). Yet belief in progress persists, especially among the middle and upper classes. When reading dire predictions like those marshaled by Lasch, I find myself saying with unfounded optimism that "need is the mother of invention" and that "science will find a way." Thus, Lasch observes, "as the twentieth century draws to a close, we find it more and more difficult to mount a compelling defense of the idea of progress; but we find it equally difficult to imagine life without it" (168). Still, for many, the disasters and calamities on every front have recast the future into a "vision of disaster" (169). Yet, as Lasch again observes, "the dystopian view of the world to come ... holds out such an abundance of unavoidable calamities that it becomes all the more necessary for people to cling to the idea of progress for emotional support, in spite of the mounting evidence against it" (169). Biblically, this "curious state of mind" is explained by the fact that God created humanity for a future with him, a future that includes both a judgment and a redemption!

26. In this regard, Lasch (ibid., 15, 226–295) points out that the Puritan and Calvinistic expressions of the faith, which Lasch calls "certain varieties of radical Protestantism,"

Accordingly, the most shocking thing about Paul's perspective for modern and postmodern people in the West is that history is going someplace beyond itself and that at the end of history stands the judgment of God. Hence, the goal of life is not the progress of pleasure on earth, but striving to please God in heaven. We live under the coming judgment of Christ. This is the lens through which Paul views life, and we must work hard to help Christians regain this fundamental perspective. Our lives should be driven by the certainty of Christ's future reign. Our hope is that in Christ we will endure the day of judgment, forgiven and clothed with the good works born of faith and done by the power of God.

The theological obstacle. This brings us to the third obstacle in this passage. Beyond the personal and cultural obstacles that make it hard to apply this text today, this passage also confronts two theological misunderstandings in the contemporary church, both of which have done much harm to the progress of the gospel in the lives of God's people: The first concerns the nature of genuine faith (5:7), the second involves the relationship between faith and obedience (5:10).

(1) In regard to the former, Paul's emphasis on his confident knowledge of the future makes clear that faith is not an irrational leap into the dark that calls for accepting the truth of something that makes no sense or has no foundation in reality. Just the opposite! Faith is trusting in God's promises for the future, not in spite of what we know, but *because of* what we know. The lack of sight in this passage does not refer to the uncertain basis of faith, but to the fact that the consummation of God's promises has not yet been realized. Paul's point in 5:7 is not epistemological (i.e., we can only know things "by faith," since we have no certain reasons for believing, i.e., no "sight"), but eschatological (i.e., we live in the present by trusting God's promises for the future, the down payment of which we are already experiencing in the Spirit). Thus, faith is an active dependence on God's promises for our future because of what God has already done for us in the past.

(2) Confronting Paul's understanding of faith raises the question of what is usually referred to as the relationship between faith and works, as if the two can be separated. On the one hand, this passage underscores that faith is not a mere mental assent to the truth of data from the past. Rather, faith is an informed act of the will by which we entrust ourselves to God's sovereign

---

worked against the American assumption of "progress." He thus views Thomas Carlyle and Ralph Waldo Emerson as "latter-day Calvinists without a Calvinist theology" (15). The key point was that people, for all their growing belief in progress, did not control their own fate or destiny. In the end, Lasch argues for the recognition of true "limits" in life in order to counter the still prevailing notions of limitless progress so dominant today. Here we see that Paul is setting up the ultimate "limit," the final day of judgment.

goodness in accord with what God has declared and demonstrated to be his intentions toward his people and the world. On the other hand, this text makes evident that Paul's walk "by faith" in 5:7 is the very means by which the good deeds of 5:10 are produced.

Paul's assumption is that whatever one trusts in for the future inevitably determines how one acts in the present. He thus sees faith as an active dependence on God's promises that inevitably expresses itself and is seen in one's actions. When one trusts God, one obeys him. We "walk by faith" (5:7) and are judged by what we do (5:10) because to trust in God's promises is to live according to his Word—the latter being the objective, public expression of the former and, as such, the basis of God's judgment. Of course, our faith-obedience is not the product of our attempt to earn God's blessing, since our hope and present obedience are the product of God's Spirit in our lives (5:5; cf. 3:7–18).

In this sense, it is impossible to separate trusting God from obeying God. Yet given our propensity to view faith as mental assent, we find ourselves satisfied with an anemic "belief" that is content with disobedience. We often hear people say or imply that they have no trouble believing God, just obeying him. For Paul, such a dichotomy is nonsense, a self-contradiction. Any attempt to separate faith from works runs aground on the fact that in one and the same passage Paul can speak of living by faith (5:7) and of being judged by deeds (5:10). Indeed, the goal of Paul's entire life as the apostle to the Gentiles is to bring them to "the obedience that comes from faith" (Rom. 1:5; cf. 15:18; 16:26; 1 Thess. 1:3; 2 Thess. 1:11), since only this kind of faith in God's promises glorifies God (cf. Rom. 4:18–25).

Every act of trust in God's promises expresses itself in an act of obedience to his commands; every act of obedience is a manifestation of trust. Conversely, every time we disobey God it is because we are not trusting him. Hence, every command of God is, in essence, a promise of God in disguise. To declare, "You shall have no other gods before me," is therefore essentially the same thing as saying, "God promises to be sufficient in all things as your sovereign Provider, Redeemer, Lord, and Judge—so trust him alone." In the same way, "You shall not covet . . . anything that belongs to your neighbor" is essentially the same thing as saying, "God promises to provide what you need in the world and in himself in order to satisfy the deepest longings of your heart—therefore trust him."

This is the framework of the Ten Commandments, which thus begins and ends with the same command (note Paul's equation of idolatry with covetousness in Eph. 5:5; Col. 3:5). All the other commands follow this pattern. "You shall not murder" is a call to trust God's promise to vindicate our cause. God's command to Moses, "Leave this place, you and the people you brought up out of Egypt, and go up to the land I promised on oath" is an expression of God's promise to give the land to Abraham's descendants (Ex. 33:1). The command to love the alien as oneself is a call to depend on God's promise that God will love us, even though we are aliens to him (Lev. 19:34). "Repent and be baptized" is built on God's promise of forgiveness and the Spirit (Acts 2:38).

With some reflection, every command can be seen to be a call to trust its corresponding promise. God commands what he commands because he promises what he promises. As a result, there is only one thing we must do to be saved on the day of judgment (i.e., "live by faith," which is to do good deeds "in the body," 5:7, 10), not two (i.e., "trust *and* obey," as if 5:7, 10 point to two different steps in the Christian's life). Paul's argument illustrates that for faith to be genuine, it must be marked by a future orientation that reveals our dependence on the promises of God (5:1), by an obedience in the present that shows our faith to be alive (5:10), and by a perseverance throughout the adversities of life in order to demonstrate that our faith is derived from the reality of the Spirit in our lives (5:5, 9; cf. 1 Cor. 15:2).[27]

Finally, the link in this passage between faith, obedience, and the presence and power of the Spirit makes clear that Paul's emphasis on judgment by works in 5:10 is not a denial of his emphasis elsewhere on justification by faith alone, nor is it a synergism in which we contribute our share to God's work. At least three additional realities make this clear:

- Paul's insistence on the inextricable link between justification and sanctification, the former of which is based on the predestining election of God and the atoning death of Christ, the latter on the power of the Spirit (cf. Rom. 8:28–30).
- Paul's understanding of God's justification of the believer as a legal act that expresses both God's imputing his own righteousness to believers because of Christ's death on the cross for them and God's consequent covenant commitment to purify his people as a result (5:5; cf. 3:7–11; 3:9; 5:21; Rom. 1:16–17; 5:17; Phil. 1:9–11).[28]

---

27. For this threefold delineation of biblical faith and for one of the best expositions of its nature and implications, see Daniel P. Fuller, *The Unity of the Bible*, esp. 269–323.

28. On the meaning of the "righteousness of God" as a dynamic concept referring to God's sovereign, covenant commitment to his people, see Bruce W. Longenecker, "Defining the Faithful Character of the Covenant Community, Galatians 2:15–21 and Beyond," in *Paul and the Mosaic Law*, ed. by James D. G. Dunn (WUNT 80; Tübingen: J. C. B. Mohr [Paul Siebeck], 1996), 75–97: "The *dikai*-root is flexible enough to connote various nuances, but all of them cohere within the broader context of the covenant relationship between the creator God and his elect people. To be marked out by righteousness, or to be justified, is primarily about having membership within the covenant people of the just and sovereign God

- Paul's conviction that obedience is the inevitable outgrowth of new life in and through the Spirit (cf. Rom. 6:5–7; 7:4; 1 Cor. 5:11; 6:9–11; 7:19; Gal. 5:16–26; 1 Thess. 1:4–5).

Love, as the fulfillment of the law, is the manifestation of genuine faith and hope (cf. Rom. 13:8–10; Gal. 5:6, 13–14; 6:2; 1 Thess. 1:3). For this reason, judgment takes place according to works, in order to vindicate publicly God's work in the hearts of those who have been changed by the power of the Spirit. Deeds are the means of evaluation in the courtroom of God's judgment, since they establish the genuine nature of the claim to trust God. In short, rather than being added *to faith*, obedience to God's will is the visible manifestation *of faith*.

In order to bring this passage into our context, we must consequently be careful never to call into question the most fundamental fact of all reality: God in Christ is the one who saves (cf. 5:16–21). Nothing we do has or ever will earn or purchase our salvation. Salvation, including our trusting God for it, is the gift of God made possible by Christ (Rom. 4:1–8; 5:8–9; 6:23; Eph. 2:8–9). We must reject all attempts to consider our works our contribution to God's saving work on our behalf. This is true whether they are the "bad works" that we think make us special or deserving in God's sight before we are saved (cf. Rom. 4:2–4), or the "good works" that God himself brings about in our lives through his Spirit (cf. Eph. 2:10). All we bring to God is our desperate need for forgiveness and deliverance from sin. All our acts in Christ are the fruit of the Spirit (Gal. 5:22) and of his own righteousness (Phil. 1:11), which therefore rebound to God's glory, not ours (cf. Matt. 5:16).

Rightfully concerned by the danger of "works righteousness," Protestantism has nevertheless been weakened by a failure to emphasize equally that the believer's good works, as the fruits of our dependence on the all-sufficiency of our God, vindicate the genuine nature of our salvation. Obedience to God's commands is what faith in God's promises looks like in everyday life. Therefore, when we are judged by our works on the Judgment Day, our deeds or obedience of faith (Rom. 1:5; 1 Thess. 1:3) will be the instrument, though not ultimate ground of our final justification. The basis of our salvation is the life and death of Jesus on our behalf, both as that which forgives us *for our sin* and that which frees us *from our sin*. Our deeds are

---

whose righteousness will be established once and for all in the eschatological in-breaking of his reign" (81). For Paul, this in-breaking of the righteousness of God's reign has already begun with the first coming of Christ, but will be consummated only at the final judgment seat of Christ. Only then will the full-orbed nature of God's righteousness, displayed in the vindication of his people as a result of the vindication of his Son, be manifest.

the public criteria of judgment, not because they contribute in some way to our salvation, but because they are, in themselves, what it means to "live by faith" (2 Cor. 5:7).

No claim to faith that is not so vindicated should be allowed to stand now, just as it will not stand before the judgment seat of Christ. This is why Paul grounds his desire to please God in his conviction that he too will one day be judged by Christ in view of his deeds (cf. 1 Cor. 4:1–5; 9:23–27). Hence, one important step toward the recovery of a full-blooded Christian life in our age of pale religious experience is to recognize afresh that emphasizing the central and essential role of obedience in judgment is not a denial of justification by faith alone, but its powerful affirmation.

LIVING IN THE LIGHT **of the future**. Paul's declarations of his confidence for the future, of his ambition in the present, and of Christ's role as universal judge are as significant today as they were in the materialistic and pluralistic world of the first century. In view of our culture's belief in some kind of universal spiritual future for all humankind, combined with a growing New Age emphasis on reincarnation, the challenge of pluralism, and the lack of consistent teaching in many churches, we must once again stake out four important boundary markers of a distinctively Christian worldview:

- There is a universal judgment to come, not just for some people, but for all, including Christians.
- Christ alone is the One who judges.
- Only those who have experienced the mercy and power of God in Christ can have confidence as they anticipate this coming day of reckoning.
- The only basis of confidence on the Judgment Day is the good deeds that constitute living by faith.

These points need to be driven home in a culture in which 85 percent of Americans consider themselves to be Christian, even though half of all adults believe you can lead a full and satisfying life without spirituality of any kind.[29] This confusion is increased when the question of final judgment is raised. As Barna reports:

---

29. According to the studies of George Barna, *Index of Leading Spiritual Indicators* (Dallas: Word, 1996), 9, 101.

Few Americans doubt that God will judge every individual. Almost nine out of ten people (86 percent) contend that "eventually, all people will be judged by God" [a poll from January, 1993].

Most Americans believe that spiritual salvation is an outcome to be earned through their good character or behavior. Six out of ten people (57 percent) believe that "if a person is generally good, or does enough good things for others during their lives, they will earn a place in heaven." This perspective has remained constant throughout the nineties [a poll from January, 1995].

Adults are evenly divided on the role played by religious beliefs in people's life-after-death experience. Forty-five percent contend that one's religious beliefs will impact their spiritual condition; another 45 percent argue that a person's beliefs will not matter. The other 10 percent refuse to take a position [a poll from July, 1994].

... Only four out of ten Americans (39 percent) believe that "people who do not consciously accept Jesus Christ as their savior will be condemned to hell" [the same poll from July, 1994].

There is a growing tendency to believe that "all good people, whether or not they consider Jesus Christ to be their savior, will live in heaven after they die on earth." The public is now evenly divided on this matter: 46 percent agree, 47 percent disagree [polls from July, 1994; January, 1992].[30]

Though vast amounts of people profess a belief in some kind of divine judgment to come, few actually operate their daily lives on the basis of such a conviction. It is also striking that few of those who say they believe in a final judgment believe Jesus Christ has any decisive role to play in it. Finally, but not surprisingly, people are optimistic about their own chances of being judged positively, just as they are confident that there will be condemnation for others. Such responses show the way in which faith has been downsized into a mere mental assent that has no tie to life, the growing distrust in the claims of Christ, and the self-reliance and self-confidence of those who feel self-justified in God's sight.

The above research also reveals the schizophrenia that exists between our culture's moral self-confidence and its ability to condemn others. This was evident in *Newsweek*'s account of the impending death and final public words of the Khmer Rouge leader, Pol Pot. In many ways the "Hitler" of the 1970s, Pol Pot was responsible for killing at least one million of his fellow Cambodians. In 1997, under house arrest, partially paralyzed from a stroke, and

---

30. Ibid., 71–72.

facing his own death with a congenital heart defect, Pol Pot granted his first interview in twenty years. During the interview he declared a number of times, "I am finished as a human being. I'm dying." But he remained unrepentant and would not apologize for his actions. So *Newsweek's* "conventional wisdom" responded with the quip, "Million-man murderer says 'mistakes were made,' but he's not sorry. Roast in hell."[31]

Who would argue with such a sentiment? But why do we think we will fare any better? Why are we so confident that Pol Pot should "roast in hell," but we should not? The answer, as Barna reads the data, is that

> the American penchant for self-reliance, achievement, and autonomy has invaded the realm of the afterlife. People are more likely to count on their own abilities and character as a means to pleasing God or otherwise earning eternal peace than they are to accept a gift . . . as taught by the Christian Church regarding the sacrificial death and subsequent atonement through Jesus Christ.[32]

Second, we have seen that Paul's argument in 5:6—8 reminds us that life in this world is not the end-all and be-all of our existence. As a Christian it sounds silly even to say such a thing, since it is so obvious. But the fact that such a conviction has risen to the level of a truism makes it all the more necessary to reaffirm it. Clichés, though so true they go without saying, are not taken seriously. But Paul's perspective in this passage, if taken seriously, challenges in no uncertain terms the contemporary cultural preoccupation with the present that pervades and cripples our churches. For in 5:8—9 Paul makes it clear that the Christian's courage derives from having the right desires for the future, which in turn leads to having the right ambitions in the present. Those who live for the present desire only what this world has to offer. Their ambition is to please themselves within the confines of the narrow pleasures of this world. But those who live for their future with God desire the life promised by God. Their ambition is to please God, since he is their true joy (cf. 4:18; 5:11—15).

Third, the resurrection-focused, Christ-centered nature of Paul's ambition, fueled by his confidence in the judgment to come, reminds us that Christians must not be fooled by the apparent confidence and nonchalance that characterizes so much of the modern disregard for the reality and finality of death. In truth, this cultural bravado merely masks our worried preoccupation with our own mortality with a drive to act heroically in the face of our own certain destruction. As Ernest Becker has so poignantly argued in his

---

31. *Newsweek* (Nov. 3, 1997), 6.
32. Barna, *Index*, 71—72.

Pulitzer Prize winning analysis of modern philosophy, religion, and psychology, *The Denial of Death*:

> The first thing we have to do with heroism is to lay bare its underside, show what gives human heroics its specific nature and impetus. Here we introduce directly one of the great discoveries of modern thought: that of all things that move man, one of the principal ones is his terror of death ... heroism is first and foremost a reflex of the terror of death.
>
> ... All historical religions addressed themselves to this same problem of how to bear the end of life. Religions like Hinduism and Buddhism performed the ingenious trick of pretending not to want to be reborn, which is a sort of negative magic: claiming not to want what you really want most. When philosophy took over from religion it also took over religion's central problem, and death became the real "muse of philosophy" from its beginnings in Greece right through Heidegger and modern existentialism.
>
> ... The fear of death is natural and is present in everyone ... it is the basic fear that influences all others, a fear from which no one is immune, no matter how disguised it may be. William James ... called death "the worm at the core" of man's pretensions to happiness.[33]

Becker's analysis of contemporary culture and thought led him to recognize finally that the fundamental problem of modern life is a religious one, to which he then offers his own, final answer:

> How ... can one be a saint and still organize scientific movements of world-historical importance? How does one lean on God and give over everything to Him and still stand on his own feet as a passionate human being? These are not rhetorical questions, they are real ones that go right to the heart of the problem of "how to be a man." ... If men lean too much on God they don't accomplish what they have to in this world on their own powers. In order to do anything one must first be a man, apart from everything else. This throws the whole splendid ideal of sainthood into doubt because there are many ways of being a good man....
>
> The most that any one of us can seem to do is to fashion something—an object or ourselves—and drop it into the confusion, make an offering of it, so to speak, to the life force.[34]

---

33. Ernest Becker, *The Denial of Death* (New York: Free Press, 1973), 11–15.
34. Ibid., 259, 285.

In earth-shaking contrast to Becker's attempt to find meaning in this life without a clear hope for the future, the answer of the gospel is a *real* resurrection in which what we have "fashioned" in our lives is judged by the One who has himself already overcome death. For the unbeliever, like Becker, the goal of life is to be "a passionate human being" apart from God by not "leaning too much on God." For the believer, the goal of life becomes learning how to "live by faith" in every circumstance, knowing that everything will be judged by the God who gives us "an eternal house in heaven, not built by human hands" (5:1).

Moreover, Paul's own life shows, without a shadow of a doubt, that living by faith leads to the kind of deep passion that offers its own life up for the sake of others as well as for the sake of Christ. Rather than destroying the drive to live passionately, it is death and eternity, once known to be real, that give life its true meaning and ambition. Carl F. H. Henry, the senior statesman of evangelical theology, thus summarizes well the basic structure of biblical theology reflected in our passage:

> The reader of Scripture will discover that the entire universe is the creation of a sovereign personal God, that God's image lifts humanity above all other orders of finite life, that a providential divine purpose governs history and moves nations toward a final judgment, that God came personally in Jesus of Nazareth who conquered death, that the divergent options of eternal damnation or eternal salvation face sinful mankind, and that forgiveness of sins and new spiritual life are even now available to the penitent—these tenets thrust themselves insistently upon every reader who samples sacred Scripture.[35]

Finally, Paul's Christ-defined, future-orientated, judgment-driven passion for the resurrection is to be contrasted with the arm-chair fascination with the after-life that is increasingly becoming a part of modern popular culture. Henry's observations again provide an insightful summary:

> Despite all the secular twaddle about nonreligious modernity, an immense wave of religiosity continues, nonetheless, to sweep over contemporary life....
>
> Scientifically gifted longer life on earth through age-retarding hormones and organ transplants is now becoming too routine to be media-dramatic, so Hollywood aggressively probes immortality as the ultimate horizon. Afterlife films leap over AIDS and senior citizenship, death, funerals, and grief to concentrate on a world beyond—which

---

35. Carl, F. Henry, "Christianity and Resurgent Paganism," *Gods of This Age or God of the Ages?* ed. R. Albert Mohler (Nashville: Broadman and Holman, 1994), 1–10 (p. 1).

often amounts to nothing more than postmortem out-of-body hankey-pankey. The movies increasingly banner that death is not final. They tell us that a spirit world is in store for us—without God, without judgment, without need of grace, without bodily resurrection, without fear of hell. Take it from Hollywood and the movie producers, our personal psyche survives the crematory or grave. Feel better about this worldly licentiousness and greed, for a pleasant Karma awaits us in the long future—on the authority of Hollywood script writers who become our generation's Scripture rewriters. Death has lost its sting . . . for we are secretly eternal quite on our own, thus saith the local theater and video store.[36]

Against this culturally defined future, made in our own image, stands Paul's insistence that Christ alone determines the character and possession of the resurrection life to come, so that Christ alone is to be pleased in this life as well. Thus, in contrast to the modern denial of a personal future determined by a personal God, who himself took on flesh and blood, listen in conclusion to Fuller's portrayal, in Pauline terms, of what it means to please God:

It has often been observed that what people hope in for a happy future, that they worship; and what they worship, that they inevitably serve. Thus Jesus, when tempted by the Devil in the wilderness, fought back saying, "Away from me, Satan! For it is written, 'Worship the Lord your God, and serve him only'" (Matt. 4:10). We worship God when we bank our hope for an eternally happy future both on the prospect of always being able to share with him his joy and on his integrity to keep his great and priceless promises. In this way we render the greatest possible honor to him, as did Abraham, who "gave glory to God, being fully persuaded that God had power to do what he had promised" (Rom. 4:20–21). So when our hearts are full of joy as we *believe* God, we will not engage in any thinking or conduct that is inconsistent with our hope being in him. And then the worship of God will inevitably lead to serving him in the sense of *obeying his commandments as laws of faith*.

This obedience that stems from faith in God's promises is the way we serve God. . . .

In the commands and wise sayings of the Bible, we who have seen the wisdom of serving God rather than money find sketched out the profile to which our lives are to conform.[37]

---

36. Ibid., 4–5.
37. Fuller, *Unity of the Bible*, 150–52 (emphasis mine).

Finally, then, when all is said and done, the bottom line is that, in order to please God and to find the happiness for which we were created, we must live by faith. The life, death, and resurrection of Jesus Christ is the only basis on which God can forgive and reconcile us to himself and still remain righteous. Jesus is the only way of salvation for the entire human race. We cannot save ourselves in any way. Like David, the only thing we bring with us when we confess our sins is our sin. We seek forgiveness for our lives, not a paycheck (Rom. 4:4–5).

Coming to God with nothing but our sin, our faith is a trusting in God to work for us, not an attempt to show God how sincere we are. Such faith overturns our sin and makes us righteous in his sight, since it honors him as the One whose word can be trusted and whose presence is to be valued more than the rewards of this world. This is why when we trust in God because of what he has already done for us, our faith is credited to us as righteousness (Rom. 4:5, 22–23). It is this last point that brings us to the next section of Paul's argument, with its focus on our reconciliation and righteousness in Christ (cf. 5:16–6:2).

2 Corinthians 5:11–6:2

SINCE, THEN, we know what it is to fear the Lord, we try to persuade men. What we are is plain to God, and I hope it is also plain to your conscience. ¹²We are not trying to commend ourselves to you again, but are giving you an opportunity to take pride in us, so that you can answer those who take pride in what is seen rather than in what is in the heart. ¹³If we are out of our mind, it is for the sake of God; if we are in our right mind, it is for you. ¹⁴For Christ's love compels us, because we are convinced that one died for all, and therefore all died. ¹⁵And he died for all, that those who live should no longer live for themselves but for him who died for them and was raised again.

¹⁶So from now on we regard no one from a worldly point of view. Though we once regarded Christ in this way, we do so no longer. ¹⁷Therefore, if anyone is in Christ, he is a new creation; the old has gone, the new has come! ¹⁸All this is from God, who reconciled us to himself through Christ and gave us the ministry of reconciliation: ¹⁹that God was reconciling the world to himself in Christ, not counting men's sins against them. And he has committed to us the message of reconciliation. ²⁰We are therefore Christ's ambassadors, as though God were making his appeal through us. We implore you on Christ's behalf: Be reconciled to God. ²¹God made him who had no sin to be sin for us, so that in him we might become the righteousness of God.

⁶:¹As God's fellow workers we urge you not to receive God's grace in vain. ²For he says,

> "In the time of my favor I heard you,
>   and in the day of salvation I helped you."

I tell you, now is the time of God's favor, now is the day of salvation.

IN 5:6–10, PAUL drew the first conclusion that comes from knowing that his eternal home was secure with Christ, the sovereign judge of all humanity. From such knowledge comes his *own* courageous ambition to please the Lord through walking by faith (5:7a, 9). In 5:11–6:2, this same awareness leads to an equally courageous commitment to persuade *others* to join him in living in a way that pleases God (5:11a, 14–15, 21). In view of Paul's self-defense (5:11b–13) and his self-understanding as "Christ's ambassador" (5:18–6:2), this persuasion has as its goal the acceptance of the gospel *as it is proclaimed and embodied in Paul's ministry.*[1]

Thus, the reference to Paul's persuading others in 5:11–12 unpacks his earlier thesis-like statements in 2:17 and 4:2 that he speaks his message in Christ before the judgment of God (cf. 12:19). Knowing the fear of the Lord, the apostle remains true to the gospel himself and seeks to persuade others of the legitimacy of his apostolic ministry in order that they too may be saved. These two are inseparable. To reject Paul, "Christ's ambassador" (5:20), is to reject Christ (cf. 2:14–17; 4:1–6, 10–12, 13–15). Hence, although Paul continues to use the plural throughout this section, his primary focus remains his own ministry. He uses the plural to indicate that he is not speaking simply for himself, but in doing so represents the apostolic office (cf. 1:3–11). His goal is to make clear how the truths of the gospel apply to his own life and calling. As a result, in seeking to persuade others of the legitimacy of his own ministry in 5:11–6:2, Paul provides one of the most profound statements of the gospel found anywhere in the New Testament.

Paul's Motivation for Ministry (5:11–15)

THE "SINCE, THEN" (*oun*, "therefore") of 5:11 indicates that Paul's commitment to persuade others of the truth of the gospel is grounded in his confidence that one day Christ will judge all people (5:10). To know that Christ is the judge of all is to fear the Lord (= Christ) above all. Though it is often suggested that this "fear" (*phobos*) should be interpreted as "reverential awe" or "respect," this softening of Paul's statement misses the seriousness of the threat in view. Nothing less than real fear is involved, since in the context Paul is referring to a strong desire to avoid the negative consequences of Christ's judgment.

---

1. Though Paul never uses the verb "to persuade" (*peitho*) to refer directly to preaching the gospel, it is used in reference to Paul's evangelizing in Acts 17:4; 18:4; 19:8, 26; 26:28; 28:23. On this point, see Ralph P. Martin, *2 Corinthians*, 121: "Thus Paul's use of *peithomen* [in 5:11] has a double flavor; he tries to persuade men and women that Christ is the means of salvation, and he attempts to persuade them of his purity of motive." My point is that the latter is intimately bound up with the former.

This is the "bottom line" motivation of Paul's ministry. He does not seek to enhance his own reputation by using fancy rhetoric in his preaching or to use his ministry to line his pockets with other people's money. Rather, the apostle seeks to persuade others to join him in fearing the Lord so that they too will escape his wrath. Fear is the flipside of faith and the gracious gift of God to his people. Only those who know Christ fear losing such a relationship, and it is this fear (the negative motivation), together with the glory of God itself (the positive motivation; cf. 3:7–18; 4:13–18), that keeps the believer persevering in pleasing God.

As a result, Paul's reference to persuasion in 5:11 is most likely also a jab at his opponents' reliance on rhetoric to support their claims. The action of "persuading men" (peitho) was virtually synonymous with the Greco-Roman rhetorical tradition as a whole, since persuasion was "the quintessential expression of the goal of rhetoric."[2] Indeed, as Hubbard points out, "so important was persuasion to the Greeks that she was deified as a goddess, and worshipped."[3] Paul does not reject the need to persuade (5:11), but he does reject relying on the persuasive techniques of rhetoric to do so, since his own reputation is not on the line, but the eternal destiny of God's people (cf. 1 Cor. 2:1–5). It is not the power of human eloquence that persuades, but the presence of God's Spirit. Conversely, it is not the desire for recognition from others, but the fear of God that motivates Paul's persuasion.

Paul goes on to make it clear, however, that though the fear of God motivates him, the goal of his persuasion is not to justify himself before God. Given his call, the integrity of his life, and his ministry of suffering and the Spirit, the legitimacy of his ministry is already "plain to God" (5:11; cf. 1:12–2:4; 2:14–17; 3:3–6; 4:1–18). Nor is he justifying himself before the Corinthians. The legitimacy of his ministry should already be "plain to [their] conscience" through the evidence of their own lives (cf. 3:1–3).[4] This is Paul's "hope" in 5:11, which points not to a "wishful thinking" (the meaning of

---

2. For a summary of this point, see Moyer Hubbard, "Was Paul Out of His Mind? Rereading 2 Corinthians 5:13," JSNT 70 (1998): 39–64 (p. 52), and esp. the works of Kennedy, P. Marshall, Buxton, Betz, Winter, and Litfin cited on pp. 50–52.

3. Ibid., 50, following R. G. A. Buxton, Persuasion in Greek Tragedy: A Study of Peithō (Cambridge: Cambridge Univ. Press, 1982), 31–48.

4. In 5:11, the perfect tenses of the verb phaneroo, "to be manifest, revealed, made known," which the NIV translates twice as "is plain," indicate a continuing state of being as the consequence of a past action, with the emphasis here on the present state. This is the so-called "intensive perfect," in which "the perfect emphasizes the present state of being, the continuing result, the finished product, the fact that a thing is.... This use approaches the meaning of the present tense" (James A. Brooks and Carlton L. Winbery, Syntax of New Testament Greek [Lanham, Md.: Univ. Press of America, 1979], 104).

"hope" in contemporary American usage), but to his "confidence for the future" (the meaning of "hope" in the New Testament).

In other words, Paul's persuasion is not an attempt in itself to win back the Corinthians, for he is confident that the majority to whom he is now writing will continue to respond positively to his polemic (cf. 1:13–14; 6:1; 6:11–7:16). Instead, the references in 5:11 to his call to be an apostle and to his ministry of suffering and the Spirit as evidence of his legitimacy, all testified to by the existence of the Corinthians themselves as Christians (cf. 3:2–3), provide the foundation for the argument to come.

Based on the affirmation of 5:11 and grounded by the argument to follow in 5:13–15, verse 12 is therefore the main point of 5:11–15. Paul's assurance before God and his hope concerning the Corinthians lead once again to the inference that he is not engaging in self-commendation, just as it did in 3:1 on the basis of 2:14–17 and 3:2–3.[5] Now, however, Paul indicates the purpose of pointing to the concrete proof of his authenticity: He is defending himself in order that the Corinthians might have the "opportunity" they need to refute those within the church who are still calling his ministry into question (cf. 1:13–14).

The word translated "opportunity" (*aphorme*) in 5:12 is a military term used to designate a strategic base of operations employed as a launching pad for mounting an attack or defense (cf. its use in 11:12; Rom. 7:8; Gal. 5:13; 1 Tim. 5:14). Paul wants to provide such a base of support so that those Corinthians who have repented of their rebellion against Paul and his gospel will be able to "boast" (NIV, "take pride") in Paul's suffering and weakness as a counter-offensive against those who still "boast [NIV, take pride] in what is seen [*prosopon*]." This contrast in 5:12 between the two objects of boasting reflects the situation that still existed within the Corinthian church when this letter was written. It also alludes to the principle of divine judgment from 1 Samuel 16:7: "The LORD does not look at the things man looks at. Man looks at the outward appearance [LXX, *prosopon*], but the LORD looks at the heart [cf. 2 Cor. 5:12]."

The issue at stake, therefore, is not a personality contest, but a struggle for the lives of those who appear to be Christian outwardly, but whose hearts are far from the Lord. In the battle for the gospel that continued to be waged in Corinth, the issue remained whether the repentant could defend their faith in Paul's ministry against the attacks of those who "peddle the word of God" (2:17). Paul's concern here is to provide them with the ammunition needed to do so.

---

5. Cf. 10:12–18 for the difference between the negative practice of *self*-commendation and the positive practice of engaging in commending *oneself*.

Paul's opponents took pride in their professional rhetorical prowess, their letters of recommendation from other churches, the payment they received for their ministry, their ethnic and spiritual pedigree, and their ecstatic spiritual experiences. These are the external things that "are seen" (5:12); that is, they are on the surface (cf. 10:7). As in 3:2 and 4:2, here too Paul maintains that his opponents' focus on such externals mask the true nature of their motives, whereas his own actions reveal the genuine nature of his "heart."

Far from being a reference to that which is not seen, kept a secret, or subjective, Paul's reference to the "heart" in 5:12 again picks up the theme of the inextricable link between the character of one's actions and the quality of one's motives (cf. 1:12—14; 2:4; 3:2; 4:2). His willing commitment to do whatever it takes to win people to Christ (cf. 1 Cor. 9:19—23), even if this entails suffering as a result of preaching for free, is the objective evidence of his love (1 Cor. 4:8—13; 9:15—18; 2 Cor. 2:17; 4:7—15; cf. 6:3—10). This is what the Corinthians can boast about to demonstrate that Paul is the rightful representative of Christ (cf. 2 Cor. 5:20). The question, then, becomes who has the real basis for boasting before God and others, Paul or his opponents.

When it came to boasting, Paul's opponents called his ministry into question not only because of his practice of preaching for free, but also because of his suffering (cf. 1:8—11; 2:12—14; 4:7—13; 6:3—10; 10:7; 11:16—33). To make matters worse, Paul made only a cautious public use of the more flamboyant gifts like speaking in tongues (cf. 1 Cor. 14:18—19) and rejected outright the impressive techniques of contemporary public orators (cf. 1 Cor. 1:17; 2:1—5; 2 Cor. 10:10; 11:6), not to mention refusing even to refer to his own spiritual experiences (cf. 12:1—7). All of this combined to make Paul look weak in the eyes of those who claimed to be spiritually strong (cf. 10:10). From the perspective of his opponents, Paul not only suffered too much, but he also exhibited the Spirit too little to be a genuine apostle. From Paul's perspective, however, the purpose of spiritual gifts is the edification of others, not the display of one's own power (cf. 1 Cor. 14:1—12). Love for others, not knowledge for oneself, is the goal (cf. 13:1—3, 8—13).

That is why persuading others rather than parading his own spiritual experiences is the "heart" of Paul's ministry. It is the "fear of the Lord," not his own reputation, that drives him (5:11). Thus, when Paul is "out of his mind" (or "beside himself"), this is done privately before God, while being in his "right mind" is maintained for others (5:13).

The word translated "out of our mind" (*existemi*) in 5:13 is used negatively in Mark 3:21 to describe the reaction of Jesus' family to his apparently deranged zeal and seemingly outrageous messianic claims. But Paul's use of this verb in reference to God indicates a different sense here. Paul would hardly say that he is demented or abnormal toward God because of his zeal to persuade others concerning the need to please Christ. Nor should we assume that Paul's opponents accused him of being out of his mind, so that he must defend himself by saying that if he is acting in a crazy manner, as they allege, then it is only toward God. If anything, Paul's opponents and those Corinthians still on their side would prize such a posture of religious ecstasy as evidence of the Spirit's power.

Rather, the contrast in 5:13 picks up Paul's earlier statements in 1 Corinthians 14:2–8, where he reminded the Corinthians that speaking in tongues takes place not "to men ... but to God" (14:2) and is therefore "unfruitful" toward others (14:14), while prophecy "speaks to men for their strengthening" (14:3).[6] To be "out of our mind" is therefore best seen as a reference to Paul's own ecstatic experiences in private worship, most likely that of tongues (cf. 14:18, 23) and visions (cf. 12:1–4).[7] Paul's point is that his love for others (here the Corinthians) causes him to consider their needs for persuasion more important than even his own spiritual, private communion with God.

Private religious experiences such as speaking in tongues are certainly valid and can even profit the church if done in proper order (cf. 1 Cor. 14:15, 26–33). Yet Paul's desire to persuade others necessitates his giving top priority when ministering to being "in [his] right mind," since people, not God, are the focus of his ministry (cf. 4:1–2). "To be in one's right mind" (*sophroneo*) refers to the "moderation, good taste, and avoidance of excess" that was desired in serious oratory and exposition of history. This passionate but measured and sober style is what Paul practiced in his preaching.[8] Read in this way, Paul's emphasis in 5:13 on his commitment to a *public* ministry explains why he adduces only objective evidence to commend his ministry, which at the same time gives the Corinthians the "answer" they need to respond to his critics (5:12; note that the *gar* ["for"] of 5:13 is not translated in the NIV).

The basis and purpose for this radical reversal from self to others is given in 5:14–15 (see the "for" of v. 14a and the purpose clause in 5:15, "that those who live ..."). In short, Paul's life is now determined by the gospel as outlined

---

6. This explains why Paul prefers prophecy to speaking in tongues, esp. when the latter was uninterpreted. Craig Blomberg (*1 Corinthians*, 269) points out concerning 1 Cor. 14:3–4: "Unlike uninterpreted tongues, prophecy edifies the whole assembly, not just the individual speaker.... Paul thus isolates two reasons why prophecy is greater: people, not just God, are addressed, and they can be more positively affected."

7. For the meaning of this same verb as "to be amazed," which would relate to the kind of impression made by such ecstatic experiences, see Matt. 12:23; Mark 2:12; Luke 8:56; Acts 2:7, 12; 8:13; 9:21; 10:45; 12:16. For a survey of these two dominant views, i.e., abnormality versus ecstatic experience, see Hubbard, "Was Paul Out of His Mind?" 40–42. For more on this view, see Appendix at the end of this chapter (p. 265).

8. So Hubbard, ibid., 59, based on the lexical work of H. North, "The Concept of *Sophrosyne* in Greek Literary Criticism," *Classical Philology* 43 (1948): 317.

in these two verses. "Christ's love ... for all," which replicates itself in Paul's love for the Corinthians, "compels" Paul to live as he does (the NIV rightly takes the genitive in "love of Christ" as a subjective genitive, referring to Christ's love, not as an objective genitive, referring to our love for Christ). Paul's giving of his life to the Corinthians is the embodiment and corollary of the lordship of Christ, who expressed his own sovereignty and love by giving himself to his people. As Paul put it in 4:5: "For we do not preach ourselves, but Jesus Christ as Lord, and ourselves as your servants for Jesus' sake" (cf. Col. 1:24–29).

Specifically, Christ's love compels Paul for two reasons. (1) He is convinced that Christ's vicarious death (i.e., "one died for all") is the true definition of what it means to be "right-minded" about life. In view of the coming judgment, Christ, moved by his love, considered the needs of others for reconciliation more important than his own glory and position with the Father. As a result, he died "for all" in order to save them (5:14b). For the same reason, and compelled by Christ's love, Paul considers the needs of God's people more important than his own, so that he does whatever it takes to persuade them of his legitimacy as "Christ's ambassador" (cf. 5:20–6:2). The needs of the Corinthians determine Paul's actions (cf. 1 Cor. 4:6–21; 9:1–27; 2 Cor. 1:12–2:4; 2:13; 4:10; 6:3–10; 7:2–13; 11:1–12; 11:28; 12:14–21). In radical contrast to his earlier days of persecuting the church, Paul now willingly suffers for those whom he once persecuted, convinced that Christ has died not merely for the Jews, but for all people, both Jews and Gentiles.

(2) Christ's death "for all" brings about the "death" of "all" for whom he died (cf. the "therefore" of v. 14c). Together with Christ's death as a model for his own behavior, this accomplished fact concerning the consequences of Christ's death "compels" Paul in his ministry. The "all died" of 5:14 must therefore be limited to God's people, otherwise Christ's death would mean that all people are now a new creation in Christ, living for him rather than themselves (5:15–17). For Christ's love-motivated death for all is not merely an *example* of what his people should do, but also the very *means* by which his followers are impelled and enabled to do it. Nor is the death of all in 5:14c merely a potential to be actualized by all people, but the compelling cause that leads those for whom Christ has died to follow him in their lives. Thus, the striking feature of Paul's statement is that all those who died in 5:14 are then identified in 5:15 as those who now live, which is surely limited to those who actually participate in God's salvation in Christ (cf. 5:21–6:1).[9] Christ died for his people.

---

9. The interpretation of "all" in 5:14–15a has given rise to various views, all of which revolve around whether the statement is real (and hence limited to believers) or merely potential (and hence applied to all humanity). As expressed above, I take it to be "real" or

Defining the content of the "all," however, is not Paul's point. Though important for our understanding of the text, Paul no doubt assumes its meaning is clear. Rather, his turn of phrase in 5:15 calls attention to the fact that those who have died with Christ to their old way of life under the power of sin are raised to a new life in him under the power of the Spirit (cf. 3:7–18; also Rom. 6:1–23; 8:1–13; Col. 2:9–15). As the second Adam, Christ's death for those now "in Christ" overturns the consequences of Adam's sin for those who remain "in Adam" (cf. Rom. 5:16–19). Second Corinthians 5:14–15 is thus the counterpoint to Romans 5:12. In our context, this new life refers to being compelled by Christ's love to live for others rather than seeking spiritual experiences for oneself or pursuing the fame and fortune that comes from self-promotion. To love like Christ, because of Christ's love, is to consider the spiritual growth of others more important than one's own status or security. To live *for* Christ is to live *like* Christ. What transforms the believer, therefore, is that the Judge (5:10–11) is also the Savior (5:14–15).

This, then, is the gospel in a nutshell: (1) The basis of the gospel is Christ's love for his people (not his people's love for Christ or any other human characteristic, act, or distinctive); (2) as a result, Christ died for them (to atone for their sin and to free them from its power); (3) therefore, they too died (to their old way of life under the power of sin); (4) the consequence of Christ's death for them and their death in Christ is a new life lived out for others.

The Consequences of Paul's Ministry (5:16–6:2)

PAUL NOW DRAWS out the consequences of the gospel he has just outlined in 5:14–15, elucidates its content, and describes how it is conveyed. The first consequence of the gospel is that Paul no longer regards anyone "according to the flesh" (lit. trans. of 5:16a). Paul's concept of the "flesh" (*sarx*) is notoriously difficult to render into English.[10] Given its various meanings in

---

"effective." Christ's death effectively initiates the new age for all those who participate in it (5:14b: Christ died for all), and his death causes the death of all those who are found in him (5:14c: "all died"). This means that the "all" in both cases must be limited to all those who "receive God's grace" (6:1). The parallels between our text and Rom. 5:15–18 are instructive. There, "the gift that came by the grace of the one man, Jesus Christ," that "overflow[s] to the many" in Rom. 5:15 is qualified in 5:17 by "those who receive God's abundant provision of grace." Hence, the statement of 5:18, "the result of one act of righteousness was justification that brings life for all men," is contextually limited to "those many who receive God's . . . grace."

10. This difficulty derives from the fact that the word *sarx* has a wide field of meaning that encompasses the whole complex of what it means to be human. In Paul's own use it can have a variety of nuances: the neutral sense of living in this world as a person with human descent (cf. Rom. 1:3; 3:20; 9:3, 5, 8; Eph. 6:5; Col. 3:22, etc.); our corresponding physical nature and ways of life (cf. Rom. 2:28; 1 Cor. 6:16; 2 Cor. 4:11; 7:1, 5; Gal. 4:13–14;

different contexts, the NIV uses forty-eight different English words or phrases to translate this one word in the New Testament! In our passage, the NIV correctly translates the phrase here as "from a worldly point of view," that is, in accordance with the standards and values that derive from living as if physical life in this world is all that exists.

Moreover, the placement of this phrase in the Greek text indicates that it modifies the verbs, not the nouns. Though awkward in English, the text reads: "We know according to the flesh no one, even if we knew according to the flesh Christ"; not, "we know no one according to the flesh, even if we knew Christ according to the flesh." The point is the contrast between two perspectives, not two aspects of a person's life, such as Jesus' earthly, historical existence versus his eschatological, cosmic identity as the "Christ." To know someone "according to the flesh" is the opposite of knowing that person "according to the Spirit," which is the mark of the age of the new covenant (cf. 3:3, 6–18). Conversion entails a converted criteria for evaluating what is valuable and true. In Christ, Paul no longer evaluates others according to the world's standards or expectations (cf. Gal. 3:28), just as he no longer evaluates Christ in this way.

Paul's statement in 5:16a most likely refers back to the practice of his opponents, who continue to criticize Paul's ministry because of its lack of worldly status due to his suffering and apparent lack of spiritual power (cf. 10:1–6, 10). Paul understands this way of thinking, since he himself "once regarded Christ in this way" (i.e., "according to the flesh"). Apart from the resurrection, Jesus' death on the cross could only mean that he had been cursed by God for his own sin (cf. Deut. 21:23; Gal. 3:13). So prior to Paul's conversion, in which the glory of the resurrected Christ made it clear to Paul that Jesus had died not for his own sins but for the sins of his people (cf. 4:6; 5:14, 21), Paul disdained the cross as a radical contradiction to Jesus' messianic claims and as a rejection of Israel's nationalistic hopes.

In the same way, Paul's opponents disdain his suffering as "Christ's ambassador" because they evaluate it to be a mark of the old age that is relegated to the past for all those who, like themselves, are truly "in the Spirit." Evidently, this rejection of Paul's ministry was tied to their corresponding appraisal of Christ, an appraisal that could lead Paul to say that they preached another Jesus (11:4). Most likely, in light of the cross, they had spiritualized their nationalistic hopes for the military and political triumph to be brought

---

Eph. 2:11; 5:29; Phil. 1:22, 24; Col. 2:5); one's self or a person (1 Cor. 1:29; Col. 2:1); and the theologically loaded concept of life in the narrowly human sphere of existence apart from the power of the Spirit, i.e., the sinful nature (cf. Rom. 7:5, 18, 25; 8:3–12; 1 Cor. 5:5; Gal. 5:13, 16–19; Eph. 2:3; Col. 2:11, 13; etc.).

about by the Messiah into a spiritual victory over this world. Though Israel's nationalistic hopes had not yet been realized, they preached that Jesus had suffered as the Messiah so that his people would no longer need to suffer themselves.

Paul too preached that Jesus' suffering as the Messiah changed his people's lives: "If anyone is in Christ, he is a new creation" (5:17a). But for Paul this change does not lead to a super-spirituality in terms of spiritual experience, but to the consequences summarized in 5:17b. Rather than still belonging to this world and its ways, all those in Christ are a "new creation," which means that they have already participated in the passing away of the old age and the arrival of the new (lit., "new things"). The "new things" that have happened in Christ, however, are not private, spiritual experiences, but a new way of life that derives from the reorientation described in 5:15. Becoming a "new creation" does not refer to becoming a new kind of "super-spiritual" human being, but to becoming like Christ. The contours of the new creation are moral, not ecstatic.

Against the backdrop of 2:14–4:18, the "new creation" of a people who live for Christ by living for others is the beginning of the restoration of God's people under the new covenant. This means that reconciliation with God through Christ (5:18–21) is the beginning of the eschatological redemption of the world, the inbreaking into this evil age of the "new creation" to come (cf. Isa. 43:18–19; 65:16b–23; 66:22–23). Indeed, in Isaiah 43:1–21 and 65:17–25 Israel's restoration from exile is described with new creation language as part of the theme of Israel's "second exodus" that is developed throughout Isaiah 40–66. Beale has therefore argued persuasively that "it is plausible to suggest that 'reconciliation' in Christ is Paul's way of explaining that Isaiah's promises of 'restoration' from the alienation of exile have begun to be fulfilled by the atonement and forgiveness of sins in Christ."[11]

This point is made abundantly clear by Paul's allusion in v. 17b to Isa. 43:18f. (LXX): "Do not remember the former things, and do not discuss *the old things. Behold I make new things*" (cf. also Isa. 66:17), which is an

---

11. G. K. Beale, "The Old Testament Background of Reconciliation in 2 Cor 5–7 and Its Bearing on the Literary Problem of 2 Corinthians 6:14–7:1," *NTS* 35 (1989): 550–81 (p. 556). Beale argues that the second exodus/restoration perspective is the basis of Paul's argument in chs. 5–7, so that the restoration motif is the foundation of his understanding of the new creation *and* reconciliation (5:17). For confirmation of this perspective, see W. J. Webb, *Returning Home: New Covenant and Second Exodus as the Context for 2 Corinthians 6:14–7:1* (JSNTSup 85; Sheffield: Sheffield Academic, 1993). Webb too views the Old Testament traditions behind Paul's argument in 2 Cor. 2:14–7:4 "under the broader rubric of 'new covenant and second exodus/return theology.'"

exhortation for Israel to forget their past sin and judgment but to look to God's work of restoration/new creation.[12]

Paul too had experienced the reality of this new creation first-hand, having been forgiven by Christ on the road to Damascus. Hence, his equating being "in Christ" with participating in the "new creation" reflects his own experience of the fact that Christ's death (5:14) inaugurates the eschatological new creation in the midst of the old (cf. 1:20).[13] For Paul, the new covenant, made possible by Christ's death, is the inauguration of the new creation.

Against its Old Testament backdrop, Paul's affirmation that the new creation is being realized "in Christ" does not refer simply to a potential for the future. It also includes the life-transforming reality that has invaded this age, determining the lives of those who are now a part of it (5:14c–15; cf. Gal. 1:4). The new creation, like the kingdom of God, is already here, but not yet here in all its glory. Within the dawning of the new creation, the revelation of God's glory among a restored people results in a life of growing obedience by the power of the Spirit, in contrast to Israel's continuing hard-heartedness and the wickedness of the nations (cf. 2 Cor. 3:14–18; 4:3–4). As an outpost of the "new creation" in Christ under the new covenant, the Corinthians testify by their obedience and separation from evil that the Spirit is truly at work among them (cf. 1 Cor. 5:1–6:20; 2 Cor. 6:14–7:1).

By implication, one can legitimately argue that the personal transformation brought about by the Spirit in 3:18 is the evidence that one is part of the new creation spoken of in 5:17. Though the consummation of the new creation is still to come, the Spirit-wrought transformation pictured in 3:18 is the foundation of Paul's assertion here that the death and resurrection of Christ have already inaugurated the eschatological "new creation." Hence, whatever the "new things" are in 5:17, they must certainly include a new life of growing obedience to God brought about by the Spirit. As the "second Adam" reflecting the image of God, Christ brings his followers back to the glory associated with Adam before his fall into disobedience. Thus, for Paul, the real evidence of the glory of the new creation is not spiritual ecstasy (5:13), but moral transformation (5:17; cf. Eph. 2:10).

---

12. Seyoon Kim, "2 Cor. 5:11–21 and the Origin of Paul's Concept of 'Reconciliation,'" *NovT* 39 (1997): 360–84 (p. 380), based on Beale's work (emphasis Kim's).

13. The key Old Testament texts concerning the eschatological "new creation" are Isa. 43:16–21; 65:16b–23 and 66:22–23. For the later postbiblical development of the expectation of a new creation, see esp. 1QH 5:1, 11–12; 7:13–17a; 11:19–23b; 19:9–14; 1QS 4:23b–26; 11QTemple 29:7b–10; *1 Enoch* 72:1; 91:15f.; *Jub.* 1:29; 4:26; *Lib. Ant.* 3:10; 16:3; 32:17; *4 Ezra* 7:75; *2 Bar.* 32:6; 44:12; 57:2.

The magnitude of what Paul has just said leads him to declare in 5:18a that the origin of all this can be none other than God himself. Only God's creative power can explain the re-creation of people who once lived according to the human sinful nature into people who live for Christ (5:15–17; cf. 4:4–6). The means of this re-creation is the redemption of God's people that comes about through their reconciliation to God through Christ (5:18b). This too comes from God. God is both the subject and indirect object of 5:18–19a: *God* reconciles the world *to himself*. Reconciliation is God's initiative and God's work, while the direction of reconciliation is also Godward. God is not reconciled with us, as if we were the point of reference and God were the transgressor (!); we are reconciled with God.

The means of this reconciliation is Christ, the One whose death makes it possible (cf. "through Christ" in 5:18 = "in Christ" in 5:19). But God uses the ministry of others to implement reconciliation in the world. For this reason, the direct object of God's reconciliation is first Paul ("us" in 5:18), then the "world" (5:19), the latter most likely being a reference to the fact that God's reconciliation includes Gentiles as well as Jews (cf. Rom. 11:12, 15; Eph. 2:16).

Once again, God is the source of reconciliation, while Paul is his instrument in bringing it to fruition. God's work of reconciling the world to himself *precedes* Paul's own reconciliation with God, just as Paul's being granted the ministry and message of reconciliation *precedes* his consequent call to others to be reconciled with God (5:18–20). It is crucial to see that the command of verse 20 is based on the prior, finished realities of verses 18–19 and 21. This view finds support in the fact that Paul's understanding of salvation as reconciliation most likely derives from his own conversion-call experience on the road to Damascus. In revealing to Paul his glory in Christ (cf. 4:4–6), God reconciled the rebellious Paul to himself and gave him a ministry of reconciliation among the Gentiles (cf. 2:14; 5:16, 18–19 with Gal. 1:12–16).[14]

It quickly becomes clear, therefore, that the center of Paul's formulation of the gospel in 5:18–19 is the concept of reconciliation. The use of this metaphor to express the significance of God's saving activity is unique to Paul.[15] Some have argued that his use of the term *reconciliation* (noun: *katallage*; verb: *katallasso*) in 5:18–21 derives directly from its secular use during that

---

14. For the development of this thesis, see Kim, "2 Cor. 5:11–21," 368–71. As Kim points out (368), the first person plurals ("we/us") in this passage, except for the general statement in v. 21, refer to Paul in his apostolic office.

15. For the specific texts, see Rom 5:10, 11; 11:15; 2 Cor. 5:18, 19, 20; Eph. 2:16; Col. 1:20, 22.

period as a diplomatic and political term referring to the harmony established between enemies by peace treaties.[16] In this view, Paul adopts this Greco-Roman backdrop as the ideal counterpart to his self-understanding as "Christ's ambassador" (verb: *presbeuo*; noun: *presbys*). As such, Paul is sent to announce that God has established a "peace treaty" with his enemies by declaring a general amnesty concerning sin (i.e., Paul's "ministry/message of reconciliation," 5:18b, 19b). Paul effects this divine peace and reconciliation as one through whom God makes his appeal (5:20).

Hence, to clarify his calling, Paul uses a secular, diplomatic word ("reconciliation") and function ("ambassador") to explain the significance of his ministry, which is an extension of his own reconciliation as a former enemy of God (5:18). What makes this reconciliation possible is Christ's death as a substitution for sin, inasmuch as the righteous Christ is made to be a sinner and dies for God's people in accordance with Isaiah 52:13–53:12 (cf. 2 Cor. 5:21). Advocates of this view argue, moreover, that there is no explicit reference to the sacrificial system in Isaiah 52:13–53:12, nor is Christ pictured in 2 Corinthians 5:21 as an atonement for sin. Hence, "reconciliation" in 5:18–21 must have a thoroughgoing political backdrop, which Paul *himself* brings together with the noncultic but Old Testament understanding of Jesus' death as substitutionary.

Though such a reading is not impossible, others have more persuasively argued that the background to Paul's self-understanding in this passage is not derived primarily from the diplomatic language of his day. Rather, it comes from the prophetic perspective of Isaiah itself, from the Old Testament and Jewish understanding of atoning sacrifice, and from the contrast between Paul's ministry and the ministry of Moses.[17]

Concerning this last point, Thrall sees in Paul's description of his being entrusted with the apostolic message ("word") of reconciliation in 5:19 a contrasting allusion to Psalm 105:26–28, where Moses and Aaron are commissioned to take the "words" of the signs of God's judgment to Pharaoh.[18]

---

16. For an extensive representation of this thesis, see Cilliers Breytenbach, *Versöhnung: Eine Studie zur paulinischen Soteriologie* (WMANT 60; Neukirchen-Vluyn: Neukirchener Verlag, 1989).

17. For a synopsis of the two views, the relevant supporting literature, and a critique of Breytenbach's position, see Peter Stuhlmacher, "Cilliers Breytenbachs Sicht von Sühne und Versöhnung," *Jahrbuch für Biblische Theologie* 6 (1991): 339–54. The adaptation of "reconciliation" language in a Hellenistic Jewish context, which Breytenbach did not take seriously enough, is seen in the use of the reconciliation terminology (*katallage*) to describe God's being reconciled to his people in 2 Macc. 1:5; 5:20; 7:32–33; 8:29; Philo, *Life of Moses* 2.166; *JosAs* 11:18; Josephus, *War* 5.415; *Ant.* 7.153, as pointed out by I. H. Marshall, quoted by Kim, "2 Cor. 5:11–21," 361.

18. Margaret E. Thrall, *The Second Epistle to the Corinthians*, 436, following the work of Bachmann and M. Wolter.

In 2 Corinthians 5:19, as in 3:7–11, Paul is contrasting his ministry of righteousness, with its message of reconciliation, with Moses' ministry of judgment. Paul's self-understanding as one who acts as an "ambassador" for Christ thus alludes back to the contrast between the ministries of Paul and Moses in 2:16–3:13. This is confirmed by the fact that Josephus and Philo also use the language of "reconciler" and "ambassador" to describe Moses (cf. Josephus, *Ant.* 3.315; Philo, *Life of Moses* 2.166; *Questions on Exodus* 2.49; *Who Is the Heir?* 205).[19]

Even more important, just as Paul's understanding of Jesus' death is significantly informed in this passage by Isaiah 52:13–53:12, so too Paul's portrayal of his own role as an apostle in 5:20 derives essentially from this same context. Paul speaks not merely as a political "diplomat," but as a prophet. As such, he brings the good news of the peace that God has established in accordance with the dawning of the reign of God announced in Isaiah 52:6–10 (cf. the parallel reference to "peace" in Isa. 53:5, Paul's use of 52:7 in Rom. 10:15, and his direct quote from the parallel passage, Isa. 49:8, in 2 Cor. 6:2). The king has come to establish God's kingdom, but he has done so as the suffering servant who gives up his life for his people. In response, Paul implores his people on Christ's behalf to be reconciled to God, knowing that God is making an appeal through his prophetic ministry.

But the suffering servant of Isaiah 53 is not enough to explain the need for or peace-creating efficacy of Jesus' death as Israel's king. In addition to a "political" backdrop, the Old Testament and Jewish understanding of atonement with God by means of a substitutionary sacrifice is the essential background for understanding *both* "reconciliation" in 5:18–20 *and* Christ's being made "to be sin" in 5:21. This backdrop is brought into view through Paul's reference to Christ's being "made . . . sin" in 5:21. Like its parallel designation "concerning sin" in Romans 8:3 (cf. Isa. 53:10), this description reflects the LXX rendering of being made a "sacrifice for sin" or "sin offering" in Leviticus 4:13–14, 20–21, 24; 5:6–7, 10–12; 6:18; 9:7; 14:19; 16:15. Accordingly, this portrayal of Christ's death as a sacrifice for sin indicates that the death/blood of Christ is the means by which God fulfills the need for atonement prefigured in the sacrifices of the Sinai covenant (cf. Rom. 3:25–26; 4:25; 5:8; 8:3; 1 Cor. 6:11; 11:23–26; 15:3–5; Col. 1:19–20 against the backdrop of Lev. 10:17; 16; 17:11).

The explicit link between the Old Testament sacrificial system and the death of Christ is found in the fact that Jesus, as the suffering servant of

---

19. For these and other parallel references to the role of angels and even the high priest as "ambassadors," see Stuhlmacher, "Sühne," 346. My understanding of Paul as prophet and of 5:21 (see below) follows Stuhlmacher's work.

Isaiah 52:13–53:12, bears the sins of God's people as their ransom (cf. Mark 8:36–37; 10:45; 14:24 against the backdrop of Isa. 43:1–4; 53:4–8, 10–12). Paul's reference to Christ as the One who "had no sin" (lit., "did not know sin"), whom God nevertheless "made ... to be sin," thus recalls the death of the "righteous servant" who did not sin in Isaiah 53:9, 11. So, without a doubt, "it is to be inferred that the efficacy of his death arises from the sinlessness of his life."[20] In his sacrificial death as the sinless Son of God, Jesus pays the penalty for our sin.

Moreover, it is this same Old Testament concept of atonement that makes clear the relationship between Christ's death (5:21) and our being reconciled to God (5:18–20). Only when Christ's death as the sinless one is seen as an atoning sacrifice for our sin does it become clear why God is able not to count his people's sins against them without compromising his own integrity and justice (cf. Rom. 3:21–26). As a result of Christ's death, not only does Christ take on our sin, we take on his righteousness. When God sees us in Christ, he sees the perfection of Christ having already been granted to us as a gift—even though our being made perfect in Christ is still to come at the consummation of the age, when we will see Christ face to face (cf. 3:18).

The process of our being transformed into the glory of God's character in this life (5:15) is simply the working out of God's glory in Christ that has already been given to us through the Spirit (cf. 4:4; Gal. 5:5–6; Titus 3:3–8). In short, Christ's atoning death (2 Cor. 5:21) effects a new creation (5:17) by making it possible for God to "not count men's sins against them" (5:19b; cf. the allusion to Ps. 32:1–2), which in turn makes it possible for his Spirit to live in their midst without destroying them (2 Cor. 3:7–18). The consequence is the "peace" with God spoken of in Isaiah 53:5, which is the conceptual equivalent of the "reconciliation" referred to in 5:19.

Paul's argument in 5:18–20 has made it clear that to be reconciled to God entails aligning oneself with Paul and his message. The Corinthians cannot claim to have received God's grace while at the same time rejecting Paul's ministry, since Paul is the one through whom God is making his appeal (5:20). As a result, Paul is concerned in 6:1 that those Corinthians who are still siding with his opponents, with their "other" Jesus, "different spirit," and "different gospel" (11:4), may have accepted God's grace "in vain." He therefore urges them "not to receive God's grace in vain" by returning to Paul's gospel. Only perseverance "with ever-increasing glory" constitutes evidence that the Spirit has really transformed one's heart (3:18). Only those who continue to live for Christ as the One who died and was raised for them

---

20. Paul Barnett, *The Second Epistle to the Corinthians*, 314.

(5:15) can be confident before the judgment of Christ (5:10). Those who begin by trusting Christ, but then fall away to another message show that their initial reception of God's grace, though it may have appeared genuine at the time, was not real.

As one of "God's fellow workers," through whose urging God himself is making his appeal to the Corinthians (5:20; 6:1), Paul himself is a divinely appointed means to overcome this danger of falling away. Thus, in 6:2 Paul identifies his own apostolic proclamation of the gospel to the church with the role of Isaiah toward Israel in Isaiah 49:8. Paul, like Isaiah, is announcing God's final deliverance and warning of the consequences of turning from it. But unlike Isaiah, for whom God's deliverance was still to come, Paul announces that it has arrived. This use of Scripture in 2 Corinthians 6:2, together with its declaration of fulfillment, is one of the strongest assertions of Paul's strategic role within the history of redemption. Paul, like Isaiah, speaks for God, and God speaks through Paul. Indeed, the reference to God's "making his appeal" (*parakaleo*) through Paul in 5:20 may recall this same verb in Isaiah 40:1 LXX (*parakaleite*, "comfort").

Furthermore, in the original context of Isaiah 49:8, the prophet is addressing Israel, who, in exile, is herself the suffering servant of Yahweh, "in whom I will display my splendor" (Isa. 49:3). For "in the time of [God's] favor" (i.e., on the future day of her salvation), Israel will become "a covenant for the people" (i.e., the means by which God will bring about his eschatological salvation among the Gentiles; see Isa. 49:8; cf. 42:6–7).

It is equally striking, therefore, that here Paul pictures the Corinthians, as the people of the new covenant/new creation, to be a fulfillment of Isaiah's expectation. As part of the history of redemption framework established in 3:6–18, the people of the new covenant, here portrayed as part of the people of God restored after the exile, are now experiencing, *in response to Paul's gospel*, the very "day of salvation" promised in Isaiah 49:8. As such, they too, as an extension of Paul's ministry, are becoming the means by which this salvation is being brought about in the world (cf. 2 Cor. 10:15–16).

Hence, to reject Paul and his message is be to cast outside the sphere of God's saving work, since Paul is now working together with God as an instrument of his eschatological salvation, here summarized as "the grace of God" (5:20; 6:1; cf. 2:15–16; 3:14–15). For this reason, because of both the fear of God (5:11) and the love of Christ (5:14), Paul "implores" (5:20) and "urges" (6:1) the Corinthians to respond to his message (cf. 10:1–2).

Finally, the drastic possibility and urgent appeal in 6:1, with its scriptural foundation in Isaiah 49:8, is grounded in 6:2b by Paul's repetition of the solemn expression "I tell you [lit., behold], now," which recalls 5:16–17, thereby emphasizing his conclusion that the day of salvation that was promised to Isaiah has indeed arrived.[21] In other words, to go back on Paul's message is to be led astray from the truth in the same way that Eve was deceived in the garden (11:3; cf. 4:4). If Paul's gospel is the inauguration of the new creation, then to doubt its truth can be pictured in terms of the Fall after the first creation. Conversely, as a "new creation" in Christ, the Corinthians must testify by their separation from evil that the consequences of the Fall are being reversed in their lives (cf. 6:14–7:1).

IN ORDER TO come to grips with this text in our day, we must recover the heart of the gospel that so motivated Paul. The fear of God that moved him to persuade others was matched by Christ's own love as that which compelled Paul to consider other's needs for the gospel more important than his own comfort (5:11–15). In 5:18b–21, Paul thus details the two means by which God brings about the new creation in Christ. (1) God reconciled Paul to himself through Christ (cf. 4:4–6), for Christ's death made it possible for God not to "count men's sins against them" (5:18b, 19b, 21). (2) God gave to Paul as an apostle "the ministry of reconciliation" (5:18b), which took place through his preaching the "message of reconciliation" (5:19b), both of which are based on God's prior act of reconciliation in Christ (5:19a). The former is the basis of reconciliation, the latter its agency.

As "Christ's ambassador" (5:20) and "God's fellow worker" (6:1), Paul's own life and ministry as an apostle embody and proclaim the "new creation" of the "new covenant," already inaugurated in Christ (5:18b, 19b). This is what gives him his mandate in 5:20–6:2 (cf. "therefore," 5:20a). Furthermore, as at the first exodus, the center of the "new creation" as a "second exodus" redemption of the world is the manifestation of the glory of God in the midst of his people. The long-awaited restoration of his people is now beginning to take place in and through the church (6:2). As the continuation of the remnant from throughout Israel's history, those Jews and Gentiles who

---

21. See Victor Paul Furnish, *II Corinthians*, 315, who points out that the expression "Behold!" (*idou*) occurs frequently in the LXX to introduce solemn pronouncements, esp. where divine promises are given, and in apocalyptic traditions, where it often introduces visions and eschatological announcements concerning the "end." As an example, he points to the same "new creation" affirmation in Rev. 21:5 against the backdrop of Isa. 42:9; 43:19; 65:17–18. Furnish (312) also points out that Paul's use of "now" (*nun*) points back to 2 Cor. 5:16, which recalls Isa. 48:6 ("the from now on . . . new things"), and is used by Paul in 2 Cor. 6:2 and in Rom. 3:21; 5:9, 11; 8:1; 11:30; 13:11; Gal. 2:20; 4:9 to refer to the time of faith and salvation.

have been reconciled with God through Christ (5:18) now encounter God's glory in Christ (cf. 3:7–18 with 4:4–6 with 5:18–19a).

This is why in 5:21b Paul can summarize the outcome of Christ's atoning death in terms of the "righteousness of God." As pointed out in relationship to 3:9, God's righteousness is his just character as demonstrated in the consistency of his actions toward his creation in accordance with his covenant promises. Specifically, those actions derive from his unswerving commitment to glorify himself by maintaining his moral standards in judgment, revealing his sovereignty in election, and showing his grace through meeting the needs of his people. God's righteousness thus includes his acts to redeem and transform his people in the midst of this evil age and culminates in the judgment of the wicked and the restoration of the righteous in the age to come (cf. 3:9, 18; 5:10, 17).

Given the sinfulness of the very people God seeks to redeem, his righteousness is revealed most dramatically in his sending his Son to be a sinless sacrifice for the sins of this people (5:21). The cross of Christ thus meets the ultimate need of God's people, that is, their need for mercy from a righteous God. On the cross, Christ takes on their sin; because of the cross, they take on God's righteousness.

The "righteousness of God" is thus both a legal quality describing his just character and a dynamic concept describing his way of acting in the world. To take on God's righteousness *in Christ* (5:21) is therefore to be declared legally righteous, in accordance with his righteous standards, because of Christ's sacrificial death on our behalf. But it is also to enjoy the new way of life as a "new creation" that Christ's death for us makes possible, on the basis of which we will be declared righteous in the judgment yet to come (5:10, 15).

These two aspects of God's righteousness are organically related. God acts righteously because he is righteous. We act righteously because God has made us righteous. As such, his righteousness is expressed in his reconciling work on the basis of Christ's death on the cross. But that righteousness is equally seen in his commitment to transform his reconciled people into his own image as seen in the "face of Christ" (i.e., by their sanctification; 3:18; 4:4, 6). Reconciliation with God enables his people to encounter his glory without being destroyed, thereby being transformed into that same glory (3:7–18; 8:9).

The character of the ministry. In reflecting on the implications of this passage in our day of privatization and age of subjectivity, we must remember that its focus is not on the validity of personal experience but on the evaluation of the apostolic ministry. Though much of Paul's perspective in this passage is common to all believers, he is representing Christian experience through the prism of his own apostolic calling. The main point of 5:11–14 in this regard is that private, spiritual experiences (even tongues and visions) do not count as a basis for ministry or constitute a criterion for its evaluation. Paul's opponents legitimized their ministries and demands for financial support by appealing to just such experiences. Paul, however, appealed to his devotion to do whatever it took to win people to Christ, even refusing their money in spite of the poverty and humiliation this entailed, since the reality of God's judgment and Christ's love, not his own comfort and reputation, ruled his life.

Paul's perspective still holds today. As Barnett put it,

> The evaluation of ministry is to be sought in the public realm, not the private. If in private [Paul] is "beside himself," this is "for God" and does not bear on his legitimacy as an apostolic minister. . . . He will make no "horizontal" or public appeal to legitimacy as a minister based on "vertical" ecstatic behavior.[22]

As a consequence, Barnett concludes that

> important and abiding principles are to be discerned in these verses. On the one hand, freedom is to be allowed to the minister or the believer to be ecstatic or nonecstatic; it is a matter of divine gift. On the other hand, in regard to the recognition of genuineness *in ministers*, the practice of ecstatic speech or behavior in itself has no bearing. Fundamental to the discernment of the authentic minister, however, is the minister's commitment to persuading people to "turn to the Lord," to "be reconciled to God." If the example of Paul is to be regarded as a yardstick, it should be noted that his life is centered on God and on others, but not on himself.[23]

The character of the gospel. If this passage is about the ministry, the focus of the ministry is the gospel of Christ's death on our behalf. In our day of "decisionism" and age of "easy-believism," it is essential that we recover our confidence in the power of the cross as the foundation of the Christian ministry and message. The contours of the gospel (cf. 5:14–15, 19, 21) make it clear that the atoning death of Christ is not only a legal act in regard to God's holiness (cf. Rom. 3:21–26), but also an eschatological act by which God breaks the rule of sin over the lives of his people. Reconciled people live reconciled lives. The death of Christ brings about already here and now God's promised "new creation."

The "therefore" of 5:14c reflects Paul's conviction that the consequences of Christ's death are not a potential that we actualize by our faith, but a real-

---

22. Paul Barnett, *The Second Epistle to the Corinthians*, 278–79, 285.
23. Ibid., 285–86, emphasis mine.

ity that God brings about in the lives of his people. Paul's point is not that Christ really died for all, therefore all *potentially* die. Paul assumes that the consequences of Christ's death are personal, powerful, and effective, not general, possible, and contingent.[24] The power of the cross is good news. The death of Christ accomplishes what it was intended to do. "Christ is a Redeemer who really does redeem."[25] As a result of his death on their behalf, all those in Christ *are* a new creation!

In proclaiming the gospel it is also important to stress, with Paul, that God's finished act of reconciliation in Christ precedes our response (cf. Rom. 5:6–11; Gal. 3:25). Paul's statement in 2 Corinthians 5:20 is a command based on the reconciliation that Christ has already accomplished for those who respond, not an "offer" that we actualize by our acceptance of it. God's people respond to God's offer of reconciliation already made real by Christ's death; they do not make it real by their own decision to have faith. The call to be reconciled is the very instrument God uses to bring about reconciliation in the lives of those who respond to it. In this text, as in so many others, God's initiative and sovereignty and our responsibility come together (cf. Phil. 2:12–13). This is no antiquated, abstract discussion between Calvinists and Arminians; rather, the very gospel itself is at stake. As J. I. Packer again puts it:

> What matters is that we should understand the gospel biblically.... And we can now see what has gone wrong. Our theological currency has been debased. Our minds have been conditioned to think of the Cross as a redemption which does less than redeem, and of Christ as a Saviour who does less than save, and of God's love as a weak affection

---

24. This understanding of the atoning death of Christ as effective and "limited" to God's people has a long history in the church. For a study of this emphasis from Augustine to Calvin, see Jonathan H. Rainbow, *The Will of God and the Cross: An Historical and Theological Study of John Calvin's Doctrine of Limited Redemption* (Princeton Theological Monograph Series 22; Allison Park, Pa.: Pickwick, 1990). Rainbow's central thesis is that "Calvin the predestinarian theologian inherited a thousand-year tradition that taught limited redemption" (p. 8). If in this text the consequences of Jesus' death are not "limited" to God's people, the only consistent conclusion would be to argue for a universal salvation, something Paul never does.

25. J. I. Packer, "Introductory Essay" to John Owen, *The Death of Death in the Death of Christ* (Edinburgh: Banner of Truth Trust, 1967, reprint of 1852), 1–25 (p. 5). Packer's essay is a classic presentation of the central importance of affirming the biblical doctrine that Christ died for God's people in particular, and not for the world in some general, potential sense. Owen's work is an extensive development of this affirmation. Packer argues that the doctrine of a universal atonement (i.e., that Christ died for all people) is unscriptural and a denial of the gospel, since it denies the power of the cross, "reduces God's love to an impotent wish and turns the whole economy of 'saving' grace ... into a monumental failure ... so far from magnifying the merit and worth of Christ's death, it cheapens it, for it makes Christ die in vain" (p. 12).

---

which cannot keep anyone from hell without help, and of faith as the human help which God needs for this purpose. As a result, we are no longer free either to believe the biblical gospel or to preach it. . . . Instead, we involve ourselves in a bewildering kind of double-think about salvation, telling ourselves one moment that it all depends on God and next moment that it all depends on us. . . .

We want to magnify the saving grace of God and the saving power of Christ. So we declare that God's redeeming love extends to every man, and that Christ has died to save every man, and we proclaim that the glory of divine mercy is to be measured by these facts. And then, in order to avoid universalism, we have to depreciate all that we were previously extolling, and to explain that, after all, nothing that God and Christ have done can save us unless we add something to it; the decisive factor which actually saves us is our own believing. What we say comes to this—that Christ saves us with our help; and what that means, when one thinks about it, is this—that we save ourselves with Christ's help. This is a hollow anticlimax.[26]

The conclusion to be drawn is clear. In transferring Paul's gospel to our present day we too must emphasize the powerful, effective, life-changing nature of Christ's death. Not to do so perverts the cross into merely a possibility created by an important event from ancient history. We must be careful not to reduce Christ's death to a transaction between God and Jesus in heaven that is intended to help people if they will only cooperate. To be reconciled to God in Christ is an act of sovereign restoration and creative power that is as magnificent and miraculous as the creation of the world (cf. 4:4–6 with 5:17).

For Paul, reconciliation is an expression of God's "new creation" by which he transforms his people's motivations and hence their way of life (cf. 5:14–16). The goal of this life-transforming reconciliation with God is to usher God's people into the new creation when it dawns in all its glory on the great and terrible "day of the Lord." Hence, Paul's awareness of the coming judgment frames this passage as its theological foundation (cf. 5:11 with 6:2). He knows that only those who are "righteous" will inherit the kingdom of God, and he is gripped by the good news that God himself has opened the way for those in Christ "to become the righteousness of God" in him (5:21).

In other words, we must recover the dynamic nature of the righteousness of God. God's righteousness is revealed not only by his considering his sinful people already righteous in Christ, but also by delivering them from this

---

26. Ibid., 13–14. Packer's essay may now be found in his *A Quest for Godliness: The Puritan Vision of the Christian Life* (Wheaton: Crossway, 1990), 125–48.

evil age and conforming them to his righteousness in anticipation of the judgment and deliverance yet to come. The righteous provision of God in Christ is both his mercy and his power. The ultimate purpose of the cross and resurrection is the pouring out of the Spirit. In this passage the cluster of consequences that result from the reconciliation brought about by Christ mutually interpret one another. Hence, not living for oneself (vv. 14–15a, 18–19) is what it means to be a new creation (v. 17), which is at the heart of what it means to become the righteousness of God (v. 21).

In our day of Christian nominalism, we must make clear the active sense of what it means to be a new creation, living under the power of the righteousness of God. This same point was emphasized by Adolf Schlatter (1852–1938), one of the most important New Testament scholars of the twentieth century, whose work, unfortunately, has been ignored far too long. Schlatter's important insights have recently been summarized and extended by Robert Yarbrough:

> As a New Testament scholar and incisive analyst of intellectual history, Schlatter argued that the Protestant Reformation had not gone far enough. It correctly repudiated the merit theology of medieval Roman Catholicism. But it failed to move far enough in the positive direction of full-orbed love for God, a love that expressed itself in joyful, and where necessary costly, obedience....
>
> Schlatter claims that the Reformers' understanding of [the righteousness of God as revealed in the gospel according to Rom. 1:17] was controlled by the burning question, Since we are hopelessly lost sinners and need righteousness, what kind of righteousness does the gospel give? Their answer: an imputed one, one that will grant to sinners the mercy that nothing else can.
>
> This answer is not wrong, Schlatter emphasizes. But it does not go far enough. "The righteousness of God" cannot be reduced to "the mercy of God." Two things result if this reduction takes place.
>
> First, the sinner's need defines the gospel's saving ministry. But this is to return to the very man-centered orientation that the Reformers were trying to break away from ... this formulation does not begin to do justice to Paul's celebrated expression "the righteousness of God." Schlatter points out: "For Paul God's work arises from God's work," not from human necessity or with human welfare exclusively in view. The gospel ushers in the powerful *positive* presence of God's kingdom-building activity, by his own hand and through his gospel-activated people, not merely the treasured but *limited* effect of conferring mercy on needy souls.
>
> Second, the stress on man's need and what the gospel provided to meet that need had a tragic practical outcome.... Head knowledge,

mere doctrinal assent, substituted for gospel reception and life trans-formation.... The living, active, transformative force of God's inbreak-ing kingdom, "the righteousness of God," was short-circuited, its power greatly reduced....

The problem is that they have contented themselves with a weak doctrine of faith, a pale facsimile of Paul's robust "righteousness of God" unleashed in believers' lives.... And if the word that proclaims righteousness is believed, that which arises is love and action.... Where that action is lacking, there is good reason to suppose the heart still languishes in unbelief. There may be assent, there may be emo-tional affirmation, there may be selective obedience to gospel imper-atives. There may even be impressive displays of religious activity.... But when Jesus called for taking up the cross and following him, he probably had something more radical in mind than motoring to an air-conditioned sanctuary, amen-ing the show, and returning to the real life of Sunday TV and family fun (after sumptuous repast at the crowded new restaurant that everyone is dying to try).... God's right-eousness is comprehensive, all-embracing, life-transforming.[27]

The character of reconciliation. If this passage is about the ministry and if the focus of the ministry is the gospel of Christ's death on our behalf, then the focus of the gospel is reconciliation with God. In our day of self-help and age of technology and technique, it is important to keep in mind that God is both the initiator and object of this reconciliation. Our propensity is to view the gospel as our opportunity to reconcile God to us by showing him how much we love him, rather than seeing it as God's act in Christ by which he reconciles us to himself by demonstrating his own love for us. The gospel is not our chance to get right with God, but God's declaration that he has already made us right with him. The gospel does not call us to do something for God that he might save us; it announces what God has done to save us that we might trust him. As Seyoon Kim has summarized Paul's statements on reconciliation,

> Paul uses the terminology never to imply that God is reconciled (or God reconciles himself) to human beings, but always to suggest that God reconciles human beings to himself or human beings are recon-ciled to God.... This distinctive usage of the terminology seems to sug-

---

27. Robert W. Yarbrough, "Biblical Authority and the Ethics Gap: The Call to Faith in James and Schlatter," *Presbyterion* 22 (1996): 67–75 (pp. 72–74). Yarbrough's summary and quotes are drawn from Schlatter's *Romans: The Righteousness of God*, trans. Siegfried S. Schatz-mann (Peabody, Mass.: Hendrickson, 1995), 22–23.

gest that Paul deliberately makes a fundamental correction of the Hellenistic Jewish conception of reconciliation between God and human beings: it is not God who needs to be reconciled to human beings, but it is human beings who need to be reconciled to God; and it is not repentance, prayers or other good works on the part of human beings that bring about reconciliation between God and human beings, but it is by his grace that God reconciles human beings to himself.[28]

Moreover, we saw in 2:5–11 that reconciliation with God entails reconciliation with those who have wronged us. In chapters 8–9 it will become clear that reconciliation with God expresses itself in a concrete commitment to meet the material needs of others. In the context of 5:11–6:2, dying with Christ leads inextricably to living for others as an expression of living for Christ. The principle in 5:14–15 is therefore applicable to a wide range of goals and activities, not just ecstatic experiences (cf. 11:7–12; 12:14–18; Phil. 2:1–3).

In the same way, Paul's understanding of his own apostolic ministry as an essential means by which the world is reconciled to God directly applies to all who are called to the ministries of preaching, teaching, and evangelism. It also applies in principle to *all* believers whenever they are in a situation in which they are able to testify to what God has done in Christ. God's people are the necessary instruments through which the world is reconciled to God. Once again, there can be no escaping Paul's operating principle that a new life with God in heaven must express itself in a new way of life in the world.

For this same reason, the gravity of Paul's plea for reconciliation can only be recovered if we maintain the underlying assumption of this passage, namely, that "the day of salvation" (6:2) is also the day of God's wrath. It is impossible to grasp the hope of God's people apart from their conviction that God will one day act to save them from the pain and suffering and injustice brought about by sin. From the biblical perspective that informs Paul's thought, the vindication of the righteous comes about in part through the judgment of the wicked (Joel 2:28–3:21; Zech. 9:1–17; Mal. 3:1–5; 4:1–6; Matt. 3:1–12; 2 Thess. 1:3–10). To be saved is not merely a state of mind or feeling. Salvation is the great act of God's deliverance on behalf of his people in which he "fights on their behalf" to rescue them from the sinful oppression of this world (cf. Ex. 14:13–14 with Gal. 1:4). It is this act of divine deliverance at the Exodus that initiates and informs the history of redemption (cf. Isa. 64:1–4). And note the "fear" and "faith" that this event was intended to bring about in the lives of God's people:

---

28. Kim, "2 Cor. 5:11–21," 362–63.

But the Israelites went through the sea on dry ground, with a wall of water on their right and on their left. That day the LORD saved Israel from the hands of the Egyptians, and Israel saw the Egyptians lying dead on the shore. And when the Israelites saw the great power the LORD displayed against the Egyptians, the people feared the LORD and put their trust in him and in Moses his servant (Ex. 14:29–31).

The history of redemption marked out by the exodus from Egypt culminates in the first and second comings of Christ, pictured in our passage as the great "second exodus" act of God that inaugurates and consummates the "new creation." The wonder of the gospel is that the goal of the first Exodus, which remained unfulfilled in Israel as a whole (their initial fear and faith in Ex. 14:31 soon gives way to the unbelief that eventually produces the idolatry of the golden calf in 32:1–8), is now being fulfilled by the people of the new covenant (see 2 Cor. 3:6–18). At the same time, we cannot escape the fact that all those outside this covenant relationship remain under the wrath of God (Rom. 1:18–32).

PREACHING THE FEAR of God. Neither the righteousness of God nor the sinful conditions of the world have changed since Paul's day. Throughout this passage, Paul's theology (God as both Judge and Savior), anthropology (humanity from the worldly point of view and as a new creation), and self-understanding (Paul as Christ's prophetic ambassador) all highlight the centrality and necessity of the proclamation of the gospel. To be redeemed *by God*, sinful people need to hear the apostolic call to be reconciled *with God* (5:20; 6:1–2). The parallel between 5:18 and 5:19 reminds us that the focal point of the *ministry* of reconciliation is the *message* of reconciliation.

Recovering this emphasis is crucial in a time when many are moving away from a focus on the Word toward more liturgical, dramatic, and experiential expressions of the faith. The recognition that reconciliation takes place in response to the retelling of what God has accomplished in Christ should caution us not to lose our emphasis on the "sacrament of the Word." What drives most people away from the preaching of the Scriptures is not preaching itself, but the weak quality of the preaching, which in turn leads to an anemic expression of praise.

One antidote to the weakness of contemporary preaching is the realization that our message is all that stands between heaven and hell. Indeed, the contemporary significance of this passage must include an appropriation of the fact that Paul's fear of the Lord drove his ministry and message, even as

Christ's love compelled it. In our culture we quickly gravitate to Christ's love. Yet the magnitude of Christ's love in this passage only comes to the fore against the reality of God's judgment. To frame our gospel within the fear of God is therefore both responsible to the text and relevant to our message.

Admittedly, this realization is not easy to recover in our culture. For although both God's character and ours remain the same today as in Paul's day, what has changed is the milieu of "felt need" into which the gospel is most often spoken in the Western world. The notion of God's wrath and the need for atonement in the face of divine judgment are foreign to our worldview, in which God, if he is thought of at all, is usually viewed as a benign teddy bear. The warning of a previous generation to "Turn or Burn!" strikes us as harsh and cruel. Even for those who accept as true the threat of God's judgment that this call signifies, the imagery of the metaphor is simply too blunt and vivid for our taste. Such a threat of God's judgment is seldom uttered today without being mocked. That God will judge the world may be true, but it is one of the best-kept secrets of the Bible.

We must remember, however, that Paul's reminder of God's coming judgment was not an attempt to scare people into heaven (though the fear of God granted by the Spirit may in fact bring about a person's repentance). Rather, it was given for those inside the church as a means of spurring them on in their life of faith (cf. 1 Tim. 5:20). Unbelievers do not fear God (Ps. 14:1; Rom. 3:18). Only believers, who have already experienced God's presence, fear losing it (Ps. 51:10–12). The fear of God, preached as an essential part of the gospel, is the gracious gift of God to keep his people persevering (Prov. 3:7; 8:13; Matt. 10:28; Acts 5:11; 2 Cor. 7:1; Phil. 2:12; Heb. 4:1; 11:7; 1 Peter 1:17). Those who fear God's judgment repent of their sin so that, trusting in God once again, they need not fear (Rom. 8:15; 1 John 4:18). Only the fear of God leads to not having to fear God (Luke 12:32; Heb. 12:28). The church is "encouraged by the Holy Spirit" even as it goes on "living in the fear of the Lord" (Acts 9:31). "The fear of the LORD is the beginning of wisdom" (Prov. 1:7; 9:10).

But where is this same sense of urgency and gravity being expressed in our churches today? Our God is so small—and our sense of self is so large. We fear God so little that we seldom sense the seriousness of our sin. And we sense the seriousness of our sin so little that we seldom fear God. Within this vicious circle, our most pressing "felt need" is not for reconciliation with God because of our sin, but for reconciliation with ourselves because of our low "self-esteem." As a result, when we hear Paul's word of judgment and call for reconciliation, our first response is to evaluate our feelings about God. Our cultural discomfort with the very thought of God's judgment has led us to emphasize the love and forgiveness of God to a fault. God is said to "like us" no matter what we say, feel, or do, to the virtual exclusion of his wrath.

The negative consequences of removing God's wrath from our portrait of God are far-reaching. As Jerry L. Walls asks, "Can we be good without hell?"[29] In other words, an ambivalence pervades the attempt to maintain traditional categories of good and evil without the context of judgment and redemption in which they find their home.

> It is the quandary faced by those who affirm traditional moral convictions but who deny the theological framework that historically provided those convictions with meaning and motivation. Without the framework, it is not clear whether or why those convictions of right and wrong are true or why they should be followed.[30]

In view of this quandary, Walls' point is an extension of Paul's presupposition in our passage:

> I do not believe there is any adequate account of moral authority or of moral motivation on secular principles. More specifically, I believe we need God, heaven, and yes, even hell, to make sense of morality. Indeed, we need to define our very selves in light of these eternal realities. If there is no God, no heaven, no hell, there simply is no persuasive reason to be moral.
>
> ... These are the resources that enable us to give a satisfying account ... of why we should not only behave morally but also be moral. For these are the best, if not the only, resources to make sense of how it is always in our best interest to be moral.[31]

We must be careful here. The issue is not morality in the narrow sense of ethical behavior within society, but the grand morality of first relating rightly to God and then of extending our reconciled relationship with God to others. God's judgment is not a utilitarian instrument to be used pragmatically to "get people" to act right. Righteousness is the natural response to knowing a righteous God, since his judgment is the natural and essential expression of his holy character. To speak of hell is not to argue for moralism, but to support the call of the gospel.

Perspectives from the past. There is no doubt that in our day we are nearsighted when it comes to perceiving the significance of God's righteous judgment and anger. The only way out of our own theological myopia may be to jump back in time. The perspectives of the past enable us to focus afresh in the present by providing us with an outside lens on ourselves.

---

29. "Can We Be Good Without Hell?" *Christianity Today* (June 16, 1997), 22–26.
30. Ibid., 22.
31. Ibid., 22–23.

Though we are often too close to see ourselves clearly, renewed clarity can be gained through looking at our own situation from a distance.

Over a hundred years ago, the great Baptist preacher C. H. Spurgeon (1834–1892) felt the same tension we do when considering the judgment of God. For example, in considering the warning of Psalm 7:12, "If you turn not, God will whet his sword," Spurgeon admitted that

> if I consulted my own feelings I should not mention it; but we must not consider our feelings in the work of the ministry, any more than we should if we were physicians of men's bodies. We must sometimes use the knife, when we feel that mortification would ensue without it. We must frequently make sharp gashes into men's consciences, in the hope that the Holy Spirit will bring them to life. We assert, then, that there is a necessity that God should whet his sword and punish men, if they will not turn.

So, like Earnest Baxter before him, Spurgeon responded to this text by preaching a sermon calling for repentance with the actual title, "Turn or Burn." His opening words reflect how little things have changed since his day:

> "If the sinner turn not, God will whet his sword." So, then, God has a sword, and he will punish man on account of his iniquity. This evil generation hath labored to take away from God the sword of his justice; they have endeavored to prove to themselves that God will "clear the guilty," and will by no means "punish iniquity, transgression, and sin." Two hundred years ago the predominant strain of the pulpit was one of terror; it was like Mount Sinai, it thundered forth the dreadful wrath of God, and from the pips of a Baxter or a Bunyan, you heard most terrible sermons, full to the brim with warnings of judgment to come. Perhaps some of the Puritan fathers may have gone too far, and have given too great a prominence to the terrors of the Lord in their ministry; but the age in which we live has sought to forget those terrors altogether . . . and if we faithfully and honestly tell our hearers that sin must bring after it certain destruction, it is said that we are attempting to frighten them into goodness . . . the cry of the age is, that God is merciful, that God is love. Ay, who said he was not? But remember, it is equally true, God is just, severely and inflexibly just! He were not God, if he were not just; he could not be merciful, if he were not just, for punishment of the wicked is demanded by the highest mercy to the rest of mankind.[32]

---

32. "Sermon XXVII: Turn or Burn," Charles Haddon Spurgeon, *Spurgeon's Sermons*, Vol. 2 (Grand Rapids: Baker, reprint of 1883 collection), 426–441 (pp. 426–27).

In going back another century, listen again to the fear of God's absolute sovereignty and wrath, so foreign today, in Jonathan Edwards' pleading with unrepentant sinners in his sermon from July 8th, 1741: "Sinners in the Hands of An Angry God," the most famous sermon ever preached in America:

> The God that holds you over the pit of hell, much as one holds a spider, or some loathsome insect, over the fire, abhors you, and is dreadfully provoked: his wrath towards you burns like fire; he looks upon you as worthy of nothing else, but to be cast into the fire; he is of purer eyes than to bear to have you in his sight; you are ten thousand times more abominable in his eyes, than the most hateful venomous serpent is in ours. You have offended him infinitely more than ever a stubborn rebel did his prince: and yet, it is nothing but his hand that holds you from falling into the fire every moment. It is to be ascribed to nothing else, that you did not go to hell the last night; that you was suffered to awake again in this world, after you closed your eyes to sleep. And there is no other reason to be given, why you have not dropped into hell since you arose in the morning, but that God's hand has held you up. There is no other reason to be given why you have not gone to hell, since you have sat here in the house of God, provoking his pure eyes by your sinful wicked manner of attending his solemn worship. Yea, there is nothing else that is to be given as a reason why you do not this very moment drop down into hell.
>
> O sinner! consider the fearful danger you are in: it is a great furnace of wrath, that you are held over in the hand of that God, whose wrath is provoked and incensed as much against you, as against many of the damned in hell. You hang by a slender thread, with the flames of divine wrath flashing about it, and ready every moment to singe it, and burn it asunder; and you have no interest in a Mediator, and nothing to lay hold of to save yourself, nothing to keep off the flames of wrath, nothing of your own, nothing that you ever have done, nothing that you can do, to induce God to spare you one moment.[33]

The hope of the gospel. Against this backdrop, the hope of the gospel burns brightly. God is the one who not only judges the world in his wrath, but also poured out his judgment on his own Son in order to reconcile the world to himself. In spite of our sin, we can still be saved! We can be forgiven! We can be set free from its power! We can be reckoned righteous in God's sight and made

---

33. From *The Works of Jonathan Edwards*, Vol. 2 (Edinburgh: Banner of Truth Trust, 1974 [reprint of 1834]), 7–12, 10. Edwards preached this sermon in Enfield, Connecticut, during the Great Awakening.

righteous as a new creation! This is the new perspective from which Paul views all humanity—not who they are in their sin, but who they can be in their Savior (5:16a). Even Christ must no longer be viewed as hanging on the cross, but as raised in his glory (5:16b). Just as Christ's death led to his resurrected life, so too Christ's death for us leads to our new way of life (5:15; cf. Rom. 6:1–23).

What makes this news so good, of course, is that all of this is accomplished not by our efforts, but by God's sovereign act of creating anew. God reconciles us to himself not because of our distinctives or accomplishments, but because of the unique distinctives of the one who was made sin even though he knew no sin (5:21). We do not reach up to God, but God reaches out to us. We are not called to make great declarations to God; rather, God has declared a word of reconciliation to us, a word of his own redeeming love, a love that stretches from the crossing of the sea to the cross of the Son of God. In Paul's words, "all this is from God, who reconciled us to himself through Christ and gave us the ministry of reconciliation" (5:18). The God-centered focus of Paul's gospel *is* the gospel. We do not save ourselves; indeed, we cannot. God saves us as the only One who can.

"It is the very heart of the gospel that it both gives everything and requires everything. The task of the preacher is to hold these together so that men and women are both released from the burden of guilt and also set free to follow Jesus."[34] Those who have been reconciled with God in Christ are called to be agents of this same reconciliation to others. To be God's "fellow worker" (6:1) is therefore not to be God's equal partner in the plan of salvation, but to be his dependent instrument through which the power of his grace and the promise of his forgiveness are illustrated and made known to others. We do not work with God; God makes his appeal through us. We do not contribute to God's cause; we share with others what God has done for us, either through the pastoral ministry of being "Christ's ambassadors," like Paul, or through living out the gospel as part of God's people, like the Corinthians (cf. 2:5–11; 8:1–15; 9:6–15).

The fear of God's judgment and the compelling nature of Christ's love express themselves in the proclamation and embodiment of the gospel, which are an expression of no longer living for oneself, but "for him who died for them and was raised again." Those who have died to themselves in Christ have now been raised with Christ, not merely to a life of personal spiritual experiences (as important as they are), but, more important, to a new life of reconciliation with God and others. As Donald Bloesch has observed:

---

34. Lesslie Newbigin, *Truth to Tell: The Gospel as Public Truth* (Grand Rapids: Eerdmans, 1991), 72–73. For Newbigin's understanding of the implications of the public nature of this gospel, see the Contemporary Significance of 6:3–13.

It is necessary to distinguish a theocentric or biblically-oriented pietism from an anthropocentric or culturally-oriented revivalism. The former places the accent on God's coming to man, whereas the latter speaks more of man's decision for Christ. The former holds that salvation is realized in a life of obedience, not simply in a crisis experience. For the classical pietist, the primary fruits of salvation are the adoration of God and love for one's fellowman. For the popular revivalist, the most cherished fruits of salvation are ecstasy and enthusiasm.[35]

Second Corinthians 5:11–6:2 thus calls us back to our fundamental commitments as followers of Christ: (1) to an awareness of the judgment of God (5:11), (2) to the proclamation of the corresponding good news of the gospel of Christ (5:14–15, 21), and (3) to the passion for others that comes about as a result (5:14, 21). Regaining these fundamentals will not be easy in our crowded day and pluralistic age.

The hustle and bustle of daily life prevents many people who see themselves as religious, and who acknowledge the significance of religion in their lives, from consciously thinking of themselves as a representative of Jesus Christ. One-quarter of adults (27 percent) say they "always" are mindful of being Christ's representatives; one-sixth (17 percent) say they are "often" aware of that mantle; and one-fourth are "sometimes" conscious of that privilege. The remaining 30 percent of the nation claim they rarely or never think of themselves in this light.[36]

What we need is not to squeeze more fleeting, religious experiences into our fast-paced lives. Rather, we need a more profound understanding of the gravity of life lived in the "fear of the Lord" (cf. 5:11), laced with a deeper joy in knowing "God's favor" (cf. 6:2). Concretely, this means taking time to focus *on Christ* as the means and model of our new life *in Christ*. The way to avoid "receiving God's grace in vain" is to get to know Christ better, that is, both his role within redemptive history and the teaching and example of his life. For our new creation takes place "in Christ" (5:17), we have been reconciled to God "through Christ" (5:18, 19, 21), and, like Paul, we are "Christ's ambassadors" (5:20). That Paul himself had such a focus can be seen in the fact that he interprets both of his motives for ministry Christologically: Paul is moved by Christ as *Judge* in 5:11 and by Christ as

---

35. Donald G. Bloesch, *Theological Notebook. Vol. 1: 1960–1964* (Colorado Springs: Helmers & Howard, 1989), 164.

36. George Barna, *Index of Leading Spiritual Indicators* (Dallas: Word, 1996), 3, based on a poll from January, 1993.

Savior in 5:14. As a result, he implores his readers "on behalf of Christ" to be reconciled with God (5:20).

But to know Christ as Judge and Savior and to realize that reconciliation with God comes through the preaching of the gospel also mean, as Barnett reminds us, that "every day in the life of the apostolic minister is judgment day."[37] The reconciliation of the righteous (5:21) is, at the same time, the day of reckoning for those who receive the grace of God "in vain" (6:1). The call of the gospel to reconciliation with God divides humanity. Even within the church, Paul's call to the Corinthians reminds us that perseverance is the sign of genuine conversion. Confessions of Christ in the past mean nothing if not matched by a continuing pursuit to live for Christ in the present. Those who begin with Christ but then turn away show themselves not to have "died" and been raised a "new creation" in Christ. Their earlier reception of God's grace is therefore "in vain" (6:1).

Yet as Paul's pleading with the Corinthians also makes clear, it is never too late to return to God (5:20; 6:2). Paul's call for reconciliation to a wayward people is God's means of rescuing his people from judgment. Paul's confidence is that those who have not accepted God's grace in vain will respond, repent, and return to the Lord. Moreover, what was true for Paul in his day is true in ours: Now is the day of eschatological salvation (6:2). And as Newbigin has pointed out, nowhere is this message more needed than in the West:

> If one is looking at the total situation of Christianity in the contemporary world, addressing European culture is the most urgent question, and for two reasons: first because it is modern, post-Enlightenment Western culture that, in the guise of "modernization," is replacing more traditional cultures all over the world, and second because ... this culture has a unique power to erode and neutralize the Christian faith.[38]

To the Western church Paul declares: "We are therefore Christ's ambassadors, as though God were making his appeal through us. We implore you on Christ's behalf: Be reconciled to God. God made him who had no sin to be sin for us, so that in him we might become the righteousness of God" (5:20–21).

Appendix

Hubbard ("Was Paul Out of His Mind?") points out that the view advocated in this commentary concerning 5:13 is the consensus today,

---

37. Barnett, *The Second Epistle to the Corinthians*, 281.
38. Quoted from Lesslie Newbigin's *Word in Season* as found in Tim Stafford's profile of Newbigin's life, "God's Missionary to Us," *Christianity Today* (December 9, 1996), 32.

though not without its difficulties. The biggest problem is that the verb usually used in contrast to being in one's right mind is *mainomai* ("to be mad/crazy"), not *existemi* (cf. its use in 1 Cor. 14:23), and it is not certain that *mainomai* and *existemi* are synonyms when used in reference to religious ecstasy (pp. 42–43). So Hubbard himself rejects the view taken here, arguing that 5:13a reflects an accusation against Paul, not Paul's own positive description of his commitment to keep his ecstatic experiences private before God. To flesh out what this accusation might have been in a way that avoids the difficulty with saying that it was excessive spiritual experience, Hubbard, 59–61, offers a new reading of the background of the text, interpreting the language of 5:13 against the backdrop of Greco-Roman rhetorical literature and practice. Hubbard argues that 5:13 reflects the accusation that Paul employed an excessive style of delivery in his public preaching, based on Aristotle's use of *existemi* in this sense in his *Rhetoric* 1408b (though Aristotle also uses it to refer to wandering from one's subject matter, cf. *Rhetoric* 1418a). Hubbard thus paraphrases 5:13 as follows: "If, as some of you complain, my speech was unpolished and excessive, credit that to God's account; if I am presently reasonable and lucid, credit that to yours" (p. 61). According to Hubbard, Paul's point is that, "In his prior visit, his personal presence was unimpressive to the Corinthians, but his writing, as the Corinthians acknowledged, is forceful and to the point (10:10)" (p. 61). The key to 5:13 is therefore 1 Cor. 2:1–5 (pp. 61–62). But was the problem with Paul's public preaching its excessive use of poetic style, i.e., that it was "too metrical and rhythmic in its delivery," as Aristotle uses the term (cf. Hubbard, 59)? When Paul refused to use professional rhetoric in Corinth, did he use excessive poetics and an overly emotional style of speech instead? As Hubbard's own quotes indicate, Aristotle's use of the term does not refer to a lack of rhetorical polish, but to too much of it, so that one gets lost in the *excessive* rhetoric! On the contrary, Paul's preaching, though not encased in professional rhetoric, was still forceful, effective, reasonable, lucid, plain, and to the point (1 Cor. 1:17–19; 2:14–16a). Moreover, it is hard to imagine that speaking before God would lead to a lack of clarity and persuasiveness. But most telling against Hubbard's suggestion is that Paul's prior mode of speaking in Corinth was not done *for God's sake*, but for the sake of the *Corinthians* (cf. 1 Cor. 2:5)! Moreover, even if God *were* the object of Paul's prior style of speaking in Corinth, Paul stands before God's judgment in his letters just as much as he does in his public proclamation (cf. 1:23; 11:11), so that it is difficult to construe Paul's point to be that a switch in audience, from God to the Corinthians, brings about a change in style. In reality, neither Paul's audience nor his style have changed. Paul's audience, i.e., his bar of judgment, whether in person or in letter, remains God alone (cf. 2:17; 12:19). And Paul's letters do not follow the patterns of contemporary rhetoric any more than his preaching did (see the commentary to 10:10). The difference between Paul's public ministry in Corinth and his letters was not his style, but the focus of his message itself, since it is in his letters Paul had to warn the Corinthians of the judgment to come against those who persist in their rebellion.

2 Corinthians 6:3–13

WE PUT NO stumbling block in anyone's path, so that our ministry will not be discredited. ⁴Rather, as servants of God we commend ourselves in every way: in great endurance; in troubles, hardships and distresses; ⁵in beatings, imprisonments and riots; in hard work, sleepless nights and hunger; ⁶in purity, understanding, patience and kindness; in the Holy Spirit and in sincere love; ⁷in truthful speech and in the power of God; with weapons of righteousness in the right hand and in the left; ⁸through glory and dishonor, bad report and good report; genuine, yet regarded as impostors; ⁹known, yet regarded as unknown; dying, and yet we live on; beaten, and yet not killed; ¹⁰sorrowful, yet always rejoicing; poor, yet making many rich; having nothing, and yet possessing everything.

¹¹We have spoken freely to you, Corinthians, and opened wide our hearts to you. ¹²We are not withholding our affection from you, but you are withholding yours from us. ¹³As a fair exchange—I speak as to my children—open wide your hearts also.

ACCORDING TO 5:18–6:2, being reconciled with God entails aligning oneself with Paul and his message. To reject his "ministry of reconciliation" (5:18) is to reject the gospel itself (i.e., the "message of reconciliation," 5:19), thereby indicating that one's own eschatological fate has been determined (6:1–2; cf. 2:15–16; 3:14–15). Yet this appeal is only as strong as the apostle who utters it. Therefore, in 6:3–13 Paul returns again to a direct apology for the legitimacy of his ministry of the Spirit, righteousness, and reconciliation (cf. 3:3–6, 7–11; 4:1; 5:18). Although it is not clear in most English translations (including the NIV), verses 3–10 are directly related to the main assertion "we urge you" in 6:1.[1] As such, Paul's catalogue of suffering delineates the *way* in which he works together with God in making the appeal not to accept God's grace in vain. He does so by

---

1. The participles *didontes* ("presenting"/"giving") and *synistantes* ("commending") in 6:3–4 are best taken as relating back to *parakaloumen* ("we urge") in 6:1.

not presenting to others a stumbling block *in anything*,[2] but by commending himself "in every way." Paul's commendation *of himself* in 6:4 supports his exhortation *to others* in 6:1.

Since the catalog in 6:3–10 supports the exhortation in 6:1, the key interpretive decision here is whether Paul's reference to "endurance" in 6:4a is a descriptive heading for all that follows, or whether it is simply another element of the catalog itself. In other words, is "endurance" the general category that is specified in what follows? Or is it simply the first of the various members in the list, all of which together modify "commending ourselves"?

In answer to this question, various translations punctuate the text differently. There are three reasons why the punctuation chosen by the NIV, which separates out "endurance" from the rest of the list, is to be preferred: (1) Paul modifies "endurance" with "great," in contrast to the unqualified designations that follow; (2) "endurance" is a singular, abstract virtue, while what follows is a list of plural adversities; and (3) it is difficult to see how hardships in and of themselves could commend Paul if they are not related to the positive virtue of endurance. As a general statement, Paul commends himself as a servant of God by his "great endurance" (cf. 12:12). Specifically, Paul's endurance takes place in the midst of the adversities that follow.

Thus, the focus of Paul's commendation in 6:3–10 is once again on his divinely enabled endurance in the midst of adversity, which embodies both Christ's "death" (= Paul's suffering) and his "resurrection" (= Paul's endurance; cf. 1:3–11; 2:14–16a; 4:7–12). At the same time, this endurance "commends" Paul as a servant *of God*, who, like Isaiah, is a mediator of God's word to his people (6:1–2). In contrast, those who lack such a divine recommendation can only engage in *self*-commendation (for Paul's other commendations of himself, cf. 4:2; 12:11; for the negative practice of self-commendation and the difference between the two, cf. 3:1; 5:12; 10:12, 18).

The catalog of those things through which Paul must show "great endurance" breaks down into four distinct units:

(1) a listing of hardships, all introduced by "in" and all in the plural (vv. 4b–5)
(2) a listing of graces, all introduced by "in" and all in the singular (vv. 6–7a)
(3) a listing of changing circumstances, the "ups and downs" of praise and blame, all introduced with "through" and given in contrasting pairs (vv. 7b–8)

2. The Greek *en medeni* in 6:3 is ambiguous. Though it could read "among anyone" (cf. NIV: "in anyone's path"), the parallel to "in every thing/way" in the next clause speaks against this rendering.

(4) a listing of divine deliverance in which Paul's suffering is the platform for the display of God's transforming power, all introduced with "as" and given in an adversative relationship (e.g., "dying and yet we live on"; vv. 8b–10).

As delineations of the prepositional phrase "in great endurance," each of these phrases form part of Paul's commendation of himself in 6:4; that is, he does so "in … in … through … as…." Moreover, as expressions of the power of God in his life, the positive elements listed are not natural attributes or self-generated virtues, nor are they the result of self-control and positive thinking. Rather, Paul's life is the product of God's "resurrection" power and presence (cf. the references to the "Holy Spirit" and the "power of God" in 6:6–7).

All of these phrases also support the conclusions and exhortation of 6:11–13 that Paul voices as the spiritual father of his "children," the Corinthians (cf. 1 Cor. 4:14–15; 2 Cor. 3:2; 11:2; 12:14–15). His use of the image of a father to describe his relationship to the Corinthians reflects the assumption that, as the people of the new covenant, the church is the family of God (cf. Mark 3:31–35). As their father in the faith, Paul's pattern of living his life for the sake of the Corinthians (vv. 4–10) points to the fact that he has conducted his ministry with open integrity and genuine affection (6:11; cf. 3:2, 12).[3]

Consequently, Paul puts the responsibility for the conflict at Corinth squarely at the feet of those Corinthians who are still in rebellion against him (6:12). All Paul wants is a fair exchange, his love for theirs (6:13a). If there has been any lack of openness, integrity, or family commitment, it has been on their part, not Paul's. Hence, they, not he, must "open their hearts" (6:13).

Looking back, it becomes clear that the prophetic exhortation to be reconciled to *God* in 5:20 and 6:1 is paralleled by the personal appeal in 6:11–13 to be reconciled to *Paul* himself as God's spokesman and Christ's ambassador. Furthermore, here too, as earlier, the Corinthians' salvation is on the line in their response. This becomes evident in the connection between 6:13 and 2:15–16, 6:1, and 13:1–10.

Paul's conviction that a person's reaction to his ministry acts to signify and further his or her destiny (2:15f.) leads quite naturally to the entreaties of 6:1 and 13:1–10. As a result, the "test" of faith becomes whether or not the Corinthians will remain loyal to Paul, not because Paul somehow stands independent of or above the gospel, but because

---

3. For explicit statements that Paul intentionally and unintentionally took up suffering on behalf of the Corinthians, see 1:3–7; 1:12–14; 1:23–2:4; 3:2; 4:5, 12, 15; 5:12; 7:3; 12:14–16, 19.

he is convinced that he is its true and genuine representative and embodiment. Hence, for Paul, it is not *his* ministry that is presently being called into question, but the genuineness of the faith of the Corinthians themselves.[4]

Our passage is thus structured in five parts: (1) an indicative statement of Paul's general point (6:3–4a), which is then supported by (2) a specific delineation of his apostolic lifestyle and manner of ministry (6:4b–10), which in turn leads to (3) a conclusion concerning the legitimacy of his relationship to the Corinthians (6:11) and (4) a conclusion concerning the illegitimacy of the Corinthians' relationship to Paul (6:12), followed by (5) the imperative implications that derive from them (6:13). Having "commended himself" as a "servant" of God by reminding his readers in verses 4–10 of the evidence in support of his apostolic claim, in verses 11–13 Paul draws out for them the implications of his ministry. Far from calling his legitimacy into question, Paul's suffering is the vehicle through which God is making himself known among the Corinthians.

As such, Paul's suffering is also the evidence of the integrity of his message, of the purity of his motives, and of the true nature of his love for his spiritual "children" (6:11). The problem in Corinth is therefore not in Paul but in the Corinthians themselves (6:12). Paul therefore addresses them as a whole in order to give everyone the benefit of the doubt concerning the genuine nature of their faith, while at the same time calling those who are still rebelling against him to respond with the same love he has already shown to them (6:13).

THE PROBLEM THAT faced Paul is much the same as that which faces many contemporary ministers in their proclamation of the gospel. Now, as then, suffering and weakness call into question the power of the Spirit. But Paul is relentless in his response: The greatest display of God's power is not the absence of pain or the presence of a miracle, but Paul's faithful endurance in the midst of adversity, through which God "makes many [others] rich" (6:10). This section's climactic appeal in 6:13 flows out of the reality of the presence of God in Paul's life, a reality that radically transforms the significance of his circumstances.

In adducing his experiences of endurance through good times and bad as a testimony to the "open" condition of his "heart" and "affection" toward the

---

4. Scott J. Hafemann, *Suffering and Ministry in the Spirit*, 75.

Corinthians (6:11), Paul is not detailing a series of cold, calculated decisions to "gut it out" for the sake of the Corinthians. Paul is not to be pitied. He is not a masochist. The Corinthians are his "boast" (1:14; cf. 7:4; 8:24; 9:2) and a great source of joy in his life (cf. 7:7). His ministry grows out of such a "depth of . . . love" for them (cf. 2:4) that Paul would even be willing to die on their behalf (cf. 7:3). And Paul is not giving a news report. His words in this section are filled with pathos. As the Corinthians' father, his appeal in this passage is pastoral and his tone affectionate. One can hear the emotion in his voice as he calls the Corinthians by name in 6:11 and breaks from his "apostolic plural" into the first person singular in 6:13. In short, Paul is speaking from his "heart."

Nevertheless, we must be careful in our subjectivist culture not to allow Paul's heartfelt apology to be interpreted as essentially emotional in nature, thereby confusing its manner with its content. He is not addressing the Corinthians as someone whose feelings have been hurt, but as their apostle, their father in the faith. Though filled with emotion, Paul's appeals derive from his self-understanding as an agent and ambassador of God's saving work in Christ. In advocating for his own legitimacy, he is not trying to recover his ego but to rescue the Corinthians from judgment. At stake is the gospel. For this reason, he does not defend himself out of a personal need to bolster his self-esteem or to be liked by others, but because of his recognition that his ministry is the means through which God is making his appeal to the world (cf. 5:20).

We must therefore make clear that Paul's reference to his "heart" in this passage, as elsewhere in his apology, speaks of the content of his character and the motives of his ministry as displayed in his life (cf. 3:2; 5:12). For Paul, the "heart" does not refer to a hidden fount of feeling, but to the value center that determines a person's character. Because of the compelling "love of Christ," Paul's "heart" is to live for the one who died for him (5:12–15). His open heart is seen not merely in the degree of his feelings, but in the depth of his endurance on behalf of the gospel and for the sake of the Corinthians.

Both Christ's death for Paul and Paul's life for Christ, lived out in suffering for the sake of the Corinthians (cf. 4:5), are historical facts that are open to scrutiny; they are not private, "religious" experiences that can only be evaluated as a matter of subjective opinion. That which compels us can be "read" by all on the pages of our behavior (cf. 3:1–2; 4:1–2). Paul's displays of deep passion on behalf of the Corinthians do not in and of themselves commend him. His divine recommendation is the public record of the ways in which Paul's "death" and "deliverance" embody Christ's own.

In the same way, Paul's exhortation in 6:13 that the Corinthians open their heart to him (cf. 7:2) is not primarily a call for renewed experiences of warm feelings toward him, though it will certainly entail such emotions. It would not be honoring to God's gospel or to his messenger for the Corinthians to be threatened into committing themselves to something for which they have no desire. To trust in Paul's gospel, one must have a certain appreciation and affection for the apostle. Still, his ultimate goal is not renewed feelings toward him as a person, but a renewed faith in the gospel that he preaches and embodies (cf. 1:24; 4:7–12). He is not trying to get the Corinthians to like him more; he is calling for their repentance. He is not conducting a personality poll; rather, he is summoning them to respond to the evidence before them.

Thus, in order to keep from reading this passage merely as Paul's baring his soul in front of the Corinthians in an attempt to get them to respond in kind, we must realize that this passage is an essential restatement of his apology for his apostolic ministry. To speak from the heart is not to call attention to the state of one's emotions, taken in isolation, but to the character of one's life as a whole, understood as the outworking of one's values. For, as Barnett has pointed out,

> [the] gospel demands that its bearer embody its central truths of death and resurrection. Thus the moral authority for Paul's ministry, which he repeatedly defends to the Corinthians, is that the death of Jesus is replicated, as it were, in "death" like sufferings incurred in ministry, and in "resurrection" deliverance from those sufferings by the power of God (1:8–10; 4:7–12; 6:3–10; 7:5–6; 12:7–9).[5]

As A CONTINUATION of the theme of Paul's apostolic suffering, the contemporary significance of Paul's apology in 6:3–13 is at least threefold. (1) It again reminds us that the call to ministry is a call to live for others as an embodiment of the One who died for them (5:15). Such a call will involve endurance and disregard for the changing circumstances and opinions of others. Through this endurance the minister exemplifies both Christ's love for his people and what it means to live for Christ in return. In K. Prümm's words, this section is Paul's "apostolic identification card."[6]

---

5. Paul Barnett, *The Second Epistle to the Corinthians*, 318.

6. K. Prümm, *Diakonia Pneumatos: Der zweite Korintherbrief als Zugang zur Apostolischen Botschaft.* II/I: *Theologie des zweiten Korintherbriefes, Apostolat und christliche Wirklichkeit* (Rome/Freiburg/Wien: Herder, 1960), 184.

Today, as then, the quality of one's life and one's willingness to endure suffering for the sake of the gospel are expressions of one's love for Christ. Paul does not shrink back from basing his appeals squarely on his character in Christ. Paul is not afraid to turn the spotlight on himself. Rather than needing to commend himself with letters of recommendation from others or with self-generated bragging (3:1; 5:12), his life as a servant of God commends his message and confirms his calling (cf. 3:1–6; 4:1; 10:16–18). The commendation that counts is the faithfulness of God in one's life, as evidenced in one's own faithful endurance. Once again, therefore, Paul can proclaim that the pattern of his life (6:4–10) does not put a "stumbling block in anyone's path" (6:3).

(2) Although those whom God calls into the ministry will often embody the gospel in a willingness to suffer for the sake of others (cf. 4:1–18), this passage reminds us vividly that it is not affliction as such that reveals God in the world. Suffering and oppression in themselves do not mark one out as representing Christ in the world. Paul has no romantic notion of suffering; he suffered too much for that. Indeed, by itself, suffering is the consequence of sin. To experience suffering is to participate in the evil of our fallen world.

Left to itself, suffering is not a noble and purifying virtue. Rather, what distinguishes the suffering of the righteous from the suffering rampant in the world is the transforming power of God's sustaining presence in their lives. Those whom God calls to suffer on behalf of others as an extension of Christ's love are not being called to masochism, but to a mission. They are not summoned to be miserable for God (God transforms their suffering into a platform for profound joy), but to be a mediator for the world. Self-denial for Christ's sake is not a sacrifice, but the pathway to gaining life itself (cf. Mark 8:34–38).

(3) Paul's admonition in 6:13 illustrates that a genuine ministry of the gospel anticipates a genuine response. The apostle is not engaging in a popularity contest with his opponents. By appealing for the affections of the Corinthians, he is fighting for their lives. Thus, his confidence in the truth of his message and in the transparency of his testimony leads him to expect that those who know God will open their hearts to Paul as well.

Today, however, such declarations of the gospel as a "public truth" that makes a personal claim on others are met with skepticism. Throughout the West there is a general mistrust of the motives and message of anyone who claims to represent God and his Word. In this regard, Lesslie Newbigin's reflections, after almost four decades as a missionary in India (1936–1974) and now twenty-three years as a missionary in England, are instructive. In returning to Birmingham, England, this great missionary-statesman discovered that ministry there

> is much harder than anything I met in India. There is a cold contempt for the Gospel which is harder to face than opposition. . . . England is

a pagan society and the development of a truly missionary encounter with this very tough form of paganism is the greatest intellectual and practical task facing the Church.[7]

As Newbigin further observed,

When the Church affirms the gospel as public truth it is challenging the whole of society to wake out of the nightmare of subjectivism and relativism, to escape from the captivity of the self turned in upon itself, and to accept the calling which is addressed to every human being to seek, acknowledge, and proclaim the truth.[8]

Not everything in postmodernism is wrong-headed, of course. Certainly, its emphasis on the cultural conditioning that impacts everyone represents a needed caution not to be cavalier or overconfident in our commitments. But instead of falling prey to its skepticism concerning knowledge, the challenge of postmodernism calls us to remain committed to the hard work of study and to the painful work of self-examination before we claim to represent Christ and the Scriptures, and then to do so with humility. Moreover, the post-modern emphasis on the ways in which interpretation and claims to the truth are often used as thinly veiled assertions of power should be taken seriously. We must scrutinize our own theological, ethical, and political presuppositions and agendas before we preach the Word to others, all the while pursuing the holiness modeled in the Word that became flesh.

Nevertheless, the necessity of being self-critical should not lead to silence. Paul, fully aware of his own faults, still calls the Corinthians to repent (6:11–14). Faced with competing truth claims, Paul gives evidence for the truth of his own position, confident that God has entrusted him with both the ministry and message of reconciliation (5:18–19; 6:3–10). Against this backdrop, the contemporary refusal to make absolute claims on others is often a false humility that exalts our private identities or subculture above the revelatory claims of Scripture. As a result, postmodernism's false humility actually politicizes all discourse, so that in the end the only arbiter of truth becomes the individual or subculture currently in power, since postmodernism's relativism calls into question the validity of common discourse.

In the face of this challenge, Newbigin has argued:

The proper answer to the charge of subjectivity is world mission, but it is world mission not as proselytism but as exegesis ... we are learning as we go. That is the only way we affirm that the gospel is not just

---

7. From Newbigin's *Unfinished Agenda*, as quoted in the insightful profile of his life by Tim Stafford, "God's Missionary to Us," *Christianity Today* (Dec. 9, 1996), 25.

8. Newbigin, *Truth to Tell*, 13.

"true for us" but true for all. The missionary action of the Church is the exegesis of the gospel.[9]

What Newbigin means by this "exegesis" of the gospel is a willingness to apply the lordship of Christ to every sector of society in all cultures, with the awareness that the implications of the gospel may not always be clear. The call to accept Paul's gospel with an "open heart" is not "a one-way promotion but a two-way encounter in which we learn more of what the gospel means."[10]

It is equally important to assert that such learning *is* possible. When proclaiming the gospel, we must avoid both a false objectivism and a false subjectivism. Paul assumes the examination of his life will lead those Corinthians in whom God is at work to change their minds. In response, we affirm that knowledge and a legitimate response to it are indeed possible for the person who, by God's Spirit, is personally committed to seeking the truth. In turn, we too, like Paul, must be willing to state our message openly before the bar of public evaluation, thereby taking the risk of being wrong.[11]

Moreover, we must be willing also to challenge publicly the ideas of others. The church cannot "continue to accept the security which is offered in an agnostic pluralism where we are free to have our own opinions provided we agree that they are only personal opinions."[12] Paul's appeal to the Corinthians in this passage, though personal, is not privatistic. It is based on a common-ground, public argument for the validity of his message. As such, it calls into question the modern and postmodern attempts to relegate "religion" to the realm of the purely subjective. Far from engaging merely in private speculation or simply sharing his feelings, Paul speaks on the basis of God's self-revelation in space and time (5:18, 20–21) and against the backdrop of the universal judgment of Christ (cf. 5:10).

(4) Finally, this text reminds us that when Paul speaks, he does so from a position of weakness before the Corinthians, not from a platform of power over them. Although a majority of the church had returned to Paul by the time he wrote 2 Corinthians, his current appeal to those still closed to him, like the "tearful letter" before it (cf. 2:1–4), rests ultimately on the convincing nature of his commendation. Under the convicting work of the Holy Spirit, Paul's only power is the persuasion of the gospel as it is embodied in his life and in the lives of those who join him in the ministry of righteousness (6:7; cf. 3:9). The same remains true today.

---

9. Ibid., 33–35.

10. Ibid., 35.

11. This is Newbigin's central thesis in response to the contemporary challenges of postmodernism; cf. ibid., 32–33, 52–53, 56–57, 59.

12. Ibid., 59.

2 Corinthians 6:14–7:1

DO NOT BE yoked together with unbelievers. For what do righteousness and wickedness have in common? Or what fellowship can light have with darkness? 15What harmony is there between Christ and Belial? What does a believer have in common with an unbeliever? 16What agreement is there between the temple of God and idols? For we are the temple of the living God. As God has said: "I will live with them and walk among them, and I will be their God, and they will be my people."

> 17"Therefore come out from them
> and be separate,
>
> says the Lord.
>
> Touch no unclean thing,
> and I will receive you."
> 18"I will be a Father to you,
> and you will be my sons and daughters,
> says the Lord Almighty."

7:1Since we have these promises, dear friends, let us purify ourselves from everything that contaminates body and spirit, perfecting holiness out of reverence for God.

THOUGH OFTEN OVERLOOKED, this passage is actually the carefully structured, closely argued, and theologically rich climax to the second major unit of Paul's letter (2:14–7:1). Its tightly-knit flow of thought falls into three sections: (1) the command of 6:14a, with its first line of support in 6:14b–16b; (2) the second line of support in the chain of Old Testament quotes in 6:16c–18b; and (3) the command of 7:1b, with its own surrounding support in 7:1a.

Thus, the command of 6:14 is restated in different words in 7:1, both of which are supported by the intervening argument from Scripture, which has its own imperative in 6:17. Everything in this section therefore supports this one exhortation, given in three forms. The main point of the passage is Paul's call to the Corinthians not to be "yoked together with unbelievers" (6:14), which is the specific application of the more general exhortation to "purify ourselves from everything that contaminates body and spirit" (7:1). This, in turn, is Paul's application of the Old Testament injunction to "touch no unclean thing" (6:17).

Nevertheless, because of the distinct style, unique vocabulary, and unusual themes found in this passage,[1] recent scholarship has questioned its origin,[2] its function within Paul's ongoing argument,[3] and its meaning.[4] However, none of the arguments against Pauline authorship of this passage is decisive, especially since this text derives its subject matter from the Scriptures. This use of the Old Testament explains why this passage would be so filled with concepts and vocabulary common to the Judaism of Paul's day. Moreover, there is no evidence that 2 Corinthians ever existed without this section.

Indeed, once the scriptural backdrop to Paul's thought in 6:14—7:1 is read against his earlier argument from Scripture in chapter 3, the integral purpose of the passage becomes apparent. Far from being a digression in his thought, these verses play a strategic role in Paul's ongoing apologetic by drawing to a conclusion the new covenant perspective introduced in 2:14—3:18. Just as 6:3—10 expands Paul's argument from his suffering in 2:14—17, so too 6:14—7:1 expands the covenant perspective first developed in 3:1—18. And just as Paul's argument from his suffering in 2:14—17 and 6:3—10 leads to the exhortation of 6:11—13, so too his argument from redemptive history in 3:1—18 and 6:14—7:1 leads to the exhortations of 6:14 and 7:1. In the present section, Paul makes explicit the implications of being part of God's new covenant people for the current controversy in Corinth. The admonition and argument from his suffering and the Scriptures in 2:14—3:18 and 6:3—7:1 thus frame his apology in 2:14—7:1.

---

1. Six of the fifty New Testament *hapax legomenon* found in 2 Corinthians occur in this passage: "to yoke together" (*heterozygeo*); "common" (*metoche*), "harmony" (*symphonesis*), "Belial" (*belial*), "agreement" (*synkatathesis*), and "that which contaminates" (*molysmos*). It is also often argued that Paul would not use the phrase "body and spirit" (7:1) in a purely nontheological way, meaning something like "outwardly and inwardly" or "the entire human person," it as means here.

2. That is, is it Pauline and written for this context, Pauline from another context but adapted by Paul for this letter, or non-Pauline, possibly from Qumran, having been interpolated by others?

3. That is, is it integral to Paul's argument, a digression from it, or misplaced and disruptive within it?

4. That is, from whom should the Corinthians separate, why, and for what purpose? For one of the clearest presentations of these issues, see Victor Paul Furnish, *II Corinthians*, 375–83. Furnish himself argues that 6:14—7:1 is of non-Pauline composition, but was incorporated by Paul himself as he wrote this letter (p.383).

The Command (6:14a)

AS OBSERVED ABOVE, this section opens up with a command, just as the last section closed with one. As "believers," the Corinthians are not to be "yoked together," in the sense of being hitched up with someone whose yoke does not fit (cf. NRSV: "mismatched"), or be "allied"[5] with "unbelievers" (6:14a).[6] But who are these "unbelievers"? Many take them to be non-Christians in general (as in 1 Cor. 5:10; cf. 6:6, 12–20; 7:12–15; 14:22–24). Others see them more specifically to be those Gentile pagans in Corinth with whom the "strong" had earlier participated in idol feasts (as in 1 Cor. 8:1–11:1; see 10:27).[7]

Both of these interpretations can succeed, however, only if 6:14–7:1 is distanced from its *current* context, in which Paul has been fighting for the legitimacy of his apostolic ministry and in which there has been no previous mention of the earlier problems facing the Corinthians. In 2 Corinthians the

---

5. In the LXX, the stem of the verb translated "to yoke together" (*heterozygeo*) occurs in its adjectival form (*heterozygos*) in Lev. 19:19, where it refers to a ban on crossbreeding animals. Though readers often point to the ban in Deut. 22:10 on yoking an ox and an ass together for plowing as the background to 6:14, the actual word does not occur there. James M. Scott, "The Use of Scripture in 2 Corinthians 6:16c–18 and Paul's Restoration Theology," *JSNT* 56 (1994): 73–99, finds only one other metaphorical use of the word outside of Paul, where it means "ally" (p. 75; see Plutarch, *Cimon* 16.10). I am indebted for much of what follows to Scott's insightful analysis of the use of the Old Testament in this passage, which points to its Pauline authorship and integral place within the argument of 2 Corinthians.

6. Based on a long-standing view of the difference between the present and aorist tenses when used in imperatives and prohibitions (i.e., the aorist was taken to indicate, "start/don't start," while the present tense meant, "keep doing/stop doing what you are presently doing"), it is often maintained that the present tense form of the prohibition in 6:14a indicates that the Corinthians were *already* engaged in such a "yoking together" with unbelievers. Recent study, however, has shown this distinction to be faulty. The force of the aorist in commands is simply to view the action as a whole, while the present views it as an ongoing process. Only context can introduce the ideas of not starting (i.e., an ingressive aorist; cf. Matt. 6:13; Luke 6:29) or stopping what one is already doing (i.e., a progressive present; cf. Matt. 19:14; John 2:16). In 2 Cor. 6:14 Paul is simply prohibiting the Corinthians from being yoked with unbelievers as a way of life, whether they have begun to do so or not. For a discussion of the Greek imperative and prohibition, see Daniel B. Wallace, *Greek Grammar Beyond the Basics* (Grand Rapids: Zondervan, 1996), 714–25.

7. Thus, Paul Barnett, *The Second Epistle to the Corinthians*, 342, interprets 6:14 to mean, "Let the Corinthians separate themselves from the local temple cults." As Barnett understands it, "Withdrawal from the Gentile cults will be their way of responding to his call to them, demonstrating that they truly are an apostolic church" (p. 341). This interpretation supposes that Paul's concern is that the Corinthian Christians are still involved in attending such idolatrous cults and that the "unbelievers" are the unconverted Gentiles who participated in them. This view owes its contemporary popularity to the influential work of Gordon D. Fee, "II Corinthians vi.14–vii.1 and Food Offered to Idols," *NTS* 23 (1977): 140–67, who argued for the equation of 1 Cor. 8:1–11:1 and 6:14–7:1, based on their similar vocabulary.

issue is not the relationship between Christians and the unbelieving world, nor is Paul concerned here, as he was in 1 Corinthians, with the Corinthians' participation in the temple cults and idolatry of Corinth. Rather, if read from the perspective of its own immediate context, Paul's command in 6:14 is the specific application of his more general command in 6:13. "Not to be yoked together with unbelievers" (6:14) is one way in which the Corinthians are to "open wide [their] hearts" to Paul.

Given the polemic situation in which Paul finds himself, "opening up" to him will necessarily entail closing themselves off from those who oppose him, whom the apostle now labels "unbelievers." This statement is shocking because "unbelievers" is not a word Paul ever uses to describe erring but still genuine Christians (e.g., those dealt with in 1 Cor. 3:10–15). Rather, "unbelievers" refers to those who are manifestly outside the sphere of God's people, even if they profess otherwise (cf. 1 Cor. 6:6; 7:12–15; 10:27; 14:22–24; 2 Cor. 4:4; 1 Tim. 5:8; Titus 1:15–16).

Thus, to make clear, in no uncertain terms, precisely what is at stake in supporting his opponents, Paul employs much of the same terminology in 6:14–16 and 7:1 that he used earlier to describe the necessity of breaking free from demon-dominated idolatry (cf. 1 Cor. 10:16–21 with 2 Cor. 6:14; 1 Cor. 8:7 with 2 Cor. 7:1). But now it describes the absolute incompatibility between those who believe (and hence support Paul's ministry) and those who are calling Paul's apostleship into question. Paul's point is stark. In the final analysis, the believers in Corinth must recognize his opponents as "unbelievers" and separate from them. Conversely, if they refuse to obey this command, they too will be considered unbelievers (cf. 13:5).[8]

Support Number One:
The Identity of the Church (6:14b–16b)

THE NECESSITY OF separating from those opposing Paul is first grounded in a series of five rhetorical questions, all of which anticipate a negative answer (6:14b–16a). Taken together, they reinforce the basic incompatibility between righteousness, light, Christ, being a believer, and the temple of God on the one hand, and wickedness, darkness, Belial, being an unbeliever, and idols on the other. The fact that in 6:14 "righteousness" is contrasted with "wickedness" (lit., "lawlessness") demonstrates once again that for Paul "righteousness" is a concept that includes both one's relationship with God in

---

8. Cf. Ralph P. Martin, 2 Corinthians, 194, 197: Paul is classing some of the Corinthians with unbelievers "to stab them awake to their condition and peril if they refuse to join him," so that his call here is aimed at "a recalcitrant group at Corinth." For a discussion of the other basic proposals concerning this passage, see Bridging Contexts.

Christ (cf. 6:15a) *and* its outworking in a life of "light" (6:14c) as a "believer" (6:15b).[9] Here "light" is not a mystical concept, but a moral designation that refers to the new life of obedience to God, engendered by trusting in Christ and enabled by the power of the Spirit.

Such "righteousness" or "light" is brought about by a reconciliation with God that is expressed both in conversion and in a converted life of continuing transformation into the image of God (cf. 3:9, 18; 4:4–6; 5:21). In contrast, the "darkness" (6:14c) of the "unbeliever" (6:15b) is associated with Satan, since, as 4:4 declares, "Belial" is the ultimate source of unbelief (cf. 2:11; 11:14; 12:7).[10]

The name used for Satan in 6:15, "Belial" ("Beliar" in some manuscripts), does not occur as a personal name either in the Old Testament or in the rest of the New Testament, though it is found as a proper name for Satan in the literature of Qumran and in apocalyptic Judaism.[11] Its creation comes from the common Jewish practice of referring to Satan and his demons by personifying negative terms or images from the Scriptures. "Beliar/Belial" is an extension of a Hebrew equivalent meaning "worthlessness" or "treacherous" (cf. Deut. 13:13; 15:9; Judg. 19:22; 1 Sam. 2:12; 2 Sam. 16:7; 22:5; 1 Kings 21:13; Ps. 18:4). Paul certainly viewed Satan's work through his opponents to be one of treachery (cf. 2 Cor. 11:13–15).

Moreover, it is significant for our present passage, in which Paul is speaking about separation from his opponents, that the name "Beliar/Belial" is often used in contexts that stress Satan's activity as an *opponent of God*. Indeed, since Paul has the sanctity of the church in view here, it is striking that in most of its underlying Old Testament uses, "Belial" "functions as an emotive term to describe individuals or groups who commit the most heinous crimes against

---

9. Cf. Rom. 6:19, where this same contrast between righteousness and lawlessness refers to two all-encompassing ways of life in which one's faith in Christ and obedience to God cannot be separated. For the same contrast between "light" and "darkness" as moral categories of motives and behavior, see Rom. 2:19; 13:12; 1 Cor. 4:5; Eph. 5:11–14; 1 Thess. 5:4–5.

10. The "dualistic" contrasts in vv. 14–15 are often associated with those found in Qumran, where "lawlessness" vs. "righteousness," and "light" vs. "darkness" are frequently contrasted (for the former, see 1QH 9:26–27; 1QS 1:4–5; for the latter, see 1QS 1:9–11; 1QM 1:1–13; cf. too *T. Naph.* 2:10; *T. Levi* 19:1). Both the early church and the Qumran community used these biblical categories to indicate their demarcation from the world and from other Jews as the true people of God (cf. Isa. 9:2; 29:15). This similarity in self-understanding between the Qumran community and the early Church derives from the fact that the Qumran congregation and the early church are the only two Jewish communities ever to portray themselves explicitly as the people of the "new covenant." This does not, however, prove dependence of one on the other.

11. See, e.g., 1QM 13:1–4; 1QS 1:18, 24; 1QH 14:21; CD 4:12–15; *Jub.* 1:20; *T. Reub.* 4:11; *T. Levi* 8:12 (where Belial is likewise opposed to the Messiah); 18:4; 19:1; *Syb. Or.* 3:63–64.

the Israelite religious or social order, as well as their acts."[12] Paul's concern to warn the Corinthian believers about his opponents, who are dividing the church as a result of being under the deluding influence of Satan (cf. 2:11; 4:3–6; 11:3, 15), may have led to his choice of this more unusual and specific designation for Satan.

If Paul's use of "Beliar/Belial" connotes Satan's opposition against God, especially God's people, then Paul's choice of the word used for "temple" in 6:16 (*naos*) highlights God's presence. *Naos* refers to the sacred worship space itself (cf. Mark 14:58; 15:29; John 2:19–20), where God's presence is manifest within the "Most Holy Place," rather than to the more general temple building or complex, the *hieron*, which is often also translated "temple" (cf. Mark 11:11; 12:35; 13:1). Naturally, beginning with the covenant stipulations given at Mount Sinai, the Most Holy Place can have no agreement with idols (2 Cor. 6:16a).[13] Paul supports this point in 6:16b: The Corinthians are not to have anything to do with "idolatry" precisely because (cf. the "for" [*gar*] of 6:16b) they are "the temple of the living God."

The fact that this reference to the temple is the climax of Paul's string of contrasts, and the only one that has its own support, highlights its significance. The most likely reason for this special emphasis is that Paul's last rhetorical question recalls the "new covenant" substructure of his apologetic as a whole, which began back in 2:14. Nowhere in the Old Testament is Israel ever identified with the temple. But the parallel between the phrase "the temple of the living God" in 6:16 and Paul's earlier reference in 3:3 to "the Spirit of the living God" indicates that he can equate the church with the temple because, under the new covenant, believers themselves are now the "location" of God's Holy Spirit on earth (cf. the same parallel in 1 Cor. 3:16).

As a result of the pouring out of the Spirit in fulfillment of Ezekiel 36:26–27 (cf. 2 Cor. 1:22; 3:3–6, 8, 17–18; 4:13; 5:5), the church, both in regard to its individual members (1 Cor. 6:19) and in its life together corporately (1 Cor. 3:16), is now the place of God's presence in the world. Paul's application of the Old Testament prohibition against idolatry to the Corinthians is based on the identification of the temple with God's people in Christ since they, like Moses, may be in God's presence without being destroyed (2 Cor. 3:6, 18).

---

12. S. D. Sperling, "Belial," *Dictionary of Deities and Demons in the Bible* (Leiden/New York: Brill, 1995), 322.

13. The prohibition against idols is a common Old Testament theme, with a corresponding New Testament development (cf. Ex. 20:4; 23:24; Lev. 26:1; Deut. 4:16, 23; 5:7–10; 27:15; 32:16, 21; Josh. 23:7, etc.; for "idolatry" in Paul's writings, see Rom. 1:22–25; 1 Cor. 5:10–11; 6:9; 10:7, 14, 19; 12:2; Gal. 4:8; 5:20; Col. 3:5; 1 Thess. 1:9). As we have seen in regard to 2 Cor. 3:7–14, Israel's idolatry with the golden calf broke the covenant and initiated her history of hard-heartedness.

Paul's point is clear. Whereas Israel as a people fell into idolatry and disobedience (cf. the vision of Ezek. 8:3–18 as the basis of Israel's judgment in the Exile), the Messiah has brought the church back into the presence of God's glory and begun the process of transforming her into the image of God himself (2 Cor. 3:16–18). The separation described in 6:14–16a that is to characterize God's people under the new covenant is thus the positive counterpart to Israel's history of syncretism under the old. Paul is therefore stunned that believers would consort with idolatry and wickedness. Here, as in 1 Corinthians 3:16–17, the identification of the church with the temple consequently contains a warning of divine destruction against all who would destroy God's people, since the Corinthians, as God's temple, are "holy" (cf. 1 Cor. 3:17 with 2 Cor. 7:1). The righteous who belong to the Messiah have been delivered from their idolatry and wickedness and brought back into the presence of God's glory.

Support Number Two: The History of Redemption (6:16c–18)

HAVING SUPPORTED HIS command in 6:14 by pointing to the "new covenant" identity of the Corinthians in 6:14b–16b, in 6:16c Paul initiates a second line of support directly from the Scriptures. His command to separate from unbelievers is not an expression of hubris or self-defensive fear. It is the immediate application of the Scriptures' expectation regarding the reality of the new covenant. Note that the chain of quotes in verses 16c–18 is introduced in verse 16c with a single citation formula, "as God has said," and closed off in verse 18c with the corresponding formula, "says the Lord Almighty." Hence, verses 16c–18 do not function to support the fact that believers are the temple of God (6:16b), but are introduced as a *single* citation, composed of six Old Testament passages, which, when read as a whole, support the command of 6:14 and its restatement in 7:1:[14] "Do not be yoked together ... as God has said ... since we have these promises [i.e., as outlined in 6:16c–18], let us purify ourselves ...."

The first Old Testament reference is taken primarily from the promise of God's covenant presence in Leviticus 26:11–12, which, however, was originally stated in the second person ("I will put my dwelling place *among you*"),

---

14. So too Scott, "Use of Scripture," 76, 83, who points to the same use of Scripture in Rom. 3:10–18, where Paul also combines six Old Testament texts into a single quotation introduced with "as it is written." There too his use of Scripture has the same threefold structure found here: beginning and ending axiomatic statements with a "concretizing parenesis" in the middle. As Scott observes, the intermediate "says the Lord" in 2 Cor. 6:17 serves to divide the quotations into two halves, with three lines each.

not the third, as it is in 2 Corinthians 6:16 ("I will live *with them*"). This alternation is due to the conflation of Leviticus 26:11–12 with the new covenant promise of Ezekiel 37:27 ("My dwelling place will be *with them*"). By interpreting Leviticus 26:11–12 in terms of Ezekiel 37:27, Paul is reflecting his conviction that the original covenant promises and the prophetic expectation of their realization after the judgment of the Exile are now beginning to be fulfilled in the Corinthian church! Furthermore, in combining these texts, Paul brings the Law and the Prophets together to make his point, unified within a promise–fulfillment, old covenant–new covenant framework.

This is confirmed by the fact that the covenant formula found in both Leviticus 26:11–12 and Ezekiel 37:27—God as the God of Israel and Israel as the people of God—occurs in only two basic contexts within the Scriptures. It is first found in relationship to the Sinai covenant instituted after the Exodus, in which God established his intention to live among his people, though this covenant was broken at the incident of the golden calf (cf. Ex. 6:7; Deut. 29:12–13; 2 Sam. 7:24; 1 Chron. 17:22; Jer. 7:23; 11:4). It then occurs in relationship to the promise of a new covenant, to be brought about by the "second exodus" redemption of Israel from the Exile, in which God will finally fulfill his purpose of living among his people (cf. Jer. 24:7; 30:22; 31:31–34; Ezek. 11:20; 36:28; 37:23, 26–27; Zech. 8:8; 13:9). Hence, Paul's conflation of Leviticus 26:11–12 and Ezekiel 37:27 intentionally reflects this correspondence between the Sinai covenant of the first exodus and the new covenant of the "second."[15]

In 6:17–18 Paul draws the scriptural conclusion (note "therefore") that flows from a covenant relationship with God: three commands from Isaiah 52:11 ("come out . . . be separate . . . touch no unclean thing") and three ensuing promises from Ezekiel 20:34, 2 Samuel 7:14, and Isaiah 43:6 ("and I will receive you, I will be a Father to you, and you will be my sons and daughters"). In its original context, Isaiah 52:11 is directed to Israel, calling her as a priestly people to separate from Babylon in conjunction with her "second exodus" redemption from captivity. Paul's application of these commands to the Corinthians again reflects his conviction that the promised restoration of God's people is already beginning to take place in the establishment of the church in Corinth.

In Romans 10:15, Paul presents the apostolic proclamation of the gospel as the beginning fulfillment of the announcement in Isaiah 52:7 of Israel's

---

15. This is confirmed by the LXX rendering of Lev. 26:11, which reads "covenant" in place of the Hebrew "dwelling." Moreover, Scott, "Use of Scripture," 82, points out that Lev. 26:12 is often used typologically in Jewish tradition in the context of the return from exile and the restoration of the broken covenant (cf. *Jub.* 1:17, which combines Lev. 26:12 with Zech. 8:8 to refer to the new covenant).

deliverance from the Exile. Here in 2 Corinthians 6:17–18 Paul portrays the church as the people of this restoration (cf. too the use of Isa. 52:15 in Rom. 15:21). Hence, if the Corinthians are part of God's new covenant people, they too, like Israel, must separate from the unbelievers around them. In fulfillment of Isaiah 52:11, Paul views the Corinthians as priests fulfilling Israel's role (cf. Ex. 19:6), so that Paul calls them to separate from what is unclean. Now, however, the "unclean" are not unbelievers outside the people of God, but unbelievers who are threatening the church from within.

Paul's argument in 6:14–17 illustrates that it is simply impossible to identify the Corinthians as a priestly people who are themselves the temple of God without drawing the moral implications that are inextricably part of it. The threefold scriptural commands of 6:17a-c lead directly to the threefold promises of 6:17d–18, which, like the commands, are also a conflation of Old Testament texts—this time Ezekiel 20:34b, 2 Samuel 7:14, and Isaiah 43:6.

In its original context, Ezekiel 20:34 is God's promise of welcome to those returning home from the Exile. Just as Isaiah 52:11 calls God's people to "come out" from the world as a result of the "second exodus," Ezekiel 20:34 promises that God will "receive" them back when they do so.[16] Its subsequent combination with the promise of a Davidic Messiah from 2 Samuel 7:14 points to the Jewish expectation that the redemption from the Exile would take place through the reign of David's long-promised "son," who is also identified as God's "Son."

In accordance with this expectation, in 6:18 Paul quotes the adoption formula from 2 Samuel 7:14, but now makes it plural ("sons") to refer to the Corinthians, in accordance with the previous texts. Finally, Paul then combines it with the reference to "daughters" from Isaiah 43:6, where the "second exodus" restoration of Israel is expressed in terms of sons and daughters (cf. 49:22; 60:4). As a result of bringing these two texts together, God's promise to become the "father" of David's "son," who came to be seen as the Messiah, is expanded to include all of God's people, who, in Christ, become God's "sons and daughters." This expansion of 2 Samuel 7:14 in terms of Isaiah 43:6 reflects the Jewish tradition of interpretation in which the regathered people of God (Ezek. 20:34) come to be seen as the adopted sons and daughters of God.[17]

Indeed, "I will be a Father to you, and you will be my sons and daughters," is the "adoption" formula that is used in Scripture to indicate the covenant relationship between God and his people. In using this formula, Paul is

---

16. For the use of the verb "receive" (*eisdechomai*) in 6:17 as a promise of deliverance from exile, see Jer. 23:3; Ezek. 11:17; 20:34; 22:19; Hos. 8:10; Mic. 4:6; Zeph. 3:19, 20; Zech. 10:8, 10 (cf. Scott, "Use of Scripture," 85n.51).

17. Ibid., 88.

reflecting the Jewish expectation that God's people would one day be "adopted" as his children by virtue of their allegiance to and incorporation in God's "adopted son," the Messiah.[18] As a fulfillment of this expectation, the Corinthians, already incorporated into Jesus as the messianic "Son" of God, are promised that they too, as God's "sons and daughters," will one day participate in the consummation of God's salvation (for the corresponding use of the concept of "adoption" [*huiothesia*], cf. Rom. 8:15, 23; 9:4; Gal. 4:4–5; Eph. 1:5). Who the Corinthians are now in the midst of history (2 Cor. 6:16) is matched by who God promises they will be at the end of history (6:18).

Again, Paul's point is as stark as it is clear. Since the Corinthians are already part of God's new covenant people in fulfillment of the prophets' hopes (6:16c-e), they must separate from the unbelievers among them (6:17a-c) in anticipation of God's final deliverance (6:18). The promise of a continuing covenant relationship and final redemption (6:18) is given only to those who keep the covenant stipulations (6:17), which in this case entail demonstrating their covenant identity by separating from impurity (6:14–16). In other words, the kingdom is here, but it is not yet here in all its fullness.

Thus, 6:16c–18 reflects the same covenant structure and "already/not yet" tension that is characteristic of Paul's theology as a whole. As members of the same covenant, God and his people belong to one another in the same family, each with their own roles and responsibilities. In this context, the emphasis falls on the responsibility of God's children to separate from those within the covenant who, in reality, do not belong and are therefore rendering it unclean.

Nevertheless, Paul's call to the Corinthians is grounded not in their own abilities, but in the present exercise of God's sovereignty to deliver and protect his people as their Father. This point is reflected in his choice of the title "the Lord Almighty" to close his quotes, which occurs only here among Paul's writings (but cf. Rev. 1:8; 4:8; 11:17; 15:3; 16:7, 14; 19:6, 15; 21:22). Paul may, however, have used this title simply because it occurs in 2 Samuel 7:8, 27 (LXX), the larger context from which 7:14 has been taken.

The Command and Its Support Restated (7:1)

IN 7:1, PAUL closes this section by restating his command, now bracketed by a summary of its support: "Since we have these promises ... [therefore] let

---

18. Ibid., 87–88, where he points out that *Jub.* 1:24 applies the adoption formula of 2 Sam. 7:14 to Israel as an extension of the covenant formula used in *Jub.* 1:17. In the same way, the adoption formula in 2 Sam. 7:14 corresponds to the covenant formula used in 2 Sam. 7:24, and Jer. 31:1 (covenant formula) corresponds to 31:9 (adoption formula). In the New Testament, cf. Rev. 21:3 (covenant formula) with 21:7 (adoption formula).

us purify ourselves ... [in that we are] perfecting holiness...."[19] Thus, the command of 6:14a is restated in different words in 7:1, both of which are supported by the argument from Scripture in the middle, which has its own command in 6:17. Everything in this passage supports this one exhortation, given in two forms. And as this carefully structured argument again reveals, inheriting God's promises in the *future* is based on keeping his commands in the *present*, which in turn is brought about by working out the holiness that has *already* been granted to those who are part of God's people (cf. 1:1). Obedience is future motivated; hope is the engine of ethics.

On the one hand, the "promises" of 7:1 refer most directly back to 6:17d–18. These covenant promises were first granted to Israel through Abraham and are now being fulfilled, albeit not yet in all their fullness, in the church's experience of the Spirit (cf. 1:20; also Rom. 4:13–17; 9:4; 15:8; Gal. 3:14, 16, 21). Having received this deposit of the Spirit, the church anticipates with confidence her final reception as God's sons and daughters. Within the framework of Paul's conviction that the "second exodus" redemption of God's people is already beginning to take place in the church (2 Cor. 6:16–18), Paul's command in 7:1 is to be read from this same "new covenant" perspective. Those who hope in God's *future* redemption purify themselves in the *present*. Specifically, the "purification" imagery in 7:1 picks up the priestly image from Isaiah 52:11 in 2 Corinthians 6:17.[20]

On the other hand, Paul's reference to "perfecting holiness in the fear of God" summarizes his earlier statements concerning the incompatibility between God's people and idolaters, with their implication that to pollute God's temple is to fall under his judgment. Just as Paul's own proclamation of the gospel was driven by his "fear of the Lord" (5:11), so too those who receive this gospel should live in light of this same reality.[21] For this reason,

---

19. Formally, 7:1 is comprised of a conjunction that indicates that it functions as the conclusion of its paragraph ("therefore," *oun*), two participial clauses, each of which summarizes a supporting point of the argument of its paragraph ("having these promises" and "perfecting" or "making complete holiness by means of the fear of God"), and a command that restates the main point of its paragraph ("Let us cleanse ourselves from every defilement of body and of spirit" as a more general restatement of 6:14: "Do not be yoked or mismatched with unbelievers"). Moreover, this command is sandwiched between the two participles, one on each side, so that the relationship between what Paul has just said and how it relates to the command he draws from it is clear: "Therefore, since we have these promises on the one hand, let us cleanse ourselves, since in doing so, on the other hand, we will be making complete our holiness by means of the fear of God."

20. Cf. esp. Jer. 23:15; 2 Macc. 5:27, where the purification imagery appears to refer to cleansing from the defilement of idols.

21. The NIV's rendering of *phobos* in 7:1 as "reverence" is too weak and misses the connection to 5:11.

Paul addresses the Corinthians in 7:1 as *agapetoi* (lit., "beloved"), which is a specifically Christian form of direct address often used in contexts of exhortation.[22] It underscores that the obedience in view is not the believer's attempt to win God's love, but the covenant stipulation or response that flows from already being loved by God in Christ (cf. its use in 2 Cor. 12:19; also Rom. 12:19; 1 Cor. 10:14; 15:58; Phil. 2:12; 4:1). Note too that Paul includes himself in the promises and command of 7:1 ("since we ... let us ..."), thereby expressing his solidarity with his church.

Thus, as in 6:14–16a, so too in 7:1 Paul takes the strong language normally used in the polemic against pagan idolatry and applies it to his opponents. This metaphorical use of purification or cleansing is not unique to Paul. In Qumran, to cleanse oneself can refer not only to an actual act of ritual purity, but also, in fulfillment of Ezekiel 36:26, to obedience to the precepts of God as that which "cleanses" one (cf. 1QS 3:8–9). In the same way, Paul's exhortation that God's people "purify themselves" recalls his earlier statements in 3:3, where the promise of the Spirit's purifying work to enable God's people to obey his statutes (from Ezek. 36:26–27) is applied to the Corinthians under the new covenant. Thus, Paul's closing admonition in 7:1 recalls his opening argumentation in 2:14–3:6. In keeping with the overarching reality of the new covenant as outlined in 3:7–18, Paul now widens his focus beyond any one particular issue and directs his command to "everything that contaminates body and spirit," that is, to anything that impacts the believer's life (cf. 1 Cor. 6:17–19; 7:34).

Within the polemical situation in which Paul finds himself, the specific application of his general command in 6:14, 17, and 7:1 is to flee anything that would keep one from being "reconciled with God" (5:20) and from accepting the grace of God in vain (6:1). *Positively*, this means having an "open heart" toward Paul (6:13; cf. 7:2–4); *negatively*, this means separating from those who reject him and his gospel (6:14; 7:1), that is, closing one's heart to Paul's opponents with their "different gospel" (cf. 11:4). For nothing less than the true gospel of the new covenant, the genuine presence of the Spirit, and the rightful identity of God's people are in the balance.

Whether or not one responds to Paul's call in 6:14–7:1 will reveal publicly whether or not one has been reconciled to God as a genuine believer (cf. 13:5–10). Conversely, as Thrall has pointed out, since the Corinthians are Paul's letter of commendation (3:2), "if they fail to maintain the holiness proper to God's covenant people (cf. Lev. 19:2), then the validity of both the message and the ministry of the new covenant will be called

---

22. The NIV's rendering of this word as "dear friends" is too weak and nontheological, since it misses the implied reference to the covenant relationship from 6:17–18.

into question."[23] Within this framework it becomes evident that 6:14–7:1 is not a later insertion into Paul's argument, but a fitting application of his covenant perspective.

The "fear of God" that motivates the believer's perseverance in holiness is therefore not simply a desire to gain rewards or an attitude of "reverence for God." Rather, as its allusion back to 5:10–11 indicates, it refers to God's judgment between believers and unbelievers, since the "fear of the Lord" is the distinguishing mark of the wise (Ps. 2:11; 5:7; Prov. 1:7, 29; 8:13). We ought not to downsize our appropriate response to the righteous and sovereign "Lord Almighty" into simply revering who he is. When we encounter God, we encounter ourselves as sinful.

STEP ONE: BEING yoked together. As we have seen, the main point of this passage is Paul's call to the Corinthians not to be "yoked together with unbelievers" (6:14), which is the specific application of the more general command to "purify ourselves from everything that contaminates body and spirit" (7:1). The first step from Paul's day to our own is to wrestle with the significance of "being yoked together." We have argued above that to be "yoked together" is not a technical term referring specifically to a legal or culturally binding act (like getting married or joining the army, though such events may indeed represent such an act). Rather, it is a metaphor referring to any kind of joint participation, formal or informal, that significantly forms one's own identity. To be "yoked together" is to take on the identity of those who are joined together for a common goal or task. It is to be someone's "ally."

For example, those involved in politics are "yoked together" when they gain their identity as members of the same party; athletes are "yoked together" on a team bearing the same name; citizens are "yoked together" by geography and civil commitments; workers are "yoked together" by function, gaining their identity from being a plumber or stock broker; members of a social class are "yoked together" by common economic status, lifestyle opportunities, and expectations. By contrast, casual, nondefining participation does not constitute such a yoke. Going to a political convention does not necessarily make one a Republican, just as playing softball periodically does not make someone a member of a team, or fixing a faucet, a plumber.

Determining whether someone is "yoked together" with someone is therefore a judgment call that depends on the degree, significance, purpose, and

23. Margaret E. Thrall, *The Second Epistle to the Corinthians*, 1:472.

level of self-identification involved in one's participation. A person can be a middle-class Republican from Chicago who is a plumber during the week, and on the weekend part of the Aces softball team. Or that same person could live like the middle class, even though rich; support a Republican candidate for election, even though an independent; live in Chicago, but be from Boston; fix a faucet without being a plumber; and play catch without being on a team. Deciding what "yokes" we wear is a matter of discernment. The key question becomes: What associations determine who I am?

Step two: defining unbelievers. This brings us to the second significant interpretive question raised by this text: Who are the "unbelievers" of 6:14 and what is the "idolatry" in view? In other words, with whom should we *not* become identified, and in what *contexts*? The answer to these questions will determine how this passage is applied in our contemporary situation.

Recent scholarship has seen three different responses to these queries. (1) Some argue that the "unbelievers" and "idols" in this passage are general terms that simply refer to becoming unduly allied with those who do not follow Christ. This passage is then applied to all areas of life, from worship and work to marriage and education, in order to maintain a purity in the world from all idolatrous defilement. As Furnish puts it, "believers are to avoid any alliance with the world that would be unworthy of a community which understands itself as the temple of the living God."[24] Although we have seen that "unbelievers" does refer to those who do not follow Christ, when taken in this way, our passage creates an unresolvable tension with 1 Corinthians 5:9–10, where Paul recognizes the necessity of participating in the affairs of this world. In fact, Paul never calls Christians to separate from "unbelievers" in the common affairs of society. Moreover, in our present context Paul is not concerned with relationships in the world, but with relationships within the church (cf. 5:11–13).

(2) On the other extreme, some take "unbelievers" and "idols" to refer specifically to the problem of eating meat offered to idols addressed in 1 Corinthians 8–10. From this perspective, Paul is once again calling the Corinthians to abstain from food that has knowingly been offered to idols and from participating in the worship of idols. Paul prohibits meat offered to idols since it violates the consciences of others; he prohibits partaking in feasts held in pagan temples because it compromises the Corinthians' own Christian commitment and identity as the temple of the living God (cf. 8:7–13; 10:14–30). Read in this way, the passage remains a concrete warning against participating in non-Christian worship. But although there are parallels in terminology between 2 Corinthians 6:14–7:1 and 1 Corinthians 8–

---

24. Furnish, *II Corinthians*, 373.

10, this interpretation does not do justice to the context of 2 Corinthians itself. There is no indication in this letter that Paul is still concerned with the spiritually strong in Corinth, who were sharing in food offered to idols. Rather, Paul is here concerned with those who are in rebellion against his authority and gospel.

(3) The position taken here is that Paul's concern is to call the Corinthians to align with his ministry by separating themselves from those who continue to side with his opponents. He drives this point home by identifying those still in rebellion against him as "unbelievers," despite their own claims to the contrary, and by framing the issue in terms of idolatry and the temple of God. For this reason, Paul calls the Corinthians of genuine faith to separate from those "unbelievers" whose lives, under the deceptive influence of "Belial," are characterized by the wickedness and darkness of unbelief (cf. 11:3–4, 13–15). The call in 6:14–7:1 for "the temple of the living God" to separate from "unbelievers" and idolatry parallels Paul's earlier warning concerning destroying the temple of God (1 Cor. 3:16–17) and his call to disassociate with anyone who bears the name of "brother" if he is guilty of immorality or idolatry (1 Cor. 5:11).

Accordingly, the issue in 6:14–7:1 is not identical with the issues of Christian discipleship outlined in 1 Corinthians (esp. 1 Cor. 6:1–20; 7:10–16). Paul is not concerned here with the need for perseverance among believers within the church, nor is he concerned with relationships between believers and unbelievers outside the church. Rather, his focus is on separation from *unbelievers* who are seeking to divide the church from within. Hence, 2 Corinthians 6:14–7:1 is not about separating from fellow believers who do not share all of our theological commitments or ministry perspectives. Only God, in the end, can decide which of us is building with wood, hay, and straw (cf. 1 Cor. 3:10–15).

In other words, Paul's concern here is that the faithful in Corinth separate from those who are not identified with Christ *at all*, despite their outward professions. Their words aside, they remain idolaters because they deny the Son with their worship of health and wealth, and unbelievers because they deny the life-transforming power of the Spirit, substituting instead a desire for spiritual ecstasy and miracles (cf. 3:3, 18; 11:4). In this sense, Paul is urging the same kind of separation from idolatry and pagan temples in 6:14–7:1 as in 1 Corinthians 10:14–22. Now, however, the pagans are not found in the temples of the Corinthian idols, but within the church herself.

This means that Paul's admonition in 6:14 does not refer to civil affairs, as if Christians should do business only with Christians, live only in Christian neighborhoods, eat only with Christians in Christian restaurants, play only on Christian sports teams, and go only to Christian schools. These are all secondary associations that are not even available in most places of the world and do not necessarily define one's primary identity as a member of God's people. Indeed, such involvements will be necessary, unavoidable, and even essential for the spread of the gospel (cf. 1 Cor. 5:9–10; 9:19–23; 10:32–33). Paul envisions no separation between believers and unbelievers in social and civil contexts, even in "mixed" marriages created by a subsequent conversion of one of the spouses, as long as the unbeliever consents (cf. 1 Cor. 7:12–15; 10:27).

Our present passage is not a call to create a Christian ghetto, but a summons to purify the Christian community. *Paul does not have in view the life of the church in the world, but the life of the world in the church.* For as we have seen, the purity of 7:1 refers to both the cultic and moral expressions of the Christian life. That which contaminates the "body and spirit" is the compromise of the gospel within the life of God's people. In 6:14–7:1, Paul is concerned with teaching, ways of life, and false expressions of worship that *defile the purity of God's people* and hence, like participation in pagan temples, must also be avoided.

Step three: the church as the temple of God. The third step is to come to grips with the implications of the fact that Paul interprets the church as "the temple of the living God" (6:16) in terms of her being "adopted" as God's sons and daughters (6:18). In fact, this identification is the key to Paul's passion in this passage. His call for separation and purity makes sense only if the church understands herself *not* to be just one more institution playing an essential role within the fabric of society. Nor is the church a social service meeting the felt needs of her neighbors. Such a domestication of the church could not be more foreign to Paul's view of God's people or to her status as a disenfranchised minority in the Roman world in which Paul lived. Instead, as the new covenant people of God, the church is the "family of God" united by a common identity in Christ and gathered around her common worship and fear of "the Lord Almighty."

To move from Paul's day to our own in this regard requires taking this point seriously. The church's horizontal relationships with one another derive from a common vertical relationship with God. Having been transformed by the presence of God in their midst (6:16; cf. 3:18), the glue that holds believers together is their common "fear of God," not their common social class, race, or cause (6:17). The imperatives of 6:14, 6:17, and 7:1 all flow from the indicative reality of already being the "temple *of God*" (6:16b), and they all lead to the indicative promise of being *God's* sons and daughters (6:17d–18). Without these realities, Paul's commands degenerate into a self-protective and isolating separatism on the one hand, or into a legalistic casuistry on the other. In order to bridge from Paul's context to our own, his family framework is therefore crucial: The church is the people of God, created by his presence, living in relationship to him, and existing for the purpose of glorifying him.

Step four: recovering the covenant perspective. The fourth step in bringing this passage to our day is to recover the covenant and eschatological perspective once again expressed in this passage (see above to 3:3–18). The realization that God's final stage in redemptive history has begun should fuel our work to purify the church. The last days of God's unfolding plan for the world are here. In the midst of this evil age, God is establishing outposts of the kingdom in anticipation of the return of Christ. God has a plan for the world—and the church is it! Believers need a bigger picture of who they are. J. B. Phillip's famous line, "Your God is too small" needs a sequel, "Your church is too small," not in terms of numbers, but in terms of her self-understanding. The people of the new covenant have cosmic significance as the people of the last days of God's unfolding plan for the world. Living between the two comings of Christ is consequently the key to Paul's emphasis on the necessity of obedience.

Many commentators are uncomfortable with Paul's insistence that the *future* reception of the divine promises in 6:17d–18 and 7:1 depends on our *present* obedience to the commands, thus apparently implying some kind of "works theology." Nothing is farther from the truth. Paul is not advocating some kind of synergism in which we cooperate with God by doing our part, now that God has done his. Salvation is his work, past, present, and future. From Paul's perspective, the promises in view in this passage have already begun to be fulfilled in the lives of God's people, even though they are not yet consummated. We should cleanse ourselves from every defilement (7:1b) because of the promises God has granted us (7:1a).

Yet these promises were themselves grounded in the reality depicted in the rhetorical questions of 6:14b–16b. God promises what he does not because his people will earn them through their obedience, but because they already belong to the church. His promises are given to his people. Paul did not say, "Obey the command in order to *become* God's people"; he said, "Obey the command because you *are* God's people." That is why all obedience is an expression of the same grace and power that saved his people to begin with.

As the references to the church as the temple of God indicate, Paul is thinking covenantally here. God's acts of deliverance in the past, which are the basis of the covenant, lead to his commands for the present, which make up the stipulations of the covenant. In turn, keeping these stipulations is tied to God's promises for the future, which are the blessings of the covenant. Thus, as we live in the present, based on what God has done in the past, our focus is on the future. The call to faith is not a call to remember the past, but to trust God in the present.

Obedience is therefore the consequence of what God has already done for us, driven by what he promises yet to do for us. The necessity of obedience is the flip side of the righteousness in Christ that forms our identity as the temple of the Holy Spirit (6:14–16). It follows then that inheriting God's promises is contingent on our obedience, because our obedience is the expression of having already begun to inherit these very promises. Moreover, the down payment of these promises is the Holy Spirit himself, who empowers us for the very obedience to which we are called. What God has already done for us in Christ and through his Spirit secures our hope for what he will do when Christ returns (1:22; 3:3, 6, 8, 18; 6:16).

So our hopes for the future and our ability to obey in the present are both founded on God's acts in the past. Christ died on the cross in order that we might become the righteousness of God and inherit this eternal home, having granted us a foretaste of his glory in the Spirit (3:9; 5:21; 6:14). This hope determines how we now live. Like all people, what we long for determines how we act. All human behavior is driven by what we think is going to happen or what we want to happen in the future. All action is goal-oriented. The past makes the present possible, but the future determines what the present actually looks like. In short, the foundation of faith is God's redemptive acts in the past; the focus of faith is his promised redemption still to come, the life of faith is depending on God to meet our needs in the meantime. Hope is the engine of ethics.

This movement from the past to the future to the present once again reflects the tension in the New Testament between what has "already" happened in Christ and what has "not yet" taken place. Christians are "saved in hope" (Rom. 8:24). Because of God's saving work in Christ, his people already experience God's presence (2 Cor. 6:16). At the same time, they look forward to that time when the kingdom will be established in all its glory (6:17d–18). The link between this present experience and future expectation is the growing purity of God's people, since it is based on what God has already done and motivated by the promises that derive from it (7:1).

In Christ, God's promises have already been granted to his people as matter of unconditional grace. But at the same time their continuing and future enjoyment is conditioned on keeping the covenant stipulations that flow from his prior acts of deliverance. Not to keep these commands is to deny the reality of God's presence and power that has been bestowed under the new covenant. Paul calls us to strive for holiness precisely because of the holiness we have already experienced through Christ. Indeed, the keeping of these commands is itself an expression of the enabling work of God's grace in our lives. Rather than "quenching the Spirit," a recovery of serious theological reflection on the nature of our covenant relationship with God and on our place within the history of redemption is therefore crucial for the life of the church. It is this reflection to which Paul drives us in this passage.

The perspective argued here is therefore distinct from those who do not take Paul's reference in 7:1 to "perfecting holiness" to signify a process of moral transformation. Instead, they interpret it to refer merely to separating from idol cults or to continuing in faith, defined as mental assent to the truth of historical data. Such views cannot accept that growth in sanctification is the necessary way by which believers purify themselves. They fear that the reading of the text argued for here introduces an insipid legalism into the gospel of grace.

This fear, however, is unfounded. Furthermore, these interpretations cannot account for the parallel between the process of transformation in 3:18 and 7:1, or for the parallel between the "fear of the Lord" in 5:11 and the "fear of God" in 7:1 (cf. too Eph. 5:21; 6:5; Phil. 2:12). These parallels indicate that the holiness in view must entail an actual progress in living according to God's will that manifests itself in deeds by which we will be judged as part of the "new creation" (2 Cor. 5:17). As part of this new creation, the Corinthians testify by their separation from evil that the consequences of humanity's fall in Genesis 3 and of Israel's idolatry in Exodus 32 are being reversed in their lives.

Against this backdrop, 6:14–7:1 is not a later insertion into Paul's argument, but a fitting application of his covenant perspective. The call to separate from unbelievers, like the calls to reaffirm their allegiance to Paul and his ministry that frame them (cf. 6:11–13 and 7:2), is grounded in the covenant formulae and their implications as quoted in 6:16–18. In the light of the new covenant, Paul's operating assumption is that it is simply impossible to be in God's presence and not manifest a transformed life (cf. 1 Cor. 6:9–11, 19–20; 2 Cor. 3:18; 5:17).

 STRIKING FOR PURITY. In drawing out the significance of this passage, the stress in 7:1 on purifying ourselves "from *everything* that contaminates body and spirit" is striking. In 6:14–7:1, Paul is concerned with teaching and ways of life that *defile the purity of God's people*. Like the Corinthians' earlier participation in pagan temples, believers must avoid such pollutants at all costs. For the Corinthians, obeying this call entailed separating from those still opposing Paul and his ministry. Today, too, any commitment, relationship, or practice that adversely impacts our identity as members of God's people must be separated from the church. Moreover, it is important to keep in mind that in this passage "purity" is first and

foremost not a ceremonial designation, but a moral one. "Righteousness" in 6:14 is contrasted with wickedness. It is the character of the Christian that is primarily in view.

As we strive for this purity, we must think anew concerning the ways in which people are "yoked together" in a society of individual isolation and private morality. Determining whether one is yoked together with others can be difficult in a culture that is less and less community-based and more and more unsure of moral absolutes. In our day, we increasingly live alone in a mass culture. The only thing that ties us together is the ever-present, all-pervasive media. As a result, our "yokes" are usually not experienced concretely with specific individuals or groups, but established privately with disembodied values. In Western society today, "yokes with unbelievers" are more readily established through TV and the shopping mall than with a neighbor. Most of us do not even know the names of our neighbors, though we know the names and family histories of dozens of movie, sports, music, and TV personalities.

The parallels in this passage between being "yoked together" and sharing things "in common," "having fellowship," creating "harmony," and being in "agreement" with unbelievers should therefore not be reduced to a narrow category of behavior that applies only to marriage and to worshiping in non-Christian ways. Neither should they be interpreted as a broad category that includes agreements between Christians and non-Christians in areas of common cultural participation. Paul is not calling for a Christian ghetto. Instead, in the words of Hauerwas and Willimon, he is calling for a Christian "colony," that is, "an island of one culture in the middle of another," a "colony of resident aliens within a hostile environment, which, in the most subtle but deadly of ways, corrupts and co-opts us as Christians."[25]

Like Paul, pastors today should consequently be "called to help us gather the resources we need to be the colony of God's righteousness."[26] At the

---

25. Stanley Hauerwas and William H. Willimon, *Resident Aliens: Life in the Christian Colony* (Nashville: Abingdon, 1989) 12, 139–40. Written from the perspective of the declining mainline churches, this study is a wake-up call to the cultural accommodation that has crept into evangelicalism as well. Such compromise can be seen in the trend among evangelical seminaries to produce clergy who, like the products of their liberal counterparts, "are agents of modernity, experts in the art of congregational adaptation to the cultural status quo, enlightened facilitators whose years of education have trained them to enable believers to detach themselves from the insights, habits, stories, and structures that make the church the church. . . . The congregation watches in befuddlement as the pastor manages to do everything but plan worship, preach well, teach, and build up the congregation. . . . The new pastors are trained to help the individual be a bit less miserable within the social status quo—just like doctors and lawyers . . ." (116).

26. Ibid., 140.

heart of this calling is the preservation of the Christian community through the cultivation of Christian character and the weeding out of wickedness. Paul's concern is that believers, who bear the name of Christ, not maintain relationships of shared values that will pollute and eventually destroy the character of God's people.

In addition, Paul's suffering on behalf of the Corinthians demonstrates that his call for separation, which strikes us today as harsh and uncompromising, is, in reality, a reflection of his deep love for the Corinthians (cf. 6:11–13; 7:2–4). For, as Hauerwas and Willimon again observe,

> how is falsehood confronted except in a manner that always seems severe to the one tangled in deceit? The cost of *not* confronting our deceit is high also: nothing less than the death of our life together. The ancient *Didache* begins, "Two ways there are, one of Life and one of Death, and there is a great difference between the two ways." The ethical stance of these early Christians ... was a concrete application of their theological assertions. The church was called to be colony, an alternative community, a sign, a signal to the world that Christ has made possible a way of life together unlike anything the world had seen. *Not* to confront lies and deceit, greed and self-service ... would be the death of this church.[27]

For the good of God's people, Paul can stomach no compromise between idolatry and the temple of God for which he has laid down his life. Paul's call for separation grows out of his profound understanding of the life-changing difference between being in the world and being in the church (6:14–16). In contrast, though confronted with a church that is yoked together with the idolatry of its culture's materialism and with the pride of its moral laxity, we have lost this moral and spiritual power because of our vacuous views of God and our consequent unwillingness to suffer for others and the gospel. As a result, our contemporary concerns over the weakness of the church, usually framed in terms of numerical growth, are often thinly veiled special pleadings for the sake of our own status and meeting the budget.

Thus, there is nothing more significant from this passage than Paul's persuasion that the church is the place of God's presence within the history of redemption. Today, however, the church is often merely "a conspiracy of cordiality," in which we refuse to confront each other out of a lukewarm definition

---

27. Ibid., 131–132. Hauerwas and Willimon make these points on the basis of the Ananias and Sapphira narrative in Acts 5:1–11. As they conclude, "Here, in struggling to be truthful about possessions, the church experienced itself as a disciplined community of truthfulness" (132).

of "love" that "keeps everyone as distant from everyone else as possible.... This accounts for why, to many people, church becomes suffocatingly superficial. Everybody agrees to talk about everything here except what matters.... The loneliness and detachment of modern life, the way we are all made strangers, infects the church too."[28] But Paul loves the Corinthians too much to settle for anything less than their being received as God's sons and daughters. Having been reconciled to God, believers are to be known by their "righteousness" as the "temple of God." Christians are a people who worship God only and trust in him alone for their future.

Hence, in order to determine the pockets of idolatry in our lives together as God's people, we must evaluate carefully the influence of our daily commitments, our social practices, and, most important, those values that we share in common with our culture. Most often, the idolatry we face is our culture's smothering covetousness, in which happiness is derived from more possessions and security comes from increasing our financial stability. As believers, we sanitize this covetousness by perverting God's power and presence into a means to some other end. Since all we need to be happy is Jesus *and* the Christian family, Jesus *and* material blessings, Jesus *and* a growing ministry, Jesus *and* my neighbor's spouse, Jesus *and* whatever it is we do not have now, we turn following Jesus into a means to these other ends. Such a perversion makes serving Jesus the means to satisfying our idolatry!

Yet, as God's people, our yoke is to the "living God" alone (6:16). We must be careful here. It is not usually our self-chosen identity labels that indicate with whom we are yoked (e.g., "I am an evangelical, Calvinistic, Baptist"). Rather, it is the "labels" that our behavior suggests to others that offer a good clue to the various "yokes" we carry and with whom we carry them. Do our lives demonstrate publicly and privately that we belong to the "colony" of the church, with its distinct subculture of righteousness, or to the dominant culture of the world around us?

We must not create churches that preach the glory of Christ while at the same time cultivate lifestyles that focus on attaining the pleasures of this world. We cannot declare the sovereignty of God and at the same time promote looking to the self-help strategies of our culture as the pathway to salvation. We cannot preach the power of God and wink at sin. The arrogant exaltation of our human egos and the love of money are the twin pillars of the wickedness and darkness that the opponent of God is using today to bring the idols of the health and wealth gospel into the church. May God grant us the strength to be his people alone.

Seeking to be the church. It is not enough, therefore, to police our private

---

28. Ibid., 138.

lives. In this passage, Paul's primary concern is for the purity of the corporate church as the temple and family of God. Like Paul, we must not shrink back either from exercising church discipline whenever it becomes evident that unrepentant idolatry exists within the body of Christ. This is not easy in modern society. Because of the church's weakened self-understanding of what it means to be the people and place of God's presence in the world, porous conceptual and ethical boundaries now exist between the church and the culture. And disciplining the church is made even more difficult by the consumer attitude that allows members to church-hop if they cannot "get along" in their former congregation.

Nevertheless, such difficulties must not deter us from working hard to sustain our identity as God's people in a particular place who, because of his presence in our lives, may live in a way the world regards as peculiar. Those who forsake living for the pleasures of this world because they pale in comparison to living for Christ will look exceedingly strange to those for whom this world is all there is (cf. 4:16–18). Our freedom from idolatry is our witness to the world.

> Christianity is mostly a matter of politics—politics as defined by the gospel. The call to be part of the gospel is a joyful call to be adopted by an alien people, to join a countercultural phenomenon, a new *polis* called church. The challenge of the gospel is not the intellectual dilemma of how to make an archaic system of belief compatible with modern belief systems. The challenge of Jesus is the political dilemma of how to be faithful to a strange community, which is shaped by a story of how God is with us. . . .
>
> This church knows that its most credible form of witness (and the most "effective" thing it can do for the world) is the actual creation of a living, breathing, visible community of faith. . . .
>
> The most creative social strategy we have to offer is the church. Here we show the world a manner of life the world can never achieve through social coercion or governmental action. We serve the world by showing it something that it is not, namely, a place where God is forming a family out of strangers. . . .
>
> The only way for the world to know that it is being redeemed is for the church to point to the Redeemer by being a redeemed people. The way for the world to know that it needs redeeming, that it is broken and fallen, is for the church to enable the world to strike hard against something which is an alternative to what the world offers.[29]

---

29. Ibid., 30, 47, 83, 94.

This acknowledgment of the desperate need to regain a living expression of what it means to be the community of God's presence is growing today across all church boundaries. For example, the concern expressed above by the Methodists Hauerwas and Willimon is echoed in the recent work of Everett Ferguson. When summarizing what it means to be the people of God, Ferguson, a Church of Christ scholar, takes his initial cues from Hans Küng, the liberal Catholic theologian, only to conclude by quoting John Howard Yoder, the Anabaptist ethicist![30] From Küng, Ferguson draws the fundamental point of our passage: "The church must be separated from the conduct characteristic of the world. Since you are God's people (2 Cor. 6:16), therefore you must live as God's people (2 Cor. 6:17) in order truly to be God's people (2 Cor. 6:18)."[31] From Yoder, Ferguson supports his own observation that Paul's understanding of the church as "true peoplehood . . . found in God through Jesus Christ (Gal. 3:28; Col. 3:11)" transcends all of the "false (and potentially sinful) principles of unity around which people organize themselves" (e.g., citizenship, race, occupation, economic status, political doctrine, social class, education, etc.).[32] In Yoder's words:

> This new Christian community in which the walls are broken down not by human idealism or democratic legalism but by the work of Christ is not only a vehicle of the gospel or fruit of the gospel; it is good news. It is not merely the agent of mission or the constituency of a mission agency. This *is* the mission.[33]

Yoder's words remind us that Paul's concern for the purity of the Corinthian church must not be construed as a desire for isolation. It is separation for the sake of mission. Just as Paul's life embodied the cross and mediated the Spirit (cf. 2:14–3:14; 4:1–18), so too the character of the covenant community *is* the embodiment of the gospel in the world. We show the all-sufficiency of God's sovereignty and our satisfaction in his presence by the way we live. In this sense, our way of life is part of our worship. We praise God by prizing him above all people and things.

Thus, Paul's admonitions in 6:14–7:1 are not only those of a pastor; they are also those of a missionary. The mission of the church is not merely to spread a message, as if the goal of the gospel were information, but to repli-

---

30. Everett Ferguson, *The Church of Christ: A Biblical Ecclesiology for Today* (Grand Rapids: Eerdmans, 1996), 90–91, referring to Hans Küng, *The Church* (London: Burns & Oates, 1968), and John Howard Yoder, "A People in the World: Theological Interpretation," in James Leo Garrett Jr., *The Concept of the Believers' Church* (Scottdale, Pa.: Herald, 1969).

31. Ferguson, *The Church of Christ*, 90 (referring to Küng, *The Church*, 122).

32. Ferguson, *The Church of Christ*, 90.

33. Ibid., 91 (quoting Yoder, "People," 274), emphasis mine.

cate itself within every people group on the globe. In this passage Paul is speaking not as someone whose feelings are hurt, but as the missionary apostle to the Gentiles. The Corinthians are not students in a classroom taking notes on theology (as important as the doctrinal formulation of the church is), but a pocket of God's presence from which Paul hopes to launch even more forays into enemy territory (cf. 10:12–18). So part of the reason Paul's call for purity in the church seems so foreign to us today is that we have lost his missionary zeal for the world. May God use us to witness to his all-sufficient power and love as the "Lord Almighty."

Living as a redeemed community. How then can we begin to recover and respond to Paul's admonitions today? (1) We must recover our sense of redemptive history. As we have seen, Paul's calls in 6:14 and 7:1 are based on his understanding of the church's place within God's saving purposes and plans. Our lives are part of his story. Indeed, "the moment that life is formed on the presumption that we are not participants in God's continuing history of creation and redemption, we are acting on unbelief rather than faith."[34] This recovery will require a concerted effort of biblical and theological study, as well as a pattern of preaching that takes the biblical canon and flow of history seriously. For as William A. Dyrness points out, we in the West have trouble conceptualizing ourselves as part of an ongoing history, since culturally "our incurable optimism has replaced history with anticipation.... Middle-class Americans seem to have lost all sense of a narrative connection with the past."[35]

Without an understanding of God's redemptive work in creating a community of faith, the church will have trouble surviving the pressure of our culture to succumb to the power of positive thinking, the assumption of progress, and the humanity-worshiping "incurable optimism" that pervades our thinking. Faith takes root not in the latest mystical experience on the market, but in the history of redemption that stretches from the covering of Adam and Eve and the call of Abraham to the exodus from Egypt and the coming of Christ.

(2) We must recover our understanding of the church as a "peculiar people." This will take a concerted effort of cultural analysis as well as a willingness to consider ourselves "cross-cultural" missionaries to our own culture.

---

34. Hauerwas and Willimon, *Resident Aliens*, 36–37. As they put it, "The church does not exist to ask what needs doing to keep the world running smoothly and then to motivate our people to go do it. The church is not to be judged by how useful we are as a 'supporting institution' and our clergy as members of a 'helping profession.' The church has its own reason for being, hid within its own mandate and not found in the world. We are not chartered by the Emperor" (39).

35. William A. Dyrness, *How Does America Hear the Gospel?* (Grand Rapids: Eerdmans, 1989), 139.

To this end, we must resist turning this text into moralism. The divide Paul makes in the world is not between those who are trying hard and those who are not; it is a fundamental divide between those who belong to Christ and are empowered by the Spirit and those who are still dead in their sin because they are living under the rule of the spirit who, as "Belial," is now working against God in the sons of disobedience (cf. 2 Cor. 4:4; Eph. 2:2). It is for this reason that God's people, who are now the Most Holy Place, can have no agreement with idols (2 Cor. 6:16).

The heart of sin is to bring an idol into the Most Holy Place (i.e., into our lives) through adopting the values and goals of the godless culture in which we live. The first commandment, "You shall have no other gods before me" (Ex. 20:3), is most likely a spatial reference to bringing false idols into the temple in order to worship them along with Yahweh, the one true God who had rescued his people from Egypt (20:1–2). Similarly, the temptation to idolatry among God's people today is not to deny God outright but to distrust his all-sufficiency and sovereignty, so that we continue to need God and something else to get us through and make us happy: God and a better job, God and a better spouse, God and a better front lawn, God and my neighbor's cottage, God and a vacation.

Again we are reminded of what Paul tells us in Ephesians 5:5 and Colossians 3:5: Covetousness is the heart of idolatry, since the first and the last commandment are, in reality, the same commandment. To say to oneself, "If I only had what Suzie or Jim had, then I could be happy," is to be an idolater who denies the sufficiency of the presence, power, and love of God to satisfy our souls (see the Contemporary Significance section of 3:4–6 and Bridging Contexts section of 5:1–10).

(3) Most important, we must recover a God-centered focus that exalts God's sufficiency in all that we do and say within the church. God alone can free us from idolatry by satisfying the deepest longings of our hearts. It is no accident that although Paul is describing the believer's entire way of life and not a gathering to worship as such, his language throughout this passage is nevertheless the language of the temple and of worship. Our willingness to forsake the happiness offered by the idols of our culture is an act of worship that exalts God through our dependence on him alone. It is also the natural magnet that draws others to God by displaying the life-changing majesty of his righteousness, moral light, and saving mercy (6:14–15). God's presence is seen in the idol-free lives of his people, who as God's temple are being transformed into his own image by virtue of his glory (6:16; cf. 3:18).

In the end, such heartfelt and heart-filled worship, expressed in separation from idols, cannot be faked or manufactured. The covenant structure of Paul's argument in 6:16–18 and 7:1 has again underscored that only those who belong to Christ now will value and long for God's promises for the future, and only those who long for God's promises for the future will be motivated to purify themselves in the present. The pathway to holiness, therefore, is not more willpower, but worship. The exaltation of God's character is the pathway to holiness since it displays the worth of being his people, as well as creating the fear of forfeiting his promises that keeps God's people persevering in faith. At the same time, such God-centered worship will expose those whose doctrine and way of life denigrate the holiness of God, the value of his promises, and the saving significance of Christ.

Hence, since it is ultimately the "fear of God" that drives Paul's concern for the Corinthians, his ethics can never be reduced to a "self-help" program of organized common sense (cf. 5:11 with 7:1). Rather, his admonitions are the expression of knowing that God walks among us as our God (6:16). For this reason, "All ministry can be evaluated by essentially liturgical criteria: How well does the act of ministry enable people to be with God?"[36] Yet, because the contemporary church has so often failed to be the place where his holiness is manifest by our idol-free lives, Paul's concern to purify the life of the church from idolatry has become almost unintelligible today. Indeed, over thirty years ago Langdon Gilkey asked, "How the church can minister to the world, which is its task, without losing itself, which is always its danger."[37] In view of Paul's argument in 6:14—7:1, Gilkey's analysis of the situation holds the answer:

> All around us we see the church well acclimated to culture: successful, respected, wealthy, full, and growing. But are the transcendent and the holy there? In the area of belief we find widespread indifference to the Bible and ignorance of its contents—and strong resentment if a biblical word of judgment is brought to bear on the life of the congregation. In worship we find notably lacking any sense of the holy presence of God and of what worship is for.... In ethics we find the cultural ideals of friendliness and fellowship more evident than the difficult standards of the New Testament or historic Christendom.[38]

Paul's words in this passage are an iron shot in the arm of the anemic church. Paul reminds us that nothing less than inheriting God's promises is at stake in how we live with God and with one another. To be received as God's sons and daughters on the day when Christ judges the world, we must

---

36. Hauerwas and Willimon, *Resident Aliens*, 138–39.

37. Langdon Gilkey, *How the Church Can Minister to the World Without Losing Itself* (New York: Harper & Row, 1964), 1.

38. Ibid., 3.

live as God's children now. This means cultivating a purity of devotion to our heavenly Father that separates from anyone or anything that would compromise our lives as those who trust in God alone for our future.

The fear of losing God keeps us close to him. The fear of falling under his judgment rather than being welcomed into his presence as his children keeps us persevering. Of course, such a fear of God, grounded in his grace, makes sense only to those in whom he already dwells, over whom Christ already reigns, and among whom the light of divine righteousness is already shining. Only believers fear God truly, since only those who have already begun to enjoy his presence can taste the horror of what it would be like to be without it. The fear of the Lord is the beginning of wisdom, just as it is the beginning of the passion for holiness among God's people. Those who fear his judgment because they love his presence put away the filth of God-compromising idolatry and wickedness from their lives, both individually and corporately.

May God grant us a fresh glimpse of his glory and a renewed vision of the splendor of his promises, that we may perfect our holiness by fearing him alone.

2 Corinthians 7:2–16

MAKE ROOM FOR us in your hearts. We have wronged no one, we have corrupted no one, we have exploited no one. ³I do not say this to condemn you; I have said before that you have such a place in our hearts that we would live or die with you. ⁴I have great confidence in you; I take great pride in you. I am greatly encouraged; in all our troubles my joy knows no bounds.

⁵For when we came into Macedonia, this body of ours had no rest, but we were harassed at every turn—conflicts on the outside, fears within. ⁶But God, who comforts the downcast, comforted us by the coming of Titus, ⁷and not only by his coming but also by the comfort you had given him. He told us about your longing for me, your deep sorrow, your ardent concern for me, so that my joy was greater than ever.

⁸Even if I caused you sorrow by my letter, I do not regret it. Though I did regret it—I see that my letter hurt you, but only for a little while—⁹yet now I am happy, not because you were made sorry, but because your sorrow led you to repentance. For you became sorrowful as God intended and so were not harmed in any way by us. ¹⁰Godly sorrow brings repentance that leads to salvation and leaves no regret, but worldly sorrow brings death. ¹¹See what this godly sorrow has produced in you: what earnestness, what eagerness to clear yourselves, what indignation, what alarm, what longing, what concern, what readiness to see justice done. At every point you have proved yourselves to be innocent in this matter. ¹²So even though I wrote to you, it was not on account of the one who did the wrong or of the injured party, but rather that before God you could see for yourselves how devoted to us you are. ¹³By all this we are encouraged.

In addition to our own encouragement, we were especially delighted to see how happy Titus was, because his spirit has been refreshed by all of you. ¹⁴I had boasted to him about you, and you have not embarrassed me. But just as everything we said to you was true, so our boasting about you to Titus has proved to be true as well. ¹⁵And his affection for you is all the greater when he remembers that you were all obedient, receiving him with fear and trembling. ¹⁶I am glad I can have complete confidence in you.

Original Meaning

JUST AS PAUL'S experience of waiting for Titus in 2:12–13 introduced his apologetic in 2:14–7:1, so too the resolution of this narrative in 7:2–16 introduces the next major section of Paul's letter in 7:2– 9:15: *The Application of Paul's Apologetic to the Repentant in Corinth.*

Because of the controversy still raging in the church, in 2:12–7:1 Paul addressed the Corinthians as a whole, focusing primarily on his self-defense. Most of the church, however, had already repented in response to Paul's previous letter (cf. 1:23–2:4; 7:5–16). Thus, in 7:2–9:15 Paul addresses this majority, focusing primarily on their responsibilities as Christians. Whereas in the first section Paul was the apologist defending the faith, here he is the pastor admonishing his flock. Hence, while his previous arguments were based largely on his legitimacy as an apostle, his arguments in 7:2–9:15 are derived largely from the legitimacy of the Corinthians' life as believers (see comments on 7:3 and 4). Beginning in 7:2 we have the legitimate minister speaking freely to those he knows to be legitimate believers. In his turning to his church, now restored in fellowship with him, we see what is often called "the pastor's heart."

Paul's Command to the Repentant (7:2–3)

PAUL'S ADMONITION IN 7:2–3 form the main point of 7:2–16, with 7:4–16 presenting an extended argument in support of this command. Although the division of the NIV supports this reading, most commentators argue that 7:2–3 (or 4) belongs to what precedes, not to what follows, or that it is a transitional text forming a bridge between the two sections.

This is not a moot point. How one decides this issue is decisive not only for interpreting chapter 7, but also for understanding the flow of the argument in chapters 6–8 as a whole. The difficulty is deciding whether 7:2–3 (or 4) provides the concluding exhortation to what precedes, so that 7:4 or 5 begins a new unit of thought, or whether the new unit begins already in 7:2–3, being supported by what follows. What makes this decision difficult is that the exhortation of 7:2–3 seems unnecessary or out of place if Paul is addressing the repentant of 7:4–16, especially in view of the *positive* description of them in 7:6–12. Paul's admonition in 7:2, "make room for us in your hearts," seems parallel to 6:13, which was given to those who were *withholding* their affection from Paul (cf. 6:11–12). Yet 7:7–16 pictures a people who are filled with longing, zeal, and obedience regarding their apostle. Why would *they* need such a command and reminder of Paul's legitimacy?

This confusion is resolved if we keep in mind that Paul's concern in 6:14– 7:1 was that the "believers" in Corinth should "open wide their hearts" to the apostle (6:13) by separating from those still in rebellion against him (see comments on 6:14–7:1). This is still the case in 7:2, where once again the way in which one "makes room" for Paul is by separating from the unbelievers. But in 6:11–13 Paul was speaking *"as to my children,"* in the hope that they would respond as such, whereas in 7:2–16 Paul is speaking to those who have already proven themselves to be among God's people by their repentance. For this reason, Paul's vocabulary is different in 7:2 than in 6:13 ("open wide" versus "make room for us"[1]). While 6:13 was a call *to repentance* to the church as a whole (cf. 6:11–12), 7:2 is aimed at those whose hearts are already "opened wide." Finally, the thematic links between 7:2–4 and their support in 7:5–16 confirm that 7:2–4 look forward to verses 5–16 rather than backward to 6:11–7:1.[2]

In 6:11–7:1, Paul gave the church as a whole the means to demonstrate that they accepted him and his gospel. In 7:2, he calls on those who have in fact repented to follow through on it, thereby effecting the separation he has just commanded. The content of the commands has remained the same, but their audience has changed. Since believers should open their hearts to Paul and his gospel (6:13), in 7:2 Paul singles out the repentant within the church because he is confident that they will obey in the present, even as they have obeyed in the past (cf. 7:15–16).

In making the transition from addressing the church as a whole in 6:11–7:1 to addressing those whom Paul knows to be believers within it, Paul is simply drawing out the implications of what it means for the believers in Corinth to be his true "spiritual children" (cf. 6:13; 12:14–15; also 1 Cor. 4:14–15). Making room for Paul will necessitate cleaning out those who are still in rebellion against him. The two cannot coexist in the affections of the Corinthian believers (6:11–13) or in the church as a whole (6:14–7:1). Those whom Paul knows to be Christian he calls to be Christian. Paul's heart is for the purity of his people.

Paul supports his command with a threefold assertion (7:2b). The Corinthians should make room for Paul because it should be clear by now that he has "wronged no one ... corrupted no one ... exploited no one."

---

1. The NIV translation, "make room for us *in your hearts*" is an unwarranted narrowing of the verb *choreo*, which simply means "to have room for, hold, contain" (cf. BAGD, 889). The only support given in BAGD, 890, for the suggestion that in 7:2 the verb has a figurative meaning, "open-heartedness," is the parallel to 6:13. But in 6:13 the verb is different (cf. *platuno*, "make wide," "enlarge") and is defined by the references to Paul's heart in 6:11 and their affections in 6:12, while here the verb is left undefined.

2. Cf. "encouragement" or "(to) comfort" (*paraklesis/parakaleo*) in 7:4 and in 7:6, 7, and 13; "joy"/"to rejoice" (*chara/chairo*) in 7:4 and in 7:7, 9, 13b, and 16, which functions as an inclusio from v. 4 to v. 16; "afflictions"/"to afflict/oppress" (*thlipsis/thlibo*) in 7:4 and in 7:5; and "boast"/"to boast" (*kauchesis/kauchaomai*) in 7:4 and 7:14.

These staccato-style statements sharply summarize his argument thus far in response to the criticisms being raised against him.

Once again Paul's use of the plural in 7:2 reflects his apostolic office, while his switch to the singular in what follows reflects his personal involvement in the situation (cf. the plural in 7:13a with the singular in the parallel statement of 7:16). Paul's behavior has been above reproach, both personally (1:12–2:11; 5:12–13; and now 7:8–12; cf. 2:14–4:18; 6:3) and in terms of his handling of the collection (2:17; cf. 11:7–11; 12:13–18[3]). His concern for the Corinthians' purity is matched by the purity of his own life before them.

In verse 3, Paul ensures the faithful that in giving this command he is not again condemning them, as he did earlier in his "tearful letter" (2:4). Unlike those addressed in 6:11–13, Paul has no doubt about their standing with him or his gospel (cf. 7:12–16). The reason for Paul's confidence is given in 7:3b, which recalls his earlier affirmation in 3:2. Far from condemning them, Paul has already declared that the repentant Corinthians are "written on [Paul's] heart" as his "letter of recommendation" (3:1–2). Here Paul reminds them that this "letter" is "read by all" in his willingness "to die and live" (lit. trans.) for their sake as their spiritual father (cf. the parallel between 7:3 and 3:2; cf. too 1:6; 6:11–12a).

Paul's reversal of the normal order of "life and death" (note that the NIV reverses Paul's order!) most likely alludes to the death and resurrection of Christ as they are being played out in Paul's own suffering and endurance on behalf of the Corinthians (cf. 1:8–11; 4:10–12; 5:14–15; 6:3–10). His willingness to suffer for their sake expresses the depth of his love for the Corinthians as fellow believers who share a common destiny (cf. 2 Sam. 15:21; Rom. 8:38–39). Far from condemning them, Paul is simply drawing out the implications of what it means for the Corinthians to be his "spiritual children" (cf. 2 Cor. 6:13; 12:14–15; also 1 Cor. 4:14–15). Hence, just as Paul's suffering shows his love for the Corinthians as their apostle (2 Cor. 2:17–3:3; cf. 11:7–11; 12:15), so too their willingness to break with his opponents will show their love for him as his people.

Paul's Disposition Because of the Repentant: Comfort and Joy (7:4)

IN VERSE 4 Paul begins his extended argument in support of 7:3 by recounting his own disposition in response to the repentant in Corinth. He does so

---

3. See the use of this same verb, *pleonekteo* ("to take advantage of, outwit, cheat, exploit"), in 2:11 to describe Satan's strategy of "outwitting" believers, and in 12:17–18 to describe Paul's denial that he and Titus "exploited" them with the collection. For its only other use in the NT, cf. 1 Thess. 4:6.

in a chain of inferences taken from his opening arguments that together form a topic sentence for what follows.[4] Paul is not afraid to call the Corinthians to action because he is convinced of their genuine standing as Christians. Hence, as a mediator of the Spirit under the new covenant, he has "great confidence" (parresia, better, "boldness of speech") toward them.[5] As the parallel in 3:12 indicates, he is speaking boldly in 7:2–3 because he is convinced that those in whom the Spirit is at work will respond to the commands of the gospel (cf. 3:3–18; 5:17). In the end, nobody can do anything against the truth (cf. 13:8). This conviction is confirmed in regard to the Corinthians by Titus's report (see 7:7–12).

Consequently, Paul's boldness leads him to "great pride" (lit., "much boasting") in the Corinthians, since they are the evidence of the Spirit-endowed character of his ministry (cf. 1:14; 3:3, 8; also 7:14; 8:24; 9:2–3; 10:12–18). The ability to boast in the Corinthians as a new creation leads Paul to be "greatly encouraged" (lit., "filled with comfort") as a result of this public testimony to God's resurrection power at work in and through his life.[6] The outworking of Paul's comfort is a life filled with joy (lit., "overflowing with joy") in the midst of his afflictions, which itself is an expression of the same resurrection power (7:4d; cf. the exact parallel in 1:4; also 4:11, 15–18; 6:10; 13:9). Paul commands the Corinthians (7:2) because he loves them (7:3), and he loves them because of the confidence, pride, encouragement, and joy he has in them as his spiritual children (7:4).

Paul's Comfort and Joy Because of God (7:5–7)

PAUL'S EXTENDED ARGUMENT in 7:5–15 supports 7:4 by detailing how God worked in the circumstances of the recent past to encourage him concerning the Corinthians. Specifically, the apostle returns to the story begun in 2:12–13 in order to show how God used his suffering as a means both to the Corinthians' salvation and to his own happiness (cf. 1:3–6).

As we saw in 2:13, Paul's anxiety over Titus's delay in returning from Corinth had caused him to push on into Macedonia in hope of hearing about the church's response to his "tearful letter." Paul's description in 7:5 of this

---

4. Victor Furnish, II Corinthians, 392–93. Furnish, however, sees 7:4 as the beginning of a new unit of thought, with the prior section extending from 6:11–7:3.

5. In view of the use of this same term in 3:12, the NIV rendering of parresia as "confidence" is possible, but not probable. In Paul's day, this semi-technical term was used to refer to a "boldness of speech" or "candor" that derived from the positive nature of one's own message (Paul speaks the truth) and from a trust between speaker and audience (Paul's relationship with the Corinthians is repaired).

6. The development of this theme in 7:7, 13 is an extension of his thought in 1:3–7; 2:14; 4:7–14. Compare too its use in 8:4, 17 to describe others in whom God is at work.

same suffering expands on the lack of peace he experienced as he waited and searched for Titus. Paul's restlessness was caused not only by external "conflicts" (cf. 2 Tim. 2:23; Titus 3:9), probably as a result of his struggles in Macedonia (cf. Phil. 1:30; 3:2), but also by internal fears concerning the fate of his coworker and the future of the Corinthians (cf. 11:28).

When Titus finally did arrive, it became evident that he was safe and that God had used Paul's letter and Titus's ministry for the good of the Corinthians. Hence, this double dose of good news, brought about by the divine hand, comforted Paul (7:6) and Titus (7:7; cf. 7:13–15). The comfort came through Titus, but its origin is God!

In spite of his suffering over Titus and the Corinthians (7:5), God used Titus's arrival, and *even more so* the comfort Titus had received from the Corinthians because of their changed attitude toward Paul, to increase his joy more than ever (7:6–7). He experiences joy and comfort when others make progress in their faith (cf. 1:24), and through Titus's ministry the Corinthians had just turned from rejecting Paul to longing for his return (cf. 7:11), having felt a deep sorrow over their past rebellion and a new zeal for his ministry. The full reason for this emphasis on Titus will become clear in 7:14 and in the transition from chapter 7 to chapters 8–9.

Paul's description in 7:6 of God as the one "who comforts the downcast" is thus the ultimate reason Paul's joy increased even more in response to the Corinthians' repentance and Titus's comfort. On the one hand, this description of God recalls Paul's opening description in 1:3–4, which provided the framework for understanding his suffering as an apostle. God is the one who comforts the suffering righteous. On the other hand, the reference to "the downcast" (lit., "the humble ones") recalls Isaiah 49:13, which points back to Paul's earlier use of 49:8 in 2 Corinthians 6:2.[7] Just as Isaiah summons all creation to rejoice over the "second exodus" deliverance of God's people, so Paul rejoices that the majority of the Corinthians have shown themselves by their repentance to be part of this redemption.[8] In heeding Paul's earlier call to repentance, they have already responded to the

7. Cf. Isa. 49:13 LXX (*tous tapeinous tou laou autou parekalesen*) with 2 Cor. 7:6 (*ho parakalon tous tapeinous*).

8. So Paul Barnett, *The Second Epistle to the Corinthians*, 369–70. Thus, Paul's vocabulary of comfort "calls to mind God's comfort of his people through the prophet Isaiah (LXX Isa 40:1; 49:13; 51:3, 12, 19; 52:9; 61:2; 66:13); the 'consolation [i.e., comforting] of Israel' (Luke 2:25) described the long-awaited messianic age. Paul's extensive use of such language within 2 Corinthians is taken to imply that this age has arrived, a view that is explicit elsewhere within the letter (see on 3:3, 6; 6:2). Thus the statement 'God . . . comforts the downcast' is not merely an edifying reflection on the gracious character of God expressed in this action; it also symbolizes God's action toward his people under the new covenant."

"day of salvation" that is declared in 2 Corinthians for the sake of those still in rebellion.

The parallel between 7:6 and 6:2 on the one hand, and 7:6 and 1:3–4 on the other, reflects Paul's conviction that his own suffering is the means by which the message of salvation announced by Isaiah and fulfilled by Christ is being made real among the Corinthians. Accordingly, Paul's comfort and joy are not merely the expressions of personal relief over his friend and his church, though they certainly are that (cf. the parallels in 1 Cor. 16:17; 1 Thess. 3:6–7). More important, they are expressions of God's presence and power, since Paul recognizes that God is the one behind the coming of Titus and the change among the Corinthians (2 Cor. 7:6; cf. 7:13a). For this reason, he rejoices even more, since he sees God as bringing about the redemption of the new creation declared in Isaiah 49:8–13. Paul's joy in meeting Titus and in hearing about the Corinthians is a joy ultimately brought about by Paul's theology.

Paul's Comfort and Joy Because of the Corinthians (7:8–13b)

THE SECOND REASON for Paul's increased joy is given in verses 8–15. Here Paul recounts the sending, sorrow, and sanctification brought about by the "tearful letter" he wrote in response to his "painful visit" (2:1, 4). In particular, verses 8–13a clarify his comfort over the Corinthians, while verses 13b–15 support his joy over Titus.

In 7:8–13b, Paul recounts how his joy increased all the more when he received word from Titus that his ministry had, in fact, born fruit among the Corinthians. Though his letter of rebuke was a reflex of his own anguish and love for the Corinthians (cf. 2:4), Paul initially regretted having sent its stark denunciation of their defiance, since he knew it would cause them sorrow (see 7:8). As part of his "fears within" (7:5), he wondered if he had been too severe and if, as he had boasted, the Corinthians really would respond. Moreover, those still in rebellion against Paul would likely interpret this letter as a hypocritical attempt to frighten the Corinthians and to "pull rank" over them (cf. 10:8–11). Nevertheless, his fears were unfounded. In response to his rebuke, the majority of the Corinthians had repented, as evidenced by their willingness to discipline the one who had led the charge against Paul (cf. 7:12 with 2:5–6).

Thus, in spite of the pain the letter caused, Paul no longer regrets sending it but rejoices (7:7, 9), since the sorrow it caused "for a little while" (7:8) was not an end in itself, but led to their repentance (7:9). "Repentance" includes both the remorse that comes from recognizing that one has wronged God and its consequent resolve to reverse one's behavior as seen in the first steps in that new direction. Therefore, though its consequences are long-term, repentance is indicated by an initial change in both attitude and action.[9]

Paul is aware, however, that not all experiences of "feeling bad" lead to repentance. People feel guilty for all kinds of reasons. The reason the Corinthians' remorse led to repentance was because they had "become sorrowful as God intended"—that is, experiencing the kind of genuine remorse that leads to a real change in one's way of life (7:9b; cf. Rom. 8:27; Eph. 4:24 for the same expression used here). Being sorrowful as God intended is feeling the deep grief that comes from knowing that our attitudes and actions have harmed our relationship with God. "Godly sorrow" feels bad because it is missing out on God.

As an expression of their repentance, the Corinthians returned to Paul and "were not harmed [lit., suffered no loss] in any way by us" (7:9c). This does not refer to Paul's concern over any emotional damage he may have done them (he knew his letter would cause them sorrow), but to the fact that their response had spared them God's judgment, which threatens all those who "accept the grace of God in vain" (6:1; cf. 5:10–11; 7:1). Paul's statement in 7:9 once again reflects the identity between the Corinthians' relationship with Paul and their relationship with God (cf. 2:14; 3:3; 4:7–12; 5:13, 20; etc.). For "Paul considered their improper behavior toward him and his apostolate as an affront to God. To mistreat God's representative placed the Corinthians in a precarious position because it involved a wrong attitude to the Gospel."[10] To oppose Paul, Christ's ambassador, was to reject Christ (cf. 5:18–6:2).

Verses 10–12 support Paul's declaration in verse 9c that the Corinthians will be spared God's judgment (of which Paul himself is an instrument; cf. 2:15–16a; 13:2; also 1 Cor. 4:21; 5:3–5; 16:22). The reason is given in 2 Corinthians 7:10a: Their repentance toward Paul leads to salvation because it was not a death-producing "worldly sorrow." Worldly sorrow is the grief that comes about because one's actions result in missing out on something the world has to offer. Worldly sorrow feels bad because it wants more of the world. Such sorrow causes us to focus even more on how hurt we are, thereby helping to bring about the death that comes from living for self rather than for Christ (cf. 5:15). At stake in the Corinthians' earlier rebellion, however, were not their feelings or their fortunes, but their future with God.

---

9. It is frequently pointed out that Paul does not often use the term "repentance"/"to repent" (*metanoia/metanoeo*) (besides 7:9–10, cf. Rom. 2:4; 2 Cor. 12:21; 2 Tim. 2:25, and the cognate, "unrepentant," in Rom. 2:5). Nevertheless, its content is everywhere present as the presupposition for the exercise of the "obedience of faith" that flows from the call of the gospel itself.

10. Ralph P. Martin, *2 Corinthians*, 30.

Paul cared deeply about the Corinthians' relationship with him not merely because he had grown fond of them, but because he was their spiritual father in the gospel. So just as their rebellion had caused him great pain, their repentance brought him great joy, since his primary goal as an apostle of the *new* covenant is not to bring God's judgment, but the joy of experiencing God's righteousness (cf. 1:24; 3:9; 13:9–10). As an apostle, Paul's happiness was bound up in the redemption of those to whom God had sent him. By their repentance, the Corinthians had shown themselves to be part of this number.

Paul's confidence that the Corinthians have indeed experienced a "godly sorrow" leading to repentance is not based on wishful thinking but on the sevenfold expression of their repentance outlined in 7:11. Heading the list and of most significance for Paul's argument is the Corinthians' renewed "earnestness" (*spoude*) in regard to his ministry.[11] What one desires is a sure sign of who one is. The Corinthians' other responses are all corollaries to this earnestness, including their indignation against the offender and against themselves for having supported him, their fear ("alarm" in the NIV is too weak) of God's judgment (cf. 5:11, 20), and their zeal ("concern" in the NIV is too weak) for Paul and his ministry. The consequence of their earnestness is that they have "proved [themselves] innocent in this matter" (7:11c).

The expression "to prove/commend oneself" (*synistemi heauton*), used here to describe the Corinthians, is the same expression Paul used elsewhere to portray his own commendation of himself (cf. 4:2; 6:4). When used positively, as it is here, it refers to demonstrating the validity of one's claims by virtue of one's actions as the visible expression of God's stamp of approval (cf. 10:12–18).[12]

Like Paul, the repentant in Corinth can point to their own attitudes and actions as evidence that God is at work in their lives. Having demonstrated genuine repentance, they prove themselves "innocent in this matter" (7:11c). The word translated "matter" (*pragma*) can be used in a technical sense to refer to a legal case (cf. 1 Cor. 6:1) and most likely carries such a "quasi-legal connotation in our present passage."[13] In their past rebellion against Paul, the

---

11. In the Greek syntax of verse 11, "earnestness" or "eagerness" (*spoude*) is set off from what follows as a matter of emphasis. The importance of the Corinthians' earnestness as a sign of their genuine faith for Paul's argument in 2 Cor. is confirmed by the fact that "earnestness" or "eagerness" (*spoude*) and its cognates are used eight times in chs. 7–8 (cf. 7:11, 12; 8:7, 8, 16, 17, 22[2x]), but only five times in all the other Pauline writings combined (Rom. 12:8, 11; Phil. 2:28; 2 Tim. 1:17; Titus 3:13).

12. The opposite of this is a "*self*-commendation" (*heauton synistemi*), in which one is forced to substitute for such hard evidence of God's approval one's own unsubstantiated claims or those of others in letters of recommendation (cf. 3:1; 5:12; 10:12, 18; 12:11).

13. Furnish, *II Corinthians*, 389.

Corinthians stood in danger of being condemned before God. But the majority has now demonstrated its "innocence" (7:11)—not on their own strength, but because of God's provision on their behalf, first in sending Christ to the cross and now in bringing them to the repentance and reconciliation with God that leads to salvation from his wrath (5:16–6:2; 7:10).

Since it is "godly sorrow" that brings repentance, Paul knew that he had to confront the Corinthians for the sake of their own salvation (7:12). He did so by reminding them that they stood "before God," i.e., in his presence as judge (cf. 2:17; 4:2; 5:10–11; 8:2; 12:19). Paul intervened in this way not because he recognized within the Corinthians a potential waiting to be realized.[14] Rather, he did so because such a confrontation for the sake of Christ, which necessarily contains a threat of God's judgment, is the way of testing the genuineness of faith. The call to repentance in view of the judgment of God is the divinely ordained means of bringing about repentance among those in whom God is at work.

It was Paul's confidence that God was at work among the Corinthians, not his confidence in the Corinthians themselves, that led to his writing of the "severe letter." Paul wrote it because he had reason to believe it would provide the stimulus needed to prove their genuineness *before God*, while at the same time exposing their true colors *to themselves* (7:12, 14). His concern was not with the fate of the one who had wronged him (cf. 2:5)[15] or with his own status as the offended one, but with the salvation of the Corinthians (cf. 2:4). The issue at stake was not his popularity but the apostolic gospel, which explains his switch to the "apostolic plural" in 7:12.

In the end, Paul's confidence in the Corinthians is confirmed. They have passed the test. As a result, he is encouraged in the midst of his afflictions (the "this" of verse 13a not only refers back to verse 12, but also picks up verses 5–6, thereby creating an inclusio back to the beginning of this larger unit of thought).

Paul's Comfort and Joy Because of Titus (7:13b–15)

JUST AS PAUL'S description of his comfort and joy over the repentance of the Corinthians in 7:8–13a unpacks 7:6, so too the recounting of his comfort and joy over the happiness of Titus in 7:13b–15 unpacks 7:7. In this way, the

14. Contra Martin, 2 *Corinthians*, 215.

15. The identity of the offender and the nature of his offense during Paul's "painful visit" (cf. 2:1) are still not resolved. Attempts to identify the offender with the man of 1 Cor. 5:1–5 or 1 Cor. 6:1–11, or with an offense against Timothy in light of 1 Cor. 16:10–11, have not been found persuasive. There is also no consensus on whether the offender was one of Paul's opponents from outside the church or a member of the church itself, though the call for reconciliation in 2:5–11 makes it highly likely that he was a member of the congregation.

theme of Paul's comfort leading to his joy is repeated at each of the major transitions in this chapter (cf. vv. 4, 6–7, and 13). Moreover, the three transitions are interrelated. Verses 6–7 and 13 explicate the general topic statement in verse 4, in which it becomes clear that Paul's comfort through the Corinthians on the one hand, and through Titus on the other, ultimately comes from God. So each major section of the chapter is marked by an emphasis on Paul's joy as a result of the encouragement he received from God's work in the lives of the Corinthians and, even more so, in the life of Titus (vv. 2–4, 4–5, 8–13a, and 13b–15).

The reason for Paul's increased joy over Titus is given in 7:13b–15. In 7:13b Paul emphasizes, as he did in verse 7, that his joy increases "even more" (NIV, "especially") over Titus than over the Corinthians in and of themselves. At first such an emphasis on Titus is puzzling. The reason becomes clear, however, in 7:14, where we learn that Paul had put himself on the line for the sake of the Corinthians. He had risked embarrassment by declaring in advance that they would respond positively to his "tearful letter" and to Titus's ministry, even though Titus himself had reservations about taking the letter to Corinth. Yet, Paul's "boasting . . . to Titus"[16] proved true. In addition, Paul's joy has increased because the Corinthians' response of obedience to him (cf. 2:9) and their reception of Titus as Paul's emissary "with fear and trembling" also increased Titus's affections for them (7:15).

In regard to the former response, the "obedience that comes from faith" is a key Pauline description of the goal of his ministry among the Gentiles (cf. Rom. 1:5; 15:18; 16:19). The Corinthians' obedience is the outward manifestation of their genuine trust in Christ; it is impossible to have one without the other. In regard to the latter response, Paul is the only New Testament author to use the expression "with fear and trembling" to describe the believer's reaction to being part of God's great salvation. He uses this expression in Philippians 2:12 and Ephesians 6:5 in connection with the believer's obedience, and in 1 Corinthians 2:3 to describe his own attitude in preaching the gospel. If obedience is the action that grows from the gospel having taken root, then "fear and trembling" is its corresponding attitude. Those who recognize that obedience is the fruit of genuine faith do not take sin lightly. Faced with God's judgment (cf. 5:9–10), perseverance in faith is a matter of life and death.

---

16. This expression (*epi* with a genitive) refers to speaking "before Titus" as the judge of Paul's claim (cf. Mark 13:9; Acts 25:9; 1 Cor. 6:1 for this same expression). Moreover, given the mixed nature of the church at this time, the "all of you" of 7:13b and the "you" of 7:14–15 are not references to the entire church, but to the repentant majority that Paul is currently addressing (cf. 2:6).

The probable source of the phrase "fear and trembling" is Isaiah 19:16, which refers to the future dread that will come over Egypt when she realizes that God is raised up against her (cf. Ex. 15:16; Deut. 2:25; 11:25; Ps. 55:5). However, when God strikes the Egyptians in the days to come, it will not be to destroy them, but so that they "will turn to the LORD," that he might "respond to their pleas and heal them" (Isa. 19:22; cf. Exod. 12:23). Unlike the first exodus, in which Moses was sent to judge Egypt, in this "second exodus" the Lord "will send them a savior and defender, and he will rescue them. So the LORD will make himself known to the Egyptians, and in that day they will acknowledge the LORD" (Isa. 19:20–21; cf. Ex. 9:14–16; 10:1–2; 14:4, 17, 31). In this great reversal, the Assyrians too will be included, thereby pointing forward to the great restoration of the nations after the Exile comes to an end (Isa. 19:23–24).

Paul's use of Isaiah 19:16 in 2 Corinthians 7:15 continues to express his conviction that the ministry of the gospel fulfills Isaiah's proclamation of this coming "second exodus" (cf. 2 Cor. 6:1–2; 6:17). God's promised redemption of the nations, even of those nations that had oppressed Israel, is now being inaugurated in the Corinthians' repentance and reception of Titus "with fear and trembling."

In Conclusion:
Confidence and Joy (7:16)

THE FOCUS THROUGHOUT this passage has been on Paul's comfort and joy because of the Corinthians, especially as this resulted in Titus's own comfort, happiness, and renewed affection toward the repentant. By way of summary, Paul's declaration of joy in 7:16 as a result of his renewed confidence in the Corinthians marks a key turning point in the letter.

On the one hand, 7:16 restates 7:4, thereby concluding the argument of 7:4–16, while at the same time picking up the theme of joy from verses 7, 9, and 13 (7:4 and 16 are supported by vv. 5–15; 7:4 and 16 support 7:2–3). On the other hand, 7:16 provides the transition to chapters 8–9 by making clear that the reason for the emphasis on Titus throughout this passage is not due only to his role in judging Paul's confidence in the Corinthians (7:14), but also to his upcoming role in the collection for Jerusalem. Titus is the one who will now bear the responsibility for completing the collection that began in Corinth over a year ago, but had stalled as a result of the intervening problems between Paul and his church (cf. 8:6). Now that a majority of the Corinthians has been reconciled to Paul, the collection can resume.

Paul's regained confidence in the Corinthians has rekindled his determination to complete the collection (cf. 7:11, 12, 16 with 8:6, 24; 9:3). The admonitions of the letter we call "Second Corinthians" are now replacing those of the "tearful letter" as the next opportunity for the Corinthians to display their faith. Just as they were obedient in response to the tearful letter (7:12, 15), so too they will manifest their faith by being obedient concerning the collection. Hence, Paul's joy as he contemplates Titus's return to Corinth to arrange for the collection foreshadows the joy he anticipates having on the Day of Judgment, when the Corinthians' deeds demonstrate, once and for all, that they have not received God's grace in vain (cf. 1:14; 5:10; 6:1–2).

 SINCE THIS PASSAGE in many ways restates the issues raised in 2:12–13 and 2:14–3:3, the reader should consult those passages for the principles involved in bringing this passage to the twenty-first century. Five additional points come to the fore in applying this particular passage.

(1) Most important, Paul's account of his recent history with the Corinthians highlights the fact that confronting sin and calling God's people to repentance are the primary instruments of sanctification in the life of a Christian. In our pluralistic, therapeutic, and privatistic culture, this kind of intervention is uncomfortable and increasingly uncommon. Paul's argument makes clear, however, that such a prophetic stance is an essential aspect of the gospel and that the courage to take such a stance is a fundamental expression of Christian love and leadership. Paul is a mediator of the Spirit, not a salesman. He is a proclaimer of the gospel, not a motivational speaker. God's Word, not self-help tips, is the tool of his trade.

(2) Paul's argument in this passage highlights once again the functional parallel between God's work of redemption and Paul's ministry of reconciliation, the former being effected through the latter. In sharing his feelings with the Corinthians, Paul is not speaking as a therapist, but as an apostle. His goal is not to empathize with the Corinthians, but to show them just how serious their sin has been. Barnett has put this point well in commenting on 7:8–12:

> Significantly, the Corinthians' reaction to Paul in this matter is inextricably connected with their relationship with God and his salvation. To have rejected Paul's authority in this matter would have been, in an ultimate sense, to have rejected their salvation ... repentance and reconciliation in regard to Paul cannot be separated from their restoration to God....

Once again we are confronted with the closeness of relationship between the gospel and the apostle who proclaimed it. . . .

To reject the apostle—as the Corinthians were effectively doing by their passivity toward the offender—was nothing less than to live as if the "day of salvation" had not come [cf. 5:18–6:2]. But repentance toward Paul, God's coworker and Christ's ambassador (5:20; 6:1), and therefore repentance toward God, confirmed the Corinthians in their salvation.[17]

Though we are no longer in the "apostolic age," the gospel still comes embodied in those who proclaim it. Nevertheless, Barnett correctly cautions us not to make the link between Paul and the modern preacher too direct.

Hermeneutically . . . it is to be doubted whether Paul's authority (10:8; 13:10) carries over in quite the same way to subsequent generations of ministers of the gospel. To be sure, a rejection of the word of God may involve rejection of the bearer of that message, as appears to be the case with the Corinthians. Let ministers and pastors be careful, however, that it is the word that is being rejected and not, in reality, some fault in them. Such rationalization is not unknown. In any case, Paul was an apostle of Christ (12:12), a revelator of the glory of God (4:2, 6), in a way that cannot be true of others outside that generation. A pastor's authority is derived from the apostles, and qualified to that extent.[18]

This high calling, together with its caution, is of importance both for those whom God has called to minister in his name and for those to whom they are sent. It is not Paul as a person whom we follow, but Paul as an apostle of Jesus Christ. The Corinthians obeyed Titus not because he was personally appealing, but because he represented Paul. In the same way, in appropriating Paul's message today, ministers must also appropriate his example of leadership by "practicing what they preach," since, as it was for Paul, the gospel is on the line in their lives. This means that they must not pervert their ministry into personality contests. Nor may ministers claim the same intrinsic authority that Paul carried. Ministers today carry apostolic authority only to the degree that they represent the apostolic gospel. Though parishioners must honor those who proclaim the gospel, they must not confuse the person of the minister with the message.

(3) Paul's analysis of the situation in Corinth highlights the power of the gospel. Paul does not minimize the fact that the rebuke of his "tearful letter"

---

17. Barnett, *Second Epistle to the Corinthians*, 372, 375n.15, 377–78.
18. Ibid., 375–76.

caused the Corinthians personal, emotional pain. But 7:8 makes clear that he is not offering an apology. Nor is Paul speaking as a counselor who is concerned with the feelings of the Corinthians and willing to share openly his own emotions by way of example.

Central to applying this passage in our contemporary "therapeutic culture" is coming to grips with the Pauline distinction in 7:10 between "godly sorrow" and "worldly sorrow." The former is that heartfelt grief over our rebellion against God that leads to a decisive turnaround in our orientation and behavior (i.e., repentance). It is a grief that leads us to view our lives the way God does and to change accordingly. Godly sorrow refers not to God's using our heartaches, but to the heartache that comes from recognizing our sin.

> In contrast to godly sorrow is the sorrow that is of the world.... This sorrow is a type that included pain and regret, similar to godly sorrow. However the result in this case is not repentance, but death.... Worldly sorrow comes about because of the unwelcome consequence of sin. The person who exhibits this response of worldly sorrow may indeed seek to avoid similar future actions and their consequences. But in no instance is the person driven to *God*, for that individual feels no deep-seated remorse over actions taken against *God*. Rather it is more a regret that one has acted foolishly or been discovered in a lapse, like king Saul's admission, "I have played the fool, and erred exceedingly" (1 Sam. 26:21). Repentance involves the whole person— knowing, feeling, willing ... and is more than an emotional reaction.... "Recognition of sin by itself is not repentance; it may be defiance. Nor is sorrow for sin repentance, if it be alone in the mind; it may be remorse or despair. Abandonment of sin, by itself, may be no more than prudence."
>
> *The criterion in evaluating the worth of an individual's "sorrow" lies in its effect.*[19]

To appreciate Paul's approach, we must therefore grasp his goal. It is not to give advice about how to get along better in this world, as if the message of Christ were the spiritual equivalent of technology. Note how Paul describes the world elsewhere as having been sold into the slavery of sin. Nor is his goal to help people sustain better self-esteem so that they can get along better with themselves, as if the gospel were the spiritual equivalent of therapy. Apart from Christ, Paul insists that people are slaves to sin. Rather, the goal of the

---

19. Martin, 2 *Corinthians*, 232–33, quoting Strachan, emphasis mine. Martin points to the contrasts between Esau (Gen. 27:38; Heb. 12:16–17) and David (Ps. 51:12–19) or between Judas and Peter (Matt. 27:3; Luke 22:31–34) as illustrations of the two types of sorrow (233).

gospel is to bring about a reconciled life with God that creates a godly life (1:22; 3:18; 4:4–6; 5:17; 7:1).

"Death," for Paul, is fundamentally an alienation from God that keeps one in the throws of sin and "blinded" to his glory, both now and in the age to come (4:2, 4). "Worldly sorrow," with its focus on the values and promises of this world, produces the same death from which it comes (2:16; 7:10b). In stark contrast, "godly sorrow" brings the repentance that leads to salvation because it has God as its source and thereby leads to life (2:16; 7:10a).

(4) The startling degree to which Paul's joy dominates this section highlights once more the proper motivation for Christian life. Paul is filled with joy because of God's work in the midst of his own afflictions (vv. 4, 16), because of Titus's arrival (vv. 5–6), because of the Corinthians' repentance and reconciliation (vv. 8–13a), and because of Titus's joy (vv. 7, 13b–15). In relating Paul's happiness to our cultural context, we must underscore, however, that Paul's comfort and joy are not merely personal or circumstantial, but deeply theological. Just as the object of true sorrow over sin is God, so too Paul is filled with joy because of what God has been doing through his own circumstances of affliction, through his ministry to the Corinthians, and through Titus's life and service (cf. 7:4, 6, 7, 13).

(5) Finally, Paul's argument here reveals his conviction that God is sovereignly at work in and through the ups and downs of life to comfort and encourage his people. When Paul sees the world, he sees the hand of God. What transpired in Corinth was not merely the unfolding of circumstances, but the unfolding of God's plan. For Paul, God is the ultimate actor in the Corinthians' response to Paul's letter (7:6–7, 9, 11; cf. Bridging Contexts of 1:3–11).

We miss the point of this passage if we miss Paul's emphasis on God. Each of his statements about himself or the Corinthians ends up being a statement about God. Paul's feelings of comfort are God's comfort to him (7:6); the Corinthians' sorrow is "godly sorrow" in accordance with God's intention (7:9–11); the Corinthians' new self-understanding takes place "before God" (7:12); and the Corinthians' repentance is God's instrument of encouraging Paul (cf. the "divine passive" in v. 13a).

For this same reason, since God is the one ultimately at work in his ministry, Paul could be confident concerning most of the Corinthians even before they received his letter of rebuke, so that he boasted to Titus in advance about their response. He was so confident

because he knew that, because they had received the word of God, the Spirit of God was active in them (1:18–22; 3:2–3, 18), and that Christ Jesus was "in" them (13:5). They had "received the grace of God" (6:1).

Paul's confidence, then, was not in the Corinthians, but in God who was so evidently at work in their lives through the Spirit.[20]

EMOTIONS. This text is filled with references to emotions—from confidence and affection to sorrow, grief, and longing. Initially, such an emphasis on emotions seems to relate easily to our contemporary sensibilities. Indeed, Roger Rosenblatt actually dubbed 1997 "The Year *Emotions* Ruled," since "even relatively small and local events evoked or involved heightened group responses."[21] As he observed, "Every few weeks in the past 12 months, something happened to invite an emotional public reaction of mass grief, panic, or elation, often wildly disproportional to the significance of the event."[22] Such emotionalism, he wrote, was the result of the cultural pendulum swinging back as the century comes to an end:

> Not all that long ago, alienation from self and others was so universally thought to be the bugaboo of modern life that it was becoming boring to mention it. To be emotionally numb to experience, to live depersonalized, was to be unhappy. Not lately. *With the notable exception of religious fundamentalism*, the past 25 years have seen an aggressive pursuit of depersonalization, a shutting off of the emotions at once so purposeful and complete that many people, the young especially, speak of envying machines—a far cry from those earlier generations that feared nothing so much as becoming machines. . . .
>
> For at least two decades, to be cool was to be "cool." And then, suddenly, it was not. As with all extreme cultural tendencies, something had to snap, and what began to show up in the mid–1990s was an insistent desire to feel passion again and show us you care. In 1995 psychologist Daniel Goleman published *Emotional Intelligence: Why It Can Matter More Than IQ*. The best-seller was embraced in educational circles because EQ (emotional quotient) offered a way to counter IQ as a standard of intelligence. But it was also a signal that the public at large might be ready, indeed eager, to return to the flagrant emotionalism of the 1960s, though fired by new and different causes.
>
> What causes were available? There was no Vietnam War to protest, no sexual revolution or drug culture to adopt (live free and die), no

---

20. Barnett, *Second Epistle to the Corinthians*, 384–385.
21. "The Year *Emotions* Ruled," *Time Magazine* (Dec. 22, 1997), 64–68 (p. 64).
22. Ibid., 64.

generation gap worth exploiting. The Gap had become a clothing store, the counterculture reduced to a few average hysterics who thought it exciting to proclaim God dead and the family expendable. As for opposing technology, it seemed out of the question. A decision had already been made to join our machines rather than beat 'em.

With no glaring cause to display mass emotions, anything that happened could qualify.[23]

Yet the contrast between the emotions described in our passage and the "hysterical packs"[24] Rosenblatt observed at the end of our century could not be more pronounced. Starved for the true joy born of godly grief and repentance (Paul's own version of the "religious fundamentalism" that Rosenblatt exempted from the recent pursuit of depersonalization), our culture increasingly lurches for whatever stimulus to emotion we can find. Our drive to protect ourselves by being detached did not deliver what it promised, producing instead an isolation and loneliness that made the cure worse than the disease.

All too often the church is likewise emaciated when it comes to experiencing deep and lasting joy in the midst of adversity because we no longer gain our identity by living within the community of faith. What we love, and therefore what we get excited about, is no longer wrapped up with the progress of God's people. The basis of our contentment is not the growing Christ-likeness of our church, but the comfort level of our personal circumstances. Conversely, we are famished when it comes to feeling grief over sin because what we hate, and therefore what we feel remorse about, no longer revolves around the reality of who God is in our midst. What makes us sad is no longer the sting of our sin, but the frustration of our failed dreams and the lack of freedom to get whatever we want.

Joy. Against the bleak landscape of modern emotions, it is striking how many times Paul refers to his own happiness and that of Titus in this passage. But it should not be that striking. As Rosenblatt observed, "religious fundamentalists" (i.e., those who hold that what they believe is true not only for them, but for everyone) are marked by their emotional engagement with life. It is natural to be emotional when life has meaning.

What *is* surprising is that Paul seems more concerned about what Titus thinks and about how they both feel about the Corinthians than about the fate of the Corinthians themselves. Such a reaction simply reveals how far we are from Paul's perspective. Today we find it hard to believe that someone's own happiness could be so wrapped up in the welfare of others that to

---

23. Ibid., 66 (emphasis mine).

24. Ibid., 64. "Mass guilt, which used to be thought of as a convenient way out of individual responsibility, was in" (65).

talk about *their* situation naturally leads to talking about one's *own* grief or gladness. Paul and Titus's own joy coalesced with the condition of the Corinthians. The focus of this text is on the joy that comes about because of another person's participation in salvation. As Jonathan Edwards summarizes this biblical logic:

> In some sense the most benevolent, generous person in the world seeks his own happiness in doing good to others, because he places his happiness in their good. His mind is so enlarged as to take them, as it were, into himself. Thus when they are happy, he feels it; he partakes with them, and is happy in their happiness.[25]

This is the miracle of a changed heart brought about by Christ. As John Piper puts it:

> The miracle of Christian Hedonism is that overcoming obstacles to love by the grace of God has become more enticing than every form of self-confidence. The joy of experiencing the power of God's grace defeating selfishness is an insatiable addiction.
>
> ... When a person delights in the display of the glorious grace of God, that person will want to see as many displays of it as possible in other people. If I can be God's means of another person's miraculous conversion, I will count it all joy, because what would I rather see than another display of the beauty of God's grace in the joy of another person? My joy is doubled in his.
>
> ... *Love is the overflow of joy in God that meets the needs of others.* The overflow is experienced consciously as the pursuit of our joy in the joy of another. We double our delight in God as we expand it in the lives of others. If our ultimate goal were anything less than joy in God, we would be idolaters and would be no eternal help to anyone. Therefore, the pursuit of pleasure is an essential motive for every good deed. And if you aim to abandon the pursuit of full and lasting pleasure, you cannot love people or please God.[26]

This radical recognition that "full and lasting pleasure" is to be found ultimately only in the enjoyment of God's glory and grace is not natural. It

---

25. Quoted by John Piper, *Desiring God: Meditations of a Christian Hedonist* (Sisters, Ore.: Multnomah, 1996), 96.

26. Ibid., 120–121, emphasis mine. In short, "How can you keep from seeking your own joy in acts of love when your joy consists in being loving?" (*Desiring God*, 98). Piper discusses a variety of biblical passages in his analysis, including 2 Cor. 8:1–4, 8 and 9:6–7, to which we will return in our next chapters. Knowing this God-given reality of human nature, Jesus appealed to our desire to be happy as the motivating drive behind discipleship (cf. Mark 8:34–38).

comes about only as the result of a supernatural transformation (cf. 3:18; 5:17). The believer has been converted to God as the source of real joy. Moreover, since our own well-being is secure in God, the outward expression of this conversion is the pursuit of our own happiness in the well-being of *others*. Because of God's loving commitment to meet *our* needs in himself (so that we love God by trusting him to do so), we are free to love our neighbor by pursuing *their* welfare.

Hence, in passages such as Romans 15:1–3; 1 Corinthians 10:24, 33; 13:5; and 2 Corinthians 5:15, Paul "does not mean we shouldn't seek the joy of edifying others, but that we should let *this* joy free us from bondage to private pleasures that make us indifferent to the good of others. Love does not seek its own *private, limited* joy, but instead seeks its own joy in the good—the salvation and edification—of others."[27]

This is especially important since, as Paul himself experienced in Corinth, love is often painful and costly, full of risk and filled with self-denial. But there is never a "sacrifice" in loving others. In giving to others, we can never outgive God, since God has given us nothing less than himself. As Paul's experience testifies, when we love God with everything we are and our neighbor as ourselves, "the gain outweighs the pain."[28]

> The obstacle that keeps us from obeying the first (vertical) commandment is the same obstacle that keeps us from obeying the second (horizontal) commandment. It is *not* that we are all trying to please ourselves, but that we are all far too easily pleased. We do not believe Jesus when he says there is more blessedness, more joy, more lasting pleasure in a life devoted to helping others than there is in a life devoted to our material comfort. And therefore the very longing for contentment which ought to drive us to simplicity of life and labors of love contents itself instead with the broken cisterns of prosperity and comfort.
>
> ... A life devoted to material comforts and thrills is like throwing money down a rathole. But a life invested in the labor of love yields dividends of joy unsurpassed and unending.[29]

Thus Paul, like Jesus, had a "holy greed for joy in God" that led him to endure the suffering for the sake of others that is so often wrapped up in love.

Grief. The joy described in this passage is the reflex of repentance. Ironically, the joy born of repentance thus owes its very existence to the grief that

---

27. Piper, *Desiring God*, 100.
28. Ibid., 111.
29. Ibid., 110. For support of this point, Piper quotes Matt. 6:19–20 and Luke 12:33.

motivates this change of attitude and action. In turn, the source and goal of such a *"godly* sorrow" is *God* (7:9–11). "Godly" is much more than an adjective thrown in for effect. The chain of Christian experience stretches back from joy to repentance to grief to *God.* Whether or not God is the qualification of our grief makes all the difference in the world—and in eternity. Unfortunately, the downsized view of God that permeates so much of modern theology makes it increasingly difficult to discern whether our grief is genuine remorse for our offenses against a holy Lord or whether it is mere embarrassment or the transitory response to a temporary loss of opportunity.

This difficulty is compounded by our contemporary substitution of sentimentality for the grief that arises according to God. As a result of this confusion, the pastoral authority and intervention exhibited in this passage are passing from the scene. For example, the chair of a pulpit search committee recently asked me if I knew of anyone with a "certain skill set" that would enable him to "speak to the congregation" without giving the impression that he was telling them what to do. This is a teddy-bear view of the pastor as someone who dispenses comfort without confrontation, for whom the Scriptures contain merely historical information and helpful advice.

It is hard to believe that we have departed so dramatically from the biblical portrait of ministry reflected in our present passage, with its joy over repentance and sorrow over sin, with its integrity in the midst of controversy and comfort in the midst of adversity, and with its prophetic voice and loving heart, all driven by a commitment to proclaim the gospel even when it hurts. But it is easy to see why, given the powerful cultural forces behind the contemporary redefinition of the pastoral office. As Hauerwas and Willimon have insightfully described it:

> One can readily understand why pastors are so ready to take up the general description of being one of the "helping professions." After all, most of us professing Christians, from the liberals to the fundamentalists, remain practical atheists in most of our lives. This is so because we think the church is sustained by the "services" it provides or the amount of "fellowship" and "good feeling" in the congregation. Of course there is nothing wrong with "services" and "good feeling"; what is wrong is that they have become ends in themselves. When that happens the church and the ministry cannot avoid sentimentality, which we believe is the most detrimental corruption of the church today.
>
> Sentimentality, after all, is but the way our unbelief is lived out. Sentimentality, that attitude of being always ready to understand but not to judge, corrupts us and the ministry. This is as true of conservative

churches as it is of liberal.... Without God, without the One whose death on the cross challenges all our "good feelings," who stands beyond and over against our human anxieties, all we have left is sentiment, the saccharine residue of theism in demise.[30]

It is no wonder, then, that in the midst of our hollow spirituality the twin pillars of Christian passion in this passage are so scarce. We seldom feel joy over the repentance of others because we so scarcely feel grief over sin. And to the degree that our grief remains self-directed when we do experience it, our joy remains saccharine sweet and on the surface. Consumed by our material circumstances, we find it hard to care enough about our real problems to feel the remorse that has God as its focus.

Repentance. Our only hope is that God will grant us a measure of his grace that we may recognize him and in so doing recognize our own sin so that we may repent. Our need, therefore, is to pray, even when prayer itself seems foreign—especially prayers of confession and repentance. We are so blind to our own faithlessness, and the vision of God's holiness is so dim, that such prayers of "godly sorrow" are hard to imagine, let alone utter. Yet God is patient with his people. As our passage illustrates so clearly, God brings us to repentance by using the lives and words of others to instruct us.

One answer to our need for instruction, perhaps may thus be found in the opening words of the Anglican *Book of Common Prayer*. This "manual" for being Christian begins each day with a confession of sin, whose profound simplicity provides an antidote to our preoccupation with ourselves and a pathway to true and lasting joy. Its pattern and content remain instructive and a starting point to our own expressions of "godly sorrow":

Almighty and most merciful Father,
We have erred and strayed from thy ways like lost sheep,
We have followed too much the devices and desires of our
    own hearts,
We have offended against thy holy laws,
We have left undone those things which we ought to have done,
And we have done those things which we ought not to have done,
And there is no health in us:
But thou, O Lord, have mercy upon us miserable offenders;
Spare thou them, O God, which confess their faults,
Restore thou them that are penitent,
According to thy promises declared unto mankind in Christ Jesus
    our Lord;

---

30. Hauerwas and Willimon, *Resident Aliens*, 120–21.

And grant, O most merciful Father, for his sake,
That we may hereafter live a godly, righteous, and sober life,
To the glory of thy holy Name. Amen.[31]

God. It is significant that this confession from the *Book of Common Prayer* culminates with a prayer for God's enabling power to repent. At the heart of "godly sorrow" is a recognition of our own inability, if left to ourselves, to please God. If we are going to live authentic Christian lives, we must share Paul's confidence that God will graciously grant his people the repentance that leads "unto salvation" (7:9–10, 14). For in the end, only God can save us. The first step is his, not ours.

The transformation of our sentimentality into a "godly sorrow" over our sins and over the sins of others will take place only as God reveals to us the glory of his sovereign majesty and the reign of his righteousness. The conversion of our surface satisfaction into lasting joy can only take place as we encounter the contentment that comes from living in his presence. Paul's consolation, sorrow, boasting, pride, joy, and confidence, like Titus's refreshment and happiness and the Corinthians' grief, longing, zeal, earnestness, and indignation, all owe their origin to God's having invaded their lives (cf. 3:12–18).

Preaching. Finally, Paul's reflections remind us that the divinely chosen vehicle for revealing God's saving presence is the instruction, example, and concern of those called to proclaim his Word. God moved in Corinth through Paul's preaching, whether in person or in his letters, backed up by his life and clothed in his love and concern. Inasmuch as we value our relationship with God through Christ, we will value those who make it possible through their patient study of the Scriptures, their struggle to live them out before us, and their willingness to confront our sin.

The passage before us makes it evident that the longing and zeal of God's people are dependent on the high calling of pastor-teachers. It is only fitting, therefore, that we give Paul the last word. As for the pastor: "Watch your life and doctrine closely. Persevere in them, because if you do, you will save both yourself and your hearers" (1 Tim. 4:16). And concerning elders in general: "The elders who direct the affairs of the church well are worthy of double honor, especially those whose work is preaching and teaching" (5:17; see also 1 Thess. 5:12–13).

---

31. *The Book of Common Prayer and Administration of the Sacraments* (Cambridge: Cambridge Univ. Press, 1922 ed.), 3.

2 Corinthians 8:1–15

A
ND NOW, BROTHERS, we want you to know about the grace that God has given the Macedonian churches. ²Out of the most severe trial, their overflowing joy and their extreme poverty welled up in rich generosity. ³For I testify that they gave as much as they were able, and even beyond their ability. Entirely on their own, ⁴they urgently pleaded with us for the privilege of sharing in this service to the saints. ⁵And they did not do as we expected, but they gave themselves first to the Lord and then to us in keeping with God's will. ⁶So we urged Titus, since he had earlier made a beginning, to bring also to completion this act of grace on your part. ⁷But just as you excel in everything—in faith, in speech, in knowledge, in complete earnestness and in your love for us—see that you also excel in this grace of giving.

⁸I am not commanding you, but I want to test the sincerity of your love by comparing it with the earnestness of others. ⁹For you know the grace of our Lord Jesus Christ, that though he was rich, yet for your sakes he became poor, so that you through his poverty might become rich.

¹⁰And here is my advice about what is best for you in this matter: Last year you were the first not only to give but also to have the desire to do so. ¹¹Now finish the work, so that your eager willingness to do it may be matched by your completion of it, according to your means. ¹²For if the willingness is there, the gift is acceptable according to what one has, not according to what he does not have.

¹³Our desire is not that others might be relieved while you are hard pressed, but that there might be equality. ¹⁴At the present time your plenty will supply what they need, so that in turn their plenty will supply what you need. Then there will be equality, ¹⁵as it is written: "He who gathered much did not have too much, and he who gathered little did not have too little."

Original Meaning

THE MOST STRIKING feature of this new section is its apparently abrupt change in subject matter. Throughout 1:1–7:16 Paul has been encouraging the repentant and arguing with the rebellious concerning the legitimacy of his ministry and message. In 8:1–9:15, Paul suddenly turns to challenge the churches in and around Corinth to resume their participation in the collection for the poverty-stricken Christians in Jerusalem (see Rom. 15:25–28; 1 Cor. 16:1–4; also the Introduction). To complicate matters further, chapter 9 appears to repeat much of what is already stated in chapter 8.

Because of this sudden switch in focus, many readers assume that Paul's train of thought breaks at the end of chapter 7, only to resume in chapters 10–13. Chapters 8–9 are considered to be a parenthesis within his larger and more pressing apologetic concerns. Indeed, some scholars argue that the break between chapters 7 and 8 is so great that chapters 8 and 9 cannot be considered part of Paul's original letter. From this perspective, Paul (or, less likely, someone else) composed chapters 8 and 9 as either one or two independent, administrative letters intended to make arrangements for completing the collection in Corinth and its environs. A subsequent editor later inserted them into the composite document we now call "2 Corinthians" (see Introduction).

In contrast to such partition or parenthesis theories, Paul's "pragmatic" discussion in 8:1–9:15 is actually a logical and necessary application of his previous arguments. The "generosity encouraged" (cf. the NIV heading to 8:1) in these two chapters is not something that Paul adds to the repentance he has just outlined, as if the Corinthians have one more hurdle to jump in order to prove themselves "innocent" (7:11). Nor is it an aside from it, an optional "add-on" for those who are really serious about their faith. Instead, their generosity in giving to the collection is to be an expression of the gospel itself in the lives of those who have already shown the kind of "godly sorrow [that] brings [the] repentance that leads to salvation and leaves no regret" (7:10).

Specifically, chapters 8–9 outline the contours of the "obedience" that the majority of the Corinthians should continue to demonstrate in response to Paul's "tearful letter" (cf. 1:24–2:6; 7:9–16). In other words, to fail to give to the collection is to expose the false nature of their professed faith! As the culmination of his ministry among them, the completion of the collection will be the final indication of Paul's renewed standing in the church. Like 2:5–11, 6:14–7:1, and 7:2–4, chapters 8–9 therefore explicate what repentance will look like among the Corinthians. Paul's confidence in 7:16 leads to his expectations concerning the collection.[1]

As the continuation of 1 Corinthians 16:1–4, whose fulfillment was interrupted by the intervening crisis within the Corinthian church, 2 Corinthians 8–9 constitutes one of four Pauline passages dealing with the collection for the believers in Jerusalem (see also Rom. 15:25–32 [written from Corinth]; Gal. 2:9–10). Now that the majority of the Corinthians had repented and were back in control of the church, it was time to resume their giving. Paul's intention was that the collection would be completed in time for his third visit (2 Cor. 8:11, 24; 9:4).

The reason for the poverty in Jerusalem at this time can only be guessed; it may have been the result of persecution (cf. Acts 11:19) and/or the consequence of bad harvests in the region during the mid A.D. 40s (11:27–30). Whatever the reason, the prototype for Paul's collection appears to be the famine relief that was sent to Jerusalem earlier from Antioch, with Paul and Barnabas as the delegates who accompanied it (cf. 11:29–30; 12:25; Gal. 2:1). The primary purpose of the collection was once again to bring economic help to the Jerusalem believers (Rom. 15:25–26, 31; 2 Cor. 8:4, 13–15, 19–20; 9:1, 12–13). After all, part of Paul's apostolic burden was to remember the poor (Gal. 2:10).

The collection, however, was more than simple charity. It had a profound theological purpose, both for the Corinthians and for the church as a whole. For the Corinthians, it was the means by which God's work of sanctifying grace would continue in their lives. Participating in the collection was a means to becoming more like Jesus (cf. 8:8–10). For the church as a whole, the collection was an act of fellowship that would solidify the unity between Jew and Gentile as one people of God (8:13–15; cf. 9:12–15). The Gentiles' sharing willingly with Jews from the abundance of God's provision was a tangible demonstration of the new covenant of the new creation (8:15). Moreover, participating in the collection was a means by which the Gentiles could repay their "debt" to the Jews for the spiritual blessings they had

---

1. Though we do not follow his view that chapters 8 and 9 were separate letters later inserted into the collage of fragments that make up "2 Corinthians," Hans Dieter Betz, *2 Corinthians 8 and 9*, 132, rightly calls the rhetoric of 8:1–15 "advisory," rather than being a letter of recommendation as such. According to Betz's analysis, it is similar in form and content to ancient administrative letters of appointment that accompanied royal envoys (cf. Acts 9:12; 15:23–29; 22:5) (133). For our purpose, it is important to emphasize, with Betz, that the focus of 8:1–15 is not on recommending *Titus*, but on motivating the *Corinthians*. For other examples of passages of commendation embedded within letters of a different genre and purpose, cf. Rom. 16:1–2; 1 Cor. 16:15–16, 17–18; Phil. 2:29–30; 4:2–3; 1 Thess. 5:12–13a; Philem.; Heb. 13:17; 3 John 12 (according to Kim, as quoted by Betz, 135n.28).

received through them, in fulfillment of the promises to Abraham (cf. Acts 24:17; Rom. 15:7–9, 27).[2]

As a result, the collection illustrates the significance of Paul's theology of grace both for the individual (having received from God, Christians give to others) and for the life of the church (having been accepted by God, Christians accept one another). Completing the collection would therefore be the theological capstone of Paul's apostolic service, bringing his ministry east of Rome to an end (Acts 19:21; Rom. 15:18–29; 1 Cor. 16:1–2, 6; Gal. 2:9).

The Example of the Macedonians (8:1–7)

PAUL BEGINS HIS discussion by using the past experience of the Macedonians (8:1–5) as an example for the Corinthians (8:6–7). The "grace that God has given to the Macedonian churches" (v. 1), which is then defined in verses 2–5, is the same "grace" desired for the Corinthians as well (v. 6), so that they too, like the Macedonians, might excel in this "grace" (v. 7; cf. 9:15, where "grace" appears again, thereby framing the entire argument with this theme). "Grace" (*charis*) is an inclusive term that refers to God's undeserved gifts or kindnesses, all of which flow from his primary expression of "grace," namely, the merciful reconciliation of sinners to himself in Christ (cf. 5:18–21, which is defined as "grace" in 6:1).

Paul's introduction in 8:1, "we want you to know," indicates that his forthcoming reference to the grace of God experienced by the Macedonians—that is, the region of Philippi, Thessalonica, and Berea—is not new information

---

2. Though often argued, it is doubtful that Paul saw the collection to be a fulfillment of Isa. 2:2–3, 60:5–6, and Micah 4:1–2, in which in the last days the Gentiles stream to Jerusalem bringing gifts. Nor does it appear that Paul thought that the Gentiles' offering would make the Jews jealous, thereby winning them to Christ and ushering in the Parousia (cf. Rom. 11:4, 25–26). For the classic presentation of these views, see Johannes Munck, *Paul and the Salvation of Mankind* (Atlanta: John Knox, 1959), 303–8. According to this view, Paul sees himself as the one on whom the consummation of the messianic age depends (cf. ibid., 33, 41, 49, 61, 66, 129–130, 247). Although a large group of Gentiles did accompany Paul (Acts 20:4, 16, 22 and 24:17 may be referring to delegates associated with the collection), there is no explicit connection made in any New Testament text between the collection and this Old Testament expectation. Paul himself expressed great concerns over whether his ministry would even be accepted, let alone be seen as the great pilgrimage of the Gentiles to Mount Zion, and his worst fears were realized (Rom. 15:30–32; cf. Acts 21:21, 27–36; 22:22–24). Finally, the order of redemption in the Old Testament is the opposite of that presented in this view: In Isa. 2:2–3; 60:5–6; Micah 4:1–2 the conversion of Israel as a people leads to the coming of the Gentiles, not vice versa. For Paul, the great conversion of Israel and the subsequent conversion of the nations pictured in these texts is still to come. At the present, only a remnant of both Jew and Gentile is being saved. For a concise exposition of this view, following the work of John Murray, see Daniel P. Fuller, *The Unity of the Bible*, 437–42.

for the Corinthians, but a reminder of what they already know (cf. the use of this same introduction in 1 Cor. 11:3; 15:1; 2 Cor. 1:8; Gal. 1:11). Paul's purpose is not to inform the Corinthians but to draw out for them the implications of what the Macedonians have experienced. The specific content of God's grace in view here is given in 2 Corinthians 8:2b, with the evidence that it was indeed a gift from God outlined in 8:2a–5. The grace of God received by the Macedonians was their ability to "well up" with a "wealth of generosity"[3] toward others in the midst of their own afflictions (v. 2b).[4] Only the grace of God can account for such generosity springing from the soil of their "extreme poverty" on the one hand, while *at the same time* issuing forth from their "overflowing joy" on the other!

The Macedonians' generosity is also evidence that they passed the "test" brought on by their afflictions (8:2; lit., "in much testing of affliction"). Such giving in the midst of adversity with joy (!) confirms that one's faith is real (for *dokime* [test, outcome of a test], cf. 2:9; 9:13; 13:3). Joyful giving to others and joy in one's good fortune, even in the midst of one's own poverty and suffering, is the sign of having received God's grace (cf. 1:24; 2:3; 6:10; 7:4, 7, 9, 13, 16). Though the Macedonians gave generously, the "wealth" that spilled over to others was not the amount that the Macedonians could give, but their joy in what God had done for them (cf. Mark 12:42–44; Phil. 4:4; 1 Thess. 1:6).[5]

In 8:3–4, Paul affirms that the Macedonians' poverty and joy combined to produce such a wealth of generosity because their giving exceeded their ability and was done "entirely on their own," that is, without being manipulated or coerced (v. 3), since it was the result of their "urgently pleading" to be involved in the collection (v. 4). The terminology used for the collection in verses 3–4 is significant. Participating in the collection is labeled a "grace" (*charis*; NIV, "privilege"), which is then equated with "sharing" (*koinonia*; cf.

---

3. Formally, the expression is "wealth in regard to generosity" (NIV, "rich generosity"). For the meaning of *haplotes* as either "single-mindedness/sincerity" (2 Cor. 1:12; 11:3; cf. Eph. 6:5; Col. 3:22) or "generosity" (2 Cor. 9:11, 13; cf. Rom. 12:8; James 1:5), see BAGD, 85–86, which suggests that the meaning "generosity" is disputed, suggesting as an alternative, "sincere concern." But the meaning "generosity" is to be retained. For the use of *perisseuo* (NIV, "well up," or better, "overflow"), see 2 Cor. 8:2, 7–8 (cf. 8:14; 9:1 for cognates); 9:8, 12.

4. On the persecution of the Macedonians, cf. Phil. 1:27–30; 1 Thess. 1:6; 2:14; 3:3–4, 7; 2 Thess. 1:4–10. For the Macedonians in Acts, see Acts 16:9–17:15; 18:5; 19:21–22, 29; 20:1–4; 27:2.

5. What Paul says here about the Macedonians he has already affirmed about his own afflictions (2 Cor. 1:4–6, 8; 2:4; 2:14 [metaphorically]; 4:8, 17; 6:4; 8:13), his God-based joy in their midst (1:3–7, 8–11, 12, 24; 2:3, 4, 7; 6:10; 7:4, 7, 9, 13, 16; 10:8; 12:9, 10; 13:9), and his own grace-inspired sincerity as a result (1:12). In 8:1–2 Paul is therefore also drawing an implicit parallel between the Macedonians and his own example: "Imitate the Macedonians as they imitate me as I imitate Christ" (cf. 8:9; cf. 1 Cor. 11:1).

Rom. 15:26), while the collection itself is called a "service" or "ministry" (*diakonia*) to the saints.

Since these terms are also found with secular meanings in administrative documents of the period,[6] Paul is possibly making a play on words, infusing them with specifically Christian connotations. What the Macedonians "administered" was the grace of God in a ministry of the gospel. This seems likely in view of Paul's use of *diakonia* in 3:7, 8, 9; 4:1; 5:18; 6:3; and 11:8 to refer to his ministry as an apostle. The "sharing" referred to in 8:4 would then be the partnership of believers as they share the gospel and its ministry.

In the same way, the use of the noun *paraklesis* in 8:4 ("with much *urging*"; NIV, "urgently"), which can also mean "comfort," recalls Paul's use of this same theme in regard to himself in 1:3–7 and 7:4–13, where it refers to the encouragement or comfort that characterizes those in whom God is at work. Here too it describes others in whom God is at work.

Finally, Paul's "Christianizing" of this administrative language is also reflected in his designation of the recipients of the collection as "saints" (cf. 1:1; 9:1, 12; also Rom. 1:7; 8:27; 12:13; 15:25–26, 31; 1 Cor. 1:2; 6:1–2; 14:33; 16:1,15; Eph. 1:1, 15, 18; Phil. 1:1). Hence, although Paul is speaking about something that happened administratively, he is not speaking as an administrator but as an apostle.

The apostolic context of this passage is made explicit in verse 5, where Paul delineates the final reason the Macedonians gave so generously. Not surprisingly, the explanation is again theological. Not only did they participate in the collection, as one might have expected, but also they gave themselves to God and to Paul in accordance with God's will.[7] The greatest expression of God's grace in a person's life is not its demonstration toward others, but its response to God and his cause. The most important thing for Paul is not that the Macedonians gave their money to others, but that they gave their lives to God (cf. 5:15; cf. Acts 15:26; Rom. 12:1–2) and to Paul as God's apostle (2 Cor. 6:11–13; 7:11–12; cf. 12:14; Rom. 16:4; 2 Tim. 4:11). Indeed, since he is the apostle who brought the gospel to Macedonia, the two cannot

---

6. See Betz, 2 *Corinthians 8 and 9*, 46. For this use of *charis*, cf. Acts 25:3. For *koinonia* as "partnership" or "fellowship," see 2 Cor. 9:13; Gal. 2:9; Phil. 1:5; 4:14–15; for *diakonia* as "charity," cf. Acts 6:1; 11:29; 12:25.

7. Verse 5 is difficult to translate because of the elided verb in the first clause. Formally it reads, "and not just as we hoped, but they gave themselves first to the Lord and to us through the will of God." The NIV rightly construes verse 5 to mean that their giving of themselves to the Lord and to Paul was not as expected. Cf. the NRSV: "and this [i.e., giving to the collection], not merely as we expected; they gave themselves first to the Lord and, by the will of God, to us." In other words, the negation refers back to their giving in the collection, but in order to establish a positive comparison to what follows: "and not *only* did they give just as we expected, but they gave. . . ."

be separated: To give themselves to the Lord means that the Corinthians gave themselves to Paul.

Of course, the two are not equal. That the Macedonians gave themselves "first" to the Lord is not a reference to a temporal sequence but to the priority of allegiance to God (contra the NIV; the word "then" is not necessarily implicit in the text). Furthermore, the designation "through the will of God" (NIV, "in keeping with God's will") is usually used in regard to Paul's apostleship. Hence, their act of giving themselves to Paul *by the will of God* is yet another pointer to Paul's status as God's appointed representative (cf. Rom. 1:1–7; 1 Cor. 1:1; 2 Cor. 1:1; Gal. 1:14, 15; Eph. 1:1; Col. 1:1; 1 Tim. 1:1). As these linguistic clues indicate, the Macedonians' participation in the collection is a reflection of God's work in their lives as well as a stamp of approval on Paul's ministry of the new covenant (cf. 2 Cor. 3:3–6).

At first glance, the transition from verses 1–5 to verse 6 is not clear. The reader must keep in mind that verses 3–5 look backward, in support of the assertion of verse 2, so that Paul's urging Titus to return to Corinth in 8:6 does not derive directly from the Macedonians' giving themselves to God and to Paul in 8:5. Rather, the Macedonians illustrate the ways in which the grace of God manifests itself in the lives of God's people. Verse 6 thus derives from verses 1–2, which have been supported by verses 3–5.

In other words, encouraged by the Macedonians' response to God's *grace* in *their* lives (vv. 1–2), Paul sends Titus back to Corinth "to bring also to completion this act of *grace* on *your* part" (v. 6). The Macedonians' "urging" (*paraklesis*) Paul to allow them to be involved in the collection (v. 4) led him "to urge" (*parakaleo*, a related verb) Titus to complete the collection in Corinth (v. 6). Paul wants God to do for the Corinthians what he has done for the Macedonians. The Corinthians had begun the collection in the past, but their rebellion had brought it to an end. With their recent repentance has come the opportunity once again to give their money to Jerusalem and to give themselves to God and to their apostle. For as the experience of the Macedonians has testified, this is what happens when the grace of God takes root in the church.

It is difficult to determine whether Titus's "earlier ... beginning" in 8:6 refers to a visit during the previous year to start the collection, so that his actions are behind 1 Corinthians 16:1–2 as well, or whether it refers to the visit mentioned in 2 Corinthians 7:5–6. The latter is to be preferred, since Titus is not mentioned in 1 Corinthians, and 2 Corinthians 7:14 seems to indicate that this was his first visit (cf. 8:6, 10; 9:2; 12:17–18). The "also" in 8:6 thus refers to Titus's earlier success as the bearer of the tearful letter (cf. 2:4). In this case, the "beginning" Titus made was the grace of God expressed in the Corinthians' restoration; the completion of this "grace" will be their recommitment to the collection.

Paul's "urging" Titus to return to Corinth does not refer, therefore, to a passionate attempt to persuade Titus, but to a fervent request to carry out an official task.[8] In 8:6, Paul is making clear to the Corinthians that in bringing his present letter to them, Titus has been commissioned to bring their recent repentance (the prior act of God's grace) to its consummation by encouraging their participation in the collection (the present act of God's grace).

The main point of the Macedonian example is made explicit in verse 7. Like the Macedonians, the Corinthians too "excel" or "overflow" in their experience of God's grace. Thus, just as the Macedonians responded by "welling up" (*perisseuo* in 8:2) in generosity, the Corinthians should overflow (*perisseuo*) in the "grace of giving" (the NIV's addition "of giving" makes the content of the grace explicit).[9]

According to 8:7, God's abundant grace toward the Corinthians is seen in their spiritual gifts of "faith … speech … and … knowledge."[10] This list parallels Paul's earlier recognition of the Corinthians' spiritual gifts in 1 Corinthians 1:5; 1:7; 12:8–10, where they were also seen as evidence that the Corinthians lacked nothing from God. In addition, Paul now points to their "earnestness" for him as evidence of God's grace in their lives (cf. 2 Cor. 7:11–12) and, in turn, to his love for them (cf. 2:4; 6:11; 11:11; 12:14–15).[11] This reciprocity of love attests to the restoration of the Corinthians (cf. 2:9; 6:12–13; 7:7, 13–16).

As elsewhere, here too we see Paul's covenantal framework come to the fore: The indicative reality of what God has already done to redeem and provide for his people grounds and necessitates the imperatives that flow from it (cf. 5:6–10; 21–6:1; 7:1; 8:8, 24). Excelling in spiritual gifts grounds and necessitates excelling in giving. Having received grace from God leads

---

8. For the use of *parakaleo* ("to urge, exhort") to refer to an urgent request, see 2:8; 5:20; 6:1; 9:5; 12:18; for the noun, cf. 8:17 and 1 Cor. 16:12; 1 Thess. 2:3. Betz, *2 Corinthians 8 and 9*, 54, argues that the verb in 8:6 has a technical meaning "to appoint," as used in administrative texts to refer to the appointment of legal or political representatives. Although the extent of the administrative tone in this passage may be debated, Betz's observation that Titus is being *appointed* as Paul's delegate, not *entreated* to be one, is a good one. For the "act of grace" as a reference to the collection see 1 Cor. 16:3; 2 Cor. 8:7, 19.

9. This thematic connection between the Macedonians and the Corinthians is obscured by the NIV's use of three different words in this context to represent the same stem (*perisse*): "overflowing" and "welled up" in 8:2 and "excel" in 8:7.

10. For "faith" as the unique spiritual gift of miracle-working faith, see 1 Cor. 12:9–10; for "speech" as charismatic speech, see 1 Cor. 12:10, 28; 14:9, 19, 39; for the gift of knowledge as special spiritual insight, see 1 Cor. 1:5, 8; 8:1–7, 10; 12:8; 13:2, 8; 14:6.

11. Contra the NIV and RSV, the textual variant "in our love for you" (cf. NRSV and NASB) is the more difficult reading and hence to be preferred over the variant "your love for us" (cf. Bruce M. Metzger, *A Textual Commentary on the Greek New Testament* [Stuttgart: United Bible Societies, 2d ed., 1994], 512–13).

to expressing grace to others. To the degree that the Corinthians are like the Macedonians in possessing a wealth of spiritual gifts (they would probably be tempted to view themselves as even more spiritually blessed than the Macedonians; cf. 1 Cor. 1:5 with 4:8), to that same degree they should be like them in the "wealth" of their generosity. The example of the Macedonians reminds the Corinthians that the reality of their spirituality will be seen in their giving.

The Example of Jesus (8:8–10)

HAVING GIVEN AN implied command in 8:7, Paul immediately qualifies it in verse 8. In calling the Corinthians to excel in giving to the collection, Paul is not speaking "in accordance with a command" (lit. trans.). The NIV wrongly translates this to mean that Paul is not commanding the Corinthians (but cf. the RSV, NRSV, NASB). This version reflects a common interpretation of this passage in which participating in the collection is viewed to be desirable, but not an obligation. As such, the collection functions as a Pauline proof or test of love in that Paul merely *advises* the Corinthians concerning what they *should* do, but does not *command* them concerning what they *must* do. The test becomes whether the Corinthians will take Paul's advice or not. This interpretation often points to Paul's emphasis on the collection as an act of "grace," assuming that, as such, it cannot be commanded. Instead, Paul's statement in 9:5 is seen to indicate that the collection must remain a free and spontaneous response on the part of the Corinthians. Those who take this position assume that participation in the collection cannot be voluntary if it is commanded, just as "grace," to be "grace," must be a free act.

In contrast to this reading, the point of 8:8 is not to deny that Paul is giving them a command, which he explicitly goes on to do in verse 11! Rather, Paul's point is that the need to complete the collection (implied in 8:7; explicit in 8:11; cf. 9:7) is not a direct command *from Christ*, but his own "advice" or "opinion" (8:10) concerning the implications of God's grace in their lives. Hence, the detail with which Paul develops his argument in chapters 8–9 derives from the fact that, as in 1 Corinthians 7:6, 25, Paul received no specific command concerning this issue from the teachings of Jesus or from the exalted Christ. As in 1 Corinthians 7:1–40, Paul himself must therefore show the inextricable link between the gospel that he was commanded to preach (cf. Rom. 16:25–26; 1 Tim. 1:1; Titus 1:3) and the implications he himself draws from it.

Far from denying that he is commanding the Corinthians, Paul's qualification in verse 8 demonstrates that what he is saying is his *own* imperative as an authoritative apostle of Jesus Christ (cf. 10:8; 13:10). The point of 8:8, therefore, is the opposite of Philemon 8–9, where Paul refrains from commanding them "in Christ," even though he has every right as an apostle to do so. Here he exercises that right!

Paul does not have a direct command from Christ concerning the collection, but he does have the example of the Macedonians on the one hand (8:1–8) and that of Jesus on the other (8:9). Since the Macedonians have graphically illustrated what an experience of God's grace looks like in the life of believers, Paul can use their "earnestness" in giving as a criterion for "testing"[12] the genuine nature of the Corinthians' recently regained "love" (8:8). This ongoing test of faith is part of the life of faith itself; such a challenge does not call the genuine nature of faith into question, but instead brings it to light (cf. 2:9; 7:12; 13:5).[13]

Moreover, the purpose of Paul's test is positive, not negative. He is not tempting them to do wrong, but giving them the stimulus to do what is right. The reference to the Macedonians in 8:1–8 is not intended to create competition between churches, but to cause the Corinthians to join their brothers and sisters in becoming like Christ. Hence, obedience to Paul's command is not to be an act of compulsion. Instead, it is to be the expression of a willing eagerness to do what is expected. Genuine obedience is an act of delight-driven duty. The greatest way to honor the one who commands is not to obey because one must, but to do what is required with joy, having willingly given oneself to his authority (cf. 8:5, 11; 9:7).

To point to the Macedonians in order to illustrate this truth is one thing; to point to Jesus is quite another. In turning his attention to Christ in 8:9, Paul wants to remind the Corinthians ("for you know") that Jesus himself is *the* example of how grace joyfully expresses itself in love. Paul's references to Jesus' being "rich" and "poor" do not signify his economic status, but his preexistence with the Father (cf. Gal. 4:4; Phil 2:6) and his entering into the humble circumstances of this world, including death (cf. Rom. 15:3; Phil. 2:7–8; 1 Tim. 3:16). Decoded, this means that Jesus underwent his incarnation (i.e., his becoming "poor"), in spite of his position in heaven (i.e., the fact that he was "rich"), in order that we might be saved (our justification through Jesus' death means our becoming "rich" through his "poverty;" cf. Rom. 10:12; 11:12; 2 Cor. 5:21; 6:10).

Jesus' incarnation illustrates that the "grace" expressed in love is the willingness to give up one's own rights for the sake of meeting the needs of

---

12. For the use of *dokimazo* to refer to putting to the test or examining something, cf. Rom. 14:18; 16:10; 1 Cor. 11:19; 2 Cor. 10:18; 13:7; for the idea of testing something to show its genuine nature, cf. Rom. 2:18; 12:2; 14:22; 1 Cor. 11:28; 2 Cor. 13:5; Gal. 6:4.

13. On test of faith, see 1 Cor. 3:13; 11:28; 16:3; Gal. 6:4; Phil. 1:10; 2:22; 1 Thess. 2:4; 5:21.

others. The "grace of our Lord Jesus Christ," which is usually a benediction (see 13:14; cf. Rom. 16:20; 1 Cor. 16:23; Gal. 6:18; Phil. 4:23; 1 Thess. 5:28; 2 Thess. 3:18; Philem. 25), is therefore employed in 2 Corinthians 8:9 as Paul's defining example of what it will mean for the Corinthians to be like Jesus in this circumstance: to consider the needs of the saints in Jerusalem more important than their own. What Christ has done for the Corinthians (the "grace of Christ" as a benediction), the Corinthians are to do for the Jews (the "grace of Christ" as a model).

Spurred on by how the Macedonians have copied Christ, in 8:10 Paul extends to the Corinthians by implication the same call to participate in the collection, now designated as his "opinion" or "judgment" (gnome; perhaps, "declaration";[14] the NIV's "advice" carries the wrong connotation). The key parallel is 1 Corinthians 7:25, which shows again that for Paul to speak of his "opinion" does not indicate that what he says is of no real consequence or obligation. On the contrary, Paul's "opinion" is his own inference from what he knows of Christ and the gospel in accordance with the leading of the Spirit (cf. 1 Cor. 1:10). Indeed, since the "test" in verse 8 is now equated with his apostolic "opinion" in verse 10, Paul's assumption is that his Spirit-led admonition will be received by those in whom the Spirit dwells (cf. 1 Cor. 2:12–14, where the Spirit's purpose is to enable believers to accept the gifts granted by God).

In line with this assumption, in verse 10b Paul expresses the basis for his giving the Corinthians his "judgment" concerning the collection. Verse 10b begins with gar ("for, because"), unfortunately omitted in the NIV. Literally, verse 10 reads: "I am giving an opinion in this matter, for [gar] this is beneficial[15] to you as those who began last year not only to give, but also to desire [to give]." The NIV's use of a semicolon after verse 10a breaks up the flow of thought at this point. Paul has expressed his opinion on this issue precisely because the Corinthians' desire to participate in the collection "last year" (i.e., before the intervening crisis occurred[16]), which had already resulted in some giving (cf. 1 Cor. 16:1–2), provided initial indications that they had truly been converted. As a result, to complete what they have started is advantageous for them as continuing evidence of God's grace in their lives. Not to complete the collection will signal that they are turning back on their earlier professed membership in the people of God.

---

14. See BAGD, 163.

15. For this same verb (symphero, to help, confer a benefit, be advantageous or profitable) and its cognates, see 12:1; also 1 Cor. 6:12; 7:35; 10:23, 33; 12:7 (cf. BAGD, 780).

16. The designation "from last year" (lit. trans.) refers to the last calendar year; it could be as little as a month or two to as much as twenty-three months ago.

Understood in this way, Paul's argument is not one of simple expediency (i.e., it is better to finish what one has begun than not to do so[17]), but another expression of his conviction that genuine faith perseveres. The Corinthians' desire to give in the past cannot substitute for a lack of desire in the present. What began earlier, if it was genuine, must and will continue on as part of their restored faith.

It is also striking that the "not only ... but also" comparison in 8:10 underscores the priority of one's intention over one's actions. Inasmuch as one can perform apparently loving acts that do not flow from love and are therefore worthless (cf. 1 Cor. 13), Paul's stress is not on the action itself but on the desire that drives it. He calls the believers in Corinth back to the collection because he has every reason to believe that their initial desire to give was an expression of the love that is born of the Spirit (cf. Gal. 5:22). For what matters in the end is whether their act of giving is an act of grace toward others, like the incarnation of Christ, and whether it flows from God's grace, like the giving of the Macedonians.

Paul's Expectation for the Corinthians (8:11–15)

THE COMMAND IMPLIED in 8:7 and 10 is made explicit in verse 11. This is the only formal command found in chapters 8–9: The Corinthians are to complete the collection so that the work of the Spirit in their lives, as seen in their "eager willingness" to give, may come to fruition. Here too the completion of the collection is tied to their desire to participate. The importance of this heartfelt motivation is seen in the repetition throughout these two chapters of the theme of "eagerness" (cf. 8:11, 12, 19; 9:2). In addition, the reference in 8:11 to giving "according to your means" picks up an important theme regarding the collection (cf. 8:3, 12–14), one that will raise the question of how to determine what one's means actually are (cf. 9:5–11).

Thus, verse 11 makes it plain that there is an obligation to give, but no call to give beyond what one can afford.[18] By comparing the Corinthians to the Macedonians, who were less well off and yet gave *beyond* their means (cf. 8:3), Paul is not trying to manipulate the believers in Corinth to do likewise. Rather, Paul's qualification that the amount given need not exceed one's ability (in contrast to the Macedonians) serves to emphasize the fundamental point that where the heart is, the will must follow. It is the condition of one's heart and the circumstances of one's life, not the attempt to measure up to the practices of others, that should determine how much a person will give. As Paul makes clear in this passage, genuine desire acts. The issue is not the

---

17. Contra Betz, *2 Corinthians 8 and 9*, 63.
18. Victor Furnish, *II Corinthians*, 406, points to Prov. 3:27–28 for the same idea.

amount given (but cf. 9:5–11), but the expression of willingness. Action without the right attitude is of no avail, but a genuine attitude inevitably results in action.

Paul's emphasis in verse 11 on the priority of one's attitude over the amount given, as well as on the inextricable link between attitude and action, is grounded in verse 12, which is itself supported by verses 13–15 (v. 13 too begins with *gar*, "for," omitted in the NIV). By way of emphasis, Paul again states in verse 12 that what makes the gift acceptable to God is the "willingness" to give in accordance with one's means, not the amount given. The Corinthians need not wait to give until they can give more, as if the size of the offering made it acceptable to God. The example of the Macedonians illustrates that proportionate giving means that even the poor can make a great contribution (cf. Luke 12:48).

The reason Paul stresses proportionate giving is because the purpose of the collection is not to relieve the saints in Jerusalem by impoverishing the Corinthians. Rather, the goal is to create an "equality" between them with reference to their basic necessities (v. 13), which is defined as a reciprocity in meeting each other's needs (v. 14; cf. Acts 2:44–45; 4:32–37; Gal. 6:10; for the only other New Testament use of "equality," cf. Col. 4:1).

A key question concerning 8:14, therefore, is whether Paul envisions that one day the Jerusalem believers will reciprocate by meeting the financial needs of the Corinthians. Though possible, this seems unlikely, given the economic disparity between the groups. Paul is probably referring to the Gentiles' present contribution to Israel as an expression of their spiritual fellowship and identity (cf. 9:14) and to Israel's ongoing spiritual "contribution" to the Gentiles as part of the eschatological redemption of the world (cf. Rom. 11:11, 12, 25–26, 30–32). If this is Paul's intention, then the reference to "the present time" is not merely temporal, but also a reference to the present period of redemptive history (cf. Rom. 3:26; 8:18; 11:5; cf. Gal. 1:4). Within the eschatological people of God, each gives what they have: The Gentiles can support the Jews financially, while the Jews can support the Gentiles with leadership and the ministry of the gospel (cf. Rom. 15:27).[19]

---

19. Again, there are those who take 8:14 to refer not to sharing financial resources, but to the conversion of the Gentiles (i.e., their spiritual "plenty;" cf. 1 Cor. 1:7) as that which contributes to the conversion of the Jews (i.e., what the Jews need in the present is Christ), which in turn brings about the final salvation of the nations (i.e., their future need; see above, n. 2). For this view of 8:14, see Martin, *2 Corinthians*, 261. However, it is difficult contextually to take v. 14 as a purely theological statement. Martin himself admits that "it has to be conceded that the turning of the Corinthians' money gift designed to help famine-racked Jerusalem into the eschatological hope of spiritual bounties at the climax of the ages seems a vast shift of thought ... " (261).

The Corinthians' participation in the collection should lead to an equality that results from proportionate and reciprocal giving. Paul's final support (v. 15) for this expectation is Israel's experience with the manna in the desert as summarized in Exodus 16:18. Far from being merely an illustrative filler for his argument, Paul's return to the Scriptures at this point highlights the importance of the collection itself and of Paul's own emphasis on its intended equality. As yet another application of the Exodus typology that has been developed throughout 2:14–7:16, Paul affirms that the "equality" of provision in the event of the Exodus is matched by an equality under the new covenant. God's promise to provide for his people, as embodied in the manna and quail, has been reconfirmed in Christ (cf. 2 Cor. 8:9 with 1:20) and applied to the Corinthians as God's people of the "second exodus."

But whereas the equality in the "first Exodus" was established miraculously by God *for the people* because of their hard hearts (cf. Ex. 16:18, 28), now it is being established *by the people themselves* through their *own* Spirit-led sharing. While God supplied Israel's physical needs with manna and quail but did not change their spiritual condition, under the new covenant God is meeting the spiritual needs of the Corinthians in order that *they* might meet the physical needs of others (cf. 2 Cor. 9:8–11). Paul's expectation in 8:11 is thus one more expression of his confidence in the transforming power of the presence of God under the new covenant (cf. 3:3, 6, 18). For this reason, Paul leaves the amount of their giving up to the Corinthians, convinced that, as a new creation in Christ (5:17), the quantity of their giving will match the quality of their changed hearts (5:15).

Hence, everything Paul says in 8:1–15 is designed to ground his explicit command to complete the collection, as their resources allow (v. 11). Rhetorically, Paul's command is sandwiched between the examples of the Macedonians and of Jesus on the one side (8:1–10), and Scripture on the other (vv. 12–15). Just as 6:14–7:1 reflects the Corinthians' status and obligations as God's new covenant people, expressed negatively ("Separate yourselves from unbelievers"), so too 8:1–15 reflects this same status and obligation, now expressed positively ("Give to believers"). The Corinthians' renewed willingness to participate in the collection will be an undeniable reflection of their repentance and restoration to Christ.

Bridging Contexts

THE VERTICAL DIMENSION. In studying Paul's discussion of the offering for the saints in Jerusalem, the reader is caught by surprise by the number of words Paul uses for it: The offering is a *logeia* (collection, 1 Cor. 16:1–2), *eulogia* (blessing, 2 Cor. 9:5), *leitourgia* (priestly service,

9:12; cf. Rom. 15:27), *koinonia* (fellowship, partnership, sharing, Rom. 15:26; 2 Cor. 8:4; 9:13; cf. the related verb in Rom. 15:27), *diakonia* (service, ministry, 2 Cor. 8:4; 9:1, 12, 13), and, most important, an expression of *charis* (grace, 1 Cor. 16:3; 2 Cor. 8:1, 4, 6, 7, 9; cf. 8:19; 9:8, 14). For Paul, the simple but profound act of giving away one's money carries a multitude of meanings.

It is therefore even more surprising that Paul's word choices for describing the collection "are all derived from the vocabulary of human relationships with God and sacred acts of worship," and *none of them make any direct mention of money*.[20] Any application of Paul's thoughts on "giving" must therefore emphasize (and be convinced of) Paul's theological justification for giving. Otherwise, people will quickly detect that our admonitions to give are nothing more than a thinly veiled plea for money. Paul's primary concern is not the "budget," but the fruition of genuine grace in the lives of believers.

We must keep this vertical dimension of giving clearly in focus. For Paul, the basis for giving to others is not what *they* have done or will do for us, but what *God* has already done for us in Christ. The foundation of giving is God's grace. Just as the language of Christ's poverty and wealth in 8:9 is metaphorical, so too the reference in 8:9 to the believer's becoming "rich" is metaphorical. Though it is already an embarrassing indictment on the modern church even to have to say this, there is no warrant for a "health and wealth gospel" in this passage. Giving to others is not planting a "seed of faith" that will bring even greater material dividends in return. Giving is the expression of faith itself, content in what God has given and will give in accordance with his own providential care.

At the same time, we must also be careful to consider the incarnation of Christ a prototype for believers, not a mandate. We do not become literally "poor" for the justification of others. Nor must believers give up their wealth entirely in order to follow Christ's example. Paul nowhere tells his congregations how much to give, nor to give until their economic status is reduced. Paul's point in 8:13 is just the opposite. And in 8:9, the example of Christ does not serve to support a universal call to become literally poor for the sake of an itinerant ministry.

Nevertheless, in 6:10 Paul does apply to himself as an apostle the principle of imitating Christ in his literal poverty in order to make others spiritually rich—so that some believers are in fact called to such a life of poverty. But this must be a matter of personal calling, not universal principle. Instead, we become "like Christ" as we act in our context in the same way as Christ acted in his: giving up our physical resources for others because of our spiritual riches in God. Paul's reference to Christ functions to support why will-

---

20. Martin, *2 Corinthians*, 251. This same thing is true of Phil. 4:16–20.

ing and proportionate giving to others is a necessary act of Christ-like love for those who claim to be Christians (8:8; cf. Eph. 5:1).

The grace behind giving. Our interpretation of this passage has emphasized that one's attitude in giving is more important than the amount of one's gift. Paul never establishes a standard *for* giving, only the standard *of* giving. He stresses that the Macedonians' generosity derived from their joy; their joy did not derive from their generosity. The progression of thought in 8:2 is from grace to joy to giving, not the other way around. Their giving was an expression of God's grace, not their own moral or spiritual virtue; they gave to others because they were already experiencing an "overflowing joy" from God. Since God's grace is the springboard for our giving, even our gifts rebound to God's glory. The only real giver is God.

Our temptation, however, is to turn giving into a display of our own benevolence rather than giving out of our contented satisfaction in God. It is easy to succumb to this temptation, since in doing so we get the credit for our gifts, rather than God receiving the praise for making them possible. Giving is not a way of showing God how much we can do for him, but a way of illustrating how much God has done for us.

Unfortunately, Paul is often interpreted to be saying that "commanding" the Corinthians to give destroys the willing and eager nature of the collection as an expression of "grace." But pitting God's commands against his grace in this way reduces grace to an abstraction divorced from its necessary impact in the lives of its recipients. As a result, Paul's admonitions become "advice," not commands, since commands are viewed as the enemy of a response that is voluntary (8:3), willing (8:11, 12), generous (8:2), eager (8:7, 8), and overflowing (8:2, 3, 7, 14). In other words, what makes the collection a matter of "grace" is that the Corinthians are left free to participate or not, as they wish, whereas a command would make giving obligatory.[21] Others who view 8:8, 10 as a qualification of Paul's argument (i.e., not a "command" but an "opinion") attribute his advice to his "permissive style of writing," showing "how he sensed the need to handle tactfully those who had just come back to his side."[22] Thus, verse 10 reflects "Paul's hesitancy in appearing too forceful," while the command in verse 11 is merely a "mild injunction."[23]

---

21. For an example of this approach, see Paul Barnett, *The Second Epistle to the Corinthians*, 388–89, 401, 404, 406, 409, 434 (on 9:5), 437 (on 9:7). Concerning 8:10, he concludes that although this is a "serious apostolic counsel" (following Furnish), "nonetheless, such 'advice' is not obligatory; otherwise their response could not be 'of grace'" (409n.28). Hence, for Barnett, Paul's emphasis on the priority of "willing" over "doing" in 8:10 reflects this same contrast (411).

22. Martin, 2 *Corinthians*, 262.

23. Ibid., 264, 265.

In stark contrast, we have argued that in verses 8 and 10 Paul is not backing away from his command, but merely indicating that his injunction is his own admonition as an apostle, not a word that he has received directly from the Lord or from Scripture. Paul is not handling the Corinthians with "kid gloves" because of their recent repentance. Just the opposite. Here too, as in chapter 7, his command is the means of demonstrating the genuine nature of repentance.

It is crucial, therefore, that we not pit the grace of God against the commands of God as part of a false dichotomy that views faith and obedience as two distinct ways of relating to God. Paul sees no conflict between God's grace and his commands. God's commands express how the experience of his grace will manifest itself in everyday life. Every command of God is a promise of God in disguise. God commands what he commands because he promises what he promises. Obedience to his commands is made possible by trusting in his promises.

Hence, obedience to the commands of God is the daily expression of our dependence on his promised provision in our lives. What makes our growing obedience an act of divine grace (i.e., God's unmerited and undeserved favor and blessing) is the *priority* of "the grace of our Lord Jesus Christ" as the all-sufficient basis of our reconciliation and righteousness (8:9), the *power* of the Spirit as the gift of grace that makes our obedience possible (cf. 1:22; 3:3, 6–18), and the *promise* of forgiveness as the expression of grace in mercy that surrounds our progressive, but not perfect sanctification (2:7–10; 7:9–10). The indicatives of verse 7a lead to the implied imperative of verse 7b, not the other way around. And in verses 10–11 it is the grace-created desire that leads to giving, not our giving that creates new desires.

Give what you've got. In the light of the full force of Paul's command in this passage, it is also important to emphasize, as a matter of principle, that Paul stresses proportionate giving. This is an important qualification, for it ensures that the force of Paul's command is felt by all, regardless of economic status. Since Christ-like giving is dependent on experiencing God's grace, not our personal resources, the amount given in comparison to others means nothing (but see 9:6–11 to determine what is a proper amount). The attitude behind the action is everything.

Moreover, the universal applicability of Paul's command is supported by the sociological makeup of the early churches. Ever since the comments of Celsus in the second century, people have often argued that the early church was a lower class movement of the uneducated, the oppressed, slaves, and the poor.[24]

---

24. See Origen, *Contra Celsus* 1.62; 3.44, 55, as discussed by Wayne A. Meeks, *The First Urban Christians: The Social World of the Apostle Paul* (New Haven: Yale Univ. Press, 1983), 51. In categorizing the Corinthians' status, I am following Meeks' discussion, 58–59, 64.

Recent studies have shown, however, that "the most appropriate conclusion about the early Christians is . . . that they represented all social classes except the aristocratic class and that the church reflected the diverse social classes to be found in the wider society."[25]

In accordance with this general picture, Paul had instructed his readers in 1 Corinthians 16:2: "On the first day of every week, each one of you should set aside a sum of money in keeping with his income, saving it up, so that when I come no collections will have to be made." As Meeks points out, "this bespeaks the economy of small people, not destitute, but not commanding capital either. This, too, would fit the picture of fairly well-off artisans and tradespeople as the typical Christians."[26] For, as Meeks observes, "the extreme top and bottom of the Greco-Roman social scale are missing from the picture."[27] In applying this text we can be confident that Paul is speaking to a church with the same kind of economic diversity reflected in most of our own.

Giving as worship. Finally, we must be careful in applying this passage and passages like it not to convert it into a lesson on the general morality of giving. "The admonition implicit in this statement is not 'Do what Christ did'; or even, 'Do for others what Christ has done for you.' It is, rather, 'Do what is appropriate to your status as those who have been enriched by the grace of Christ.'"[28] Paul is not advocating an abstract, moral duty, but a theology. His goal in stirring up the Corinthians to give is to verify the genuine nature of their love as Christians (8:8, 11). This is why he emphasizes the earnestness that must characterize their giving. For "ancient thought on public fundraising exhibited particular concern to maintain the voluntary nature of subscriptions. This had its cause in the frequent abuse of putting pressure on the contributors."[29]

Such an emphasis is as important in our day as it was in Paul's. Today, too, the amount of money means little (8:12); the motivation means everything

25. Derek Tidball, *The Social Context of the New Testament: A Sociological Analysis* (Grand Rapids: Zondervan, 1984), 98. See, e.g., the presence in the church of the wealthy Gaius and prestigious Crispus (1 Cor. 1:14), Erastus, with his high civic status (Rom. 16:23; 2 Tim. 4:20), the independent artisans and homeowners Prisca and Aquila (Rom. 16:3–5; 1 Cor. 16:19), and the description of the majority of the people in 1 Cor. 1:26, some of whom must have been slaves (cf. 1 Cor. 7:20–24).

26. Meeks, *First Urban Christians*, 65. Nevertheless, because of the fragmentary and opaque quality of our sources concerning the nature of social status and class in the ancient world in general and in the church in particular, Meeks' caution is well taken: "We cannot draw up a statistical profile of the constituency of the Pauline communities nor fully describe the social level of a single Pauline Christian" (72).

27. Ibid., 73.

28. Furnish, *II Corinthians*, 418.

29. Betz, *2 Corinthians 8 and 9*, 59.

(8:7, 11–12; cf. 9:5). This becomes shockingly clear when we compare this passage to Paul's famous words in 1 Corinthians 13:3: Even giving away everything we have, without love, will gain us nothing—except to prepare us for God's judgment. Giving to others may or may not be an act of love, depending on whether it is motivated by the overflowing joy that flows from having been made "rich" by Christ (8:1, 5–7, 9, 10–12). Hence, nobody has captured the theological principles at work in this passage with more passion and precision than John Piper, who is worth listening to at length concerning the nature of Christian love as expressed in our passage:

Love Is the Overflow of Joy in God

2 Corinthians 8:1–4, 8 shows that Paul thinks of genuine love only in relation to God. . . . He writes 2 Corinthians 8 and 9 to motivate the Corinthians to be generous. The crucial thing for our purpose is to notice that in 8:8 he says this is a test of their *love*. . . .

The clear implication of 8:8 (especially the word "also") is that the Macedonians' generosity is a model of love that the Corinthians "also" should copy. By recounting the earnest love of the Macedonians, Paul aims to stir up the Corinthians to genuine love *also*. So here we have a test case to see just what the love of 1 Corinthians 13 looks like in real life. The Macedonians have given away their possessions just as 1 Corinthians 13:3 says ("If I give away all I have"). But *here* it is real love, while *there* it was not love at all. What makes the Macedonian generosity a genuine act of love?

The nature of genuine love can be seen in four things:

First, it is a work of divine *grace* (8:1). . . . The generosity of the Macedonians was not of human origin. Even though verse three says they gave "of their own accord," the willingness was a gift of God— a work of grace.

You can see this same combination of God's sovereign grace resulting in man's willingness in 8:16–17. . . . God put it in [Titus's] heart. So he goes of his *own* accord. The willingness is a gift—a work of divine grace.

Second, this experience of God's grace filled the Macedonians with joy (8:2). . . . Note that their joy was not owing to the fact that God had prospered them financially. He hadn't! In "extreme poverty" they had joy. Therefore the joy was a joy in God—in the experience of his grace.

Third, their joy in God's grace *overflowed* in generosity to meet the needs of others (8:2). . . . Therefore the liberality expressed horizontally toward men was an overflow of joy in God's grace.

Fourth, the Macedonians begged for the opportunity to sacrifice their meager possessions for the saints in Jerusalem (8:3–4). . . . In other words, the way their joy in God overflowed was in the joy of giving. They *wanted* to give. It was their joy!

Now we can give a definition of love that takes God into account and also includes the feelings that should accompany the outward acts of love: *Love is the overflow of joy in God which gladly meets the needs of others.*

Paul did not set the Macedonians up as a model of love just because they sacrificed in order to meet the needs of others. What he stresses is how they *loved* doing this (remember Micah 6:8!). It was the over-flow of JOY! They "begged earnestly" to give. They found their plea-sure in channeling the grace of God through their poverty to the poverty in Jerusalem. It is simply astonishing!

This is why a person can give his body to be burned and not have love. Love is the overflow of joy *in God!* It is not duty for duty's sake, or right for right's sake. It is not a resolute abandoning of one's own good with a view solely to the good of the other person. It is first a deeply satisfying experience of the fullness of God's grace, and then a doubly satisfying experience of sharing that grace with another person.

When poverty-stricken Macedonians beg Paul for the privilege of giving money to other poor saints, we may assume that this is what they want to do, not just ought to do, or have to do, but really long to do. It is their joy—an extension of their joy in God. To be sure, they are "denying themselves" whatever pleasures or comforts they could have from the money they give away, but the joy of extending God's grace to others is a far better reward than anything money could buy. The Macedonians have discovered the labor of Christian Hedonism! It is the overflow of joy in God which gladly meets the needs of others.[30]

WILLIAM DYRNESS HAS observed that in many respects American identity is estab-lished in material terms. We define ourselves by our relation to our material environment, perhaps more than our relation to other people (or even to God). That this has resulted in great material prosperity and great technological accomplishment we can readily acknowledge. But we [note] a dark side

---

30. John Piper, *Desiring God: Meditations of a Christian Hedonist* (Sisters, Ore.: Multnomah, 1996), 102–4.

as well: Americans invariably tend to endow material means with ulti-mate or final value. Owning a home, for example, is seen as one of the ends of life rather than as a means to other ends. Meaning is attached to accumulating an estate far beyond any conceivable use.[31]

The point Dyrness makes is that this cultural backdrop has permeated our preaching of the gospel. In his words:

> Communicating the gospel in America will invariably reflect these emphases. On the one hand, it will tend to affirm the quest for achieve-ment. It might emphasize that God loves us and seeks to help us real-ize our potential or our gifts (He "has a wonderful plan for our life"). On the other hand, it will encourage a practical no-nonsense kind of faith, a "faith that works" ... it will in general affirm the goodness and value of the person and the created order. As a rule, Christians in America will feel the need of affirmation rather than of deliverance.[32]

The question must be raised whether this adaptation to our culture is not a syncretism that compromises the gospel itself. Is God the great "supporter of my goals," the assistant assigned to help me realize my potential? Is the call to give merely an affirmation of my duty within society as part of a mutu-ally interdependent created order? Is my giving an expression of my inher-ent goodness as a person? Sloppy thinking about this crucial area of our lives as Christians will open the door for an invasion of American self-serving materialism and self-congratulating moralism.

The smorgasbord of values. This confusion of our culture with the gospel struck me with new force recently in a series of flyers that we received at our church on the subject of "smart giving."[33] Not surprisingly, they appeared in our bulletins over several weeks toward the end of the year, when most peo-ple do the greatest percentage of their giving. What surprised me, however, was their mixed message. They reminded us that regular giving is a Chris-tian characteristic *and* that at the end of the "tax year," there "may be appro-priate tax motivations to make a gift now and receive an additional charitable deduction." Moreover, the many sound, biblical insights scattered through-out the material were not integrated with its "practical" content within any kind of coherent theological framework. Instead, the flyers were filled with "sound bytes" on giving.

---

31. William Dyrness, *How Does America Hear the Gospel?* (Grand Rapids: Eerdmans, 1989), 132–33.

32. Ibid., 133.

33. I have removed the name of my church to protect the innocent! The bulletin flyers were copyrighted by Willing Way, Inc., 1996, 1997.

Because of this lack of biblical evaluation and theological grounding, there was much in the material that smacked of American, self-help pragmatism. For example, at the end of the lead brochure we were rightly told that "responsive giving is an outward evidence of God's grace in the Christian's life" (referring to 2 Cor. 8:7). But it was hard to square this with the rationale for giving presented at the beginning. After calling us to "consider God as the Original Giver and His giving," the flyer promised: "Your Christian life will be enriched and be more successful when you have a proper giver's perspective." True, but "enriched" and "successful" in what sense? The brochure never said. So, in the context of giving money and without a careful, God-centered explication, one can easily guess what definition will naturally be given to these all-important terms!

Furthermore, in the middle of the first flyer we were rightly enjoined to give willingly and proportionately (citing 2 Cor. 8:11—12) and reminded that "giving Christians evidence God's existence to the world." But we were also told that as part of the "essence of giving" we "transfer treasure from earth to heaven" (citing Matt. 6:19—21; Phil. 4:17—18). Again, this could be a helpful biblical perspective. Yet without a theological framework, such ambiguous affirmations give the impression that generous giving on earth is part of an eternal investment policy in which we store up material "treasure" in heaven. There was no reference to giving as an instrument by which we learn to recognize that the kingdom of God and its righteousness are themselves the real and only treasure worth having! Giving is not a way to transfer earthly treasure into heaven (as if being in God's presence were not enough), but a way of demonstrating that earthly treasures cannot compare to those of heaven. According to Matthew 6:19—21, we are not to transfer our treasure, but to seek a new one! What this illustrates is that when biblical reflection is missing, godly motivation is left wanting.

The flyers presented in the following weeks exhibited this same dangerous lack of biblical evaluation. One flyer asked and answered the question, "*How* can I give?" The responses, in this order, were: "Cash or check" (prized first because it is "simple and easy" and "readily usable"), "Stocks, bonds," etc. (prized because one avoids capital gains tax), "Bargain Sale," "Property," "Employer Match," "Business Gift," "Cheerfully," "Willingly," "Proportionately," "Regularly." What bothered me was not the call to exercise wisdom in managing our assets. What was troubling was that giving "cheerfully" and "willingly" was on the same conceptual level as a "bargain sale" and that these conditions of the heart were not listed first, but last (together with "proportionately" and "regularly").

Moreover, there was no theological narrative to place these answers in any kind of context. This smorgasbord approach to answering the question of how to give leaves the impression that there is an array of ways to give and that we should pick the one that fits us best, whether "cash" on the one hand or "willingly" on the other, as long as we give.

The other flyer asked and answered the question, "*Why* give?" In doing so, it ticked off the following answers, in this apparently random order: "Worship God," "Praise God" (one wonders what the intended distinction between worshiping and praising God was), "Love God," "Invest in changing lives," "Family participation," "Pay dues" (with the explanation that one is expected to contribute for the services rendered by the church), "See your investment at work," "Integrity in management," "Giving breaks the chains of money and materialism" (which may or may not be true, of course), "God commands it," "Giving blesses the giver," and "You'll enjoy it!" Although in this case the worship of God was first, we were still encouraged to take our choice of motivations— whether paying our dues, making an investment, or simply enjoying the fact that our money was being well managed, all the while getting blessed. Such a deal!

It is staggering that when it comes to giving, the church spends so little time and theological energy addressing our most cherished cultural values, namely, the materialistic accumulation of money and the idolatrous status and security that come through material possessions. When we do speak about giving, we are quick to adopt the motivational strategies and mores of our culture. The fact that Paul devotes so much of 2 Corinthians, his letter of restoration and apologetic for the truth, to the issue of the collection should be a sober reminder of the significance of this aspect of our Christian life. Nowhere is our materialism challenged more directly, and nowhere do we skirt the issues more often, than when it comes to expressing the genuine nature of our faith and the unity of the church through our giving.

Learning from the Macedonians. The example of the Macedonians is still instructive today. In a radical role reversal of the world's values, the abundance of their *poverty*, fueled by the *riches* of their joy in God, led to a *wealth* of generosity. We usually think of "fund raisers" as encouraging those who can afford to give to give more; in the Macedonian churches those who had nothing begged to give. Why? Paul's answer is the grace of God. Indeed, the "also" of 8:7 shows that giving is just as much a spiritual gift of grace as any of the other charismatic gifts the Corinthians had received. Giving is not merely an expression of compassion for the needy. Nor is it simply a reflection of our own concern. Rather, the spiritual gift of giving to others is to be the reflex of our own joy in the grandeur of God's gift to us in Christ. As we have seen, the Macedonians' joy led to giving, not the other way around. For this reason, throughout Paul's discussion, the collection is termed a "grace" and a "ministry!"

Thus, following Paul, giving is not motivated by trying to convince people of how "smart" and "responsible" and "enjoyable" it is to give. By participating in the collection the Macedonians were not trying to pay their dues or make a wise financial investment. Instead, they were savoring and seeking the kingdom of God. Only the greater treasures of the kingdom of God can free us from clinging to the competing treasures of this world (cf. Jesus' call to do some "comparison shopping" in Matt. 6:19–21). Only the deeper satisfaction that comes from spending ourselves for others can defeat the sinfully natural impulse to use others for our own ends. And giving up ourselves for others can take place only when our own security needs have already been met in the Christ who spent himself for us (8:9). Hence, rather than focusing merely on more effective ways to advertise the benefits and obligations of giving, we need to pray for the pouring out of God's Spirit on his people. Instead of bigger fund-raising campaigns, we need a bigger picture of God.

Paul's discussion of the collection makes clear how much we have been lulled to sleep by the materialistic, self-seeking ethos around us. Our culture's mythology of "deserving what we have earned" has often led to a culturally compromised Christianity. Under the lure of our materialism, this sense of deserving what we have earned expresses itself by "rewarding" ourselves through spending our surplus on luxury. As a result, we find it almost impossible to be countercultural when it comes to money.

We lack models of that kind of joyful, "Macedonian" giving that comes from a profound experience of God's grace. As a result, we struggle against a nominalism that chokes out voluntary, sacrificial giving as an unsavory example of religious fanaticism. What could be more "fanatical" in our day than to live below one's level of income for the sake of giving away as much money as possible? In today's world, the Macedonians' giving out of their poverty serves as a wake-up call in the midst of our self-satisfying slumber.

Listening to William Law. Such nominalism is nothing new. In the early eighteenth century, William Law (1686–1761) faced the same lack of godliness within the church that we face today, despite (or, as he argued, because of) the "Christian" culture that dominated much of England at the time. In 1728 he responded by publishing *A Serious Call to a Devout and Holy Life.*[34] In

---

34. William Law, *A Serious Call to a Devout and Holy Life: Adapted to the State and Condition of all Orders of Christians*, Introduction by G. W. Bromiley (Grand Rapids: Eerdmans, 1966). Though Law himself remained within the Church of England his entire life, J. H. Overton observed in the introduction to the 1898 edition that the great Evangelical Revival, beginning in 1738, "owed its first impetus to this book more than to any other" (ix). Law wrote his *Serious Call* to those who professed to be Christians but who showed little evidence of being Christian in the affairs of everyday life. As Overton points out, the purpose of Law's call "to live more nearly as they prayed," was "to convince their minds of the absurdity of believing one thing, and doing another" (xii). In what follows, all quotes are taken from this edition and cited first by original chapter number and then by page number in the Eerdmans edition. The emphases are mine.

it, Law issued a plain but profound plea to consider what knowing God means in *every* aspect of life. He called for this consistent examination since, by definition, the devout person "makes all the parts of his common life, parts of piety, by doing everything in the name of God, and under such rules as are conformable to His glory" (ch. i, 1).[35]

Law recognized that central to this concern for godliness is the issue of money. Like Paul, he perceived that our attitudes and actions toward our possessions reveal the reality of God's grace in our lives. It is not accidental that when Paul moved to apply his gospel to the repentant, he immediately turned to the collection. As Jesus said, "For where your treasure is, there your heart will be also.... You cannot serve both God and Money" (Matt. 6:21, 24). So too, after Law outlined the nature, obligation, and obstacles to devotion in general (chs. i–v), the first specific issue he takes up, and then develops in detail for three entire chapters, is "the great obligations, and the advantages of making a wise and religious use of our estates and fortunes" (ch. vi, 50). For as Law observes, our attitudes toward and use of money influence almost every area of our lives: "Because the manner of using our money, or spending our estate, enters so far into the business of every day, and makes so great a part of our common life, that our common life must be much of the same nature as our common way of spending our estate" (ch. vi, 50).

So Law's theological concern is imminently practical: The way we spend our money determines the character of our lives, even as the character of our lives determines how we spend our money. In short, we know who we are by how we spend our money. In Law's words:

> Every exhortation in Scripture to be wise and reasonable, satisfying only such wants as God would have satisfied; every exhortation to be spiritual and heavenly, pressing after a glorious change of our nature; every exhortation to love our neighbour as ourselves, to love all mankind as God has loved them, is a command to be strictly religious in the use of money. (ch. vi, 53)

Like Paul in 2 Corinthians 8:9, Law's call was to apply the cross to our money.

> The Christian's great conquest over the world is all contained in the mystery of Christ upon the cross. It was there and from thence that

---

35. "If we are to be in Christ new creatures, we must show that we are so, by having new ways of living in the world. If we are to follow Christ, it must be in our common way of spending every day. Thus it is in all the virtues and holy tempers of Christianity, they are not ours unless they be the virtues and tempers of our ordinary life. ... If our common life is not a common course of humility, self-denial, renunciation of the world, poverty of spirit, and heavenly affection, we do not live the lives of Christians" (ch. i, 7).

He taught all Christians how they were to come out of and conquer the world, and what they were to do in order to be His disciples. And all the doctrines, sacraments, and institutions of the Gospel are only so many explications of the meaning, and applications of the benefit of this great mystery.

And the state of Christianity implieth nothing else but an entire, absolute conformity to that spirit which Christ showed in the mysterious sacrifice of Himself upon the cross. (ch. xvii, 196)

Further, like Paul in 2 Corinthians 8:6–7, Law saw that conformity to Christ in giving was not an option or merely good advice, but the necessary outworking of what it meant to be Christian itself.

Every man, therefore, is *only so far a Christian as he partakes of this spirit of Christ.*

... The necessity of this conformity to all that Christ did and suffered upon our account is very plain from the whole tenor of Scripture.

... If "we suffer with Him, we shall also reign with Him." ...

It was for this reason that the holy Jesus said of His disciples, and in them of all true believers, "They are not of this world, as I am not of this world." Because all true believers conforming to the sufferings, crucifixion, death, and resurrection of Christ live no longer after the spirit and temper of this world, but their life is hid with Christ in God. (ch. xvii, 196–198)

Thus, just as God calls the Christian to forgive his brother "seventy times seven" (Matt. 18:21–22, RSV), Law saw this "rule of forgiving" to be "the rule of giving" as well. In his words, "it is as necessary to give to seventy times seven, to live in the continual exercise of all good works to the utmost of our power, as it is necessary to forgive until seventy times seven, and live in the habitual exercise of this forgiving temper" (ch. vi, 56).

Law knew that the loophole in such a call is our propensity to spend luxuriously on ourselves so that we are not "able" to give to others. So Law went to the jugular vein of our compromised values in order to cut the life-blood of materialism: To spend needlessly on ourselves at the expense of others is a denial of our salvation itself. For Law, as for Paul in 8:8, the test of genuine faith was a willingness to give and the adoption of a lifestyle that makes giving possible.

It is as much the best use of our money to be always doing good with it as it is the best use of it at any particular time; so that that which is a reason for a charitable action is as good a reason for a charitable life.

... If, therefore, it be our duty at any time to deny ourselves any needless expenses, to be moderate and frugal, that we may have to give to those that want, *it is as much our duty to do so at all times*, that we may be further able to do more good.

... Either, therefore, you must so far *renounce your Christianity* as to say, that you need never perform any of these good works; or you must own that you are to perform them all your life in as high a degree as you are able. There is no middle way to be taken, any more than there is a middle way betwixt pride and humility, or temperance and intemperance.

... Hence also appears the necessity of renouncing all those foolish and unreasonable expenses which the pride and folly of mankind have made so common and fashionable in the world. For if it is necessary to do good works as far as you are able, it must be as necessary to renounce those needless ways of spending money, which render you unable to do works of charity.

... When, therefore, any one tells you of the lawfulness of expensive apparel, or the innocency of pleasing yourself with costly satisfactions, only imagine that the same person was to tell you that you need not do works of charity, that Christ does not require you to do good unto your poor brethren as unto Him, and then you will see the wickedness of such advice; for to tell you that you may live in such expenses as make it impossible for you to live in the exercise of good works, is the same thing as telling you that you need not have any care about such good works themselves. (ch. vi, 56–58)

This is indeed a "serious call." Law realized that he was living in a dangerous day. He saw clearly that the values of the secular world, "with its passions of sensuality, self-love, pride, covetousness, ambition, and vain-glory" (ch. xvii, 200), had infiltrated the nominal "Christian world." Law also recognized that this posed an even greater threat to the faithful than direct persecution:

And indeed the world, by professing Christianity, is so far from being a less dangerous enemy than it was before, *that it has by its favours destroyed more Christians than ever it did by the most violent persecution*.

... We must guard against it as a greater and more dangerous enemy now than it was in those times.

It is a greater enemy, because it has greater power over Christians by its favours, riches, honours, rewards, and protections, than it had by the fire and fury of its persecutions.

It is a more dangerous enemy by having lost its appearance of enmity....

Whilst pride, sensuality, covetousness, and ambition had only the authority of the heathen world, Christians were thereby made more intent upon the contrary virtues. But when pride, sensuality, covetousness, and ambition have the authority of the Christian world, then private Christians are in the utmost danger not only of being shamed out of the practice, but of losing the very notion of the piety of the Gospel. (ch. xvii, 200–202)

It is therefore not surprising that the litmus test for whether one has capitulated to the authority of the secular, "Christian world" is money: "How can a man be made more incapable of the spirit of Christ than by a wrong value for money; and yet how can he be more wrong in his value of it than by following the authority of the Christian world?" (ch. xvii, 202). How we spend our money is no innocent matter:

Now this is truly the case of riches spent upon ourselves in vain and needless expenses; in trying to use them where they have no real use, nor we any real want, we only use them to our great hurt, in creating unreasonable desires, in nourishing ill tempers, in indulging our passions, and supporting a worldly, vain turn of mind.

... So that money thus spent is not merely wasted, or lost, but it is spent to bad purposes, and miserable effects, to the corruption and disorder of our hearts, and to the making us less able to live up to the sublime doctrines of the Gospel. It is but like keeping money from the poor to buy poison for ourselves. (ch. vi, 52–53)

We must be careful here. Law's call is uncompromising: We are to live in order to give. But it is by no means a summons to a self-destructive "sacrifice" or joyless martyrdom. Law's extended treatise on devotion and happiness makes it clear that just the opposite is true. There he argues that "great devotion fills our lives with the greatest peace and happiness that can be enjoyed in this world" (ch. xi, 102). Accordingly, Law's "serious call to a devout and holy life" is a serious call to be happy. As he put it:

As there is no foundation for comfort in the enjoyments of this life, but in the assurance that a wise and good God governeth the world, so that the more we find out God in every thing, the more we apply to Him in every place, the more we look up to Him in all our actions, the more we conform to His will, the more we act according to His wisdom, and imitate His goodness, by so much the more do we *enjoy* God, partake of the divine nature, and heighten and increase *all* that is *happy* and *comfortable* in human life. (ch. xi, 102)

Understood in this way, the Christian faith teaches believers how to use everything God has granted them, so that they "may have always the pleasure of receiving a right benefit from them" (ch. xi, 110). Specifically,

it shows [a person] what is strictly right in meat, drink, and clothes; and that he has nothing else to expect from the things of this world but to satisfy such wants of his own, and then to extend his assistance to all his brethren, that, as far as he is able, he may help all his fellow-creatures to the same benefit from the world that he hath.

[Conversely] it tells him that *this world is incapable of giving him any other happiness*, and that all endeavours to be happy in heaps of money, or acres of land, in fine clothes, rich beds, stately equipage, and show and splendour, are only *vain* endeavours, *ignorant attempts after impossibilities*; these things being no more able to give the least degree of happiness than dust in the eyes can cure thirst, or gravel in the mouth can satisfy hunger; but like dust and gravel misapplied, will only serve to render him more unhappy by such an ignorant misuse of them. (ch. xi, 110)

Hence, if we are told,

"sell that thou hast, and give to the poor," it is because there is no other natural or reasonable use of our riches, no other way of making ourselves happier for them. . . . For if a man has more food than his own nature requires, how base and unreasonable is it to invent foolish ways of wasting it, and make sport of his own full belly, rather than let his fellow-creatures have the same comfort from food which he hath had? It is so far, therefore, from being a hard law of religion to make this use of our riches, that a reasonable man would rejoice in that religion which teaches him to be happier in that which he gives away than in that which he keeps for himself; which teaches him to make spare food and raiment be great blessings to him than that which feeds and clothes his own body. (ch. xi, 112)

Paul's argument in 8:1–15 is reasonable because it is based on the reality of the all-satisfying grace of God. The Macedonians are no fools for giving out of their poverty. But neither are they great religious heroes. It is not the Macedonians who are praised in this passage, but the God who brought about their giving by first having given them joy in himself in the midst of their poverty in this world.

2 Corinthians 8:16–9:15

THANK GOD, who put into the heart of Titus the same concern I have for you. [17]For Titus not only welcomed our appeal, but he is coming to you with much enthusiasm and on his own initiative. [18]And we are sending along with him the brother who is praised by all the churches for his service to the gospel. [19]What is more, he was chosen by the churches to accompany us as we carry the offering, which we administer in order to honor the Lord himself and to show our eagerness to help. [20]We want to avoid any criticism of the way we administer this liberal gift. [21]For we are taking pains to do what is right, not only in the eyes of the Lord but also in the eyes of men.

[22]In addition, we are sending with them our brother who has often proved to us in many ways that he is zealous, and now even more so because of his great confidence in you. [23]As for Titus, he is my partner and fellow worker among you; as for our brothers, they are representatives of the churches and an honor to Christ. [24]Therefore show these men the proof of your love and the reason for our pride in you, so that the churches can see it.

[9:1]There is no need for me to write to you about this service to the saints. [2]For I know your eagerness to help, and I have been boasting about it to the Macedonians, telling them that since last year you in Achaia were ready to give; and your enthusiasm has stirred most of them to action. [3]But I am sending the brothers in order that our boasting about you in this matter should not prove hollow, but that you may be ready, as I said you would be. [4]For if any Macedonians come with me and find you unprepared, we—not to say anything about you—would be ashamed of having been so confident. [5]So I thought it necessary to urge the brothers to visit you in advance and finish the arrangements for the generous gift you had promised. Then it will be ready as a generous gift, not as one grudgingly given.

[6]Remember this: Whoever sows sparingly will also reap sparingly, and whoever sows generously will also reap generously. [7]Each man should give what he has decided in his heart

to give, not reluctantly or under compulsion, for God loves a cheerful giver. [8]And God is able to make all grace abound to you, so that in all things at all times, having all that you need, you will abound in every good work. [9]As it is written:

"He has scattered abroad his gifts to the poor;
   his righteousness endures forever."

[10]Now he who supplies seed to the sower and bread for food will also supply and increase your store of seed and will enlarge the harvest of your righteousness. [11]You will be made rich in every way so that you can be generous on every occasion, and through us your generosity will result in thanksgiving to God.

[12]This service that you perform is not only supplying the needs of God's people but is also overflowing in many expressions of thanks to God. [13]Because of the service by which you have proved yourselves, men will praise God for the obedience that accompanies your confession of the gospel of Christ, and for your generosity in sharing with them and with everyone else. [14]And in their prayers for you their hearts will go out to you, because of the surpassing grace God has given you. [15]Thanks be to God for his indescribable gift!

THE IMPORTANCE OF the collection within the argument of 2 Corinthians (not to mention within Paul's theology) is often underestimated. Far from being a digression in Paul's thought, the practical point of 2 Corinthians as a whole is actually expressed in these chapters: Those Corinthians who have not accepted the grace of God in vain (6:1–2), as evidenced by their repentance (7:9–11), are to prepare for Paul's third visit (cf. 13:1) by purifying the church (6:14–7:1) and by completing the collection (8:1–9:15).

There is also an important apologetic motive behind these chapters: Paul wants to demonstrate his integrity regarding this sizable sum of money (7:2; 8:20; 11:20; 12:15–18) and to pave the way for transferring it to Jerusalem, since its favorable reception was by no means guaranteed (see Rom. 15:30–31; cf. Acts 21:15–26; 24:17). Thus, when it comes to the collection for Jerusalem, both the status of the Corinthians and the reputation of the apostle are on the line (cf. 1 Tim. 5:8).

In 8:1–15, Paul argued theologically and ecclesiologically for the resumption of the collection. Now in 8:16–24, Paul commends the three-man delegation that he is sending to Corinth to administer it: Titus, the chief delegate (vv. 16–17), and two other unnamed brothers (vv. 18, 22). The main purpose of this commendation is the corresponding admonition in 8:24 that his readers respond to them and to their task appropriately. But inasmuch as the apostle is always a pastoral theologian, his recommendation is not merely a matter of administrative detail. Rather, it is laced with theological and scriptural argumentation, while as a whole it unfolds under the rubric of praising God (8:16a), which once again is the literary and theological formula Paul uses to open up a new section of his letter (cf. 1:3 and 2:14).

The paragraph in 9:1–15 directly supports the command of 8:24 by outlining why the collection in Achaia must be completed before Paul arrives and by supporting this necessity theologically (Rom. 15:26 indicates that Achaia did in fact respond!). Hence, rather than being a fragment from a separate letter that was subsequently incorporated into what we now call 2 Corinthians, chapter 9 requires chapter 8 in order to be understandable. The reference to the brothers in 9:3 builds on 8:16–23, and the need to complete the collection before Paul arrives requires the obligation stated in 8:7–15 (cf. 9:5 with 8:20; 9:1–2 with 8:24).

Paul wants the collection completed before he returns in order to avoid any possibility of coercing the collection by his presence (9:5), since he knows that when he returns, it will be to judge the church (cf. 10:2–6; 13:1–4). Paul does not want people participating in the collection because of their last-minute fear of being judged by God, but because of the continuing grace of God in their lives. Paul's concern is to show that giving is not a way to *stay* in the church under the threat of punishment, but a way of demonstrating that they *belong* to the church because of their continuing trust in what God has done, is doing, and will do for them.

The anticipation that God will be praised through the generosity of his people (9:11), the main point of 9:1–15, also reflects this same theocentric focus. For this reason, Paul's discussion of the collection ends where 8:16 began, with thanksgiving to God (9:15). Hence, not to participate willingly in the collection as an act of worship to God does not remove one from the church; it merely indicates that one is not part of God's people to begin with.

The Necessity of Sending the Delegation (8:16–24)

LIKE ITS PARALLEL in 2:14, Paul's praise to God in 8:16 introduces a new literary unit. Moreover, in the same way that 2:14 introduced Paul's commendation for himself, 8:16 introduces Paul's commendation for Titus and the two brothers from Macedonia. Just as having the Corinthians in his "heart" commended Paul in 2:14–3:3 (cf. 3:2), so too the "concern" (or better, "eager-ness," cf. NRSV) in Titus's "heart" regarding the Corinthians commends him (8:16). These parallels support the NIV's decision to interpret the "same" eagerness or concern in 8:16 to be a reference to Titus's sharing the same con-cern Paul had for the Corinthians, rather than drawing a comparison between Titus's concern and the Corinthians' concern for Paul (cf. 7:11–12; 8:7) or that of the Macedonians (8:8). Paul himself is the point of comparison.

The evidence of Titus's eagerness was his willingness to accept Paul's assignment and the "enthusiasm" and "initiative" with which he took it up (8:17). In the light of Paul's argument in 8:1–15, this zeal to complete the col-lection is a zeal for the good of the Corinthians themselves. Though such a willingness to serve is often mentioned in Hellenistic letters as the most important qualification for administrators,[1] Paul's point in 8:16–17 is that, as with the Macedonians (cf. 8:1), *God* is the one who put the desire to help the Corinthians in Titus's heart. Titus is commended not because of his own innate qualities, but because of the way in which God has worked in his life. This is why Titus is commended, but God is praised (cf. Matt. 5:16).

Verses 18–21 concern the sending of the second brother, who remains unnamed. Though all attempts to identify him remain pure conjecture, sug-gestions have ranged from Luke (cf. Col. 4:14; 2 Tim. 4:11; Philem. 24), Barnabas, or Apollos (Acts 18:24–28), to one of the men listed in Acts 19:29; 20:4. Paul's designation of this person as simply "the brother" (8:18) indi-cates that he is a Christian, but that within the delegation he probably has less status than Titus. Whereas the latter was sent on Paul's own recommen-dation, this brother is sent because of his reputation among "all the churches" in Macedonia, Achaia, and Asia (cf. 11:28; also Acts 20:3–4; 1 Cor. 7:17; 14:34). He is praised for his "service to the gospel," which likely refers to his work as an evangelist (cf. Rom. 1:9; 10:14–15; Eph. 4:11; 1 Thess. 3:2; 2 Tim. 4:5), though it may simply denote his support for the evangelistic work of others (as in Phil. 1:5; 4:3).

As these designations indicate, though this "brother" is sent by Paul, he is not Paul's personal envoy but a chosen delegate of the churches. The word translated "chosen" in 8:19 is a technical term for being elected by the rais-ing of hands in the assembly (cf. Acts 14:23; Titus 1:9). Paul is lending his apos-tolic authority to the decision of the local church (for this same procedure, see 1 Cor. 16:3). As 2 Corinthians 8:19 indicates as well, the churches com-missioned this brother to travel to Jerusalem with Paul and the collection before it was decided to send him to Corinth too (here again, the collection is referred to literally as a "grace" [*charis*]; cf. 8:1, 4, 6, 7, 9; 9:8, 14, 15).

---

1. Hans Dieter Betz, *2 Corinthians 8 and 9*, 58nn.140–41, 70.

Thus, Paul is simply expanding this brother's appointment to include preceding him to Corinth in order to help complete the collection. The presence of this respected brother will help certify the integrity of the enterprise both before God (8:20) and, more important (since God knows of its integrity), before others (see in 8:21; cf. Prov. 3:4; Rom. 12:17). Paul sends the delegation to ward off all suspicion that he is somehow using the collection to line his own pockets (cf. 2 Cor. 2:17; 4:2; 6:3; 7:2–4; 11:7–12; 12:16–18).[2]

It is significant, therefore, but not surprising, that in a passage detailing the sending of church delegates to ensure the purity of the offering, we again encounter Paul's self-understanding. He relates everything he does to his role as an apostle. Accordingly, in 8:19–20 he says that the collection is "ministered by us," using the same Greek phrase as found in 3:3 to describe his new covenant ministry of the Spirit (the NIV obscures this parallel with its translation, "administer"). For Paul, the collection is not simply a practical matter or merely an application of his message. Instead, it is an integral part of his ministry of the gospel itself. This is reflected in the purpose of the collection as stated in 8:19: "in order to honor the Lord himself [lit., for the glory of the Lord] and to show our eagerness to help."

In other words, the collection is an essential aspect of Paul's ministry precisely because it glorifies God and demonstrates the reality of the Spirit through Paul's enthusiastic willingness to meet the needs of others (cf. 3:18; 4:15; 9:12–13; Rom. 15:7; 1 Cor. 10:31; Phil. 1:11; 2:11). Indeed, the latter accomplishes the former. Once again, Paul himself models the same God-glorifying quality of Spirit-given "eagerness" that he calls for in the Corinthians (cf. 2 Cor. 8:11–12; 9:2).

The third member of the delegation is introduced in 8:22. Paul's description of him as "our brother" suggests that he too, like Titus, has been appointed directly by Paul, not the churches, though his responsibility is not to represent Paul per se, but the concerns of the congregations (cf. 8:23b). Like Titus in 8:16–17 and Paul himself in 8:19, this brother's key qualification was his being "zealous" or "eager to help." When Paul appoints someone to represent

---

2. As the background to Paul's commitment to the collection and to his arrangement for Gentile envoys to accompany it to Jerusalem, commentators often point to the Old Testament expectation that, in conjunction with Israel's final restoration, Gentiles will come to Mount Zion bearing gifts. But there are no allusions or references to these texts in chapters 8–9 and no mention of any eschatological expectations. Rather, the Gentiles accompany Paul simply to ensure the fiscal integrity of the collection. A more appropriate parallel is the practice of sending envoys of the highest repute with the yearly offerings of the Diaspora Jews for the temple treasury (cf. Philo, *Embassy to Gaius* 216; *Special Laws* 1.78; Josephus, *Antiquities* 16.172). For this point and the linguistic parallel to 8:20, see Victor Paul Furnish, *II Corinthians*, 423; Paul Barnett, *The Second Epistle to the Corinthian*, 426n.65.

the ministry of the gospel, he looks for this tangible sign of the Spirit's work (cf. its presence in the Macedonians in 8:8). The greatest fruit of the Spirit is love, since "love is the overflow of joy in God which gladly meets the needs of others."[3] Indeed, according to 8:22b, this man's zeal to serve the Corinthians had been fueled all the more by the renewed, Spirit-induced zeal of the repentant Corinthians themselves (cf. 7:11–12; 8:7). Love begets love.

In 8:23–24 Paul draws two conclusions; the first concerns the delegation (v. 23); the second, derived from the first, is aimed at the Corinthians (v. 24). (1) Given what Paul has said about Titus in 8:16–17, he now describes Titus as his "partner and fellow worker" (8:23), a "formula of authorization" designating him as Paul's own representative.[4] "Fellow worker" is Paul's favorite description of his associates in ministry.[5] In contrast, the two brothers of 8:18–22 are designated "representatives" (lit., "apostles"; cf. 1:1 in contrast to Phil. 2:25), not of Paul but "of the churches" (8:23). As such, they are "an honor to Christ" (lit., "a glory of Christ").

Paul's equation of the two brothers with the "glory of Christ" reflects his earlier assertion in 3:18 and 4:4–6 that those who encounter the glory of God in the face of Christ are transformed into that same glory. Since Christ is the one who creates in them their eager desire to serve the Corinthians, these "apostles," like *the* apostle Paul (cf. 1:1), are manifestations of Christ's life-changing glory. This means that to reject their work among the Corinthians is to reject the reality of Christ in his church and within her apostles.

(2) Given the representative status of the delegation, Paul concludes this section by calling the Corinthians to respond appropriately to its presence and purpose among them (8:24). The delegation that has just been commended is, of course, the very one that has delivered the letter they are now reading (i.e., our 2 Corinthians) and are at work completing the collection. The Corinthians must therefore demonstrate the reality of their renewed love for Paul and his gospel by complying with the call to contribute. Just as the Macedonians are an example to the Corinthians (8:1–7), the Corinthians are to be a reciprocal example to them, demonstrating that the same expression of God's grace they experienced is now being replicated among the Corinthians.

Paul has boasted that the majority of the Corinthians, having genuinely repented, would indeed respond. Now it is time for them to confirm that confidence by living out what they have confessed (cf. 8:2, 8; 9:13). To dis-

---

3. John Piper, *Desiring God: Meditations of a Christian Hedonist* (Sisters, Ore: Multnomah, 1996), 103. This was the climactic point in Bridging Contexts with regard to 8:1–15.

4. Betz, *2 Corinthians 8 and 9*, 79–80.

5. See 1:24; Rom. 16:3, 9, 21; 1 Cor. 3:9; 16:10, 16; Phil. 2:22, 25, 30; 4:3; 1 Thess. 3:2; Col. 4:11; Philem. 1, 17, 24.

cipline their own is one thing, but to reach out across ethnic, social, religious, and cultural boundaries to the Jews in Jerusalem will be the ultimate test of their "earnestness," "eagerness," and "concern" (7:11–12). For as will become clear in 10:12–18, one can only legitimately boast about those things for which there is concrete evidence that God has been at work. This explains why Paul's boasting concerning the Corinthians in 8:24 is the ultimate ground for the praise to God with which this section began: His boasting is, at the same time, a declaration of thanksgiving to the One who made their lives possible.

The Necessity of Completing
the Collection in Advance (9:1–5)

DESPITE THE CHAPTER division in our Bibles, 9:1–5 is a direct support for Paul's admonition in 8:24, not the introduction of a new topic, much less the beginning of a separate letter fragment (note the *gar* ["for"] in the Greek text, unfortunately not translated in the NIV).[6] Paul calls the Corinthians to respond to the three-man delegation (8:24) because its task is to ensure that their earlier desire to give will be fulfilled before he arrives (9:3) and that their giving itself will express God's blessing in their lives (9:5). His point in 9:1–2, therefore, is that his command in 8:24 does not concern participating in the collection as such, since they have already shown their "eagerness" or "enthusiasm" to do so (in 8:7–15 the issue is their generosity and completion of the project, not their desire to participate per se). Rather, Paul's burden is that the Corinthians respond positively to the delegation by completing the collection before he himself returns.

So Paul really has "no need" to write to the Corinthians about "this service to the saints" itself (9:1). This qualification is more than merely a rhetorical device intended to gain their goodwill. Paul had already boasted about their desire to give in response to Titus's previous initiation of the collection last year, before all the trouble had begun (8:6, 10, 24; cf. 7:4, 14). Indeed, their earlier willingness had proved to be an example to the very Macedonians who were now providing an example for those in "Achaia" (9:2; cf. 8:1–7).

Most likely, Paul employs the geographical designation of "Achaia" here to match his corresponding reference to the "Macedonians," especially since Corinth was the senatorial and provincial capital of Achaia. Paul's concern is not only with the central church in Corinth but also with all the churches

---

6. It is often pointed out that Paul uses the construction *peri de* ("now concerning") to introduce a new subject or section in his letters (cf. 1 Cor. 7:1, 25; 8:1; 12:1; 16:1, 12; 1 Thess. 4:9; 5:1). But here we have *peri gar* ("for concerning"), which introduces a subheading within the ongoing argument.

or believers in the wider environs (cf. 1:1; 11:10; also 1 Cor. 16:15).[7] His point in 2 Corinthians 9:2 is that their renewed readiness (*paraskeuazo*, a military term describing preparation for military actions; cf. 1 Cor. 14:8[8]) should now be brought to fruition, since their desire must be matched by action for it to be considered genuine (cf. 8:11–12).

Despite their readiness, past and present, Paul has nevertheless sent the three brothers[9] in order to ensure that his boast concerning the collection, which is the visible fruit of his ministry among them, will not be "emptied" (9:3; NIV, "prove hollow"). The verb used here (*kenoo*) belongs to the same stem as the noun used in 6:1 to refer to the danger of the Corinthians' accepting the grace of God "in vain" (*kenos*).[10] This parallel is not accidental. As we have seen, the genuine nature of the Corinthians' renewed repentance is at stake in completing the collection (cf. 8:8). Repentance must bear fruit.

This means that the character of the Corinthians will soon be evident to all. For what was only a possibility in 1 Corinthians 16:3–4 has now been decided. A delegation of Macedonians will accompany Paul with the collection, which means that they will also be with him when he returns to Corinth on his way to Jerusalem (2 Cor. 9:4; cf. 8:19; Acts 20:2–4; Rom. 15:25–28). This, then, is the final basis for Paul's concern that the collection be completed before he arrives. He is well aware of the shame both he and they will incur if these Macedonians, to whom Paul has boasted about the church in Achaia, find the Corinthians unprepared (9:4b).[11]

---

7. Contra those who, like Betz, *2 Corinthians 8 and 9*, 52, argue that chapter 9 is addressed to a different group of churches than chapter 8. In his view, "Paul also seems to have had an exceptionally good relationship with the Christians of Achaia. So far as we can tell, the Corinthian crisis was limited to Corinth, while the other Achaian churches maintained an untroubled and loyal relationship to the apostle. For this reason, Paul turned to them when he needed assistance in bringing the collection for Jerusalem to a conclusion. He trusted that the Achaians would be wise enough to ensure that the collection would be not only a financial, but also a spiritual success...."

8. Ibid., 92.

9. The NIV's "I am sending" reflects Paul's use of the aorist tense here (*epempsa*, "I sent"), to depict an event that is past by the time the letter is being read, since the brothers are now in Corinth with this letter. For this same use of the "epistolary aorist," see 8:17 (Gk. "he came" = "he is coming"), 18 (Gk. "we sent" = "we are sending"), 22 (Gk. "we sent" = "we are sending").

10. Cf. Paul's use of these same words in Rom. 4:14; 1 Cor. 1:17; 9:15; 15:10, 14, 58; Gal. 2:2; Eph. 5:6; Phil. 2:7, 16; Col. 2:8; 1 Thess. 2:1; 3:5.

11. Following Furnish, *II Corinthians*, 427–28; Ralph P. Martin, *2 Corinthians*, 284–85, who, against the NIV, argue that the Greek in 9:4 should not be rendered "having been so confident," but rather "in this project" or "undertaking" (cf. NRSV), or "eventuality." Cf. this same terminology in 11:17; Heb. 1:3; 3:14; 11:1; Jer. 23:32 (LXX); Ezek. 19:5 (LXX), where it never means "confidence."

Paul's positive purpose in sending the brothers in advance of his arrival is made clear in 9:5: If the collection is completed before he arrives, the suspicion presently being cast on his motives will be dispelled (cf. 8:20), and no one will be able to say that the collection was extracted from the Corinthians under the fear of judgment. In other words, the collection will remain what it is called here and what it ought to be—namely, a "blessing" (*eulogia*; NIV, "generous gift"), and not something given "grudgingly" (9:5).

Paul's choice of the word "blessing" in 9:5 to describe the collection reflects his earlier argument in 8:6–9 that the Corinthians' giving is to be a response to God's grace in their lives. At the same time, it points forward to his explication in 9:6–15 of the specific nature of this response (cf. esp. 9:6, 8, 14). By contrast, its antonym, *pleonexia* (which the NIV translates "grudgingly given"), refers to the covetousness or idolatrous greed that parts with money only when forced to do so (cf. this terminology in Rom. 1:29; 1 Cor. 5:10–11; 6:10; Eph. 4:19; 5:3; Col. 3:5; 1 Thess. 2:5). Paul's purpose in sending the delegation is to preserve the former and to avoid tainting the collection with the latter.

In 9:5, Paul is consequently pointing to two opposite ways of giving: the kind of generosity that flows from experiencing God's blessing and from trusting in the sufficiency of God's grace, versus the kind of begrudging greediness and self-reliance that selfishly seeks to keep as much as possible for oneself. The former realizes that everything is a gift of grace and that God can be depended on for the future (cf. 1 Cor. 4:7; 2 Cor. 4:14, 18); this is the pathway of salvation. The latter views everything as a deserved reward to be hoarded out of insecurity and self-gratification, which are fundamental acts of unbelief in the faithfulness and goodness of God (8:7–8; 9:6–8, 11; cf. Luke 12:13–34). Some argue that in 9:1–5 Paul is playing one church off against another; others posit that he is merely trying to keep the Corinthians from losing face. But, as 9:5 indicates, the apostle is concerned with their souls.

The Theological Ground and Purpose of the Collection (9:6–15)

IN 8:1–9:5, PAUL dealt with the necessity of completing the collection; in 9:6–15, he addresses why this participation must be characterized by generosity and joy. In short, giving must be generous and joyful because only such giving is an expression of faith in God as the one who provides the gracious means to being righteous (9:8–11a). As a result, it brings his approval (9:6–7) and leads to gratitude to him (9:11b). Ultimately, then, such grace-driven generosity, through meeting the needs of others, redounds to God's glory (9:11b–15).

Within Paul's ongoing argument, 9:6–15 therefore serves to support 9:5, the main point of 9:1–5, by expressing the collection's theological basis (God's abundant grace) and purpose (the praise of God's glory). In order to do so, the goal of 9:6–15 is to make clear why the Corinthians' gifts must be an expression of "blessing" rather than being wrenched out of greedy hearts by the threat of God's impending judgment.

Paul's argument begins in 9:6 with a proverbial statement, variations of which are common in Israel's wisdom tradition: "You reap what you sow."[12] But Paul expands this basic principle in a chiastic (ABBA) structure that emphasizes the respective degrees of reward associated with sowing and reaping respectively. In doing so, he again uses the terminology of "blessing" (*eulogia*; NIV, "generously") to describe the nature of the giving, thereby making the link between 9:5 and 9:6 explicit. Formally translated, 9:6 thus reads: "The one who sows sparingly, sparingly will he also reap, and the one who sows with/because of blessings, with/because of blessings will he also reap."

The point here is not how much one gives, but that one gives as freely as possible, knowing that the "return" will be of like kind. Since the manner of one's giving reflects the character of one's heart, there is a principle of divine retribution here. God gives back "blessings" to those who give as a matter of "blessing," but withholds his blessings from those who withhold from others.

The logical conclusion to be drawn from this maxim is Paul's counsel in 9:7 that "each man should give what he has decided in his heart, not reluctantly or under compulsion" (for an illustration of cheerful giving, see Acts 11:29). Paul's exhortation echoes Deuteronomy 15:10, an admonition to lend and give freely to the poor without being reluctant or grieving in one's heart, knowing that the Lord will bless such actions. The original context of this passage concerns the "Sabbath year of remission" in which, in remembrance of their deliverance, Israel was to forgive all debts (cf. 31:10–11). This year of remission every seventh year pointed forward to the fiftieth year (after seven times seven years of remission), the "year of Jubilee," which was to be a symbol of the ultimate redemption of God's people (cf. Lev. 25:8–55, cf. esp. vv. 38, 42, 55).

Paul's use of Deuteronomy 15:10 is yet another indication that he understands the church, as the continuation of the faithful remnant within Israel, to be the eschatological people of God (cf. Lev. 25:20–22, where keeping the year of remission, like the Sabbath, was a call to exercise faith in God's ongoing provision). Therefore, what was given to Israel to do every seventh

---

12. See Job 4:8; 31:8; Ps. 126:5; Prov. 11:21 (LXX); 22:8; Jer. 12:13; Mic. 6:15; Sir. 7:3; Matt. 6:26 par.; 25:24, 26; Luke 19:21; John 4:36–37; Gal. 6:7–9; Rev. 14:15–16.

year is now, under the new covenant, to be the *daily* pattern of those in Christ. The symbol has been replaced by its reality, albeit not yet in all its fullness. In giving freely to the poor, the church continually celebrates her own "year of remission" by remembering her deliverance at the cross, while at the same time anticipating her final redemption on that "year of Jubilee" when Christ returns. The kingdom is here, but not yet here in all its glory.

The rule of divine recompense that was the basis for giving in 9:6 is restated as a matter of principle in 9:7c: God rewards those who, because they belong to the new covenant in Christ, give freely and generously, "for God loves a cheerful giver." Put negatively, there is no divine approval for giving to others merely out of duty. Instead, obedience, in order to count before God, must flow from a happy reliance on and contentment in God's gracious gifts to his people.

Here Paul is most likely alluding to Proverbs 22:8 (in the LXX; this passage does not occur in the Hebrew text; cf. also Rom. 12:8). His statement differs somewhat from the LXX, which reads, "God blesses a cheerful and giving man," though the LXX of Proverbs 22:8 also contains an expression of the "sowing" and "reaping" maxim as found in 2 Corinthians 9:6. Paul's choice of "loves" over "blesses" is likely influenced by Proverbs 22:11 (LXX, "The Lord loves pious hearts"), where, as here, "loves" carries the sense of "approves" and where, as in 9:7, the concept of the "heart" is also found. Hence, Paul combines two related texts from the same context in order to make his point: The Lord approves of those who show by their willingness to give cheerfully to the poor that their hearts are holy (cf. Prov. 22:9).

Verses 8–9 continue to ground Paul's call to give by indicating why God approves only of those who give cheerfully (9:7c). Note 9:8: The foundation and focus of faith is that God has the power to do what he has promised (cf. Rom. 4:21; 14:4). Specifically, as an expression of his grace, God is able to provide for his people whatever it is they need in order to provide for others. Giving to others is simply what trusting in God's promises looks like in a different dress. As a consequence of these promises, believers will always have "all that you need"[13] (*autarkeia*; lit., "contentment"; cf. 1 Tim. 6:6 and a related adjective in Phil. 4:11), a virtue that the Cynics and Stoics of Paul's day prized as well.

The Hellenistic ideal, however, linked this contentment to a self-reliance brought about by self-discipline that led to a passive detachment from external circumstances and people. In striking contrast, Christian contentment, relying on God's promised provision, leads to doing "every good work" for

---

13. The NIV's "all that you need" gives the false impression that God promises his people material blessings.

the sake of others. Among the ancients, the motive for giving was to show one's moral superiority. For Paul, the motive was to glorify God for his grace (see 9:11–13, 15; cf. 4:15; Acts 14:15–17; 17:25).

The quote in 9:9 from Psalm 112:9 is intended to provide scriptural support for Paul's affirmation in verse 8, especially its assertion that, given God's provision, God's people "will abound in every good work."[14] Such an expectation is in full accord with the description of the righteous man of this psalm, whose righteousness is manifest in his providing for the poor. This righteousness, having shown itself to be genuine through giving, "remains forever"—that is, beyond the Day of Judgment, just as Paul asserted in 3:9 (cf. 5:21; 6:7).[15]

Neither Psalm 112:9 nor Paul, however, is advocating a works righteousness in disguise. The righteous act of giving to others does not merit or earn God's blessing. Within its original context, the vindication of the righteous man in the psalm, in view of his "good works," is based squarely on the "good works" of the Lord manifest in the divine provisions of redemption and food outlined in Psalm 111. The "righteousness" of the one who gives to the poor "endures forever" (Ps. 112:9) *only because* it is created and sustained by the Lord's "righteousness," which also "endures forever" (111:3). All human righteousness owes its existence to and is an expression of God's righteousness. According to 112:9, the righteous person is the one who is gracious in his giving to the poor *because* he fears the Lord and delights in his commandments (cf. 112:1, 5).

Hence, while 2 Corinthians 9:9 quotes Psalm 112:9, 2 Corinthians 9:8 reflects the point made in Psalm 111. Paul's argument follows the argument of the two psalms exactly. Believers "abound in every good work" (2 Cor. 9:8), as the psalmist declares, since the righteous work of God on their behalf ensures that their righteousness, manifest in this good work (along with many others), will also endure forever (9:9; cf. Phil. 1:6, 11; 4:17; 1 John 3:7, 10, 17; Rev. 22:11). Paul's insistence that the collection be completed before he arrives (2 Cor. 9:5), supported by his call to give from the heart (9:7), are therefore both grounded in his concern for the salvation of the Corinthians themselves.

---

14. Cf. 1 Cor. 15:58. For Pauline references to "good work" in the singular, see Rom. 2:7; 13:3; 2 Thess. 1:11; 2 Tim. 2:21; 3:17; Titus 1:16; 3:1. For the plural, "good works," see Eph. 2:10; 1 Tim. 2:10; 5:10, 25; 6:18; Titus 2:7, 14; 3:8.

15. Many commentators, such as Barnett, *Second Epistle to the Corinthians*, 440n.26, maintain that 9:9 is not referring to the righteous man of Ps. 112:9 but to God, since God is the subject of 2 Cor. 9:8a and 10 and since Ps. 111:3 speaks of the righteousness of God remaining forever. Hence, Barnett argues that Paul took the language of 2 Cor. 9:9 from Ps. 112:9, but the content from Ps. 111:3. But once 2 Cor. 9:9 is seen to support 9:8c, there is no reason to violate the original context of Ps. 112:9.

Paul summarizes the point of 9:8–9 in verse 10 by alluding to two more passages from Scripture, Isaiah 55:10 ("he who supplies seed to the sower and bread for food") and Hosea 10:12 ("the harvest of your righteousness"). The God who supplies what believers need will also ensure that his provision brings about its desired consequences: Their "seed" will increase and their "harvest of righteousness," that is, their good works, will grow.

This summary is important for two reasons. (1) These Old Testament texts make clear that the "seed" and "harvest" that God supplies and promises to be multiplied cannot simply be equated with material provisions. The context of both Isaiah 55:10 and Hosea 10:12 is the provision of God's Word (i.e., the seed), which brings about the final redemption of his people. God's promise in 2 Corinthians 9:10 is not to make his people rich but to use them as instruments of his presence for the salvation of others. (2) In making this point, Paul's summary in 9:10 provides a transition from the purpose of the collection in regard to the Corinthians themselves, as the manifestation of their righteousness in Christ (9:8–9), to the significance of their righteousness for others, that is, its "harvest."[16] It is this latter point that Paul goes on to outline in verses 11–14.

In the original text, verses 10–14 form one long, complex sentence. Verses 11–14 support verse 10 by detailing the way in which God will "enlarge" the Corinthians' "harvest": God will provide for the Corinthians "in every way" so that they can be generous to others (vv. 11a, 12a, 13a). These people in turn will give thanks and pray to God (vv. 11b, 12, 13b), for God is the one who makes all this possible (v. 14b; cf. 1:11; 4:15 for this same principle, there applied to Paul). The Corinthians' own "harvest of righteousness" will increase as their lives are blessed through being instruments for the praise of God and as recipients of the love and prayers of those whose needs they meet. For as we have seen, the righteousness of God is his just character as demonstrated in the consistency of his actions toward his creation.

God's righteousness consists, therefore, in his unswerving commitment to glorify himself by maintaining his moral standards in judgment, by revealing his sovereignty in election, and by showing his loving mercy through meeting the needs of his people. Hence, to those in rebellion against him, his righteousness is revealed in judgment. But on behalf of his people it begins with their redemption and transformation in the midst of this evil age and culminates in their final restoration in the age to come (cf. 3:9, 18; 5:21). In 9:10–14, we see clearly that one divinely orchestrated means to

---

16. Others take this "harvest" to refer to the final redemption of the Jews in response to the Gentiles' participation in the collection (see 8:14 and n.2 above; cf. Rom. 11:12, 15). But in 2 Cor. 9:11–14 Paul explicitly says that the consequence of the collection will be thanksgiving and prayers to God among Jews who are *already* believers, not the large-scale conversion of Israel that will mark the return of Christ.

revealing this divine righteousness within the church is the creation of the kind of interdependent relationships among God's people that flow from their primary dependence on God as the one who meets their needs.

Since Paul is speaking of giving money to those in need, in 9:11 he uses the terminology of wealth to describe God's commitment to meet the needs of his people ("you will be made rich"). But Paul's own suffering as an apostle and his argument throughout 2 Corinthians both make it evident that in speaking of such "wealth," he does not have material prosperity in view (cf. 1:5–6; 2:14; 4:8–10, 17–18; 6:10; 8:9, 14). The Corinthians may have financial resources at this point in time, but there is no promise from God, and hence no guarantee, that such circumstances will continue. What they *can* be assured of is that God will sustain his people by meeting their needs in himself, at the same time providing for them circumstantially, for the sake of others, as he deems wise (cf. 1:10; 4:13–14, where this principle is applied to Paul).

In that the Corinthians' righteous giving is the manifestation of God's righteousness, in 9:12 Paul can describe their participation in the collection as "the ministry [*diakonia*] of this service [*leitourgia*]" (lit. trans.). *Diakonia* refers here to the administration of that with which one is entrusted, namely, the collection, and recalls Paul's earlier use of this same terminology to refer to the ministry of the old and new covenants (cf. its use in 3:7–9; 4:1; 5:18; 6:3). *Leitourgia* (cf. Rom. 15:27, where this word is also used for the collection) can refer to any act of public service (cf. Rom. 13:6), including the specifically religious ceremonies conducted by priests (cf. this religious connotation in Luke 1:23; Phil. 2:17, 30; Heb. 9:21; cf. also Phil. 4:18).

The combination of this terminology in 9:12 reflects Paul's conviction that giving to fellow believers in Jerusalem is an essential part of the ministry of the gospel and a genuine expression of worship. Indeed, the collection is a ministry of the gospel precisely because it brings about worship. Its purpose is praise and prayer among those to whom it is ministered, the two essential elements of magnifying God's character: We praise God for what he has done in the past, and pray for what we depend on him to do in the future.

Verse 13 indicates the twofold manner by which this praise (vv. 11b, 12) and prayer (cf. below, v.14) will actually be brought about: "through the proof/evidence (*dokime*) of this ministry" (lit. trans.; NIV, "because of the service by which you have proved yourselves"; cf. 2:9; 8:22; 13:3). The Corinthians will express the genuine nature of their own faith by "the obedience that derives from[17] [their] confession of the gospel of Christ" (lit. trans.), here

---

17. This trans. takes *tes homologias hymon* ("of your confession") to be a subjective genitive; but cf. NRSV, which renders it an objective genitive, "obedience to the confession." The NIV rendering, "accompanies your confession," is ambiguous. For Paul's other uses of "confession," see 1 Tim. 6:12–13; for the verb, see Rom. 10:9–10; 1 Tim. 6:12; Titus 1:16.

interpreted in terms of their generosity. Just as the righteous one in Psalm 112:9 gives to the poor out of a delight in God's righteousness (2 Cor. 9:9), so too the Corinthians' willingness to contribute to the needs of the saints expresses their righteousness (9:10), for they are obeying a command that derives "from their confession of the gospel of Christ" (9:13). At the same time, the Jews in Jerusalem will praise God for this manifestation of his righteousness in the Corinthians. Moreover, their participation in the collection, here identified as the Corinthians' "ministry," is also concrete evidence of the validity of Paul's ministry among the Gentiles (cf. 8:8, 24).

In 9:14, Paul draws out the second consequence of the Corinthians' generosity: The saints in Jerusalem will pray for them out of the longing created by their newly formed unity in the gospel. Paul anticipates a deep bond being formed between those in whom God's "surpassing grace" has been poured out. Thus, for example, in 7:7, 11, the Corinthians' longing for Paul was evidence that God's grace was indeed at work in their lives.[18] This is the final step in his argument in support of 9:6, 10. Those who sow generously because of God's blessing will reap generously because of God's blessing, both in their own lives and among others. The collection will bring this about "because of the surpassing grace of God" that has, through their giving, been demonstrably granted to them (9:14b).

This reference in 9:14 to God's grace at work in the Corinthians picks up the thread that Paul has woven throughout this unit (cf. 8:4, 6, 7, 9, 16, 19; 9:8) and repeats the point with which he began (cf. 8:1), thus cementing chapters 8 and 9 together. Furthermore, the parallel between 9:14 and 8:1 indicates that Paul is anticipating that the grace granted to the Corinthians will be no less than that given to the Macedonians, since God's "grace" is the basis of all giving (cf. again 9:8).

The reason for Paul's expectation is that he understood deeply that God's "surpassing grace" toward his people in 9:14 is the manifestation of his "surpassing glory" as described in 3:10.[19] There Paul argued that God's glory under the new covenant is "surpassing" that of the old, not in terms of quality or quantity, but in terms of its life-transforming impact as it encounters those whose hearts and minds are no longer hardened (cf. 3:16–18; 5:15–17). Paul's point here is that the transforming impact of the "surpassing glory" of God's "surpassing grace" under the new covenant is seen in the Corinthians' giving to others.

18. Cf. Paul's use of this same terminology of "longing" in Rom. 1:11; Phil. 1:8; 2:26; 1 Thess. 3:6; 2 Tim 1:4 to describe his own desire and that of Epaphroditus for those in whom Christ is being formed.

19. For Paul's other descriptions of God's "surpassing" gifts toward his people, see Eph. 1:19 (his power); 2:7 (the riches of his grace); 3:19 (his love that surpasses knowledge).

This is why the "surpassing grace" being poured out on the Corinthians by God is described in 9:12–13 in terms of the Corinthians' own "ministry," which not only meets the needs of the saints, but also becomes the vehicle through which "many expressions of thanks to God" are "abounding [NIV, overflowing]" (cf. 3:9b for this same use of the verb, trans. "is" in NIV). As in 3:9b, here too the "ministry" (*diakonia*) of the gospel is pictured in terms of its function as that which "abounds" in its manifestation of the "glory of God." And where God's glory is made known, praise and prayer result.

It is therefore fitting that in 9:15 Paul draws 8:16–9:15 to a close by returning to the thanksgiving with which he started. That the Corinthians' giving to others (8:24; 9:3; 9:5), which begins in God's grace (8:4, 6, 7, 9; 9:8), will also rebound to their own blessing from God (9:6–10) in response to the praise and prayers of others (9:11–14) is an amazing "gift" of grace worthy of praise (9:15). God's gift is "indescribable"; it exceeds our most profound attempts to portray it (though attempt we must!), while at the same time evoking our deepest praise. In the end, Paul's theology inevitably leads to doxology (cf. Rom. 11:33–36).

ISSUES OF GIVING in the ancient world. In Paul's day, like our own, participation in charitable giving and the administration of financial affairs were matters of public concern and conversation. It is not surprising, therefore, that each of Paul's three major themes finds echoes in his contemporary culture: (1) a concern for the integrity of the collection, as reflected in the need to send the delegation (8:16–24); (2) a concern that giving be uncoerced and generous, as seen in the necessity of completing the collection in advance (9:1–5); and (3) a concern for maintaining the proper purpose of the collection, as expressed in Paul's emphasis on the theological character of the collection as a response to the grace of God (9:6–15).

On the issue of integrity, the Roman orator and statesman Cicero (106–43 B.C.) declared that "the chief thing in all public administration and public service is to avoid even the slightest suspicion of self-seeking."[20]

In regard to motivation, Paul's admonition in 9:5, 7 to willing and generous giving out of a joy-filled heart, though directly fueled by the Old Testament and Jewish tradition, parallels the longstanding wisdom of the ancient world in which giving, to be genuine, had to be a matter of the heart. Note, for example, Hesiod's statement (eighth/seventh century B.C.): "For when a man gives willingly, though he gives a great thing, yet he has joy of his gift

---

20. *On Moral Obligation* 2.21.75, quoted in Furnish, *II Corinthians*, 434.

and satisfaction in his heart, while he who gives way to shameless greed and takes from another, even though the thing he takes is small, yet it stiffens his heart."[21]

Similarly, Paul's contemporary, Seneca (d. A.D. 65), states: "Let us give in the manner that would have been acceptable if we were receiving. Above all let us give willingly, promptly, and without hesitation."[22] Seneca's first support for this principle is that "no gratitude is felt for a benefit when it has lingered long in the hands of him who gives it, when the giver has seemed sorry to let it go, and has given it with the air of one who was robbing himself." His reason for emphasizing willing and prompt giving parallels Paul's principle in 9:5: "For, since in the case of a benefit the chief pleasure of it comes from the intention of the bestower, he who by his very hesitation has shown that he made his bestowal unwillingly has not 'given,' but has failed to withstand the effort to extract it." Seneca therefore enjoins one to give as promptly as possible for the joy it will bring: "One who acts thus readily leaves no doubt that he acts willingly; and so he acts gladly, and his face is clothed with the joy he feels."

Hence, as Betz points out, Paul's concept "that gifts offered as sacrifices are the human response to blessings received from the god, and that the human response expresses the expectation of receiving still more" (cf. 9:8) corresponds to ideas that "have become commonplaces in oratory."[23] Clearly, when it came to public behavior, Paul shared fundamental starting points with the prevailing culture of his day, especially since it was predominantly religious in its worldview and it often understood the link between outward actions and inner states of being.

The modern culture of independence and isolation. The parallels between the method and motivation for charitable giving in the ancient world and in Paul's own thought remind us that Christian conduct in every age takes place within a cultural framework that reflects, rightly or wrongly, on the same set of fundamental issues, since Christian concerns are basic to the fabric of society itself. The same set of questions confronts believers and unbelievers alike. There are, of course, many exceptions to every cultural norm. Nevertheless, understanding the particular culture in which we live is crucial for understanding the implications of what it means to be Christian in our world. Such an analysis will inform the church concerning where she must resist the values that surround her, where she has already been compromised by them,

---

21. *Works* 357—60, quoted by Betz, *2 Corinthians 8 and 9*, 105n.122.

22. This statement and those that follow from Seneca derive from his work, *On Benefits* 2.1.1—2, as quoted by Betz, *2 Corinthians 8 and 9*, 107; the last quote comes from Furnish, *II Corinthians*, 441.

23. Betz, *2 Corinthians 8 and 9*, 109, including n.150.

where she must adapt to them for the sake of witness, and where she may build on them profitably. Fundamental to these concerns is the basic question of whether and why we should give of our own resources to others, since this question goes to the heart of our modern self-understanding.

Accordingly, when it comes to addressing the Christian call to give, it is important to keep in view that the dominant cultural practices in the West stand in sharp contrast to those both of the ancient world in general (at least in its philosophical reflection—the views of the common person are largely lost to us) and of Paul in particular. In contemporary culture, an emphasis on personal integrity as essential for the success of public projects has taken a back seat to pragmatic efficiency. And Paul's concern for the integrity of the collection, which led to his sending the delegation to Corinth, is often replaced with a concern that everything be done "legally" (to avoid being sued), regardless of the "hidden" motives of the heart (which are beyond litigation).

Even within the church, generosity in giving has often become a "tax advantage," an opportunity for self-actualization, or an expression of one's "indebtedness to society," rather than an expression of the blessings of God. Paul's comparison of the Corinthians to others in whom God is at work as a basis for evaluating and encouraging moral acts (cf. 9:2–4) has consequently given way to a "none of your business" privatization of all such acts. The church today, for the most part, no longer shares Paul's working assumption that God's grace is inevitably expressed in the public behavior of God's people. As a result, comparison to others among God's people as a means of self-examination (cf. 9:2–4) is no longer considered appropriate.

Such attitudes and actions within the church are not biblical, but derive in large part from the self-understanding of human independence and isolation that still runs through contemporary culture. With the dawn of the "modern world," the predominantly religious worldview in which Paul lived gave way to a pervasive naturalism that rendered humanity merely a product of its own abilities to manage and cope with its environment. Humanity was separated from its Creator and put in competition with itself. And, if anything, the current move toward a postmodern emphasis on humanity's cultural embeddedness has only served to heighten this sense of separation from a God who is outside of us and from those who do not share our particular social location.

As a result, the prevailing assumption of Paul's day that all people have received gifts from a deity and are part of a larger community has been replaced by the conviction that we control what we possess because we have earned it "on our own." At the most, we may admit that the circumstances of our birth and the opportunities afforded by our race or social location may have played a role in acquiring the status and material benefits we enjoy.

But even then, we are quick to attribute our wealth to our own hard work, either as the expression of our own will or as the embodiment of our cultural values. When all is said and done, we are convinced that we possess more than others because we work harder. God may provide the "raw material," but it is up to us to make the most of the opportunities he brings our way.

Thus, the Enlightenment emphasis on independence and isolation from God and others, whether expressed in the modern view of the self-determining individual or in the postmodern emphasis on our cultural captivity, has led to a self-understanding in which contemporary men and women view their "hard-earned" resources as their own possessions to do with as they please.[24] Add to this the suffocating materialism of our age and Paul's worldview and words in this passage go through our culture, and our churches, like an electric shock. Indeed, nowhere is the myth of having "pulled ourselves up by our own bootstraps" more powerful than in our attitudes toward the acquisition and disposition of our personal resources. Any basic commonality that Paul could assume with the culture of his day has evaporated.

The countercultural context of Christian giving. But even in his day, Paul was not merely parroting his culture. The parallels between the dominant culture of Paul's day and his own Christian convictions serve to highlight all the more the distinctive aspects of Paul's biblical frame of reference. The religious worldview of Paul's day makes the unique features of his "religion" all the more apparent. Paul does not approach the topic of giving from the standpoint of being "religious," but from his perspective as an apostle of Jesus Christ, called to be a minister of the new covenant. When he speaks of God, Paul is not referring to some general spiritual consciousness of an undefined higher being, nor to one's own favorite form of the deity, but to the God of Israel, who made himself known supremely in Jesus as the Christ, the Son of God. Thus, when Paul speaks of "blessings," he does not mean some nondescript sense of "having it good," but the specific acts of the one true God on behalf of his people.

Paul's God is not a privatized version of the Self. Nor for Paul are all visions of the deity equally valid. God is the One who has revealed himself to us from *outside* of us. Thus, giving to the needs of the poor in Jerusalem was rooted in the character of God as made known in his works on our behalf. This specifically theological ground becomes critical whenever we speak about the necessity of giving. We must keep in mind that within our context Paul's relating every aspect of giving to God is inherently countercultural. As David Wells observes:

---

24. For an insightful summary of the cultural and religious consequences of this self-understanding, granted to us by the effects of modernity, see David Wells, *Losing Our Virtue: Why the Church Must Recover Its Moral Vision* (Grand Rapids: Eerdmans, 1998).

Ours is the first major civilization to be building itself deliberately and self-consciously without religious foundations. Beneath other civilizations there have always been religious foundations, whether these came from Islam, Hinduism, or Christianity itself. Beneath ours there are none, and it is no surprise to learn that 67 percent of Americans do not believe in the existence of moral absolutes and that 70 percent do not believe in absolute truth. . . . We are building a world of the most marvelous ingenuity and intricacy but it is arising over a spiritual vacuum.[25]

[As a result] we have also rewritten the religious question. That question was always how we might be consoled in our journey through this valley of tears. Socrates found consolation in the good, the beautiful, and the true; the New Testament finds it in Christ's redemption; Marx and liberation theology found it in the journey toward a more just world. But we find it simply in ourselves. We have become both our own patients and therapists, deeply committed to the gospel of self-fulfillment.[26]

Faced with the recent attempts to fill such a spiritual vacuum with the Self, it is imperative that we cultivate the theological tenets of the Christian counterculture if we intend to live in ways that honor God. If we fail to do so, the values of our culture will simply sweep us away as they rush in to fill the void. This is certainly true when it comes to spending our money. In moving from Paul's day to our own, the issues are more pervasive and profound than simply replacing one set of actions with another. There is, of course, nothing wrong with possessions in and of themselves, though they are an extremely dangerous temptation (cf. 1 Tim. 6:3–10, 17–19). Nor is it illegitimate to take a tax deduction for giving, to be concerned to do things legally, or to want to be fulfilled. Instead, what is needed is an evaluation of all that we do, including our giving, from a consistent and thoroughgoing *theological* perspective.

God the Giver. The structure of Paul's argument in this text makes clear that the starting point for applying this passage is the distinctive theological context from which he interprets the wisdom of both his tradition and his culture. This same theological perspective must be brought to bear on our own cultural attitudes and actions. As even Hans Dieter Betz, who emphasizes above all the similarity between Paul and his Greco-Roman environment, concludes, "Both Paul and Seneca were concerned with the same group of ideas, but they treated them quite differently in both length and concep-

---

25. Ibid., 26.
26. Ibid., 107.

tuality."[27] Most important, Paul differed from the mainstream of Greek philosophy in that he did not think that the goal was to attain "inner freedom" from possessions in order to be truly self-sufficient.[28]

Paul's goal was not to attain an inner detachment from material things through some sort of Stoic self-mastery, but a recognition that God is the giver of *all* things. Perhaps nothing today is more radical than to assert that God, not our own "Self," is responsible for all that we are and have. Our resources originate from him as a blessing, not from us as an expression of what we deserve. This insight is as profoundly life-changing as it is simple. That God is the giver of everything is the foundation of our giving to others. The key to generosity is not caring less about what we have in the world, but caring more about God's purposes in granting to us his gifts.

Wealth is a gift of God, freely given as an expression of God's commitment to his people; hence, for those who trust in him, it can be freely given away. "Cheerful givers" are not so by nature. Only those who realize that they have received great benefits from God have both the material means and inner disposition to become cheerful givers.[29]

Giving as an act of grace to the glory of God. Since our giving is an expression of God's having already given all things to us, we must follow Paul's lead by focusing on God's grace as the basis for giving. This entails resisting the cultural temptation to turn the necessity of giving into a voluntary opportunity "to do something great for God." Giving to others should not become yet another way of contributing back to God for what he has done for us. God does not need our money to further his causes. He is not dependent on us. God gives out of his sovereign self-sufficiency and love, not in order to receive back, as if he needed anything (Acts 17:24–25).

Nor should we give "in order to show God how thankful we are." Our job is not to prove our sincerity to God. Those who recognize God to be the giver of all things *are* thankful, and God knows our hearts. Instead, in chapter 9 the motivation for giving is as radically God-centered as its foundation. Far from being our contribution back to God or our way of showing God the depth of our gratitude, giving to others is a response to what *God* has already done for us in the past and a demonstration of our continuing confidence in what he has promised to do for us in the future. Giving is an act of faith in response to God's grace. As such, our giving is not a decision to participate in the projects of the church, but an expression of the fact that we *are* the church—that is, that we belong to God and hence to one another.

---

27. Betz, *2 Corinthians 8 and 9*, 107.
28. Ibid., 110.
29. Ibid., 111.

This is why integrity is such a key issue for Paul, why he can call the collection itself an act of "grace," and why the collection becomes for him part of the "ministry" of the gospel. For in it, God's own righteous character is being displayed in the faith-driven righteousness of his people (cf. 8:16, 19, 23; 9:9, 11—14). For Paul, participation in the collection was not a "practical" outworking of faith as something done in addition to trusting in God; it was an expression of faith itself. Paul wanted the Corinthians to see that they could not claim to trust in God and then give begrudgingly only when threatened or put on the spot.

The reality of the Spirit is to be seen precisely in their eager willingness, like that of Titus, to meet the needs of others. Paul therefore models the same God-glorifying, Spirit-given "eagerness" that he calls for in the Corinthians (cf. 8:11, 12; 9:2). For in the end, eager participation in the collection is a ministry because it reflects and glorifies God's eager participation in our lives (8:16; 9:15).

The new covenant context of giving. Since the goal of life is the glory of God, Paul is not interested in theology in a detached or speculative sense. Nor does he engage in cultural analysis for the sake of speaking to society at large. Paul speaks as an apostle to the church. In doing so, he approaches giving, as he does all aspects of the Christian life, from within the biblical framework of the new covenant. He views all of life, even giving money to the poor in Jerusalem, through the lens of what God has done, is doing, and will do for his people as a result of the life, death, and resurrection of Christ.

That Paul's argument in 9:6—15 presupposes the framework of the new covenant becomes evident in that his reference to the "surpassing grace of God" in 9:14 recalls his earlier reference to the "surpassing glory" of the new covenant in 3:10 and the "surpassing greatness" of the light of the knowledge of the glory of God on the face of Christ in 4:6. It also picks up the same terminology in 4:17, where the "eternal weight of glory" literally translates "surpasses beyond surpassing." Thus, to describe something as "surpassing" is, for Paul, tantamount to describing it as part of the reality of the new covenant.

Against this backdrop, the "ministry" (*diakonia*) of the collection is pictured as that which "abounds" in its manifestation of the glory of God because the grace it reveals as part of the new covenant is "surpassing." The implication is clear. Not to contribute means that one is blind to the reality of the surpassing glory of God now being mediated under the new covenant (3:10, 14—18; 4:3—4). Conversely, since the themes of chapter 9 derive from the realities of the new covenant, giving to others, especially cross-cultural and cross-ethnic giving, becomes a manifestation of the glory of God on the face of Christ (4:4, 6).

Since believers, as God's sons and daughters in Christ, are the temple of God's Spirit through whom the surpassing glory of God's grace is now being revealed in the world (cf. 3:18; 4:15; 5:15, 17; 6:14–18), it is not surprising that in the present context Paul develops these new covenant themes in direct relationship to the ministry of the Corinthians. In 9:14, that which is "surpassing" refers to the grace of *God* that has been given to the Corinthians. The parallel in 9:13 demonstrates, however, that this surpassing grace is at the same time a reference to the *Corinthians'* "obedience to [their] confession of the gospel of Christ" (see comments on this in Original Meaning section)—in this case, their generous giving.

Moreover, in 9:12 this "surpassing grace" *toward* the Corinthians is described in terms of the Corinthians' *own* "ministry of service" *toward others*. Of course, the principle that the surpassing sufficiency of God's grace is demonstrated in a willingness to meet the needs of others is not Paul's idea, but an extension of the wisdom teaching of the Scriptures from Proverbs 22:8 (LXX; cf. 2 Cor. 9:7) and Psalm 112:9 (cf. 2 Cor. 9:9).

The new covenant context of these general maxims comes to the fore in that Paul applies both of these texts to the Corinthians in fulfillment of the promise of eschatological salvation from Isaiah 55:10 (see 2 Cor. 9:10). Here too, as in 3:3–18, 5:11–6:2, 6:14–7:1, Paul's understanding of his own situation and that of his congregation is informed by his conviction that, in Christ, God has inaugurated the new age of the new creation under the new everlasting covenant (cf. Isa. 55:10 with the context of 55:1–5). As part of this new creation, the "seed for the sower and bread for the eater" of 55:10 is identified in 55:11 as God's Word, which, having been sent out, will not return without accomplishing its designated task.

Often our appeals for money appear anemic because we have lost sight of the gravity of what God is now doing in the world in and through his people. When God's people give to others within the body of Christ, they mediate his glory as it is now being revealed under the new covenant. In so doing, God's Word is embodied and proclaimed to the ends of the earth. To give is to be an outpost of the kingdom of God. Hence, the only way to talk about money biblically is to talk about money in relationship to God and his purposes.

God and money. If our analysis is correct, the foundation of Paul's appeal for money is the history of redemption. Paul's call to the Corinthians to give is driven by his conviction that under the new covenant God is now revealing himself in and through the lives of his people. As the temple of God (6:16), "God is most glorified in us when we are most satisfied in him.... 'We shall bring our Lord most glory if we get from Him much grace. If I have much faith, so that I can take God at His Word ... I shall greatly honor my

Lord and King.'"[30] One grand expression of the satisfaction in God's grace that brings him great glory is giving freely and generously to others.

For this reason, Paul's pastoral theology in regard to those Corinthians who have already repented climaxes with the collection. For as his discussion of the collection reveals, the ground and purpose of Paul's apostolic ministry matches God's own design throughout history, namely, the manifestation (cf. 3:7–18) and praise (cf. 9:12–15) of God's glory. In 9:15, Paul thus ends this section not only how he began it in 8:16, but also how he introduced each major section of his letter, with praise to God (cf. 1:3 and 2:14a). In turn, the adequacy of our own attempts to bridge from Paul's context to our own can be measured by the degree to which our talk of money resounds to the glory of God for who *he* is, what *he* has done, what *he* is doing, and what *he* will do as the Sovereign Lord of history and Savior of his people.

THE CONTEMPORARY SIGNIFICANCE of these major themes is straightforward. Fueled by a biblical understanding of God and of our own role within redemptive history, giving to other believers should be characterized by an integrity that is beyond reproach, a willing generosity that reflects the grace of God, a proclamation of the gospel, and joy.

Integrity. Paul could have managed the collection himself. His decision to send the delegation instead reminds us, therefore, that the church must meet the standards for honesty and accountability that are found not only in the Scriptures, but also in the society around us. Note Paul's stress on this point in 8:21, where "also in the eyes of men" receives the emphasis! Betz has rightly argued that Paul's terminology itself confirms this emphasis on acting in accordance with society's norms, since "Paul's letters share the administrative practices and legal terminology of the day."[31] This was because "the integrity and credibility of the churches as administrative agencies depended to a great degree in these early years on the extent to which they were able to conform to current practices in the conduct of official business."[32]

The same is true today, in a time when many people are rightly skeptical concerning the motives of "organized religion." Barnett summarizes this point well:

Edifyingly, Paul's exercise of the "ministry of service . . . for the saints" was conducted with careful forward planning (8:10; 1 Cor. 16:1–4),

---

30. John Piper, *Future Grace* (Sisters, Ore.: Multnomah, 1995), 9, quoting Charles Spurgeon.
31. Betz, *2 Corinthians 8 and 9*, 134.
32. Ibid.

with prudent attention to detail (8:16–24), with sensitivity to matters of probity (8:20), with perseverance in the face of difficulty and disappointment (8:6–12), and, not least, in unswerving devotion [to] the doctrine [of] the grace of God (8:1–9:15 passim).[33]

Generosity. The New Testament does not teach a doctrine of tithing (i.e., the mandatory giving of 10 percent of one's income). Nor does Paul define what constitutes giving generously. He does not even provide a target number or general guidelines. The only rule is to give freely and generously as an expression of our continuing trust in God's grace (9:5–8). Paul simply assumes that believers will give all they can to meet as many needs as they can in order to glorify God as much as they can. The point of 9:6 is that one should give as freely as possible, knowing that the "return" will be of like kind. There is a principle of divine retribution here, since the manner of one's giving reflects the character of one's heart. God gives back blessings to those who give as a matter of blessing, but withholds his blessings from those who withhold from others. We must be careful here, however. The "payback" is not material, but the prayers of God's people and the enjoyment of God's glory (cf. 9:12–15).

At the same time, while giving must be done freely, it is not optional. The ministry of the gospel requires that this point be made strongly and consistently, especially in a culture drowning in materialism. Unfortunately, many pastors are afraid to mention giving too often, lest the congregation think that the "church just wants our money." Such fears are misplaced theologically and often reflect our cowardice in the face of the reigning idols of our day. To speak about our need to give is to emphasize that we are God's people through whom God glorifies himself. The Corinthians' participation in the collection was not "for the church," but evidence that they were the church. Indeed, to give to others is a manifestation of the righteousness of God, apart from which there is no salvation (9:9–11). The fact that believers often ask how much they should give reveals that they have not yet grasped Paul's perspective. Besides, our problem is usually not that we are in danger of harming ourselves by giving too much!

If grace-driven generosity is a thermometer of our spiritual health, Tim Stafford has provided a troubling analysis of our current temperature. As he points out, Americans as a whole give more to charitable organizations, and at a higher percentage of their income, than any other industrial society (except, perhaps, Israel). Moreover, of all Americans, Christians give and volunteer the most:

33. Barnett, *The Second Epistle to the Corinthians*, 450.

> More than income, age, race, or education, faith predicts giving and volunteering. . . . American Christians are the core reason why Americans can be described as "generous."
>
> Christians—not just nominal Christians, but believing, practicing Christians—are the backbone of virtually all charitable causes in America.[34]

While only 38 percent of Americans attend religious services weekly, they give two-thirds of all charitable contributions, while two-thirds of the donations to nonreligious organizations also come from church members. And of all American Christians, conservative or evangelical Christians are the most generous.

This sounds like good news, but we should not take too much comfort in such comparisons. The bad news is that, though certainly "rich" by the living standards of even our own grandparents,[35] Christians today contribute only between 1.1 percent and 3.4 percent of their annual income to religious and nonreligious organizations combined (for the past forty years Americans as a whole gave away between 1.5 percent and 2.0 percent of their income). Such statistics show just how much materialism has gripped both us and the culture in which we live (31 percent of American households say they give away no money at all).

This is even more sobering since this pattern of giving includes not only our participation in the United Way and March of Dimes, but also our involvement with the people and mission of the church. From 1985 to 1993, the average per-member contribution to evangelical churches actually shrank when measured in constant dollars, from $651 per year to $621, while the percentage of income given in evangelical churches dropped from 6.19 percent in 1968 to 4.27 percent in 1993.

In short, Christians spend the vast majority of their money on themselves. This is most true of the middle class, since those who earn under $20,000 or over $100,000 a year give away the highest percentage of their income. In view of these trends and in recognizing the undeniable fact that the "good American" is the "*Christian* Good American," Stafford raises the question of whether we are more American than Christian. As he recounts, studies of American Christians reveal that

> they believe in hard work and decency more than they believe in distinctly Christian behavior. They support evangelism only when it is

---

34. Tim Stafford, "Anatomy of a Giver," *Christianity Today* (May 19, 1997), 20–24 (pp. 22, 24). The following information is taken from Stafford's article.

35. Stafford (ibid., 21) points out that after adjusting for inflation and taxes, the average American in 1997 earns almost four times what the average American earned in 1921, while real incomes have nearly doubled since the late 1950s.

done by someone they are absolutely sure won't embarrass them. They give generously, but not sacrificially. As they have gotten wealthier they have been able to live better, but they give about the same, proportionately. Their affluence is indistinguishable from their neighbor's. . . . They think charity begins at home—they are less and less eager to send money overseas for a missionary cause that seems distant and never-ending. Above all, Good Americans don't talk about money. Their money is their own, to do with what they like. It is a private matter, and they don't want it talked about too much in church.[36]

So when it comes to giving away our money, we have on the one hand the American code of silence and privatization. On the other hand, we have the apostle Paul's public and sizable discussion of the collection, forged out of the spiritual urgency that surrounded the Corinthians' willingness to participate generously in giving cross-culturally for the support of the church.

Proclamation. The issue of giving away money evokes two diametrically opposed responses among conservative Christians: an awkward timidity among mainstream evangelicals and an "in-your-face" boldness among the health and wealth movement. In the first case, mainstream evangelicals are offended by "too much" talk about money, fearing that it may contaminate true spirituality. The real reason for seeking this silence, however, is subtle but clear: Too much emphasis on the spiritual *necessity* of giving as a matter of our salvation directly confronts our materialism and the individualistic privatization of our lives. The call to give is a call to flee the idolatrous worship of the Dollar and the Self by trusting in God's grace alone for our happiness and security. To talk about money *is* to talk about God.

To make matters worse, the propensity to downplay discussing money is strengthened by our embarrassment over the way in which giving is constantly discussed among those who advocate a health and wealth gospel. Having divorced spirituality from money on the one extreme, we recoil from the way in which they have *identified* money with spirituality on the other. When we say, "The preacher should talk about God," we mean that the preacher should *not* talk about money (since, for us, giving is a private affair that has nothing to do with being blessed spiritually). When they say, "The preacher should talk about God," they mean that the preacher *should* talk about money (since, for them, giving money is the way to getting money, which *is* the spiritual blessing). Simply put, the health and wealth gospel looks down on the lack of emphasis on money among the evangelical mainstream as a lack of faith in God's promise to prosper his people financially.

---

36. Ibid., 24.

We rightly find such theology repulsive. We reject the perversion of giving into a pathway to getting more money for ourselves, thereby blatantly caving in to the idolatrous materialism of our culture. Nevertheless, we must be careful that in judging others, we are willing to judge ourselves. The difference between the silence of most evangelicals and the noise of the health and wealth gospel is often only a matter of emphasis. Both extremes purport to give as a matter of faith. But while evangelicals give out of gratitude for what God has *already* given them, the health and wealth movement gives out of gratitude for what God *will* give them. The former give by looking back at what they already have, the latter give by looking forward to what they hope to receive. Evangelicals typically emphasize the past; the health and wealth gospel looks to the future.

In neither case, however, is Paul heard. For Paul, faith is trusting in God to meet our needs in the *present* that we might give to the needs of others.[37] As such, faith encompasses the past and future as we live them out day by day before God. We give to others, therefore, as an expression of our trust in God to meet our needs *today*. We should not give simply out of our surplus from the past, nor should we give in the hope of getting more in the future. Rather, not worrying about tomorrow and trusting God to sustain us through the trouble of today (Matt. 6:34), we are free to share our daily bread with others. Indeed, Paul calls us to give freely and generously, supremely because of our riches *in God himself*, past, present, *and* future, quite apart from our current economic status (remember the Macedonians), and without any thought of future financial recompense (Paul never promises a financial reward for giving).

Ironically, then, both the prevailing silence concerning giving that characterizes mainstream evangelicals and the equally constant discussion of giving among those who advocate a health and wealth gospel are generated by the same underlying source. Both see giving as a response to the amount of money God has granted or will grant his people. Moreover, since both groups have spiritualized the act of giving, gratitude, not the giving itself, becomes the "true" act of faith. This allows both groups to remain comfortable with

---

37. This is not a denial of the essential, future-focused nature of faith (faith as banking our hope on God's promises), nor that faith in the present is based on God's actions in the past (we trust God today because of what he had done for us in the past, esp. in the cross and pouring out of the Spirit). It merely recognizes that a focus on the future can take place only in the present and that faith is not wishful thinking, since its confidence for the future is based on what God has already done for us in the past. Cf. 2 Cor. 1:8–11: Paul hopes in the present for deliverance in the future because God has delivered in him the past. As the future unfolds, Paul's trust in God will continue to be based on what has happened in the past as this now encompasses what is happening in the present.

their own spirituality (after all, we are grateful for our material blessings!), all the while keeping or seeking wealth itself. In the end, both are driven by the idolatrous belief that money, not knowing God and participating in the spread of his kingdom, is the real, tangible expression of his blessing and therefore the essential ingredient in making us happy.

Joy. In stark contrast to this worship of money stands Paul's conviction that the basis and purpose for giving is to maintain joy in God himself (9:7). Reluctantly giving to others reflects an insecurity that fundamentally denies the very thing Paul affirms in 9:8–11. Likewise, giving to others in order to get more money in return is a crass and idolatrous rejection of God's all-sufficiency in Christ. It denies the very thing Paul affirms in 9:12–15.

Since joy and security in God should be our motives for giving, it is striking that Paul does not point to our gratitude per se as the basis for giving. Rather, it is God's grace in our lives that forms the foundation of faith-filled giving. We give because of what God has done to secure our joy in him, not because of how we feel about being secure in God's grace. We give because we are happy in God, not because we are thankful to be happy in God. A study of 2 Corinthians 8–9 consequently confirms John Piper's helpful observations that

> the Bible rarely, if ever, motivates Christian living with gratitude. Yet this is almost universally presented in the church as the "driving force in authentic Christian living." ... Gratitude is a beautiful and utterly indispensable Christian affection. No one is saved, who doesn't have it. But you will search the Bible in vain for *explicit* connections between gratitude and obedience.... Gratitude was never designed as the primary motivation for radical Christian obedience.... Could it be that *gratitude for bygone grace* has been pressed to serve as the power for holiness, which only *faith in future grace* was designed to perform? [38]

If our grateful response to what we have *already* received from God were the primary foundation for giving to others, our willingness to give would become a reflection of our own moral character as people who are grateful, not of the God who gives.

Thus, if gratitude were the motive, the focus of attention would fall on trying to become more grateful in order to be able to give more, thereby throwing ourselves back on ourselves, since God has already done enough to make us grateful for all eternity. Furthermore, if gratitude, not faith, is the

---

38. John Piper, *Future Grace*, 11 (italics in original). See Piper's biblical defense on pp. 31–49 for rejecting a "debtor's ethic" that tries to pay God back for what was received as a matter of grace.

motive, then giving becomes a futile attempt to "pay God back" as a debtor to grace—which is impossible, since it cuts at the heart of what God's grace means in the first place. The grace of God, from creation to the mercy of the cross, is something we have received and continue to receive "without price or payment."[39] Though we certainly must be and can only be grateful for God's grace, it is our trust in God's grace that grounds our giving.

> In the debtor's ethic the Christian life is pictured as an effort to pay back the debt we owe to God. Usually the concession is made that we can never fully pay it off. But "gratitude" demands that we work at it. Good deeds [like giving to others] and religious acts are the installment payments we make on the unending debt we owe to God.[40]

Thus, rather than deriving our giving from our gratitude, Paul points to our continuing trust in God's continuing grace as the fountain of generosity. His focus is not on trying to be more grateful but on learning to trust God more. And as Piper recognizes,

> this is not nit-picking or incidental; it is amazing.... Gratitude is a beautiful thing. There is no Christianity without it. It is at the heart of worship.... But when it comes to spelling out the spiritual dynamics of how practical Christian obedience happens [like giving money], the Bible does not say that it comes from the backward gaze of gratitude, but that it comes from the forward gaze of faith.[41]

Surely gratitude is evidence that God has transformed the human heart. Indeed, the heart of sin is a failure to glorify God by giving thanks for all that he has done for us (Rom. 1:21). But gratitude, like giving, is itself a response to God's grace, and not the source of faith-filled obedience. Gratitude is itself a virtue produced by grace, not the source of other Christian virtues. God and God alone is the source of all Christian emotion and activity.

Viewed in this way, our willingness to give becomes a reflection not of our feelings toward God, but of what God is doing for us now and promises to do for us in the days to come. Giving, in order to honor God, must be an act of dependence on God. As believers, our confidence in God for the future makes it possible for us to give to others in the present (cf. again 9:8). We will never give away more money than our comfortable 2 percent unless we are convinced that God will take care of us tomorrow, just as he has taken care of us in the past and is now taking care of us in the present. This is why

---

39. Ibid., 31.
40. Ibid., 33.
41. Ibid., 43.

Paul supports his call to give by pointing to the joy that accompanies it (9:7) and to the righteousness from faith that is expressed through it (9:9–10).

This is also why the admonition to give in 9:5 is supported in 9:6–15 not by a reference to what giving will say about *us* (i.e., that we are filled with gratitude), but by a reference to what giving will say about *God* (i.e., that his grace is and will be sufficient, no matter what; cf. 12:9). The ground of our giving is God's continuing, abundant grace and the purpose of our giving is the praise of God's glory as manifest in the "indescribable gift" that is God himself in Christ. Our ability to give is a declaration about God.

Thus, 9:6–15 make it clear why the Corinthians' gifts must be given as an expression of blessing and joy rather than being pried out of their greed by the threat of God's impending judgment. Only generous, joyful giving is an expression of the faith and contentment that brings God's approval (9:6–7). As Paul makes clear in 9:7, there is no divine approval for a giving to others that does not flow from a happy reliance on and satisfaction in God. For since God's power and commitment to do what he has promised provides the continuing means to be righteous through giving (9:8–11a), only such grace-driven generosity, evidenced in our willingness to meet the needs of others, redounds to God's glory (9:11b–15).

In conclusion, we therefore turn once again to John Piper, who has captured well the contemporary significance of 9:7 ("God loves a cheerful giver") for establishing a God-honoring motivation in giving, the only motivation that will fulfill the "ministry" and "grace" of giving:

> I take this to mean God is not pleased when people act benevolently but don't do it gladly. When people don't find pleasure (Paul's word is "cheer"!) in their acts of service, God doesn't find pleasure in them. He loves cheerful givers, cheerful servants. What sort of cheer? Surely the safest way to answer that question is to remember what sort of cheer moved the Macedonians to be generous. It was the overflow of joy in the grace of God. Therefore, the giver God loves is the one whose joy in him overflows "cheerfully" in generosity to others. . . .
>
> If love is the overflow of joy in God that gladly meets the needs of other people, and if God loves such joyful givers, then this joy in giving is a Christian duty, and the effort not to pursue it is sin.
>
> . . . Love is the overflow of joy in God which *gladly* meets the needs of others. It is the impulse of a fountain to overflow. It originates in the grace of God which overflows freely because it *delights* to fill the empty. Love shares the nature of that grace, because it too *delights* to overflow freely to meet the needs of others. . . .
>
> The contentment of a Christian Hedonist is not a Buddha-like serenity, unmoved by the hurts of others. It is a profoundly dissatisfied

contentment. It is constantly hungry for more of the *feast* of God's grace. And even the measure of contentment that God grants contains an insatiable impulse to expand itself to others (2 Corinthians 8:4; 1 John 1:4). Christian *joy* reveals itself as dissatisfied contentment whenever it perceives human need. It starts to expand in love to fill that need and bring about the joy of faith in the heart of the other person.[42]

---

42. Piper, *Desiring God*, 104–7 (emphasis mine).

2 Corinthians 10:1–18

B Y THE MEEKNESS and gentleness of Christ, I appeal to you—I, Paul, who am "timid" when face to face with you, but "bold" when away! ²I beg you that when I come I may not have to be as bold as I expect to be toward some people who think that we live by the standards of this world. ³For though we live in the world, we do not wage war as the world does. ⁴The weapons we fight with are not the weapons of the world. On the contrary, they have divine power to demolish strongholds. ⁵We demolish arguments and every pretension that sets itself up against the knowledge of God, and we take captive every thought to make it obedient to Christ. ⁶And we will be ready to punish every act of disobedience, once your obedience is complete.

⁷You are looking only on the surface of things. If anyone is confident that he belongs to Christ, he should consider again that we belong to Christ just as much as he. ⁸For even if I boast somewhat freely about the authority the Lord gave us for building you up rather than pulling you down, I will not be ashamed of it. ⁹I do not want to seem to be trying to frighten you with my letters. ¹⁰For some say, "His letters are weighty and forceful, but in person he is unimpressive and his speaking amounts to nothing." ¹¹Such people should realize that what we are in our letters when we are absent, we will be in our actions when we are present.

¹²We do not dare to classify or compare ourselves with some who commend themselves. When they measure themselves by themselves and compare themselves with themselves, they are not wise. ¹³We, however, will not boast beyond proper limits, but will confine our boasting to the field God has assigned to us, a field that reaches even to you. ¹⁴We are not going too far in our boasting, as would be the case if we had not come to you, for we did get as far as you with the gospel of Christ. ¹⁵Neither do we go beyond our limits by boasting of work done by others. Our hope is that, as your faith continues to grow, our area of activity among you will greatly expand, ¹⁶so that we can preach the gospel in the regions beyond you. For we do not want to boast about work

already done in another man's territory. ¹⁷But, "Let him who boasts boast in the Lord." ¹⁸For it is not the one who commends himself who is approved, but the one whom the Lord commends.

IN 1:3–7:1, PAUL defended his apostolic ministry in order to strengthen the faith of those who had recently repented. In doing so, he drew out the implications of his gospel (cf. 6:14–7:1), while at the same time establishing a foundation for his final appeal to those who were still rebelling against him (cf. 5:16–6:2). In 7:2–9:15, Paul then applied his gospel to the repentant by calling them to complete the collection. Giving to the saints in Jerusalem would be the test of their own experience of God's grace to them (cf. 9:6–11).

Against this backdrop, Paul's appeal to the Corinthians in 10:1 begins the last of the three main sections of his letter: *The Application of Paul's Apologetic to the Rebellious in Corinth.* Just as chapters 8–9 apply Paul's apologetic and gospel to the repentant, chapters 10–13 apply this same apologetic to those who persist in their rejection of his ministry.

The dual audience of 2 Corinthians thus contributes to its complexity, since Paul must encourage the faithful majority, while at the same time try to win back the recalcitrant minority. Though one emphasis may predominate over another in any given passage, neither group is ever far from view. At the same time, James Scott has insightfully pointed out that there is a chronological progression to 2 Corinthians: Chapters 1–7 reflect on past events, chapters 8–9 prepare for the completion of the collection in the present, and chapters 10–13 look forward to Paul's third visit in the future.[1] Hence, though each of the three main sections prepares for his third visit in some way, chapters 10–13 confront head-on the persistent problem posed by his opponents. The ambassador of reconciliation (cf. 5:18–6:2) now becomes the warrior against rebellion (cf. 10:1–6).

In response to the accusations leveled against Paul, the argument of 10:1–18 is presented in three parts (see the headings, below). Clearly, this development is an extension of his earlier apologetic concerning the nature and foundation of his apostolic ministry. As such, both the structure and content of the argument are derived from Paul's thesis-like statement in 2:14–3:3. It follows, therefore, that 10:1–18 does not represent a general intellectual confrontation between Paul and his opponents. Rather, he is responding

1. James M. Scott, 2 Corinthians, 208–9.

once again to their criticism of his self-humiliation as a result of his suffering (cf. 2:14–16).

At one level, Paul's opponents were, of course, right. Both his suffering and the criticism of others had been exacerbated by his decision to support himself in Corinth (2:17; cf. 1 Cor. 9:1–18).[2] Nor was Paul's "reputation" helped in the eyes of many by his withdrawal when attacked during his previous visit, by his change of plans, by his writing of the "tearful letter" (1:15–2:4), or by his refusal to employ the professional rhetoric of his day (cf. 1 Cor. 2:1–5; 2 Cor. 10:10).

Here, as in 2 Corinthians 2:14–3:3, the issue in 10:7–11 is once again whether Paul's suffering as an apostle corresponds to the spiritual nature of the new covenant (cf. 3:1–3). The summary statement in 2:14–3:3 thus becomes the framework for reading 10:1–18, as confirmed by the structural parallel between the two passages. Paul's discussion of his "weakness" in 10:1–11 leads to the theme of self-commendation in 10:12–18, just as his earlier reference to suffering in 2:14–17 led to this same theme in 3:1–3. In 10:1–18, however, Paul extends the points of 2:14–3:3 by drawing out their direct implications for those who continue to call his ministry into question.

Paul's Warfare on Behalf of his Authority (10:1–6)

PAUL BEGINS THE last section of his letter by again "appealing" (10:1) and "begging" (10:2) the Corinthians to respond to his apologetic on behalf of his gospel. Now, however, with his eye directly on his opponents, his earlier appeal (5:20) and urging (6:1) to be reconciled to God become an explicit admonition to reaffirm their loyalty to Paul himself (Paul uses the same verbs of "appealing" and "begging" in 10:1–2 as in 5:20; 6:1). Paul's self-identification with his gospel, implicit in his earlier chapters, is now made explicit.

At the same time, it is striking that in introducing this section Paul uses the verb "I appeal" (*parakaleo*), since he only does so when his authority is viewed as unproblematic.[3] Hence, even though he is now directly addressing the rebellious minority, Paul still writes knowing that the Corinthians as a whole are basically on his side. This is confirmed by his use of the emphatic expression "I, Paul," which is itself an assertion of authority (cf. 12:13; Rom. 9:3; 15:14; Gal. 5:2).

Moreover, this stress on his authority is not an attempt to compensate for the criticism being leveled against him. Instead, Paul begins this final section

---

2. For the arguments in favor of this reading, see Abraham J. Malherbe, "Antisthenes and Odysseus, and Paul at War," *HTR* 76 (1983): 143–73.

3. Following Ralph P. Martin, *2 Corinthians*, 302, based on Bjerkelund's study of *parakaleo* in Paul's writings.

of his letter by boldly asserting his authority because he is about to announce his third and final visit, which will bring God's judgment on those who at that time have not yet repented (cf. 10:6; 12:14, 20–21; 13:1–2, 10). Paul is being bold now so that he will not have to be "bold" when he arrives (10:2), since verse 6 makes it clear that the boldness in view is the punishment of the disobedient.

The stress on Paul's authority and the severe warning vented from the beginning of this section have often caused readers to wonder how these polemical chapters can be an expression of his appealing to the Corinthians "by the meekness and gentleness of Christ" (10:1).[4] This is all the more problematic when we realize that 10:1 is an oath formula intended to support the validity of his following admonitions (for the use of this same formula, see Rom. 12:1; 15:30; 1 Cor. 1:10; Philem. 9).

As 10:1b itself indicates, the question of how Paul's actions are said to be carried out "by the meekness and gentleness of Christ" is nothing new. Already in his own day his opponents had accused him of duplicity or cowardice because of the discrepancy between the powerful threats in his previous writing(s) and his apparent powerlessness or "timidity" when it came to carrying them out in person. In their view, Paul's change in demeanor, like his change of plans as outlined in 1:15–2:4, was evidence that he was living "by the standards of this world" (v. 2). The NIV rendering here makes good sense of the original, which formally translated reads, "walking according to the flesh" (cf. Paul's defense of his apparently "fleshly actions" in 1:12–22). In other words, Paul's opponents took his vacillating and the apparent contradiction between his words when absent and his actions when present to be evidence that he lacked the Spirit (i.e., "walked according to the flesh"). From their perspective, 2 Corinthians itself could be viewed as another example of this duplicity and lack of courage.

From Paul's perspective, of course, the accusation reported in 10:1b is ironic (hence the NIV's correct decision to put "timid" and "bold" in quotation marks). Paul's use of "timid" here (lit., "humble") carries the negative connotation of being servile, humiliated, despised, or demeaned, though normally humility is a positive virtue.[5] According to his detractors, his being "bold" when absent was a coward's threat, while for the apostle his boldness was an expression of his confidence from Christ (cf. its use in 5:6, 8; 7:16). So his

---

4. For representative expressions of Christ's meekness and humility, see Matt. 5:5; 11:29; 18:4; Mark 9:35–37; Luke 18:14; John 13:14–17; Phil. 2:8.

5. For Paul's positive use of humility (*tapeinos, tapeinoo*) as a virtue, cf. 7:6; 11:7; 12:21; Rom. 12:16; Phil. 2:8; 4:12. Cf. too James 4:6, 10; 1 Peter 5:5–6; and related concepts in Eph. 4:2; Phil. 2:3; Col. 3:12; 1 Tim. 6:11.

goal was to show them that his boldness when absent was just as much an expression of the "meekness and gentleness of Christ" as his humility when present.

It is true that Paul had been "timid" when he was attacked during his second visit, but "bold" when he subsequently wrote his "severe" or "tearful letter" (cf. 1:13; 2:3–4, 9; 7:8, 12). His opponents criticized him for this apparent contradiction because they did not understand the role of warnings, mixed with mercy, in the life of faith. In 10:1–2, Paul therefore restates this apostolic strategy, since his current letter also contains a strong apologetic and ends with a forceful warning to those who persist in their rejection of him and his message. For, ironically, in confronting one last time those who are still in rebellion against him, Paul is actually attempting to *avoid* the very kind of consistency that his opponents apparently desire (i.e., being "bold" both in letter and in person, cf. 10:11)!

This means that Paul's strong appeals and warnings flow from "the meekness and gentleness of Christ" not in the sense of a specific tone of voice or failure to confront. Rather, the meekness and gentleness of Christ can be seen in his patient restraint from pronouncing judgment, as he did before in 1 Corinthians 5:1–5. Like Christ, Paul is giving the Corinthians one last chance to repent (cf. 1 Cor. 4:21; 2 Peter 3:8–10). The messianic backdrop to his actions is reflected in the fact that the word translated "meekness" (*praütes*) in 2 Corinthians 10:1 is also used in the LXX of Psalm 132:1 of David, and in Psalm 45:4 and Zechariah 9:9 to describe the messianic king (cf. Matt. 11:29; 21:5). As the Davidic Messiah, no one should confuse Christ's meekness in his first coming with a lack of resolve to judge when he returns. Far from timidity, his "meekness" is his slowness to anger; far from lacking conviction, his "gentleness" is his forbearance, in contrast to being vindictive (cf. Acts 24:4; Phil. 4:5; 1 Tim. 3:3; Titus 3:2; James 3:17; 1 Peter 2:18).

In the same way, when Paul found himself under attack during his earlier visit to Corinth, he felt it better to leave rather than bring God's judgment on the church (cf. 2:5; 7:12). In doing so, he expressed Christ's "meekness and gentleness." Far from being an act of cowardice, Paul's "timidity" in the past was an act of mercy (cf. 1:23; 2:1). His "weakness" was an expression of the "weakness" of Christ. Moreover, the Corinthians were aware that in their immaturity in the past, Paul had treated them tenderly and with patience as their loving, spiritual father (cf. 1 Cor. 3:1–2; 4:18–21).

But just as Christ's meekness must not be misinterpreted to mean that he winks at sin, so too Paul's restraint must not be seen as cowardice. As the messianic king, Jesus will vindicate his name by judging those who presume upon his mercy by not repenting (cf. 5:10–11). In the same way, whereas

Paul's opponents viewed his "tearful letter" as a cowardly attempt to assert his authority at a distance, in reality it was a prophetic act of warning aimed at bringing about the repentance of the Corinthians (cf. 2:5–11; 7:5–7, 13–16). For as an apostle of Christ, Paul too will come to judge those who have presumed on God's grace and scoffed at his warnings (cf. 10:6; 13:10). Thus, in 10:1 Paul "cites [the opponents'] estimate while retaining in a double entendre his own self-estimate based on the model of the incarnate Lord."[6]

Despite their vigor and confrontational character, Paul's self-defense and threats in chapters 10–13 are therefore *themselves* also an expression of the "meekness and gentleness of Christ." Just as Christ's primary purpose in his first coming was to establish and extend mercy to God's people, so too Paul's purpose in not being "bold" in person is to extend mercy to the Corinthians. Viewed in the light of Christ's meekness and gentleness, Paul was being truly humble by not judging them in the past or even at the writing of 2 Corinthians, but instead warning them for a final time. Like Christ, Paul desires that they will all respond so that he will not have to be "bold" by judging them when he returns for his third visit. But inasmuch as he considers such judgment to be a real possibility against "some people" (10:2; i.e., his opponents), the specific content of his appeal is that he "begs" the Corinthians for reconciliation now so that none of them will have to suffer God's wrath then.

Once again, therefore, one's relationship to Paul himself becomes the criterion by which judgment will be meted out. To impugn his weakness and suffering, some of which has been caused by the Corinthians themselves, is to impugn the weakness of Christ himself, whose character the apostle has embodied in Corinth. Far from living by the standards of the world (10:2), he has been acting "in Christ" and by the power of the Spirit (cf. 1:5; 2:14, 17; 5:14).

In 10:3–6, Paul plays off the accusation from verse 2 that he conducts himself "by the standards of this world" by developing a military metaphor to support his strategy of writing boldly from afar in anticipation of not having to act boldly when he arrives. Specifically, Paul is using a prophetic, Christ-like strategy of warning for the purpose of repentance, rather than pronouncing judgment immediately. In doing so, he is not "waging war as the world does" (lit., "according to the flesh"), even though he is still "living in the world" (lit., "in the flesh"; 10:3; cf. 1:12; 4:7–5:15; 6:4–10; 11:23–33; Gal. 2:20; Phil. 1:24).

Though Paul concedes that he "lives in the world," his battle plan is not worldly (10:3) because his "weapons" (10:4) are not worldly; by implication, they are expressions of the power of the Spirit (the NIV omits the "for" [*gar*]

---

6. Martin, *2 Corinthians*, 303.

at the beginning of 10:4a).[7] Instead of reacting with immediate wrath when offended, as the world would do, Paul's weapons have "divine power" (i.e., the power of the Spirit[8]) for bringing about the genuine repentance and endurance in faith that escapes the wrath of God (10:4b; cf. 3:2–3; 6:14–7:1; 7:8–12).

In particular, Paul's weapons are the manifold proclamation of the truth of the gospel in the power of the Spirit, embodied in and mediated through his own life of suffering as an apostle (cf. 2:14–17; 6:6–7; 1 Cor. 1:18, 23; Rom. 1:16; 1 Thess. 5:8; Eph. 6:14–17). Their purpose is to "demolish strongholds," an allusion to the bulwarks erected by citizens to protect their city from invaders (10:4b; cf. Lam. 2:2; 1 Macc. 5:65; 8:10; Luke 19:43–44). The truth of the gospel will overcome anything or anyone standing in its way.

Paul's metaphorical reference in 10:4 to demolishing "strongholds" (ochyroma) likely looks back to Proverbs 21:22, where the wise man is said to destroy the strongholds (ochyroma) in which the ungodly trust. Like the wise man of the Proverbs, Paul's purpose is to destroy the defenses of self-confidence and self-exaltation that have been erected by the self-commendations of those who oppose the progress of the gospel (cf. 10:12, 17–18; 11:4). Many commentators suggest that these "strongholds" were embodied in the powerful rhetoric of Paul's opponents, who, like the Sophists of their day, were more concerned with impressing the Corinthians with their style of presentation than with the truth of its content (cf. 10:10). Though their concern for style over substance was certainly part of the problem, the issue was not merely their methods. Paul is on the offensive primarily because he knows that his opponents preach a "different gospel" altogether (cf. 11:4).

What renders their personal appearance so dangerous is that it makes their false "gospel" so appealing. Hence, as a true apostle of Christ, Paul's goal, like an invading army laying siege against its enemy in order to destroy the bulwarks of their city, is to destroy both their manner *and* their message. Having been conquered by Christ himself (2:14), Paul now wages war on Christ's behalf (10:3–4). Having been made a minister of the new covenant of the Spirit (3:4–6), Paul's apostolate is a conquering army that can overcome any and every foe.

---

7. Though helpful in terms of interpretation, the NIV translation of *sarx* as "world" in 10:3–4 rather than "flesh," obscures the typical Pauline flesh/Spirit contrast implied in vv. 2–4. In Paul's conception, to act or be in the flesh is, by definition, to be devoid of the Spirit (cf. 1:18–22; 3:2–3; 5:14–6:2).

8. The phrase rendered by the NIV "they have divine power" is lit., "powerful to God," which is best taken with the NIV as a Semitism meaning "divinely powerful." For this view, see Paul Barnett, *The Second Epistle to the Corinthians*, 464n.46. The other options are to render it as a dative of advantage ("powerful for God's cause") or as a dative of subjective judgment ("powerful in the eyes of God"). But the contrast to "fleshly" in verse 4a best supports the idea of two kinds of weapons: those devoid of the Spirit and those possessing divine power.

Verse 5 details the two ways in which Paul wages his war on behalf of the gospel. (1) He demolishes the "arguments" and "pretensions" (lit., the "heights" from which the defenders opposed the besieging army) that his opponents have raised against "the knowledge of God" being revealed through his own preaching and suffering (cf. 2:14–17; 4:4–6; 8:7; 11:6; 13:8). The arguments in view here are the objections being raised against his apostolic authority and message (the "arguments" [*logismous*] of 10:4 recall the "thinking" [*logizomenous*] of "some people" in 10:2). Paul overcomes them by a clear presentation of the gospel and its implications, surrounded by an unabashed appeal to his own life as its verification.

(2) Once he has destroyed the enemy defenses, Paul takes every thought of the enemy "captive" by evaluating it in view of his own ministry of the cross and resurrection of Christ. Specifically, Paul argues for his conviction, and supports it evidentially, that as a true apostle of the crucified and risen Christ, he reveals the power of God (cf. 2:17; 3:2–3; 4:1–6; 5:11–12; 11:2; 12:19; 13:3–4) in and through his weakness (cf. 1:3–11; 2:14–16; 4:7–12; 6:4–10; 11:23–12:10). As a result, his presentation and embodiment of the truth also reveal the satanic nature of those who oppose his "treasure" because it comes in a "jar of clay" (4:7; cf. 2:11; 3:14; 4:4; 11:3). This is Paul's twofold strategy throughout 1 and 2 Corinthians.

After demolishing the defenses of his enemies and taking captive their counterattacks, Paul will punish those who remain in rebellion. But he will only do so once the repentant, by their obedience, have shown themselves to be on his side (10:6). Note the emphasis in 10:6 on the Corinthians' obedience being "complete" as the qualification for meting out punishment. Paul wants to give them every opportunity to surrender to the gospel before he executes God's judgment, and he will not do so until all who will repent have done so. This is why he has delayed returning in the past and why he has now written his present letter (cf. 10:2). He is confident that when they receive 2 Corinthians, those genuine believers who are still unrepentant will be brought back to Christ, showing their remorse by joining the majority in withdrawing from the rebellious (6:14–7:1) and by participating willingly in the collection (chs. 8–9).

Paul's choice of this warfare metaphor in 10:3–6 is itself an indication of the seriousness of the present situation: He is at war for the eternal destiny of the Corinthians.[9] To win the battle, Paul intends to destroy the defenses of the enemy by demolishing the arguments they raise against the knowledge

---

9. The warfare/siege metaphor in vv. 3–6 is the most extensive use of military imagery in Paul's letters. For other uses of this sort of imagery, see 2:14; 6:7; Rom. 13:12–13; 1 Cor. 9:7; Phil. 1:30; 2:25; Eph. 6:10–17; 1 Thess. 5:8; 1 Tim. 1:18; 2 Tim. 2:3; Philem. 2.

of God (vv. 4b–5a). Specifically, his goal in these last four chapters is to show how his enemies contradict the person and message of Christ (10:5b). Nevertheless, though the issue may have been the nature of the gospel, the explicit point of contention in Corinth was the legitimacy of Paul as an apostle (cf. 10:1–2, 7–11). For this reason, Paul switches from speaking about himself in 10:1–3 to speaking about God and Christ in 10:5, in order to underscore once again the identification of his own person and message with the knowledge of God and Christ being revealed through them (cf. 2:14–16a; 4:7–12; 5:18–6:2; etc.).

The Purpose of Apostolic Authority (10:7–11)

IN THIS NEXT section Paul unpacks his exhortation from 10:1–2 in view of the war that he is presently waging against the enemies of the gospel. In doing so, he draws out three implications of his battle against those who are opposing his ministry: (1) the implication for the *Corinthians* (v. 7), which supports (2) the implication for how one should view *Paul* (v. 8), which in turn supports (3) the implication of Paul's argument for his *opponents* (vv. 9–11). Concretely, this section issues a command to the Corinthians (v. 7a), which leads to a command concerning Paul (v. 7b), which in turn supports a command, albeit indirectly, to Paul's opponents (cf. v. 11).

This reading of the passage is based on taking the verb "look" in verse 7 to be an imperative ("Look!" as in the RSV, NRSV, and NIV footnote), rather than an indicative statement ("You are looking," as in the NIV and NASB), or an interrogative ("Do you look?" as in the KJV). Though all three meanings are possible and the decision is a difficult one, elsewhere Paul always uses this form of the verb "to look" (*blepete*) as a command (cf. 1 Cor. 1:26; 8:9; 10:18; 16:10; Gal. 5:15; Eph. 5:15; Phil. 3:2; Col. 2:8; cf. the singular in Col. 4:17). Moreover, within this context, an indicative or interrogative would expect a contrast in 2 Corinthians 10:7b, not a supporting statement.[10] Finally, as the extension of his "begging" them from 10:2, in verse 7 Paul is most likely not simply describing or questioning what the Corinthians *are* doing, but stating what he wishes they *would* do. Having begged them to avoid judgment in 10:1–6, he now calls them to do so by evaluating

---

10. Following Victor P. Furnish, *II Corinthians*, 465. The strongest argument against this reading is that when *blepete* is used as an imperative elsewhere, it always stands first in its clause, whereas when it is an indicative statement it is placed elsewhere (as in 10:7; cf. Matt. 11:4; 13:17; 24:2). For this argument in favor of taking it to be a statement, see Timothy B. Savage, *Power Through Weakness*, 184n.109. But the unusual word order here may simply reflect Paul's emphasis on the fact that they must examine things *as they appear*. The phrase rendered by the NIV "on the surface of things" (lit., "according to the face") is the same phrase rendered "face to face" in 10:1, both of which refer to what is clearly evident.

things as they readily appear to the Corinthians themselves, rather than listening to Paul's opponents.

When Paul's life is compared to others in Corinth who claim to be Christ's (10:7b), the transparent nature of his belonging to Christ becomes his support for the command of 10:7a: "Look at the obvious facts."[11] In making this comparison, Paul still has his apostleship in view. To speak of being a Christian is, for him, to speak of being an apostle, since his calling to Christ and his calling to be an apostle were one. Nevertheless, interpreting verse 7b as a reference merely to his role as an apostle in comparison with other apostles is too narrow. When the office alone is in view, Paul uses the explicit designations "apostle of Christ" or "servant of Christ" (cf. 11:13–15, 23 and the comparisons in 11:5; 12:11).

The use of "anyone" in 10:7b is a generic designation that most likely refers either to Paul's opponents or to all in Corinth who question his integrity as a Christian, rather than to people in general (cf. this same use in 1 Cor. 3:12, 18; 8:2–3; 14:37). The purpose of this reference is to indicate that those who question his apostleship are in reality also calling into question his very status as a believer. But Paul's mediation of the Spirit, through his lifestyle of suffering, is ample proof of the legitimacy of his ministry and hence of his belonging to the Lord (cf. 1:1; 3:2–3; 4:7; 6:4). If the Corinthians are children of God, then Paul too must be, since he is their father in the faith, the Corinthians' having received the Spirit through his preaching and ministry. If they deny Paul, they are denying their own standing in Christ (cf. 10:7 with 3:1–3).

Moreover, the legitimacy of Paul's ministry is confirmed by his own confidence in his authority as a servant of the new covenant. This confidence is derived from the new covenant expectation of Jeremiah himself (cf. 3:6), to which Paul alludes in 10:8 (cf. 13:10). In fulfillment of Jeremiah's promise, the Lord (i.e., Christ) gave Paul authority to be a minister of the new covenant "for building you up rather than pulling you down," whereas under the old covenant the emphasis of Jeremiah's ministry was just the opposite (Jer. 1:10; cf. 24:6; 42[LXX 49]:10; 45[LXX 51]:4). This is why Paul's role as a minister of the new covenant is to mediate the Spirit, since as an apostle his primary purpose is the salvation of God's people, not their judgment (cf. 2 Cor. 1:11, 23–24; 2:3; 3:6–11, 17–18; 4:6, 13–15; 5:13–15; 6:2).

Though Jeremiah and Paul were each called both to save and to judge, their *primary* purposes within redemptive history have been reversed. As the introduction to the promise of the new covenant puts it (Jer. 31:27–28):

---

11. For the expression "[to be] of Christ" as a reference to belonging to Christ as a believer, see Rom. 14:8; 1 Cor. 3:23; 15:23; Gal. 3:29; 5:24; cf. Mark 9:41.

"The days are coming," declares the LORD, "when I will plant the house of Israel and the house of Judah with the offspring of men and of animals. Just as I watched over them to uproot and tear down, and to overthrow, destroy and bring disaster, so I will watch over them to build and to plant," declares the LORD.

For this reason, the theme of "building up" becomes a common Pauline description of the call to build churches and strengthen the faith of believers (cf. Rom. 14:19; 15:2, 20; 1 Cor. 3:9–10, 12, 14; 8:1; 14:3, 5, 12, 26; 1 Thess. 5:11).

Therefore,[12] since the Corinthians themselves are evidence of Paul's rightful standing in Christ (v. 7), he will not be ashamed before the judgment of God if he boasts exceedingly concerning his apostolic authority (v. 8a; cf. 2:17; 12:19).[13] Paul's boasting in chapters 10–13 is not the exercise of an uncontrolled ego, but the expression of his love and calling as a "minister of the new covenant" (3:2–6). Since the Lord is the One who gave him this authority, he will not be ashamed in invoking it, for in doing so he is simply using part of the means God has ordained to bring about the conversion and renewal of God's people (cf. Rom. 1:14–16). Hence, as a minister of the new covenant in fulfillment of Jeremiah's promise, Paul declares that "everything we do [including his self-defense] . . . is for your strengthening [building up]" (2 Cor. 12:19).

In verses 9–11, Paul expresses the purpose for his boasting and warnings that are to come in the chapters ahead. He is aware that his opponents have accused him of trying in his previous letter(s) to frighten the Corinthians with empty threats from a safe distance (v. 9). Indeed, Paul *had* threatened destruction to the destroyer of God's people (1 Cor. 3:16–17) and exclusion from the kingdom to those whose lives show no evidence of God's grace (6:9–11), not to mention calling for judgment within God's people (5:1–5; 2 Cor. 2:4–11; 7:8). Thus, we can only guess at the strength of his previous "tearful letter," but it must have been considerable (cf. 2 Cor. 8:8).

Moreover, the fact that Paul is once again being "bold" by letter could play into the hand of his opponents. He knows that the apparent contradiction between his "weighty and forceful" letters and his personal weakness and suffering has been used against him as proof that he lacks the power of the

---

12. Taking the conjunction *gar* in 10:8 not to introduce a ground or causal clause, with the meaning "for" (as in the NIV), but to be inferential, with the meaning "therefore" (cf. the NRSV's rendering, "now"); cf. BAGD, 152. Paul's confidence before God does not logically support his confidence in belonging to Christ, but is derived from it.

13. For explicit references to "boasting" in chs. 10–13, cf. 10:8, 13, 15, 16, 17; 11:10, 12, 16, 17, 18, 30; 12:1, 5, 6, 9; see also in chaps. 1–9, 1:12, 14; 5:12; 7:4, 14; 8:24; 9:2, 3, 12.

Spirit (v. 10). Nevertheless, he has made it clear throughout 2 Corinthians that his decision to support himself in Corinth, his ministry in the midst of his weakness and suffering, his change in travel plans, his "weighty letters," and his simple, "unimpressive" manner of presenting the gospel (remember that part of Moses' insufficiency was his speech defect, Ex. 4:10; cf. 2 Cor. 2:16; 3:4–5) are all expressions of his apostolic commitment to the Corinthians.

As part of this commitment, according to 10:10, Paul's speech could be considered to "amount to nothing" (cf. Gal. 4:14, where the same verb describes Paul himself because of his suffering). This reflects the truth that God chooses the things that "amount to nothing" (1 Cor. 1:28, where the same verb occurs) in order that all people might rely on God's power and gifts (2:5) rather than boast in their own distinctives (1:28–31).

Thus, Paul's opponents should be put on notice that he is more than prepared to carry out his threats of judgment when he arrives (10:11). Since he is an apostle of the new covenant, his primary goal, unlike Jeremiah's, is to be an instrument of the Corinthians' repentance. But inasmuch as there is also judgment under God's covenant for those who do not repent, Paul will carry out this "secondary" responsibility as well. The contrast that began in 10:1–2 between Paul's presence and absence is therefore brought to a conclusion in 10:10–11. The consistency his opponents purport to desire will become a reality when the apparent inconsistency of God's mercy, expressed in Paul's patience, gives way to his final judgment in Corinth.

The main point of verses 10:1–11 is verse 9. Paul is begging those Corinthians who are still rebelling to be reconciled to him (10:1–2) because he is fighting a Spirit-empowered war on behalf of the gospel (10:3–6). He consequently calls them to examine his claims to authority in view of what is clearly evident to them (10:7–8), in order that his letter might not merely frighten them from afar (10:9). For in spite of the fact that his opponents accuse him of duplicity and cowardice (10:10), Paul *will* execute the threatened judgment of God when he arrives (10:11).

The Basis of Apostolic Authority (10:12–18)

THE FUNDAMENTAL ISSUE at stake in Corinth was the gospel itself, as it had been preached and embodied by Paul. Nobody could dispute what Paul had accomplished: He had founded the Corinthian church and performed signs and wonders in their midst. What made the issue of his apostolic ministry so acute was that despite his role in founding the church, his opponents were claiming that they themselves, not Paul, were the ones who now had the right to exercise apostolic authority *in Corinth*. In their view, Paul's suffering had disqualified him as an apostle. They were the ones who should now lead the Corinthians in their faith.

In 11:1–12:13 Paul will address the more fundamental question of whether his opponents should be considered apostles at all. But first, having argued for the legitimacy of his apostolic ministry in general, he must reestablish his claim to apostolic authority over the Corinthians in particular (10:8). Otherwise, his call to repentance in view of his coming judgment will be considered irrelevant (10:9). So Paul's burden in 10:12–18 is twofold: (1) to define the proper criterion for determining what is, in fact, a proper boast or claim to apostolic authority in Corinth, and (2) to demonstrate that his boast, not that of his opponents, actually meets this criterion.

Paul accomplishes these purposes by introducing a negative comparison between his opponents' practice of commendation (10:12) and his own (10:13–18).[14] Just as Paul's discussion of his suffering in 1:3–2:13 had led him to compare himself *positively* to Moses in 2:14–3:18, so too the issue of his suffering in 10:1–11 leads him to compare himself *negatively* to his opponents in 10:12–18. Paul is like Moses, but with a different ministry; he is unlike his opponents, though they claim to have the same ministry. His statement in 10:12 that he lacks the courage to compare himself with his opponents is therefore most likely ironic: In spite of the "boldness" attributed to him by his opponents, he does not "dare" to put himself in their class or to join them in their kind of self-commendation.

To engage in comparisons was a common rhetorical practice in Paul's day. So his hesitancy does not come from the practice itself; he himself does so without qualification (cf. 1 Cor. 15:10). Here, however, he refuses to participate with those who commend themselves because their *means* of comparison is faulty from the start: They measure themselves *by themselves* and compare themselves *with themselves*, thereby revealing that they are without understanding (10:12).

We must be careful here. The problem with Paul's opponents is not that they are boasting, as many suggest, since for Paul the act of boasting is not negative in and of itself. Whether boasting is legitimate wholly depends on the *object and validity* of the boast itself. Nor is the problem that they boast too much, as others sometime argue. There does not seem to be a limit on boasting in what is appropriate. Paul himself boasts "freely" about his authority (10:8). Nor is Paul's refusal to join them due to their commending themselves, since Paul too commends himself (cf. 2:17; 4:2; 6:4–10; 11:1–12:10 as implied in 12:11; see below, Bridging Contexts).

What Paul does object to is the criterion they use in attempting to substantiate their claim to apostolic authority in *Corinth*, namely, themselves.

---

14. The following analysis of the theme of "self-commendation" in 2 Corinthians closely follows and often reproduces my earlier work, "'Self-Commendation' and Apostolic Legitimacy in 2 Corinthians: A Pauline Dialectic?" *NTS* 36 (1990): 66–88.

From Paul's perspective, to support a claim to apostolic authority in Corinth by pointing to one's own abilities, spiritual power and experiences, and/or rhetorical prowess is to be without understanding; such factors are simply irrelevant to the question at hand. Regardless of whatever personal qualifications and experiences his adversaries may have had (for the moment Paul grants the validity of such claims), his opponents lack the commendation needed to establish their authority over the Corinthians. This particular commendation does not come by comparing oneself to others; it comes from the Lord.

Thus, in the words of 10:13, translated formally, Paul will not join them in boasting "beyond proper limits," but will boast "according to the measure of the canon concerning which God apportioned to us a measure, namely, to reach even as far as you." The key to this passage is to determine what Paul means by the "measure" (*metron*) God has granted to him in accordance with the divinely established "canon" (*kanon*). This statement is notoriously difficult because of the uncertainty that exists over the precise meaning in this context of *kanon* and *metron*, and over whether they are being used as synonyms or refer, in fact, to two distinct entities.

These two words can signify either the means or standard by which something is measured (e.g., the "canon" or "measure" used to determine which books belong in the Scriptures), or the thing itself that has been measured (e.g., the "canon" or "entity" of the New Testament). Often the two words are simply taken to be synonyms. Read in this way, Paul is referring either to the single means of measuring his ministry[15] or to the one thing measured.[16]

Although these readings are possible, Paul's repetition of the word *metron*, together with his modification of it with the second word *kanon*, seems to suggest that in this context he is differentiating between the two concepts. If *kanon* were merely a restatement of what Paul means by *metron*, then the repetition of *metron* in the following relative pronoun clause would simply be a tautology (i.e., "according to the *measure* of the *measure* concerning which God apportioned to us *a measure*"). It seems therefore best to take *metron* in its common meaning as a reference to "what is measured as the result of measuring,"[17]

---

15. This interpretation is reflected in the RSV rendering, in which both words are taken together and translated by the one word "limits": "But we will not boast beyond limit, but will keep to the limits God has apportioned to us."

16. This interpretation is reflected in the NIV and NRSV rendering, in which both words are taken together and translated by the one word "field": We will "confine our boasting to the field God has assigned to us."

17. K. Deissner, "μέτρον," *TDNT*, 4:632–34 (p. 632). See too H. W. Beyer, "κανών," *TDNT*, 3:596–602 (p. 599n.12). For its use elsewhere in Paul, see Rom. 12:3; Eph. 4:7, 13, 16, where it also carries this meaning.

while retaining the typical meaning "standard" or "norm" for *kanon*. Taken in this way, 10:13 reads as follows: Paul will only boast "according to what is measured by the standard by which God apportioned to us that measure, namely, to reach even to you."

In contrast to his opponents, who measure themselves by themselves (10:12), Paul asserts in 10:13–15 that he will not boast beyond "proper limits," that is, beyond what God has apportioned for him. Instead, he will boast in accordance with the "measure" he has been granted by the "norm" established by God himself: that he was the one who reached Corinth with the gospel (10:13c, 14c; cf. 1 Cor. 4:15). The "standard of judgment" (*kanon*) that determined Paul's apostolic authority in Corinth—and hence the validity of his boast in this regard—is the simple fact that he founded the Corinthian church. That Paul was the one through whom the Corinthians received the Spirit (cf. 3:1–3) indicates clearly that he, not his opponents, is the one to whom God has delegated apostolic authority in Corinth. As 10:13bc makes explicit, God himself determined who would bring the gospel to Corinth. Since Paul was that selected one, he alone can boast in this divine "measure" or "limit." He is therefore not "going too far" in asserting his apostolic authority over them (10:14; the NIV leaves the *gar* ["for"] untranslated here).

Hence, the unexpressed premise of Paul's argument is that this founding function is the only appropriate and divinely instituted "canon" for determining apostolic authority in a particular church. Paul's boast is therefore based on his own divinely established "work" (10:15a). Thus, the three negative contrasts in verses 13–15a all carry a double meaning. In establishing these affirmations about himself, the apostle is at the same time affirming that his opponents are "boasting beyond proper limits" and "going too far" (10:13a, 14a) in their attempt to assert apostolic authority in Corinth. They have no relevant evidence to back up such a claim. Unlike Paul, they are "boasting of work done by others" (10:15a).

In stark contrast, Paul has no need to boast in the work of others. Instead, his hope is that, as the church in Corinth grows in faith, his legitimacy and authority in Corinth "will be magnified greatly among them" (NIV, his "activity among them will greatly expand") in accordance with his own "canon" (NIV, "our area")[18]—that is, in accordance with God's having granted Paul missionary success in Corinth (10:15b). Here he is once again alluding to his

---

18. The NIV obscures the point of v. 15b by translating *kanon* as "our area of activity" and making it the subject of the sentence. It is actually part of an adverbial prepositional phrase modifying the verb "to be increased" or "expanded." The subject of the infinitive "to be magnified" or "increased" is Paul himself. The formal translation of 10:15 is as follows: "not boasting beyond measure in other's labors, but having hope, as your faith grows, to be increased/magnified to a vast extent among you according to our canon."

opponents' desire for letters of recommendation from the Corinthians (cf. 3:1). By contrast, the Corinthians themselves are Paul's recommendation (3:2–3). His opponents wanted letters verifying their own spiritual power; Paul's spiritual power could be seen in the growing faith of the believers in Corinth (cf. 1:24; 8:7; 13:5).

Note the emphasis on "growth" in 10:15. It is not enough that the Corinthians have manifested faith in the past. They must persevere in the midst of the challenges now facing the church. Paul hopes that their growth in faith, manifested in their rejection of his opponents (6:14–7:1) and participation in the collection (chs. 8–9), will send him on approved and recommended. He desires that the solidifying of his work in Corinth will lead to an expansion of his apostolic ministry beyond Achaia (10:16, most likely a reference to Rome and Spain; cf. Rom. 15:24–29).[19]

It is not clear whether Paul means by this that as their faith grows, he will be able to use Corinth as a base of operations for his mission to Rome and Spain, or whether he has no right to expand his ministry elsewhere until his labor among the Corinthians is completed. The latter is more probable. Paul cannot move on toward the West until his work in the East has been solidified, which includes the fortification of his congregations and their unification with Jerusalem through the collection.[20]

In 10:13 Paul asserted that, in contrast to his opponents, his own boast is not beyond the measures God has established. In 10:14–16 he supported this assertion by reminding the Corinthians of what constitutes the canon of apostolic authority. In 10:17–18 he undergirds this canon by declaring the corresponding object of legitimate boasting: Since the Lord is the one who determines the measure of one's ministry, the only true object and ground of boasting is the approval that comes from the Lord's commendation. And the Lord commends his people as his people by working in their lives. His commendation of Paul's apostleship in Corinth was the fact that he had brought the great missionary to Corinth as the church's founding father in the faith. In the end, therefore, the ultimate foundation of Paul's apologetic is that the only genuine boast and basis of authority is "boasting in the Lord" (10:17, quoting Jer. 9:22–23 LXX). For what matters is not the Corinthians' approval (cf. 2 Cor. 2:17; 12:19), but God's commendation (10:18).

Accordingly, in order to understand Paul's argument we must map out what it means to "boast in the Lord." Paul's quotation of Jeremiah 9:22–23 in

---

19. For Paul's ministry as his "labor," cf. Rom. 16:6, 12; 1 Cor. 3:8; 15:10, 58; 16:16; Phil. 2:16; 1 Thess. 5:12.

20. For more on this and on the relationship some scholars see here to Gen. 10, see the Appendix to this chapter (p. 418).

2 Corinthians 10:17 is the positive counterpart to the negative point made in 10:14–16: False boasting is boasting either in one's own self-proclaimed and irrelevant accomplishments (assuming for the moment their genuineness) or in the labors of others. Legitimate boasting, by contrast, is boasting "in the Lord." To boast in the Lord is to exalt in what the grace of God has accomplished in one's life. This divine action on one's behalf is God's commendation.

In this context, this meant pointing to God's having established Paul's mission territory (10:13–16). In general, however, boasting in the Lord refers to boasting in the fact that God has granted his people wisdom, righteousness, sanctification, and redemption in Christ (cf. Paul's other use of Jer. 9:22–23 in 1 Cor. 1:31; cf. Rom. 2:29). The Christian's calling (2 Cor. 10:7) is based solely on this divine mercy, so that no one may boast that one's spiritual status, strength, or gifts are a result of one's own wisdom or might (cf. 1 Cor. 1:26–29; Eph. 2:4–10).

This is the point of Jeremiah 9:23–24 (cf. 1 Sam. 2:10). There Jeremiah calls the wise, the strong, and the rich not to boast in their own distinctives but in the God who is known by the mercy, judgment, and righteousness he exercises on earth, since these are the things in which he delights. The prophet's criticism of the wise, the strong, and the rich is not that they are wise, strong, and rich per se, but that they act as if their wisdom, strength, and wealth came from them. Moreover, they esteem these things of more value than God's mercy, justice, and righteousness. Jeremiah's point is that God is the sole origin of humanity's distinctives and that his actions alone are of ultimate value.

Following Jeremiah's admonition, in 1 Corinthians 1:31 Paul boasts in the saving activity of Christ as the expression of God's mercy, justice, and righteousness. The issue is not whether one boasts or not (we all do!), but whether the object of our boast is God. The call to boast from Jeremiah 9:23–24 is a summons to acknowledge God for his gracious acts and provisions.[21] It is consequently striking, but thoroughly consistent with the original meaning of the text, that in 2 Corinthians 10:17 Paul modifies Jeremiah 9:23–24 by substituting "in the Lord" for Jeremiah's list of what the Lord provides. Paul introduces this shorthand because he is following the biblical conviction that God is known by what he does and gives. As a result, God's actions in Jeremiah 9:24 can be equated with the Lord himself.

---

21. This meaning of Jer. 9:23–24 and its significance as the "key text" for Paul's boasting in 2 Cor. 10–12, esp. his boasting in his weakness in 11:1–12:10, has been presented in detail by Ulrich Heckel, *Kraft in Schwachheit: Untersuchungen zu 2.Kor 10–13* (WUNT 2.Reihe 56; Tübingen: J.C.B. Mohr [Paul Siebeck], 1993), 162–214. For the point made above, see esp. his 165–67.

In view of this Old Testament injunction, to "boast in the Lord" is not to cease from boasting but to boast only in what God himself has actually accomplished in one's life. It is this sort of boasting that marks one out as legitimate before God and others. In 10:18, Paul is applying the same standard of approval to himself that he has applied to others and to the Corinthians (cf. 2:9; 8:2, 8, 22; 9:13; esp. 13:3–7). To "boast in the Lord" (10:17) is the human counterpart to being commended by the Lord and hence "approved" by him (10:18).

Accordingly, when Paul points to his bringing the gospel to Corinth, he is, in reality, boasting in the Lord, since God is the one who enabled and determined Paul's ministry in this regard (cf. 10:13b).

> Paul's opponents may be able to point to great displays of spiritual power and rhetorical expertise when they measure themselves by themselves and compare themselves with themselves (10:12), but all such personal qualities remain irrelevant to the question at hand: whom has the *Lord* commended for apostolic authority in Corinth? Regardless of their value for demonstrating the validity of one's apostolic ministry *per se* (presupposing their genuine nature), the opponents' boasts therefore simply become empty ... the *kanōn* ("canon") being used by his opponents to measure their claim (and his!) to apostolic authority is simply illegitimate.[22]

In commending themselves, Paul's opponents are "not wise" (10:12). They fail to understand the nature of divine approval. The opponents' claim to authority *in Corinth* is merely an exercise in *self*-commendation, since it lacks the divine accreditation appropriate to that claim: having brought the gospel to Corinth. For this reason, if the Corinthians continue to fall prey to the illegitimate boasting of Paul's opponents, they will become the real "fools" (cf. 11:1, 16–19, 21; 12:6, 11). Paul is striving to spare them this, for he knows that they too, like he himself, stand before the judgment of God (cf. Jer. 9:25–26; 2 Cor. 5:10).

THERE ARE AT least four tenets from this text that can help us apply Paul's concern to "wage war" against his opponents to our own battlefields: the issue at stake, the purpose of Paul's response, the manner of Paul's response, and the criteria for response.

The issue at stake in the "war." From Paul's perspective, the issue at stake between him and the Corinthians is the gospel, since to reject his claims is

---

22. Hafemann, "Self-Commendation," 83–84.

tantamount to rejecting Christ. But as the Corinthians see it, the problem is Paul himself. Scholars of the social world of Paul's day have pointed out that what is at stake culturally in 2 Corinthians 10 was Paul's *honor*, one of the central virtues of the period. As Bruce Malina has observed, one's honor is called into question when the support for his or her claim does not correspond to what the social peer group considers to be reputable.[23] Or, as Arthur Dewey has put it, a person's honor is called into question when "the individual has not balanced his verbal claims with socially understood reality."[24] Hence, since Paul's opponents maintain that his weakness and suffering are not reputable grounds for his claim to be an apostle, Paul's honor is being called into question.

Since the dispute is a matter of personal honor, calling Paul's apostleship into question also meant questioning his very identity and social status in the Christian community. According to his opponents' understanding of the Spirit, Paul was living "by the standards of this world" (i.e., "according to the flesh," 10:2). "There were 'objective criteria' for determining the validity of such claims to authority: letters of recommendation, ecstasy, wonder-working, rhetorical and interpretive competence"—which Paul "evidently did not meet."[25] Rather than boasting about his authority over the Corinthians, Paul should be shamed by his behavior.

The dynamics of honor and shame in Paul's day remind us that we too determine what is "reputable" according to the standards that derive from our own social context. In most of our circles, the honor of a Christian is no longer determined by an absence of suffering in and of itself, since the social reality of most believers today does not revolve around displays of the miraculous. Most churches do not expect that their pastors must be able to accredit their message and the legitimacy of their ministry with a miracle, nor do the members of the congregation measure the depth of their own spirituality by the presence of miracles in their lives.

True, in some churches the miraculous is a measure of the Spirit's presence and power. For them, being sick or in financial difficulty is, in the end, due to a lack of faith. But what most churches today expect is a correspondence between what the pastor preaches and the way in which he lives. A significant conflict between the two would be a serious issue, since our understanding of the social reality of the Spirit, both for our leaders and for ourselves, includes moral integrity and consistency.

---

23. Bruce J. Malina, *The New Testament World: Insights from Cultural Anthropology* (Atlanta: John Knox Press, 1981), 27–29.

24. Arthur J. Dewey, "A Matter of Honor: A Social-Historical Analysis of 2 Corinthians 10," *HTR* 78 (1985): 209–17 (p. 210).

25. Ibid., 212–13.

Again, there are some churches where this is not the case, and ironically they are often the same churches that stress the miraculous as the sign of the Spirit. In their view, if one can perform miracles, then that person is obviously "anointed by the Spirit," regardless of the disconfirming evidence of his or her character. Among evangelicals, a similar argument is sometimes mounted in terms of salvation itself: If someone has said a "sinner's prayer" and "accepted Jesus as his Lord and Savior," then he or she is a Christian, regardless of the disconfirming evidence of one's character. When it comes to leadership, the argument is often the same: If God has "used" a pastor in the past (which usually means that his church has grown numerically), then the ministry of that person is surely legitimate, regardless of the disconfirming evidence of character.

So in making application of this passage, we must map out carefully what constitutes an honorable claim to be "spiritual." This is especially arduous, since all Christians are still in the *process* of sanctification, so that perfection of character cannot be the criterion. It therefore requires wisdom to determine what constitutes a match between our standards in Christ and how we live. Paul's discussion forces us to reflect deeply on the criteria by which we consider a claim to Christian leadership, not to mention Christian identity itself, to be honorable. This chapter is driven by the fact that Paul, like his opponents, believed that such evaluations could and must be made. As such, it provides a case study for evaluating competing claims to God's approval.

The purpose of the battle. Paul's model in this passage presents a call to "test the spirits," as well as a caution that in doing so our criteria and goals be biblical. In this regard we have noted that although Paul is "waging war" against his opponents, he nowhere addresses his adversaries directly. Paul's primary interest is not the defeat of his enemies but the renewal of the Corinthians (10:8). He knows that only if they come to a clear understanding of the issues at stake for themselves will they be able to maintain their faith (10:15). More than merely defeating his opponents, Paul wants to fortify the Corinthians for the future by teaching them the spiritual discernment they need in order to remain faithful to the gospel (see again the broad terms in which he defends his ministry in 10:3–6). As Barnett has observed, "Typical of his pastoral method, Paul has kept this issue and the critics in question separate within the letter (vv. 1–2) in order that he may reflect theologically upon it for the sake of his readers."[26]

Paul is a great model here as we confront conflicts and theological challenges today. Like the apostle, we too must examine our motives and strategy in order to maintain the proper focus for our apologetics: Are they aimed at

---

26. Barnett, *Second Corinthians*, 462.

strengthening the church for her mission or merely at scoring points off our opponents for the sake of boosting our own reputations? Paul is concerned for his honor not for his own sake, but for the sake of the Corinthians.

The manner of Paul's warfare. Many scholars suggest that in this passage Paul is parodying the practice of self-praise that was common among the teachers and Sophists of his day. In pointing to the stark change in tone between chapters 1–9 and 10–13, they suggest that it corresponds to common rhetorical conventions of the period, in which a strong emotional appeal was needed near the end of a speech in order to win one's audience.[27] As an example, in Demosthenes's *De Corona* 278 we read that vehemence is required when adversaries beset one's people. "It was likewise rhetorically obligatory for Paul to resort to *pathos*, irony, invective, sarcasm, parody, and the like if he really believed that his converts were endangered by adversaries."[28] And Paul does so at the end of his letter since this is the "propitious moment" in which to influence the Corinthians by leaving a strong and lasting emotional appeal.[29] Witherington even goes so far as to declare that "the key to grasping the real character of the argument is recognizing Paul's anti-Sophistic approach to self-praise."[30]

Certainly, both Paul's approach and content have nothing in common with such Sophistic self-praise. It is also probable that part of the reason the Corinthians have fallen so easily for the theology and practice of Paul's opponents is that their message feeds into the health and wealth, entertainment mentality of Greco-Roman culture.[31] It is by no means clear, however, that Paul's opponents have self-consciously availed themselves of the Sophistic criteria of evaluating his presence and oratory. Nor can it be demonstrated that he is offering a philosophical critique of the Sophist mentality by intentionally employing the rhetorical practices of his day. His change in tone in chapters 10–13 may simply be the result of theological "common sense," since Paul realizes the gravity of the situation. His deep emotion reflects his awareness that time is running out for the rebellious and that this is his last opportunity to reach them for Christ.

In writing chapters 10–13, Paul is not calmly employing rhetorical strategies as a literary artifice, but reacting in the only way that would be natural,

---

27. See now Ben Witherington III, *Conflict and Community in Corinth: A Socio-Rhetorical Commentary on 1 and 2 Corinthians* (Grand Rapids: Eerdmans, 1995), 431, relying on work of Danker, and Young and Ford.

28. Ibid., 431.

29. Ibid.

30. Ibid., 434.

31. See the summary of Savage's cultural analysis in the Bridging Contexts section of 4:1–18.

given his prophetic desire to win back his readers. The pathos of his argument is not the result of consciously following the rules of rhetoric, his knowledge of which is itself questionable.[32] It comes from the passion of his heart.

In fact, Weima rightly emphasizes that "even if Paul did know or had been trained in ancient rhetoric, there is evidence that he deliberately chose not to engage in such oratory practices."[33] Indeed, as 10:10 makes clear, the unprofessional manner of Paul's public presentation, compared to the popular philosophers and entertainers of his day, has not been lost on his opponents (cf. 11:6 for Paul's acknowledgment that he is untrained in professional rhetoric). Finally, since there is no evidence that the rules of public rhetoric were ever intended to be applied to literary works in the first place,[34] it is unlikely that what Paul disavows in person he then uses in his letters. What makes Paul's letters "weighty and forceful" is not their rhetorical character but their content.

Because Paul assumes that everyone boasts in something, the real debate between him and his opponents is not one of style but of substance. Paul is passionate in this passage not simply because he is concerned about how his opponents carry themselves, but because he realizes that the gospel is at stake. The issue is not simply a philosophical debate over which way of life and ministry best corresponds to the gospel—that is, Paul's weakness and lack of oratorical performance or his opponents' image of strength and captivating public presentations. The fight is over the gospel itself.

The fundamental question, in other words, is whether the Spirit is being manifested in Paul's apostolic ministry. His opponents insist that Paul's physical weakness and lack of flashy rhetorical techniques are signs that he lacks the presence of the Spirit. Paul's "weighty" letters of warning are an attempt

---

32. For a helpful summary and critique of the method of analyzing Paul's letters according to the ancient rules of rhetoric, see Jeffrey A. D. Weima, "What Does Aristotle Have to Do with Paul? An Evaluation of Rhetorical Criticism," *CTJ* 32 (1997): 458–68. As Weima concludes, "There is no concrete evidence that Paul knew or was ever trained in ancient rhetoric" (464).

33. Ibid., 465. For the textual support for this assertion, see again 1 Cor. 1:17; 2:1–5, 13.

34. Weima (ibid., 463–64) points out that neither the relevant epistolary handbooks nor the rhetorical handbooks of Paul's day advocate applying the rules of oral discourse to written discourse. In fact, in the rhetorical handbooks, letters are "virtually always" contrasted to oratory; to interpret Paul's letters as if they were speeches is therefore to mix genres. Weima thus concludes (464) that "the evidence of both the epistolary handbooks and the rhetorical handbooks seriously calls into question the common practice of using the ancient Greco-Roman rules of rhetoric as a key to interpret Paul's letters. As Traugott Holtz observes, 'The application of rhetorical theory to epistolary literature stands methodologically on uncertain feet.'"

to compensate for his lack of personal strength (10:2, 10). For them, the power of the Spirit should be seen in the power of the person. For Paul, his weakness and refusal to employ contemporary methods of entertainment are the very means by which God makes known the power of the Spirit through the gospel.

How then does Paul "demolish arguments and every pretension" and "take captive every thought to make it obedient to Christ"? By proclaiming the gospel of the crucified and risen Christ and by embodying it in his own life of voluntary suffering on behalf of God's people. One does not "demolish arguments" and "take thoughts captive" by majoring in philosophy per se, though this may be helpful as a way to delineate carefully where the battle lines are currently being drawn. Rather, one does so by getting a clear vision of who Christ is and what he has done on the cross in order that one's own life may reflect Christ's character in word and deed (cf. 5:14–15). It is Paul's suffering in the Spirit and his proclamation of Jesus as Lord that forms his counterattack against his opponents, recognizing that God himself must win the battle (cf. 2:14–17; 4:1–6; 6:7; 7:2–3). The battle in 10:1–5 is not intellectual, but spiritual, and the power of the Spirit is seen in the transformed lives of God's people (3:18; 5:17; 6:14–7:1; 7:8–13; chs. 8–9).

The weapons of Paul's attack. At the time of 2 Corinthians, however, it is still simply Paul's word against theirs. Hence, the foundation to Paul's apologetic is his understanding of what constitutes a divine commendation (10:12–18; cf. 3:1–3), not the style in which he writes. The ultimate weapon of his warfare is not to compare personalities or passions, expertise or experiences, but to challenge the Corinthians to examine the work of God in *history*, both in regard to Christ as the Messiah, who inaugurates the new covenant, and to Paul as his minister.

Thus, the theme of "self-commendation" versus "commendation of oneself" because of "God's commendation" is in many ways the heart of Paul's apologetic throughout 2 Corinthians (cf. 3:1; 4:2; 5:12; 6:4; 12:11). For God commends his servants by working in and through their lives in accordance with the claims being made. God commends the claim to be Christian by moving believers to life-changing repentance; God commends those who claim to be apostles in a given place by moving them to establish the church. For this reason, the theme of "commendation" both initiates and concludes Paul's defense of his apostolic ministry in 2:14–6:13 (cf. 3:1; 6:4), as well as appears at the two strategic transitions within this section (cf. 4:2; 5:11–12). In the same way, the theme of self-commendation frames chapters 10–13, where it both introduces and concludes the "fool's speech" of 11:1–12:10 (10:12–18 and 12:11).

We have also seen an apparent inconsistency in Paul's development of this theme. In 3:1–3 and 5:12 Paul denies that he is engaging in self-commendation, only to commend himself in 4:2 and 6:4–10. This same apparent conflict exists between Paul's criticism of his opponents' self-commendation in 10:12–18 and his own commendation of himself in 11:1–12:10. Indeed, this letter as a whole functions in part as Paul's commendation of himself. How then can we reconcile the apparent contradiction in Paul's apologetic between what he asserts and what he denies?

Given the two distinct ways in which Paul himself uses the theme of self-commendation, the conflict between him and his opponents cannot simply have surrounded who in fact has commended themselves. It is not as if the mere practice of commending oneself is wrong in and of itself, always being an expression of pride or boasting in the negative sense. If it were, then Paul becomes his own worst enemy. Nor can the difference between Paul's self-commendation and that of his opponents be their distinctive content (e.g., the opponents' power versus Paul's weakness). In addition to boasting in his weakness, Paul has also pointed to the purity of his motives and actions (1:12; 4:2; 6:12; 7:2), his authority and power (10:7–11), his preaching free of charge (2:17; 11:10), and his signs and wonders (12:11–12). Rather, the distinction between Paul's commendation of himself and his opponents' self-commendation is expressed in 10:18: Only the one whom the Lord commends is approved in his claims. Paul's boast concerning his authority is merely the counterpart to the Lord's commendation on which it rests.

Thus, the crucial question in 10:12–18 is what constitutes a divine commendation. The problem with Paul's opponents has been their attempt to commend themselves without the divinely granted "canon" or attestation to support it. They have claimed authority over the Corinthians without God's "stamp of approval" for such a boast. Instead, they have introduced irrelevant achievements and abilities to support their claims. In contrast, when Paul points to his bringing the gospel to Corinth, he is following the Old Testament admonition to boast in the Lord, since God is the one who enabled and determined that he would have this success (10:13). To "boast in the Lord" or to engage in a proper "commendation of oneself" is not to cease from boasting, as is commonly argued, but to boast only in what God himself has actually accomplished in one's own life as it relates to what is being claimed.[35]

---

35. For the demonstration of this principle in regard to the Corinthians, see 7:9–12, where the Corinthians have rightly commended themselves by virtue of their divinely enabled repentance and punishment of the offender (cf. 2:5–11).

Based on the principle of 10:18, Paul's seemingly contradictory statements concerning commendation can now be brought together. In 3:1, Paul denies that he is presenting a *self*-commendation or that he needs the corroboratory evidence of letters of recommendation, since he can point to his suffering (2:14–17) and to his mediation of the Spirit (3:2–3) as the Lord's commendation of his ministry (3:4–6). In 5:12, Paul denies that by seeking the Corinthians' approval he is engaging in a *self*-commendation, since his own work in the Lord testifies to the fact that he has been called by God and is pleasing to him (cf. 5:9, 11).

Yet in 4:2 and 6:4–10 Paul does commend himself by pointing to the kinds of behavior and results that are evidence of God's attestation of his apostolic ministry (6:4) and message (4:2) *in general*. In the same way, in 10:12–18 he points to the evidence that confirms his specific claim to apostolic authority *in Corinth*. Moreover, we have seen that Paul marks this distinction between a legitimate and illegitimate "commendation" linguistically. Whenever the commendation in view is negative, he front-loads the reflexive pronoun (cf. *heauton synistanein* in 3:1; 5:12; 10:12, 18); whenever it is positive, he places it behind the verb (cf. *synistanein heauton* in 4:2; 6:4; 7:11; see too 12:11). In our own discussion, we have followed this convention by distinguishing between a negative "*self*-commendation" and the positive "commendation *of oneself*."

The culmination of the theme of commendation in 10:1–18 provides a strong impetus to rethink the cleavage often posited between justification by faith and Paul's insistence that judgment is by works. What holds true for Paul as an apostle holds true for all Christians. Paul consistently argues from the external evidence of the Spirit in the life of the believer to the genuineness of one's standing before God, just as he argues here from the external evidence of his apostolic work in Corinth to the legitimacy of his authority over that church (cf., e.g., Rom. 1:5; 8:3f.; 15:18; Gal. 5:16–26; 1 Thess. 1:3–6; Phil. 1:6, 11; 2:12–13; see comments on 2 Cor. 13:5).

In Paul's thinking, we will be judged according to our deeds, since they are the expression of our faith and the fruit of the Spirit in our lives (5:10; cf. Rom. 2:6–13, 25–29; 1 Cor. 4:3–5; Gal. 6:4–5). From our perspective, faith in God's promises unfolds in obedience to God's commands; from God's perspective, the pouring out of his Spirit gives birth to a new way of life. For this all-important reason, inasmuch as our boasting in our works is, at every point, a boast in the *Lord*, such an emphasis never degenerates into a boasting in oneself. There is no "easy believism" for Paul, just as there is no works-righteousness. In order to be valid, sure signs of God's transforming work in our lives must match our boasting in the Lord. At the same time, our commendation from the Lord must never become a *self*-commendation.

PAUL'S FIGHT TO "take captive every thought ... to Christ" (10:5), which epitomizes this chapter, is often misapplied in our contemporary context. The issue in view is not Paul's private struggle with his own "thought life," as important as it is to make sure that we are thinking in ways that honor Christ. Paul is not striving to control his worry or lust or arrogance or tempting thoughts. Nor is it a criticism of philosophy or of intellectual pursuits as such, though it does contain an implied warning that all truth-claims must be subjected to the constraints of the gospel and its worldview.

Rather, Paul's concern in 10:1–18 is with a public dispute over the content of the gospel and the true nature of God's commendation of those who preach it. His self-defense is not the expression of a hurt ego, but the necessary response against those who deny the gospel by their lifestyles and teaching. To take captive every thought to Christ is to evaluate every teaching concerning who Jesus is and what it means to follow him in order to ensure that whatever is said and thought conforms to the character and purposes of Christ himself.

The need for apologetics and church discipline. As a continuation of Paul's own "warfare," this passage calls us to engage in apologetics and church discipline whenever the gospel is being denied or diluted. Paul's affirmation that his future ministry was linked to the spiritual growth of those who under his authority had already confessed Christ (10:6, 15) is a sober reminder that quality, not quantity, reigns supreme in the ministry of the gospel.

In a recent Barna Research Group opinion poll, 82 percent of Americans say they consider themselves to be Christians, while 50 percent of those who say they are Christians describe themselves as "absolutely committed to the Christian faith."[36] One wonders what the noun "Christian" means in contemporary American English. Paul's apologetic in his passage reminds us that genuine salvation is marked by perseverance in the truth. He makes it clear that those who confessed Christ in the past but now persist in rejecting Paul's gospel in word or deed stand under the judgment of God. Today we must fight again for the recognition that a growing faith, not a past decision, is the sign of the presence and power of the Spirit.

Paul's argument also makes clear that the way to combat the denial of the gospel (10:5) and to strengthen the faith of believers (10:15) is to present the basis of apostolic authority (10:7–11) and its divinely granted commendation (10:12–18). In confronting those who opposed him, Paul's urgent appeal

---

36. As reported in *Viewpoint* 2 (1988): 9.

(10:1–6) was therefore based on the obvious fact of his apostolic authority (10:7–11) and the undeniable evidence of God's approval (10:12–18). As a result, Paul's "manner" and "weapons of warfare" present us with our own need to strengthen the foundation of scriptural authority (10:8, 13–15) and to seek divine approval, not in self-authenticating claims to be spiritual, but in lives of integrity that attest to God's power (10:17–18). Both are imperative for the life of God's people.

The need for spiritual substance over style. In defending himself, Paul does not argue from style, one way or the other, to substance. His argument is not, "I am weak and unimpressive in speech, *therefore* I am legitimate." Paul's concern is not to pit one way of acting publicly against another, as if the goal were simply to counter the image of the Sophists, who emphasized personal persona, self-praise, and eloquence. Paul is not engaged here in the common dispute of his day over the public appearance of the wise, though he certainly believed that the pouring out of the Spirit through his ministry was inextricably tied to his calling to suffer as an apostle (cf. 2:14; 4:7–12; 6:3–10).

Rather, Paul argues from substance to style: "God has called me (10:8) and commended me in Corinth (10:13–14); *therefore*, my weakness and contemptible speech are legitimate expressions of my apostleship, of the validity of my message, and of my authority in Corinth." In the end, his argument for legitimacy is not rhetorical, philosophical, or cultural, but evidential. To reduce his argument to a debate over the proper public manner of a minister misses the force of his reference to his own call as a Christian and to the evidence of the Corinthians themselves. Paul's point is that *his* legitimacy is based on *God's* work in Christ and through his own ministry.

If we miss this all-important emphasis on God as the one who commends his people, we will end up evaluating ministries and ministers based on what *we* think is an effective style and appropriate manner. For most, this will mean choosing leaders who have a forceful public personality and an "uplifting message," since they will no doubt often have a more popular ministry. After all, the assumption is that if God's Spirit is powerfully at work among his people, the church will "grow" numerically. Hence, we assume that those churches that draw a big crowd must, by definition, have a God-ordained ministry. The bigger the church, the bigger the blessing. If a church is growing numerically, the pastor must be doing something *right*. It is difficult for us to keep in view that Paul's opponents, with their compromised gospel, were very appealing because of their personal strength and powerful public speaking.

For others, however, applying Paul's "warfare" metaphor will mean creating a ministry style that almost purposely drives people away. Here the assumption is that, given the power and pervasiveness of sin, all genuine ministries will grow slowly. Those in this camp are convinced that the

remnant of those who truly believe is always small. Big churches, by definition, are therefore superficial, not spiritual. Only a compromised gospel can
draw a crowd. After all, for a church to be large it must have capitulated to
the prevailing culture. Thus, if a church is growing numerically in dramatic
ways, it must be doing something *wrong*. Yet this passage reveals not only
God's work in commending his people, but also Paul's passion for reaching
the lost, his expectation for the spiritual growth of the church, and his plan
for the expansion of his apostolic ministry. Precisely because God is at work,
Paul never assumes that "enough" people have been saved or that they have
already grown "enough" in their faith.

In contrast to both of these approaches, Paul's emphasis is that, although
he is doing the fighting (10:1–6), *God* is the one who calls his people and
causes their growth (10:17). Our responsibility is not to decide what we can
do to "grow the church," but to be faithful to God (10:5), to be passionate
for the effective proclamation of the gospel (10:8, 15), and to be utterly
dependent on God's commendation of our work through his Spirit (10:18).
In short, our job is to "boast in the Lord" (10:17). God's sovereign will, not
our techniques, determines the number of God's people in a given place,
large or small.

Though many of the Corinthians had come to faith when Paul founded
the church in Corinth, so that he was ready to move on, God commanded
him to keep on speaking and promised him the protection needed to do so
because *God* had "many [more] people in this city" (Acts 18:9–10). As a
result, Paul stayed for a year and a half. In contrast, the Bereans were more
receptive than the Thessalonians (17:11–12), in Athens only a few believed
Paul's message (17:34), and in Ephesus, when the Ephesians asked Paul to
remain longer, Paul declined, saying, "I will come back if it is God's will"
(18:21). These examples illustrate that the mark of God's blessing is the genuine conversion (2 Cor. 10:13–14) and sustained spiritual growth (10:15) of
God's people, not the size or length of one's ministry. Whatever the Corinthians may have thought about "ministry styles" from their culture, Paul's point
is that *God* has commended him through their own conversion. His boast is
in God as the source of all things. Any "gospel" that contradicts this boast
must be called into question.

Rather than arguing back from the "popularity" or "purity" of our style to
the credibility of our ministry, we must be careful to adduce the only evidence
that counts: Does the authentic work of the Spirit in the conversion (10:13–
14) and growing faithfulness (10:15) of God's people attend our gospel and
way of life? This will demand discernment as we sort out the distinction
between differing, but equally God-honoring styles of ministry on the one
hand, and different gospels on the other. This will not always be easy, but it

is necessary nonetheless. Today, as in Paul's day, the stakes are high. The issue in Corinth was not merely a disagreement over legitimate cultural preferences. The Corinthians were being seduced, not realizing that the opponents' difference in style also revealed a "different gospel" (cf. 11:4, 6).

The need for the proclamation of the gospel. Regaining Paul's confidence that God is the Lord of his church is crucial for evaluating ministries in our day and age. It is equally important that we regain Paul's conviction that God does his sovereign work *through his people*. As in Paul's day, what is needed today are those who preach the gospel out of lives shaped by its truth and commended by God's power (cf. 10:4–5). On the one hand, this will mean fighting against the temptation to become what Hauerwas and Willimon call "an accommodationist church." Such a church, "so intent on running errands for the world," actually gives the world

> less and less in which to disbelieve. Atheism slips into the church where God really does not matter, as we go about building bigger and better congregations (church administration), confirming people's self-esteem (worship), enabling people to adjust to their anxieties brought on by their materialism (pastoral care), and making Christ a worthy subject for poetic reflection (preaching). At every turn the church must ask itself, Does it really make any difference, in our life together, in what we do, that in Jesus Christ God is reconciling the world to himself? As anybody knows, such a question is hard to keep before us. Atheism is the air we breathe.[37]

Paul's insistence that God does not approve those who commend themselves by their own achievements, but only those whom he himself commends through the active display of his own power, condemns such atheism.

The need for a truth-saturated, life-embodied proclamation of the gospel will also mean not falling into the trap of becoming a "ghetto church." Rather than giving the world little to disbelieve, such a church, though priding itself on being filled with faith, takes away the opportunity for others to believe at all. Instead of "running errands" for the world, this church withdraws from it. Instead of becoming atheistic, the ghetto church seeks to contain God within its own walls, like the territorial gods of the ancient world. Instead of trusting God to work through their message and manner of life as the instruments of his grace, citizens of the ghetto act as if God's election of his people means that he will "zap" their hearts while they sit and watch behind the barriers of their isolated subculture. They pat themselves on the back for

---

37. Stanley Hauerwas and William H. Willimon, *Resident Aliens, Life in the Christian Colony*, 94–95.

their faithfulness, all the while being dangerously content with their lack of evangelism, since they live with the allusion that God acts sovereignly in the world apart from his people.

Those in the ghetto rightly fear slipping into the practical and triumphant atheism of the accommodationist, who manufactures "belief" by programs. But if the accommodationist fears the world too little, the ghetto-dweller fears the world too much. Within the ghetto, the courage to break out ebbs away. Instead, their fear leads to a self-justifying quietism that acts as if God's sovereign grace negates the call to share the gospel with the world in ways it can understand, not to mention the need to wage war on behalf of those who already confess Christ. The ghetto mentality cannot accept the fact that in 10:15–16 Paul is anticipating the growth and purification of a church still partly in rebellion against him, and that it will come about precisely through his own teaching. Nor does it feel Paul's passion to establish the church further through his preaching of the gospel to complete strangers.

On the one extreme, the accommodationist church is characterized by a free-will theology gone to seed in its attempt to win others by meeting their "felt needs." On the other extreme, the ghetto church is characterized by a passive "hyper-Calvinism" (even though they may not be Calvinistic at all) that has lost sight of the desperate need for spiritual warfare (10:3–6) and for preaching the gospel throughout the world (10:15–16). If the accommodationist church tries to offer what it does not have by taking the place of God, the ghetto church refuses to offer what it possesses by not taking its place as God's people. Following Paul, our challenge (and it is not an easy one) is to remain true to the gospel as the power of God, while at the same time passionately waging war as his soldiers on behalf of the gospel in order to protect the church and reach the world.

Appendix

Some commentators see the demarcation of ministries in Galatians 2:7–10 to be behind Paul's argument in 2 Corinthians 10:13–16. They argue that the "canon" in view is the "field" of Gentiles over against Jews, so that the problem in Corinth is that Paul's Jewish opponents have trespassed into his Gentile region. But there is no mention of the "canon" of being a "founding father" in Galatians 2 or of the accord between Paul and the pillar apostles in 2 Corinthians 10. The demarcation in Galatians 2:7–10 is not geographical, but ethnic, while the "field" in 2 Corinthians 10:13–16 is determined by who plants the church, not by the location or ethnic distribution in the church. It is not as if Paul had to count noses to see who could minister in a given congregation.

Furthermore, even in predominantly Gentile regions, Paul first goes to synagogues and to the Jews, while his churches typically consist of both Jews and Gentiles (see Acts 18:1–8, 18 for this practice and for the mixed nature of Corinthian church).

Thus, the two passages are not dealing with the same issue: Galatians 2:7–10 concerns respective spheres of ministry, whereas 2 Corinthians 10:13–16 concerns apostolic authority in a particular local church. In line with this latter "measure" of authority, Paul does not attempt to establish his own church base in Rome, even though it is the capital of the Gentile world (Rom. 15:20–21). Moreover, the problem in 2 Corinthians 10–13 is not just the arrival of Paul's opponents, but their arrival with a false gospel (11:4), so that Paul would not want them ministering among the Jews either. The issue is their building on Paul's foundation with a different gospel, that is, their claiming apostolic authority to establish a distinct message. In contrast, Paul did not object to Peter and Apollos working in Corinth, only to the way in which the Corinthians used their work to create divisions within the church (cf. 1 Cor. 1:12–13; 3:4–9).

More recently, James Scott has argued extensively that 2 Corinthians 10:13–16 reflects Paul's Jewish mindset concerning the Corinthian region as part of the "nations" outlined in the "Table of Nations" from Genesis 10 (cf. 1 Chron. 1:1–2:2; Ezek. 27; 38–39; Dan. 11; Isa. 66:18–20). Based on this view of the world, Paul defends his apostolic right to a territorial jurisdiction over the Corinthians, since, as an apostle to the Gentiles, Paul had been called to these nations, a calling confirmed at the apostolic council.[38]

In Scott's view, Galatians 2:7–9 thus reflects the council's decision that the apostles were to observe the territorial jurisdictions that are mapped out according to the three sons of Noah in Genesis 10. It was this "Table of Nations" that provided Israel's understanding of her place as central among the nations, both now and in the eschaton. Hence, in Scott's reading, all the churches of Paul's jurisdiction, whether founded by him or not, stand under his authority, which is declared in Romans 1:5–6. Specifically, according to this "Table of Nations" tradition, "the Corinthian church falls within the swath of (Japhethite) territory from Cilicia to Spain that has been divinely allotted to Paul."[39]

---

38. Scott, *2 Corinthians*, 8–9, 206–7, based on his extensive work, *Paul and the Nations: The Old Testament and Jewish Background of Paul's Mission to the Nations with Special Reference to the Destination of Galatians* (Tübingen: J.C.B. Mohr [Paul Siebeck], 1995). For a similar view, see Martin, *2 Corinthians*, 316–17.

39. Scott, *2 Corinthians*, 206.

As such, Corinth was in the midpoint of Paul's westerly expanding mission (cf. Rom. 15:19). As a result, Paul's opponents were overstepping the limits of their commission geographically and nationally by usurping Paul's God-given apostolic territory.

Of course, it is a question of much debate whether Galatians 2:7–10 reflects Acts 10 or an earlier meeting between the apostles. Moreover, in Galatians 2:9 it is God's grace, not the pillar apostles, that gives Paul his ministry and jurisdiction. The specific content of his commission is not determined by their understanding of the world, but by the limits of God's grace in Paul's life as seen in the churches he establishes.

The primary problem with this territorial view, therefore, is that in 2 Corinthians 10:13–14 Paul likewise points explicitly to his having reached Corinth with the gospel as the basis for his divinely granted authority, not a prior geographical distribution that was granted by the Jerusalem council. Paul too would have been overreaching his apostolic authority in Corinth if he had not founded the church there. His sphere grows by virtue of the fact that his ministry is blessed by the pouring out of the Spirit as manifested in the establishment and solidification of a church, not by virtue of a static geographical demarcation. Galatians 2:7–10 is primarily about the grace of God among Jews and Gentiles, not geography.

2 Corinthians 11:1–33

I HOPE YOU will put up with a little of my foolishness; but you are already doing that. ²I am jealous for you with a godly jealousy. I promised you to one husband, to Christ, so that I might present you as a pure virgin to him. ³But I am afraid that just as Eve was deceived by the serpent's cunning, your minds may somehow be led astray from your sincere and pure devotion to Christ. ⁴For if someone comes to you and preaches a Jesus other than the Jesus we preached, or if you receive a different spirit from the one you received, or a different gospel from the one you accepted, you put up with it easily enough. ⁵But I do not think I am in the least inferior to those "super-apostles." ⁶I may not be a trained speaker, but I do have knowledge. We have made this perfectly clear to you in every way.

⁷Was it a sin for me to lower myself in order to elevate you by preaching the gospel of God to you free of charge? ⁸I robbed other churches by receiving support from them so as to serve you. ⁹And when I was with you and needed something, I was not a burden to anyone, for the brothers who came from Macedonia supplied what I needed. I have kept myself from being a burden to you in any way, and will continue to do so. ¹⁰As surely as the truth of Christ is in me, nobody in the regions of Achaia will stop this boasting of mine. ¹¹Why? Because I do not love you? God knows I do! ¹²And I will keep on doing what I am doing in order to cut the ground from under those who want an opportunity to be considered equal with us in the things they boast about.

¹³For such men are false apostles, deceitful workmen, masquerading as apostles of Christ. ¹⁴And no wonder, for Satan himself masquerades as an angel of light. ¹⁵It is not surprising, then, if his servants masquerade as servants of righteousness. Their end will be what their actions deserve.

¹⁶I repeat: Let no one take me for a fool. But if you do, then receive me just as you would a fool, so that I may do a little boasting. ¹⁷In this self-confident boasting I am not talking as the Lord would, but as a fool. ¹⁸Since many are boasting in the way the world does, I too will boast. ¹⁹You gladly put up with

fools since you are so wise! [20]In fact, you even put up with anyone who enslaves you or exploits you or takes advantage of
you or pushes himself forward or slaps you in the face. [21]To my
shame I admit that we were too weak for that!

What anyone else dares to boast about—I am speaking as
a fool—I also dare to boast about. [22]Are they Hebrews? So
am I. Are they Israelites? So am I. Are they Abraham's descendants? So am I. [23]Are they servants of Christ? (I am out of my
mind to talk like this.) I am more. I have worked much harder,
been in prison more frequently, been flogged more severely,
and been exposed to death again and again. [24]Five times I
received from the Jews the forty lashes minus one. [25]Three
times I was beaten with rods, once I was stoned, three times I
was shipwrecked, I spent a night and a day in the open sea, [26]I
have been constantly on the move. I have been in danger from
rivers, in danger from bandits, in danger from my own coun-
trymen, in danger from Gentiles; in danger in the city, in dan-
ger in the country, in danger at sea; and in danger from false
brothers. [27]I have labored and toiled and have often gone
without sleep; I have known hunger and thirst and have often
gone without food; I have been cold and naked. [28]Besides
everything else, I face daily the pressure of my concern for all
the churches. [29]Who is weak, and I do not feel weak? Who is
led into sin, and I do not inwardly burn?

[30]If I must boast, I will boast of the things that show my
weakness. [31]The God and Father of the Lord Jesus, who is to
be praised forever, knows that I am not lying. [32]In Damascus
the governor under King Aretas had the city of the Dama-
scenes guarded in order to arrest me. [33]But I was lowered in a
basket from a window in the wall and slipped through his
hands.

THE CENTRAL QUESTION driving this complex section is what constitutes valid evidence for establishing a servant of Christ. Since Paul answers
this question by taking on the persona of a fool
(cf. 11:1; 12:11), all of 11:1–12:13 is often referred to as Paul's "Fool's Speech."
Actually, however, the speech itself occupies only part of 11:21b–12:10 (cf.
the other references to being "foolish" and a "fool" in 11:16, 17, 19; 12:6).
Moreover, many commentators consider Paul's "foolishness" to be a literary

or rhetorical device designed to establish his own legitimacy as a servant of Christ by mocking or parodying the boasting of his opponents.

Paul certainly uses many rhetorical devices in this passage (e.g., irony, sarcasm, plays on words, and parodies). Yet there is no evidence that he crafted his argument according to a distinct genre or literary form, whether from among those employed in the debates between the philosophers and the Sophists or from the arsenal of professional oratory.[1] Paul himself denies that he uses those kinds of technical, academic approaches in his ministry (cf. 11:6; cf. 1 Cor. 2:1–5). Rather than trying to categorize the type of rhetorical speech Paul employed, the most fruitful approach to this passage is to trace the flow of Paul's argument.

Most commentators argue that Paul's "foolishness" consists in his boasting in and of itself. In contrast, we will argue that Paul's "foolishness" in 11:1–12:13 consists *only* in his being forced to boast in his "strength," which, after preparing his readers at length for such a ridiculous act, he nevertheless does in 11:21b–23b and 12:1–4. But he does so reluctantly and in a manner as curtailed and oblique as possible. Furthermore, the reason Paul considers such boasting to be foolish is not because he is thinking of the role of the fool in Greek comedy, Stoicism, or professional rhetoric. Rather, he has in view the picture of the fool portrayed in Jewish wisdom tradition, who refuses to acknowledge or praise God, and the false boasting of the arrogant, which is condemned by the prophets as an affront to God's glory.[2]

Consequently, Paul's criterion for determining what is "foolish" is not Greek philosophy or the theater, but "not talking as the Lord would" (11:17; lit., "not according to the Lord") and instead "in the way the world does" (11:18; lit., "according to the flesh"). In other words, foolish boasting does not conform to the principle established in Jeremiah 9:23–24, as already

---

1. On the question of Paul's use of formal rhetoric, see again Jeffrey A. D. Weima, "What Does Aristotle Have to Do with Paul?" 458–68. See too Paul Barnett, *The Second Epistle to the Corinthians*, 494, who rightly argues that this passage is an ironic parody of the self-praise of Paul's opponents, though Paul is not consciously following the specific forms of parody or the catalogues of suffering found in the Cynic-Stoic tradition. Indeed, as Barnett, 495, observes, boasting in weakness "appears to be without literary precedent."

2. For the "fool" in the wisdom tradition, see Job 1:22; 2:10; Ps. 14:1; 53:1–2; 74:18, 22; 92:6; 94:8; Prov. 9:13–18; 19:3; 27:1; Isa. 32:5–6; Sir. 9:16; 11:4; Wisd. Sol. 1:16–2:20. For the false boasting of the arrogant, cf. Jer. 9:23–24 with 2 Cor. 10:17–18; also 1 Sam. 2:3, 10; Ps. 74:4; Judith 7:2. For the development of this backdrop to Paul's argument, see Ulrich Heckel, *Kraft in Schwachheit: Untersuchungen zu 2.Kor 10–13*, 144–214. Heckel demonstrates that the Hellenistic backdrop merely illuminates the general rejection of self-praise in the ancient world that is also common in the Scriptures and Judaism. But it cannot explain Paul's positive boasting in God's glory in response to the inappropriate boasting of his opponents (cf. Deut. 10:21; 1 Chron. 16:35; 29:13; Ps. 5:12; 32:11; 106:47; 149:5; Jer. 17:14).

applied to Paul's opponents in 2 Corinthians 10:17–18. Thus, the boasting in 11:21b–23a and 12:1–4 is foolish because it focuses on Paul's human distinctives and private spiritual experiences instead of calling attention to the Lord as the giver of all things in Christ (cf. 1 Cor. 1:26–31).[3]

The rest of Paul's boasting, however, is focused on his "weakness," which is *not* the act of a fool but an essential aspect of his legitimate apology for being an apostle (11:23–33). As we will see in the next chapter, Paul's boasting in his weakness is also the appropriate means for glorifying God's grace and power in his ministry (12:5–10). So if forced to boast about himself at all, Paul will do so concerning his weakness (cf. 11:30; 12:5, 9). Thus, 11:23–33 and 12:5–10 are part of Paul's *positive* self-commendation as seen earlier in 1:3–11; 2:14–17; 4:7–12; 6:3–10.

Although most commentators take all of 11:21b–12:10 as Paul's playing the fool, it is crucial for understanding his argument to recognize that his foolishness is identified only with boasting in what his *opponents* boast in (i.e., their Jewish pedigree in 11:21b–23b and their visions and revelations in 12:1–4). The issue is the object of one's boast, not the act of boasting itself (cf. 10:12–18).[4] Indeed, it is Paul's boasting in his weakness, not boasting per se, that unmasks his opponents' foolishness and falsity.[5]

There is, therefore, a *double* irony in this passage. On the one hand, Paul considers it foolish to boast in the very things his opponents think are appro-

---

3. The importance of 11:17–18 to Paul's argument is highlighted by Heckel, *Kraft*, 195, 198–202. But like many commentators, Heckel fails to make a clear distinction between Paul's foolish boast in his Jewish distinctives and his legitimate boast in his weakness. Heckel therefore concludes that *all* of Paul's boasting in 11:21–12:10 is both not according to the Lord and *at the same time* according to the Lord. Thus in the end, Paul is really not a fool when he boasts, even in his Jewish distinctives, which is the opposite of what Paul himself says.

4. This is contrary to those who, like Jan Lambrecht, S. J., "Strength in Weakness: A Reply to Scott B. Andrews' Exegesis of 2 Cor 11.23b–33," *NTS* 43 (1997): 285–90, argue (289) that "although all boasting is foolish and dangerous, there are degrees." According to Lambrecht's view, boasting in one's Jewish and Christian titles in 11:22–23 is acting "according to the flesh" and is the most dangerous, boasting in one's "utter weakness," as in 11:32–33, is less foolish and dangerous, while boasting in one's hardships and labors is in the middle. But there is no indication of such a gradation in Paul's catalogues, only the distinction between weakness and strength. Moreover, since Paul's boast in his weakness reveals the power of Christ, there can be nothing foolish or dangerous in this, since it fulfills the principle of 10:18.

5. Contra those who, like Barnett, *Second Corinthians*, 534, see Paul's boasting itself to be his "madness" or "foolishness," "which is the 'foolishness' and 'madness' of Christ himself;" and James M. Scott, *2 Corinthians*, 214: "These boasts are doubly foolish, since boasting itself is foolish, and, by the opponents' standards, suffering and weakness do not count as meritorious qualities."

priate. On the other hand, he gladly boasts in those things that his opponents think are foolish. While Paul's opponents point to their ethnic identity and spiritual experiences, Paul lists his sufferings. He calls foolish what they think is wise (i.e., the strength of their Jewish pedigree and revelatory experiences) and boasts freely in what they consider foolish (i.e., his weakness). Read in this light, 11:1–21a is not part of the "fool's speech" itself, but prepares its way by setting out why it has become necessary for Paul to engage in such foolish boasting. Paul then concludes his discourse in 12:11–13 by declaring why such boasting should not have been necessary in the first place.

Here, too, Paul's "thesis statement" in 2:14–3:3 is central for the development of his argument.[6] Earlier, when addressing the repentant majority, Paul moved from a discussion of his weakness in 2:14–17 to his ministry of the Spirit as the founder of the Corinthian church in 3:1–3. Now the order is reversed. In addressing those who still question his apostleship, he moves from the "canon" of his founding function in 10:12–18 to a discussion of his weakness in 11:1–12:13. Paul's purpose in doing so is to offer an extended apologetic for his legitimacy as an apostle by unpacking his earlier affirmation that his "being led to death" is the very means by which God is revealing himself through Paul's ministry (2:14–17; cf. 4:7–12; 6:3–10). His goal is to confront the accusations of the rebellious head-on, both those within the church and his opponents from outside the church; the former he addresses directly, the latter, indirectly.[7]

In 11:23b–33, Paul details the ways in which "the sufferings of Christ flow over" into his own life as a "jar of clay" and "servant of God" (1:5; 4:7; 6:4). He does so in order to tackle the claim that since he lacked commendations from others, he had no recourse but to commend himself (cf. 2:16a; 3:1). According to his opponents, Paul lacked such commendations because he was insufficient for the apostolic ministry, as indicated by his suffering. Just the opposite is true. Paul's suffering *itself*, as the vehicle for the mediation of the Spirit and embodiment of the gospel, is an essential aspect of his letter of recommendation (3:2–6; 4:2; 5:12; 10:18).

Thus, Paul's argument in 11:1–12:13 is not new but builds on the case he has already demonstrated earlier in his letter (cf. 1:8–11 in support of 1:3–7; 4:7–12 in support of 4:1–6; 6:3–10 in support of 5:11–6:2; 10:12–18 in support of 10:1–11). What *is* new is the forceful way in which he now applies this argument to his opponents in order to win back those who are

---

6. So too Barnett, *Second Corinthians*, 534, who rightly argues that Paul's boasting in weakness "must be read with the antitriumphalism of the striking prisoner-of-war image at the beginning of the excursus on new covenant ministry."

7. The Corinthians are addressed directly in 11:4, 6, 7, 8, 9, 11, 19, 20; 12:11, 13; Paul's opponents are addressed indirectly in 11:4–5, 12–15, 20–23a, 26; 12:1, 11.

still under their influence. This is Paul's last attempt to rescue them and hence his most pointed. Indeed, he is so desperate for their sake that he willingly joins his opponents in acting like a fool by boasting in his own Jewish distinctives and heavenly visions (cf. 11:22; 12:1). But before doing so, he must prepare his readers for what he considers to be an act that is so foolish and dishonoring to God that someone would have to be "out of [his] mind to talk like this" (11:23).

The Necessity of Paul's Boast (11:1–21a)

DESPERATE SITUATIONS DEMAND desperate measures. Paul knows it has become necessary to boast like his opponents. Nevertheless, boasting "in the way the world does" (11:18; lit., "according to the flesh") makes him extremely uncomfortable. This is reflected in that his justification for engaging in such foolish boasting lasts from 11:1–21a, while his initial expression of foolish boasting itself occupies only two verses (11:21b–23b)!

The danger in Corinth (11:1–6). In 11:1–4, Paul begins his justification for boasting like a fool by expressing his desire that the Corinthians "put up with" him as he does so for the reasons given in verses 2–4.[8] Since they are already "putting up with" the false apostles so easily, they should bear with Paul too (see vv. 4, 19, 20). This is irony. Paul does not really want them to be so patient with foolishness. But if they can "put up" with the opponents, who are truly fools, then they should be able to "put up" with Paul when he plays the fool.

In mounting this plea, Paul is not expressing jealousy over being rejected. As their "father" in the faith (cf. 1 Cor. 4:15; 2 Cor. 6:13; 12:14), he supports this drastic request by reminding the Corinthians that he has pledged them to be Christ's bride (2 Cor. 11:2). It is Paul's "paternal" relationship to the Corinthians and their ensuing "marriage" to Christ, not their rejection of him in and of itself, which explains his "jealousy." According to Jewish betrothal customs in the New Testament era, a father pledged his daughter to her future husband and was then responsible for her purity until the marriage took place (cf. Deut. 22:13–24). In the same way, Paul is fighting for the faithfulness of the Corinthians because of their current temptation to commit spiritual adultery.

Paul's portrayal of the Corinthians as engaged to Christ in 11:2 recalls the Old Testament representation of Israel as betrothed to God (cf. Isa. 50:1–2;

---

8. In 11:1, the first pronoun (*mou*) is better taken as the object of the verb ("put up with me"), as indicated by its position in the sentence and in accord with this same usage in the next sentence, than as modifying "foolishness" (see the NRSV, contra the NIV). The next sentence is better rendered as a command than as a statement of fact (see the NRSV, contra the NIV). The Corinthians are not bearing with Paul but with the false apostles (cf. 11:4, 20).

54:1–8; 62:5; Jer. 3:1; Ezek. 16:23–33; Hos. 2:19–20; for Israel as God's "bride," cf. Isa. 49:18; 54:5–6; 62:5). Moreover, Paul's use of this metaphor reflects his conviction that the church is now living between her engagement to Christ and the consummation of her "wedding," which is yet to come (cf. 4:14). Hence, Paul is jealous for the Corinthians since he regards them as God's people under the new covenant (cf. the jealousy of God that brings about the final redemption of his people in Isa. 9:7; 26:11; 37:32; 42:13; 59:17; 63:15–16; Joel 2:18; Zech. 1:14; 8:2). As such, unlike Israel's history of adultery toward God (cf. comments on 2 Cor. 3:7–18), they must keep themselves pure for Christ (cf. 5:1–10; 6:16–18). Like God's jealousy for Israel (cf. Ex. 20:5; 34:14; Deut. 4:24; 5:9; 6:15), Paul is jealous with a *"godly jealousy"* for the Corinthians.

In spite of his intervention, however, the apostle fears that those who are still in rebellion may be falling prey to Satan's temptation, even as Eve did in the garden (11:3; cf. 1 Tim. 2:14). Just as the devil deceived Eve by calling into question the sufficiency of God's provisions (Gen. 3:1–13), so too he is seeking to undermine the Corinthians' purity of devotion to Christ by enticing them with "another Jesus," as if the Christ of Paul's gospel were not enough. Satan tempts God's people by presenting a substitute savior: In the garden it was the false promise that they could provide for themselves without consequence; in Corinth it was the promise that the real "Christ" would provide for them health and wealth. Paul's argument thus moves from portraying the rebellious in the church as the counterpart to Israel under the law in verse 2 (i.e., reduplicating the "fall" of Israel; cf. 3:14), to portraying them as the counterpart to Eve at creation in verse 3 (i.e., reproducing the "fall" of humanity; cf. 4:4).

The reference to the Fall reveals just how serious the danger facing the Corinthians really is. It is a warning that, in reality, his opponents are "servants of Satan" who are seeking to destroy the Corinthians' marriage with Christ in the same way that Satan spoiled Eve's relationship with God (cf. 11:14–15).[9] As in the garden, the goal of their deception is to create a new way of thinking among the Corinthians that no longer agrees with God's will.[10] But those who are truly God's people will resist this satanic temptation to idolatry and strife (cf. 2:11; 6:14–7:1; also Rom. 16:17–20). In this way they show themselves to be "new creatures" in Christ, who are being transformed by God's

---

9. So too Ernst Baasland, "Christus und das Verlorene Paradies: *noēma* ein Schlüsselbegriff im 2.Korintherbrief?" *Text and Theology: FS Magne Sæbø*, ed. Arvid Tångberg (Oslo: Verbum, 1994), 67–94 (p. 73).

10. Following Baasland, "Christus," 74. The focus of Paul's argument is thus on Satan's cunning as it is being replicated in his servants in Corinth. For a comparison of Paul's use of Gen. 3 with its development in post-biblical Judaism, see his pp. 82–86.

glory in their midst (2 Cor. 3:18; 5:17). Like Paul, their lives will be characterized by sincerity and purity toward Christ (for sincerity as evidence of the grace of God in one's life, cf. 1:12; 2:17; on purity, cf. 6:6).

The instrument of Satan's deception is the opponents' preaching of another "Jesus," a "different [S]pirit," and "a different gospel" (11:4). Paul's use of the generic singular in 11:4 ("if someone comes") could refer to the leader of the opposition, but it is more likely a collective reference to the opponents as a whole (cf. 3:1; 10:12). There is no consensus among scholars concerning the origin, identity, and theology of these adversaries.[11] The key to this question is not to drive a wedge between "Judaizers" and "pneumatics" within the early church. Instead, the appeal of the Judaizers' demand that the Gentiles keep the old covenant resided in the promise of the Spirit that undergirded it (cf. 3:1–18 with Gal. 3:1–5[12]). Paul's opponents promised more of the Spirit (i.e., health, wealth, and ecstatic experiences) to those who would keep more of the law (i.e., adding the stipulations of the old covenant to those of the new). For, in their view, Jesus suffered in order that we might not have to do so ourselves.

It is therefore important to keep the three issues of 11:4 together. The proper understanding of the mission of Jesus, the proper understanding of the role of the Spirit (not simply a human "spirit," contra the NIV[13]), and the proper understanding of the relationship between the gospel of the new covenant and the role of the old are inextricably linked together. The central question is what Jesus accomplished in his ministry, how one receives and grows in the Spirit as a result, and what the conditions are for belonging fully to the people of God. In short, the issue is "what constitutes a proper manifestation of the Spirit in the ministry of the gospel. A *mistaken* emphasis on the miraculous by these so-called super-apostles (11:5) resulted

---

11. Though there have been many suggested variations, the basic proposals have identified Paul's opponents either as Judaizers or as some kind of pseudo-charismatic pneumatics, whether they be Gnostics, self-styled divine men, or simply a group that emphasized spiritual experiences. For the problems inherent in attempting to reconstruct the identity of Paul's opponents and a solid proposal concerning the method for doing so (i.e., one that is text-based in its starting point and minimalist in its extrapolations), see Jerry L. Sumney, *Identifying Paul's Opponents*, and my review of his work in *JBL* 111 (1992): 347–50. Sumney himself concludes, with Käsemann, that Paul's opponents are some type of pneumatics.

12. Charles H. Cosgrove, *The Cross and the Spirit: A Study in the Argument and Theology of Galatians* (Macon, Ga.: Mercer Univ. Press, 1988), has shown most clearly that the argument with the Judaizers in Galatians revolved around the basis for the reception and continuing experience of the Spirit.

13. The inclusion of "Spirit" between "Jesus" and the "gospel" suggests what is at stake is the faithful witness to the message of salvation; cf. Linda L. Belleville, "Paul's Polemic and Theology of the Spirit in Second Corinthians," *CBQ* 58 (1996): 281–304 (294n.43).

in a construal of the Spirit as a wonder-worker rather than a guarantor of the kerygma."[14]

Whereas Paul preached and embodied the fact that the Spirit of God is experienced in and through the suffering of this age, his opponents maintained that the Spirit of God, if truly present, delivers one from such suffering. For Paul, the cross is still central to the gospel. He carries in his body the *death* of Jesus (cf. 4:7–12). In his opponents' "different gospel," the cross is merely a matter of history, having been replaced by the resurrected Lord.

This may explain Paul's use of "Jesus" in 11:4 without the title "Christ," since the debate in Corinth revolved around different conceptions of what Jesus had in fact accomplished in his earthly ministry as the Messiah. The opponents maintained that Jesus brought the kingdom in its fullness; Paul preached that the kingdom had been inaugurated but is not yet consummated. In the imagery of our text, the opponents claimed to be married to Christ already, whereas Paul saw the church as betrothed but still waiting for her wedding day.

This reading of the conflict between Paul and his opponents is confirmed by his designation of their message as proclaiming a Jesus "other than the Jesus we preached," which recalls Paul's earlier argument in 4:5.[15] There Paul made it clear that the true gospel of Jesus' lordship, in contrast to the monetary and personal demands of his opponents, is embodied in a Christ-like "slavery" to the needs of his people. Sumney has therefore rightly emphasized that in 2 Corinthians 10–13 "the central issue at Corinth is the appropriate way of life for apostles."[16] Hence, Paul's implied critique of his opponents in 4:5 and 11:4 becomes explicit in 11:20. Paul's opponents do not preach Jesus as the Lord who is embodied in the suffering of his apostle.

As a result, Paul's willingness to be a slave of all stands in stark contrast with their having made the Corinthians *their* slaves. That his opponents preach "another Jesus" is clearly revealed in their refusal to take up their cross on behalf of the Corinthians (cf. comments on 4:5). Rather than following in the footsteps of the crucified and then risen Lord (cf. 4:7–12 with 4:13–18),

---

14. Belleville, "Paul's Polemic," 297, emphasis mine. In contrast to the position taken here, Belleville identifies the "super-apostles" of 11:5 with the false apostles of 11:13. She also rejects the hypothesis that Paul's opponents were "Judaizers," because of the traditional polarity that is assumed to exist between a call for obedience to the law and experiences of the Spirit on the one hand, and because of the lack of explicit references in this letter to circumcision and the law on the other (cf. 296–97).

15. I owe this insight to Timothy B. Savage, *Power Through Weakness*, 156.

16. Sumney, *Paul's Opponents*, 162. Though Sumney believes chapters 1–9 and 10–13 to be separate letters, he argues that the issue facing Paul in both was essentially the same, namely, the dispute over the "proper criteria for identifying legitimate apostles" (182).

they preach an "exalted" figure that they wrongly assert is reflected in their assertions of superiority and the demands that they lord over the Corinthians. Nevertheless, the Corinthians gladly "put up" with such mistreatment because the opponents' Jesus promises the power of the Spirit over all sickness and financial want to those who will accept their gospel. To do so, however, is to go back on the true Jesus, gospel, and Spirit as first preached by Paul.

Against this backdrop, the meaning and flow of Paul's argument from 11:4 to 11:5 has been a matter of much debate. The NIV opts for one side of the debate by translating verse 5 as a *contrast* to verse 4 ("but") and rendering those to whom Paul compares himself as "those 'super-apostles.'" Read in this way, the "super-apostles" of verse 5 are equated with the opponents of verse 4, with the title itself understood to be ironic or sarcastic (note the quotation marks). By using this designation, Paul is reflecting his opponents' inflated view of themselves, while Paul himself is viewed as going back on his prior resolve not to compare himself with his opponents. As Witherington puts it, this gives "a dialectic character to this whole section since Paul refuses to compare himself with his rivals and then proceeds with the comparison."[17]

From this perspective, the peddlers of God's Word in 2:17 and those "recommending themselves" in 10:12–16 become equated with the "super-apostles" in 11:5 (cf. 12:11), who are then identified as the "false apostles," "deceitful workmen," and "servants of Satan" in 11:13–15. Paul's point is that he is not inferior to his opponents, regardless of the fact that they hold themselves to be "super-apostles."

It would be highly unusual, however, for the conjunction introducing verse 5 (*gar*) to indicate a contrast. Its most common function is to introduce a ground or support (i.e., "for" or "because"). Moreover, it is difficult to imagine that Paul would go back on his resolve not to compare himself with others or that he would try to establish his authority by comparing himself *positively* to Satan's servants![18] This objection takes on special force in light of 11:12, where Paul refuses to allow his opponents to be compared to himself. Furthermore, the Greek text need not be translated as "those super-apostles" but can be rendered simply as "the highest ranking apostles"[19] or "superlative"

---

17. Ben Witherington III, *Conflict and Community in Corinth*, 446.

18. This objection, first pushed forcibly home by Ernst Käsemann, "Die Legitimität des Apostels: Eine Untersuchung zu II Korinther 10–13," *ZNW* 41 (1942): 33–71, esp. 38–39, 41–43, 45–49, has not been satisfactorily met by those who read 11:5 as a comparison to Paul's opponents. For the major supporter of the position taken here in the English-speaking world, see the various works of C. K. Barrett, esp. his "Paul's Opponents in II Corinthians" *NTS* 17 (1971): 233–54, and his *A Commentary on the Second Epistle to the Corinthians*, 30–35.

19. So Martin, *Corinthians*, 342.

or "eminent apostles" (cf. NASB). Rendered in this way, in 11:5 Paul is not comparing himself to his enemies but to the authority and status of the leading apostles of the early church, namely, to the acknowledged "pillar apostles" of Galatians 2:9 and those within their sphere of authority.

Hence, the "most eminent apostles" of 11:5 and 12:11 should not be equated with the false apostles of 11:4 or 11:13–15. Paul is not continuing his discussion of his opponents and their "gospel" from verse 4, but is switching focus in verse 5 by introducing the reason why the Corinthians are in such danger if they accept Paul's opponents (11:2–4) and why they ought to "put up" with Paul instead (11:1). In turning their backs on him, the Corinthians must remember that in his message and ministry he is in no way inferior to those acknowledged to be the church's most eminent apostles but that he carries their same authority and status. Those who reject Paul are therefore rejecting the one common, apostolic gospel (cf. 1 Cor. 15:3, 8–11). By comparing himself positively to the "pillar apostles," Paul is driving a wedge between his gospel and the subsequent claims of his opponents, who may have supported their message by boasting that they came with the Jerusalem church's stamp of approval. In reality, however, Paul is the one who represents the apostolic tradition.

Paul's equality with the leading apostles means that even if he is an amateur in the art of professional rhetoric and public oratory, his knowledge of the gospel is not second rate (11:6). Indeed, he has manifested this knowledge to the Corinthians "in every way," that is, by both word (i.e., his preaching) and deed (i.e., his suffering), a clear reference back to 2:14. Paul's statement in 11:6 also recalls 1 Corinthians 15:11, where Paul stated that it was of no significance whether the Corinthians heard the gospel from Paul or from any of the other apostles, since they all represent the same message. Paul's reference in verse 6 to his "knowledge" makes this same point: His knowledge is on a par with any of the apostles, just as he himself shares their apostolic authority in every way.

The necessity of Paul's boasting in his weakness (11:7–15). Earlier, Paul moved from a general statement concerning his manifesting the knowledge of God through his suffering in 2:14 to his practice of self-support in Corinth as a specific example of such suffering in 2:17.[20] Now he moves from a general statement of his mediating the knowledge of God in 11:6 to the specific instance of "lowering himself" for the sake of the Corinthians by

---

20. For Paul's hard labor for the gospel, cf. Acts 18:3; 20:34–35; 1 Cor. 4:12; 9:18; 15:10; 2 Cor. 6:5; 11:23, 27; Eph. 4:28; 1 Thess. 2:9; 2 Thess. 3:7–8. The suffering incurred by Paul's practice of self-support included experiencing the cultural disdain that the upper classes had for manual labor.

preaching the gospel for free in 11:7–12 (cf. 12:13–18). Once again, his point is that his willing practice of self-support (i.e., his lowering himself), which his opponents consider a "sin,"[21] is in reality the very means God has used to manifest himself to the Corinthians. Paul's lowering himself has led to his elevating the Corinthians because of his love for them (11:7, 11; cf. 1 Cor. 4:8–15; 9:12–23).

Paul returns to the theme of his self-support in 11:7–12 because his voluntary humiliation and suffering are at the heart of the debate among those still questioning his apostleship. From Plato through Paul's day, the Sophist philosophers and professional orators charged fees and took money for their teaching, since a free or cheap message implied that the message itself was not worth much (cf. the discussion to 2:17).[22] We might call this the "Harvard principle" of charging fees in accordance with one's perceived status (though the actual quality of the instruction may or may not match the price tag). Hence, Paul's refusal to solicit support from the Corinthians could be viewed as casting an aspersion on his teaching: He gives his gospel away because nobody will pay for it. In his opponents' view, Paul's refusal to accept money is not an expression of Christ-like love for the Corinthians but a tacit admission of the inferior nature of his apostleship.

At the same time, Paul's self-support is an affront to the pride of the Corinthians, who most likely want to be viewed as Paul's benefactors or patrons, with him as their client. But as an apostle, Paul is *their* patron, representing *his* true Patron, Christ. Far from calling his ministry into question, his preaching for free represents God's gift in Christ. Christ's humbling himself in the "poverty" of his incarnation, suffering, and death (cf. 8:9) leads to Paul's humbling himself in the "poverty" that results from supporting himself for the sake of the Corinthians (11:7).

Given the precarious situation of itinerant craftsmen in Paul's day, 11:8–9 reports that Paul's ministry of self-support in Corinth was made possible in that the Macedonian churches supplemented Paul's income when needed. Thus, the Macedonians' generosity as an expression of God's grace (cf. 8:1), combined with Paul's self-support as an extension of the gospel of Christ (cf. 1 Cor. 8:13; 9:19–22; 10:24, 33; 2 Cor. 2:17), made it possible for him not to "burden" the Corinthians. There is therefore no basis for his opponents'

---

21. The exact nature of the "sin" attributed to Paul by his opponents is not clear. His refusal to demand money for his ministry could have been seen as cheapening the gospel itself (i.e., a sin against the gospel), or as an expression of his shame concerning what he preached (i.e., a sin against the Corinthians by falsely representing himself).

22. For a survey of the attitudes toward charging fees for one's teaching from Plato through Lucian (ca. 125–180 A.D.), see my *Suffering and Ministry in the Spirit*, 106–25. The main lines of my understanding of 11:6–12 have been developed in *Suffering*, 145–54.

---

accusation that Paul is somehow using the ministry or the collection to serve his own ends (cf. 12:16–18). His "robbing" other churches for the sake of his ministry in Corinth was not a scam but an expression of Christ-like love, both on Paul's part and on the part of those who gave.[23] This is why Paul pledges to continue his practice of not relying on the Corinthians financially—he will not put any stumbling block in the way of the gospel.

The two oath formulas of 11:10 and 11[24] undergird Paul's resolve to continue his boast of preaching the gospel for free in Achaia. No criticism can stop him from doing so (cf. v. 7), since his boast is an expression of the truth of Christ in his life. He can equate his commitment to preach for free with the truth of Christ because the humiliation and suffering that his practice of self-support entails derives from his love toward the Corinthians, as God himself can attest (cf. 2:4; 3:2; 5:14; 6:6; 8:7; 12:15).

The bold assertions of 11:10–11 thus reiterate what Paul has already argued in detail in 1 Corinthians 9:15–18. There Paul made it clear to the Corinthians that he would rather die than give up his practice of self-support, since giving up his right to financial support was an essential part of that "boast" for which he would be rewarded by God. As a slave of Christ entrusted with the gospel, he has no choice but to preach. For this there will be no reward; to preach is Paul's duty. But his practice of self-support in doing so goes beyond the call of duty for the sake of the gospel. So what his opponents called a "sin" (2 Cor. 11:7) is the very thing for which Paul expects to be rewarded by God. For Paul's practice of self-support demonstrates without further argument that he loves the Corinthians.

There is a second reason why Paul will not stop supporting himself in Corinth. It is also his way of exposing the fraudulent motives of his opponents. Paul's preaching for free makes it impossible for his opponents to compare their missionary practice favorably with his own. In so doing, it removes their "ground" (11:12, *aphormē*, a military term referring to the base from which an attack can be launched). Indeed, that Paul willingly suffers like

---

23. The money needed to supplement Paul's wages was most likely brought by Silas and Timothy (Acts 18:5; 1 Cor. 4:12; 1 Thess. 2:9). Barnett, *Second Corinthians*, 515nn.16, 18, points out that the verb "to rob" (in the sense of plundering a defeated enemy) and the noun "wage" (in the sense of a soldier's rations or provisions; cf. 1 Cor. 9:7; Luke 3:14) are both military metaphors. This underscores Paul's earlier portrayal of his ministry as warfare in 10:3–6. Phil. 4:15 implies that Paul accepted no support from the Macedonians while still with them, but only after he had left. The money from the Macedonians was therefore a gift in support of ministry elsewhere, not a wage for services rendered to them. For Paul's desire was not to be a burden in the ministry (see 1 Thess. 2:9; 2 Thess. 3:8; 1 Tim. 5:16); for the practice of paying pastors, see 1 Cor. 9:3–14; Gal. 6:6; 1 Tim. 5:17–18; 2 Tim. 2:6.

24. For other examples of oaths in Paul's writings, see 1:18, 23; 2:10; 11:11, 31; cf. Rom. 9:1; Gal. 1:20.

Christ for the sake of others calls into question the dictum of the health and wealth gospel that Christ has suffered so that his people need not do so. That is why the opponents are denigrating Paul; they realize that his practice of self-support calls their own ministry into question. His refusing support as evidence of his love for the church destroys his opponents' ability to demand support under the pretense of claiming to be the ones who really love the Corinthians.

Many commentators argue that Paul engages in boasting because the opponents are comparing themselves to Paul in order to assert their own superiority. But in 10:12 the opponents are said to be comparing themselves *to themselves*, not to Paul. Their tactic is not to compare themselves with Paul, but to generate commendations from one another without the kind of evidence that counted in Corinth (cf. 10:13—18). As 11:12 makes clear, the opponents are actually afraid to compare themselves to Paul because of the clear testimony that his practice of self-support gives to the sincerity of his motives. It is Paul, not the opponents, who therefore initiates the comparison in chapters 10—13.

Thus, in 11:12 Paul goes on the offensive by turning his opponents' criticism on its head and exposing it for what it really is: an attempt to get Paul to compromise his convictions so that they will not look so bad by comparison. The decisive issue is whose gospel and way of life are truly motivated by love: Paul's willingness to support himself for the sake of the Corinthians as the "slave of all" (cf. 1 Cor. 9:12, 17; 2 Cor. 4:5), or his opponents' attempt to "enslave" the Corinthians by demanding that they support them (cf. 11:20). Paul maintains that his message and ministry are the true criteria of legitimacy by which the opponents are to be measured, not the other way around.

Paul must set himself up as the criterion for true apostleship because of the deceptive nature of his opponents, who are "masquerading as apostles of Christ" (11:13). This is no innocent misunderstanding on their part. The verb translated "masquerading" signifies the idea "to change the form of, transform … change or disguise oneself into or as something."[25] It is best taken here to signify "disguising oneself." The opponents are *"deceitful* workmen" in that, though false or pseudo-apostles, they are pretending to be genuine apostles.[26]

---

25. BAGD, 513.

26. Scott, 2 *Corinthians*, 205—9, 237, argues that, in view of the parallels between Moses and Paul established in 2:16 and 3:4—18, Korah's rebellion recounted in Num. 16—17 (cf. Ex. 19:6; 29:45; Deut. 7:6; 14:2; 26:19; 28:9) should be the framework for understanding Paul's view of his opponents here and throughout the letter (cf. 1:24; 2:6—7, 15, 17; 3:1). Just as Korah and his followers were called "outsiders" in Num. 16:40, and just as Jewish tradition accuses Korah of rejecting the revealed Torah (cf. *Ps-Philo* 16; *Num. Rab.* 18:12; *b. Sanh.*

Paul is not surprised by this, since Satan too "masquerades as an angel of light" (11:14). This exact designation for Satan is not found in the Old Testament or Judaism, though the idea is certainly there (cf., e.g., Job 1:6–12; Isa. 14:12–15; *Life of Adam and Eve* 9:1; *Apocalypse of Moses* 17:1–2). The point of designating Satan as a false "angel of light" is to highlight his counterfeit nature as a messenger of God. Satan pawns himself off as the real messenger of the light—that is, Christ[27]—in contrast to the true apostles, who mediate the "light of the gospel of the glory of Christ" and the "light of the knowledge of the glory of God in the face of Christ" (cf. 4:4, 6). Note the focus on Christ. The opponents disguise themselves as "apostles of Christ" even though they serve Satan, who presents himself as the one who truly reveals the glory of God. As prisoners of Satan's deceit, these opponents preach a "different Jesus."

As a result, just as God made Paul competent to be a "servant" (*diakonos*) of the new covenant "ministry [*diakonia*] of righteousness" (3:6, 9), so too Satan's "servants" are masquerading as "servants [*diakonoi*] of righteousness" (11:15). Their deceptive, satanic claim is that Christ's life and death are not sufficient to bring about the righteousness of God, but must be supplemented with the stipulations of the old covenant. Keeping the old covenant in addition to the new is consequently trumpeted as the way to experience the fullness of the Spirit, the sign of which was health, wealth, and supernatural experiences.

110a), so too Paul's opponents come from outside the congregation and preach a different gospel. Conversely, in order to resist his opponents, Paul, like Moses, has to demonstrate that he is the one whom the Lord has called and sent (cf. Num. 16:11, 28, 30). Moreover, when charged with lording his authority over the Israelites, Moses declares that he has never taken tribute from anyone (Num. 16:15). In the same way, Paul refuses to accept financial support from the Corinthians (11:7). Just as Korah and his followers were jealous of Moses, claiming an equal holiness and priesthood (Num. 16:3, 8–11), so too Paul refuses to allow his opponents to compare themselves favorably with him (11:12). Scott even suggests that Paul's reference in 11:12 to "cutting the ground from under" his opponents "may recall" Korah's followers being swallowed up by the ground in Num. 16:31–35, though this seems an improbable parallel given the military connotation of 11:12. Finally, Scott suggests that if Korah's rebellion attempted to eliminate Moses and Aaron as mediators of divine revelation, since Israel had received a direct revelation at Sinai, then Paul's opponents may have maintained that he is that much more superfluous under the new covenant. Scott's observations are interesting, though in the absence of any direct verbal parallels between the two passages, the certainty of this backdrop cannot be established.

27. For "light" as a metaphor for God, the gospel, and the realm of the kingdom, cf. 6:14; Job 33:28–30; Ps. 18:28; 27:1; 119:105; Isa. 9:2; 60:1, 19–20; Acts 26:18; Eph. 5:11–14; 6:12; Col. 1:12–13; 1 Thess. 5:5; 1 Tim. 6:16; 1 Pet. 2:9; 1 John 1:5; 2:8. The designation may also recall Jesus' own claim to be the light of the world (John 1:7–9; 3:19–21; 8:12; 9:5; 12:36, 46).

This insistence on the continuing validity of the old covenant brings with it, in reality, a conviction that the Christ proclaimed by the apostles is insufficient to bring about God's promises—that is, they represent "another Jesus" (cf. 4:4–6). The opponents' overrealized emphasis on the glorified Christ therefore includes a false understanding of what God has promised by pouring out his presence in the midst of this evil age; that is, they promise a "different Spirit" (cf. 3:3–6). As a result, they are ministers of a gospel that cannot save; that is, they proclaim a "different gospel" (cf. 5:16–6:2). Those who preach such a false message will be rewarded "according to their works" (NIV, "what their actions deserve;" cf. 5:10; Rom. 2:6; 3:8; Gal. 6:7–9; Eph. 6:8; Phil. 3:18–19; Col. 3:24; 2 Tim. 4:14), a sober reminder of the principle of 1 Corinthians 3:17: "If anyone destroys God's temple, God will destroy him."

The foolishness of boasting in one's strength (11:16–21a). Paul knows where his argument is leading, that is, that he is about to boast in his human distinctives. Again, desperate situations demand desperate measures. But before he goes down this path, Paul hesitates yet again in 11:16–21a in order to make it clear just how inappropriate such boasting actually is. Understood in this way, Paul's statement in 11:16 refers back to 11:1.[28] Despite the fact that he is about to boast in himself, no one should take him to be a real "fool" for doing so. He understands what he is doing and why he must do it. If the Corinthians do take him to be a fool, they should do so only for the sake of allowing him to boast "a little" (i.e., just enough to make his point).

Indeed, 11:17 indicates that Paul is well aware that his boast will be that of a fool, since it will not be the kind of boasting that honors the Lord by exalting in his grace and gifts. In Paul's words, it will not be talking "according to the Lord" (NIV, "as the Lord would"), that is, in accordance with who the Lord is (cf. 1:14; 10:17–18; Rom. 5:11; 15:17–18; 1 Cor. 1:26–31; Gal. 6:14; Phil. 3:3; 1 Thess. 2:19). Instead, the foolish boast takes pride in its own distinctives, spiritual endowments, and/or leaders, as if these were not all gifts from God (cf. 1 Cor. 3:3; 4:5–7). As a result, the boast that is "according to the Lord" is the opposite of boasting that is "according to the flesh" (NIV, "the way the world does"). Such boasting is rooted in the world's values, devoid of the Spirit.

Nevertheless, Paul feels compelled to conform to such boasting for the sake of winning back the Corinthians, since they are gladly bearing with

---

28. Contra Martin, *2 Corinthians*, 360, who takes 11:1 to mean, "Bear with me in my folly," while 11:16 is interpreted as, "Do not think me to be a fool" (since Paul knows that the Corinthians already consider him to be one). But there is no evidence that they already view Paul to be a fool, only that they have rejected his weakness, persecution, suffering, self-support, and theology of the cross as the means for experiencing the Spirit. It is Paul, not his opponents, who introduces the theme of foolishness into the debate.

Paul's opponents, the real fools (11:18–19a). This description in 11:18 of the boasting to come as being done "according to the flesh" indicates that the "fool's speech" cannot be extended to include all of 11:21–33, but must be limited to 11:21b–23b (i.e., his "little boasting," 11:16). It is difficult to imagine that Paul would characterize his extended boasting in his weakness as "fleshly" or "worldly," since it is precisely his suffering through which the power and glory of Christ are made known in the Spirit (cf. the thesis statements in 2:14; 3:2–3; 12:5, 9–10).

In contrast to Paul's foolishness, in 11:19 those Corinthians who remain enamored with his opponents are pictured, ironically, as the "wise." The irony is that those claiming to be "wise" are the real fools for accepting such fools. Having introduced this irony, Paul develops it further. Since the Corinthians are the "wise" ones, their acceptance of the real fools must be an act of condescension (cf. 1 Cor. 4:10). But if they can accept Paul's opponents (the real fools), then surely in their "wisdom" they can accept Paul's foolish boasting too. If the opponents' "strength" qualifies them to be apostles, then Paul too must be accepted under this criterion, since he too can boast in his "strength." Certainly the Corinthians will be "wise" enough to see this!

Paul unmasks his irony in 11:20–21a. The progression of abuse the Corinthians have suffered from the false apostles details why they are not really wise but fools for accepting his opponents. As we have seen, the reference to the opponents' "enslaving" the Corinthians recalls Paul's characterization of his own ministry as being enslaved *to the Corinthians* (cf. 1:24; 4:5). So too, the fact that his opponents "exploit" (lit., "devour") the believers in Corinth for their own gain recalls Paul's own willingness to be spent *for them* (cf. 2:17; 4:11, 15; 6:4–5; 12:14). The insulting "slap ... in the face" received from his opponents most likely refers to their denigrating the Corinthians as second class citizens in the kingdom—unless, of course, they side with the opponents, who pride themselves on their Hebrew and Israelite heritage (cf. 11:22).

In stark contrast stand Paul's pride in, affection for, and willingness even to die with the Corinthians (1:14; 6:12; 7:3–4, 14, 16; 11:11). In yet another statement of biting irony, even sarcasm, Paul therefore admits to the "shame" he feels over being too "weak" to act like his opponents (11:21a; cf. the earlier reference to his physical weakness in 10:10). His "weakness" is the strength of his apostolic calling and character; his opponents' supposed "strength" reveals the weakness of their claims and the sinfulness of their attitudes and actions.

Paul's Boast in His Weakness and the Boasting of a Fool (11:21b–33)

THE IDENTITY BETWEEN Paul's person and his proclamation is spelled out in the twofold boast of verses 21b–23b and verses 23c–33. Nevertheless, the former is the boasting of a fool, the latter that of the true apostle of Christ. Since to boast in one's strength is, in reality, to be a fool, Paul would be "out of his mind" to take refuge in his pedigree (11:23b). In line with this, his "fool's speech" includes only his boasting in his Jewish heritage in 11:21b– 23b, framed by declarations of his foolishness in 11:21b and 23b.[29]

By contrast, Paul, like the suffering righteous of the Old Testament, is no fool when he boasts in his suffering. His rightful boast unmasks the ridiculous behavior of his opponents. Paul's *genuine* boast in his weakness is what his opponents' deplore; his *foolish* boast in his distinctives is what they do. In both cases, his boast becomes an indictment of their own. Thus, Paul's declaration of "daring" to boast in 11:21b is most likely an ironic reference to a slogan of his opponents, who bragged about being "bold" enough to boast about their ethnicity and accomplishments. Of course, to be daring in this way is to be a fool, so Paul must once again qualify what he is about to do lest the Corinthians think he puts any stock in such posturing.

The boasting of a fool (11:21b–23b). Paul's litany of boasts in verses 21–33 is arranged in an ascending order of emphasis. First, Paul marshals in increasing force his "foolish" claims to apostolic authority, climaxing with his boast in being a "servant of Christ" (v. 23). He then turns to his suffering, from his labors as an apostle to his being exposed to death, in which the generalized statements first given in 11:23c are unpacked in the details that follow.[30]

In verses 22–23b Paul matches his opponents' foolish boast element for element. Paul too can boast in his ethnic identity as a Jew (he is a member of the Hebrew nation; cf. Phil. 3:5), in his religious identity as a member of God's chosen people (he is an Israelite; cf. Rom. 1:4; 11:1), and in his identity as part of the remnant who have received the Spirit as the true descendants of Abraham (cf. Rom. 9:6–9; 11:1–6; Gal. 3:8, 16, 29). If heritage makes one an apostle, then Paul can claim the heritage of the most esteemed Jewish apostles.

In fact, if this is the way his opponents are prepared to argue, then Paul can claim to be "more" a servant of Christ than they are. Nobody can top his well-known pedigree and his former life of zeal for the law and the Pharisaic

---

29. Contra Witherington, *Conflict and Community*, 444. Witherington argues that although Paul engages in a "little foolishness" beginning in 11:1, he does not assume "the full mantle of the 'fool' until 11:21b," since his catalog of suffering is meant to be an ironic comparison to the Emperor Augustus's *res gestae*, rather than Paul's real, genuine boast.

30. I owe this insight to Martin, *2 Corinthians*, 369. See too Barnett, *Second Corinthians*, 541, who points out that the four general categories of suffering listed in v. 23b summarize in advance the specifics to come: the physical and Christian labors in v. 27, the imprisonments and floggings in vv. 24–25a, and the experiences of death in vv. 25b–26.

traditions (11:23b; cf. Gal. 1:14; Phil. 3:4–6). But this way of arguing is mad-ness. It denies the very basis of apostolic authority itself: the call of the risen Christ to take on the character of the crucified Christ.

The boasting of Christ's apostle (11:23c–33). It is striking that the Greek text of 11:23c continues on without indicating much of a break, if any. Because of the absurd and sinful nature of such boasting in one's self, Paul abruptly cuts it short and turns to the suffering outlined in 11:23–33 as the real proof and ground of his apostleship. Paul's reference in verse 23 to his greater labors recalls the way he has spent himself for the ministry (cf. 1 Cor. 15:10), as well as the suffering that surrounded his supporting himself for the sake of the gospel (cf. 1 Cor. 4:12; 9:15–23; 2 Cor. 2:17; 11:7–9; 12:14). Both of these are "boasts in the Lord" (cf. 10:17), since his willingness to work and suffer manifest God's grace and calling in his life (cf. 10:18).

Likewise, Paul's various arrests, imprisonments, and punishments referred to in verses 23–26 were suffered as an apostle for the gospel (cf. 6:5; Acts 16:23–30). His more severe beatings (2 Cor. 11:23) refer both to the Jew-ish punishment of thirty-nine "lashes" (v. 24) and to the Gentile punishment of being beaten with rods (v. 25a). Five times Paul received synagogue pun-ishment, which, among other things, was inflicted for false teaching, blas-phemy, and seriously breaking the law. It was the most severe beating Scripture allowed (cf. Deut. 25:1–3). Paul's receiving such punishment five times attests that the synagogue continued to be a strategic focus of his min-istry. He went to the Jews first, even though they often accused and convicted him of false teaching and/or breaking the law for his witness to Jesus as the Messiah and for his ministry among the Gentiles (cf. Acts 9:20; 13:5, 14–43; 14:1; 17:1–3, 10–21; 18:4, 19; 19:8).[31]

That Paul submitted to these punishments rather than separating himself from the Jewish community is an indication both of his self-understanding as an apostle and of his amazing love for his people (cf. Rom. 1:16; 9:2–3). He suffered for his mission to the Gentiles while never abandoning his com-mitment to his own people (cf. 1 Cor. 9:19–23). For him to live like a Gen-tile for the sake of his mission and yet to remain within the Jewish community "was to incur the virtual necessity of regular punishment in order to maintain

---

31. Of the three most probable crimes worthy of such a lashing (doctrinal heresy, blas-phemy, and serious offenses against Jewish customs), Harvey argues that most likely Paul was whipped for either profaning the Sabbath, working on the Day of Atonement, or com-mitting offenses against food and ritual purity regulations (cf. *m. Makk.* 3:2; 3:15; *m. Ker.* 1:1). These are the kind of Jewish crimes that would have come about because of his ministry among the Gentiles; see A. E. Harvey, "Forty Strokes Save One: Social Aspects of Judaiz-ing and Apostasy," *Alternative Approaches to New Testament Study,* ed. A. E. Harvey (London: SPCK, 1985), 79–96 (p. 84).

his Jewish connections. It was a heroic course, of a piece with all those other ordeals which Paul underwent for the sake of the gospel."[32]

Paul's ministry as the Jewish apostle to the Gentiles also caused rifts within the Jewish and Gentile social fabric as a whole. Hence, three times the Romans punished Paul for disturbing the peace by beating him with rods, a form of punishment usually reserved for noncitizens and slaves (11:25a; cf. Acts 16:22–23, 35–38; 22:25–29; 1 Thess. 2:2).

Finally, Paul's repeated exposure to death (v. 23c) includes his being stoned in Lystra (cf. Acts 14:5–19), the most common form of execution in the Bible,[33] his three shipwrecks, and the manifold dangers he encountered as part of his missionary journeys (vv. 25b–26).[34] Of special note is the fact that within Paul's listing of his various dangers, "'dangers from false brothers' stands alone and unpaired at the foot of the list, thus giving it preeminence in the catalogue of hazards to Paul's life."[35] By calling special attention in this way to the danger posed by false brothers as the climax of all his dangers, Paul is subtly reminding the Corinthians of the serious peril they themselves are now facing by embracing his opponents (cf. Gal. 2:4 for Paul's only other reference to "false brothers," where it refers to the Judaizers, thus supporting a similar identification here).

In verse 27 Paul returns to the suffering caused by his practice of self-support. He does so in a carefully structured list of three doublets ("labored and toiled," "hunger and thirst," "cold and naked") that are separated by references to going without sleep and food, a consequence that recalls his earlier catalog in 1 Corinthians 4:11–12 (cf. 15:10; 2 Cor. 6:5; 1 Thess. 2:9; 2 Thess. 3:8). Paul labored day and night in order to support himself and preach (cf. Acts 20:9–11, 31), while the uncertainties of his work and travel meant days of hunger and thirst. His sleeplessness could refer to late nights he spent writing and studying, as well as to the consequence of his pressing concern

---

32. Ibid., 93.

33. I owe this observation to Scott, 2 Corinthians, 218. Scott points out that stoning was used for apostasy (Lev. 20:2; Deut. 13:10–11; 17:2–7), blasphemy (Lev. 24:14, 16, 23; 1 Kings 21:10), sorcery (Lev. 20:27), Sabbath violations (Num. 15:35–36), misuse of the devoted things (Josh. 7:25), a disobedient son (Deut. 21:21), and adultery (Deut. 22:21–24). Cf. John 8:5; 10:31–33; 11:8; Acts 5:26; 7:58; Heb. 11:37.

34. For references to these various "dangers," see Acts 9:23–25, 29; 13:8, 45, 50; 17:5, 13; 18:6, 12; 19:9, 23–41; 20:3, 19; 21:11, 27, 30–31; Rom. 15:31; 1 Cor. 15:32; 2 Cor. 1:8; Gal. 2:4; 5:11; 1 Thess. 2:14–16, not to mention the dangers inherent simply in traveling during Paul's day. Paul suffered at the hands of Jews and/or Gentiles in Pisidian Antioch, Iconium, Lystra, Thessalonica, Corinth, and Ephesus, plus, no doubt, other places not mentioned in his writings or in Acts.

35. Barnett, Second Corinthians, 545.

for his churches.[36] Paul's being "naked" is probably a metaphor representing the shame of being afflicted and disgraced, which he certainly was in the eyes of the world (1 Cor. 4:13; 2 Cor. 6:8; cf. Gen. 2:25; 3:7–11; Ezek. 16:8; Nah. 3:5; Mic. 1:11; Rev. 3:18[37]). Here too, what others considered shameful Paul *boasts in* as legitimating expressions of his calling and commitment to the ministry.

In 11:28a, Paul concludes his list properly by summarizing the other physical afflictions he could have listed with the phrase, "besides everything else." He moves on at this point to his personal struggles on behalf of the gospel, passing "over what he might have mentioned in order to come to what he needs to say to the Corinthians."[38] As Barnett rightly observes, "This suggests that the privations listed are illustrative, not exhaustive, and that his anxiety for the churches was the greatest suffering of all."[39] Paul's catalog of affliction reaches its climax not with any of his specific sufferings but with a reference to the "daily ... pressure of [his] concern for all the churches" (v. 28).

This too is part of Paul's apostolic suffering, since the pressure he feels is brought about by his identification with the weak and by his indignation over those who lead others into sin (v. 29). Normally, such concern or anxiety is considered negative, since it expresses a lack of confidence in God's care and a lack of satisfaction in God's provision (cf. Matt. 6:25–34; Mark 4:19; 1 Cor. 7:32–34; Phil. 4:6; 1 Pet. 5:7). In these cases, however, the anxiety is directed toward *oneself*. Paul's anxiety, in contrast, is not for himself but for the welfare of others as an expression of his love (cf. 1 Cor. 12:25; Phil. 2:20). The Corinthians must have realized that in this context he was talking about them. The apostle is emphatic in stressing that his continual concern over the Corinthians, a recurrent theme throughout the letter, is more difficult than any of his physical sufferings (cf. 2 Cor. 1:6; 2:4; 2:12–13; 4:12, 15; 7:3, 5; 11:2; 12:20–21; 13:9). Paul's greatest boast is his constant worry over their welfare.

Paul's main point is clear. Contrary to what his opponents maintain, Paul is "weak" not because of his own inadequacies, but because of his willingness to identify with those to whom he has been sent with the gospel (11:29). His

---

36. A. Plummer, *Second Epistle of St. Paul to the Corinthians* (ICC; Edinburgh: T. & T. Clark, 1978 [1915]), 328, points to the prologue to Sirach and to 2 Macc. 2:26, where the word for "without sleep" in 11:27 (*agrypnia*) is used of sitting up at night writing, while Sir. 38:26–30 uses it to refer to laborers working at night. In Sir. 36(31):1, 2, 20; 42:9 it is used of sleeplessness caused by anxiety or discomfort.

37. Pointed out by Martin, *2 Corinthians*, 380.

38. Ibid., 381. Martin renders v. 28a: "the remainder, which I have omitted as too incidental," suggesting that what he goes on to say "stands at the high point of the 'list of trials.'"

39. Barnett, *Second Corinthians*, 548n.41.

reference to his weakness in verse 29 returns us to the comparison with his opponents established in 11:20–21. Whereas they lord their status over the Corinthians in order to exploit them, Paul gives his up in order to match their weakness with his own. Since the mark of a true apostle is a willingness to suffer for his people as a representative of the crucified Christ (cf. 13:4), Paul's weakness is his boast.

The counterpart to Paul's weakness is his strong anger over the thought of someone falling away from Christ (11:29bc).[40] The reference to his "burning" in verse 29 is therefore an apt metaphor for the intense passion he experiences over those who are led astray (cf. 1 Cor. 7:9). Far from being a self-defense, the very letter the Corinthians are now reading is another example of Paul's burning zeal for their salvation (cf. 12:19). His boasting in 11:23c–29 leaves no doubt that his weakness, brought about by his unrelenting concern for the welfare of his people, is the primary support for his apostleship.

Paul's argument concludes with the principle stated in verse 30, which is illustrated one last time by the story recounted in verses 31–33: If forced to boast, he will do so concerning his weaknesses. Of course, Paul's list in verses 23–29 has already made this point by way of illustration. But its surprising nature leads him to underscore the veracity of his declaration with yet another oath in verse 31. As in 11:10, he again swears an oath in order to testify to the validity of his boast that his weakness is the divinely ordained vehicle of God's self-revelation (cf. 2:14–17). His oaths earlier in this chapter were by the truth of Christ (11:10) and the knowledge of God (11:11). Now he brings the two together. Moreover, the interpretation of God's character in terms of his relationship to "the Lord Jesus" reflects Paul's specifically Christian worldview, in which Jesus, under the authority of the Father, is the direct sovereign over his people.

To illustrate his boast one last time, Paul recalls his experience in Damascus after his conversion when he escaped from the Nabatean governor who was serving there under the reign of Aretas IV (cf. Acts 9:8–25).[41] Aretas IV ruled Nabatea from 9 B.C. to A.D. 40, whose capital was in Petra. He was the father-in-law of Herod Antipas, who became infamous as the one who divorced Aretas's daughter to marry Herodias. The governor in view here was most likely the head of the Nabatean community in Damascus, albeit

---

40. The "sin" in view in v. 29 is that of "being caused to stumble" or "fall" (skandalizo) over the cross of Christ (cf. the use of this vb. in Matt. 5:29–30; 11:6; Mark 9:42–47; Rom. 14:21; 1 Cor. 8:13; etc., and the corresponding noun, "stumbling block" (skandalon), in Rom. 9:33; 14:13; 16:17; 1 Cor. 1:23; Gal. 5:11.

41. This corresponds with dating the crucifixion around A.D. 33 and Paul's conversion between 34–39. Paul was in Damascus twice, at his conversion and after his return from Arabia (cf. Acts 9; 22; 26:12–21; Gal. 1:17).

under Roman jurisdiction, since there is no evidence that the Nabateans were in direct control of either the city or the region during this period. Moreover, "had the Nabateans been in control of Damascus they would, surely, have arrested Paul openly and would not be reduced to the expedient of keeping watch over the city."[42]

The introduction of this incident at this point is abrupt and seemingly out of place. Moreover, none of the other sufferings Paul lists has either this detail or specificity. It is not surprising, therefore, that scholars have offered various theories concerning why Paul chose this particular event as a capstone to his litany of suffering. Some posit that he chose it for thematic reasons, in order to emphasize a humbling "descent," as a matter of contrast to the "ascent" into heaven portrayed in 12:1–4. But the transition in 12:1 makes this unlikely (see next sec.). Others suppose that Paul's opponents were using this incident against him, so that he chose it for polemic reasons. Though perhaps true, it does not explain how the incident functions in this context.

Others give a theological reason for 11:31–33, viewing it as an allusion to Proverbs 21:22 (cf. 2 Cor. 10:4–5), in which Paul contrasts his life of weakness with "the scaling of cities" done by the wise.[43] Yet this allusion is not strong enough to be convincing; in 11:32–33 Paul is describing the event in its own terms, not those of Proverbs 21. Still others compare it to the Roman military honor, *corona muralis*, which was awarded for valor to the first soldier to scale the defender's wall during an attack upon a city. Read against this backdrop, Paul is "parodying the images of what it means to be truly heroic in a culture saturated with Roman imperial propaganda.... Paul is saying that while the typical Roman hero is first up the wall, he is first down the wall."[44] Nevertheless, the absence of warfare motifs in 11:32–33 and the difficulty of seeing how portraying himself as a coward could fit into Paul's self-defense (for Paul, being weak is not the opposite of being a hero) render this suggestion untenable.

The most likely reason for Paul's adducing this experience at this point in his apology is that, as a result of his conversion-call on the road to Damascus, it was the initial and foundational example of his newly granted weakness as

---

42. Mark Harding, "On the Historicity of Acts: Comparing Acts 9:23–5 with 2 Corinthians 11:32–3," *NTS* 39 (1993): 518–38 (p. 531). Harding points out that this is the consensus among present scholarship, as seen in Knauf's conclusion that the governor (Gk. *ethnarches*), like a consul, represented the Nabatean interests in Damascus that likely centered around a Nabatean trading colony (531n.41).

43. Martin, *2 Corinthians*, 385, writes: "They scaled the city walls of the mighty; he only managed to be let down in a fish-basket." In other words, they were victorious; Paul suffered defeat.

44. Witherington, *Conflict and Community*, 444, 459, following the work of Judge.

an apostle. As such, it stands in stark contrast to the strength in which he had originally left for Damascus to persecute the believers—the same foolish "strength" his opponents continue to boast in (11:22). But the one who left for Damascus to persecute Christians left Damascus as a persecuted Christian. Given the fact that his weakness is now his strength, this experience also provided the platform for his increasing "power" in regard to preaching Jesus as the Christ (cf. Acts 9:16, 22). This is why Paul structures his sentence to emphasize that this experience took place in "Damascus," the place associated with his conversion call (the NIV rightly follows the Greek, which has the prepositional phrase "in Damascus" standing at the beginning of 2 Cor. 11:32 for emphasis).

Hence, to wrap up his boasting in his weakness as the consequence of his calling to be an apostle, Paul provides one final and especially poignant example of his suffering. Like his suffering in Asia recounted in 1:8, his opponents may well have used this incident against him as an example of his cowardice. But from Paul's perspective, his narrow escape in Damascus, like his despairing even of life (cf. 1:8–11), serves to highlight God's deliverance and sustenance. It forms a paradigm of his calling to suffer for the sake of Christ and the gospel. In Heckel's words, Paul's flight from Damascus is the "counter-history to the vision that brought about Paul's calling."[45] Paul's litany of suffering in 11:23–29 is nothing new; weakness was the contour of his calling from the very beginning of his apostleship.[46]

Bridging Contexts

THE IMPLICATIONS OF this passage derive primarily from Paul's self-understanding as an apostle. Most of the issues involved in moving from his discussion of his own suffering and practice of self-support to our day have been taken up in earlier chapters when these themes were first introduced (cf. the discussions to 1:3–11; 2:14–17; 4:7–18; 6:3–10). In applying this particular passage, the contemporary interpreter should keep in mind the two essential themes that emerge anew from this text: the content of "foolish" boasting and the issue at stake in Paul's speaking as an amateur.

The content of "foolish" boasting. Paul's boasting in his weakness is the main point and central theme of this section. There have been two pre-

---

45. Heckel, *Kraft*, 39.

46. So already A. Schlatter, *Paulus, der Bote Jesu: Eine Deutung seiner Briefe an die Korinther* (Stuttgart: Calwer Verlag, 1969[4] [1934]), 657: Paul gave this memory in more detail than all the others "because it was an especially clear illustration of the way in which weakness and strength, danger and deliverance were bound together in his work from the very beginning."

---

dominant interpretations of this theme in Paul's letters: (1) the psychological interpretation, associated with the work of C. H. Dodd, in which Paul's boasting is part of his own struggle for recognition, and (2) the theological interpretation, associated with Rudolf Bultmann, in which Paul's boasting indicates the basis of the believer's confidence before God.[47] Paul's argument in 11:1–12:13 clearly involves both dynamics, since the nature of one's boasting before others, rightly or wrongly, reflects the nature of one's relationship with God. Paul boasts because his legitimacy as an apostle is being attacked, but the nature of his boast is determined by his understanding of the way in which God commends his servants (cf. 10:12–18).

Driven by his experience "in Christ" and by the content of the gospel itself, Paul's boasting in his weakness is not simply a parody of his opponents, as often argued. It is a positive expression of his own apostolic calling. This priority of theology over practice is crucial for evaluating the content and validity of boasting today, whether in our personal lives and churches or in the quality of our ministries and ministers. Regardless of cultural pressures to do otherwise, we must boast only in what God has done in and through us, giving credit to God for *all* that we are and do, since everything is a gift from him. There is no synergism in the life of faith, in which we add our contributions to what God has done. Rather, the scriptural principle crystallized in Jeremiah 9:23–24 provides the key both to the positive practice and content of Paul's boast and to the contours of our own.

This means that the "foolishness" in which Paul is forced to participate (11:1, 16–19, 21; cf. 12:6, 11) does not consist in the fact that he "boasts" per se.[48] What makes Paul a "fool" is the *content* of what he boasts in, that is, when he boasts in his Jewish pedigree, in a self-generated claim to be an apostle, or in private, spiritual experiences (cf. 11:22–23a; 12:1–5). As we will see, when he concludes in 12:11–12 that he has become foolish, he is referring to the two times he felt compelled to engage in such boasting about his "strength"—that of his spiritual heritage and of his spiritual experiences. Both are true factually, but neither one is relevant to the issue at hand. In view of the principle summarized in 11:30 (cf. 12:9–10), such things are simply useless for establishing the validity of Paul's apostolic authority, since the grace of God and power of Christ are revealed in his weakness.

As a result, to point to such things is to boast "according to the flesh" (11:18; NIV, "in the way the world does"), while only the work of the Spirit

---

47. These views are surveyed by C. K. Barrett, "Boasting (*kauchasthai, ktl.*) in the Pauline Epistles," *L'apôtre Paul: Personnalité, style et sonception du ministère,* ed. A. Vanhoye (BETL 73; Leuven: Leuven Univ. Press, 1986), 363–68.

48. This summary is taken from my previous work, "'Self-Commendation' and Apostolic Legitimacy in 2 Corinthians: A Pauline Dialectic?" 86–87.

can authenticate one's validity as a Christian (10:7) and the genuineness of one's ministry (10:17–18). To boast in such human distinctives and private experiences is therefore to be "out of [one's] mind" (11:23). It evidences a desire to "push [oneself] forward" (11:20) and can be exploitative (11:20). It denies that Christ is the one who determines his servants (11:23). It erects barriers between believers based on human distinctives (11:22). In the end, if it persists, such boasting in ourselves reflects a different gospel (11:4).

Thus, by boasting in such things, Paul's opponents are the real fools. In turn, by accepting such boasting, the Corinthians are being led astray from their devotion to Christ as the ultimate and all-sufficient provision from God (11:3). In contrast, suffering and the Spirit are the true signs of apostolic authority and the true marks of the gospel. In order to apply this passage, it is therefore imperative to keep in view the distinction Paul makes between a "foolish boast" and the boast in weakness. The former is irrelevant and arrogant when it comes to making spiritual claims (cf. 11:21–23a; cf. 12:1–5), the latter is the appropriate counterpart to boasting in God's power (cf. 11:23b–33; cf. 12:5b, 9–10).[49]

Paul's speaking as an amateur. As we have seen, Paul's opponents criticized him for failing to reflect the sophisticated style and flashy rhetorical forms that were characteristic of professional entertainers and orators in first-century Greco-Roman culture. It is important that we understand just what was at stake in this issue if we are to respond appropriately today to the same pressures to measure up to the popular "media" that Paul faced. As Duane Litfin has pointed out,

> Paul simply did not measure up to the rhetorical standards the Corinthians had come to expect. They were used to the polished eloquence of the orators of the day, in comparison to which Paul's preaching was found lacking. He was, as he himself admitted in 2 Corinthians 11:6, only a "layman" when it came to public speaking.[50]

---

49. See Scott B. Andrews, "Too Weak Not to Lead: The Form and Function of 2 Cor 11.23b–33," *NTS* 41 (1995): 263–276 (p. 266), who points out that according to the ancient rhetoricians, catalogs of hardship contained three elements: the items of hardship, the reaction to the hardships, and the resulting implications for one's status. Those who endure suffering were considered noble and worthy of praise. For in ancient philosophical literature, endurance of hardships revealed one to be a wise man or sage, since the sage was marked by his "self-sufficiency" and "freedom from passion" (p.267). But in contrast to the view presented here, Andrews argues that Paul inverted this ancient perspective. Rather than enduring or overcoming hardships, which would provide one with a noble social status, he suggests that Paul willingly submits to weakness in order to lower himself socially to the level of a populist leader, thereby claiming authority in Corinth (pp. 275–76).

50. Duane Litfin, "An Analysis of the Church Growth Movement," *Reformation and Revival* 7 (1998) 57–77 (p. 59). Litfin's analysis in this article is built on his extensive comparison of

Training in Greco-Roman rhetoric constituted the crown of a liberal education in the ancient world, and the orators it produced became the movie stars of their day. The people of the first century loved eloquence and lionized those who could produce it. Eloquence was perhaps their primary entertainment, and it was ubiquitous throughout the Roman Empire. Audiences consisted of avid and sophisticated listeners who knew what they liked and what they disliked. But the orators were willing to risk their displeasure for the sake of gaining their approval and the rewards that accompanied it (61).

In short, with its goal of informed entertainment, "ancient rhetorical education was designed to train an orator in the art of persuasion" (61). For this reason, the ancient orator was always adapting to his audience in order to achieve his goals. Since the orator's desired results and audience were variable, his methods were equally variable (62). Rhetorical education was therefore designed to enable the speaker to evaluate his audience and to determine his desired results in order to adapt his efforts to that particular situation. Hence,

the persuader's stance is both audience- and results-driven, and is methodologically uncommitted. . . . That is why so much attention is paid in the ancient rhetorical literature to the mindset of the audience, to their belief systems, to their likes and dislikes, and to what it takes to win particular responses from them. . . . This ability to mold one's efforts to the demands of the given situation in order to achieve a particular result with an audience was what ancient rhetorical theory and training were designed to teach. (62–63)

In order to apply Paul's model to our contemporary situation, Paul's refusal to utilize the rhetorical approaches of his day for the reason he did so takes on great significance. He intentionally remained an "amateur" when it came to public speaking because he viewed his calling to be proclamation, not persuasion. He did whatever it took not to be confused with an entertainer or professional speaker. "In the literally dozens of places in Paul's writings where he refers to his own preaching, the apostle scrupulously uses the language of the herald . . . language which plays no part in the rhetorical literature because it describes non-rhetorical behavior" (64–65).

Though Paul's audience may change, his methods were fixed, since they were determined by the message that had been given to him to proclaim (cf. 1 Cor. 2:2). Regardless of the responses he received, his message also

---

ancient Greek rhetoric to the style and purpose of Paul's preaching (cf. his *St. Paul's Theology of Proclamation* [SNTSMS 79; Cambridge: Cambridge Univ. Press, 1994]). In what follows, the page numbers of the quotes from Litfin's article are indicated in the body of the text.

remained the same, since it was the Holy Spirit, not his own power of persuasion, that brought about the desired results. "Paul was determined to depend upon the spiritual dynamic of the cross rather than the human dynamic of the persuader" (64).

Paul's concern was "the possibility of obtaining false, human-centered results . . . (1 Cor. 2:5)" (64). Consequently, his "efforts are neither results-driven nor audience-driven; they are obedience-driven" (65). Indeed, as Savage points out, "in the first century the cross was simply too repugnant to be exploited for personal gain."[51] How different it is today when Christ's cross, often reduced to a piece of polished jewelry, has become nothing more than a vague religious symbol and those who represent the crucified Christ come across as polished showmen.

 LIKE THE CORINTHIANS, we too long for immediate gratification and personal autonomy rather than finding our delight in learning to depend on God in the midst of suffering and affliction, weakness and woe. Like Paul's opponents, our leaders are drawn to models of cultural power and prestige. Like all people, we gravitate to promises of health and wealth and to messages that puff us up rather than glorify God. In a word, we have become "worldly." As David Wells makes clear:

> This "world" . . . is the way in which our collective life in society (and the culture that goes with it) is organized around the self in substitution for God. It is life characterized by self-righteousness, self-centeredness, self-satisfaction, self-aggrandizement, and self-promotion, with a corresponding distaste for the self-denial proper to union with Christ.[52]

As Satan's "servants"(11:15), all who deny the gospel do so, in the end, by selling the "Self" or some trinket of this world as more reliable, sufficient, and satisfying than knowing and living for God.

Over against these temptations to sin stands Paul's gospel of the glory of God in the crucified Christ on the one hand, and Paul's boast in his weakness on the other. Though they both confront our sin, Paul's message and experience also contain a great promise for God's people. What God did for Paul, he will do for all who boast in the Lord and in their own weaknesses. This will mean, however, keeping Paul's priorities clearly in view.

---

51. Savage, *Power Through Weakness*, 168.

52. David F. Wells, *God in the Wasteland: The Reality of Truth in a World of Fading Dreams* (Grand Rapids: Eerdmans, 1994), 40.

Not church growth, but the growth of God's glory. Paul's boasting in his weakness, emphasized all the more by his temporary "boasting as a fool," calls us to keep our own personal and ministry priorities pure for the sake of the gospel. More and more, modern management strategies, personal and church growth techniques, and therapeutic messages are infiltrating into every area of life. These Self-saturated approaches make it increasingly difficult to boast in God alone as the one whose goal it is to glorify himself by working in and through the weak lives of his people. God's purpose of revealing his sovereign and loving self-sufficiency as all-sufficient for his creation is blunted by our own "foolish boasting."

As a result, we are tempted to feel and act as if God may have made our lives and ministry possible, but it is now up to us to make them successful. Deep down we believe that the success of the gospel in our own lives and in the world around us is dependent on our creating ever new and culturally appealing ways to attract and satisfy our ever-changing interests. Rather than holding on to, cherishing, and giving ourselves to the study of God's self-revelation in the Scriptures, we look for what the Christian publishing industry calls the latest "Bible product" on the market. Rather than following Paul's example of focusing on the content of the gospel and its implications, we fall into the trap of thinking that the progress of the gospel is determined by the preacher's own powers of persuasion. After all, everyone loves a great speaker.

As it was for Paul, today too the pressure on pastors to be successful according to the standards of contemporary culture is intense. And as it did for Paul, today too this pressure comes not from the world but from the worldliness within the church. The temptation is to respond by boasting in one's strength. For in our day we find it difficult, if not impossible, to believe that God is at work through the proclamation of his Word if the number of people in our Sunday morning services is not growing exponentially.

In our "size is success" culture, it is almost beyond our ability to resist determining the measure of God's blessing by the numbers in our congregation. We confuse the ability to draw a crowd with the establishment of a people known by their "sincere and pure devotion to Christ" (11:3). Accordingly, we look to the size of our parking lot rather than to the size of our church's heart for God, for his people, and for the lost world in which she lives. The result is, as Thomas N. Smith points out, that the "dreadful treadmill" of competition and self-comparison over the size of our churches characterizes so much of modern ministry.[53] Yet, as he reminds us:

---

53. See Thomas N. Smith, "A Shepherd's Heart: So You Pastor a Small Church. Congratulations!" *Viewpoint* 4/1 (2000): 7.

Caring for a smaller church is no less a sacred stewardship than doing the same for a larger one. 'Me irrascible John McNeill purportedly told a young minister who lamented the smallness of his congregation, "Tha's a'right, laddie. In the Great Day it will be the least of your worries that ye've only eighty souls to give an account for!"

... Evangelicals have not begun to discern the potential of ambition, recognition, popularity, fame, and power to corrupt men. But, while sex and money have slain their thousands, ambition and its unholy siblings have slain their tens of thousands.[54]

There is no doubt that Paul wanted to distance himself from the professional orators of his day. He did not preach for the money and he did not teach to entertain. Nor did he determine his method by the needs and tastes of his audience, as if being persuasive, in and of itself, were his goal. Paul's method of presentation was determined by his message. His primary goal was to proclaim and embody the gospel, not to move his audience. Nevertheless, instead of resisting the "success" methods of the day, as Paul did (1 Cor. 1:17; 2:1–5, 13), even though he was severely criticized for doing so (2 Cor. 10:10; 11:6), many churches seek a ministry that, like ancient rhetoric, is determined by the felt needs and cultural appetites of its audience. If we do so, our church may grow, but we may not. To quote Duane Litfin again:

> We should note that the apostle is working here with a principle that has much wider application than to preaching alone, a principle that he is merely *applying* to his ministry of preaching. What Paul is working out here is a principle so fundamental that it deserves to shape our entire philosophy of ministry. The results- and audience-driven approach Paul rejects is one we all understand and take for granted. It is quintessentially American and wonderfully useful and practical. Indeed, it is the most natural thing in the world. But it is also an approach to ministry the apostle was required by his own theology to reject, precisely because it is so "natural" (1 Cor. 2:14). It is the product of a merely anthropocentric way of thinking and doing and as such is out of concert with God's way of working. Moreover, it is fraught with the potential for obtaining false, merely "natural," results.[55]

It is certainly true that we owe a great debt to the "Church Growth Movement" for its driving emphasis on evangelism and for its insistence on culturally relevant communication. Litfin rightly warns us, however, that

---

54. Ibid.
55. Litfin, "An Analysis of the Church Growth Movement," 66 (the next quotes have page numbers in text).

the Church Growth Movement remains vulnerable to accusations that it has largely embraced the persuader's stance. If one looks, not to what can merely be found written somewhere within church growth literature, but *to the constant and distinctive emphases of the Church Growth Movement*, what one finds is a characteristically pragmatic, method-ologically-neutral stress upon audience-driven, results-oriented strate-gies that "work." Despite the inevitable disclaimers, it is an approach which does seem to show the telltale signs of the persuader's stance....

In their fierce pragmatism they evaluate strategies only on the basis of their ability to generate results. (68, 71)

Since Paul's opponents were so successful in Corinth because they "met the needs" of the Corinthians, Litfin is careful to point out that ministry methods are not simply neutral tools, but must be rooted in our under-standing of God himself and of God's own way of working in the world (72).

Paul did not disavow the persuader's stance because it was *immoral*; he rejected it because it was based *upon a purely human dynamic which produced human results*. Has the Church Growth Movement adequately come to grips with these two issues?...

If Paul was so exercised about avoiding methods which engen-dered merely human results, why aren't we? (72–73)

We cannot assume that as long as we avoid immoral, unfair, or fraudulent methods, we are free to use whatever other means will "work."

For a Christian there exists a crucial added dimension which the audi-ence- and results-driven approach largely ignores. It is the concern for driving out the divine work of God by unduly crowding our human methods into the process....

For example, while Paul was aghast at the thought of basing his approach to ministry on the pragmatic insights of classical rhetorical the-ory, the church growth movement seems to harbor no such reserva-tion. In fact, the movement often appears to be sold out to classical rhetoric's closest modern counterpart, the world of advertising and mar-keting, and leans upon it constantly for advice and strategy. (73–75)

Paul was being compared to his opponents, who advertised themselves as the true apostles by pointing to their self-aggrandizing "gospel" and way of life. But Paul resisted this pressure to compromise to the norms of his cul-ture, even when it appeared for a while that he would lose his church to Satan. In their place, he stood for truth and instituted his own basis of com-parison, namely, his willingness to lay down his life for his people, by which he demonstrated that he was the one who, like Christ, truly loved the Corinthians (11:7–12).

Wells observes that the reason churches today are so quick to adopt the strategies and worldview embodied in modern marketing, with little if any regard for truth as her primary message, is because they have been convinced that "the church must define its services in terms of contemporary needs just as any secular business must."[56] The church, rather than resisting its culture and offering another standard of measurement, has herself become a market-driven company in the "business" of selling relationships with Jesus. Wells warns us, however, that

> allowing the consumer to be sovereign in this way in fact sanctions a bad habit. It encourages us to indulge in constant internal inventory in the church no less than in the marketplace, to ask ourselves perpetually whether the "products" we are being offered meet our present "felt needs." In this sort of environment, market research has found that there is scarcely any consumer loyalty to particular products and brands anymore. The consumer, like the marketeer, is now making fresh calculations all the time. And so it is that the churches that have adopted the strategy of marketing themselves have effectively installed revolving doors. ... People keep entering, lured by the church's attractions or just to check out the wares, but then move on because they feel their needs, real or otherwise, are not being met.
>
> ... What is going to happen when churches meet all of the felt needs of their consumers and then realize that they have failed to meet the genuine need for meaning? Meaning is provided by the functioning of truth—specifically biblical truth—in the life of the congregation.
>
> ... A business is in the market simply to sell its products; it doesn't ask consumers to surrender themselves to the product.... Businesses offer goods and services to make life easier or more pleasant; the Bible points the way to Life itself, and the way will not always be easy or pleasant. [57]

Paul's concern in his boasting was to remain true to Jesus, to the work of the Spirit, and to the message of the apostolic gospel (11:4–6). Thus, his example drives us to ask why, when we "advertise" our church, we do not "promote" the death of Christ for sinners, boast in God in what we say and do, highlight our own weaknesses, and call attention to the voluntary suffering of our role models? Why do we seek instead to portray an image of our-

---

56. Wells, *God in the Wasteland*, 74.
57. Ibid., 75–76.

selves as successful and "normal"?.The reaffirmation of Paul's principle from 11:30 is just as essential today as it was in his own: "If I must boast, I will boast of the things that show my weakness." The goal of the ministry is not attaining numerical growth, but fostering a growing experience of depending on Christ's grace and power, knowing that the one who gives the grace receives the glory, which is God's own purpose in all that he does as the Giver of all things. Thus, Ron Man, a pastor of worship, draws the right conclusion that

> as believers, our ultimate motivation in all of our endeavors is His glory ("Whatever you do, do all to the glory of God," 1 Cor. 10:31)....
>
> If this is true in all of life, it is even more important to have this perspective when we undertake the work of the Church. Human theories, techniques, ideas, systems, tastes, structures—all must be submitted to a compelling and overriding passion for the glory of God. How quickly we forget whose work, whose church, whose worship service it is! How quickly we seek to supplement the revelation of Scripture with human ingenuity, demographic studies, and how-to seminars. How anxious we are to find gimmicks which will attract people and keep them coming back! Our single-minded focus in worship must be on recognizing, reflecting, declaring, and celebrating the glory of God! [58]

No new images, but the image of integrity. As the corollary to Paul's boasting in his weakness, his refusal to employ professional rhetoric also calls us to examine whether there is a direct link between what we say we believe and the actual manner of our ministries. Both Paul and his opponents were convinced that the "medium was the message." This is why they carried themselves so differently in public. Hence, inasmuch as the character of their ministries differed so dramatically, so too they must be preaching different gospels.

Yet the real proof was in the pudding. The opponents' use of rhetoric was merely emblematic of their values as a whole. From Paul's perspective, the gospel of the crucified and risen Christ could not be mediated to the Corinthians by a lifestyle or manner of presentation that implicitly promised health and wealth, success, and an escape from suffering. The contrary values embodied in the ministry style of Paul's opponents thus revealed that their preaching, no matter how persuasive it was rhetorically, was, in reality, poison. They proclaimed themselves to be servants of Christ (11:13, 15), but their way of doing so made it clear that they were serving their own egos. And their corresponding unwillingness to serve the Corinthians unmasked

---

58. Ron Man, "Soli Deo Gloria. To Him Be Glory in the Church!," *Viewpoint* 4/1 (2000), 5.

the hollowness of their profession. Instead of meeting the needs of the Corinthians, they made the Corinthians their slaves (11:18, 20).

This is why Paul did not respond to his opponents' charges by arguing for the "correct" way of praising oneself inoffensively. The question was not simply whether one could boast and how such boasting was to be carried out publicly. Nor did Paul engage his opponents on the question of rhetorical style per se, even though his opponents had made their differing styles a major point of contention. For Paul, the deciding issue was not a distinct manner of speaking. Paul knew that he was not engaged merely in a personality contest in Corinth. As important as it is, the debate, in the end, was over theology, not technique.

Paul's mode of argument in this chapter again reflects his conviction that our public manner inevitably reveals our private character (cf. 1:12–14). He therefore focused his polemic on what his manner of preaching revealed about the character of his person and the content of his proclamation, which he backed up by pointing to his practice of self-support (cf. 2:17; 4:1–2). The heart of the issue is that the gospel we believe will invariably be expressed in the image we portray, and vice versa, so that the integrity of the gospel and its messenger must be our primary concern. A right heart produces appropriate habits, even in the pulpit.

When all is said and done, rhetorical skill can never make up for unbelief. Paul preaches himself as the Corinthians' slave because he preaches the crucified Christ as the glory of God (cf. 4:4–6). So too, if our focus remains centered on faithfulness to the gospel, our concern for a proper image, style, and way of life, though important, will be met when approached with a measure of scriptural and sober self-evaluation. There are no "how to" chapters in the Bible on the technique of public ministry. We can be confident, however, that if we seek to love Christ, we will serve others in ways that honor him, not ourselves.

As a result, because Paul's opponents believe in "another Jesus," they preach themselves as lord and enslave the Corinthians. As Savage points out,

> Far from being humble servants, the opponents actually exploit, take advantage of, assume airs over and insult members of the Corinthian church (11:20). It is clear that in Paul's mind the opponents are patently not proclaiming Jesus as *Lord.*
>
> ... Their self-regarding ambitions represent the exact antithesis of the self-giving gospel of Christ. For this reason, Paul unleashes his most scathing invective on the intruders at Corinth. They are false apostles, workers of deceit, ministers of Satan (11:13–15).[59]

---

59. Savage, *Power Through Weakness*, 157.

Today we often fail to penetrate Paul's argument, thinking that the primary purpose of this passage is to call us to rethink our public image. Indeed, the focus on style and circumstance in this passage may be misleading. Ultimately, however, Paul is not concerned with himself at all. He must spotlight himself in order to expose the darkness of his opponents. That Paul, like Christ, would lower himself in order to exalt the Corinthians (11:7; cf. 4:5; 8:9) reveals the genuine nature of his apostleship. Paul's simple rhetoric, his willing self-support, and his daily suffering for his churches all indicate that his ministry in Corinth, unlike that of his opponents, was aimed at benefiting the Corinthians, not himself. By doing so, Paul's rejection of flashy rhetorical practices and his boasting in his weakness expose those who "masquerade as servants of righteousness" (11:15).

2 Corinthians 12:1–13

I MUST GO on boasting. Although there is nothing to be gained, I will go on to visions and revelations from the Lord. ²I know a man in Christ who fourteen years ago was caught up to the third heaven. Whether it was in the body or out of the body I do not know—God knows. ³And I know that this man—whether in the body or apart from the body I do not know, but God knows—⁴was caught up to paradise. He heard inexpressible things, things that man is not permitted to tell. ⁵I will boast about a man like that, but I will not boast about myself, except about my weaknesses. ⁶Even if I should choose to boast, I would not be a fool, because I would be speaking the truth. But I refrain, so no one will think more of me than is warranted by what I do or say.

⁷To keep me from becoming conceited because of these surpassingly great revelations, there was given me a thorn in my flesh, a messenger of Satan, to torment me. ⁸Three times I pleaded with the Lord to take it away from me. ⁹But he said to me, "My grace is sufficient for you, for my power is made perfect in weakness." Therefore I will boast all the more gladly about my weaknesses, so that Christ's power may rest on me. ¹⁰That is why, for Christ's sake, I delight in weaknesses, in insults, in hardships, in persecutions, in difficulties. For when I am weak, then I am strong.

¹¹I have made a fool of myself, but you drove me to it. I ought to have been commended by you, for I am not in the least inferior to the "super-apostles," even though I am nothing. ¹²The things that mark an apostle—signs, wonders and miracles—were done among you with great perseverance. ¹³How were you inferior to the other churches, except that I was never a burden to you? Forgive me this wrong!

Original Meaning

As WE SAW in the last chapter, the majority of Paul's boasting in 11:1–12:13 is focused on his weakness. As such, it is *not* "foolish" but forms an essential aspect of his apology for being an apostle (11:23–33). Such boasting is also the appropriate means for glorifying

God's grace and power in Paul's ministry (12:5–10). Thus, 11:23–33 and 12:5–10 are part of Paul's *positive* self-commendation as developed earlier in 1:3–11; 2:14–17; 4:7–12; 6:3–10. Conversely, Paul's foolishness is identified *only* with his temporarily joining his opponents in boasting in their Jewish pedigree (11:21b–23b) and in their visions and revelations (12:1–4). The issue is the object of one's boast, not the act of boasting itself (cf. 10:12–18). Indeed, it is Paul's boasting in his weakness, not his boasting per se, that unmasks his opponents' foolishness. So if the polemic situation forces him to boast about himself, he will gladly do so concerning his weakness (11:30; cf. 12:9–10).

In 11:21–33, when forced to boast about his personal distinctives, Paul boasted in his weakness. What supported his claim to be an apostle was not his ethnic pedigree and service to Christ but his suffering for the sake of the gospel and on behalf of God's people. In 12:1–10, Paul now applies the principle of 11:30 to the other major object of his opponents' boasting, namely, their spiritual experiences. But before he boasts in his weakness with regard to his own spiritual experiences, he feels compelled once again to act like a fool, this time by boasting in his revelations themselves (cf. 11:16–21). Just as his opponents' boasting in their ethnic pedigree had forced Paul into the foolish boasting of 11:22, so too their boasting in their spiritual pedigree makes it necessary for Paul to boast foolishly of his own "visions and revelations from the Lord" (12:1).

Paul's Boast in His Weakness and the Boasting of a Fool (12:1–6)

PAUL THUS BEGINS 12:1 exactly as he began 11:30 (the NIV obscures the parallel between these two, both of which begin with the condition, "if it is necessary to boast"), only to complete it this time with a reference to his visions and revelations. However, since such boasting is foolish, he immediately qualifies it as useless; that is, "there is nothing to be gained" from it (cf. 11:23). This is the only reference to a "vision" or "visions" within Paul's writings, and only here and in the parallel reference in 12:7 do we find the plural, "revelations."

The striking absence of references to visions and revelations in Paul's letters demonstrates his lack of interest in sharing such private, spiritual experiences. He viewed them as without benefit either for establishing his authority as an apostle or for building up the church (cf. 1 Cor. 13:1–2; 14:18–19).[1] Indeed, that Paul would refer in 12:1 to his "surpassingly great"

---

1. Elsewhere, "revelation" (*apokalypsis*) refers to the coming of Christ (Rom. 16:25), to the return of Christ and final redemption (Rom. 2:5; 8:19; 1 Cor. 1:7; 2 Thess. 1:7), to

visions and revelations (12:7) and then only recount one of them is itself a reflection of his conviction that such experiences are tangential to a genuine boast in the Lord (cf. 10:17–18).

This same hesitancy to boast in his visions is also reflected in Paul's use of the third person to describe his own being caught up into heaven (12:1–5: "I know *a man* in Christ . . . *this man.* . . . *He* heard inexpressible things. . . . I will boast about *a man* like *that*").[2] He is trying to report his experience while at the same time not reporting it. He wants the Corinthians to evaluate him only on the basis of what they themselves can see and hear from him directly, not on the grounds of personal reports of private mystical experiences (12:6; cf. 1:12–14; 5:11–12; 10:13–15). For this same reason, Paul leaves the circumstances surrounding this experience and its content obscure, telling the Corinthians only that it took place "fourteen years ago." This places it sometime between A.D. 42–44, assuming that 2 Corinthians was written about A.D. 55/56. During this time, Paul was most likely in or around Tarsus or Antioch, prior to his first missionary journey with Barnabas (Acts 9:29–30; 11:25–26; Gal. 1:21).

In line with Paul's commitment not to talk about such things, no known experience or event can be associated with this vision. The closest visions—that is, the call to Jerusalem (Gal. 2:2) and the call to his missionary journeys (Acts 13:1–3)—took place around A.D. 47. Moreover, these words from the Lord were public declarations of his apostolic call and itinerary, not private experiences of God's presence. Indeed, the very fact that he had been quiet about his rapture into heaven for fourteen years demonstrates that he considered such private experiences unimportant for his ministry. In the almost two years that he had spent with the Corinthians, he apparently never mentioned it. In contrast, Paul repeatedly referred to his conversion experience as an essential part of his preaching (cf. 1 Cor. 9:1; 15:1–11; 2 Cor. 2:14–16; 3:4–6; 4:5–6).[3]

---

knowledge given for the sake of others (1 Cor. 14:6, 26), to Paul's public experience of Christ on the road to Damascus (Gal. 1:12; Eph. 3:3; cf. Acts 9:3–9; 22:6–11; 26:12–19; 1 Cor. 9:1; 15:8), to his instruction to go to Jerusalem (Gal. 2:2), and to the knowledge of God's power in our redemption, past and future (Eph. 1:17). For Paul's other recorded visions and revelations prior to the writing of 2 Corinthians, see Acts 16:9–10; 18:9–10 (given at the founding of the church in Corinth, instructing him to continue preaching in that city!); 22:17–21; for those after, see 23:11; 27:23–24. All of these recorded visions and revelations have to do not with Paul's private illumination, but with revealing his missionary itinerary.

2. Contra those who argue that Paul uses the third person simply to follow contemporary rhetorical conventions surrounding self-praise or in accordance with the conventions associated with visions in Jewish pseudepigraphical writings. Nor do I follow C. R. A. Morray-Jones, "Paradise Revisited (2 Cor. 12:1–12): The Jewish Mystical Background of Paul's Apostolate, Part 2: Paul's Heavenly Ascent and its Significance," *HTR* 86 (1993): 265–92, who interprets Paul's use of the third person as possessing a "deeper mystical significance" (273).

3. Ulrich Heckel, *Kraft in Schwachheit*, 59.

The experience Paul describes in 12:2–4 was a personal rapture into the "third heaven," which is equated with being "caught up to paradise" (for the verb used here [*harpazo*], see Acts 8:39; 1 Thess. 4:17; Rev. 12:5). The Judaism of Paul's day could view the heavenly realm as consisting of various numbers of levels (e.g., three, five, seven, or ten).[4] In this case, the parallel between the "third heaven" and "paradise" indicates that Paul's reference is to the highest spiritual realm, where one encounters the very presence of God.[5]

Although Paul is unsure *how* this experience took place—that is, whether he was actually transported there "in the body" or went there in a vision "out of the body"—he is sure *that* it took place. This is underscored by his twofold testimony to *God's* knowledge of the mechanics of the event, since the "divine passive" in verses 2 and 4 indicates that God was the agent who brought it about. Paul "was caught up [*by God*] to the third heaven," which is to say that he "was caught up [*by God*] into paradise." Hence, even here Paul is careful to give God the credit for his experience, thereby boasting in the Lord even as he shares what happened to himself.

In recent scholarship, Paul's experience has been associated with the Jewish tradition of "*merkabah* mysticism" (*merkabah* is the Hebrew term for the chariot associated with Ezekiel's vision in Ezek. 1:15–20). As a result, Paul's experience has also been compared to the later rabbinic parable of the four individuals who entered into a paradise "garden" (*pardes*), but only one, Rabbi Aqiba, returned unscathed.[6] But Paul does not use the language of the

---

4. For the New Testament and other Jewish conceptions of the levels in heaven, see Luke 23:43; Rev. 2:7; *1 Enoch* 14:8–25; *2 Enoch* 8:1–3; *Apoc. Moses* 35:2; 37:5; 40:1; *T. Levi* 3:4; 18:10; *T. Abra.* 10 B; *Asc. of Isa.* 3:13; *4 Ezra* 4:7–8. The idea of a threefold heaven (i.e., the atmosphere; the place of the stars; and the abode of God) is apparently built on 1 Kings 8:27; 2 Chron. 2:6; 6:18; Neh. 9:6; Ps. 148:4.

5. Based on the use of the plural in 12:1 ("visions and revelations") and the use of "and" in 12:3, some commentators suggest that 12:1–4 reports two distinct experiences, one of the third heaven and one of paradise. But the parallel between 12:1 and 4 and the single time reference in 12:2 speak against this view. The description of heaven as a "paradise" is based on the use of the Persian loan word "paradise" (*paradeisos*) in the LXX to refer to the garden of Eden (cf. Gen. 2:8–10; 13:10; Isa. 51:3; Ezek. 28:13; 31:8–9). The word originally meant an enclosure or nobleman's walled-in park and comes to mean simply a "park"; for a helpful discussion of this theme, cf. J. Jeremias, "παράδεισος," TDNT, 5:765–73.

6. In Jewish tradition, *pardes* is used for the abode of God within the heavenly temple, which is parallel to the Most Holy Place in the earthly temple as an extension of the Garden of Eden. For the primary sources, see *t. Hag.* 2.1; *y. Hag.* 77b; *b. Hag.* 14b–15b; *Cant. R.* 1.28; *Hekhalot Zutarti* §§338–46; and *Merkabah Rabbah* §§ 671–73. For an application of this tradition to 2 Cor. 12:1–4, see James M. Scott, *2 Corinthians,* 221–25. The view taken here, however, is that although their roots may have something in common (e.g., a basic apocalyptic experience of God in visions and dreams and a common reference to heaven in terms of a garden paradise), beyond such basic elements the two traditions diverge

throne-chariot in this passage. Furthermore, rather than describing any trance-inducing techniques, as is common in *merkabah* mysticism, he simply refers to God's supernatural action of transporting him to heaven.[7] His preaching does not derive from these mystical experiences but from his encounter with Christ on the road to Damascus, from his reception of the traditions of the early church, and from the Scriptures.

This is confirmed by Paul's report in 12:4 that while he was in God's presence, he heard "inexpressible things, things that man is not permitted to tell." Note once again Paul's use of the divine passive: "man is not permitted [*by God*] to tell." Thus, these things were "inexpressible" not because they were unintelligible or because of any inferiority in Paul himself as a mediator, but because God forbade Paul to speak of them. By doing so, God ensured that the basis of apostolic authority did not become ecstatic, mystical experience. The Corinthians must content themselves with what they see and hear in Paul's "earthly" ministry. This stands in stark contrast to his opponents, who evidently were sharing their revelations as a key to their gospel and as a basis of their authority.

Having "boasted" about his own visions and revelations in 12:1–4, albeit indirectly, Paul concludes in verse 5 that this is as close as he will get to declaring his spiritual pedigree, since there is nothing to be gained by such self-promotion based on private experiences (cf. 12:1). If Paul is to boast about himself, he will do so only concerning his weaknesses (v. 5; cf. 11:30). Thus, his reason for not boasting in his visions and revelations is not that he has none (contra the accusations of his opponents). If he were to boast in such things, he would not be a "fool" for doing so, since he would only be stating what is true (12:6a). Nevertheless, he refuses to boast in them because they are useless when it comes to edifying others or establishing his apostolic authority.

Accordingly, Paul restrains himself from such boasting so that no one will brag about him *beyond what can be evaluated objectively* (cf. 5:12–13; 10:7, 11–

---

greatly. What the merkabah mystical texts discuss *at length* (e.g., the manner, purpose, technique, divine names, divine language, legitimating function, and character of the heavenly temple and glory, not to mention the chariot imagery itself), Paul is silent about. Conceptual parallels to Paul, if any, must therefore be suggested with the greatest caution. Moreover, the earliest forms of the Jewish mystical tradition are very late, being attested only in talmudic and early medieval texts. Whether they preserve traditions that extend as far back as the first century remains a contested question. For a *non*-mystical interpretation of the earliest form of the tradition concerning the parable of the four individuals who entered into paradise, see Alon Goshen Gottstein, "Four Entered Paradise Revisited," *HTR* 88 (1995): 69–133. Indeed, Gottstein argues that the point of the Tosefta version of this parable is that a spiritual gluttony for mystical experiences will cause one to fall away from the Torah (p. 116)! In this sense, the rabbinic parable *is* teaching exactly the same point as Paul.

7. I owe this point to Heckel, *Kraft*, 60.

14, 17–18). As we saw in 11:16–33, it is not boasting per se that is foolish, but boasting in those things that are not true, do not edify others, or are irrelevant for establishing the point at hand; what counts is what others can observe concerning his words and deeds (12:6). What the Corinthians *can* see and boast about is Paul's weakness on their behalf, through which they received the Spirit (12:5; cf. 2:14–3:3; 10:11–18). What they *can* hear and boast in is his proclamation of the gospel (12:6; cf. 1:19; 2:17; 4:5; 5:11; 11:3–4; cf. 1 Cor. 1:17; 2:1–5; 4:9–13).

Paul's Strength in His Weakness (12:7–10)

IN 12:7–10, PAUL turns his attention to his appropriate object of boasting. In doing so, the contrasts between the report about the third person in verses 1–6 and the first person account in verses 7–10 are stark. From an opaque description of the highest possible heavenly revelations, Paul moves to a specific declaration of what Christ said about Paul's earthly afflictions. Whereas he was forbidden to speak about what he saw in heaven, he can quote Christ verbatim concerning Paul's life on earth. As a result, Paul's silence over his revelations is broken only by his boast in his weakness, a boast that once again answers the accusations of his opponents (cf. 10:10). The strength of Paul's visions remains "weak" when it comes to revealing God, while Paul's weakness becomes the place of God's power.

In 12:7a, Paul states explicitly his concern that if he did share his private experiences, others would go beyond boasting in his apostolic work to glorifying him as an apostle; that is why he has restrained himself. Because of the great magnitude of his revelations,[8] Paul knew that to boast in his visions, as his opponents were doing, would lead to exalting himself in a way that would cut out the very heart of the gospel. So, rather than causing him to trumpet his visions aloud, the fact that his revelations were "surpassingly

---

8. That is, 12:6b–7 should read as follows: "I refrain, so no one will think more of me than is warranted by what I do or say and [*kai*] because of these surpassingly great revelations. Therefore [*dio*], in order to keep me from becoming conceited, there was given me a thorn in my flesh, a messenger of Satan, to torment me, to keep me from becoming conceited." This reading follows the punctuation represented in the NA²⁷, which rightly takes the beginning of v. 7 ("and because of these surpassingly great revelations") with v. 6 and begins a new sentence with *dio*. In contrast, the NIV connects the beginning of v. 7 with what follows. But to do so, it must ignore the "and" (*kai*) of v. 7a and rearrange the order of the clauses in v. 7ab so that the sentence begins with the "therefore" (*dio*) of v. 7b. Moreover, the NIV does not render the second purpose (*hina*) clause of v. 7, which repeats word for word the first for the sake of emphasis. Keeping Paul from being conceited is derived directly from the granting of the thorn and the tormenting of Satan, which in turn are derived from the magnitude of Paul's revelations.

great" kept him from boasting in them, both for his own sake (cf. 12:5) and that of others (cf. Col. 2:18).

Paul's restraint, however, was not the result of his own moral willpower. In 12:7b, he makes it clear that God kept him from such conceit by granting him "a thorn in [or against] his flesh," that is, "a messenger of Satan" sent to batter or torment him. Once again, Paul uses the divine passive in this verse: "There was given me [by God] a thorn in my flesh." Both Paul's rapture and his thorn are the work of God. As Ralph Martin observes, "The importance of the passive verb, *edothē*, 'was given,' can hardly be exaggerated. God is the unseen agent behind the bitter experience."[9] Paul's use of the divine passive in regard to his receiving this "messenger" as well as for his rapture into heaven may be intended to correct the accusation of his opponents that his "thorn" was the work of Satan alone, not of God. From their perspective, Paul's inability to overcome it thereby called his legitimacy into question.

The exact nature of this "thorn" or satanic messenger has been a matter of much debate. Nonetheless, Ulrich Heckel has convincingly demonstrated that Paul's "thorn in the flesh" in 12:7 and the parallel reference to his "weakness" (*astheneia*) in 12:9 are best taken to refer to some personal sickness.[10] The other options are to understand them as referring to his inner temptations (a view that no longer finds much support) or to his being persecuted by his opponents (a view first found among the Fathers, beginning in the fourth century A.D.). Those who favor this last view emphasize that it was not a thorn *in* the flesh, but a thorn *against* the flesh.[11] They also advocate a parallel between the "messenger of Satan" in 12:7 and the "servants" of Satan in 11:15 and point to the use of the image of a "thorn" in the LXX of Num. 33:55 and Ezek. 28:24 to refer to the enemies of Israel.[12]

---

9. Ralph P. Martin, *2 Corinthians*, 416.

10. Ulrich Heckel, "Der Dorn im Fleisch: Die Krankheit des Paulus in 2Kor 12,7 and Gal 4,13f.," *ZNW* 84 (1993): 65–92. Heckel (84) points out that Paul could have already been suffering under the same illness mentioned in 12:7 at the time of his original preaching in Galatia, referred to in Gal. 4:13. For if Paul received the "thorn in the flesh" at the same time he had his vision, then according to 2 Cor. 12:2 it was present fourteen years earlier than the writing of this letter, ca. 42 A.D. For the image of the thorn as something physical, cf. Ps. 32:4, which is a psalm Paul quotes in Rom. 4:7–8 (the LXX of this verse trans. lit.: "I was tormented when the thorn pricked me"). Luke 13:10–17 (cf. Mark 3:22–30) refers to a "spirit of weakness" (NIV "crippled by a spirit"), which would correspond to Paul's reference here to a demon that causes sickness.

11. The text reads, *skolops tē sarki*, a dative of disadvantage; the locative would be *en* + dative. For this point, see Martin, *2 Corinthians*, 412–413, following Plummer.

12. Against the view that the thorn was Paul's sickness, Paul Barnett, *The Second Epistle to the Corinthians*, 569–70, points as well to the following arguments: (1) *angelos* is generally per-

Yet the "thorn" image in the Old Testament does not always refer to one's enemies (cf. Hos. 2:6; Sir. 43:19). Moreover, the parallel between 2 Corinthians 11:15 and 12:7 is not exact. Satan's servants in 11:15 and the thorn/messenger (Gk. *angelos*, angel) in 12:7 have different functions, so that Paul's response to them is also different. In 11:14–15, Satan appears as an angel of light whose servants, Paul's opponents, must be *opposed* (cf. 10:4–6; 11:4). In chapter 11, Paul therefore fights against his opponents as part of the eschatological battle between Satan and Christ, while in 12:7–10 Paul *accepts* Satan's messenger as the demonic angel who does God's bidding. This is confirmed by the contrast between 12:7–10 and 1 Thessalonians 2:18, where persecution leads to a hindering of Paul's work, not to an education in dependence and humility. Furthermore, in 2 Corinthians 10–11, Paul faces *many* opponents (see 10:12–16; 11:5, 12–15, 18, 22–23; the use of the singular to refer to the opponents in 10:7, 11, 18; 11:4, 20 is collective), whereas in 12:7–10 he faces a *single* messenger.

Finally, the context of 2 Corinthians itself speaks against taking Paul's "thorn" as a reference to his opponents. In 11:13–15, he is not speaking about opponents in general, but about a specific group of false apostles who arrived in Corinth after writing 1 Corinthians (i.e., in the mid-50s A.D.). In 12:7–10, however, Paul's thorn apparently goes back to about A.D. 42.[13] This same emphasis on the fourteen-year-long continuation of the thorn as one of Paul's weaknesses speaks against those who have argued that the messenger was a demon who attacked Paul during his mystical experience because Paul was not worthy to see the throne of God.[14] While there is no doubt that the two units of 12:1–4 and 7–10 are related thematically, the "thorn" should not be limited to Paul's visionary experience. The "thorn" persisted for fourteen years; it was not a onetime experience that accompanied his rapture to the third heaven.[15]

Whatever its exact referent, Heckel has rightly argued that Paul's silence in 12:7 concerning the nature of his "thorn" is intentional. He is not interested in the medical diagnosis of his weakness but in its theological origin (sent by Satan but given by God), in its cause (Paul's great revelations), and in its purpose (to afflict Paul in order to keep him from becoming

---

sonal in Paul's other uses; (2) "to buffet" or "to beat with a fist" (12:7) is an act generally performed by a person (Matt. 26:67; Mark 14:65; 1 Peter 2:20; but see 1 Cor. 4:11, which he himself points to as an exception); (3) the New Testament elsewhere uses the verb in 12:8 "to take away" (*aphistemi*) of persons; and (4) the difficulty of imagining how Paul's exhausting missionary endeavors could have been carried out under such continual sickness.

13. See Heckel, "Dorn," 70, 74–75.

14. For this view see Scott, *2 Corinthians*, 228.

15. I owe this point to Ben Witherington III, *Conflict and Community in Corinth*, 461.

conceited).[16] Hence, rather than calling his divinely granted authority into question, Paul's ongoing weakness is itself proof of the revelations granted to him as an apostle, since they are the ground for his receiving a thorn in the flesh. In 12:7, Paul therefore turns his opponents' argument on its head. The more they call attention to the severity of Paul's weaknesses as a "sick charismatic," the more they themselves point to the exalted nature of his revelations!

At first, Paul reacted to his "thorn in the flesh" as would be expected from one who knew of God's sovereignty over evil and of God's love for his children: He prayed that the Lord would remove the "thorn" (12:8). Paul is no Stoic, who sees the thorn as an opportunity for self-mastery and endurance. Nor is he a theological masochist, who glorifies suffering itself. When suffering hits, Paul prays for deliverance. What is striking is that Paul directs his prayer for deliverance in 12:8 to Christ himself, since such a practice is not common for him.[17]

Paul utters his prayer to Christ despite his own affirmation in 12:7 that the source of his sickness is God's will. Still, the context and content of his prayer make Christ the natural recipient of his request (cf. the stress in 11:31 on the sovereignty of Christ). The One whom the Father raised from the dead, establishing him to be the Lord, is the One to whom Paul prays for his own deliverance from suffering.

That Paul prayed "three times" may simply be a conventional way to emphasize that the prayer was repeated (cf. Ps. 55:17, where the psalmist utters his complaint three times a day[18]). In this case, Paul is simply saying that he prayed repeatedly about the matter. The problem with this reading is that Paul stopped praying after the third time. The reference to "three times" is therefore better taken as signaling an event that is now over and done with, having gone through its beginning, middle, and end.[19] Read in this way, Paul's threefold prayer parallels Jesus' threefold prayer in the Garden of Gethsemane, which also culminated in confidence that the prayer had been answered, even though the cup of suffering remained (Mark 14:32–41).

---

16. Heckel, "Dorn," 80. In view of Paul's silence in 12:7 and elsewhere, all attempts to determine the nature of Paul's sickness remain purely speculative. The main suggestions have been: epilepsy, an eye sickness, a speech impediment, malaria, leprosy, hysteria, or depression (cf. "Dorn," 80–92). Heckel's own best guess is that Paul suffered from debilitating migraine headaches, given the link between the verb used in 12:7, *kolophizo* ("to strike [the head]"), and the related noun *kolaphos* ("a buffet"). This was also Tertullian's understanding (160–220), who says he inherited it from earlier oral tradition (Heckel, 76).

17. That "the Lord" of v. 8 is equal to Christ in v. 9 is seen in the parallel in v. 9 between "my grace," "my power," and "Christ's power." For other examples of prayer to the resurrected Lord, see Acts 7:59–60; 1 Cor. 1:2; 16:22; 1 Thess. 3:12–13.

18. So Scott, *2 Corinthians*, 229.

19. I owe this insight to Heckel, *Kraft*, 84.

God's answer to Paul's prayer in 12:9a and Paul's response in 12:9b–10 form the conclusion both to Paul's experience of his thorn in the flesh (vv. 7b–8) and to his refraining from boasting in his own "surpassingly great revelations" (vv. 5–7a). Instead of removing the thorn, Christ declared that his own grace would be sufficient for Paul in the midst of his suffering, for his weakness would provide the platform for perfecting the Lord's power (v. 9a).

Paul's sufferings can never outstrip God's supply of grace (cf. 1:8–11). For this reason, he will "all the more gladly" boast in his weaknesses instead of his revelations, in order that the power of Christ may dwell on him (v. 9b; cf. 1:9–10; 11:30; 12:5). The promise of God's grace and power leads Paul to be pleased in his sufferings (v. 10a) rather than continuing to pray for their removal, because he now knows that "when" he is weak, "then" he is strong (v. 10b). *Thus, the revelation of Christ's power in Paul's weakness (v. 9b) and Paul's consequent contentment (v. 10a) form the high point of his argument in this passage and, in doing so, provide a summary of the theological substructure of 2 Corinthians as a whole.* To comment on these verses in our words is to risk detracting from their own profundity.

The contrast between Paul's thorn and God's word of grace is yet another expression of the principle established in Jeremiah 9:23–24 and applied to Paul's ministry in 10:17–18. In 10:17–18 "boasting in the Lord" referred to Paul's apostolic ministry of the Spirit (cf. 3:1–3), whereas in 12:9–10 it refers to Paul's suffering (cf. 2:14–17). Just as his founding of the church in Corinth is a boast in the power of God's Spirit, so too his ministry in the midst of weakness is a boast in the power of God's grace (note the parallel between grace and power in 12:9; cf. 4:7–12; 6:3–10). Paul's weakness makes it clear that his apostolic ministry, in all its glory, can only be attributed to the Lord (1:12; 3:4–6; 5:14, 18; 10:8).

Paul is a jar of clay (cf. 4:7). His weakness is the occasion for God's sufficient grace and power. His reference in 12:9 to "Christ's power . . . resting on me" recalls the earlier affirmation in 3:7–18 that under the new covenant the glory of God is being revealed in Christ "unveiled." Here too Paul is reflecting the contrast between his own ministry of the Spirit and the veiled glory on Moses' face and in the tent of meeting, tabernacle, and temple (cf. Ex. 25:8; 40:34; Ezek. 37:27; John 1:14; 2 Cor. 6:16; Rev. 21:3). Christ's declaration and Paul's response in 12:9 are yet another affirmation that the apostle is a mediator of God's transforming presence under the new covenant ministry of the Spirit.

Instead of calling that ministry into question, Paul's various weaknesses (listed in 11:23b–33 and now summarized in 12:10) are therefore his only legitimating boast as an apostle, since they are the means by which God makes known his glory in Christ among the Corinthians (cf. 1:3–11; 2:14–

16a; 3:7—4:6; 4:13—18).[20] For this reason, Paul boasts in the very things that cause others to slander him. His strength in 12:10b is not his personal strength, but the strength that derives from his divinely granted ability to endure adversity for the sake of the gospel (cf. 4:7—18). This then is Paul's strongest argument for the legitimacy of his apostleship: His weaknesses are the basis of Christ's power. For to boast in his weakness (11:30; 12:5, 9—10) is, at the same time, to boast in what the Lord is doing by his grace and power (Jer. 9:22—23).

The Superfluous Nature of Paul's Boast (12:11—13)

IN 12:11, PAUL closes his apology by returning to the point with which he began in 11:1. He has become a fool by boasting in his personal distinctives and private revelations. A desperate situation has called for desperate measures. This is the tragedy of the situation. The need to match his opponents in their boast should not have been necessary in the first place, since the Corinthians themselves should have commended Paul as his "letter of recommendation" (cf. 3:2; 5:12; 7:12; 10:7, 14; also 1 Cor. 9:2). They should have recognized him as of equal standing with the eminent apostles of the church (cf. 2 Cor. 11:5). Here too his positive comparison of himself to these "super-apostles" in support of his legitimacy indicates that the apostles in view in 12:11 are not his opponents, but the leading "pillar" apostles from Jerusalem. To be equal to the false, satanic "apostles" of 11:13—15 would hardly qualify one for commendation by the church.

That Paul has the pillar apostles in view is confirmed by his following disclaimer at the end of 12:11 that such equality is asserted "even though he is nothing." Many commentators think that in saying this, Paul is ironically parroting a taunt from his opponents, who have accused him of being of no account. However, if in 12:11 Paul is comparing himself to those who were apostles before him, then his disclaimer is intended to remind the Corinthians of what he had taught them previously in 1 Corinthians 15:8—9. Paul is "nothing" because he was the "last of the apostles," having previously persecuted the church. Nevertheless, because of God's grace in his life, he worked harder than the rest (1 Cor. 15:10; cf. 2 Cor. 11:23—29), with the Corinthians themselves being the concrete evidence of God's commendation of his ministry (cf. 2 Cor. 3:1—2; 4:2; 6:4; 10:18). Paul *is* nothing, because everything he is and accomplishes are the result of God's power in his weakness (3:4—6; cf. 1 Cor. 3:5—9). Yet, because of this same power, Paul is also no less than the most eminent apostles.

---

20. Paul's argument in 12:9—10 shows the difficulty in maintaining that his boasting in his suffering is also part of his "fool's speech."

In 12:12, Paul supports his assertion of equality by affirming that in addition to his weaknesses, the "things that mark an apostle" (lit., "the signs of the apostle") had also accompanied his ministry. The force of his argument derives from his assumption that this too, as part and parcel of his founding the church in Corinth, was common knowledge among the Corinthians (cf. 3:2–3; 10:12–18; cf. 1 Cor. 4:15).

Moreover, Paul uses the divine passive in 12:12 yet again (the signs of the apostle "were done [by God]") to signal that God was the one who performed these signs through Paul, thereby accrediting his apostolic ministry of the new covenant. The "signs" themselves are the outpouring of the Spirit and its attendant circumstances, especially the conversion and gifting of the believers, as that which characterizes the genuine ministry of the new covenant (cf. 2:17–3:3; 1 Cor. 1:18–2:15; 15:1–11). This interpretation is confirmed by their having been performed "with great perseverance," a reference to Paul's endurance in the ministry in the midst of his weakness and adversity (cf. 6:4).

In addition to the signs of an apostle, Paul goes on to speak of *other* "signs, wonders, and miracles" that accompanied these signs. This distinction between these two sets of signs indicates too that the former signs are not miracles in the narrower sense of that word (*semeion*).[21] In other words, "the things that mark [lit., signs of] an apostle" were done (lit.) "*with* signs, wonders and miracles," which is a threefold description of various miraculous acts, not a reference to three neatly differentiated types of miracles. Paul's point is that the pouring out of the Spirit as the primary sign of apostleship was done among the Corinthians, the authenticity of which was further attested by other miraculous works (cf. Rom. 15:18–19; note Paul's miracles and exorcisms in Acts 13:11; 14:10; 15:12; 16:18; 19:11–12; 28:3–6, 8).

The divine certification of the pouring out of the Spirit with signs, wonders, and miracles was an important part of the apostolic ministry (cf. Acts 2:22, 43; 4:30; 5:12; 14:3; Gal. 3:1–5; Heb. 2:4). Nevertheless, the key sign of apostleship remained the establishment of the church, since false apostles may do counterfeit signs and wonders, but they cannot fake the Spirit's work in conversion (cf. 2 Thess. 2:9 with 1:3–4; also Deut. 13:1–4) In addition, Paul reminds the Corinthians of the triad of "signs, wonders and miracles" in order to "tie the apostle to God's great redemptive event under the new

---

21. The NIV obscures the difference between the (lit.) "signs [*semeia*] of the apostle" and the subsequent reference to the attending, but distinct "signs [*semeia*], wonders and miracles." The NIV rendering gives the impression that the "signs of the apostle" are these "signs, wonders and miracles" themselves. But the change to the dative case in the second instance and the second use of "signs" together with "wonders and miracles" indicates that Paul has two different realities in view.

covenant, focused on Christ's death and resurrection. 'Signs and wonders' mark the Exodus; 'signs, wonders and miracles' mark the death and resurrection of Jesus as at the first Easter and its apostolic proclamation."[22]

Hence, Paul did not treat the Corinthians in any way as inferior to any other church, since he brought to them the same gospel that the apostles did (11:15; 12:11; cf. 1 Cor. 15:9–11). Likewise, this gospel was empowered by the same Spirit and validated by the same confirming miracles of the "second exodus" redemption in Christ (2 Cor. 12:13a). What is more, like Christ, the validity and power of the gospel manifested in these signs were embodied in Paul's willingness to suffer on behalf of the Corinthians, the most poignant example of which was his self-support for the sake of his witness (cf. 11:7–9; 1 Cor. 9:7–18). Thus, in a declaration steeped in irony, Paul acknowledges that the *only* way in which he treated the Corinthians as "inferior" to other churches was that he did not "burden" them financially, a "wrong" for which he now asks to be "forgiven" (12:13b; cf. 2:17). In reality, however, the only one who has been wronged is Paul himself (cf. 2:5–11; 7:12).

WHAT IS THE contemporary significance of Paul's visions, revelations, and rapture into heaven (12:1–4)? What lesson is being taught by Paul's "thorn in the flesh" (12:7–10)? How we understand the function of Paul's experiences within his own cultural and theological context will determine to a large degree how we answer these crucial questions today.

The significance of Paul's experiences in the Spirit. When making the move from Paul's day to our own, it is increasingly common to answer this first question by picturing Paul as a model mystic. There is no doubt, of course, that he had profound visionary experiences. This should not be denied or played down. The important issue, however, is the role they played in Paul's ministry. What must be emphasized is that Paul never derived his authority or the content of his message from such supernatural experiences. Even when the polemic situation in Corinth forced him to speak about them, which he considered the act of a fool, he still refused to mention their content.

Paul's gospel does not come from his experience in heaven, but from the history of redemption recorded in the Scriptures, from early Christian tra-

---

22. Barnett, *Second Corinthians*, 581. For the phrase "signs and wonders" in connection with the Exodus, see Ex. 3:20; 7:3; 8:23; 10:1–2; 15:11; Num. 14:22; Deut. 4:34; 6:22; 7:19; 26:8; 29:3; 34:11; Josh. 3:5; 24:17; Neh. 9:10; Ps. 78:43; 105:27–36; 135:9; Jer. 32:21 (581n.18). For this link in the New Testament, see Acts 7:36.

dition concerning the life, death, and resurrection of Christ, and from his own encounter with the resurrected Christ on the Damascus road. Paul provides no support for a personalized, subjective approach to the truth of the gospel, not to mention the common move in our culture to consider private, immediate experience of more value than God's objective self-revelation in time and space. As important as such experiences were for Paul personally, his private visions never became the subject of his teaching, nor are they held up as a model for others. In this sense, Paul was no mystic.

This conclusion is controversial today not only in the pews but also in the pages of scholarship. For example, Morray-Jones is convinced that the Jewish mystical traditions derived from Ezekiel's vision of the chariot (*merkabah* mysticism) are a source of Paul's perspectives in 12:1–12. As a result, he argues that the "signs and wonders" of an apostle (12:12) are "clearly connected in [Paul's] mind with the 'visions and revelations' by which this authority was conferred upon him."[23] In this view, Paul is echoing the mystical tradition in which "supernatural power and authority are conferred upon the one who attains to the vision of the merkabah, and this person functions as God's emissary and (eschatological?) judge of both Israel and the angels. . . . The visionary ascent to heaven of which Paul is driven to boast seems, then, to be of crucial importance to his claim to apostolic authority and power."[24] "'Merkabah mysticism' was, therefore, a central feature of Paul's experience and self-understanding."[25]

Yet, Paul's refusal to boast in his visions, in contrast to his ready and repeated references to his Damascus road experience, demonstrates the opposite of Morray-Jones' thesis. There is no evidence that Paul derived any aspect of his teaching from a mystical experience. Though his visions may have been a central feature of his personal experience, he kept them to himself, at best viewing them as confirmatory but not determinative of his public ministry. It was not Paul's private, visionary experiences that established his apostolic authority and formed his self-understanding (he mentions them only because is he forced to do so by false apostles). Rather, the "Lord's commendation" (10:18) is seen in Paul's public call, his suffering in public, his public work of the Spirit among his churches, and his public performance of the signs of an apostle, which the Corinthians could see and hear (12:6).

Morray-Jones calls the view "that Paul's visions were important for him personally, but irrelevant to his apostolic claim or Christian belief," as absurd, part of a "hidden agenda . . . to produce a portrait of Paul that conforms to

---

23. Morray-Jones, "Paradise Revisited, Part 2," 274.
24. Ibid., 276–77.
25. Ibid., 283.

rationalist Protestant presuppositions" and "a distortion of the context in which 2 Corinthians 12 occurs."[26] Notwithstanding this objection, the context of chapter 12 is clear: In naming his rapture into heaven, Paul is forced to speak of what otherwise would have remained unsaid. The evidence of his letters concerning the source of his apostolic instruction is equally clear: It derives from sources outside of himself. That he ever taught things he learned in mystical experiences remains a matter of speculation. Like his experience of speaking in tongues (cf. 1 Cor. 14:18–19), such visionary experiences occupied a secondary place in his ministry.

The reason for Paul's silence is that when God makes himself known for the salvation of his people and the judgment of the world, he does not do so mystically in the private experiences of the individual. Rather, God's self-revelation takes place historically in the redemptive events that take place in space and time as they are interpreted and reflected on in the Scriptures. The Word of God is the record and interpretation of the acts of God. The climax of God's self-revelation is therefore the gospel of God's self-revelation in the Word of God become flesh. As its corollary, Paul does not boast in his private experiences but in the Christ who died for his sins and sustains him in the midst of his suffering. Paul's foolish boast in his spiritual experiences consequently reflects and provides support for Emil Brunner's study of the "Central Doctrine of the Christian Faith," in which he characterized Christianity as

> the "absolute opposite" of any religion that views God as disclosing himself immediately to mankind: "In the one form of religion it is claimed as fundamental that God reveals Himself directly to the human soul, in the other as fundamental that God reveals Himself through the Mediator. This is the fundamental distinction."
>
> Requiring personal faith in Jesus Christ, Brunner continues, Christianity affirms that "a real event in time and space . . . is the unique final revelation, for time and for eternity, and for the whole world. . . . Faith in the Mediator—in the event which took place once for all, a revealed atonement—is the Christian religion itself. . . . In distinction from all other forms of religion the Christian religion is faith in the one Mediator. . . ." The fact of the Mediator, Brunner adds, is "the characteristic and final token of the contrast between general religion and the Christian faith."[27]

---

26. Ibid., 284 (cf. n65, following Tabor).

27. As quoted and commented on by Carl F. H. Henry, *God, Revelation and Authority. Vol. III: God Who Speaks and Shows, Fifteen Theses, Part Two* (Wheaton: Crossway, 1999 [1979]), 48, from Brunner's work, *The Mediator* (1947), 30, 40, 456.

We must be careful here. To deny that Paul was a mystic when it came to knowing and communicating the truth of the gospel does not entail denying that the very core of Christianity is its supernaturalism. We are not arguing for a Protestant rationalism. In fact, it has been Protestant rationalism that has most often stressed the priority of private, religious experience as the only locus of truth. If one denies the supernatural acts of God's self-revelation in history and the veracity of his inspired Word, all one has left is general religious experience. To deny history is to be left only with the heart. But as Carl F. H. Henry has emphasized throughout his magisterial work on the centrality of divine revelation to biblical faith, mysticism is to be rejected as the model of experiencing God's truth precisely because God reveals himself miraculously in time and space. In Henry's words:

> Instead of veiling God's person with transcendent mystery or mere probabilities, the Old Testament and New Testament alike offer and define divine revelation and authority as their hallmark. . . .
>
> To bring about [a] significant face-off between Christianity and secularism Christianity must reaffirm its claim of the self-revealed supernatural. Like the ancient Greeks and Romans before them moderns recoil before such biblical claims; Scripture exposes them for the rebellious sinners they are and calls them to moral and spiritual commitments that they resent and resist. . . .
>
> In view of the self-revelation of the living God, Judeo-Christian religion challenges contemporary theology to break its silence concerning the supernatural. . . . The fact should sober us that, as eternity will disclose, modern scientism for all its probing of the universe actually compressed the parameters of reality by deflecting interest from Supernature.
>
> Harry Blamires remarks that [a] "supernatural orientation" is "a prime mark of the Christian mind." "Modern secular thought . . . treats this world as the Thing. . . . Whenever secularism enters the Christian mind, either the Christian mind will momentarily shake that (this worldly) rootedness, or secularism will seduce the Christian mind to a temporary mode of converse which overlooks the supernatural. . . . The Christian mind, thinking christianly, cannot for a moment escape a frame of reference which reaches out to the supernatural."
>
> For Judeo-Christian religion the Supernatural is the one and only personal Supernatural, the living God.[28]

---

28. Carl F. H. Henry, *God, Revelation and Authority. Vol. VI: God Who Stands and Stays, Part Two* (Wheaton: Crossway, 1999 [1983]), 33, quoting Harry Blamires, *The Christian Mind*, 67ff.

The significance of Paul's suffering. We must therefore be careful not to turn Paul's spiritual experiences into a model of mysticism as the foundation of our faith. Paul considered himself a "fool" to boast in such things. In the same way, we must be careful to distinguish his argument concerning his *legitimate* boast from the Stoicism of his day and from its descendant in our own, "the power of positive thinking."[29] Paul was *no* fool to boast in his weaknesses, and God kept him from pride precisely through granting him an unrelenting "thorn in the flesh." Stoics, however, whether ancient or modern, repudiate the reality of external circumstances by affirming a human or semidivine power within them that can "overcome" such "thorns." For the Stoic, this power was usually an impersonal force, like the divine or human "will" or one's own spiritual essence. For the power of positive thinking, this power is the ability to overcome one's circumstances through fighting the negative thoughts they produce.

In stark contrast, when Paul boasts in his weakness, he is not engaging either in the self-mastery of the ancient Stoic or in the reinterpretation of events that is common to the modern "power-of-positive-thinking" movement. For Paul, weakness is not the result of failing to control our passions or being unable to fight negative thoughts or influences. Weakness for Paul is a real suffering and powerlessness because of our existence under the real power and circumstances of sin. The Self cannot subdue sin on its own. Weaknesses cannot be escaped simply by thinking differently. What is needed is not more willpower, but the power of God's grace. When confronted with his thorn in the flesh, Paul does not try to think positively; he prays. His contentment does not come from a renewed ability to exercise his will but from receiving God's grace. He is not seeking a higher virtue of contentment but a supernatural act of deliverance.

Indeed, when confronted with his suffering, Paul can complain to God and call out for help, while Stoics and the power of positive thinking cannot.[30] Paul's threefold prayer for deliverance is an expression of his godliness; for the Stoic it would be a failure of nerve and willpower. The answer to Paul's prayer is in God himself, while the answer for the power of positive thinking is in the Self. Whereas Stoics try to save themselves by relying on their natural endowments, what Paul needs is God's grace. The power of positive thinking says, "I am stronger than fate"; Paul says, "God's power is stronger than the circumstances he himself has orchestrated." The Stoic's goal is self-mastery, and this is what makes him content in the midst of his circum-

---

29. This section is based primarily on the work of Heckel, *Kraft*, 279–88.

30. Heckel, *Kraft*, 96, 99n.226–27, points to the lament Psalms as the key backdrop to Paul's cry to the Lord for deliverance (e.g., Ps. 6:4–5; Jer. 15:10–21; Lam. 3:55–57; esp. Ps. 6:2; 32:11; 106:47, in which the lament leads to a boasting in God). Paul's complaint is therefore itself an expression of his faith.

stances; Paul's goal is the glory of God, and this is what causes him to rejoice in the midst of his suffering (12:10).

That Paul's faith is not to be confused with self-mastery or the power of positive thinking means that suffering is a means to an end rather than the necessary condition to that end. Paul does not glorify suffering as the necessary condition for spirituality, though all people will suffer to varying degrees. Instead, he recognizes its presence as a (not *the*) platform for the revelation of God's grace. This is why he can pray for its removal.

This is also why Paul's point in 12:10 is that *whenever* he is weak, then he is strong; not *if* he is weak, then he is strong. Weakness is a ground of Christ's power, not its one and only condition. The experience of Christ's power is not a reward or payment for suffering, nor must we seek suffering in order to experience his grace. By boasting in hardships and persecutions, Paul is not laying the foundation for a theology of martyrdom as the goal of spirituality; he is boasting in Christ's sufficiency for every situation.

For this reason, it is important to note that the sufferings Paul lists here are all passive. He does not seek to suffer. Even his voluntary practice of self-support was softened, when possible, by the contributions of other churches (cf. 11:8–9). His point is not that the weaker he is, the stronger he is, which would wrongly lead to seeking suffering for the sake of a supposedly deeper spirituality. Rather, Paul's point is that Christ's power is present *in* his suffering, whenever and wherever and however such suffering should, in God's providence, come his way.

Paul acknowledges the presence of suffering, and its essential role as part of his apostolic calling is presupposed, but there is no universal call to suffer in Paul's theology. Even for the apostle himself, it is not his weakness as such that provides the seal of his apostleship but the power of Christ at work in his weakness, a power manifested in the establishment of the Corinthian church. It is only the power of Christ that makes Paul content with his suffering.

In 12:5, 7–10, Paul is not teaching an imitation of Christ in his suffering. Suffering does not make one a Christian or an apostle, Christ does. It is crucial not to confuse the role of suffering in Paul's life as an apostle with the universal call for humility before the sovereign God. His thorn in the flesh was God's particular prescription to keep him from being conceited (12:7); it may not be ours. It is the universal need for humility as it expresses itself in dependence on God's sovereignty and love, not weakness and suffering per se, that Paul has in view in this passage.[31] Not all who suffer are humble and not all who are humble suffer.

---

31. See Timothy B. Savage, *Power Through Weakness*, 167: "It is axiomatic in the OT that God 'dwells with the contrite and lowly of spirit' (Isa. 57:15), 'looks to the humble' (66:2) and 'is near the broken hearted' (Ps. 34:18). Where there is humility there, too, will be the power of God."

Contemporary Significance

AS WE HAVE seen, when Paul concludes in 12:11–12 that he has become foolish, he is referring to the two specific times he felt compelled to engage in boasting about his "strength": in regard to his spiritual heritage (11:22–23a) and concerning his spiritual experiences (12:1–4). As A. T. Lincoln has put it, "What is ... specifically at issue in II Corinthians 12 is what is to count as evidence for the legitimacy of claims to apostleship.... Paul will rely on the evidence that is plainly before the Corinthians' eyes (cf. also 10:7; 11:6)."[32] What the Corinthians can see is Paul's perseverance in suffering for the sake of the gospel as a testimony to the grace of Christ itself.

Nonetheless, like the Corinthians, we are often tempted to exchange Paul's gospel for one of Stoic self-reliance and willpower or pseudo-charismatic experientialism. We find ourselves prone to glorify suffering as the pathway to spirituality rather than accepting it as part of the God-ordained fabric of living in a fallen world. Nevertheless, Paul's experience embodied the truth that both the thorn in the flesh and the power of God's presence to endure it come from the gracious hand of God's sovereignty for the good of his people. Paul's experience, portrayed so profoundly in 12:9–10, is not a call to suffering per se but an expression of God's promise to all Christians whenever they too, like Paul, are led into situations of weakness and hardship (cf. 2:14). The good news of the gospel is that those who find themselves weak but boast in God can expect the same message from Christ that Paul received: "My grace is sufficient for you, for my power is made perfect in weakness" (12:9a).

The question of whether or not experiences of rapture like that of Paul's still happen today is therefore irrelevant. If they do, those who experience them are to keep it to themselves. Such experiences have value only for those who have them. Our only source of divine revelation remains the all-sufficient Word of God and Word of God become flesh. Our only boast, like that of Paul's, is in our weakness as the platform for the display of Christ's power and grace.

Not experience, but emptiness! This passage poses at least three challenges to the contemporary church. First, Paul's boasting in his weakness because of the all-sufficient grace of Christ challenges our current propensity to create Christian celebrities based on their "spiritual experiences" and "power" and to mimic their mysticism. From his experience week in and week out among God's people, Pastor Arturo Azurdia has pointed out the dangers of such foolishness for the life of the local church.

32. A. T. Lincoln, "'Paul the Visionary': The Setting and Significance of the Rapture to Paradise in II Corinthians XII.1–10," *NTS* 25 (1979): 204–20.

Two serious concerns should be aroused within us related to these "Holy Spirit experiences." Firstly, from a *pastoral* perspective, we need to be concerned that the spiritual development of well-meaning Christians can become vulnerable to the law of diminishing returns. That is to say, the maturing of a Christian will be consistently impaired if devotion to Jesus Christ is determined by fresh experiences of spiritual ecstasy. Why is this the case? Because one's sensation of being overpowered by God will need to steadily intensify. The ordinary will give way to the unusual. The unusual will surrender to the extreme. The extreme will topple to the ridiculous. Often, the inevitable consequence is spiritual emptiness.[33]

Azurdia goes on to quote Gardiner's helpful insight that

the seeker for experience goes back through the ritual again and again, but begins to discover something; ecstatic experience, like drug-addiction, requires larger and larger doses to satisfy. . . . Eventually there is a crisis and a decision is made; he will sit on the back seats and be a spectator, "fake it," or go on in the hope that everything will eventually be as it was. The most tragic decision is to quit and in the quitting abandon all things spiritual as fraudulent. The spectators are frustrated, the fakers suffer guilt, the hoping are pitiable and the quitters are a tragedy.[34]

Even more important, there is a *doctrinal* concern raised by Paul's example. Those who seek such spiritual experiences as the focus of their seeking God do so because they operate with an expectation concerning the ministry of the Holy Spirit that is "Christian-centered rather than Christ-centered."[35] Paul's example, however, reveals that the role of the Holy Spirit is to glorify the all-sufficiency of the grace of Christ in the midst of the very adversity and suffering, weakness and persecution that would seem to call it into question. As Azurdia summarizes it, "the vitality of the Spirit is His effectual work of glorifying Jesus Christ through fallible men who faithfully proclaim the Christocentric scriptures."[36] Thus, to be effectively glorifying God, "the preacher must recognize, and even revel in, his own human inabilities."[37] And what is true for our apostles and pastors is true for us as well.

---

33. Arturo G. Azurdia, *Spirit Empowered Preaching: The Vitality of the Holy Spirit in Preaching* (Geanies House, Fearn, Rosshire, Great Britain: Christian Focus Publications, 1998), 49.

34. George Gardiner, *The Corinthian Catastrophe*, 55; quoted by Azurdia, *Spirit Empowered Preaching*, 49.

35. Azurdia, *Spirit Empowered Preaching*, 50.

36. Ibid., 66–67.

37. Ibid., 143, commenting on 1 Cor. 2:3–5; 2 Cor. 4:7; 12:7–10.

The life of Charles Haddon Spurgeon, whose power in the ministry was embedded in a life of emotional and physical suffering, is a profound example of Paul's principle that Christ's power is perfected in the weakness of his servants. Spurgeon suffered recurring bouts of depression throughout his adult life. Because of his own popularity and the unpopular stands he took against the theological liberalism of his day, Spurgeon also had to endure constant ridicule from others, including other pastors. Added to this was his need to provide relentless care for his wife, who was an invalid for most of their marriage. As if this were not enough, Spurgeon spent a third of his last twenty-seven years of ministry out of the pulpit because of his own physical illness. There was hardly a weakness, insult, hardship, or difficulty (12:10) that Spurgeon did not know personally.

Nevertheless, this was Spurgeon's response to his suffering and weaknesses as a minister:

> Instruments shall be used, but their intrinsic weakness shall be clearly manifested; there shall be no division of the glory, no diminishing of the honor due the Great Worker. The man shall be emptied of self, and then filled with the Holy Ghost.... My witness is, that those who are honored of their Lord in public, have usually to endure a secret chastening, or to carry a peculiar cross, lest by any means they exalt themselves, and fall into the snare of the devil.... Such humbling but salutary messages our depressions whisper in our ears; they tell us in a manner not to be mistaken that we are but men, frail, feeble, apt to faint.[38]

Listen to this same testimony concerning the life of the believer in general from the German monk Thomas à Kempis (1379/80–1471):

> It is good that we sometimes have griefs and adversities, for they drive a man to behold himself and to see that he is here but as in exile, and to learn thereby that he ought not put his trust in any worldly thing. ... Therefore, a man ought to establish himself so fully in God that, whatever adversity befall him, he will not need to seek any outward comfort.[39]

Not exalting self, but exposing God! Second, Paul's boasting in his weakness challenges our preoccupation with our Self, whether positively or negatively. In regard to the latter, Paul's call to carry the treasure of God's glory

---

38. From Spurgeon's *Lectures to my Students*, quoted by Azurdia, *Spirit Empowered Preaching*, 145–46, from whom I also learned of the amount of time Spurgeon was sick.

39. Thomas a Kempis, *The Imitation of Christ*, ed. Harold C. Gardiner (Garden City: Image Books, 1955) 43–44.

in a "jar of clay" (cf. 4:7) did not lead him to a life of self-pity. Concerning the former, his boasting in his weakness did not lead to an attitude of exalting sacrifice, in which he paraded before others how much he had "given up for God." Instead, his experience moved others to join him in trusting and praising the "God of all comfort" (1:3, 6, 11). Everywhere that God led Paul to death, his suffering revealed "the knowledge of God" (2:14). Hence, knowing that God was using Paul's suffering to reveal his grace, he "gladly" boasted in his weaknesses and "delighted" in his hardships. In turn, such joy in the midst of adversity magnified the very sufficiency of Christ that he proclaimed (12:9–10).

We must therefore not subvert Paul's passion for the power of Christ into a modern Stoicism of self-control, willpower, and positive thinking. In boasting in his weakness, Paul is not boasting in his own patience and ability to endure tribulation. By boasting "gladly" in his hardships, Paul is confessing in word and deed his contented dependence on the grace of Christ. Suffering is not praised for itself, but because it carries with it this promise of Christ's power. It cannot be overemphasized that God refused to remove Paul's thorn in order to teach Paul this fundamental truth: *"God is most glorified in us, when we are most satisfied in him."*[40]

To that end, God would not allow Paul to become self-assertive, self-dependent, self-satisfied, or self-glorifying because of the great revelations he had received. Suffering strips away second-rate sources of happiness, even divinely granted spiritual experiences and revelations, driving us to depend on God alone to satisfy the deepest longings of our heart. For this reason, Paul's example reminds us that our public ministry, pulpit presence, programs, and personal lives should all communicate our utter dependence on and satisfaction in God, rather than calling attention to our own strength, experiences, and, if we are in the ministry, "professionalism." This will be difficult, given the cultural pressure around us to do otherwise. Paul too was conscious that he did not meet the cultural expectations of the Corinthians, but he refused to do so for the sake of the gospel.

Paul's example in 12:1–10 certainly carries the general application we have drawn from it above. But 12:11–13 makes it clear that Paul's primary focus here is on his own ministry as an apostle (for the issue of money in the ministry and Paul's practice of self-support, cf. our earlier discussions of 2:17; 11:7–12). The primary application of this passage will thus be to our leaders and ministers of the gospel.

At this point, we thus turn our attention directly to the issue of style in the pulpit. Though not mentioned explicitly in 12:1–13, it is clear from the

---

40. John Piper, *Desiring God*, 50.

larger context that the false teachers' boasting in their spiritual experiences was an essential aspect and extension of their self-exalting use of rhetoric (cf. 10:10; 11:4–6). Their self-commendation was a complex mixture of word and deed, with their boasting in their "strength" no doubt being matched by their "strong" persona as professional "public speakers." Today, as in Paul's day, "boasting in our weaknesses" (12:5, 10) will consequently mean turning our back on all attempts to cultivate a manufactured "rhetorical presence" in the pulpit, since doing so will cloud the presence of Christ's power and grace in our weakness. So, having already looked to Spurgeon for the role of suffering in the life of the minister, it is only fitting that we turn to him as well for counsel on the public task of preaching.

Given Paul's battle with his opponents over the public image of the pastor, it is striking that Spurgeon's two published lectures on preaching focus on "posture" and rhetorical techniques in the pulpit, not on theology per se (though he certainly taught plenty of that!). Like Paul, Spurgeon takes up this topic because he knew how significant the image of the preacher can be for the promulgation of the gospel. As Spurgeon observed, posture and actions are comparatively small aspects of the preaching process, but "in the service of God even the smallest things should be regarded with holy care."[41]

Spurgeon himself was known for his drama, wit, and movement in the pulpit. He was certainly not against using a style that forcefully communicated the power and passion of the Scriptures. His concern, like Paul's, was that the persona of the preacher be genuine and that it fit the content of the message rather than being theatrical or rhetorical for their own sake or for the sake of making an "impression." As a result, Spurgeon insisted that his students rid themselves of any mannerisms or quirks that distracted others by calling attention to themselves instead of to their message. In Spurgeon's words, "It is not so much incumbent upon you to acquire right pulpit action as it is to get rid of that which is wrong" (273).

Because of his concern for authenticity and effectiveness in the pulpit, Spurgeon admonished his students that "we should never advise you to practice postures before a glass, nor to imitate great divines, nor to ape the fine gentleman; but there is no need, on the other hand, to be vulgar or absurd" (274). Rather, the point is to be oneself when preaching, so that the pastor's passion for God comes through naturally. Spurgeon was convinced that to feign passion or to produce a gesture self-consciously "at just the right time" contradicts the inherent power of the message and reveals the pastor's lack

---

41. C. H. Spurgeon, "Posture, Action, Gesture, etc.," *Lectures to My Students* (Grand Rapids: Zondervan, 1972), 272–304 (p. 272). The page numbers for the quotes from his lectures are given in the body of the text.

of conviction. Instead, the pastor "goes to work with all his heart, and drops into the positions most natural to an earnest man, and these are the most appropriate.... Unstudied gestures, to which you never turned your thoughts for a moment, are the very best" (279). It follows, then, that "perhaps a man is nearest to the golden mean in action when the manner excites no remark either of praise or censure, because it is so completely of a piece with the discourse that it is not regarded as a separate item at all" (284).

Part of why Paul was so angry with the false teachers is that preaching must not be an act. Whether preaching or listening to the preaching of others, we are to "loathe all affectation ... all tricks and stage effects are unbearable when the message of the Lord is to be delivered. Better a ragged dress and rugged speech, with artless, honest manner, than clerical foppery. Better far to violate every canon of gracefulness than to be a mere performer, a consummate act, a player upon a religious stage" (301). Just as Paul remained an "amateur in speech," Spurgeon taught his students that they were to "shun the very appearance of studied gesture ... your pulpit manner is only worth a moment's thought because it may hinder your success by causing people to make remarks about the preacher when you want all their thoughts for the subject" (302).

By "success" in the pulpit, Spurgeon means the successful communication of the *gospel*, not the successful mastery of rhetorical techniques: "The whole should be, not for the winning of honor to ourselves, but for the glory of God and the good of men; if it be so there is no fear of your violating the rule as to being natural, for it will not occur to you to be otherwise" (302). Hence, by "natural," Spurgeon means being spontaneously filled with wonder over the glory of God and with heartfelt humility over what God has done for his people. "Above all, be so full of the matter, so fervent, and so gracious that the people will little care how you hand out the word; for if they perceive that it is fresh from heaven, and find it sweet and abundant, they will pay little regard to the basket in which you bring it to them" (303–304).

For this reason, Spurgeon maintains that the most essential quality for success in the ministry is earnestness: "Men prosper in the divine service in proportion as their hearts are blazing with holy love."[42] The application of 2 Corinthians 11:1–12:10 to the ministry is clear: "Let mere actors beware, lest they be found sinning against the Holy Spirit by their theatrical performances.... To sham earnestness is one of the most contemptible of dodges for courting popularity; let us abhor the very thought."[43]

---

42. C. H. Spurgeon, "Earnestness: Its Marring and Maintenance," *Lectures to My Students* (Grand Rapids: Zondervan, 1972), 305–20 (p. 305).

43. Ibid., 308.

Not tomorrow, but today! Finally, Paul's boasting in his weakness challenges our very definition of spirituality. In view of Christ's own death and resurrection, we should not consider it a strange providence of God that, like Paul, our own greatest experiences of Christ's grace and power often (though not always) come through our experiences of suffering and difficulties. Indeed, Paul's testimony that Christ's "power is made perfect in weakness" (12:9) has been confirmed throughout the ages. John Piper's "Meditation on Psalm 119:71," entitled, "Luther, Bunyan, Bible and Pain," is a poignant reminder of this truth.

From 1660 to 1672, John Bunyan, the English Baptist preacher, and author of *Pilgrim's Progress*, was in the Bedford county jail. He could have been released if he had agreed not to preach. He did not know which was worse—the pain of the conditions or the torment of freely choosing it, in view of what it cost his wife and four children. His daughter, Mary, was blind. She was 10 when he was put in jail in 1660.

"The parting with my Wife and poor children hath often been to me in this place as the pulling of the Flesh from my bones . . . not only because I am somewhat too fond of these great Mercies, but also because I . . . often brought to my mind the many hardships, miseries and wants that my poor Family was like to meet with should I be taken from them, especially my poor blind child, who lay nearer my heart than all I had besides; Oh the thoughts of the hardship I thought my Blind one might go under, would break my heart to pieces."[44]

But this broken Bunyan was seeing treasures in the Word of God because of this suffering that he would probably not have seen any other way. He was discovering the meaning of Psalm 119:71, "It is good for me that I was afflicted, that I may learn Your statutes."

"I never had in all my life so great an inlet into the Word of God as now [in prison]. The Scriptures that I saw nothing in before are made in this place to shine upon me. Jesus Christ also was never more real and apparent than now. Here I have seen him and felt him indeed. . . . I have seen [such things] here that I am persuaded I shall never while in this world be able to express. . . . Being very tender of me, [God] hath not suffered me to be molested, but would with one scripture and another strengthen me against all; insomuch that I have often said, were it lawful I could pray for greater trouble for the greater comfort's sake."[45]

---

44. John Bunyan, *Grace Abounding to the Chief of Sinners* (Hertfordshire: Evangelical Press, 1978), 123.

45. Ibid., 123.

In other words, one of God's gifts to us in suffering is that we are granted to see and experience depths of his Word that a life of ease would never yield. Martin Luther had discovered the same "method" of seeing God in his Word. He said there are three rules for understanding Scripture: praying, meditating and suffering trials. The "trials," he said, are supremely valuable: they "teach you not only to know and understand but also to experience how right, how true, how sweet, how lovely, how mighty, how comforting God's word is: it is wisdom supreme." Therefore the devil himself becomes the unwitting teacher of God's word: "the devil will afflict you [and] will make a real doctor of you, and will teach you by his temptations to seek and to love God's Word. For I myself ... owe my papists many thanks for so beating, pressing, and frightening me through the devil's raging that they have turned me into a fairly good theologian, driving me to a goal I should never have reached."[46]

I testify from my small experience that this is true. Disappointment, loss, sickness and fear send me deeper into God and his Word than ever. Clouds of trifling are blown away and the glory of unseen things shines in the heart's eye. Let Bunyan and Luther encourage us to lean on God's Word as never before in times of affliction. I know that there are seasons when we cannot think or read, the pain is so great. But God grants spaces of some relief between these terrible times. Turn your gaze on the Word and prove the truth of Psalm 119:71, "It is good for me that I was afflicted, that I may learn Your statutes."[47]

If our weakness is the platform for the revelation of Christ's grace and power, then what do we reveal to the world? In answer to this question, the same Spurgeon who suffered so much himself told his congregation that one of the central points of 2 Corinthians 12:9 is that God's grace is *now* sufficient for whatever need we may face. In the end, Paul's boast in his weakness summons us to trust in the sufficiency of Christ today.

> It is easy to believe in grace for the past and the future, but to rest in it for the immediate necessity is true faith. ... At this moment, and at all moments which shall ever occur between now and glory, the grace of God will be sufficient for you. This sufficiency is declared without any limiting words [in 12:9], and therefore I understand the passage

---

46. Martin Luther, *What Luther Says*, Vol. 3 (St. Louis: Concordia, 1959), 1360.

47. John Piper, *The Bethlehem Star* (Minneapolis: Bethlehem Baptist Church, January 19, 1999), 4.

to mean that the grace of our Lord Jesus is sufficient to uphold thee, sufficient to strengthen thee, sufficient to comfort thee, sufficient to make thy trouble useful to thee, sufficient to enable thee to triumph over it, sufficient to bring thee out of it, sufficient to bring thee out of ten thousand like it, sufficient to bring thee home to heaven. Whatever would be good for thee, Christ's grace is sufficient to bestow; whatever would harm thee, his grace is sufficient to avert; whatever thou desirest, his grace is sufficient to give thee if it be good for thee; whatever thou wouldst avoid, his grace can shield thee from it if so his wisdom shall dictate. . . . Here let me press upon you the pleasing duty of taking home the promise personally at this moment, for no believer here need be under any fear, since for him also, at this very instant, the grace of the Lord Jesus is sufficient.[48]

---

48. C. H. Spurgeon, "Strengthening Words from the Saviour's Lips," a sermon on 2 Cor. 12:9 delivered on April 2, 1876, now in *The Metropolitan Tabernacle Pulpit*, Vol. 22 (London: Passmore & Alabaster, 1877), 193–204 (pp. 196–97).

2 Corinthians 12:14–13:14

❧

NOW I AM ready to visit you for the third time, and I will not be a burden to you, because what I want is not your possessions but you. After all, children should not have to save up for their parents, but parents for their children. ¹⁵So I will very gladly spend for you everything I have and expend myself as well. If I love you more, will you love me less? ¹⁶Be that as it may, I have not been a burden to you. Yet, crafty fellow that I am, I caught you by trickery! ¹⁷Did I exploit you through any of the men I sent you? ¹⁸I urged Titus to go to you and I sent our brother with him. Titus did not exploit you, did he? Did we not act in the same spirit and follow the same course?

¹⁹Have you been thinking all along that we have been defending ourselves to you? We have been speaking in the sight of God as those in Christ; and everything we do, dear friends, is for your strengthening. ²⁰For I am afraid that when I come I may not find you as I want you to be, and you may not find me as you want me to be. I fear that there may be quarreling, jealousy, outbursts of anger, factions, slander, gossip, arrogance and disorder. ²¹I am afraid that when I come again my God will humble me before you, and I will be grieved over many who have sinned earlier and have not repented of the impurity, sexual sin and debauchery in which they have indulged.

¹³:¹This will be my third visit to you. "Every matter must be established by the testimony of two or three witnesses." ²I already gave you a warning when I was with you the second time. I now repeat it while absent: On my return I will not spare those who sinned earlier or any of the others, ³since you are demanding proof that Christ is speaking through me. He is not weak in dealing with you, but is powerful among you. ⁴For to be sure, he was crucified in weakness, yet he lives by God's power. Likewise, we are weak in him, yet by God's power we will live with him to serve you.

⁵Examine yourselves to see whether you are in the faith; test yourselves. Do you not realize that Christ Jesus is in you—unless, of course, you fail the test? ⁶And I trust that you

will discover that we have not failed the test. ⁷Now we pray to God that you will not do anything wrong. Not that people will see that we have stood the test but that you will do what is right even though we may seem to have failed. ⁸For we cannot do anything against the truth, but only for the truth. ⁹We are glad whenever we are weak but you are strong; and our prayer is for your perfection. ¹⁰This is why I write these things when I am absent, that when I come I may not have to be harsh in my use of authority—the authority the Lord gave me for building you up, not for tearing you down.

¹¹Finally, brothers, good-by. Aim for perfection, listen to my appeal, be of one mind, live in peace. And the God of love and peace will be with you.

¹²Greet one another with a holy kiss. ¹³All the saints send their greetings.

¹⁴May the grace of the Lord Jesus Christ, and the love of God, and the fellowship of the Holy Spirit be with you all.

SECOND CORINTHIANS 12:14–21 is the last section of Paul's extended defense of his legitimacy as an apostle, which extends from 10:7–12:21. Having completed his argument, Paul returns in 13:1– 10 to the exhortations with which he began in 10:1–6. The admonitions of 10:1–6 and 13:1–10 thereby frame the apologetic of 10:7–12:21. Moreover, these last two sections of Paul's letter, both of which are introduced by a reference to his third visit (12:14; 13:1), do not introduce new material but conclude Paul's letter by recalling earlier discussions. In doing so, Paul highlights what he considers the central issues in the conflict. In 13:11–14, he then ends his letter with a final word of exhortation and a closing benediction.

Paul's Final Appeal Regarding His Legitimacy as an Apostle (12:14–21)

IN 12:14, PAUL once again takes up the theme of his travel plans by explicitly announcing his upcoming, third visit to Corinth (cf. 1:15–2:1; 9:3–5).[1] His current readiness to return reflects the changed situation in Corinth. Now that the majority has repented in response to his "tearful letter" (2:4, 9; 7:4–16), the apostle will return to solidify the faithful (6:14–7:1; 7:2), com-

---

1. Paul's first visit was his founding visit (described in Acts 18); his second was the "painful" visit recounted in 2 Cor. 2:1.

plete the collection as evidence of their repentance (chs. 8–9), and sift out those still in rebellion against him (cf. 10:1–6; 13:1–4). Accordingly, the paragraphs before us are Paul's last attempt to keep this rebellious minority from the judgment of God to come.

Given these purposes, it is not surprising that in announcing his impending visit Paul emphasizes one last time his commitment to support himself in Corinth (12:14–18; cf. 2:17; 11:7–12; 12:13). This theme, above all, encapsulates his own claims as an apostle, while at the same time calling into question the counterclaims of his opponents. Paul's self-support was a dramatic expression of his call to suffer on behalf of his churches (2:14; 4:7–12; 6:3–10; 11:23–33). For this reason, he refuses to stop boasting in this practice in order to expose the motives of his opponents (11:9–12, 20–21). Paul maintained that his opponents' demand for support revealed the true character of their hearts (cf. 2:17; 11:12, 20). To them, however, Paul's self-support revealed that he preached a second-class message of no value and created a "pious" smokescreen for his attempt to defraud the Corinthians through the collection (7:2; 8:18–24).

Hence, in spite of their criticism and in accordance with his principle of self-support for the sake of the gospel (1 Cor. 9:18), Paul will continue not to "burden" the Corinthians with his monetary needs when he returns for his third visit (12:14). Unlike his opponents, he is not interested in benefiting financially from them. Instead, he "wants [lit., seeks] the Corinthians" themselves (12:14b). In stark contrast to the false apostles, Paul does not lord his authority and status over the Corinthians for his *own* material benefit. Instead, as *their* slave, he works to support himself because he desires their welfare (cf. 4:5). Specifically, Paul is referring to the fact that all of his ministry, including his upcoming visit, is aimed at solidifying their faith for the sake of their own happiness (cf. 1:24).

In 12:14b–15a, Paul supports his affirmation that he is seeking the Corinthians' welfare, not his own, by returning to the imagery of parenthood to describe his relationship with the church. Because he is their spiritual father, Paul is responsible to give to his "children," not the other way around, even if this means pouring out his life on their behalf (cf. 1 Cor. 4:14–15; 2 Cor. 2:14; 3:3; 4:10–12; 6:11–12; 7:3).

James Scott goes so far as to suggest that Paul's refusal to accept support from the Corinthians reflects his evaluation of them as still in their infancy as believers (cf. 1 Cor. 3:1), since grown children can be expected to provide for their parents (Ex. 20:12; 21:17; Mark 7:8–13).[2] This would explain why Paul was willing to receive financial support from churches he considered

---

2. James M. Scott, *2 Corinthians*, 243–44.

more mature in their faith (cf. 2 Cor. 11:8–9). It could also explain why the Corinthians could interpret Paul's refusal to take their money to mean that they were "inferior" to his other churches (cf. 12:13).

Paul's practice of self-support, however, is not a putdown. Even if their continuing struggles do show that the Corinthians have not yet grown up in Christ, Paul gives up his life for the Corinthians because he feels the love of a father for his children (cf. 2:4; 6:13; 11:11). And to continue to support himself is no drudgery. As their father in the faith, Paul "gladly spends" himself for the Corinthians (12:15a).

Thus, with yet another jab at his opponents, Paul uses a rhetorical question in verse 15b to draw the only conclusion that can possibly follow from this concrete evidence of his fatherly love toward the Corinthians. Paul's loving them "more" than his opponents by refusing to take their money should not cause the Corinthians to love him "less" than those who *demand* their money. The Corinthians must reject the model of patronage advanced by his opponents, in which the false apostles purport to "honor" the Corinthians by relying on their financial support, while the Corinthians gain the self-satisfaction of being their benefactors. The Corinthians are not Paul's patron; rather, he is their parent in the faith. He is not dependent on the Corinthians as their client; rather, they are dependent on Paul as his children.[3] If the Corinthians want to show the maturity of their faith by giving away their money, they should do so by contributing to the collection for Jerusalem (chs. 8–9).

In 12:16–18, Paul presses home his point. Those Corinthians who are still rebelling against him must now make a final decision. Are they right that Paul's practice of self-support was simply a smokescreen to cover up his attempt to defraud them, an accusation that Paul parodies in 12:16 (cf. 8:20–21)? Was Paul skimming off the collection to line his own pockets? Regardless of the Corinthians' perspective on Paul's practice of self-support ("Be that as it may," v. 16), they cannot deny that Paul did not burden them by asking for their money (12:16a).

Titus's careful handling of the money and Paul's sending of the well-respected "brother" to Corinth also speak concretely against his opponents' accusation (12:17–18; cf. 8:6, 16–24).[4] Since Paul is the one who gave Titus

---

3. Following the emphasis of Paul Barnett, *The Second Epistle to the Corinthians*, 585–86: "Let the Corinthians understand that his self-support by manual labor is not motivated by a lack of love, as if to demean them. To the contrary, his sacrifice expresses the depth of his love (cf. 2:4; 8:7; 11:11). . . . In his ministry Paul replicates the sufferings of Christ as he gives himself for the people."

4. Paul's failure to mention the second brother sent with Titus is probably due to the famous nature of the first unnamed brother, whose presence is of most importance (cf. 8:17–19). There is no need to see a distinction between 12:18 and chapter 8, with chap-

and the brother their mandate, he can argue from their integrity to his own (12:18a). The two rhetorical questions in 12:18 make it clear that an examination of Titus's behavior and of Paul's own precautions against suspicion should lead the Corinthians to the only appropriate conclusion: Titus's honesty is merely a reflection of "the same spirit" and conduct in Paul (cf. 7:2).

In 12:19, Paul's rhetorical questions continue. This time he leads his readers to a surprising conclusion, given the lengthy apologetic that runs throughout 2 Corinthians. Lest the believers in Corinth misunderstand his purposes, Paul wants it clear that his confidence in the integrity of his ministry means, in reality, that his "apologetic" is not a *self*-defense before them at all (12:19a). By recalling his earlier argument in 2:17, in 12:19b Paul reaffirms that, as one "in Christ," he "has been speaking in the sight of *God*," a reference to the fact that God is the judge of his proclamation, not the Corinthians (cf. 5:10). Furthermore, the apostle is confident of God's approval (cf. 3:1–6; 4:1–6; 6:3–10; 10:12–18)!

Thus, in defending himself, Paul has not been seeking the approval of the Corinthians but fighting to strengthen their faith (12:19c). He does so as the outworking of his calling to be Christ's ambassador (5:20a). Since God is making his appeal through Paul (5:20b), for him to fight for his own legitimacy as an apostle is to fight for the faith of the Corinthians. Conversely, given the identity in his life between the message and the messenger, to reject him is to reject the gospel and hence to be rejected by God himself. Thus, Paul is fighting for the faith of the Corinthians because his ultimate goal is to remain faithful to God in Christ, who loves his people and has entrusted the apostle with the ministry and message of reconciliation (5:18–19). Controlled by Christ's love and knowing the fear of God's impending judgment, Paul defends his ministry before God for the sake of the Corinthians (5:11, 13–15).

The basis of Paul's concern for the Corinthians' welfare, therefore, is his fear that the continuing rebellion of those who have not yet repented, as evidenced in their sinful lifestyles,[5] will lead to their being condemned by God

---

ter 12 taken to be part of a later letter. The past tense of the verbs in both passages are best taken as epistolary aorists—a use of the aorist that portrays Paul's current action at the time of writing as in the past when it is read (cf. "I urged," "I sent" in 12:18 with "we urged" and "we sent" in 8:6, 18). For this reason, the NIV renders 8:18 in the present tense.

5. Some commentators take the sexual sins of 12:21 together with the various sins against the community described in 12:20 as examples of the continuing problems within the church. Others argue that they describe two separate problems, the latter aimed at Paul during his second visit and feared to reoccur when he comes again, and the former problem endemic to the church herself. Solving this issue need not detain us. In either case, the sins described in these verses, whether their source was the Corinthians themselves or the influence of the false apostles, would reveal the unrepentant hearts of those so engaged, to which Paul will have to respond in judgment.

through Paul's hand (12:20–21). Apparently, the rebellion against Paul's authority, fueled by the arrival of his opponents, included an unwillingness to repent from the kind of sexual immorality that had been a problem in Corinth from the beginning (cf. 1 Cor. 5:1–2, 9–11; 6:9, 15–20). That Paul mentions these sins for the first time at the end of his argument indicates that such sins were not the direct problem, but symptomatic of the larger issue still facing the church: the continuing rejection of Paul's apostolic gospel for a different Jesus and Spirit (cf. 11:4). This fundamental acceptance of an alien message had led to the Corinthians' continued lives of rebellion.[6]

Paul's reference to sexual immorality at this point in his letter also serves to remind the Corinthians of the punishment to come. Just as Paul had the sexually immoral person put out of the church in 1 Corinthians 5:1–13, so too the judgment for such habitual sins will be excommunication from the church when he returns. Since the church is the temple of the Holy Spirit, where God's glory is now being encountered, unveiled, on the face of Christ (2 Cor. 3:7–18; cf. 1 Cor. 3:16; 6:19), to be cast out of the church is to be given back over to Satan (1 Cor. 5:5; 2 Cor. 6:14–7:1).

It follows, then, that those who adhere to the false apostles, Satan's servants, will be given over to Satan to suffer with him and his servants the judgment they deserve (11:15). As Paul closes his last appeal, the situation in Corinth demands such a drastic verdict since he attributes the continuation of such a pattern of unrepentant sin to the absence of the Spirit, thereby testifying to the unregenerate nature of their lives as those still outside the new covenant. When faced with such sin, only repentance indicates that one belongs to the body of Christ, the temple of the living God (12:21; cf. 6:14–16; 7:8–13).

This is what Paul means by the reference in 12:20 to his not finding the Corinthians as he wants them to be when he returns. By continuing to follow the false teachers and to live in sin as a result, the rebellious among them are not "perfecting holiness out of reverence for God," which is the work of the Spirit in the lives of those whose hearts have been created anew in Christ (7:1; cf. 3:18; 5:17). At the same time, when Paul returns they will not find

---

6. Scott, 2 *Corinthians*, 247, suggests that as part of "Paul's portrayal of himself as a Moses figure who confronts a Korah-like rebellion in Corinth," the sins listed in 12:20 all find parallels in or apply to the rebellion of Numbers 16–17. On the association of quarreling and jealousy with the rebellion of Korah, see Ps. 106:16–18; Sir. 45:18; Josephus, *Ant.* 4.14; on "outbursts of anger," see Sir. 45:18; on slander, see Num. 16:3, 13–14; Josephus, *Ant.* 4.15; on pride or arrogance as Korah's "fundamental fault," see Num. 16:8–11; Josephus, *Ant.* 4.14–19, 23 (pp. 247–48). Since such attitudes and actions can be characteristic of any insurrection and rebellion, Scott's suggestion, though tempting, remains speculative, since there are no direct verbal parallels between 2 Cor. 12:20–21 and Num. 16–17.

him as they want him to be either, that is, still willing to tolerate their sinful rebellion against the gospel. Those whom Paul does not find repentant when he comes this "third time" will not find him willing to withdraw yet again in order to spare them (cf. 1:23). In writing this final warning, he is aware that as an apostle he is the instrument of both life and death (cf. 2:14–16a). He is also aware that how the Corinthians react to him will consequently reveal the condition of their hearts.

Nevertheless, all is not lost for those still in rebellion against Paul and his gospel. The danger seen in the pattern of their lives described in 12:20–21 need not be the last word. The writing of 2 Corinthians 10–13 itself demonstrates that Paul is still committed to working for the Corinthians' joy in the faith by giving them yet one more opportunity to be restored (cf. 1:24; 2:3). Indeed, he does so even though he knows that his continued patience and mercy could mean yet another humbling experience for himself (12:21a).

When Paul had been with them in the past (10:1), the opposition in Corinth had accused him of being "lowly" (tapeinos; NIV, "timid"), especially because of the lowly state brought about by his practice of self-support (11:7: emauton tapeinon; NIV, "to lower myself"). While waiting for news from Titus about the Corinthians' reaction to his earlier call for repentance, Paul had again been "humbled" or "made low" (tapeinos; NIV, "downcast") by their plight (7:6). Now, he fears that "God will humble [tapeinose] him" once again, this time by using Paul as a grieving instrument of their excommunication (12:21).

The sorrow Paul felt over their rejection during his second, "painful visit" (cf. 2:1, 5–11) will be matched by the mourning he will feel over their upcoming punishment. To be forced finally to judge them when his primary mission is their salvation and joy (cf. 1:24; 10:8; 12:19; 13:10) would be yet another humbling experience. There is no glee in Paul's contemplating this possibility, nor is there a spirit of revenge. Instead, given his love for the Corinthians, both their rejection of him and his eventual rejection of them can be described equally as his being humbled before them. In this last case, such humiliation will express itself in grief over all who continue to presume upon and spurn God's grace (cf. 5:20–6:2).

Paul's Final Appeal for the Repentance of the Rebellious (13:1–10)

IN VIEW OF God's judgment against the unrepentant (12:21), in 13:1 Paul introduces the last major section of his letter with a final announcement of his impending third visit (cf. 12:14 with 13:1). In doing so, he refers to the legal requirements from Deuteronomy 19:15 for accepting evidence in a trial: Everything must be corroborated "by the testimony of two or three witnesses." The necessity of meeting this qualification in conjunction with his visit indicates that his arrival will initiate a judicial act within the congregation against all still in rebellion against him (cf. Matt. 18:16–17; 1 Tim. 5:19 for the application of this principle in the church).[7]

Paul's promise to fulfill this legal mandate is his final scriptural word to the Corinthians. When he arrives, he will make his case against his opponents and those who follow them, which, as an application of 6:14–7:1, will be verified by multiple witnesses from within the congregation itself, and all those found guilty will be punished. This is, of course, a harsh declaration. For this reason, Paul warns them in advance, as he did on his second visit, that when he returns the period of patience will come to an end (cf. 13:2a with 1:23–2:2). As God did not "spare" (*pheidomai*) his own Son the judgment required by sin (Rom. 8:32), so too Paul will not "spare" (*pheidomai*) those who reject Christ (2 Cor. 13:2b). Like the return of Christ, when Paul returns it will be to judge. According to 13:2, this judgment will take place against those who have sinned earlier during his painful visit and[8] against any others who have joined their cause since then.

The theological foundation of Paul's warning, unfolded throughout chapters 10–13, is crystallized in 13:3–4. When he arrives, Paul will not spare the Corinthians, "since [they] are demanding proof that Christ is speaking through [him]" (cf. 2:17; 5:20). Believing that Christ was not "weak" but "powerful" among them, the Corinthians insisted that Christ's apostles should manifest such power as well (13:3b).

Most likely, this reference to Christ's power among the Corinthians is a quote from Paul's opponents, who have portrayed the believer's relationship to the risen Christ in a triumphalistic way. They then used this picture to critique Paul's weakness and to justify their own emphasis on health, wealth, and the miraculous as expressions of Christ's "power" in their midst (cf. 1 Cor. 4:8). Paul turns the tables and uses their own emphasis against them. If they want

---

7. Contra Victor P. Furnish, *II Corinthians*, 575, who, with Calvin, Windisch, Bruce, Barrett, etc., rejects the idea that Paul has such a formal hearing in view. Furnish takes the reference to Deut. 19:15 to be merely "'a sort of proverb,'" with Paul's impending visit the third of the three witnesses. In this view, the first two witnesses are either his first two visits, which is difficult since the first visit was Paul's founding visit, not a time of accusation and warning, or his second sorrowful visit (2:1) and his present letter. Furnish himself points out, however, that such a view does not "strictly speaking, satisfy the requirement (Paul) himself quotes. They still represent the testimony of just one witness, Paul" (p. 575). Nevertheless, Furnish still opts for this view, taking the point to be simply that Paul has warned the Corinthians two or three times before. But Paul's direct quotation of Deut. 19:15, its reference to distinct witnesses, its use in the early church elsewhere in this regard, and the prior references to such formal proceedings in Corinth itself (cf. 1 Cor. 5:1–5; 6:1–6; 2 Cor. 2:5–11) speak against such a view.

8. *kai*. The NIV translation "or" in 13:2 is not to be preferred.

---

to see the power of Christ, then it will come in judgment, even as the return of the risen Christ will mean the judgment of the world.

Paul could not agree more that the resurrected Christ is acting powerfully in the midst of the Corinthians. Christ "lives by God's power" (13:4). At the same time, Paul will not concede that his suffering and endurance as an apostle are not just as much a revelation of Christ's resurrection power (1:3–11; 2:14; 4:7–15; 6:3–10; 11:23–33; 12:7–10). Paul carries the glory of God and the life of Christ in a clay pot (4:7). Hence, in affirming Christ's resurrection power in 13:3, the apostle reintroduces the cross in 13:4 in order to remind the Corinthians that Christ too was "weak" for the sake of his people.

Specifically, Paul grounds his reference to Christ's power among the Corinthians in 13:3 (cf. "for," *gar*, in v. 4) by portraying Christ's cross as the counterpoint to the resurrection in 13:4: Christ is powerful among the Corinthians *because* "he was crucified in [Gk. *ek*, "out of" or "because of"] weakness, yet he lives by God's power." For Christ too, as for Paul, his "weakness" is the platform for God's power, culminating in the resurrection.

Christ's "weakness" in 13:4 is best understood as a reference to his human, bodily existence, which he willingly took on in order to humble himself by becoming a servant to God's people and by dying on a cross for their sins (cf. 8:9; Phil. 2:7–8).[9] In the same way and as the consequence of Christ's own experience of death and resurrection (13:4a), Paul too is weak in Christ, "yet by God's power . . . will live with him toward you (13:4b)."[10]

---

9. Following Ulrich Heckel, *Kraft in Schwachheit*, 124–30. Heckel shows how the history of interpretation has tried to soften this text, so that Christ himself is not identified with weakness. Some have interpreted v. 4 as a reference to *our* sins/weakness, so that Paul's point is taken to mean that Christ dies representatively because of our weakness (already Ambrosiaster, Origen). In the light of 1 Cor. 1:18–25; 2:14, others take "weakness" to refer to *unbelievers* who view the cross as folly (Chrysostom). Still others read it to mean that Christ was crucified *"in* weakness" rather than *"from* weakness" (so Furnish, Käsemann, Bultmann; but cf. "from [the] power of God" in the same verse). Finally, others take it to refer to the freewill and obedience of Christ, so that Christ's weakness is that which comes from his obedience to God, reading 2 Cor. 8:9 and Phil. 2:6–8 in this way as well (Black; but Heckel points out that this view cannot do justice to 10:10 and 12:7).

10. The movement of Paul's thought from 13:4a to 4b is at first puzzling, since 4b cannot serve as the basis of 4a, as if *Paul's* suffering and experience of God's power grounded *Christ's* death and resurrection. I prefer to take Paul's statement in 13:4b concerning his own weakness and God's power in his life as *deriving* from 13:4a (reading the *gar* of 13:4b as an inference), which then together with 13:4a supports Paul's statement in 13:2 concerning why Paul will finally not spare the Corinthians. Paul's argument thus runs like this: Christ was crucified and lives from the power of God among the Corinthians (13:4a); *therefore* Paul too is weak and will live with him from the power of God *toward the Corinthians* (13:4b), so that he will give *them* the proof they are seeking (13:3a) by not sparing *them* (13:2). Read in this way, 13:2 and 13:4b say essentially the same thing in different terms.

The rendering of the end of 13:4 in the NIV as "to serve you" (Gk. *eis hymas*, "toward you") gives the wrong nuance; in this context the expression of God's power "toward" the Corinthians is now not to serve but to judge them. Since they seek proof of the power of the resurrected Christ in Paul's life, Paul's living with Christ from the power of God will be seen in his not sparing the Corinthians upon his return. Just as the crucified, weak Jesus gives way to the resurrected Christ who lives by God's power and will come again in judgment, so too the suffering Paul will give way to a Paul who "lives" to return to Corinth in judgment. In this way, Paul pictures his return to Corinth as participating in the resurrection power of God already displayed in Christ.

Paul's portrayal of his return to Corinth in these terms seems at first strange to our ears. He intends by it to remind the Corinthians that the judgment he will bring on his third visit is an inauguration of the final judgment to come. To "live with Christ" is clearly an eschatological designation that refers to experiencing the final resurrection.[11] The surprising thing is that Paul declares that he is *already* experiencing the resurrection and will do so in a dramatic fashion when he returns to Corinth. As we have seen throughout this letter, his endurance for the gospel in the midst of adversity replicates Christ's resurrection as an inauguration or foretaste of the resurrection still to come (cf. esp. 4:7–12; 6:3–10).

Thus, the parallels established between Christ and Paul in 13:4 show how Christ's power is made perfect in Paul's ministry (cf. 12:9). His primary purpose as an apostle is to mediate through his suffering in Christ the knowledge of God and the transforming power of the life-giving Spirit (2:14–3:18; 4:1–15). This is the way in which Paul usually mediates the power of Christ's resurrection. But toward those who reject the cross and power of Christ as embodied in his suffering and endurance, the resurrection power of Christ will be made known through his acts of judgment within the church. If Paul is an agent of God's redemption, he must also be an agent of God's judgment (cf. 2:15–16a; 4:4; 6:1–2). Those who reject him in his suffering will face him in his judgment, just as those who reject the cross of Christ will one day face Christ in his resurrected glory. Christ's power is the power of his resurrection, which vindicates his weakness and vanquishes his foes (v. 4a).

In view of Paul's imminent return to bring God's judgment to Corinth, his commands in 13:5 again contain a severe warning. In the past, he postponed his return in order to give the Corinthians time to repent, since his primary goal as an apostle of the new covenant is the ingathering of God's people (cf. 1:23–2:4; 5:18–20; 10:8; 12:19). In his next visit, however, Paul will carry out

---

11. Following Heckel, *Kraft*, 133 and n.70, pointing to Rom. 6:8; 8:17, 29; 2 Cor. 4:14; Phil. 1:23; 3:21; Col. 3:4; 1 Thess. 4:14, 17; 5:10; 2 Tim. 2:11.

both aspects of his apostolic calling by being a fragrance of both life *and* death to those he encounters with the gospel (cf. 1 Cor. 1:18 with 2 Cor. 2:15–16a). Like the prophets of the old covenant, Paul thus announces the coming judgment in advance in order to bring about the repentance of those who are truly God's people (cf. 10:1–6). He does so by calling the rebellious in Corinth "to examine" or "test themselves" to see if they are truly "in the faith" (13:5). The goal of the test is to make it clear that Christ is indeed in them (cf. 7:11–12; 8:7–8).

The means by which the test is performed is Paul himself. Allegiance to him as their apostle is the criterion that determines whether Christ is present in their lives, since Paul is confident that he himself has already passed the test (13:6).[12] To accept *Paul's* message of reconciliation is to accept *God's* message of reconciliation (cf. 5:18–20). For this reason, because they have responded to Paul and his preaching in the past, he gives them the benefit of the doubt that Christ is in fact in them (13:5b).

In view of their current rebellion, however, the Corinthians must confirm the reality of their conversion by responding once again to Paul's person and proclamation. His call for repentance is therefore based on the assumption that those in whom God *is* at work by his Spirit *will* recognize that Paul's holiness, sincerity, and way of life all derive from the same grace of God that Paul is now calling them to accept (cf. 1:12 with 6:1–2).

This assumption also means that those in whom Christ is present will not continue in the lifestyles of rebellion characterized in 12:21. Where Christ is, there is a life of growing holiness. To encounter the glory of God on the face of Christ is to be transformed by it (3:18). Conversely, to continue in lives of disobedience is to fail the test of Christ's presence. In 13:7, Paul thus prays that the Corinthians will "stand the test" by "not doing anything wrong."

Put positively, this means showing support for Paul's ministry by manifesting the life of the new creation that flows from trusting his gospel (5:17). Paul prays this not for the sake of his own reputation but for their good.[13]

---

12. Note Paul's use of the apostolic plural in 13:6–9. For his confidence as an apostle, cf. 1:1, 12–14; 2:17; 3:4–5; 4:1; 5:18–6:2; 6:4; 7:2; 10:7, 14–18; 11:5, 23; 12:11–12, 19.

13. Contra those who, like Scott, *2 Corinthians*, 254, argue that "the Corinthians are in a position to unravel Paul's whole mission in the east (to say nothing of the lost prospects for the west), if they consider that he has failed the test of apostleship. . . . In this dire situation, in which the legitimacy of Paul's apostleship depends on the Corinthians' reaction to him, Paul resorts to prayer." In contrast to this view, Paul's legitimacy and missionary success depend ultimately on God's call, not the Corinthians' acceptance; hence, Paul's concern is their welfare, not what outsiders may think of him, since what the Corinthians think about Paul is paramount to their welfare, not his! Moreover, the situation is no longer dire. The repentance of the majority has already reestablished Paul's authority in Corinth; now it is a matter of dealing with the rebellious minority.

Indeed, he desires this for them even if their repentance at this last hour will make him look as if he has failed again, for it will mean yet another change of plans, from his announced coming in judgment to an arrival filled with mutual acceptance (13:7; cf. again 1:23–24). Although such an arrival may look as if Paul does not mediate the visible power of Christ, nothing is farther from the truth. The primary "proof" of the power of the Spirit in Paul's ministry is the conversion and moral transformation of the Corinthians. This is Paul's true "letter of recommendation" (3:2–6, based on 3:7–18).

Paul's confidence in 13:6 and his corresponding prayer for the Corinthians in 13:7 are both buttressed by the conviction that the truth of the gospel will prevail over all contenders (13:8; cf. 4:2; 7:14; 11:10; 12:6). Not even Paul's inadequacies and infirmities can do anything against it. *Therefore* Paul rejoices whenever he is "weak," but the Corinthians are "strong" (taking the *gar* of 13:9a, untranslated in the NIV, as inferential). The apostle is glad whenever, as an extension of the cross, he is being led into suffering on their behalf (i.e., whenever he is "weak") so that, as an expression of the resurrection, they are being consoled and encouraged in their faith (i.e., they are "strong"; cf. 1:4–7; 2:14; 4:10–12, 15; 11:29). Just as Paul's weakness leads to his own strength in Christ (12:10; cf. 1:8–11; 4:11), so too his weakness leads to the strength of others as they learn from his experiences to trust God's grace (1:3–7; 4:12).

This is why Paul prefers to be "weak" for their sake and why he prays for the "restoration" or "completion" (*katartisis*)[14] of those who have begun with Christ but have now been led astray by the false apostles (13:9b). Paul takes no pleasure in having to judge the Corinthians. This is also why he is writing "these things" (13:10)—a reference to the present letter, especially chapters 10–13 (cf. 10:1–6, 11; 12:19; 13:2).

Paul's desire is that he will not be forced to exercise his authority harshly when he comes again to Corinth (13:10b). For in fulfillment of Jeremiah's promise that God will one day "build" his people, Paul's ministry under the new covenant, in contrast to Jeremiah's under the old, is predominantly for "building . . . up, not for tearing . . . down" (13:10c, alluding to Jer. 24:6; cf. Jer. 1:10; 31:4, 28; 33:7). Paul used this same definition of his ministry in 2 Corinthians 10:8, thereby beginning and ending the last major section of his letter by reflecting on the nature of the new covenant ministry. The link between chapters 10–13 and the thesis statements of 3:3–6 is clear.

That chapters 10–13 are framed by this allusion to Jeremiah 24:6 is not accidental. Paul intentionally ends the final section of his letter by recalling

---

14. Cf. BAGD, 417–18. The NIV rendering, "perfection," does not adequately communicate that Paul is referring here to the repentance of those still in rebellion and to the restoration of the unity of the church.

the pastoral purpose with which he began in order to put his third visit in per-spective. He views the necessity and purpose of his exhortations, like all else in his ministry, through the lens of redemptive history and the Scriptures. This means that his primary goal as an apostle of Christ is the building up of the church in fulfillment of the promise of the new covenant.

At the same time, Paul makes it clear that God's act of deliverance in Christ includes both the salvation of the righteous *and* the judgment of the wicked (2:14–16a; 4:1–6; 6:14–17; 10:4–6; 11:15). The message of the cross is the power of God to those being saved, but it is foolishness to those who are perishing (1 Cor. 1:18–25). Hence, if judge he must, then in this way too Paul will be acting "for the truth" of the gospel (2 Cor. 13:8).

Paul's Final Words of Exhortation and Benediction (13:11–14)

JUST AS HE did in his opening, Paul closes his letter by following the con-ventions common to ancient letter writing. In the past, modern readers largely ignored Paul's letter closings, viewing them as simply standard con-ventions used to say "good-by." Indeed, Weima's survey of Hellenistic and Semitic letters has shown that there were a number of standard epistolary conventions that belonged to the closings of ancient letters, though they were rarely all utilized at once.[15] Paul too uses these conventions to end his letters.

This is where the similarities end, however. Unlike other ancient letters, in which the closings were curt and only linked to the body of the letter in a general way, Paul expands the letter closing significantly, strategically employing it to echo specific themes from his letter. Paul's closings are not merely ways to end his letters; they are summations of his arguments. As Weima puts it:

> Every one of Paul's letter closings . . . relates in one way or another to the key issue(s) taken up in their respective letter bodies. . . . The clos-ings serve as an hermeneutical spotlight, highlighting the central con-cerns of the apostle in his letters and illumining our understanding of these key themes and issues.[16]

---

15. Jeffrey A. D. Weima, *Neglected Endings: The Significance of the Pauline Letter Closings* (JSNTSup 101; Sheffield: Sheffield Academic, 1994), 55. These elements included a farewell wish, a health wish, secondary greetings, an autograph, an illiteracy formula, the date, and a postscript. Of these, only the farewell wish was considered essential. For the literary fea-tures of Paul's closing, I am following Weima's work closely, who demonstrates these points throughout Paul's letters; cf. his treatment of 2 Cor. 13:11–13 (pp. 208–15).

16. Ibid., 238.

The closing to 2 Corinthians supports this thesis. Paul closes his letter with additional commands (13:11), greetings (13:12), and two farewell benedictions, one for peace and one for grace (13:11, 13). In each case, his closing highlights a main theme of his letter.

As in 1 Corinthians 16:13–14, here too Paul begins his closing with five commands: to rejoice,[17] to aim for restoration,[18] to encourage one another,[19] to be of one mind, and to live in peace. The first three commands focus on the Corinthians' relationship with Paul as their apostle; the last two refer to their life together as those who have been reconciled to God.

In particular, the commands to rejoice and to aim for restoration pick up Paul's reference in 13:9 to his own joy over the strengthening of the Corinthians' faith and to his prayer for their restoration. In the former case, Paul calls them to manifest their unity with him as their apostle by joining him in rejoicing over the strength they have derived through his weakness. In the latter, his exhortation that they be restored becomes the instrument by which his own prayer to that end will be fulfilled. So too, Paul's call that they encourage or admonish one another recalls his earlier appeals in 5:20; 6:1; and 10:1.

We must be careful not to gloss over these commands, as if they were merely some "closing remarks" thrown in only to fulfill a rhetorical or literary purpose. From Paul's perspective, there is much at stake in issuing these exhortations. Moreover, the structure of his closing again reveals the structure of his theology. In particular, the movement from the admonitions of verse 11a to the benediction in verse 11b demonstrates that God's continuing presence among the Corinthians is inextricably linked to the purification and repentance of his people (cf. 6:14–7:1). Even in his closing Paul wants to make it clear yet again that the blessing of God's presence is contingent on the obedience of his people.

This does not mean that the obedience of God's people earns or merits his presence. Note how Paul begins his final exhortations by reminding the Corinthians that in Christ they are all "brothers," a reference to their stand-

---

17. *chairete*. This reading goes against the NIV and RSV and other commentaries, which take it to mean "good-by" or "farewell." Weima, ibid., 210–11n.2, argues convincingly that here the verb is an imperative, meaning "to rejoice," because it is part of a string of commands, its use in 13:9 clearly means "rejoice," and its parallel use as an imperative in 1 Thess. 5:16 also carries this meaning.

18. *katartizesthe*. My translation again follows Weima, ibid., 210n.1, who takes it as a middle rather than passive. As a middle it can mean, "aim for restoration" (so too Ralph Martin), "mend your ways" (RSV), or "pull yourselves together" (so Barrett). The NIV rendering, "aim for perfection," misses the reference of this verb to the situation in Corinth.

19. *parakaleisthe*. The NIV's "listen to my appeal" takes it as a passive (so too the RSV and other commentators such as Plummer and Furnish). We are taking it as a middle; so too Barrett, Martin, Bruce, et al., including Weima, *Neglected Endings*, 211n.2.

ing as believers. Keeping the commands of 13:11 does not make one a Christian; rather, being a Christian means that one will keep these commands. The obedience of the believer is the link between the reality of God's presence that he or she already enjoys, as a matter of grace, and the continuing reality of God's presence in the future.

Hence, both are matters of grace, since the *future* blessing of God's presence is predicated on an obedience that has been brought about by God's blessing his people in the *past*. This explains why Paul calls the Corinthians "brothers" at the beginning of the first two major sections of the letter, where he is primarily addressing the repentant (cf. 1:8 and 8:1), but not in chapters 10–13, where he directly addresses those in rebellion against him. "Brothers," because they are "brothers," do not rebel against the gospel but respond to its call. Against this backdrop, it is striking that Paul closes his letter by addressing the whole church in this way. He is expressing his hope that all in Corinth may be considered his "brothers" when he returns.

Paul's own greeting in verse 11 is matched by two final greetings in verses 12–13, both of which continue his emphasis on unity within the church by stressing its local and universal dimensions respectively. Paul first calls for a greeting of "one another with a holy kiss," a practice unique among believers that signified their mutual acceptance and oneness as a family (cf. Rom. 16:16; 1 Cor. 16:20; 1 Thess. 5:26[20]).

Next, Paul extends to the Corinthians a greeting from "all the saints," thereby emphasizing their oneness with the church at large. Taken together, these greetings implicitly emphasize that to reject Paul's pleas will put one not only outside the church in Corinth, but also outside the church universal (cf. 6:18). For Paul's speaking on behalf of "all the saints" also "alludes to [Paul's] own apostolic authority and, thus, indirectly to the obligation that the Corinthians have to obey his exhortations in the letter."[21]

This emphasis on unity in Paul's closing, which is unique to 2 Corinthians, is carried through in Paul's two farewell wishes (vv. 11b, 14), which for him become benedictions of God's blessing on the church as a whole as she

---

20. See William Klassen, "Kiss," *ABD*, 4:89–92, who points out that "nothing analogous to it is to be found among any Greco-Roman societies, nor indeed at Qumran.... In the Second Temple period it is quite probable that among Jews the public kiss was not generally practiced.... Greco-Roman society treated the public kiss, both hetero- and homosexual, with considerable reticence," except in times of reunion of loved ones after times of separation, or to signal special occasions of acceptance or joy or honor, or as a formal greeting (p. 91). Paul "was the first popular ethical teacher known to instruct members of a mixed social group to greet each other with a kiss" (p. 92). Thus, "the 'holy kiss' is a public declaration of the affirmation of faith: 'In Christ there is neither male nor female, Jew nor Greek, slave nor free' (Gal. 3:28)" (p. 92).

21. Weima, *Neglected Endings*, 212.

lives together under the gospel. In contrast to the formula found in his other letters ("May the God of peace . . ."), Paul's benediction in 13:11b is the only one that combines "love" with the wish for "peace." Likewise, the dramatic grace benediction in 13:14 is the only one in Paul's letters that is Trinitarian in structure. It is also the only one that combines the wish for grace with wishes for "love" and "fellowship," all of which come from God (taking all three genitives to be genitives of source): grace *from* the Lord Jesus Christ, love *from* God, and fellowship with one another *brought about by* the Holy Spirit.[22]

Paul also adds "all" at the end to stress further the inclusive unity of the church. Moreover, as with his use of the direct address "brothers" in 13:11, this emphasis on love and fellowship recalls themes from chapters 1–9 not found in chapters 10–13.[23] In so doing, Paul again subtly indicates his goal of incorporating those who are still in rebellion against him back into the church as a whole. Paul's benedictions thus stress the implications of what it means to be in the presence of God: grace from Christ and love and peace from God necessarily include the fellowship with one another brought about by the Spirit.

Paul's letter closing in 13:11–14 is much more than simply a pious platitude included as a necessary literary convention. The closing admonitions, greetings, and benedictions all reflect the reconciliation for which Paul longs (5:20–6:2; 6:13; 10:1–2; 11:2), prays (13:7) and labors as a minister of the new covenant (2:17; 6:3–10; 12:19), and toward which he has written this letter (13:10). Indeed, the structure of his closing benediction signifies the blessing of the new covenant itself, in which the grace of Christ has made it possible to experience God's love, poured out in the Holy Spirit.

It is not accidental, therefore, that Paul's letter climaxes with a reference to the fellowship brought about by the Spirit. The pouring out of the Spirit on God's people is *the* gift of the new covenant (cf. 3:3–18). So in closing, Paul prays as a minister of the new covenant that God will grant to all those in the church the unity of the Spirit that he has worked so hard to mediate.[24]

---

22. Following the comparison of the structure and content of the various benedictions provided by Weima, ibid., 80, 89, 209–10. For the other "peace benedictions," see Rom. 15:33; 16:20a; Gal. 6:16; Phil. 4:9; 1 Thess. 5:23; 2 Thess. 3:16. For the other "grace benedictions," see Rom. 16:20b; 1 Cor. 16:23; Gal. 6:18; Eph. 6:24; Phil. 4:23; Col. 4:18; 1 Thess. 5:28; 2 Thess. 3:18; 1 Tim. 6:21; 2 Tim. 4:22; Titus 3:15; Philem. 25.

23. I owe this insight to Weima, ibid., 214. For Paul's earlier references to "love," see 2:4, 8; 5:14; 6:6; 8:7, 8, 24; but see the verbal forms in 9:7; 11:11; 12:15. For the references to "fellowship," see 1:7; 6:14; 8:4, 23; 9:13.

24. As Weima, ibid., 214–15, observes, "every one of the closing conventions of this letter has been written and/or adopted in such a way that it relates directly to Paul's preoccupation in the letter for his Corinthian converts to reject the divisive influence of his opponents and to restore peace and harmony both within the church and with him."

For after everything is said and done, and despite all her flaws and growing pains, the church remains the temple of the living God.

THE SUMMARY NATURE of this closing passage brings us back to the interpretive principles and perspectives suggested throughout our study. Perhaps the most important point to be made in closing is that Paul's appeal for repentance, both here and throughout his letter, and the direct link between this repentance and the blessing of God rest on Paul's confidence in the power of the Spirit being unleashed through the gospel *as proclaimed in this very writing* (cf. 13:10). In short, from beginning to end, Paul speaks and writes as a minister of the new covenant of the Spirit (1:22; 3:5–6; 13:14).

Keys to applying Paul. To bring this passage from Paul's day to our own, we need to recapture his confidence in the authority of his writings and in the power of the Spirit. A key to this recovery will be a deepened understanding of the significance of our place as Christians in the continuing flow of redemptive history. Inasmuch as the church is "the temple of the living God" (6:16), contemporary readers must take seriously that nothing less than the very presence of God among his people is at stake in Paul's appeals (cf. 13:11, 13).

To this end, we must be careful not to paint Paul as an egotist with an exaggerated sense of his own importance, who cannot "get over" the fact that not everybody is bowing to his authority. In 2 Corinthians, Paul is not defending himself but working for the joy and strengthening of the Corinthians' faith (1:24; 4:5; 12:19).

Nor should we make him into a moralist who is concerned with the reformation of human character for the good of the family, the church, and society. Paul's self-understanding and his concern for the Corinthians are not the result of new moral insights. His goal is not to "improve" the world. Rather, Paul's life and writing are the consequence of having come face-to-face with the Christ who "was crucified in weakness" but now "lives by God's power" (13:4; cf. 4:6), and of experiencing the power of the Spirit that raised him from the dead (13:14c; cf. 1:22). So too the grace, love, and fellowship Paul wishes for the Corinthians in 13:11, 14 come from Christ, God the Father, and the Holy Spirit. In other words, when everything is said and done, Paul's final desire for the Corinthians is that God himself might be with them. Paul's theology was driven by the reality of the presence of the living God.

Paul's covenant perspective. Given Paul's emphasis on the transforming power of God's presence, it is also important to keep in mind when applying this passage that the manner of Paul's "self"-defense for the sake of the Corinthians reminds us that he is no mystic either. His experience of the risen Christ and the unleashing of the power of the Spirit in his ministry do not lead him to a private spirituality with a personal code of ethics. Paul does not trumpet his spiritual experiences as a model for others. What he teaches does not derive from his "visions and revelations" (12:1).

Instead, Paul's experiences as an apostle cause him to realize that he stands before the judgment of God (2:17; 5:10; 12:19), so that he too is called to act in accordance with the revealed truth of God (13:8). Even in closing, Paul quotes from and alludes to the law and prophets (13:1, 10). The authority of the Scriptures and of Christ himself, not Paul's spiritual experiences per se, drive his exercise of his own authority, to which his letters now belong. As a continuation of this scriptural and Christological authority, Paul's own writing now becomes an instrument by which Jeremiah's promise is to be fulfilled (cf. 13:10).

At the same time, Paul's closing defense, appeal, and benedictions make it clear that in mediating God's glory to his churches, the apostle was not simply transferring a data bank of information. The urgency and passion of his writing reveal that his theology and authority derive from a burning love for his people. Paul does not write as the Corinthians' boss but as a parent who is willing to spend his very life for their welfare (12:14–15).

The presence of God in the gospel is mediated to others not least through the love of those who have encountered the living Christ. Our doctrinal purity in allegiance to Paul must be matched by a love like Paul's that rejoices whenever he can serve others for the sake of their joy and faith in God (13:9). As Paul anticipates his third visit to Corinth, he is not gloating over the chance to get even with his enemies. Instead, he longs for the salvation of those for whom he has suffered so much (13:4–5, 10).

Finally, to apply 13:1–14 properly will entail placing it within its larger context, both in terms of 2 Corinthians itself and in terms of Paul's basic "covenant" theology. We have seen that this passage embodies and brings to a head the purpose of his argument in chapters 10–13: to provide the means, one last time, of instigating the "godly grief" that leads to repentance (cf. 7:8–11). Paul's conviction is that, "in Christ," the consequences of humanity's fall into sin (Gen. 3) and of Israel's idolatry with the golden calf (Ex. 32–34) are both being reversed in the lives of those who are truly members of the "new covenant" (cf. 2:14–3:18; 6:14–7:1). If "Christ Jesus is in [them]" (13:5), he will make himself known in their repentance and growing obedience, since they are now a "new creation" (5:17) and the "temple of the living God" (6:16; cf. 3:3; 7:2–16).

Hence, a growing transformation into the image of God himself marks the lives of those on whom God has "set his seal of ownership" by pouring out his Spirit in their hearts (1:22; 3:18). God's presence and power bring about the "godly sorrow" over sin that "leads to salvation and leaves no regret" (7:10). "All will appear before the judgment seat of Christ, that each one may receive what is due him for the things done while in the body, whether good or bad" (5:10). At that time, God's people will stand firm in this judgment, since God himself "makes [his people] stand firm in Christ" (1:21).

Paul's warning in 13:1–10 is the final application of this covenant perspective. The call to test one's faith, like the call to reaffirm one's allegiance to Paul (5:20–6:1; 6:11–13; 7:2; 10:1–7), to separate from unbelievers (6:14–15 and 7:1), and to participate in the collection (chs. 8–9), is grounded in the reality of what God has done for his people in establishing the new covenant in Christ. The framework of Paul's thinking is that the new covenant brought about by the redemption in Christ is the inauguration of the new creation in which God once again dwells in the midst of his people (3:7–18).

The commands of God—from the command to be reconciled to God in Christ (5:20) to the commands to forgive others (2:7) and to give away one's money (8:7, 11)—are nothing other than explications and applications of what the grace of God has brought about and continues to bring about in the lives of God's people. To obey God's commands is what trusting in God's provisions in Christ looks like in everyday situations. To "accept Christ" is to obey God's call to be like Christ. As Jonathan Edwards put it, the "acts of a Christian life," that is, our "evangelical obedience," all imply and are expressions of faith. Hence, they

> may be looked upon as so many acts of reception of Christ the Saviour. . . . The obedience of a Christian, so far as it is truly evangelical, and performed with the Spirit of the Son sent forth into the heart, has all relation to Christ, the Mediator, and is but an expression of the soul's believing union to Christ. All evangelical works are works of that faith that worketh by love; and every such act of obedience, wherein it is inward, and the act of the soul, is only a new effective act of reception of Christ, and adherence to the glorious Saviour.[25]

Therefore, from Paul's perspective as a minister of the Spirit who makes us alive (3:6), it is simply impossible to be in God's presence and not manifest a transformed life (cf. 3:18; 5:17). Conversely, only those who are experiencing the transforming power of the glory of God in the face of Christ (4:4–6) can be considered members of the new covenant community. Paul

---

25. Jonathan Edwards, "Five Discourses on Important Subjects, Nearly Concerning the Great Affair of The Soul's Eternal Salvation: Discourse I. Justification by Faith Alone," *The Works of Jonathan Edwards: Vol. One*, revised and corrected by Edward Hickman (Edinburgh: Banner of Truth Trust, 1974 [1834]), 622–54 (pp. 640, 642).

simply assumes that those whom he calls "brothers," if they are indeed part of the family of God and thereby deserving of a "holy kiss," *will* respond to his commands. In doing so, they *will* enjoy the "fellowship of the Holy Spirit" that exists within God's people (13:11, 12, 14). This means that to preach the gospel Paul must also test the Corinthians' faith by calling for their obedience (13:5). The same will be true for all those who preach the gospel today.

FOR PAUL, THE reality of "Christ Jesus [being] in you" (13:5) means that there is no cheap grace in the gospel, no easy believism in the biblical definition of faith, no repentant-less forgiveness in the cross, no powerlessness in the Spirit, and no absence of judgment in the future. Put positively, those in whom Christ is present will pass the "test"; those who claim Christ without the repentance- and obedience-producing power of the Spirit in their lives will not.

The expectation of godliness. In an age of disappointment over the lives of high profile leaders in the church, such an expectation seems unrealistic, being openly mocked by the daily news. Such disappointment over others is matched by our own slow progress in the faith, in which some sins seem to haunt us forever. We are also aware of the rank nominalism of the church at large and of the shallowness of so much of contemporary worship, in which the weekly emotionalism of the "praise service" is separated by days of lifelessness. As a result, modern readers of Paul are often put off by his spiritual and moral enthusiasm, which calls for and anticipates a real difference in the everyday lives of those whom God has encountered.

Paul's conviction that the power of God is being unleashed in the gospel seems abstract and utopian when confronted with the diluted nature of what it means to be "Christian" in our post-Christian culture. During the 1990s, 39 percent of adults in the United States called themselves born-again Christians, 68 percent claimed they had been in the presence of God at some time in their lives, 65 percent claimed they had made a personal commitment to Jesus Christ that was still important to them, and 85 percent considered themselves to be Christian.[26] Can Paul's claims be taken seriously? Is the practice of church discipline a relic of an unrealistic and overly zealous past?[27] Is there any hope this side of heaven?

---

26. According to surveys taken in the mid-1990s and reported by George Barna, *Index of Leading Spiritual Indicators* (Dallas: Word, 1996), 4, 5, 8, 9.

27. Concerning church discipline, Barnett, *Second Corinthians*, 596–97, deduces from 1 and 2 Corinthians that there was "some kind of congregational procedure" involved in this discipline (cf. 1 Cor. 5:4; 2 Cor. 2:5–6, 10). "Evidence would be heard, with no fewer than

In answer to these questions, Paul's letters offer several important perspectives.[28] (1) Paul recognized that sanctification is a matter of progress over a lifetime, not of perfection overnight (cf. Phil. 1:25; Col. 1:10; 1 Thess. 4:1; 2 Thess. 1:3). When it comes to completing the work he himself has begun in our lives, we cannot put God on our timetable. Both justification *and* sanctification are a matter of grace. Often the slow rate of change is itself part of our school of faith, teaching us to be wholly dependent on the only One who can free us from our sin. Patience with the slow progress of others, not to mention with our own, is often needed. If 2 Corinthians reveals anything about Paul, it reveals his long-suffering patience with God's people.

(2) Yet the fact that 2 Corinthians is written in preparation for Paul's third visit, in which he plans to judge those who continue in rebellion against him, reveals that eventually patience comes to an end. Some of those addressed in 12:20—21 *may* have been Christians, albeit "infants in Christ" (cf. 1 Cor. 3:1—3). If they were "spiritual," Paul fully expects them to grow up, an expectation encapsulated in the final admonitions of 2 Corinthians 13:11 (see 1 Cor. 1:10; 3:18—22; 4:7, 16; 5:1—2; 6:4—8, 18; 11:17—22; 14:20). Moreover, Paul expects those who are already strong in the faith to get even stronger (e.g., 1 Cor. 8:11; 10:24, 31; 11:1; 14:1; 2 Cor. 8:7—8, 24; 9:3, 13; cf. Rom. 14:13—21). Talk is cheap; perseverance is the only evidence of a genuine conversion.

(3) The sober nature of Paul's conclusion to 2 Corinthians does not derive from a religious moralism or a belief in human potential, but from the life-transforming reality of Christ that Paul himself had experienced (3:4—6; 4:6; 5:16—6:2; cf. Phil. 2:12—13; 2 Thess. 2:14—15). Paul's expectations for the Corinthians are expectations for God. His admonitions to them are expressions of his confidence in what God can do in the lives of sinners. He can be demanding because, as the "worst of sinners" (1 Tim. 1:15), he knows from his own life that there is no deception or pattern of behavior that God cannot overcome. Every command of God is a promise of deliverance in disguise. There is hope for all who trust in Christ. Perseverance is not reserved for a Christian elite but is promised to *all* who belong to God. A reconciled way of life is the necessary implication of having experienced the love, peace,

---

two or three witnesses (13:1), perhaps preceding a congregational vote (cf. 2:5 [sic]—'the majority'). A judgment would be passed (1 Cor. 5:3), followed by 'punishment' (cf. 2:5 [sic]), apparently some kind of separation or exclusion of the erring member (cf. 1 Cor. 5:11, 13). Such a procedure, as best we are able to reconstruct it from fragmentary data scattered through 1 and 2 Corinthians, was to provoke the sinner's repentance with a view to his restoration to the community of faith (1 Cor. 5:5; 2 Cor. 2:10—11; Gal. 6:1—2)."

28. This section is adapted from my essay "Paul's Understanding of Perseverance," *SBJT* 2 (1998): 68—71.

grace, and fellowship that come from God the Father, Christ, and the Spirit (13:11–14).

This means that the "carnal Christian" of 1 Corinthians 3:1–4 is not a third class of humanity that exists somewhere between being a non-Christian and being a "Spirit-filled Christian." Just as the designation "Spirit-filled Christian" is a needless tautology (Rom. 8:9, 14), "carnal Christian" is an oxymoron that cannot endure for long. In 1 Corinthians 3:3, Paul places the behavior of those "acting like mere men," who are still "infants in Christ," in the category of those who do not have the Spirit at all. In the same way, those who refuse to repent after receiving 2 Corinthians will have failed the test of Christ's presence in them, despite their professions of faith (13:5). To claim to be Christian while at the same time gladly remaining in baby-like states of immature sin such as described in 12:20–21 is a contradiction in terms.

Real sin, real redemption, real prayer. Inherent in Paul's closing admonitions, therefore, is the recognition of real sin and the promise of a real redemption. We must recover this recognition and promise if we are to remain faithful to the witness of the gospel in the modern–postmodern world. If the church is to speak to the culture around it, whose "moral fabric is rotting," David Wells has rightly observed that

> it will have to become courageous enough to say that much that is taken as normative in the postmodern world is actually sinful, and it will have to exercise new ingenuity in learning how to speak about sin to a generation for whom sin has become an impossibility. Without an understanding of sin ... there can be no deep believing of the Gospel.
>
> Second, the Church itself is going to have to become more authentic morally, for the greatness of the Gospel is now seen to have become quite trivial and inconsequential in its life. If the Gospel means so little to the Church, if it changes so little, why then should unbelievers believe it?
>
> It is one thing to understand what Christ's deliverance means; it is quite another to see this worked out in life with depth and reality, to see its moral splendor.... That is what makes the Gospel so attractive. The evangelical Church today, with some exceptions, is not very inspiring in this regard.... Much of it, instead, is replete with tricks, gadgets, gimmicks, and marketing ploys as it shamelessly adapts itself to our emptied-out, blinded, postmodern world. It is supporting a massive commercial enterprise of Christian products, it is filling the airways and stuffing postal boxes, and it is always begging for money to fuel one entrepreneurial scheme after another, but it is not morally

resplendent. It is mostly empty of real moral vision, and without a recovery of that vision its faith will soon disintegrate. There is too little about it that bespeaks the holiness of God. And without the vision for and reality of this holiness, the Gospel becomes trivialized, life loses its depth, God becomes transformed into a product to be sold, faith into a recreational activity to be done, and the Church into a club for the like-minded.[29]

Here is where "the greatness of the Gospel" is so crucial. In the light of Paul's critique of the Corinthians and his conviction concerning the transforming power of the glory of God in Christ, the sting we feel from such an analysis is not a summons "to try harder" but to pray. The majesty of the message Paul preached about God and the radical nature of his corresponding expectations for God's people can both be seen in the simple fact that Paul ends his pleas with prayer. He knows the magnitude of his demands, and he knows that they cannot be met from our own spiritual or moral resources. For this reason, Paul pours out his life for the Corinthians, while at the same time praying that *God* will keep the Corinthians from doing wrong, that *God* will restore them, and that *God* will grant them the benefits of his presence (cf. 13:7, 9, 11–14). In the end, the apostle knows that only God himself can bring about the repentance he calls for. What is needed is the "godly grief" that only God can create (7:10).

Our tendency today is to skip over these references to prayer as mere platitudes of an obligatory religious piety. We do so because this is what prayer has so often become for us. Rather than a cry of desperation, prayer becomes a duty performed for God. The power of God's presence is a theological doctrine, but not a theological reality in our lives. Giving lip service to our need for God, we quickly turn to the latest technique, self-help program, or growth group. To quote David Wells again, "The fundamental problem in the evangelical world today is that God rests too inconsequentially upon the church. His truth is too distant, his grace is too ordinary, his judgment is too benign, his gospel is too easy, and his Christ is too common."[30]

In stark contrast, Paul ends his letter by praying because only God can enable the Corinthians to pass the test that Paul has given, for the goal of the test is the presence of God himself. Accordingly, his final word is that the love, peace, and fellowship he calls for in the commands of 13:11 all come from the presence of God he prays for in 13:14. Paul does not take such a

---

29. David F. Wells, *Losing Our Virtue: Why the Church Must Recover Its Moral Vision* (Grand Rapids: Eerdmans, 1998), 179–80.

30. David F. Wells, *God in the Wasteland: The Reality of Truth in a World of Fading Dreams* (Grand Rapids: Eerdmans, 1994), 30.

prayer for granted. He offers it because of the promise of the new covenant, under which God's people, in Christ and by the power of the Spirit, may enter into God's presence without being destroyed (3:7–18). If the Corinthians are to keep the commands of 13:11, it is only because God has answered the prayers of 13:7, 9, 14.

The real God. Though implicit, it becomes evident that the interplay between Paul's prayers and his closing admonitions reflects the same covenant structure that has informed his thinking throughout 2 Corinthians (cf. 3:6; 6:14–7:1). God's prior act of grace in the mercy of the cross, by which he grants to us his presence in Christ, through the Spirit, is the all-sufficient ground of our relationship with him. Moreover, God's presence with his people here and now brings with it his promise to sustain them through this life and to bring them into his presence in the age to come. God is faithful; he will not forsake his people. Our response is to trust God for our future, no matter what may come our way. As his people, we trust him with our lives.

Paul again makes clear in closing his letter that the expression of this faith is always obedience to God's commands. To know God is to live a life of believing obedience or obedient faith. The two cannot be separated. Nor can our obedience ever be construed as earning or meriting the blessing of God's presence. Believing obedience to God's commands flows from and is made possible by his presence in our lives, granted to us by an act of his gracious mercy. Faith-driven obedience is therefore the only evidence that "Christ Jesus is in us" (13:5).

Conversely, obedient faith is the condition that must be met for God to remain with us (13:14). God's *continuing* presence with us flows from and is made possible by his *present* dwelling with us, the "test" of which is faith-driven obedience. This is why Paul's benediction in 13:11b is based on the obedience called for in 13:11a. Only those who obey can be promised God's love and peace, because only they have already received them. As "a new creation" in Christ (5:17), we "are transformed into his likeness with ever-increasing glory" (3:18).

In sum, Paul commands what he does and prays as he does because God rests heavily on his daily life and experience. As moderns and postmoderns, perhaps we can best learn what this means by listening to someone from the past, such as Augustine, seeing that our own age of autonomy, self-reference, and self-sufficiency so clouds our vision. Augustine was a "premodern" man, who knew with a profundity not often matched in our own day that he was utterly dependent on God for everything, including any obedience he might render to God's commands. The entirety of Augustine's most famous and influential work, his *Confessions*, is a desperate prayer for help. In his words:

My entire hope is exclusively in your very great mercy. Grant what you command, and command what you will.... He loves you less who together with you loves something which he does not love for your sake. O love, you ever burn and are never extinguished. O charity, my God, set me on fire ... grant what you command, and command what you will.... But remember, Lord 'that we are but dust' (Ps. 102:14).... Paul had no power in himself because he was of the same dust as we, but he said these words [Phil. 4:11–12] under the breath of your inspiration and I loved him for it.... Strengthen me that I may have this power. Grant what you command, and command what you will ... it is by your gift that your command is kept.[31]

Augustine's prayer reflects Paul's conviction that God grants what he commands by mercifully revealing the all-consuming and incomparable nature of his divine love, a love that eclipses all other objects of desire and takes them into its shadow. To obey God in all things, God must have no competitors. One must love all other things for God's sake, glorifying the Giver by receiving them as gifts with thankfulness and by using them in accordance with his will.

Yet, to love all things for God's sake, we must know the supremacy of God's own "burning love." This is why Augustine, like Paul, prays when confronted with the need for restoration and obedience. Augustine had learned what we need to learn afresh, that such a "holy desire" for God cannot be manufactured or willed into existence. Such a desire for God comes not from our latest techniques or therapies, but from encountering the superiority and ravishing goodness of God himself. We will desire God enough to trust him only if we have first experienced him.[32]

Augustine prayed for the power to obey because he knew that only *God* could reveal himself in such a way that the joy and peace to be found in his beauty, holiness, and love would drive out all lesser pleasures. Compliance

---

31. St. Augustine, *Confessions*, trans. Henry Chadwick (Oxford: Oxford Univ. Press, 1991), 10.29–31 (pp. 202–6).

32. Note Augustine's summary of his conversion in *Confessions*, 10.27 (p. 201), a passage that Chadwick says summarizes the central themes of the *Confessions*: 'The lovely things kept me from you, though if they did not have their existence in you, they had no existence at all. You called and cried out loud and shattered my deafness. You were radiant and resplendent, you put to flight my blindness. You were fragrant, and I drew in my breath and now pant after you. I tasted you, and I feel but hunger and thirst for you. You touched me, and I am set on fire to attain the peace which is yours." This is a poetic expansion of the same thought expressed by Paul about his own conversion in 2 Cor. 4:6. The negative flipside of this insight is that those who reject the gospel do so because they are blind to Christ's glory (2 Cor. 4:3).

to God's will does not derive from our own willpower, but from a new thirst and love created by encountering God himself. In this sense, we are prisoners of God. Only God can make himself known to us; he cannot be manipulated by our designs. As Augustine put it to God in his last confession:

> What man can enable the human mind to understand this? Which angel can interpret it to an angel? What angel can help a human being to grasp it? *Only you can be asked, only you can be begged, only on your door can we knock* (Matt. 7:7–8). Yes indeed, this is how it is received, how it is found, how the door is opened.[33]

The only antidote to the preoccupation with technology and technique that dominates the contemporary church is to return to the God-centeredness that runs throughout 2 Corinthians, from the opening word of praise for the comfort of God's sovereignty in 1:3 to the closing benediction for God's presence in 13:14. The hope of the church is not a new program but God's invasion of our lives. Nothing else can save us from the health and wealth gospel that threatens so much of contemporary Christianity, just as it did the Corinthians in Paul's day. The only cure for the cancer of modern materialism now growing in our hearts, with its insatiable desire for ever-multiplying pleasures on earth, is the surpassing and profound pleasure of knowing the God of love and peace (13:11).

In reality, Paul's moral "enthusiasm" is an enthusiasm for the all-surpassing and life-transforming grandeur of the eternal glory of God that far outweighs all the afflictions and affections of this world (4:16–18). In our cramped modernity, Paul's God seems too big to us because our god is too small. May Paul's last word to the Corinthians in 13:14 be fulfilled in our lives as well.

> O My Saviour,
>   help me.
> I am so slow to learn, so prone to forget, so weak to climb;
> I am in the foothills when I should be on the heights;
> I am pained by my graceless heart,
>   my poverty of love,
>   my sloth in the heavenly race,

---

33. Ibid., 13.38 (pp. 304–5), emphasis mine. I am indebted to John Piper for calling my attention to this theme in Augustine's thought. For a moving and insightful analysis of Augustine's understanding of the role of desire and joy in God in the Christian life, see Piper's "The Swan Is Not Silent: Sovereign Joy in the Life and Thought of St. Augustine," unpublished paper from The Bethlehem Conference for Pastors (Feb. 3, 1998), 10–11, 15, available on tape or in print from Bethlehem Baptist Church, Minneapolis, Minnesota.

    my sullied conscience,
    my wasted hours,
    my unspent opportunities.
I am blind while light shines around me:
    take the scales from my eyes,
    grind to dust the evil heart of unbelief.
Make it my chiefest joy to study thee,
        meditate on thee,
        gaze on thee,
        sit like Mary at thy feet,
        lean like John on thy breast,
        appeal like Peter to thy love,
        count like Paul all things dung.
Give me increase and progress in grace so that there may be
    more decision in my character,
    more vigour in my purposes,
    more elevation in my life,
    more fervour in my devotion,
    more constancy in my zeal.
As I have a position in the world,
    keep me from making the world my position;
May I never seek in the creature
    what can be found only in the creator.
Let not faith cease from seeking thee until it vanishes into sight.
Ride forth in me, thou king of kings and lord of lords,
that I may live victoriously, and in victory attain my end.[34]

---

34. "A Disciple's Renewal," *The Valley of Vision: A Collection of Puritan Prayers and Devotions,* ed. Arthur Bennett (Edinburgh: Banner of Truth Trust, 1975), 184.

Scripture Index

1 Corinthians

Scripture Index

Scripture Index

Subject Index

Subject Index

First Corinthians, purpose of, 29

giving, necessity of, 344–45, 352–55, 362, 381; theological basis of, 341–43, 345, 348–50, 365–66, 375, 376–77; trends in contemporary practice of, 381–84

glory (of God), as goal of ministry and life, 13–14, 19, 35, 63, 65, 66, 73–74, 85, 101, 188, 195, 359, 361, 370, 372, 377, 379–80, 387, 453, 477; transformative effect of, 124, 142, 144, 150–51, 161–63, 165–66, 176–77, 180–81, 188, 213, 244, 248, 251, 283, 304, 362, 371, 378, 427–28, 498, 500–502, 505–6, 507–8

God, character of, 66, 71–72, 84, 91, 327, 505–7; mercy of, 87, 95–96; sovereignty of, 59, 61, 66, 71, 74–77, 115, 118, 286, 320–21, 416, 442, 462, 464

gospel, nature of, 62, 77, 84–85, 93–94, 96, 162, 177, 239–41, 250, 252–53, 262–63, 317, 429, 470

grace (mercy), of God, 331, 465, 506; future aspect of, 202–5; transforming nature of, 47, 81–82, 83–84, 91, 97, 101, 332–37, 339, 343–44, 350, 359, 365, 371–72, 465, 466, 474, 482, 497, 498, 501, 503; as goal of gospel, 88–90, 93, 98, 249

gratitude, as improper motive for obedience, 385–86

health and wealth gospel, 383–84, 435, 448, 508; challenged by Paul's suffering, 28, 77, 121–22, 182, 194, 199–200, 434

heaven, 190–91, 200–201, 215, 217, 220; absence of longing for in contemporary church, 218–19

hedonism, Christian, 73, 99–101, 194, 202–5, 313, 320, 322–24, 332, 337, 339, 343, 347, 351, 355–56, 367, 385, 387–88, 507–9

Holy Spirit, 13, 86, 123–24, 149–51, 161–62, 187–88, 197, 214, 244,

294, 488, 498; mediated by Paul, 115–17, 119, 126, 145, 162–63, 175, 183, 309, 398, 410, 428, 494, 499

honor, social virtue of, 407–8, 486

hope, 65, 68, 74, 97, 197–98, 229, 232, 236–37, 287, 294

interpreting the Bible (hermeneutics), 51–52, 54–55, 164, 167–73

Israel, 156–59, 165

Jesus Christ, as fulfillment of God's promises, 85–86, 91–93, 435–36; as image (glory) of God, 177–78, 180–81, 435; as last Adam, 190, 210–11, 241, 244; as model, 90–93, 240, 337–38, 341–42, 393–94, 464, 468, 490; as object of prayer, 464

judgment, of God (Christ), 87, 94–96, 115, 119–20, 139–40, 213, 216–17, 219, 223, 227. 235–36, 257, 258–62, 287–89, 303–4, 312, 393–94, 488–89, 492, 501; by works, 216–17, 225–26, 413, 436; modern conceptions of, 227–29

katargeo, meaning of, 147–48, 152–53

law (of Sinai), 117, 142–45

law/gospel contrast, 130–31, 146

letter/Spirit contrast, 130–33, 142

love, nature of, 69, 87–88, 97, 100–101, 346–47, 362; necessity of, 500

ministry, Paul's view of, 67–68, 128–30, 149–50, 178–79, 235, 245, 250–52, 494; true nature of, 102, 120–21, 130, 302–3, 317, 319, 325, 452–54

modernism, 52–53, 55, 198, 220–21, 276

Moses, 30, 118, 127–28; ministry of, 142–50, 154–55, 158–59, 401, 434–35

mysticism, merkabah, 459–60; role of in Christian life and ministry, 468–72, 475, 500

Bring ancient truth to modern life with the
NIV Application Commentary series

Covering both the Old and New Testaments, the **NIV Application Commentary** series is a staple reference for pastors seeking to bring the Bible's timeless message into a modern context. It explains not only what the Bible means but also how that meaning impacts the lives of believers today.

Exodus
The truth of Christ's resurrection and its resulting impact on our lives mean that to Christians, the application of Exodus is less about how to act than it is about what God has done and what it means to be his children.

Peter Enns
ISBN: 0-310-20607-3

Esther
Karen H. Jobes shows what a biblical narrative that never mentions God tells Christians about him today.

Karen H. Jobes
ISBN: 0-310-20672-3

Ezekiel
Discover how, properly understood, this mysterious book with its obscure images offers profound comfort to us today.

Ian M. Duguid
ISBN: 0-310-20147-X

Available at your local Christian bookstore

ZondervanPublishingHouse
Grand Rapids, Michigan 49530
http://www.zondervan.com

Daniel

Tremper Longman III reveals how the practical stories and spellbinding apocalyptic imagery of Daniel contain principles that are as relevant now as they were in the days of the Babylonian Captivity.

Tremper Longman III
ISBN: 0-310-20608-1

Mark

Learn how the challenging Gospel of Mark can leave recipients with the same powerful questions and answers it did when it was written.

David E. Garland
ISBN: 0-310-49350-1

Luke

Focus on the most important application of all: "the person of Jesus and the nature of God's work through him to deliver humanity."

Darrell L. Bock
ISBN: 0-310-49330-7

Acts

Study the first portraits of the church in action around the world with someone whose ministry mirrors many of the events in Acts. Biblical scholar and worldwide evangelist Ajith Fernando applies the story of the church's early development to the global mission of believers today.

Ajith Fernando
ISBN: 0-310-49410-9

Available at your local Christian bookstore

ZondervanPublishingHouse
Grand Rapids, Michigan
http://www.zondervan.com

1 Corinthians

Is your church struggling with the problem of divisiveness and fragmentation? See the solution Paul gave the Corinthian Christians over 2,000 years ago. It still works today!

Craig Blomberg
ISBN: 0-310-48490-1

Galatians

A pastor's message is true not because of his preaching or people-management skills, but because of Christ. Learn how to apply Paul's example of visionary church leadership to your own congregation.

Scot McKnight
ISBN: 0-310-48470-1

Ephesians

Explore what the author calls "a surprisingly comprehensive statement about God and his work, about Christ and the gospel, about life with God's Spirit, and about the right way to live."

Klyne Snodgrass
ISBN: 0-310-49340-4

Philippians

The best lesson Philippians provides is how to encourage people who actually are doing quite well. Learn why not all the New Testament letters are reactions to theological crises.

Frank Thielman
ISBN: 0-310-49340-4

Available at your local Christian bookstore

ZondervanPublishingHouse
Grand Rapids, Michigan
http://www.zondervan.com

Colossians/Philemon

The temptation to trust in the wrong things has always been strong. Use this commentary to learn the importance of trusting only in Jesus, God's Son, in whom all the fullness of God lives. No message is more important for our post-modern culture.

David E. Garland
ISBN: 0-310-48480-4

1&2 Thessalonians

Paul's letters to the Thessalonians say as much to us today about Christ's return and our resurrection as they did in the early church. This volume skillfully reveals Paul's answers to these questions and how they address the needs of contemporary Christians.

Michael W. Holmes
ISBN: 0-310-49380-3

1&2 Timothy, Titus

Reveals the context and meanings of Paul's letters to two leaders in the early Christian Church and explores their present-day implications to help you to accurately apply the principles they contain to contemporary issues.

Walter L. Liefeld
ISBN: 0-310-50110-5

Hebrews

The message of Hebrews can be summed up in a single phrase: "God speaks effectively to us through Jesus." Unpack the theological meaning of those seven words and learn why the gospel still demands a hearing today.

George H. Guthrie
ISBN: 0-310-49390-0

Available at your local Christian bookstore

ZondervanPublishingHouse
Grand Rapids, Michigan
http://www.zondervan.com

James

Give your church the best antidote for a culture of people who say they believe one thing but act in ways that either ignore or contradict their belief. More than just saying, "Practice what you preach," James gives solid reasons why faith and action must coexist.

David P. Nystrom
ISBN: 0-310-49360-9

1 Peter

The issue of the church's relationship to the state hits the news media in some form nearly every day. Learn how Peter answered the question for Christians surviving under Roman rule and how it applies similarly to believers living amid the secular institutions of the modern world.

Scot McKnight
ISBN: 0-310-49290-4

2 Peter, Jude

Introduce your modern audience to letters they may not be familiar with and show why they'll want to get to know them.

Douglas J. Moo
ISBN: 0-310-20104-7

Letters of John

Like the community in John's time, which faced disputes over erroneous "secret knowledge," today's church needs discernment in affirming new ideas supported by Scripture and weeding out harmful notions. This volume will help you show today's Christians how to use John's example.

Gary M. Burge
ISBN: 0-310-486420-3

Available at your local Christian bookstore

ZondervanPublishingHouse
Grand Rapids, Michigan
http://www.zondervan.com

Revelation

Craig Keener offers a "new" approach to the book of Revelation by focusing on the "old." He stresses the need for believers to prepare for the possibility of suffering for the sake of Jesus.

Craig Keener
ISBN: 0-310-23192-2

Available at your local Christian bookstore

ZondervanPublishingHouse
Grand Rapids, Michigan
http://www.zondervan.com

Praise for the NIV Application Commentary Series

"This series promises to become an indispensable tool for every pastor and teacher who seeks to make the Bible's timeless message speak to this generation."

—Billy Graham

"It is encouraging to find a commentary that is not only biblically trustworthy but also contemporary in its application. **The NIV Application Commentary** series will prove to be a helpful tool in the pastor's sermon preparation. I use it and recommend it."

—Charles F. Stanley, Pastor, First Baptist Church of Atlanta

"**The NIV Application Commentary** is an outstanding resource for pastors and any-one else who is serious about developing 'doers of the Word.'"

—Rick Warren, Pastor, Saddleback Valley Community
Church, Author, *The Purpose-Driven Church*

"**The NIV Application Commentary** series shares the same goal that has been the passion of my own ministry—communicating God's Word to a contemporary audience so that they feel the full impact of its message.

—Bill Hybels, Willow Creek Community Church

"**The NIV Application Commentary** series helps pastors and other Bible teachers with one of the most neglected elements in good preaching—accurate, useful ap-plication. Most commentaries tell you a few things that are helpful and much that you do not need to know. By dealing with the original meaning and contemporary significance of each passage, **The NIV Application Commentary** series promises to be helpful all the way around."

—Dr. James Montgomery Boice, Tenth Presbyterian Church

"If you want to avoid hanging applicational elephants from interpretive threads, then **The NIV Application Commentary** is for you! This series excels at both original meaning and contemporary signficance. I support it one hundred percent."

—Howard G. Hendricks, Dallas Theological Seminary

"**The NIV Application Commentary** series doesn't fool around: It gets right down to business, bringing this ancient and powerful Word of God into the present so that it can be heard and delivered with all the freshness of a new day, with all the im-mediacy of a friend's embrace."

—Eugene H. Peterson, Regent College

"This series dares to go where few scholars have gone before—into the real world of biblical application faced by pastors and teachers every day. This is everything a good commentary series should be."

—Leith Anderson, Pastor, Wooddale Church

"This is THE pulpit commentary for the 21st century."

—George K. Brushaber, President, Bethel College & Seminary

"Here, at last, is a commentary that makes the proper circuit from the biblical world to main street. **The NIV Application Commentary** is a magnificent gift to the church."

—R. Kent Hughes, Pastor, College Church, Wheaton, IL

Look for the NIV Application Commentary *at your local Christian bookstore*

ZondervanPublishingHouse
Grand Rapids, Michigan 49530
http://www.zondervan.com

"We want to hear from you. Please send your comments about this
book to us in care of the address below. Thank you.

ZondervanPublishingHouse
Grand Rapids, Michigan 49530
http://www.zondervan.com